Law in Social Work Practice

Consulting Editor: Charles Zastrow
University of Wisconsin-Whitewater

Law in Social Work Practice

Andrea Saltzman, M.A., J.D.

David M. Furman, M.S.W., J.D.

University of Denver

BROOKS/COLE
CENGAGE Learning

Australia • Brazil • Japan • Korea • Mexico • Singapore • Spain • United Kingdom • United States

BROOKS/COLE
CENGAGE Learning™

Law in Social Work Practice
Andrea Saltzman, David M. Furman

Project Editor: Steven M. Long

Typesetter: E. T. Lowe

Cover Art: *Blue Room and Yellow Room* by N. Sistler

For product information and technology assistance, contact us at
Cengage Learning Customer & Sales Support, 1-800-354-9706.

For permission to use material from this text or product, submit all requests online at **www.cengage.com/permissions**. Further permissions questions can be emailed to **permissionrequest@cengage.com**.

Library of Congress Control Number: 98039712

ISBN-13: 978-0-8304-1517-5
ISBN-10: 0-8304-1517-3

Brooks/Cole
10 Davis Drive
Belmont, CA 94002-3098
USA

Cengage Learning is a leading provider of customized learning solutions with office locations around the globe, including Singapore, the United Kingdom, Australia, Mexico, Brazil, and Japan. Locate your local office at: **www.cengage.com/global**.

Cengage Learning products are represented in Canada by Nelson Education, Ltd.

To learn more about Brooks/Cole, visit **www.cengage.com/brookscole**.

Purchase any of our products at your local college store or at our preferred online store **www.ichapters.com**.

Printed in the United States
10 11 12 13 14 15 12 11

CONTENTS

CHAPTER 6
PROSECUTION AND PUNISHMENT OF ADULT OFFENDERS   159

CHAPTER 7
ADJUDICATION AND TREATMENT OF JUVENILE OFFENDERS   193

SECTION III ▪ THE CHILD, THE FAMILY, AND THE LAW

CHAPTER 8
PROTECTION OF CHILDREN   221

Whatever the nature of your social work practice, knowledge of the law may be helpful to you and your clients and you may play a variety of roles within the legal system. Since the earliest days of the profession, social workers have been learning the law to benefit their clients and have worked within the legal system to further their clients' interests. Through the years, the involvement of social workers with the legal system, including the number and types of roles they play in it, has been steadily growing.

In the course of reading this book, you will learn many roles that social workers play within the legal system. You will learn that, whatever your speciality as a social worker, you may be able to assist your clients by working in the legal system. You may not be doing all you can for your clients if you do not make use of all available resources—including the legal system. And even if you are never actively involved with the legal system in your career as a social worker, you still have to learn about the law for several reasons:

- The law may shape and regulate your social work practice. In many States, the law defines who can practice social work and specifies the tasks a social worker may perform. The law in these and other States may give social workers certain legal rights, may impose certain legal obligations, on social workers, or may make social workers accountable for certain actions they take on their jobs. For example, laws in some States give social workers a right and an obligation to keep client records confidential; laws in every State obligate social workers to report suspected child abuse; and laws in most States allow the clients of social workers who believe they were injured through poor practice to sue their social workers for monetary damages. In other words, whatever form your social work practice takes, the law may govern your actions. Equally important, the law may govern the actions of your clients. This leads to another reason you need to know the law.

- The law may shape and restrict your clients' actions. Social workers have to be aware of the laws that affect their clients in order to assist them effectively. For example, in order to arrange for a patient's aftercare, a hospital social worker may have to know whether or not the law allows an adult child to admit a parent to a nursing home against the parent's will. And, in order to help a battered woman make an appropriate decision, a social worker in a shelter for battered women should know whether or not the woman risks losing custody of her children if she temporarily leaves them with her husband.

While the law may influence the choices of social workers' clients, social workers should not act as lawyers and may not dispense legal advice to their clients. However, social workers must know when the law affects their clients and when it is necessary for their clients to consult lawyers. This brings us to another reason why you must know the law.

- Knowledge of the law will enable you to recognize certain of your clients' problems as legal. Recognizing a client's problem as legal and helping a client find a lawyer may be the most important service a social worker can perform for a client. As has been stated, "Too many clients in the past have endured the painful consequences of festering or unsolved legal problems because neither they nor the social worker recognized the problem as a legal one or knew what to do about it."[1]

Moreover, people who seek the assistance of social workers or whom social workers are assisting often have legal problems in addition to their social problems. A client's legal and social problems may be intertwined; they may not be able to be resolved independently. For example, a social worker cannot effectively assist a woman with Alzheimer's disease who has come to him for help in coping with the disease without discussing the need for a legally appointed guardian who can make decisions for the woman when she can no longer make them herself. The social worker may even want to help the woman find a lawyer to advise and assist her in obtaining a guardian. Another example is that of an alcoholic who may have several legal problems that will affect his treatment for alcoholism and his well-being. He may be facing a charge of drunk driving and eviction from his home because of his alcoholism. He needs the assistance of both a lawyer and a social worker to resolve these problems. This interdependence of legal and social problems is another reason you should know the law.

- Knowledge of the law will help you work effectively with lawyers to resolve your clients' problems. The interdependence of legal and social problems may require lawyers and social workers to work together to resolve mutual clients' problems. Working with lawyers is easier if social workers understand what lawyers are doing and why they are doing it. Such an understanding can facilitate cooperation and the successful resolution of a client's problems. In addition, social workers must be able to communicate with lawyers in order to work successfully with them. The social worker must speak the lawyer's language. That language is the law.

Sometimes, social workers and lawyers may not be working together for mutual clients but may seem to be working against each other for clients with opposing interests. For example, a social worker may be working to pro-

---

1. Michael Zander, *Social Workers, Their Clients and the Law* (Sweet & Maxwell: London, 1981), p. vi

tect a child who she believes has been abused by a parent and a lawyer may be working to protect the rights of the parent who denies any abuse. Even when lawyers and social workers are working for the same client, they may be working against each other. For example, a social worker may be seeking to protect a mentally ill client by having the client committed to a hospital for treatment while a lawyer may be seeking to protect the client's rights by preventing the commitment.

Whether working with or against a lawyer, you will be more effective in your work if you have a knowledge of the law, including the legal rights that the lawyer may be acting to protect. And even if no lawyer is involved in your work, knowledge of your clients' legal rights will help you be more effective. The need to know your clients' rights is still another reason you need to know the law.

- Knowledge of the law enables you to recognize and respect your clients' rights. The law clothes social workers' clients with certain rights. Clients may be forced to shed these rights, but only in accordance with the law and in conformity with legal procedures. For example, a drug addict has a right to refuse to enter a treatment program; her social worker may only be able to force her to enter the program if certain legal standards are met and certain legal processes are completed. To give another example, an unwed teenaged mother has a right to keep her child; her social worker may only be able to place the child for adoption if certain legal standards are met and certain legal procedures are followed.

If social workers do not know the law, they may ignore their clients' rights. If social workers ignore these rights, they may not be able to assist their clients effectively. For example, arranging a treatment to which a client will not consent may mean the client will get no treatment. Social workers also may not be able to assist their clients effectively if they ignore the rights of others who may be affected by their actions or the actions of their clients. This is one more important reason you need to know the law.

- Knowledge of the law enables you to recognize and respect the rights of those who may be affected by your actions. Social workers need to know the law not only because the law gives their clients certain legal rights but also because it gives others whose lives are affected by social workers' actions certain legal rights. Social workers cannot ignore these rights. For example, even if an unwed mother agrees to allow her child to be adopted her social worker may not arrange for the adoption without considering the rights of the child's father. If his rights are ignored, any adoption arranged by the social worker may be invalid.

In short, whatever your field of practice as a social worker, you should know the law to help your clients and to do your job effectively and legally. Unfortunately, the law on a given subject is rarely a simple rule that can be easily unearthed and understood. The law is a complex web of concepts, principles, rules, standards, tests, practices, customs, traditions, and modes of thinking and reasoning. It is a vast body of material coming from many sources that must be interpreted before it can be applied. It is more process than precept. It is more reasoning than rule.

Even laws that appear simple rarely provide simple answers to your questions. Some seemingly simple laws are difficult to apply in different situations and are not easily used to resolve certain problems. Some seemingly simple laws have hidden qualifications, exceptions, and conditions. Think about the commandment: "Thou shalt not kill," which translates into the law that killing another person is a crime called homicide. This seemingly simple law has many exceptions, and leaves many questions unanswered. For example, is it homicide for a woman to kill a man who raped her? Is an eleven-year-old boy who kills a friend guilty of homicide? Can a doctor who heeds a patient's wish to disconnect life support systems be prosecuted for homicide?

Even those simple laws that provide unqualified answers to legal questions may be difficult to understand or apply. These laws may be written in language completely unfamiliar to you or may depend on concepts that are totally unknown to you. Think about the California law: "Homicide is excusable . . . [w]hen committed by accident and misfortune . . . and without any unlawful intent."[2] To understand this law, you must know how the law defines *intent*. While you might know what *misfortune* is, you might not know what it means in this context.

Thus, you will not know the law essential to your practice if you are simply handed a few laws or are provided with the key to a law library. Learning the law is a more complex and difficult process.

Similarly, learning how the legal system operates and how those who run the legal system (i.e., lawyers) think is difficult. The American legal system is complex. It is made up of many different legal systems, each of which is as complex as the law that creates it and governs its operation. The American legal system is often mysterious to those outside of it. It operates in a way that is quite different from other institutions with which social workers are familiar. Lawyers have a unique way of thinking and of approaching their work, which differ from the way social workers are taught to think and approach their work.

Although learning about the law and the legal system may be difficult, achieving an understanding of both is far from impossible. Many social workers assume that because the law is complex and is often written in unfamiliar language, it is unknowable. Many social workers assume that because the legal system is complex and is run by lawyers, the veils shrouding this system are impossible to lift. Neither assumption is accurate. The law can be found, read, and understood by nonlawyers. You, like many social workers in the past and in the present, can lift the veils shrouding the legal system and play important roles in it.

This book is designed to make the law and the operation of the legal system less mysterious to you. It is also designed to improve your legal skills and practices so that you can work effectively in the legal system. To these ends, the book begins by providing, in the first section, an overview of American law and the American legal system. In the course of providing this overview, the book attempts to:

---

2. California Penal Code § 195.

- define basic legal concepts and terms;
- demystify the operation of the legal system;
- decode the process known as legal reasoning;
- delineate the hearing process;
- dispense practical guidance for performing the various roles of the social worker in the hearing process, including testifying effectively; and
- describe the fundamentals of legal research.

In other words, the first section of the book sets forth the how, what, where and why of the law and the legal system. The information provided in these introductory chapters should give you the grounding necessary to understand the areas of the law that are most relevant to social work practice. These areas of the law are then presented in the next three sections of the book, which cover respectively 1) constitutional and criminal law; 2) the law related to children and the family; and 3) the law related to mental and physical health. In the last section, the book concludes by discussing the laws that directly regulate the practice of social work.

Throughout the book, general principles, basic concepts, issues, problems, and trends are emphasized. The book does not simply set forth a series of laws or descriptions, summaries or paraphrases of laws. However, to give you practice in understanding the law as you will find it in your work, excerpts from actual laws—mostly court opinions and statutes—are often presented.

This book is designed to enable you to find, figure out, and use the law by yourself. Through the approach taken by this book, you should learn how to recognize when a law may be significant to your practice, how to find this significant law, how to understand it when you find it, and, most important, how to use it in your practice. The approach is somewhat like giving you a good roadmap to enable you to get around in unfamiliar territory instead of giving you detailed directions.

This approach is not easy. It can be frustrating. But in the long run it is the best approach to the study of law and the legal system for several reasons.

As we have said, the model of the law as a collection of simple rules that can be committed to memory is far from reality. Further, any rules that do exist may differ from place to place and may change over time. In addition, there are so many laws that may be relevant to social work practice that presenting them all would be impossible for this book and learning even those relevant to your particular practice would be difficult for you. With a basic understanding of the law and of legal principles, however, you should be able to absorb current laws necessary to your practice quickly and easily.

As we have also said, the American legal system is a complex system made up of many different legal systems that take on different forms in different places and that change over time. You will only gain an understanding of this complex system and be able to operate effectively within it if you have a basic understanding of the law and of the general principles that control the legal system's functioning, regardless of how many specific laws relevant to your work and how much about court procedures you may have learned in your classes or on the job.

Finally, and perhaps most important, skills acquired in locating, analyzing, and interpreting the law remain long after specific laws fade from memory; you can still understand the law after you have forgotten particular laws.

Commenting not only on the approach of this book, but also on how you can use the book most profitably is necessary.

First, you should use this text in conjunction with the laws from the State in which you practice or intend to practice. As we have said, laws may differ significantly from place to place. We will provide examples of laws from many States in this book, but the laws of the State in which you practice, not the laws given to you as examples in this book, will govern your practice. It is essential that you be familiar with your State's laws.

Second, although learning the law requires that you learn many unfamiliar terms, this book does not provide you with a traditional glossary. A law dictionary would thus be a valuable asset. This book does, however, put all unfamiliar legal terms in boldfaced print the first time they appear or whenever they are defined for you. All such terms are then included in a special glossary index. When you next encounter the terms, you can use this glossary index to locate the definitions and see how the terms are used in context. Seeing unfamiliar terms used in context may be more useful to you than reading a standard glossary or law dictionary definition.

Last, while this book includes many excerpts from statutes and court opinions to help you become familiar with legal writing and reasoning, the excerpts are substantially edited. You may want to read the full statutes and opinions to get a fuller picture. Further, you should understand how we excerpt court opinions so you will not be confused when you read real opinions.

When we excerpt a court opinion for you (and even when we give you relatively short quotations from court opinions), we will delete most citations to authority and most footnotes. These deletions will not be indicated. Other deletions within sentences will be indicated by ellipses (i.e., three dots like this . . .). Deletions of whole sentences, paragraphs, or even several pages will not be indicated. What appears as one sentence or paragraph may actually be drawn from two sentences or several paragraphs, but the order of sentences and paragraphs will not be altered. Substitutions of terms and explanatory matter will be placed in brackets [like this]. Where there is only a substitution of terms, no deletion will be indicated. Where a sentence begins with a bracketed capital letter (as "[T]he"), there has been a deletion at the beginning of the sentence. Footnotes from the opinion that are retained will be indicated with an asterisk (*). Long explanatory matter we have written will be included in a footnote instead of in brackets and will be numbered as other footnotes to the text. Text of particular importance within the excerpts will be emphasized. Any emphasis by the court in the original opinion will be underlined in addition to being emphasized. Although most court opinions are replete with quotations, and even quotations within quotations, we will generally not include internal quotation marks or otherwise indicate when a court is quoting another court's opinion or other authority.

SECTION I

AN OVERVIEW OF
THE LEGAL SYSTEM
AND THE LAW

INTRODUCTION TO SECTION I

This section of the book sets forth some of the basic concepts and principles that shape the law and the legal system. It also provides you with some tools that you may use when you encounter the law in your practice, whatever its nature. Whether you are working in a public agency doing child protection or as a private marriage and family counselor, whether you need an answer to a question on the education of disabled children or on health care, or whether you are asked to testify in a criminal trial or a mental health commitment, you need to know some basic concepts and principles and you need to have certain skills. For example, you must know how to find the applicable law and how to translate it when you find it. This section of the book is designed to provide you with the necessary knowledge and skills.

While this section may seem very general and broad, it is actually narrowly focused on the concepts, principles, and tools necessary for effective social work practice. It is not designed to give you the necessary grounding for an understanding of all areas of the law. Rather, it is designed to give you the grounding necessary for you to understand the specific areas of the law that are most relevant to social work practice and that are discussed in the next sections of the book.

For example, if you do not understand the relationship between the federal and the State legal system or how the jurisdiction of a State court is limited, you may not understand the discussion in Section III on the problems arising when a parent in one State seeks to collect child support from a parent in another State. Thus, this section explains the federal-state relationship and the limits on a State court's jurisdiction—but only to the extent necessary for you to understand the problems associated with interstate collection of child support or other issues that may arise in your social work practice. To be effective in your social work practice, you probably do not have to understand the aspects of the federal-state relationship that cause problems when one State wants to tax or regulate an interstate corporation headquartered in another State, or how the limits on a State court's jurisdiction affect litigation arising from plane crashes. Accordingly, this section is not designed to provide this understanding.

Despite this section's limited focus, the information it provides on the federal-state relationship, on State court jurisdiction, and on a variety of other concepts and principles could be helpful to you in areas of the law that you might encounter in your practice but that are not discussed in this book. For example, to be effective in your practice, you may have to know and understand welfare law. An understanding of the federal-state relationship is crucial to an understanding of this topic. While this book does not discuss welfare law and while its discussion of the federal-state relationship is limited, this section does provide basic information on the federal-state relationship that can help you understand welfare law.

1

Basic Legal Concepts and Principles for the Social Worker

This chapter introduces you to the American legal system. It describes the ways laws are produced by this system and the kinds of laws that are generated. It also tells you how you can change the laws that affect your clients.

WHAT IS THE LAW?

Law can be defined as those standards, principles, processes and rules—usually written down in some manner—that are adopted, administered, and enforced by a governmental authority and that regulate behavior by setting forth what people may and may not do and how they may do what they can do. Put more simply, the law consists of "those guides to social conduct which are created and enforced by public officials."[1]

The keys to these definitions of the law are the phrases "by a governmental authority" and "by public officials." The involvement of government is what makes laws unique among rules of behavior. There are many rules that guide behavior, but only those rules that are adopted and backed by the authority of the government are rules of law. For example, you probably obey the rule that you must wash your hands before you serve dinner, the rule that you should wipe your mouth on your napkin not your sleeve while you eat dinner, and the rule that you may not make love with your neighbor's spouse after you finish dinner. But these are rules of health, etiquette, and morality, not rules of law prescribed by a government. You

may obey these rules not because of any government sanction, but because of your training, social pressure, habit, personal morality and beliefs, or a myriad of other reasons. Sometimes, rules that you obey for such reasons are also rules of law. For example, a city ordinance may require restaurant employees to wash their hands before serving food, and a statute may make adultery illegal. But these rules do not become rules of law unless and until a governmental authority adopts them and they are backed by the authority of government. They are not considered part of the law until this occurs.

Laws are generally adopted when it is believed that rules of behavior should be backed by governmental authority either because the rules serve an important societal purpose or are necessary for the safe and healthy functioning of society. Laws should change when beliefs change or society changes. As stated by Justice Oliver Wendell Holmes: "It is revolting to have no better reason for a rule of law than that it was laid down in the time of Henry IV. It is still more revolting if the grounds upon which it was laid down have vanished long since, and the rule simply persists from blind imitation of the past."[2]

Laws do not work when the people do not believe in them or they do not fit well with the functioning of society, but sometimes laws should mold, rather than reflect, public opinion or should operate to change the functioning of society. For example, laws forbidding discrimination on the basis of race may be adopted to change beliefs about the races and to end

1. James L. Houghteling, Jr., *The Dynamics of Law* (Harcourt, Brace & World Inc: New York, 1968), p. 5.

2. Oliver Wendell Holmes, "The Path of the Law," *Harvard Law Review*, Vol. 10 (1897), p. 496.

the widespread practice of discrimination.

Laws may be categorized in a variety of ways. First, they may be categorized in terms of how they regulate behavior. When you think about the law, you probably think about those rules that are enforced by the coercive power of the government, that is, laws that make certain behavior illegal and establish the punishment for the behavior. But many laws merely authorize certain behavior, with no penalties imposed if someone chooses not to engage in the behavior. And some laws may induce certain behavior by rewarding those who choose to engage in the behavior, not by penalizing those who do not. For example, you may be punished if you drive a car without a driver's license, but you would not be punished if you chose not to drive and not to obtain a driver's license. The law permits you to drive if you obtain a driver's license, but it does not require you to obtain a driver's license if you choose not to drive. If you do choose to drive and you drive carelessly, the law may require you to pay damages to anyone you injure. The law attempts to make you drive carefully by imposing such a sanction. It may also induce you to drive carefully by requiring your insurance company to reduce your premium if you have no accidents.

Second, laws may be categorized in terms of whether they impose a duty, accord a right, or grant a power. Laws that impose a **duty** (i.e., an obligation) may take the form of a command or a proscription. For example, a law may be phrased either "You shall drive less than 65 m.p.h. on the highway" or "You are forbidden to drive more than 65 m.p.h. on the highway." Usually, if someone has a duty to do

something, someone else has a right to insist that the duty be done. The term **right** is also used to refer to privileges or liberties the law accords to all or to certain people. For example, Americans have a right of freedom of speech. Rights are rarely absolute; they may also be withheld from certain people. Thus, for example, the right of free speech does not allow a person to incite violence, to tell lies about someone else, or to utter obscenities; a witness in an investigation may not have a right to talk about his or her testimony if there is a need for secrecy. **Powers,** like privileges, allow someone to do something, but powers differ from privileges in that they create new rights or duties in others. For example, adults have a privilege to drive; this privilege creates no rights or duties in others. On the other hand, adults have the power to contract for driving lessons; any such contracts create rights and duties in those providing the lessons. Most commonly, powers are accorded to public officials, but private citizens also have certain powers, such as the power to sell their homes, which create rights in others, like the right to buy a home that has been put on the market. Powers, like rights, are rarely absolute. The power of one person is often limited by the rights of another. For example, while a woman who is renting her house has the power to refuse to rent it to someone, civil rights laws may prohibit her from refusing to rent her house to a man merely because he is African American.

Third, laws may be categorized as procedural or substantive. **Procedural laws** set forth how one must proceed to obtain certain results from the legal system. **Substantive laws** set forth the possible results and, more important, how one must behave in everyday life. In other words, procedural laws set forth how something is to be done within the legal system while substantive laws set forth what may be done within the law or must be done by the law. To illustrate, a law that sets forth how to obtain a driver's license is procedural while a law that requires one to obtain a driver's license before driving is substantive.

Finally, laws may be categorized as **criminal** or **civil**. Procedural criminal laws regulate the operation of the criminal justice system. All other procedural laws are civil laws. Substantive criminal laws regulate behavior; they impose duties on people and specify that any violation of these duties may be prosecuted and punished by the government and only by the government. All other substantive laws are civil laws. Substantive civil laws may also regulate behavior and impose duties on people, and the government may also take action against violators of civil laws, but the government may not punish the violators of civil laws; it is mainly private citizens who take action against the violators. Certain acts may be violations of both criminal and civil laws and may have both civil and criminal consequences. For example, a person who drives while intoxicated and injures another person may be criminally prosecuted and punished by the government and civilly sued for damages by the injured person.

WHAT IS THE LEGAL SYSTEM?

The **legal system** encompasses both the governmental systems that produce, administer, and enforce the law and the body of law that is produced, adminis-

tered, and enforced. America has a complex legal system made up of many different individual legal systems. There are many laws of many different types produced, administered, and enforced by many different branches, levels, and types of governments. There are federal laws produced by the federal government, that is, the government of the United States as a whole. There are also at least fifty different sets of State laws produced by the States.[3] And, there are thousands of different sets of local laws produced by the thousands of local governments, such as counties, cities, and special purpose agencies, like school districts.[4] There are constitutions, statutes, regulations, ordinances, executive orders, and court opinions, all of which are considered law.

---

3. Lawyers and those discussing the legal system frequently use the word *state* as a synonym for the word *government* or *governmental*. When lawyers so use the word *state*, it usually is uncapitalized. This book will follow that usage. Hereafter, if the word *State* is capitalized in this book, it should be understood as referring to the particular unit of government known as a *State*, such as the State of Nebraska. However, you may sometimes see the uncapitalized word *state* used for this purpose in laws excerpted in this book.

In this book, the capitalized term *State* should be understood to encompass American territories and special jurisdictions, like Puerto Rico or the District of Columbia, unless the text otherwise indicates. Thus, there may be more than fifty States. The term *State* should also be understood to encompass units of local government within a State, like cities. Thus, a statement like "No State may discriminate on the basis of race " should be understood as meaning no State, city, or other local government within a State may discriminate. Of course, if the uncapitalized word "state" is used as a synonym for "government," it may refer to any type or level of government, whether federal, State, or local.

4. According to the *World Almanac and Book of Facts* (World Almanac Books: New Jersey, 1997), in 1996, there were 84,955 units of local government, of which 38,978 were general purpose agencies, like cities, towns, villages, and counties.

There are laws produced by constitutional conventions; by the United States Congress, State legislatures, and local legislative bodies; by the President of the United States, the governors of the States, and the mayors of cities; by federal, State, and local agencies; and by federal and State courts. All of these laws are administered and enforced by various federal, State, and local governmental entities.

TYPES AND SOURCES OF LAW

Despite the complexity of the American legal system and the vast number of laws coming from so many different sources within the legal system, you should usually be able to determine what the law is on a particular subject. You may not be able to predict the resolution of a legal problem with absolute certainty, but, frequently, neither can a lawyer. What the lawyer—and the social worker—can do is determine with some degree of certainty what is an acceptable and legal course of conduct and how to achieve a particular goal within the legal system.

Understanding the types and sources of law should help you make such determinations. Therefore, the main types of law and their sources will be reviewed.

Constitutions

Constitutions are laws that usually are drafted by special conventions and adopted by the people who are to be governed by them. There is a constitution for the United States as a whole and all the States have constitutions. Local govern-

ments also may have constitutions that may be called **charters** or some other term.

Constitutions are very general documents that provide the framework for all the other laws within their jurisdictions. In other words, constitutions set forth the fundamental principles, procedures, and procedural rights that serve as guides for the enactment of other laws and for the making of legal decisions within their jurisdictions. Constitutions generally do not regulate people's conduct directly. Rather, they set up the governmental entities that will regulate it. They set forth what laws can be enacted, by whom, and how, specifically, the U.S. and State constitutions. They create the legislative bodies that will be primarily responsible for enacting the law. They create the courts that will enforce the laws enacted by legislative bodies and that also may make some law themselves. They grant power to executives to administer the laws enacted by legislative bodies and also to make some law themselves. In other words, they establish the three branches of the federal and State governments: the legislative, the judicial, and the executive.

Constitutions also set the limits of governmental authority and establish the basic rights of those within their jurisdictions that cannot be infringed by government.

The Constitution of the United States, that is, the federal constitution, is the supreme law of the land.[5] This means it

---

5. For simplicity, this book uses the capitalized term *Constitution* standing alone to refer to the United States Constitution. If the word *constitution* is not capitalized, it should be understood as referring to any constitution. If a particular constitution other than that of the United States is being referred to, the word *Constitution* will also be capitalized but, additionally, the jurisdiction governed by the Constitution will be identified (e.g., the California Constitution).

prevails over all other kinds of law. A law in conflict with the Constitution—whether it be a State constitutional provision or a State or federal statute or other law—is invalid and without legal force. One may not freely disregard such a law, however, unless and until a court declares it unconstitutional.

State constitutions' relationship to other forms of law in their States is similar to the Constitution's relationship to all other forms of law. In other words, State constitutions are supreme as compared to all other laws in their States.

Legislation

The chief law-making entity of any government in America is its elected and representative legislative body.[6] A law passed by a legislative body, whether Congress, a State legislature, or a local legislative body is called **legislation.** When you think of legislation, or, indeed, when you think of the law, you probably think of **statutes,** a type of legislation passed by Congress or State legislatures, but statutes are, as we shall see, only one piece in the puzzle of the law and only one type of legislation. **Ordinances,** that is, legislation passed by local legislative bodies, and resolutions, that is, legislation

of limited authority, are other common forms of legislation. Statutes are, however, the most important kind of legislation and we will focus on them.

How Is a Statute Enacted? The process for enacting a federal statute is summarized below. Most State legislatures follow a similar process for the enactment of State statutes.

What eventually becomes a statute begins as a **bill** in one of the two branches of Congress, the House of Representatives or the Senate.[7] Only a member of Congress, that is, a representative or a senator, may introduce a bill.

Let us assume for the purpose of understanding the process, that a representative has introduced a bill in the House. The bill is first "read" (i.e., set forth on the record) on the floor of the House. It is then assigned to a committee of the House, which is concerned with the subject of the bill (like health or labor). The committee may hold public hearings or conduct investigations on the wisdom or necessity of the bill. After the committee has considered the bill, it votes on it. If the committee votes unfavorably on the bill, the bill dies. If the committee votes favorably on the bill, the bill may go to another committee for consideration or back to the full body for a vote. There typically will be a debate on the bill on the floor of the House followed by a vote.

If the bill passes in the House, it will go through this whole process in the Senate.

---

6.   The legislative body for the federal government is known as the United States Congress. The legislatures in the States have a variety of names, such as General Assembly or simply Legislature, but never go by the name Congress. Thus, whenever this book refers to Congress, it should be understood as referring to the federal legislature.

Local legislative bodies also have a variety of names, like city council, board of aldermen, or school board, and also never go by the name Congress.

---

7.   Like Congress, all but one of the fifty State legislatures (Nebraska's) are bicameral, that is, they have two branches, a smaller branch, usually called a senate and a larger branch, often called an assembly or a house of representatives.

(If the bill had started and passed in the Senate, it would have to go through the whole process in the House.) If the bill passes both the House and the Senate, it goes to the President who may sign it or veto it. If the President vetoes the bill, Congress may override the veto with a two-thirds vote. The bill becomes a statute (also called an **act** or a **code**) and thus the law, either when the President signs it or the President's veto is overridden.

The process is not always as simple as we have presented it. Amendments may be introduced both in committee and on the floor of the entire body. If a bill is controversial, there may be many amendments, parliamentary maneuvers, and referrals to different committees. The bill might be assigned to one or more subcommittees before it is considered by a committee as a whole. Hearings and debates might be extensive. Further, the House and the Senate may pass similar, but not identical, bills. In such a case, the differences in the bills must be reconciled before the bill can be sent to the President.

How Can a Social Worker Influence Legislation? You or any other social worker can intervene at several points in the legislative process. First, you can propose bills to legislators. Second, you can help legislators draft bills. Third, you can submit written statements to committees on bills or seek to orally testify at committee hearings on the bills. Sometimes, testimony or statements are solicited by committees, particularly from social workers who work in government agencies. Fourth, you can communicate your views to legislators in person or by telephone, electronically, or in writing when floor debates and votes are occurring. No one but a legislator can speak during a floor debate, but anyone can communicate views on a bill to a legislator before a vote is taken. Finally, you can communicate your views to the chief executive officer who must sign or veto a bill that is before him or her.

At times, your involvement may seem quite direct. You may be communicating directly with legislators or at least members of their staffs. You may be testifying at hearings. But you can only influence the process indirectly. Only a legislator can introduce or vote on a bill. Your influence thus depends on your ability to influence a legislator.

Although attempting to influence the legislative process as an individual is possible for you, most social workers rely on the efforts of groups with which they are affiliated. For example, the National Association of Social Workers (NASW) solicits views on needed legislation from its members, develops positions that express the views of the members, and employs lobbyists who communicate these positions to legislators and attempt to convince them to accept NASW's positions. NASW, in turn, works with other groups who have similar interests to it, such as the Children's Defense Fund or the American Association of Retired Persons, to influence legislation.

There are more opportunities for individual involvement in the State legislative process than in the federal process. The State process is closer to home, and State senators and representatives have fewer constituents and experts on whom to rely. Social workers have more opportunity to testify in a hearing before a State legislative committee than to testify before a congressional committee. Thus, at the federal level, social workers rely more on the groups with which they are affiliated to influence legislation than at the State level.

At both the federal and State level, many bills are introduced at the initiative of public agencies. For example, a State agency with responsibility for mental health services often has its own legislative agenda and works closely with legislators who are interested in the care of the mentally ill. The State agency might suggest bills changing commitment standards or establishing greater local control of services. Or a federal agency that administers a federal welfare program may report to Congress that there is a need for wider coverage and suggest ways to broaden the program. Social workers who have leadership positions in public agencies therefore have a powerful opportunity to influence the law.

What Can a Statute Do? A statute can create a social program and tax citizens to raise the money for the program. A statute can create an administrative agency to enforce and produce the law on its own. A statute can establish new rights and obligations of citizens or can outlaw certain conduct and provide sanctions for engaging in the conduct. The only limitation on a statute is that it cannot be inconsistent with the Constitution and, in the case of a State statute, the State constitution.

Statutes, however, are rarely self-enforcing. Usually, statutes need to be implemented, but a legislature cannot implement a statute. For example, a legislature can enact a statute authorizing the collection of taxes and the spending of the money raised by the tax for a particular purpose, but the legislature itself cannot collect the taxes or spend the money. Or a legislature can make certain behavior a crime and establish the punishment for it, but the legislature cannot itself prosecute and punish those who engage in the behavior. Administrative agencies, the executive, or the courts usually have to actually enforce statutes in accordance with the will of the legislature as expressed in the statutes.

Statutes also are rarely detailed enough to answer all questions that may arise. Sometimes, statutory language is unclear. Sometimes, statutes conflict with one another. Filling in the details of statutes, interpreting their terms, or choosing the controlling statute among several statutes is often necessary. This may be the job of a court. In other words, a court may have to decide what a statute or several statutes really mean.

A court decision that fills in the details in a statute, determines its scope, or interprets its language merges with the statute. The statute alone is no longer the law. You will not know the law if you know only the statute; you must also know all authoritative judicial interpretations of the statute.

In addition to courts, administrative agencies may also fill in the details of a statute or interpret a statute. They will do this in **regulations.** You will also not know the law on the subject if you know only the statute and the authoritative judicial interpretations of a statute; you must also know the applicable regulations. The following section discusses regulations.

A Note on Ordinances. Local legislative bodies, like city councils and county boards, also enact laws. These laws, which cover matters of local concern, are generally called **ordinances.** The enactment process for ordinances may be somewhat like that for statutes. That is, there may be a proposal for an ordinance made by a member of the body, a referral of the proposal to a committee, debate and possibly hearings in committee, and then a vote in committee. If the committee passes the proposal, there will be a debate and a vote by the full body. There is usually an opportunity for public input in committee and an opportunity at the time of debate and vote by the full body to lobby but not to have direct input.

Constitutions and State statutes provide the framework for and establish limits on ordinances. No ordinance may conflict with the Constitution or the constitution and statutes of the State in which the local government is located. Further, ordinances may not be allowed on subjects that are fully covered by State statutes, that is, in which State statutes have **occupied the field** or which the State government has **preempted.**

Regulations

The executive branch of government also makes law. Administrative agencies, which are part of the executive branch, at the federal, State, and local levels produce laws that are generally called **regulations** or are simply known as **rules.** Sometimes, regulations or rules are referred to as **delegated legislation** because a legislative body delegates its power to create law to an agency. Sometimes, the process of producing regulations is called **promulgation.**

Why are unelected bureaucrats permitted to make law in our democratic system? Why would elected officials delegate their law-making power to the bureaucrats in administrative agencies?

First, as has been stated, legislative bodies do not and cannot fill in all the details in their laws. Congress can, for example, create a program to provide cash benefits to those who are disabled and unable to work, but Congress cannot draw fine lines delineating who should be considered disabled and what it means to be unable to work. It has neither the time nor the expertise to do this. Thus, it must authorize some other government entity to draw the lines.

Second, as has been noted, most legislation is not self-enforcing. Administrative agencies generally must administer the programs created by legislatures. Allowing the agency that administers a program to develop its own rules of operation and having it work out the details of the broad general legislation establishing the program makes sense. The agency has the time and expertise that the legislature lacks.

Third, legislators are elected to determine policy, not to concern themselves with the day to day functioning of government. The public only expects legislators to enact legislation that sets forth broad policy statements and that leaves the interpretation and effectuation of these policy statements to others. Bureaucrats in administrative agencies cannot be given unbridled discretion to make law, but if legislatures clearly define and establish limits on the discretion of administrative agencies to adopt regulations and if they give the agencies clear policy guidance on their exercise of discretion, the electorate is satisfied.

Administrative agencies must follow

proper procedures in promulgating regulations. Further, they may only promulgate those regulations that are within their statutory or constitutional authority. Moreover, any regulations they promulgate must be within or consistent with legislative intent or, in other words, any policies and purposes of the legislature that are revealed in any legislation.

If an administrative agency follows proper procedures in promulgating a regulation, if the regulation is within the authority of the agency, and if it is consistent with the legislative intent revealed in any authorizing legislation, the regulation has the same force and effect as a statute. That is, the regulation is "the law" and, as such, is binding on agency personnel and the public. It can, however, be overruled or changed by the legislative body that authorized its promulgation at any time. For example, at one time, a properly promulgated and authorized regulation allowed the immediate discontinuance of social security disability benefits if it was decided that a beneficiary was no longer disabled even if the beneficiary disputed the decision and requested a hearing. When the hardship caused by this practice received a great deal of publicity, Congress, by statute, mandated that, under most circumstances, social security disability benefits must be continued if a hearing is requested. Congress, thus, forced the Social Security Administration to change the regulation.

A court can also invalidate a regulation if it is not properly promulgated, if it is not within the authority of the agency, if it is inconsistent with legislative intent or, as with a statute, if it is unconstitutional. For example, many years ago the Supreme Court decided that a regulation that allowed the immediate discontinuance of welfare benefits—even if the recipient disputed the grounds for discontinuance and requested a hearing—was unconstitutional. The regulation was, thus, invalidated and was no longer the law.[8]

Further, as with a statute, a court may interpret a regulation or fill in details left out of a regulation by the administrative agency. The court's decision then merges with the regulation. You will not know the full law on the subject if you know only the regulation.

How Is a Regulation Promulgated? Most States and the federal government have statutes that set forth the process by which regulations are to be promulgated. These statutes may be found in something called an **Administrative Procedures Act** (the name used by the federal government and many States) or the like. Usually, these statutes provide that after a regulation is drafted by agency personnel (generally with no public input although nothing would prevent such input), it must be published in a designated publication for written public comment. After publication, there may or may not be one or more public hearings required. There may or may not be a requirement that one or more other government entities, such as a budget agency, a government management office, or a legislative committee, review the regulation for cost, necessity, wisdom, or consistency with authorizing legislation. After the required procedures are completed, a final version of the regu-

---

8. Because of differences between welfare and social security, the Supreme Court did not decide that the regulation allowing immediate discontinuance of social security disability benefits was unconstitutional and it required Congressional action to force the Social Security Administration to change it.

lation is written and, if it is approved by the appropriate agency official or board, the regulation is published in a designated publication.

How Can a Social Worker Influence Regulations?

Some social workers who work in public agencies at the supervisory level may be responsible for drafting regulations, either alone or with agency legal staff. Therefore, social workers can have a direct role in the process of promulgating regulations. But most social workers will not have this direct role. They will only have the indirect role in the process of promulgating regulations that they have in the process of enacting statutes. And very few will have this role.

Despite the usual requirement that proposed regulations be published for public comment, the process of promulgating regulations is much less visible than the legislative process. Most social workers are not aware that a regulation relevant to their practices has been drafted and do not know where to obtain copies of proposed regulations. Although the wide use of the Internet by administrative agencies is making the process of promulgating regulations more visible, few social workers know of or review the publications or Web sites where proposed regulations are published. As a result, few social workers impact the process—even though regulations may be of critical importance to social workers. To give just two examples, most rules for the administration of social welfare programs and most licensing standards, such as those for child care facilities and extended care facilities, are found in regulations. Social workers certainly have a vital interest in such regulations.

Perhaps the best way for you to learn of proposed regulations is to be a member of an interest group that monitors certain public agencies and informs its members of actions proposed or taken by the public agency. Examples are associations of private child care agencies, client advocacy groups, and associations of social workers. Such associations will often inform their members of proposed regulations and identify persons to whom comments should be directed. In addition, such associations will often be proactive, proposing regulatory changes to State and federal officials. Many associations are also posting proposed regulatory changes on the Internet.

Once you know that a regulation has been proposed, you can formally offer your comments in writing or seek to testify at any hearings on the regulation. Moreover, you can suggest possible regulatory changes either to an agency directly or to the interest groups with which you are affiliated.

What Should Be Promulgated as a Regulation?

Many agency rules, practices, and policies are not formally promulgated as regulations. Agencies have operation guidelines, statements of policies and plans, and internal directives that are never promulgated as regulations and, indeed, may not even be written down. These unpromulgated rules make things difficult for those outside the agency who must deal with the agency. If you have ever been thwarted by a government bureaucrat on the basis of an unknown, unwritten rule, you surely understand the problem. There have been many lawsuits in which it has been argued that an agency rule cannot be followed in a given case because it was never formally promulgated as a regulation. If the court in such a suit determines that the rule should have been promulgated as a regulation, the suit will be successful and the unpromulgated rule cannot be applied in the case, for example, to deny benefits or cause sanctions. Thus, if agency personnel wish a rule to be followed, they may have to promulgate it as a regulation. However, determining what rules must be formally promulgated as regulations is difficult. A general rule would be: rules of general applicability that would have a significant impact on members of the general public should be promulgated as regulations. A word of advice for social workers working in public agencies who may be responsible for drafting regulations would be: when in doubt, promulgate.

A Note on Executive Orders and Rules of Court Chief executives of governments, like the President, governors, and mayors, may also enact law by issuing **executive orders.** Executive orders are somewhat like regulations except that there may be no official promulgation process or officially designated publication in which they are published.

The executive may be specifically authorized to issue executive orders on a particular subject by a legislative body or may issue executive orders pursuant to the general powers inherent in the office of the executive. Executive orders prohibiting discrimination in awarding government contracts are examples of the latter.

Courts may also make laws, usually called **rules of court,** which are somewhat like regulations. Rules of court are formal, published rules regulating the operation of certain courts by, for example, prescribing the form of notice to use in a par-

ticular kind of lawsuit or setting forth the amount of a filing fee. Like regulations, rules of court may interpret or fill in the details of legislation.

Court-Made Law

The judicial branch of government sometimes makes law in the course of resolving disputes that go to courts. This court-made law is very important in America. We tend to think that judges do not and should not make law and, indeed, that it would be undemocratic for them to do so, but judges do make law. They do it all the time, and they have always done so in our country and in England, the source of our legal system. They do it in two main ways.

First, in the course of resolving a dispute, a court may have to interpret or add to laws that apply to the dispute. That is, a court may have to determine the meaning and scope of an applicable constitutional provision, statute, regulation, or other form of law; resolve a conflict between several applicable laws; or fill in the gaps in an applicable law. The process of interpreting existing laws in which a court engages is often called **construction.** When construction occurs, the courts make law. As we have said, the courts' construction of the law merges with the existing law, and the existing law alone is no longer the complete law on the subject.

Second, a dispute before a court may involve a novel fact situation or problem not addressed by any existing constitutional provision, legislation, regulation, or other law. To resolve the dispute, the court must make law. There are many areas of the law in America that have been totally developed by the courts in this way; there is no legislation on the subject but, over the years, court decisions have created a body of law on the subject. For example, most of the civil law relating to one person's liability for injuring another person, often referred to as **tort** liability, has been developed by the courts.

To understand the two main ways in which courts make law, consider the following example. In every State, based on law developed by the courts and found in statutes, doctors are liable for damages if their careless treatment injures their patients. This type of tort liability is known as **malpractice** liability. Now assume that a State has a statute that provides that an injured patient cannot sue a doctor for malpractice more than two years "after an injury."[9] Further assume that a patient from the State has been injured by a doctor's careless treatment but that the injury did not become apparent until three years after the treatment. In other words, as is not at all uncommon, the adverse effect of the treatment only appeared after the time to sue under the statute of limitations ostensibly had passed. Finally, assume the patient sued the doctor anyway, asserting that the statute of limitations can be read to allow a patient injured by a doctor's careless treatment to sue within two years of the time that the injury first appeared. To decide whether the patient's lawsuit should be allowed, the court in which the suit was filed must interpret the language of the statute of limitations. In doing so, the court makes law in the first way noted earlier. Whatever the court decides, its decision may become law.

Now assume that a social worker who works as a family therapist carelessly treated a client, causing the client psychological damage, and that the injured client sued the social worker for malpractice. It is clear in the State where the social worker treated the patient and where she was sued by him that if she were a medical doctor, she could be sued for malpractice, but no one has ever sued a therapist who was not a medical doctor for malpractice before in the State and there is no law on the subject. To decide whether or not the client's lawsuit should be allowed, the court in which the suit was filed must make law. In deciding if clients can sue social workers for malpractice, the court will be making law in the second way mentioned previously.

Law made by courts in the second way, particularly law that was developed by the courts in England and later brought to America and adapted to American needs, is often referred to as the **common law.** Law made in the first or second way may be called **case law** or **precedent.**

There are limits on courts' ability to make law. First, unlike legislative bodies and administrative agencies that may make law at any time, courts may only make law in the course of resolving disputes that are before them. Second, judges may not make law on the basis of their view of what is right and what is wrong while legislators and administrators can make law on this basis or on the basis of whim, prejudice, public opinion, pressure, political expediency, and so on. Courts may only make law based on a process called common-law reasoning, which will be explained later in this chapter. Third, courts are limited in the kind of law they can make. They cannot

---

9. This kind of statute is known as a **statute of limitations** because it establishes limits on bringing lawsuits. Statutes of limitations are quite common.

appropriate money. They cannot establish social programs. They cannot establish regulatory schemes like social work licensing laws or toxic waste transportation rules. And, they usually cannot mandate how something must be done. They may determine that something was done improperly and what the consequences should be, but they will not specify how it can be done properly.

Despite these limitations on courts' ability to make law, a court can exercise a powerful influence on other law-making entities. For example, although a court cannot appropriate money or create a social program, a court decision that counties are obligated to provide shelter for the homeless may force county boards to appropriate money and establish a shelter program. To give another example, a court cannot establish a regulatory program, but a court decision that social workers may not be sued for malpractice may make a legislature enact a social worker licensing law.

Moreover, courts may review and invalidate the laws and actions of the other branches of government. They have the final authority to decide what is and what is not constitutional, thus, they can invalidate actions or legislation as unconstitutional.

Case law is the law, but, like a regulation, it may be overruled by legislation—except insofar as it interprets a constitution. The courts are the ultimate interpreters of constitutions and the legislative or the executive cannot force their own interpretation on the courts. For example, assume a State court rules that a battered woman who kills her husband may not use the battered woman syndrome as a defense to a charge of murder. This ruling will be the law in the State. If, however, the State legislature disagrees with this ruling and be-

lieves that the battered woman syndrome should be allowed as a defense, it may pass a statute to this effect and thus overrule the court decision. But if the court had ruled that the battered woman syndrome is a constitutionally mandated defense, the legislature could not pass a statute that overruled the court decision by saying the defense could not be allowed.

Before you can fully understand how courts make law and the law they make, understanding the structure of the court system in America is necessary. And before you can fully understand the structure of the court system, you must understand the relation between the federal and State legal systems. Let us, then, turn to those subjects.

THE FEDERAL AND STATE BALANCE

The relationship between the federal and State governments is established by the Constitution. This relationship is often misunderstood. Many people think that the federal government may make law on any subject it chooses and that any law the federal government may make is superior to the law made by State governments on the subject. The former is not true, however, and the latter is often not the case. Apart from the supremacy of the Constitution over all State (and other federal) law, all areas of the law fall into one, and only one, of the following four categories:

Category One: There is exclusively federal law on the subject.

Category Two: There is both federal and State law on the

Category Three: subject, with the federal law superior. There is both federal and State law on the subject, with neither law superior.

Category Four: There is exclusively State law on the subject.

Determining which category an area of the law falls into is not always easy (even for lawyers), but a few basic constitutional principles and some simple guidelines may prove helpful.

It is a basic constitutional principle that the federal government may only act in those areas in which it has been given a power to act by the Constitution. It is also a basic constitutional principle, expressly set forth in the Tenth Amendment to the Constitution, that the "powers not delegated to the United States by the Constitution nor prohibited by it to the states are reserved to the states respectively, or to the people." In other words, the United States has a system of dual sovereignty with different powers resting in the federal government and the States.

Because the Constitution gives the federal government only a few specific powers (like providing for the national security and establishing a national system of currency), most of the sovereign powers rest with the States and, thus, most areas of the law fall into category four (i.e., the law is exclusively State law). However, many areas of the law fall into category three (i.e., there is both federal and State law in the area, with neither law superior) because the Constitution gives Congress, the chief lawmaking body of the federal government, some general powers

that have been broadly interpreted to allow Congress to legislate in areas traditionally reserved to the States.

For example, Article I, Section 8, of the Constitution gives Congress the power to "provide for the general welfare of the United States" and to "make all laws necessary and proper" to execute its specific powers. Pursuant to these general powers, particularly the welfare power, since the 1930s, beginning with Roosevelt's New Deal, Congress has been enacting more and more social legislation covering subjects traditionally reserved for the States, such as foster care or substance abuse treatment.

Congress's general powers are not seen as unlimited, however, and claims of "States' rights" have inhibited the federal government from making law in areas traditionally reserved for the States. If the federal government does enact a law in any of these areas, the law probably only covers a small aspect of the law in the area. For example, almost all law governing the care and support of children has traditionally been and remains State law, but the federal government has enacted a law to aid in collection of child support across State lines and to ensure that children receiving federal welfare benefits get child support.

Thus, the States continue to make almost all of the law in the areas traditionally reserved to the States and in which the federal government may only act pursuant to Congress's general powers. And although Article VI of the Constitution provides that both the Constitution and "the Laws of the United States" are "the Supreme Law of the Land," the limited federal law in these areas is generally not considered superior to State law. This is because the courts are often reluctant to find federal supremacy in an area of the law traditionally reserved to the States and because there often is no need for consistency between federal and State laws or for uniformity among the States in a particular area of the law. Even if there is extensive federal law in an area of the law (such as in criminal law), inconsistent federal and State laws may exist side by side and the laws may differ from State to State without causing any problems. Federal supremacy may yield because there is no need for it.

There are, however, areas of the law in which federal and State law can and should both exist, but there is some need for consistency between federal and State law and for uniformity among the States. Laws in these areas fall into category two (i.e., there is both federal and State law in the area, but federal law is superior). For example, both the federal government and the States may appropriately make laws related to occupational health and safety, but because many employers operate in more than one State or are involved in interstate commerce, there is some need for consistency and uniformity. Thus, federal law on this subject is superior.

Laws also fall into category two if the federal government, pursuant to its general or specific powers, puts conditions on a State's receipt of federal funds for a specific purpose or establishes the rules for a State's participation in a federal program. Federal law will be supreme to the extent that the State has accepted the funds or is participating in the program.

For example, a State that has accepted federal highway funds must set the drinking age in the State at twenty-one years because this has been made a condition

on the receipt of federal highway funds by Congress. To give another example, over the years, the federal government has established many programs providing cash benefits or special services to those in need of financial or other kinds of assistance. These programs are often administered and partially funded by the States and the States have been free to adopt or reject the programs. But if a State adopts a federal program, its laws relating to the administration of the program must be consistent with federal law.

This type of supremacy of federal law (i.e., one linked to federal funds or a federal program) is limited, however, to the specific terms of any condition on the receipt of federal funds or to any specific program in which the State is participating. And inconsistencies between State and federal law that cause no problems and that do not defeat the purposes of federal law may be tolerated.

For example, a State can have any drinking age it wants but, as has been stated, if a State wants federal highway funds, it must set the drinking age at twenty-one years. However, just because the federal government has legislated on the drinking age, federal law is not supreme over other State laws related to drinking (e.g., laws establishing when bars close and who can go to bars) or over other State laws related to age (e.g., the age to marry or quit school).

Consider another example. If a State is receiving federal funds to operate a special substance abuse program, it must have eligibility rules that are consistent with the federal laws governing this program, but a State can have its own substance abuse programs that have their own eligibility rules as long as the programs are not funded by the federal government. And a State may be able to establish its own eligibility rules for a federally funded substance abuse program and serve those who are not eligible under federal law as long as it does not use federal funds to provide the services. A State may even be able to impose special eligibility requirements in the federally funded part of its special federal substance abuse program as long as the eligibility requirements do not conflict with the federal law and serve the federal purpose.

Even where an area of the law falls into category two not because of a link with federal funds or a federal program but because there is an overall need for consistency between federal and State law and uniformity among the States, some inconsistencies and differences between federal and State law may not cause any problems and do not defeat the purposes of federal law. These inconsistencies and differences may be tolerated. As with category three, federal supremacy may yield, but, in category two, federal supremacy yields only for specific laws within the area of law, not the whole area of the law.

For example, the federal law on occupational health and safety is supreme, but this law does not apply to small employers who are not in interstate commerce. The States may make their own laws for such employers without regard for federal standards. And, even for larger, interstate employers, the States may be allowed to impose certain standards that are more stringent than federal law. Similarly, federal law establishes a minimum wage for most employees, but States may establish a higher minimum wage for these employees and may establish a lower wage

for any employees not covered by the federal law.

Whether an area of the law falls into category two because of the need for consistency and uniformity or because of federal funding and federal programs, the federal law on the subject may be extremely limited and most of the law in the area may be State law. This also depends on how broadly you define an "area" of law. For example, although there is federal law on occupational health and safety and establishing a minimum wage, and although there is important federal law relating to discrimination in employment, the bulk of the law governing the employment relationship is State law. And, although there are federal programs for treatment of substance abuse, most law relating to treatment for physical and mental health problems, including substance abuse, is State law.

Only a few areas of the law fall into category one (i.e., the law in the area is exclusively federal law). Laws fall into category one in those limited areas where the federal government has an express power to act or where the States should not act because there should be only one uniform law on the subject for the whole country. For example, only the federal government can and should regulate immigration from other countries. Thus, State laws on immigration that may impact federal immigration policy, like State laws keeping American born children of illegal immigrants from public schools, are generally not allowed. Congress can, however, allow State laws on immigration or on any subject within the power of Congress.

Laws also fall into category one in a few other areas in which the courts have determined that the federal government has **occupied the field** so that there is no room for conflicting or even consistent State law. Another way to say this is that federal law has **preempted** State law. Total federal preemption is rare, particularly in areas of the law of interest to social workers. Most of the areas of law that have been preempted relate either to interstate business (like labor union law or bankruptcy) or relations with other countries (like immigration or international trade) and are areas that traditionally have not been within the sovereign power of the States.

To summarize, most laws fall into category four (i.e., they are exclusively State laws). More and more law is falling into categories two and three (i.e., there is both federal and State law on the subject), but the federal law in these categories is often quite limited and not considered superior to the State law. In particular, if a federal law is enacted pursuant to Congress's general powers in an area that has traditionally been exclusively reserved to the States, if there is no need for consistency between federal and State law or uniformity among the States in this area of the law, and if the federal law is not tied to a specific federal program or federal funds, the federal law is probably not supreme. In other words, more laws fall into category three than category two. Only a few laws fall into category one.

When specific areas of the law are discussed in this text, we will tell you in which category the areas fall. In your practice, you can use the guidelines provided in this section to try to determine if federal or State law applies. In doing so, you should remember that there may not be, and, in fact, probably will not be fed-

eral law on a subject and that, if there is federal law, it probably will not govern State law unless the federal law is tied to funds given to the States.

THE AMERICAN COURT SYSTEM

In America, there is a federal court system and more than fifty State court systems.[10] These systems all have different features, but all of them are basically alike. In all of these systems, there are **trial courts** and **appellate courts** that perform certain distinct functions.

Trial Courts

Trial courts resolve disputes. Each separate dispute that a trial court resolves is called a **case** or **suit.** With very rare exceptions, as between trial and appellate courts, cases begin in trial courts. With no exceptions, trial courts: 1) only decide cases that are brought before them by those involved—they do not initiate cases; 2) do not decide cases when there is no actual dispute between real individuals or entities—they do not issue so called advisory opinions; and 3) will not decide cases brought by persons who do not have a real interest in the case or if a court decision is not yet required to resolve a dispute. This necessary interest of a party bringing a case is referred to as **standing**; the necessity of a court decision is called **ripeness.**

---

10. Remember, the term *State* in this book encompasses areas like the District of Columbia and Puerto Rico.

Consider this example to help you understand these concepts and terms. Imagine that a big lumber company has bought some land in northern California that contains an old-growth redwood forest. A judge in southern California may believe that the company intends to log the forest and that logging would violate a law restricting logging of old-growth redwoods, but she cannot initiate a case against the company in her official capacity. She would also not be able to pursue a case against the company as a private citizen if she has no interest in the land or the redwoods except the interest of any other concerned citizen. She would have no standing to challenge any logging on the land. And even if she or another citizen had standing, unless the company had made its intention to log the forest clear, there would be no actual dispute and the court would not decide a case against the company simply to issue an advisory opinion on the legality of logging the land. Moreover, even if the company had made its intention to log the land clear, the court would still not decide a case against the company if the company has to obtain a permit to log the forest. Because the company might not get the permit, a court decision might not be necessary and the case would not be ripe.

Cases must be initiated in a proper court, both in terms of the geographical reach of the court and the ability of the court to rule on the matter in dispute. Both the geographical reach of a court and its authority to rule on the matter in dispute are referred to as the court's **jurisdiction.** Jurisdiction is an important concept in law. In order to consider a case, a court must have at least two different kinds of jurisdiction: **subject matter jurisdiction,** that is, jurisdiction over the type of issues involved in the dispute; and **personal jurisdiction,** that is, geographical or territorial jurisdiction over the parties to the dispute. Courts must also have geographical jurisdiction over any property or other matters in dispute (such as a house that is sought by both parties to a divorce or a child who is the subject of an adoption petition).

Federal trial courts have extremely limited subject matter jurisdiction. They may only resolve disputes in a few kinds of cases. Of particular importance, they may decide cases in which the federal government is involved or there is a **federal question** (i.e., a question of federal law). They may also decide some cases in which the parties are from different States, that is, there is **diversity of citizenship.** Because, as we said, federal law is limited, federal question jurisdiction is limited. Diversity jurisdiction is also quite limited to certain disputes about money.

State trial courts usually have subject matter jurisdiction over every kind of case, including those that may involve federal law, except for a few types of cases that are exclusively federal, such as bankruptcy cases. Many States, however, have two levels of trial courts. Their lower level trial courts usually have jurisdiction only over less serious criminal cases and over cases involving disputes about money of less than a certain amount, while their higher level trial courts usually have jurisdiction over all other cases. Further, some States have one or more specialized trial courts that have jurisdiction only over special kinds of cases, while other trial courts have jurisdiction over all but these special kind of cases. For example, some States have special trial courts that only hear cases involving family law; other trial courts in these States have no jurisdiction over such cases. If a State has two levels of trial courts, there may be specialized courts at either or both levels. Some typical specialized courts of importance to social workers are: 1) **family courts**—courts that hear divorces, adoptions, and other family matters, and in some States, such as New York, juvenile matters; 2) **probate courts**—courts that deal with estates after death and often with guardianships, and in some States, like Michigan, juvenile matters and commitments of the mentally disabled; 3) **chancery courts** or **courts of equity**—courts that resolve civil cases involving claims for something other than money damages, like an injunction; 4) **courts of claims**—courts that resolve claims for money against the government; 5) **small claims courts**—low-level courts that resolve disputes between individuals involving small amounts of money and that typically have simplified procedures so that lawyers may not be necessary (indeed, in some States, like California, lawyers are not even allowed); and 6) **housing courts**—low-level courts that resolve simple landlord-tenant matters.

Sometimes, trial courts resolve the cases that are brought before them as a matter of law without having a trial. If they conduct a trial, they resolve a case by deciding the facts and by applying the law to the facts they have decided. They decide facts by listening to testimony, looking at documents and examining objects—in other words, by receiving **evidence.** They determine what evidence to receive, how it must be presented, and the facts in accordance with the law.

Appellate Courts

A party who believes a trial court made an error in deciding a case generally has a right to **appeal** the final judgement in the case to a higher court (i.e., to have the decision reviewed by an appellate court). The party who appeals generally argues that the trial court made an error of law in the way it decided the facts or applied the law or that the facts do not support the conclusion. Appellate courts do not receive evidence or decide facts (except for those rare instances when they act like trial courts in cases of great importance). They look at the record that was made of the proceedings in the trial court and decide questions of law based on this record. An appellate court may decide that a trial court had insufficient evidence to determine a certain fact or that a trial court failed to make a determination on a relevant fact, but, even in these situations, an appellate court will not receive additional evidence or decide the facts itself. Instead, if the trial court's error was significant, the appellate court will overturn (or **reverse**) the trial court's decision and send the case back to the trial court to decide it again. If the trial court made no significant mistake, the appellate court will sustain (or **affirm**) the trial court's decision.

In the federal system and most State systems, there are two levels of appellate courts: an intermediate court, usually called a **court of appeals**; and a court of last resort, usually called a **supreme court.** A court of appeals generally must hear all properly appealed cases (i.e., cases in which there is a timely appeal of an order or judgment from which an appeal is allowed). However, a supreme court generally has discretion to refuse cases. Because most supreme courts are asked to decide many more cases than they have time to decide, a supreme court's decision to accept or refuse a case may have nothing to do with its view of the correctness of the lower court's decision; it may only reflect its view of the importance of the decision.

Generally, cases are appealed from a trial court to an intermediate appellate court and from there to the supreme court of a jurisdiction. A few cases may be appealed directly from a trial court to the supreme court. In some States that have two levels of trial courts, cases heard in the lower-level trial court may be appealed only to the higher-level trial court. When hearing such appeals, the higher-level trial court acts as an appellate court.

The Federal and State Court Systems

The State and federal court systems are parallel systems. Cases do not go back and forth from one system to another. A party may never appeal from a State trial court to a federal appeals court. However, if a party is not happy with a decision of a court of last resort in a State court system and if there is a federal question raised by the case, the party may seek review in the United States Supreme Court.

Most cases are filed and remain in State court systems. As has been noted, federal courts have limited jurisdiction. They may hear far fewer cases than State courts. Furthermore, many disputes that may be heard in federal courts may also be resolved in State courts, at the option of the parties. Moreover, even if the parties chose to go to federal court or a federal law is involved in a case, a federal court may de-

cline jurisdiction if State law is of prime importance in the case. Declining jurisdiction to let a State court decide is known as **abstention.** Finally, even if a federal court has and accepts jurisdiction over a civil case, it may not be able to give the parties complete relief and may not be able to resolve the case fully. Federal courts cannot make many types of orders that people regularly seek in civil court actions, such as orders for a divorce, an adoption, an appointment of a guardian for a developmentally disabled relative, and so on. Usually, only State courts may make such orders.

Diagram 1.1. may help you understand the relationship between the State and federal courts in America and how the State and federal courts are structured. Some State court systems have structures different than what is shown on the diagram. For example, they may only have one level of appellate courts or, as has been stated, they may have two levels of trial courts with the higher level functioning as an appellate court for cases from the lower level.

As shown in the diagram, federal trial courts are called **United States District Courts.** There is at least one District Court in every State. There may be several judges and court buildings for each District Court. The bigger States may have several districts and District Courts, each of which may have several judges and several court buildings. For example, the federal trial court in Charlotte, North Carolina, is known as the United States District Court for the Western District of North Carolina. It has two judges and encompasses several cities and areas of North Carolina outside of Charlotte, including Asheville, which, like Charlotte, has a federal courthouse. There are also

Diagram 1.1

THE AMERICAN COURT STRUCTURE

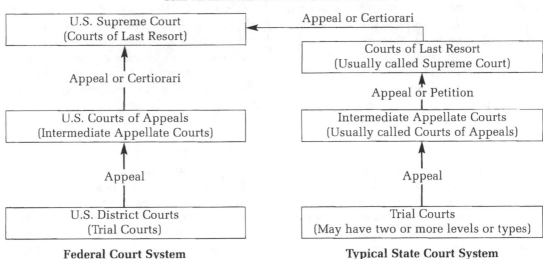

Federal Court System

Typical State Court System

Eastern and Middle Districts of North Carolina encompassing Raleigh (and other cities). By way of contrast, South Carolina has only one district, but it has judges and courts in several cities.

State trial courts have different names in different States. In many States with two levels of trial courts, the lower-level courts are called **district courts, city courts,** or **municipal courts,** and the higher-level courts are called **circuit courts, county courts,** or **superior courts.** The names of any specialized trial courts also differ from State to State.

As in diagram 1.1, federal intermediate appellate courts are called **United States Courts of Appeals.** They are also sometimes referred to as **Circuit Courts of Appeals** because there are thirteen divisions, known as **circuits,** of the United States Courts of Appeals. Eleven of the circuits cover particular geographical regions en-

compassing several States or territories. One circuit covers the District of Columbia. In addition, there is a special Circuit Court of Appeals for special kinds of cases.

There are many appellate judges in each circuit of the United States Court of Appeals. Usually, only three judges in the circuit, selected on a random or rotational basis, hear and decide each appeal. The judges who hear a case are known as the **panel.** If all the judges hear a case, it is said to have been decided **en banc.**

State intermediate appellate courts are usually divided into divisions, districts, or circuits. As with United States Courts of Appeals, there may be many judges in each division, but usually only three or some other small number of judges serve as the panel for each appeal.

There is only one United States Supreme Court. It has nine judges who are referred to as **justices** (as are many State appellate judges). All nine generally hear and decide each case. To have a case heard and decided by the Supreme Court, depending on the nature of the case and the court from which review is sought, one either appeals to the Court or asks the Court to grant discretionary review through something called a **petition for a writ of certiorari.** The Supreme Court only takes a tiny percentage of the cases in which certiorari is sought.[11]

All of the States but Texas have only one court of last resort, usually called the supreme court. State supreme courts usually have nine or fewer justices. While the State supreme court is the last court to which one can appeal on questions of State law (shown in diagram 1.1), one can appeal to or seek a writ of certiorari from the Supreme Court in State cases raising federal constitutional or federal law questions.

Court Opinions

For the most part, when they decide cases, trial courts do not write opinions setting forth their reasons for deciding as they did. If they do write opinions, generally they will not be published in books available to the general public. (Federal trial courts and higher-level trial courts in New York, known as supreme courts, and in a few other States sometimes write and publish their opinions.) Appellate courts usually do write opinions that are published in books available to the public. Only published opinions create law that affects people in addition to the parties to

a case. This law is created using the common law reasoning process discussed below.

COMMON LAW REASONING

The starting point in deciding a case for any court, whether a trial or an appellate court, is to determine if there is any existing law that controls the result. The court must look first for an applicable constitutional provision, legislation, or regulation. If it finds none, it looks to **case law** or **precedent**, that is, the law which is found in published court opinions. It examines and applies this law by using the common law reasoning process.

The common law reasoning process is a process of reasoning by analogy. When using this process, a court looks for previously published cases with facts similar to the facts of the case it is currently deciding. It follows the rulings of law in these similar cases in deciding the case before it. Judges are required to follow rulings in similar cases in deciding the cases before them by the doctrine of *stare decisis,* which means "stand by decisions." Under the doctrine of *stare decisis,* if a prior case has significant facts that are analogous to the facts of the case before a court, a court in the same jurisdiction as the court that decided the analogous case and lower in the hierarchy is required to follow the rulings of law in the analogous case and come to the same result. The earlier analogous case establishes the precedent. A court in a different jurisdiction or at the same or a higher level in the hierarchy than the court that decided an analogous case is not required

---

11. Hereinafter, the capitalized term *Supreme Court,* standing alone, will be used to refer only to the United States Supreme Court.

to follow the case under the doctrine of *stare decisis* but generally will do so unless substantial considerations dictate a different result. Such a case is considered persuasive, although it is not binding.

Stare decisis is not an absolute principle; courts may depart from precedent on occasion. Yet, *stare decisis* is the rule in the vast majority of cases for two important reasons. Because of *stare decisis,* like cases are treated alike and people can know in advance the consequences of their actions. To the extent that a court deviates from *stare decisis,* it is not treating like cases alike and is changing the rules after people have acted, which would be contrary to most people's conception of justice.

The difficulty in using the doctrine of *stare decisis* is determining what facts in a prior case are significant and if they are analogous to the facts in the case before the court. No two cases are ever exactly alike. Only if it is determined that the facts are sufficiently similar in a prior case and the case before the court, and only if these similar facts are determined to be significant, should the prior case serve as precedent. But these determinations may not be easy. This difficulty, and the entire process of common law reasoning, may best be understood by using one case as an example.

Assume that Ms. Green, who lives in an apartment building in State X, was injured when she was assaulted in the public hallway of her apartment building. Although no statute, regulation, or ordinance in X provides that a tenant may sue a landlord for such injuries, Green sued her landlord, Mr. Black. She claimed that Black had a duty to make the building safe, that he breached this duty, and that

he was, thus, liable to her for her injuries. The trial judge ruled that Black had no duty to keep Green safe from criminals and decided the case in favor of Black. Green appealed the judgment to the X Court of Appeals.[12]

To decide Green's appeal, since no legislation or regulation applies, the justices would look for analogous cases from X. Cases from other States would only be persuasive, not binding. And, since the duty of a landlord to a tenant does not present a federal constitutional or statutory issue, the court would not look for federal cases, including Supreme Court cases. The court would probably look first for opinions of the X Supreme Court and then for cases from its division of the X Court of Appeals. In many States and in the federal system, courts are only bound by *stare decisis* to follow the opinions of the courts of appeals in their own divisions. Each division is treated, in effect, as its own jurisdiction.

Assume that the court finds only one decision mentioning a landlord's duty to a tenant in the common areas of an apartment building, *Blue v. Brown.* In *Blue,* a tenant, named Blue, sued his landlord, named Brown, when he was injured falling on a broken step leading to the building. The X Supreme Court ruled that a landlord has a duty to keep the common

---

12. This example is based on a case called *Kline v. 1500 Massachusetts Avenue Corporation,* from the District of Columbia. The citation to this case is: 439 F.2d 447 (D.C. Cir 1970). We will explain citation form in chapter 4. We will also discuss case names in chapter 4. For now, you should know that a case name often takes the form of the names of the opposing parties separated by a *v.,* meaning versus, and that the name is always underlined or put in italics. Thus, Green's case would probably be known as *Green v. Black.*

parts of an apartment building in reasonably safe condition and that Brown was, thus, liable for Blue's injuries.

Although the *Blue* facts are somewhat similar to those in *Green,* the court may not be bound by *stare decisis* to follow *Blue. Blue* dealt with dangerous physical conditions of a building, not its security. Moreover, in *Green* there was an intervening criminal act by a third person. The *Green* court would have to decide if these differences were significant. Whatever it decides, it will make law. Either the *Blue* precedent will be **extended** to the *Green* facts, and landlords in X will have a duty to keep their property safe and secure, or *Blue* will be **distinguished,** and landlords in X will have a duty only to keep their property free from dangerous physical conditions. Either way, *Green* will establish a new precedent that must be followed in later analogous cases.

This new precedent will not have come out of thin air. The new precedent established by *Green* must follow logically from *Blue.* The common law reasoning process and the doctrine of *stare decisis* allow courts to make law but only by building on previous law. There must be a sound and principled reason for the *Green* justices to extend or distinguish *Blue.* Judges should not decide cases based on their own notions of right and wrong. They may refer to history, custom, common sense, logic, and social policy, but their primary reference should be to prior cases. Even if no prior cases are binding as precedent, prior cases contain general principles that provide guidance to courts. Courts may not depart from the accumulated wisdom found in the common law, which should develop slowly, incrementally, and logically, not by great leaps and flights of fancy. Changes in the law should be firmly grounded in existing law.

Nevertheless, the justices' personal beliefs as to what is right or wrong can influence decision making. Even if a court finds a precedent that logically points in a particular direction, the court is not likely to extend that precedent to the case before it if the result will produce a decision that is contrary to the justices' view of the "correct" decision. If past precedent is clearly analogous, the justices' determination of law has largely been made for them. Thus, if instead of *Blue,* the *Green* court found the case of *White v. Tan,* in which the X Court of Appeals ruled that a landlord, named Tan, was liable to a tenant, named White, who was attacked in the parking area of his duplex, the court would have no choice but to follow *White*—even if *White* was decided decades ago and the *Green* justices would not have reached the same result if the case were before them as a matter of first impression. *White* is just not distinguishable from *Green.* But precedent is not always as analogous as *White,* or even *Blue,* is to *Green.* A court may be able to distinguish past cases and need only be bound by their general principles. And these principles may point in different directions, allowing the court to decide as it wishes. For example, if instead of finding *Blue* or *White,* the *Green* court found *Orange v. Gray Bank,* in which the X Supreme Court ruled that a bank was liable when a customer was injured during a bank robbery, and *Red v. Azure Inn,* in which the X Supreme Court ruled that a hotel was not liable when a guest was injured by a drunk driver who drove into the pool area, the *Green* judges could probably decide *Green* as they chose. Both *Orange* and *Red* are distinguishable from *Green,* but could provide guidance to the *Green* justices. The guidance in *Orange,* however, could lead to a different result in *Green* than the guidance in *Red.*

Moreover, in extraordinary circumstances, a court equal to or above the court that decided a precedent could decide that the precedent was indistinguishable but nevertheless refuse to follow it. The court could **overturn** or **overrule** it as precedent. *Stare decisis* requires adherence to past precedent without regard to a court's view of the precedent's correctness. A court would, however, be justified in overruling a prior case if its rationale is no longer sound because of scientific developments or changes in society, or if it is based on assumptions that have been proven inaccurate or on societal beliefs that no longer prevail.

Thus, a court has some freedom in deciding cases, but the justices' ability to make law is restricted by the common law reasoning process and by the doctrine of *stare decisis.* Moreover, a court's creative capacity is limited by the doctrine of *stare decisis* to the particular fact situation before it. If judges reach out and address questions not presented by the cases before them, their answers to the questions will not make law. *Stare decisis* requires adherence only to courts' **holdings,** that is, their rulings as to those matters that had to be settled to decide cases. A holding is limited to the facts before the court. Comments made by a court that are not essential to deciding the case before it are called *dicta* (or, in the singular, *dictum*). *Dicta* are not binding on later courts under the doctrine of *stare decisis.*

To illustrate, *Blue v. Brown,* previously mentioned in the *Green* example, dealt with unsafe physical conditions, not security measures. Thus, *Blue*'s holding was only that a landlord has a duty to repair dangerous physical conditions. Since the issue of security measures was not before the *Blue* court, any judicial comment about security measures in *Blue* would have been unnecessary to the court's ruling. Even if the *Blue* court had thought about security measures and commented on them in rendering its decision, the comments would be *dicta* and *stare decisis* would not apply to them. The *Green* justices could ignore these comments.

The common law reasoning process, as described in the *Green* case, was used in the situation where there was no legislation, regulation, or constitutional provision available to help decide the case. But, a court may also have to use the common law reasoning process when such law is available. For example, precedent may be used to determine the meaning of a general constitutional provision, to determine the scope of a statute, or to interpret a regulation.

We will look at the use of precedent in interpreting the Constitution in chapter 5. Let us now look to the common law reasoning process when a statute or several statutes appear applicable to a case. The process would be the same for other forms of legislation and for regulations.

If a statute's applicability to a case is obvious, if its language is clear, and if it is sufficiently detailed to resolve the case, the common law reasoning process will not be necessary. But this is not often the situation. Several different and conflicting statutes might all seem to apply to a case. The "plain meaning" of a statutory provision is not always plain; frequently, there will be several conflicting interpretations that can be reasonably drawn from statutory language. Few statutes are detailed enough to answer all questions that may arise. Thus, even though a statute or several statutes appear applicable to a case, the court may have to look beyond the statutory language to resolve the case. The first place the court would be required to look is at the purpose of the legislature in enacting the relevant statutes, that is, the **legislative intent.**

To determine the legislative purpose for federal statutes and for statutes of a few States, courts may use the **legislative history** provided by recorded debates and committee reports. In most jurisdictions, however, such recorded history will not be available. Even if it is available, it may not be dispositive. Often, legislatures have never considered a situation that has arisen. Courts, thus, must infer the legislative intent. They may infer it from their reading of the statute as a whole, from their understanding of the societal claims and demands that gave rise to the statute, and from their determination of the overall objective of the entire statutory scheme in which the statute is found, if any. But often a court will infer the legislative intent by examining precedent interpreting similar statutes, dealing with analogous situations, or establishing general principles of the law. This is where the common law reasoning process and the doctrine of *stare decisis* come in.

For example, assume that after full debate, all of which was recorded and has been maintained, the legislature in the State of X adopted a statute providing that landlords have a duty to keep their buildings "safe." Seemingly, this statute would resolve the *Green* case, but the word "safe" is unclear. The landlord in *Green* may argue vigorously that the legislature did not mean "safe" to include "secure." Recorded legislative history is no help to the court in deciding if the landlord is correct. The legislature was not thinking about security measures when it passed the statute and nothing was said about them. The legislature only discussed dangerous physical conditions. Thus, the court must determine what the legislature would have done if it had thought about security measures. It does this by looking at the entire statutory scheme related to landlords, at other statutes talking about duties to keep people safe, and at precedent—specifically at cases that establish general principles that can guide its determination of the meaning of the word *safe*. In other words, the court will use the common law reasoning process to infer the legislative intent and interpret the statute.

The process of common law reasoning and the doctrine of *stare decisis* may seem difficult or confusing to you now, but common law reasoning is really a simple process of reasoning by analogy and *stare decisis* is really a simple rule that a court must follow the law as stated in previous cases in the court's jurisdiction—even when a court is developing new law. The process and the rule will become clearer to you as you read more court opinions.

The Hearing Process

As part of their professional responsibilities, many social workers will play a role in a hearing in a trial court or before an administrative agency in the course of their career. Social workers often describe their roles in hearings as challenging and stressful or express frustration with the hearing process and the attorneys who dominate it. If you understand the basic nature and mechanics of the hearing process and the roles you and other participants may play in trial court or administrative hearings, however, you can perform your role effectively and confidently. In addition, if you understand how trial courts operate you can better understand the case law that develops from appeals of trial court decisions. This chapter is designed to acquaint you with the hearing process in courts and before administrative agencies, while the next chapter will focus on your possible roles in the process.

THE BASIC NATURE OF THE HEARING PROCESS

The basic nature of court and administrative hearings in America stems from the principles embodied in three terms: **adversarial, accusatorial,** and **fair.** Thus, in order to understand the hearing process, examining each term is necessary.

Adversarial

Courts in America resolve legal disputes through an adversarial process. With such a process, each party to a dispute presents and argues its case and a neutral decision maker (either a judge or a jury) decides who should prevail in light of the opposing presentations and arguments. At the trial level, the parties to a dispute each present their version of the facts to the decision maker who determines the "true" facts. The parties also present their opposing views on what law should be used to resolve the dispute to the judge who determines the "correct" law and then either applies this law to decide the facts or directs the jury to apply this law to decide the facts. At the appellate level, the parties do not present evidence to establish their version of the facts and the decision makers (who are a panel of appellate justices) do not determine the facts, but the parties do argue that certain facts are or are not significant, that certain facts were or were not established by the evidence, and that certain characterizations of the facts are or are not accurate. And, at the appellate level, the parties present their opposing views on what law should have been used by the trial judge to resolve the dispute to the justices who determine the "correct" law and then apply this law to decide if the judge made any errors.[1]

Whether at the trial or appellate level, in an adversarial system the opposing parties act as advocates for their positions. Each party is given the opportunity to present its side of the story, that is, to

---

1. Of course, in America, the parties generally act through an attorney. The lawyers rather than the parties themselves present evidence or argue the law, particularly in appellate courts. However, for convenience and because, as we shall see, the parties are not always represented by an attorney, in this chapter we will just say the parties must do or are doing something.

have its "day in court." The opposing parties frame the issues, advance their interpretation of the law, and, at the trial level, seek out and choose the evidence that they will present. The decision makers do not develop the case. An assumption is made that material presented by the opposing sides will fully develop the relevant facts, accurately present the law, and permit the decision makers to reach an impartial and rational conclusion.

An adversarial system operates fairly only if each side has the capacity to present its case fully and if the opposing sides have roughly equal capacities. A primary criticism of the system is that neither this capacity nor this equality always exists, particularly if one party is poorer than the other or a government agency opposes an ordinary citizen. The government, critics argue, has so many resources that it can overpower all but a few private opponents, and a rich opponent can generally overpower a poor one.

The American adversarial system is also criticized because partisan advocacy is not seen as the best way to arrive at the truth. Some people point out that partisans may suppress evidence that hurts their case or take other actions to prevent a determination of the truth. People who are accustomed to the scientific method cannot accept that the truth will be revealed through the unscientific process of partisan advocacy. Further, the formality and rigidness of the rules that determine what the parties may present as evidence in a trial and how this evidence may be presented (i.e., the **rules of evidence**) are seen by many people as artificial barriers to truth-seeking and contribute to the perception of a trial as something other than a truth-seeking process. The rules of evidence may make a trial seem more like a game than a way to reveal the truth.

The adversarial system is also criticized because it is not seen as the best way to achieve a just outcome. Critics state that when emphasis is placed on winning or losing, compromises may be ignored and creative solutions to problems will not be sought. Some say that victory is the goal rather than justice; they see the process as more like a battle than a problem solving method. And, they say that the winner of the battle may be the party with the best lawyer who best manipulates the rules—not the party with the best case.

The O. J. Simpson case highlighted these criticisms of the adversarial system, but the case was an exception in many ways. In the usual case, these criticisms are not wholly justified or may be counterbalanced by other considerations. There are advantages to an adversarial system, and partisan advocacy, like that seen in the O. J. Simpson case, is not the only way legal disputes are resolved in America.

Most trials in America are not jury trials and most legal disputes, including criminal cases, are settled without any kind of trial. Indeed, many legal disputes are resolved before they even become lawsuits. Further, **alternative dispute resolution** methods (often referred to as ADR), like **mediation** and **arbitration**, are being used more of the time and in more situations to resolve legal disputes before or after they become lawsuits.[2]

---

2. *Mediation* is an attempt to resolve disputes in a nonadversarial fashion, with a mediator facilitating the resolution, not deciding the issues. *Arbitration* may be similar to mediation, but the arbitrator will decide the facts or may be like an informal trial with the arbitrator acting like a judge and jury.

If a legal dispute does become a lawsuit and if the lawsuit is not settled before a trial, partisan advocacy will be used to resolve the case. Such partisan advocacy may be the best way to protect and promote the parties' interests at the trial. If the parties had to rely on others to present their stories, their stories might not be told. If the parties had no one to act as their advocates, their desires might be ignored, which would be the case particularly when an ordinary citizen was involved in a dispute with the government.

In an **inquisitorial system,** a system used instead of an adversarial system, there is no partisan advocacy and the "judge has the responsibility to 'arrive at the truth by his own exertions in conjunction with those of the official prosecutor.' "[3] In such a system, in a case involving the government, the government gets to present, not only its own side of the story, but also its opponent's side—and gets to act as the judge and jury. This seems unfair and, in fact, experimental studies have shown that "an adversary form of presentation, in contradistinction to an inquisitorial presentation, counteracts bias in decisionmakers."[4]

Partisan advocacy, thus, may lead to the best outcome. And, people may have the greatest confidence in the decision-making process if they know they may argue for their positions and present their cases as they wish—without relying on the government.

Finally, although the rules of evidence may sometimes seem to restrict the ability of a decision maker to arrive at the truth, most of the rules have been designed, not to obscure the truth, but to reveal it. And those that are not so designed have been designed instead to keep trials fair, to prevent the imbalance that results when one party has a greater capacity to present his or her side of the story, or to serve other equally important purposes. For example, in a criminal case, it is considered an error for the government to present a coerced confession. This rule was designed to deter police from coercing confessions. But a coerced confession may not be a true confession and excluding coerced confessions also balances the power of the government over the usual criminal defendant.

Appreciating why we have an adversarial system based on partisan advocacy may be difficult for social workers because, typically, social workers do not perform a partisan or advocacy role in the legal system. The role of the social worker in the system is generally different than the role of the lawyer. When lawyers are representing a client, they must be concerned with what their clients *want*. They advocate for their clients' positions even if they do not agree with these positions; they seek to protect their clients' rights even if they believe their clients or society might be better off if these rights were not protected. On the other hand, social workers typically are concerned with what their clients (and possibly the other parties) *need*. Social workers try to work out the best solution to a problem even if those involved may not agree it is the best; they work to further their perception of the parties' and society's best interests—even if these interests do not coincide with the parties' desires.

---

3. Ralph Slovenko, *Psychiatry and Law* (Little, Brown & Co.: Boston 1973), p. 19.
4. *Id.*

There are some advocacy roles for social workers in the legal system, such as acting as legal representatives of clients before administrative agencies, but, in the typical legal case involving a social worker, the social worker will be focusing on the parties' *best interests* and any lawyers will be focusing on their clients' *rights*. Of course, the best solution to a problem would generally be one that both serves the parties' best interests and protects their rights.

Accusatorial

Courts in America use an accusatorial process of proof as well as an adversarial system of decision making. The key to an accusatorial process is that one party, usually the party bringing the case to court, has the **burden of proof** or, in other words, bears the burden of proving that the case has merit.

You can see the accusatorial process in its purest form in the criminal system where the government accuses someone of committing a crime. The government has the burden of proving that the accused is guilty. The accused need not prove his or her innocence but can simply sit back, produce no evidence whatsoever, and be assured of exoneration if the government does not meet its burden of proving guilt.

Although you may not see the accusatorial process in such a pure form in the civil system, the civil system in America is also accusatorial. To get a dispute before a court, a party to the dispute must initiate a lawsuit. To win the case, the initiating party usually has the burden of proving that his or her claims have

merit. The opposing parties need not prove that the initiating party's claims have no merit or that their own claims have merit, but can prevail if the initiating party does not meet his or her burden of proof.

The accusatorial process sometimes makes legal disputes quite hostile. One party to the dispute is accusing another party of wrongdoing in some manner. A party who is being accused often responds in kind. But the accusatorial process is probably the fairest way to allocate the burden of proof. Making the parties who initiate legal actions prove the validity of their claims is only fair; the parties being sued, who may be completely free of any wrongdoing, should not be given a burden of proof simply because they were sued. It is not fair to require someone to prove innocence, particularly since it is usually extremely difficult to prove a negative. Keeping these reasons for the accusatorial process in mind, may enable you to minimize some of the hostility in cases in which you are involved.

Fair

The adversarial system and the accusatorial process were developed to make our system of resolving legal disputes fair. Adjustments are constantly being made to them, and to other aspects of our legal system, to keep the system fair. Most rules of procedure and evidence were developed, and are constantly being revised, to ensure that our legal system is, and remains, fair to *all* participants. For example, because the government in a criminal case has far greater resources than the ordinary defendant, the burden of proof not only is placed on the government but also is made extremely high. A high burden of proof is also seen as fair because of what is at stake for a criminal defendant. And, because of a concern with fairness to the victim in recent years, changes have been made to the criminal justice system to give victims a voice.

THE MECHANICS OF THE HEARING PROCESS

In order to understand the court hearing or trial process, understanding the process for resolving a legal dispute from the time it is first brought before a court until it comes to trial and beyond is necessary. A discussion and explanation of the technical aspects of this whole process, including the hearing or trial process, for a **civil case** follows. Throughout the discussion, key terms are defined for you. The process and the terms may differ for different types of civil cases and in different jurisdictions, but the process is generally as described.[5]

Initiating a Case

To initiate a civil case in a trial court, one party to a dispute files a document generally called a **complaint** or a **petition.** If it is a complaint, the party filing it is generally called the **plaintiff,** while if it is a petition,

the party filing it is generally called the **petitioner.** The opponent of a plaintiff is typically called a **defendant,** while the opponent of a petitioner is typically called a **respondent.** Whether one files a petition or a complaint depends on the jurisdiction and the type of case. Petitions are used more frequently than complaints in most cases involving social workers.[6]

There may be several plaintiffs and defendants on each side in one case. Furthermore, a defendant may file complaints against one or more of the plaintiffs in the case or even against others not originally parties to the case. These complaints of defendants, known as **cross-complaints** or **counterclaims,** become part of the original case.

A single case may involve several related disputes. Each dispute would be set forth separately in the petition as a separate **cause of action, count,** or **claim.** As with petitions and complaints, the term used depends on the jurisdiction and the type of case.

Petitioners may have several different reasons, grounds, or theories why they are entitled to win a case, which could be set forth in one cause or in separate causes of action. The causes of action in a petition may be cumulative, alternative, or even inconsistent. All petitioners may not join in all causes of action; all respondents may not be named in all causes of action.

To illustrate, a single complaint against a marriage counselor who engaged in sex with the wife of a couple he was counseling and who stole money from the couple could have different claims alleging malpractice, undue influence, battery, theft,

---

5. The process and the terms do differ significantly in a **criminal case.** The whole process, including the hearing process, for a criminal case and the different terms for criminal cases will be discussed and explained in chapter 6.

6. These two sets of terms will be used interchangeably throughout this book.

invasion of privacy, breach of contract, intentional infliction of mental distress, and fraud. The husband could bring some of the claims and the wife others; some could also be against the counselor's supervisor and his agency on the theory that they were responsible for some of the actions.

The petition always asks for something, generally called **relief** or the **remedy,** in something generally called a **prayer.** A petition may seek several different, alternative, or cumulative kinds of relief. Different causes of action may also seek different kinds of relief. To illustrate, using our previous example of the marriage counselor, the couple could seek: 1) money damages to compensate for the distress caused by the sexual misconduct, to pay for therapy needed because of the distress, and to make up for the theft; 2) an order from the court requiring the counselor to return the stolen money, preventing the counselor from contacting the wife, and requiring the counselor to give up his license to practice; and 3) an order requiring the agency to provide appropriate training for all its counselors to prevent future incidents.

Often, petitions are simply preprinted forms from the court that the petitioner has filled in, or the petitioner simply uses forms obtained from a book, stationery store, or computer program. Sometimes, petitions are long, typed documents that are drafted for a particular case. Either type of petition may use highly formal language and must contain certain necessary formal allegations. You should ask to see petitions from cases like the ones in which you might be involved before you begin your involvement. In addition, documents filed with a court in most cases, including the petitions, are generally available to the public (although the documents filed in some cases, like those involving juveniles, may be confidential); most lawyers have sample or form petitions (and other legal documents) they can show you; there are books of sample forms available in law libraries; and most agencies keep a supply of forms for cases in which they are frequently involved. Courts will tell you if there is a court form that can or must be used for a given type of case and, if there is, will provide you with the form.

Petitions must be filed in courts that have jurisdiction over the case and the parties. If a court does not have this jurisdiction, it usually will dismiss a case rather than transferring it to a court with jurisdiction. If the time period set by a statute of limitations elapses before the cases have been filed in courts with jurisdiction, the cases may not be allowed to proceed.

Several courts may have geographical and subject matter jurisdiction over a case, but one of these courts may be in the most appropriate location to hear the case. This court is said to have **venue** to hear the case. If a case is filed in a court with jurisdiction but not venue, it may be transferred to a court with venue or heard in the court without venue, but it generally would not be dismissed.

Usually, plaintiffs must pay fees to file a case. If plaintiffs cannot afford these fees, they may ask courts to permit them to file without paying the fees, which is known as filing **in forma pauperis.**

A copy of a petition must be given to the respondent. The delivery of a copy of a petition or court paper to the other parties is known as **service.** Service of the petition is the responsibility of the petitioner, not the court. The method of service depends on the nature of the case and the location of the respondent. **Personal service** (i.e., actually handing someone the papers) is not always required. Service by mail or even service by publishing a notice in a newspaper may be sufficient. Service may usually be done by any adult who is not a party to a case, although the parties may prefer to have a professional process server or a government agent, such as the sheriff, do the service for them for a fee.

Pre-Trial Actions

A defendant must respond to a complaint within a certain amount of time. If the time to respond has passed and the defendant has failed to respond, the defendant is said to have **defaulted.** The plaintiff can inform the court that the defendant has defaulted and, depending on the type of case, the plaintiff may be granted the relief sought in the complaint without further action or the court may hold a hearing to determine the relief. Defendants who have defaulted are not entitled to further notice of the proceedings and cannot appear to argue their positions but may ask to be relieved of their default for a good reason.

A response usually must be written but, in some cases, only an oral or both an oral and a written response are required. A written response to either a petition or complaint is generally called an **answer,** but a written response to a petition may also be called a **return** or simply a **response.** Sometimes, the defendant must pay a fee to file a written response to a complaint. If there is a fee and the defen-

dant cannot afford the fee, the defendant may request to file in forma pauperis. The petition and the written response together are known as the **pleadings.**

An oral response is made by **appearing** in court. At the time a petition is filed or soon after, the petitioner may ask the court to set a date and time for the appearance and possibly, at the same time, the hearing on the petition. Except for jury trials, getting a date for an appearance or hearing (typically from the court clerk, not the judge) is generally the responsibility of the parties.

If a defendant has a legal argument that the case has some legal flaws or should not go forward for some reason, for example, because the court has no personal jurisdiction over him or her, because the statute of limitations has passed, or because the case was filed in the wrong venue, the defendant may make a motion raising the argument instead of answering. Common motions made instead of answering are **motions to dismiss** (also known as **demurrers**), which argue that even if the petitioner proved everything alleged in the petition, the petitioner would not be entitled to relief under the law, or **motions to quash service,** which argue that there was faulty service or that there is no personal jurisdiction over the defendant.

These and other motions are argued at court hearings, but these hearings are not like full trials. Usually, no one testifies at hearings on motions. Instead, the parties simply argue about the law before the judge and submit written arguments and evidence, like affidavits or copies of relevant documents.

A defendant is usually not considered in default if he or she has made a motion within the time for an answer instead of answering. However, if the motion is denied, the defendant would have to answer in a time set by the court or be considered in default.

After a defendant has answered, there may be **discovery,** a process by which each side determines the facts known to the other side and the facts the other side will seek to prove. A common type of discovery is submission of written questions, known as **interrogatories,** to the other side. Another common type of discovery is taking a **deposition,** that is, questioning a witness in person with an opportunity for both sides to do questioning. A court reporter or stenographer is usually present at a deposition to administer oaths and to make a written record, that is, a **transcript,** of the proceedings.

There may also be motions filed asking for some legal issues to be resolved before trial or that the case as a whole be resolved without a trial. Motions for a **summary judgment** or for a **judgment on the pleadings** are common. These motions argue that, based on what has been revealed by the pleadings and the discovery, there are no significant disputes as to the facts and that, applying the law to the facts, the moving party should win the case.

In some jurisdictions for some kinds of cases, there may be mandatory settlement conferences or referrals to arbitration, mediation, or other alternative dispute resolution (ADR) method. For example, mediation or arbitration may be required in child custody cases or in cases involving wage claims. Even without laws requiring or encouraging settlement or ADR, some judges are very active in attempting to settle cases or to resolve them without a court trial.

The Trial

If a case has not been settled or otherwise resolved, such as through a motion or ADR, it will go to trial. As has been stated, however, most cases are settled or otherwise resolved prior to trial.

The rules of evidence, which will be discussed later in this chapter, and the specific rules of procedure of each jurisdiction will control the conduct of the trial. Generally, however, the party who initiated the case has the burden of proof and goes first. This party presents his or her case by submitting evidence, that is, the testimony of witnesses, documents, actual objects, and anything else that may be submitted to a court to establish a fact under the rules of evidence. After this party completes his or her case, the opposing parties may present their evidence or simply argue that the initiating party has not met his or her burden of proof, that is, has not presented enough evidence to win. Usually, if a party without the burden of proof presents evidence, the party with the burden of proof may present further evidence to rebut this evidence.

A civil trial is often not before a jury. Whether or not there is a jury at a trial is determined by the type of the case and the wishes of the parties. One is usually entitled to a jury in cases seeking money damages that involve personal injuries or contracts but, in many States, one is not entitled to a jury in many of the kinds of civil cases that would involve social workers, like family law, mental health, or juvenile matters. Further, any party who has a right to a trial by a jury may choose not to have a jury and may ask, instead, to have the case tried before a judge. In other words, the party may **waive** his or her right to a jury. The other party may, however, be able to insist on a trial with a jury. A trial with only a judge is called a **bench trial.**

Juries are supposed to be impartial and representative of the community, but creating such juries may be difficult. Courts have prohibited the systematic exclusion of certain types of prospective jurors from the **jury panel** or **venire,** that is, the group of people from which a trial jury is chosen. Thus, random selection is the basis on which most jury panels are chosen. Making the random selection from lists, such as voter registration lists or lists of utility connections, however, may serve, just as much as systematic exclusion, to exclude large classes of potential jurors, such as the poor.

The judge or the lawyers may question the members of the jury panel before a trial to determine if anything would prevent them from being impartial. This questioning is called **voir dire.** If jurors would not be impartial, they are **excused for cause.** Usually, both sides may also excuse a certain number of prospective jurors without stating a reason. This is called a **peremptory challenge** or **challenge without cause.**

While juries traditionally have twelve people and while jury decisions, known as **verdicts,** generally must be unanimous, there is now a trend to have smaller juries or majority verdicts in some or all kinds of civil cases (and even in some criminal cases).

If there is a jury trial, the jury will decide the facts. If there is a bench trial, the judge will decide the facts. Whether or not there is a jury, only the judge will decide what law to apply to the facts and how to apply it. If there is a jury, the judge will instruct the jury on the applicable law and on how to apply it.

The Judgment

Whether a case is decided with or without a trial or by a judge or a jury, the judge will render or enter a **judgment.** Sometimes, there are jury trials, but the judge will grant a motion to take the case away from the jury and enter a judgment for the moving party. This action will be used if the judge determines that, as a matter of law, the moving party must win the case. Sometimes, the judge decides that a jury verdict is erroneous and grants a motion for a judgment **notwithstanding the verdict.**

Plaintiffs usually seek judgments awarding them **damages,** that is, monetary compensation for an injury or wrong. Plaintiffs may additionally or alternatively seek special kinds of orders, including a **declaratory judgment** (i.e., judgment declaring a law invalid or valid, stating the meaning of a document, or setting forth the respective rights and obligations of the parties to the litigation); an **injunction** (i.e., an order commanding defendants to do something or, more commonly, to refrain from doing something, like polluting the air or enforcing an invalid law); a **writ** (i.e., a special kind of legal order that, like an injunction, commands people to do something or to refrain from doing something); or a **decree** (i.e., an order that creates a new legal status or changes a legal status, like a divorce decree, a decree of adoption or an order appointing a guardian).

Writs, injunctions, and declaratory relief are frequently sought against government officials and agencies. Writs, injunctions, and other special orders or decrees are generally sought in petitions; money damages are generally sought in complaints. While a jury may decide entitlement to and the amount of damages, a judge usually decides entitlement to and the nature of any special orders.

Special orders, writs, or injunctions may also be sought before judgment, either as temporary measures to preserve the status quo or to prevent irreparable injury pending final resolution of a case. Common orders issued before judgment include: **stays** or **temporary restraining orders** (TROs), which are issued on an emergency basis to prevent someone from doing something for a short amount of time until some kind of hearing can be held; **preliminary injunctions,** which are issued after a hearing but before a full trial; or **writs of attachment,** which prevent someone from disposing of or using property in dispute until trial.

Special orders or writs may further be sought after judgment, either, as a means of enforcing a judgment or as a special way to appeal from it. For example, writs of attachment or **writs of execution,** that is, orders seizing property or assets, are often sought to enforce money judgments, while landlords in eviction actions may seek **writs of possession** or **writs of restitution.**

While a party may seek several alternative or cumulative remedies in a complaint, the party generally will not be entitled to receive alternative or cumulative remedies. A party may, however, be awarded more than one nonalternative, noncumulative remedy. For example, a landlord may get a writ of possession commanding a tenant to give up possession of her apartment, a judgment for past due rent

(framed as an order to pay the rent or as a judgment for damages), and a judgment for money damages to repair the damage to the apartment caused by the tenant.

Post-Judgment Actions

A judgment is usually the final and complete resolution of a case at the trial level, but some parts of a judgment, like a child custody order, may be modifiable in the future and sometimes matters collateral to the main case, like whether the losing party should pay the winning party's attorney's fees, are resolved after judgment.

The usual method of protesting a judgment is an appeal to an appellate court, asking it to reverse or modify the trial court's judgment. But, sometimes protests are made in the trial court by motions, like a **motion for a new trial, a motion to reconsider,** or a **motion to vacate,** or review is sought in an appellate court through a petition for a writ rather than an appeal.

If an appeal is taken, the party that appeals is usually called the **appellant,** while the other side is called the **respondent** or the **appellee.** A party seeking review in an appellate court through a writ is usually called the petitioner and the other side called the respondent. The writ may be called a **writ of certiorari** or a **writ of error.** The effectiveness of a judgment may be stayed (i.e., delayed or stopped) pending appeal or resolution of a writ by the trial court or the appellate court.

If a trial court has made no significant errors of law in reaching its judgment, the appellate court will **affirm** the judgment (or deny a writ if review is sought by a writ). If the trial court has made significant errors of law, the appellate court will **reverse** the judgment. It may also affirm one part of a judgment and reverse another part or may modify a judgment. Whether the appellate court affirms, reverses, or modifies a judgment, the case will probably be **remanded,** that is, sent back to the trial court to take all actions necessary in light of the appellate decision. The trial court, not the appellate court, will make all orders and take all actions necessary to enforce an affirmed judgment.

THE PARTICIPANTS IN THE HEARING PROCESS

Important participants in the hearing process include the judge, the jury, the parties, the attorneys, the guardian *ad litem,* and the witnesses. Every hearing may not include each of these participants and, indeed, you may encounter some of these participants relatively rarely, but you nevertheless should understand each of these participants' role in the hearing process.

Judge

The judge performs at least three important roles in any court hearing: 1) presiding over the hearing; 2) deciding what law to apply and how to apply it; and 3) either deciding the facts or instructing the jury on how to decide the facts. In performing these roles, the judge is always guided by the law.

To illustrate, in the course of presiding over a trial in a case seeking to commit a mentally disabled man for treatment, the judge may have to decide if a social worker's evaluation can be used at the hearing, that is, make a decision about the admissibility of evidence under the law. The judge will also decide what standard to apply in determining if the man should be committed, that is, decide the applicable law, and, assuming there is no jury, will decide if the man meets the standard for commitment, that is, decide the facts in light of the law.

In summary, the judge is the primary *legal* decision maker in a hearing and may also be the *factual* decision maker.

Jury

If there is a jury at a trial, the jury will decide the facts based on the evidence the judge permitted the parties to present. It will then reach a verdict based on these facts in accordance with the judge's instructions on the proper law to apply and the proper legal standard to use. The jury will be the primary *factual* decision maker, but it will never decide the law.

Parties

All people involved in a legal dispute should be named as parties in the pleadings. Usually, they should be named as petitioners or respondents by the petitioners or respondents. When petitioners or respondents are government entities, agencies, private associations, or corporations, depending on technical rules, the entity or organization may be named as a party or a person in charge of the entity or organization may be so named.

In some cases, a party who is named as a petitioner or respondent has no real stake in the case but must be named for technical reasons. Sometimes, a person with the real or the biggest stake in the case is not appropriately named either a petitioner or respondent but might be named as the **real party in interest.** For example, a welfare department might bring an action against the father of a child on welfare to obtain support for the child. The welfare department might be named as the plaintiff, but the child would be named as the real party in interest. To give another example, a woman may seek a writ against a court to get it to change a decision to commit her to a mental hospital. The petition for a writ may name the court as respondent, but the man who petitioned the court to have the woman committed in the first place would be named as the real party in interest. This man, not the court, would defend the court's action.

Sometimes, individuals who have a legitimate and direct interest in a case, for example, a natural father in an adoption action, are not named as parties in any pleadings, but they may be granted **party status** by a statute or by the court. Other individuals, who are not named as parties or granted party status but who have a stake in the outcome of a case, may move to be made parties or, in other words, to **intervene** in a case.

In some cases, known as **class actions** or **representative suits,** one or more named parties act as representatives of unnamed parties who are similarly situated to the named parties. A class action may be used if there are too many similarly situated people to name as parties or all the similarly situated people are not known. For example, two women who are employed by a State social welfare agency with thousands of employees may use a class action to sue the agency if they believe it discriminated against them and all other women employees in setting salaries and making promotions. If the named parties in class actions prevail in their suits, the unnamed parties also prevail. If they lose, the unnamed parties also lose and may never be able to bring suit on their own. Thus, using the above example, if two women sue the agency that employs them for discriminating against women in a class action on their own behalf and on behalf of all other women employees and if they win their case, the other women employees would be entitled to the same relief as the named plaintiffs (like back pay or promotions). If the named plaintiffs lost their case, however, other unnamed women employees would get no relief and probably would never be allowed to sue the agency for discrimination.

All parties to a case who have not defaulted, including real parties in interest, intervenors who have been made parties, and persons with party status, must be served with all pleadings, motions, and other important papers; must be given **notice** (i.e., notified) of all court dates and court actions; and have a right to be heard at any hearings. Unnamed class members may also be entitled to notice and to be heard.

Attorneys

All parties to a case will not necessarily be represented by an attorney. Whether or not a party has an attorney depends on the party's wishes, the party's ability to afford an attorney, and the type of case. Sometimes, parties do not wish to have attorneys because they choose to represent themselves. Sometimes, they wish to have attorneys, but cannot afford to hire one. The Constitution expressly grants defendants in criminal cases the right to the assistance of counsel. The right to the assistance of counsel, however, does not necessarily mean that a lawyer will be provided free of charge to a party who cannot afford to pay for a lawyer and the Constitution says nothing about the right to the assistance of counsel in civil cases. Nevertheless, the Constitution has been interpreted to provide that a party to litigation is entitled to the appointment of counsel at no cost in serious criminal cases (but not all criminal cases) and in a few civil cases. The States may grant a right to the assistance of counsel and a right to appointment of counsel at no cost in further matters under their constitutions or statutes or as a matter of common law.

A party that does not have an attorney and that represents himself or herself is described as being *in pro per* or as *pro se.*

Guardian *ad Litem*

In certain cases, instead of or in addition to appointing an attorney for a party, judges may be either required or permitted to appoint a **guardian *ad litem,*** meaning a guardian at law, for the party. A guardian *ad litem* acts in a given case to protect a party to the case who is assumed to be unable to protect himself or herself because of age or disability. Guardians *ad litem* are typically appointed to represent children who are

the subjects of juvenile court actions or custody disputes or adults alleged to be incompetent.

Guardians *ad litem* may or may not be attorneys, but even if they are attorneys, they do not act like attorneys in the usual sense. The role of the attorney is to represent the client's interests *as defined by the client.* The guardian *ad litem,* on the other hand, *defines the interests* of a person thought unable to do so. In other words, a guardian *ad litem* presents to the court what he or she thinks is best for the party—not what the party wants to present. In a sense, the difference between the roles of the guardian *ad litem* and the attorney in a case is the same as the difference between the usual roles of the social worker and the attorney in the legal system.

The difference between the attorney's and the guardian *ad litem*'s roles can be illustrated by a case of a man whose relatives seek to have him declared incompetent. The court may appoint an attorney to represent him, and if he wants to object to the allegations of incompetence, the attorney must do so, and should do so vigorously, whatever she thinks about the man's competence. But if the court appoints a guardian *ad litem* for the man, the guardian *ad litem* may conduct an investigation and may recommend a finding of incompetence because she believes it is in the man's best interests—even if he objects.

Unlike other kinds of guardians appointed by courts, the guardian *ad litem* represents the interests of the party only in the particular case in which he or she was appointed; he or she is not a guardian of the party's interests in any other context or for any other purposes.

Witnesses

Witnesses are those people who present evidence to the fact finder, whether it be a judge or a jury, at a hearing. Under oath and under penalty for **perjury** (i.e., lying under oath), witnesses typically present information about what they have seen, heard, and done through responses to questions from attorneys. In short, they tell what they know to be the facts through **testimony.** So-called **expert witnesses** may also present their opinions. We will discuss expert witnesses in greater depth in the next chapter.

All witnesses, whether expert or not, must be found competent to testify. This means the judge must determine, among other things, that a witness understands the obligation to tell the truth and either has personal knowledge of the facts or, in the case of an expert witness, is qualified by virtue of training or experience to give an opinion on a subject beyond the knowledge of the ordinary person.

In some hearings, there may be no witnesses present. Either there may be only a dispute about the law, and thus no testimony is needed, or the facts may be presented through written statements made out of court but under oath and under penalty for perjury. Such written testimony may be called **affidavits** or **declarations.** Transcripts of depositions and responses to interrogatories may also be submitted in some cases. The rules of evidence in a jurisdiction determine the admissibility of such written testimony with admissibility generally depending on the nature of the hearing and the nature and purpose of the testimony.

THE USE OF EVIDENCE IN THE HEARING PROCESS

Evidence is everything, exclusive of argument, that is offered to a court to prove the facts. Whether the offered evidence will be allowed to be presented to the trier of fact (i.e., will be admitted into evidence) or can be considered by the trier of fact, as we have said, depends on the rules of evidence.

Legal evidence should be distinguished from **social evidence.** Evidence of importance to social workers in writing a social history or working with a client may be of no legal significance. Evidence of importance to a lawyer in proving a case may be of no significance to a social worker. For example, evidence that a defendant charged with stealing from his employer was an alcoholic would probably be of no legal significance but it might be important to the social worker, while evidence that the defendant in a murder case had been threatened by the victim in the past might be legally significant but might not be important to the social worker. Recently, however, the lines between social evidence and legal evidence have blurred in criminal cases as more criminal defendants present social evidence, such as that they were victims of sexual abuse or battered wives, to explain or excuse their conduct.

Evidence may be direct or circumstantial. **Direct evidence** proves a fact without the need to draw an inference or make an assumption. For example, if John testifies "I saw Jim shoot Jane," this testimony is direct evidence that Jim killed Jane. **Circumstantial evidence** requires an inference or presumption. For example, if John testifies "I saw Jim standing over Jane's body with a smoking gun in his hand," this testimony is circumstantial evidence that Jim killed Jane. Circumstantial evidence is not "bad" evidence; it is just not direct proof of a fact.

Evidence may be real, documentary, or testimonial. **Real evidence** (also called **demonstrative evidence**) is a tangible object that is itself the fact to be proven (e.g., the gun, the marijuana). **Documentary evidence** is, as the name implies, some kind of document that commemorates a fact. It may be, for example, a writing sample or a photograph. In some instances, documents may be real evidence. For example, an x-ray that a doctor in a malpractice case allegedly misread would be real evidence, while an x-ray showing a person's injury from an accident would be documentary evidence. **Testimonial evidence** is testimony made under oath by a witness. Testimonial evidence is usually oral, but sometimes written evidence, like an affidavit or declaration under penalty of perjury, may be offered to a court as testimonial evidence.

The Rules of Evidence

The **rules of evidence** determine what may be presented as evidence and how evidence must be presented. The rules of evidence differ from jurisdiction to jurisdiction although the basic principles are the same throughout America. Where the rules of evidence are found also differs from jurisdiction to jurisdiction. In some jurisdictions, most of the rules of evidence, including the basic rules are found in case law. In other jurisdictions, the basic rules of evidence are found in a single **code,** that is, a group of statutes on a

particular topic. Whether the basic rules of evidence are in case law or a single code, most jurisdictions have rules of evidence contained in statutes on other subjects. For example, a statute related to child abuse may specify the evidence that may be admitted in a hearing in a case involving an abused child and the burden of proof in such a hearing. As this example demonstrates, the rules of evidence in a particular jurisdiction may differ depending on the type of case. They may also differ depending on the nature of a hearing or the type of court.

Admission of Evidence

Not everything the parties seek to introduce as evidence at a trial will be admitted into evidence. In order to be admitted into evidence, all documentary and real evidence must be properly identified and authenticated. Certain formalities may be required to authenticate some documentary evidence (e.g., notarizing). Usually a witness must identify and authenticate documentary or real evidence through testimony.

As has been stated, before testimonial evidence can be admitted into evidence, the witness must be found **competent** to testify. Competence may be a substantial issue in the case of children and persons with mental or developmental disabilities. A court may have to determine whether a child or a disabled witness knows what it means to tell the truth. As we shall see in the next chapter, competence may also be a substantial issue in the case of expert witnesses.

Even if documentary or real evidence that is offered into evidence is authenticated or a proposed witness is found competent to testify, the offered evidence may not be admitted into evidence and the witness may not be allowed to testify under the rules of evidence. Two important rules that keep evidence from being admitted (i.e., the rules that exclude evidence) in every jurisdiction are that evidence must be relevant and that hearsay cannot be admitted into evidence.

Relevance. To be admitted, evidence must be **relevant.** Another word for relevant that is often used is **material.** Almost any fact may be related to almost any other fact if we pursue a process of reasoning long enough, but courts must save their time for the determination of the case. Thus, only facts determined to be legally relevant or material to a particular case will be admitted in the case.

Evidence is relevant and material if it establishes the facts essential to proving the parties' cases. It may also be enough if the evidence sheds light on the parties' cases. But, often social evidence of importance to social workers, such as evidence about a person's background and ethnicity, is not considered legally relevant and is, thus, not admissible.

Hearsay. **Hearsay** is a statement made orally or in writing outside of the courtroom that is offered to prove the truth of the matter asserted in the statement. For example, if Jane testifies "John told me he saw Jim hit his baby," this testimony is hearsay if it is offered to prove that Jim hit his baby. It would not be hearsay if it were offered to prove that John is not always truthful or that John is antagonistic towards Jim.

Hearsay is excluded because the person who made the hearsay statement (the **hearsay declarant**) is not in court and cannot be questioned by the opposing side and, thus, the truthfulness of the declarant cannot be assessed by the trier of fact. Rather than letting Jane testify about what John said he saw, John should testify about what he saw so that John can be questioned and so that the trier of fact can determine if John is telling the truth.

Despite these valid reasons for excluding hearsay, there are many exceptions to the hearsay rule. Many oral or written out-of-court statements may be admitted into evidence to prove the truth of matters asserted in the statements. Most of the exceptions arise because the rule unduly burdens the truth-seeking process and the circumstances are such that the hearsay is likely to be truthful. For example, if John is unavailable to testify about what he saw, the only way to put the crucial evidence of what he saw before the trier of fact may be to allow Jane to testify as to what he said to her. Jane may be allowed to testify, especially if John made his statement to Jane at a time and in such a way as to indicate it was truthful. Thus, dying declarations, admissions against interest, excited utterances, and statements of physical sensations may all be admissible if the declarant is unavailable to testify and even in some instances where the declarant is available. There may also be exceptions to the hearsay rule to allow social workers or others to testify about children's statements in cases involving their alledged abuse.

Client files, records, or reports, including those of a social worker, are written statements made out of court. Thus, they would be hearsay if a party seeks to have them admitted into evidence to prove the truth of their contents. Even reports made for a court would be hearsay if a party seeks to admit them to prove the truth of something contained in them. If, however, the reports make recommendations to a court and do not attempt to establish facts, the reports may be considered by a judge. They may be considered, but they are not considered for the purpose of establishing the facts and they are not admitted into evidence. And many files, records, and reports can be admitted into evidence as exceptions to the hearsay rule even if a party seeks to admit them to prove the truth of their contents.

The most commonly encountered exception to the hearsay rule for written out-of-court statements is that for **business records.** Business records are admissible to prove the truth of facts contained in them if they are made in the ordinary course of business, at or near the time of the event that they record, and in circumstances that indicate their trustworthiness. The "business" maintaining the record need not be a commercial or industrial concern that operates for a profit. Public agencies and nonprofit organizations, like hospitals or counseling centers, are considered businesses for the purpose of this exception. If a party seeks to admit business records into evidence, the person in charge of the records (i.e., the custodian of the records) will usually have to testify about how the records were made and maintained. We will discuss the business record exception for social work records in greater depth in the next chapter.

There is also a **public records** exception to the hearsay rule. Public records are official government documents, like birth certificates or marriage licenses, created and maintained for specific governmental purposes. The records kept by social workers who work for public agencies would ordinarily not qualify as public records, but these records may contain public records, like a court order removing a child from her parents or a child's birth certificate.

A record or report that is admissible into evidence as a business record or a public record may contain hearsay or even "double hearsay," like a notation that "Jane said John said he saw Jim hit his baby." Just because the record is admissible into evidence, the hearsay within it would not be admissible. The inadmissible hearsay, and any other inadmissible evidence, will be stricken before the record or report will be admitted into evidence.

Other Rules Excluding Evidence. In addition to the relevance requirement and the hearsay rule, there are numerous other rules of evidence that operate to exclude evidence that you may consider relevant and trustworthy. The evidence may be excluded for a variety of reasons. For example, logically the character of an individual may be an excellent indication of what a person did or did not do in a given situation. Yet the law usually excludes evidence of character because of the danger of prejudice, because the jury might give such evidence undue weight, and because such evidence will tend to complicate the case with collateral issues and lengthen any trial unduly. To give another example, confidential communications to certain professionals, like clergy or psychotherapists, are generally excluded from evidence even if they are not considered hearsay. The communications are excluded in order to encourage full disclosure.

You would probably agree on the necessity for the rule of evidence excluding confidential communications. This rule of evidence, which is of great importance to social workers, will be discussed in chapter 18. Other rules excluding certain evidence are less significant and will not be discussed in this book.

Presentation of Evidence

In addition to operating to exclude certain evidence from a hearing, the rules of evidence establish how real and documentary evidence is presented and the form of the questions that may be used to elicit testimony. Questions may not be compound (i.e., contain several parts) and may not call for a narrative (i.e., a long, unstructured answer). Further, questions by the party that called someone as a witness generally may not be leading. A **leading question,** such as, "You left your child alone all day, didn't you?" suggests its answer.

The rules of evidence also establish the order in which parties to a case present evidence (i.e., the **burden of going forward**). More important, the rules establish which party must present evidence to prove an essential fact or to win the whole case and how much evidence that party must present (i.e., the **burden of proof**).

If a party with the burden of proof in the case produces enough evidence to meet the burden, without regard to how convincing the evidence is, the party is said to have established a ***prima facie case.*** If the party with the burden of proof fails to establish a *prima facie* case, the opposing party will win without having to produce any evidence.

While the party with the burden of proof must establish a *prima facie* case in order not to lose the case, establishing a *prima facie* case may not be enough to win. In order to win a case, the party with the burden of proof usually has to present enough evidence to meet a certain **standard of proof** (also called the **burden of persuasion**). The standard of proof, which is generally encompassed within the burden of proof, depends on the nature of a case, but there are three basic standards.

The normal standard of proof is a **preponderance of the evidence.** Under this standard, the party with the burden of proof merely has to prove that his or her version of the facts is more likely true than not true. If both sides present evidence, the party with the burden of proof needs a mere majority of the evidence to win.

The highest standard of proof, used primarily in criminal cases, is **beyond a reasonable doubt.** Under this standard, the party with the burden of proof only wins if his or her evidence establishes the necessary facts to a very great degree of certainty (in fact, some courts say to a "moral certainty") and the fact finder has no doubts, based on reason, on the facts.

The intermediate standard is called many things but usually is called **clear and convincing evidence.** This standard is used in cases where there is a great stake in the outcome, like a loss of an important right, but not as great a stake as in a criminal case.

As we shall see, one of the two higher standards of proof may be constitutionally or otherwise required in certain types of cases.

Sometimes, the parties can meet their burden of proof or of persuasion through the use of presumptions. A **presumption** is a rule of law that allows one to presume the truth or the existence or nonexistence of a fact (or facts) after another fact (or several facts) is established. Presumptions are either **conclusive** (i.e., irrebuttable) or **rebuttable.** For example, if it is proven that a woman driving a car had a blood alcohol level higher than a certain amount set forth in the law, she may be conclusively presumed to have been driving while intoxicated or she may be allowed to rebut the presumption that she was intoxicated. But even if the presumption of intoxication is rebuttable, the party with the burden of proof on the issue may satisfy the burden simply by establishing the blood alcohol level.

Not all facts in a trial require the presentation of evidence to be proved. The parties will **stipulate** to some facts (i.e., they will acknowledge their truth). Courts will also take **judicial notice** of some facts (i.e., the judge will accept some facts, such as matters of common knowledge, public laws, or the laws of nature, as true without proof or a stipulation). For example, a judge may take judicial notice of the fact that Abraham Lincoln was assassinated, that people born in America are U.S. citizens, or that it is dark at night.

ADMINISTRATIVE HEARINGS

Courts are not the only government entities that resolve disputes through a hearing process. Administrative agencies also resolve disputes through a hearing process that, sometimes, is similar to the hearing process in a court.

There are two types of disputes that are generally resolved by administrative

agencies through an administrative hearing process: 1) disputes that individuals have with the agency; and 2) disputes that are within areas of the law that the agency administers. An example of the first type of administrative dispute resolution is found in the hearings conducted by the Social Security Administration. People who have been denied social security benefits by the Social Security Administration may have the denial reviewed by requesting an administrative hearing run by the Administration. An example of the second type of administrative dispute resolution can be found in the hearings conducted by the National Labor Relations Board (NLRB). If a union claims an employer engaged in an unlawful labor practice, the union makes its claim against the employer in an administrative hearing run by the NLRB.

Administrative hearings are like court trials in that a dispute is resolved by determining the facts and applying the law to the facts. They are unlike court trials, however, in that they may not be adversarial, they may be quite informal, and the rules of evidence may not apply. Moreover, the judge may not be a lawyer, there may be no lawyers involved, and there usually is no jury (although there might be a panel of judges).

More social workers may be involved and have more roles in administrative hearings than in court trials. In many administrative hearings, a party may be represented by someone who is not a lawyer, such as a social worker. Social workers who work for agencies may also represent their agency's position at administrative hearings, or even act as judges at such hearings.

Some administrative agencies have appellate bodies that hear appeals of hearing decisions. Usually, parties to administrative hearings may appeal to a court if they are dissatisfied with a hearing decision or any administrative appellate decision. A party that is appealing a federal administrative agency decision to a court would go to a federal court in accordance with the procedures set forth in either the federal Administrative Procedures Act or in a federal act that applies to the particular kind of hearing involved. A party that is appealing a State administrative decision to a court would appeal to a State court in accordance with a general State administrative procedures act or a particular State act that applies to the particular kind of decision involved. You might better understand where one appeals from an administrative hearing decision if, in diagram 1.1., you visualize various federal administrative tribunals below federal trial courts and various State administrative tribunals below State trial courts.

Someone who is seeking court review of an administrative decision, whether in State or federal court, usually goes to a trial court, but the trial court generally operates more like an appellate court than a trial court. That is, the court generally does not receive evidence and decide facts but rather reviews the administrative record and decides if the law was correctly applied.[7]

Often, one may not go to court to resolve a dispute without first going to an administrative agency for a decision. In other words, one must go through the administrative hearing process and any administrative appeal process before going to court. This process is called **exhausting administrative remedies.** When exhaustion is required, one can go to court if, and only if, one has exhausted all administrative remedies. For example, a woman who has been denied social security benefits cannot go to court directly to protest the denial but must first seek an administrative hearing before the Social Security Administration. If she is denied benefits by the administrative law judge after the hearing, she still cannot go to court; she must then appeal to the Social Security Administration's appeals board. If she is still denied benefits by this board, she can go to court in accordance with the procedures set forth in the Social Security Act.[8]

Which types of cases require exhaustion, which courts hear appeals from which types of administrative decisions, and whether a person who appeals a certain type of administrative decision gets a trial *de novo* or an appellate type of review may be established by a general administrative procedures statute, by statutes covering particular subjects, or by case law. Generally, where one has a dispute with an administrative agency or where a type of dispute is generally handled by an administrative agency, exhaustion will be required.

The proliferation of administrative agencies and the increased demand on

---

7. In a few types of cases, a party that appeals from an administrative decision to a court may get a new evidentiary hearing, usually known as a **trial *de novo,*** in the court. In a few types of cases that might have an impact on many people, such as a utility rate case, a party may appeal an administrative decision directly to an appellate court.

---

8. Because social security is a federal program and the Social Security Administration is a federal agency, she would appeal to a federal trial court, that is a U.S. District Court.

administrative agencies to make and enforce the law has meant that administrative agencies are being called on more often to resolve disputes and that the doctrine of exhaustion of administrative remedies has become increasingly important. And because many social workers will work for administrative agencies or on cases involving administrative agencies, exhaustion is an important concept for them.

The Social Worker in the Hearing Process

As we shall see, social workers play many roles in the hearing process. Social workers probably appear most often as witnesses, offering facts or giving an opinion, but they are sometimes petitioners, asking the court to take action in a given case. Less frequently, they may be respondents. They may also act as judges or work directly for judges and, in some administrative hearings, they may act as advocates. A common role for social workers is the role of guardian *ad litem*.

This chapter is designed to explain the possible roles of social workers in the hearing process and to provide some guidance on effective ways to perform these roles. However, one should remember that the roles social workers play *related to* the hearing process may be far more important than the roles they play *in* the hearing process. Because of their continuing relationship and involvement with their clients, social workers are in a unique position to interpret the legal system, particularly the hearing process, for their clients, to otherwise assist their clients with the hearing process, and to help their clients live with the outcome of hearings. This chapter is also designed to provide some guidance on effective ways social workers can perform these roles related to the hearing process.

ROLES PLAYED BY SOCIAL WORKERS IN THE HEARING PROCESS

Witness

As witnesses, social workers provide vital information in many hearings. At times the social worker who acts as a witness may be avowedly partisan, testifying for a certain position. But, more often, even though social workers might desire a certain outcome, they are simply providing objective information learned in the course of their work in response to questions from the attorneys. The social worker's task as a witness is not to persuade the court but to inform the court. To give several examples: in a case charging a mother with criminal neglect of her daughter, a social worker might provide information from her investigation of the mother; in a guardianship proceeding brought by the relatives of an elderly man, a social worker might provide information obtained while working with the man on his adaptive behavior; and, in a divorce action involving the custody of a child, a social worker might provide information, obtained during evaluative interviews, on the child's relationship with her parents.

Some of the information provided by the social worker in these examples and in other instances is somewhat subjective. But the element of subjectivity does not negate the primary point—the role of the social worker as a witness is that of information provider.

Social workers as witnesses may be asked to make recommendations based on the facts or to state conclusions about the facts. They may be asked, for example, whether or not placement with a grandparent would be a good placement for a child found to be abused, what services are available and appropriate for a person who is involuntarily committed, or if a child custody plan is workable. The fact that the social worker is asked to make a recommendation or state a conclusion also does not change the social worker's primary role as a witness. The social worker's task is still to inform, not to convince; any recommendation or conclusion must be firmly grounded in facts known to the social worker to be credible and useful.

Sometimes, social workers are asked to make recommendations or state conclusions when they are performing the special role of **expert witness.** Expert witnesses are those people who, by virtue of their training or experience, may assist courts to understand matters beyond the knowledge of the ordinary person. The qualifications to be an expert witness may differ from case to case and court to court.

As expert witnesses, social workers may give their opinions on the basis of their professional expertise in addition to testifying only on facts known of their personal knowledge. They may even give their opinions in cases in which they have no direct or personal knowledge of the facts. Unlike ordinary or lay witnesses, expert witnesses may testify on or give opinions about matters outside of their personal knowledge. For example, as an expert witness, a social worker might testify on the probable effects of joint custody on a child with whom he is familiar or on a child he has never met.

Whether or not a social worker knows the specific individuals involved or is personally familiar with the facts, as an expert witness, the social worker's role is still to inform the court. Social workers as expert witnesses still provide information—based on their general knowledge and experience, if not their personal knowledge of the facts.

Petitioner

Social workers who work in child welfare agencies are often in the position of asking a court to take action in a case. They may prepare and file the petition themselves or they may ask a government or agency attorney to do it for them. In either case, the social workers are petitioners and perform a different role than that of witness. Social workers as petitioners want to persuade courts that a specific course of action is needed.

Other social workers may also act as petitioners and may also want to persuade a court to take a specific action. For example, medical social workers may petition for guardianship or commitment of a patient when family members are unwilling or unable to do so. Social workers who work in community mental health or other mental health facilities may also petition courts for involuntary commitment of clients.

The social worker who is a petitioner may at some point act as a witness in the case. As a witness, the social worker's task is, as has been stated, not to persuade but to inform—despite his or her status as the petitioner.

Respondent

Social workers occasionally are respondents in court cases. This role occurs most often when the social worker's performance is called into question, for example, in suits for violation of civil rights, for malpractice, or to release records.

Social workers who work for an agency may also be individually named as respondents when something their agency has done is called into question or may be asked by their agency to act as the respondent in court or administrative cases against the agency. Social workers named as or acting as respondents may have had no involvement with the action in question but nevertheless are considered responsible because of their supervisory authority or because of the nature of their work with the agency.

Like a petitioner, a respondent may be a witness in a case.

Judge

Social workers occasionally act as judges. In a few jurisdictions, some court hearings, like those involving juveniles, may be presided over by nonlawyer judges. In appropriate cases, these nonlawyer judges (usually called something other than a judge like a **referee**, **magistrate**, or **commissioner**) may be social workers. More commonly, nonlawyers may act as judges in administrative hearings. Again, in appropriate cases, these nonlawyer judges (often called **hearing officers**) may be social workers. For example, in some jurisdictions, social workers serve as hearing officers at institutions for the mentally disabled, reviewing the validity of continuing mental health commitments. Or medical social workers serve as the presiding officers of hospital ethics committee cases, deciding whether or not life support can be removed from terminally ill patients.

Social workers sometimes work directly for judges. They may be regularly employed as court officers, assisting judges with certain kinds of cases or problems, like adoptions, child custody cases, bail determinations, criminal sentencings,

or child support determinations. Alternatively, they may work as part-time or occasional consultants to judges, assisting judges when requested to do so. Usually, the social worker's role, whether as court officer or consultant, is to make recommendations to the judge in the form of written reports or oral testimony, but sometimes social workers assist judges by performing other roles. For example, they may act as referees in hearings, may mediate contested cases, or may perform what may be described as traditional social work functions, like divorce conciliation or other counseling of those involved in court cases.

Guardian *ad Litem*

In some cases, courts may appoint social workers as guardians *ad litem*. A social worker would be appointed as a guardian *ad litem* most typically in a case where a party is not represented by an attorney or where a party might not be able to communicate with an attorney. As a guardian *ad litem*, the social worker may conduct an investigation of the case or may ask others to do the investigation. It is also common for attorneys who act as guardians *ad litem* to employ social workers to conduct assessments and offer recommendations and for social workers appointed as guardians *ad litem* to have attorneys appointed to represent or assist them.

Advisor and Advocate

Clients often have legal problems in addition to the social and personal problems that have brought them to a social worker.

At times, these legal problems are quite independent of the problems the social worker is addressing. At other times, the legal problems might be intertwined with the problems being addressed by the social worker or might even be the reason for or the result of the social worker's involvement. Whatever the source of the legal problems, social workers are in a position to recognize that the problems are legal—even when the client does not recognize them as such. The social worker cannot give the client legal advice but can advise clients of the need to obtain legal services and help them do so. In a few situations, the social worker may even act as an advocate or legal representative for a client in an administrative setting.

Even this limited advisory role may be problematic for many social workers, particularly those working for a government agency. The advocacy role may be even more so. But given the nature of the legal system, these roles are not inconsistent with other roles social workers play. For example, if you are working with a parent who is alleged to be neglectful, informing the parent that legal action may be taken and strongly suggesting that the parent retain an attorney is your responsibility. Doing so will not harm the children who are involved and may even facilitate a more satisfactory outcome. To give another example, if you are working with a disabled client who has serious financial problems, you should advise the client of his possible eligibility for social security disability benefits. If the client is denied these benefits, you might assist him with an appeal, even going so far as acting as his representative in an administrative hearing. Whether it would be appropriate for you to do so and whether you would

be the best representative for the client depends on your position and the circumstances of the case.

Interpreter

Legal proceedings are complicated, confusing, and frightening to many people. All too often, attorneys and social workers assume that the proceeding is understood by the client when in fact it is not. Social workers, because of their relationship with the client, are in a position to explain the proceeding, what is likely to occur, what the possible outcomes are, and what alternatives might exist. This is not to suggest that the social worker should act as an attorney and provide legal advice; to do so would be improper and a disservice to the client. But it is proper for the social worker to provide information in terms understood by the client without trying to advise the client to pursue a certain course of action. A social worker can also help a client formulate questions to ask an attorney or can accompany a client to an attorney's office.

Consider the case of a woman brought to an emergency room during a psychotic episode. Assume the attending psychiatrists believe continued hospitalization is necessary and initiate commitment proceedings. The woman would probably have been informed of her rights at the time of admission, and later she will be informed of the pending hearing and her rights related to the hearing. But it cannot be assumed she understands what might happen because she has been told once and given some information to read. A knowledgeable social worker can be invaluable in providing her with information in terms she can understand. Moreover, a social worker who has continuing contact with the woman can repeat information and answer questions as they arise. To be told once is often not enough. Finally, a social worker could help the woman communicate with her attorney.

The social worker can perform the role of interpreter, not only with the client, but also with the client's friends and family members. Friends and family members may be in a position to help the client, but they are often overlooked in the legal process. If they are not informed, they cannot be involved and cannot help the client. Social workers often know who these significant others are and can provide them with information in behalf of the client—as long as the social workers are mindful of the client's right to confidentiality.

As will be discussed in chapter 18, releasing information about a client to third parties without the client's consent may be unethical, or even illegal, for a social worker. Before social workers discuss a case with a client's family, friends, or anyone else—even when they are trying to assist the client—they should obtain the client's consent. And if the client does not consent, a social worker may not be free to interpret the case or the client's position to anyone.

Keeping the requirements of confidentiality in mind, social workers can provide a further valuable service to clients involved in legal proceedings by speaking to other parties in a case. Attorneys for one party cannot ethically talk to other parties, except through their attorneys, but social workers, who are not partisan advocates, may speak with other parties and perhaps explain the proceedings to them. Of course, social workers should not take it upon themselves to persuade other parties to go along with their clients' wishes or interfere in any way with attorneys' relationships with their clients or with attorneys' handling of cases, but social workers may help facilitate cases in their role as interpreters.

Counselor

What happens after the hearing is over? The judge calls the next case, the attorneys return to their offices, and the client is left to live with the outcome. In most cases, the attorneys will have little subsequent contact with the client, but any social worker involved in the case may continue to be involved. This continuing contact can enable the social worker to help the client accept the outcome and comply with any orders imposed by the court.

This aspect of litigation is often overlooked, but it is an important aspect for several reasons. First, even though a judge has handed down a decision, a dispute is not truly resolved until the resolution is accepted by the parties. Anyone who has been involved in continuing custody battles knows this fact only too well. Closure must be reached psychologically as well as legally. Second, in many cases one family member has taken action against another, engendering feelings of guilt. For example, a woman who has sought an order keeping her battering husband away from their family or a man who has asked to be named guardian of his elderly mother, might be quite ambivalent about their actions; they might need help in dealing with their feelings about the actions. Third, in many cases the court imposes orders with which a party must comply. These orders may require substantial changes in a party's life. This is true in most juvenile court cases. Yet, a party may not fully understand an order or the duty to comply. A party may further experience difficulties in complying. The social worker can help the parties comply by explaining the orders and working with them on compliance.

In sum, the social worker who continues to be involved with the client after a court case is over can help the client reach closure, sort out reactions to what has occurred, and comply with court orders—in other words, to move on with life.

EFFECTIVE PERFORMANCE OF THESE ROLES

Many social workers feel unprepared for and fearful of their roles in the hearing process, particularly when they involve appearing in court. Testifying is especially frightening. While each case in which you might have to play a role or have to appear in court is somewhat different, there are some general principles you can learn for any role and some steps you can follow to prepare for any court appearance. These general principles and steps can make the process less frightening and your work more effective. In addition, some of what is said on testifying can also enable you to assist clients who may be called to testify. Testifying can be even more frightening for the client than the social worker, particularly if the client is a child. While preparing witnesses for testifying is the attorney's role, attorneys often neglect to prepare witnesses psychologically, which is something a social worker can and should do.

Determining Whether or Not to Initiate a Court Action

In many situations, social workers' involvement in cases begins long before they have to appear or testify. The social worker may have been actively involved in deciding whether to initiate the court action and, as has been stated, may even have been the person who actually initiated the action by filing a petition.

Initiating a court action can be thought of as one type of intervention. It is, however, an intervention that has profound consequences for your clients and that may have a significant impact on your work with your clients. Therefore, it is an action that should never be undertaken lightly. You must determine whether or not initiating a court action is the best intervention before attempting to initiate one.

There are no hard and fast rules to determine if a court action is desirable, but you can ask yourself certain questions that will help you make such determinations. First, what do you hope to achieve? Second, can the desired result be achieved in any other way? Third, is the desired result likely to be achieved through court action? Fourth, does there appear to be sufficient evidence for the court to act as you hope? Fifth, how have the attorneys and judges who are likely to be involved responded in similar cases?

To illustrate these points, consider the case of a confused, elderly man found wandering outside in freezing temperatures. What you want to do is protect the man; you believe his health is endangered and he is unable to act to protect himself. Appointment of a guardian might thus be indicated. But, can the man be protected without appointment of a guardian? And will the appointment of a guardian assure that he will be protected? Moreover, under the law in your State, does there seem to be evidence sufficient to support a determination that a guardian should be appointed? And are the attorneys and the judge likely to take the action you want to take?

These last two points—your assessment of the sufficiency of the evidence and your evaluation of the willingness of court officials to act as you would like them to act—need further comment.

On the first point, the suggestion that you assess the sufficiency of the evidence is not a suggestion that you should practice law. The assessment of the evidence is the responsibility of the attorney who will pursue the case either at your request or the request of someone else. Moreover, only the attorney can assess the admissibility of the evidence. However, before going to the attorney, you should consider how strong your case appears to be. Returning to the example of the elderly man, one or two incidents of being found outside, especially in the absence of other information about the man, would probably not be enough to warrant appointment of a guardian. You risk frightening the man and embarrassing yourself by going to an attorney or a court without more evidence.

On the second point, your assessment of the response of court officials should not determine what you do. It simply prepares you for what you might encounter. Again using the example of the elderly man, the fact that judges in a given area are reluctant to appoint guardians should

not prevent you from requesting this action if you believe it is truly necessary.

Presenting Admissible, Credible, and Persuasive Evidence

As we have said, the **rules of evidence** determine what may and may not be presented as evidence in a hearing, that is, what is **admissible**. Admissibility is primarily the concern and responsibility of the attorneys for the parties. In preparing cases, the attorneys must determine what will be admissible, how they can make helpful evidence admissible, and how they can convince a judge that harmful evidence is not admissible. During any hearings, the attorneys must object to evidence offered by the opposing side if they want to keep it out of evidence.

Evidence may be admissible but it may not be given much weight or even be believed by the trier of fact. That is, admissible evidence may not be persuasive or credible. As a social worker, you cannot be expected to know if evidence you might present will be admissible although you should have some general knowledge of admissibility and some general ideas on making your evidence admissible. However, you can be expected to know what evidence will be both persuasive and credible and how you can be a witness that is both persuasive and credible.

What is meant by *credible*? Simply put, credible evidence is believable. Evidence is believable if it is consistent with facts that have already been established in a case, consistent with common experience, and consistent with itself. What makes you a credible witness? You are credible as a witness if you have a professional demeanor, appear to be unbiased, are familiar with the facts of the case, and demonstrate expertise in the area involved in the case—in other words, if you have done a good job in a case prior to testifying.

What is meant by *persuasive*? Persuasive evidence or testimony is the kind of evidence or testimony that influences decisions; it is convincing. While we have said that the social worker as a witness is primarily concerned with providing information, you certainly want your testimony to be given due weight by the trier of fact. You do not want to be an advocate, and, indeed, becoming an advocate for a position may weaken the persuasiveness of your testimony, but there is no point to testifying if your testimony has no influence on the decision made by the trier of fact.

What makes you a persuasive witness? If your testimony is credible, it may also be persuasive, but sometimes more than mere credibility is necessary. Just because your testimony is believed, it will not necessarily exert an influence on the trier of fact. A professional demeanor contributes not only to credibility but also to persuasiveness. The conviction with which you testify plays a large part in persuasiveness as does the manner in which you present yourself. And, the less you try to persuade and the more natural and knowledgeable you are on the witness stand, the more persuasive you will be.

The desire to be credible and persuasive should influence your work as you prepare to testify and as you testify. It should also influence your work long before that point. Any of your written work that may be admitted into evidence should be credible and persuasive, including your notes and files, the records you have maintained, and the reports you have written for yourself, your supervisors, the court, or the parties.

An emphasis on credibility and persuasiveness, as you work on a case, as you prepare to testify, and as you testify, does not mean that you should have no concern about admissibility. As has been stated, the lawyers in a case are primarily responsible for the admissibility of evidence, but you can better investigate and assess a case if you are somewhat aware of what evidence may and may not be admissible. Moreover, you want what you have to say and what real evidence you want to present to the court to be admissible. After all, credible and persuasive evidence that is not admissible serves no purpose.

You can take two steps to increase the probability that your evidence will be admissible and your testimony will be accepted. First, in your records, reports, and testimony, you can and should attempt to communicate what is known directly to you, not secondhand or hearsay information. Second, you should not present conclusions that you cannot support with facts or with your professional expertise. Evidence presented by social workers is probably most often criticized because it is full of hearsay and conclusions, not facts.

As was stated in the discussion of hearsay in chapter 2, there are many exceptions to the rule excluding hearsay, but hearsay is generally not admissible. And even if it is admissible, it may not be as persuasive or credible as firsthand information. Thus, you want to avoid hearsay whenever possible.

Conclusions can be thought of as judgments you make. Conclusions may not be admissible because they take the responsibility away from the trier of fact to decide the case and place it with the witness.

Conclusions may also be mere opinion. With the exception of certain matters that are rationally based on the perception of a witness and that are generally expressed in the form of an opinion, like the speed of an automobile, only the opinions of expert witnesses are admissible into evidence. But even if you are qualified as an expert witness in a particular case, and thus allowed to give your opinion on a matter, or even if you are permitted to give an opinion on a certain matter as a lay witness, your testimony will be more credible and persuasive, and more likely to be admissible, if you avoid conclusions and testify as to the facts instead.

To illustrate, in most jurisdictions, lay witnesses can give their opinions as to whether or not someone they observed was drunk; in all jurisdictions, experts on the effects of alcohol use on human behavior would probably be allowed to testify that someone was intoxicated. Thus, you could probably testify in a case, "In my opinion, Mrs. Smith was drunk." But much more persuasive and credible testimony, and testimony that is even more likely to be admissible, would be: "Mrs. Smith's speech was slurred and she bobbed her head and rolled her eyes when she talked. She was unsteady on her feet and her hair and clothes were disheveled. I smelled alcohol on her breath." To further illustrate, instead of testifying, "Mr. Jones seemed nervous," you would be more credible and persuasive, and your testimony would more likely be admissible, if you testified that: "Mr. Jones's hands shook when he spoke to me and he kept avoiding my eyes. I noticed perspiration on his upper lip. His voice wavered and he kept stuttering."

Documenting Your Work

If you wait to prepare for court until right before you are required to appear or even until you are first asked to appear, you have waited too long. The credibility, persuasiveness, and even admissibility of any evidence you might present can be dependent on the quality of the documentation of your work. This documentation includes your personal case notes, the files and records you have maintained, and, occasionally, audio and video tapes of interviews.

Social workers often believe that a given case will never involve court action. This, combined with a dislike of record-keeping, can result in little or no documentation or vague documentation. Without good documentation, important information, such as the dates of contacts, with whom contacts were made, and what was observed and said during contacts, may not be remembered. This can be a problem whether or not you have to go to court, but poor documentation is particularly damaging if you do have to appear in court. You cannot always rely on your memory. If your memory fails and you do not have good documentation, you could weaken or destroy a good case. However, if you kept good, contemporaneous records while working on a case even if you do not remember anything about the case or forget aspects of the case, your records may be admissible under one of two exceptions to the hearsay rule known as **past recollection recorded** and **present recollection refreshed**.

And, even if your memory is good, poor documentation may make your evidence less credible and persuasive. Good records can provide good support for what you say in court.

What should you record? You should record specific information about the dates, places, times, and substance of client contacts or contacts with other persons related in some way to the case. The information should be written in a style that is factual, objective, specific, clear, to the point, and without jargon.

As you record, it is wise to remember that ultimately all your records might be viewed by judges, attorneys and your clients—despite your expectations of confidentiality. As we shall see in chapter 18, in many States the confidentiality of social workers' and agency records is not protected, and you may be required to allow your client, your client's attorney, and others involved in a case to read your personal notes as well as your agency's records. But even if the confidentiality of your notes and records is protected, it is good practice to be honest, but to record as if anything you write might eventually be read by your client or by your client's attorney.

Recording events as soon as possible is also good practice. The more contemporaneous your records are, the more reliable, credible, and persuasive they will be. Moreover, records made long after an event may not be admissible under an exception to the hearsay rule. For example, the business records exception only applies to contemporaneous records.

You should note that many jurisdictions permit expert witnesses to base their opinions on records prepared by other people, even if the records would be inadmissible or contain inadmissible portions. This is because experts need not rely only on admissible evidence in forming their opinions. Thus, your records may not be admissible and you may not

be appearing in a case, but your records may be examined by an expert and may form the basis of the expert's testimony. This is another reason to take care in preparing your documentation.

Writing Court Reports

Before a social worker ever appears in court on a case, the social worker is likely to have written one or more court reports related to the case. The content and the form of the reports vary according to their purposes and the jurisdiction in which they will be used.

Types of Court Reports. Social workers who expect to be called to testify might write a report for personal use simply to prepare for a hearing. For example, a child welfare worker who has investigated a complaint of child neglect and who expects to be called to testify might prepare a summary of his personal contacts with the child, the child's parents, and the collateral informants. In preparation for a hearing based on a child's truancy, a school social worker might prepare a list of dates of the child's absences, the dates and times of her contacts with the child and the child's parents, and what occurred during the contacts.

Social workers can usually take this type of report into hearings and use it to refresh their memory during testimony. Such a report would not typically be given in advance to any attorneys who are involved nor would it be admissible into evidence. However, an attorney or the judge can properly ask to inspect the report if it is used during testimony. You should therefore not include any information in such a report that you do not want others to read.

Social workers, particularly those working in child welfare agencies, might also write reports to inform an attorney about a case. For example, in a case of child abuse, a social worker might write a report for the attorney responsible for filing or presenting child abuse cases for the agency. Such a report not only would provide information about the child welfare worker's personal observations of the child and the child's parents but also would identify other individuals who have knowledge of the case, such as physicians, teachers, day care center staff, and others, and would briefly summarize what information the social worker expects them to provide. This report helps the attorney decide whether or not to file a case and forms a basis of the attorney's efforts to build the case.

Even though these reports are written for a specific attorney, they may be given to other attorneys who are involved. This may occur informally or it may occur through discovery. Such reports may be protected from discovery by the so-called **work product rule**, which protects an attorney's work from discovery, but, as with routine case recording, you should work under the assumption that anything you write may be seen by other people.

Social workers also frequently write reports to inform the court. Reports you write to prepare to testify and reports you write to inform an attorney are, in a sense, informal reports. Their content and form are not determined by any particular rules, but by your own preferences and perhaps by local custom. The content and form of many reports whose primary purpose is to inform the court may, however, be deter-

mined either explicitly or implicitly by law. Two examples illustrate this point.

First, in many States, the factors a judge should consider in awarding child custody as part of a divorce action are specified in a statute which, typically, also provides that the judge can or should consider all or any other relevant factors. Other statutes may allow the judge to ask a social worker to conduct an investigation of the divorcing parents when custody is disputed and to submit a report of the investigation to the judge. Given that certain factors to be considered in decision making are specifically mentioned in a statute, both the judge and the attorneys will focus on these factors. To be most useful, the social worker's investigation and the report on the investigation should cover these factors but should also cover all the factors that the social worker thinks are relevant in this particular case. Ignoring something that would be clearly relevant to the court's decision because it is not specifically mentioned in a statute limits the usefulness and the persuasiveness of a report.

Second, in many States, a statute provides that before committing a mentally ill adult to a hospital, a judge must consider a report on alternatives to hospitalization. The report, which is often done by a social worker employed in a mental health facility, must contain certain information that may have to be presented in a certain way or in a certain format.

Any court report may have to contain certain information. The required information might be presented to the court in narrative form, but an approved court form, which the person making the report can simply fill in or which has boxes that can be checked, might also be available.

The courts expect and are used to any court forms, and their use is strongly preferred although perhaps not required.

Principles to Follow in Writing Court Reports. No matter what the type of report you are writing, the style of writing should be the same—factual, objective, specific, to the point, and without jargon. Statements such as "they appear to have a co-dependent relationship," "his affect was sometimes depressive," "home maintenance was deficient," or "her school attendance was good" say little that is useful to anyone.

Any report you write must clearly distinguish between what you know from your first hand observation and what you have learned from other sources. When you obtain information from other sources, your report should, to the greatest extent possible given the law and professional ethics concerning confidentiality, fully identify the sources.

In writing reports where the content is determined or suggested by law, clearly including the specified content is important. If the practice or requirement in a given court is to use a certain format, you should use that format. A general rule is to provide information in the format that those who will use it expect to see.

You should carefully proofread any report you write, and any report you submit should be a "clean" report. Misspelled words, typographical errors, poor punctuation and grammar, and excessive erasures not only detract from readability but leave the impression that the writer is careless at best and not intelligent at worst. In short, a poor presentation can mask good information and detract from a report's credibility and persuasiveness.

Admissibility of Reports. Depending on the type of case and on the nature and purpose of a report, it may or may not need to be admitted into evidence and may or may not be admissible evidence. In general, you should keep in mind that a report, even a report prepared at the request of a court, is an out of court statement that constitutes hearsay if it is being used to establish the truth of its contents. As such, it would be inadmissible unless an exception to the hearsay rule applies.

As with records, admissible reports may contain hearsay within them. For example, an admissible report might state: "Mr. Smith told me he saw Mrs. Jones hit Jane." The report might be admitted into evidence with the hearsay portions stricken or the whole report may be rendered inadmissible because of the hearsay within it. You make your reports more credible, more persuasive, and more likely to be admitted into evidence if you remove hearsay yourself. Of course, you must indicate if information has been obtained from others and is not of your personal knowledge.

Reports contained in your records that are not prepared for courts or for any court case, such as reports for your supervisor, are also written out of court statements that are hearsay if they are being admitted to establish the truth of matters contained in them. Reports in your records might, however, be admissible, with all inadmissible portions stricken, under the business records or another exception to the hearsay rule.

Responding to Discovery

As was noted in chapter 2, **discovery** (i.e., formal and informal investigation of a case by the lawyers for each side) may occur in many cases before any trials. As part of discovery in a case in which you have been involved, you may be asked to respond to **interrogatories** (i.e., written questions from a party to which you must respond in writing) or may have your **deposition** taken (i.e., may have to respond orally to questions from an attorney).

You should always respond to interrogatories with the assistance of a lawyer. In fact, usually your lawyer will actually write the answers after questioning you or will write the final answers after you write draft answers; you will only approve the answers and sign the interrogatories. You should make sure the answers are accurate before signing.

If you are only a witness and not a party to a case, you may not have a lawyer available to assist you in a deposition. You should, however, treat a deposition as any other form of testifying and follow the advice given later in this chapter. Despite the informality of some depositions and the fact that no judge is present, you should take depositions seriously. Many cases are settled based on testimony in depositions and, in some cases, transcripts of depositions may be admitted into evidence instead of having the person deposed (i.e., the **deponent**) testify. Further, deposition transcripts or portions of them may be submitted in support of motions.

Testifying

The Mechanics of Testifying. If you understand the mechanics of testifying, testifying may be a little less mysterious to you and thus a little less frightening. These mechanics will be discussed and some of the key terms related to testifying will be defined. The actual terms may differ from jurisdiction to jurisdiction, but the terms we use are the usual terms.

You will be notified of the hearing in which you will testify in one of several ways. An attorney might call and ask you to appear on a certain date or you might receive a formal written request for you to appear, usually called a **summons** or a **subpoena**. Oral requests and informal written requests do not require you to appear, while a summons or subpoena usually requires you to appear. If you fail to appear as directed, the court may issue a warrant ordering your arrest or may hold you in contempt of court.

Usually, a summons or subpoena will tell you to appear at the time a hearing is scheduled to begin, but you will probably not testify at that time. Often, several cases will be scheduled to be heard at the same time and each hearing may not begin on the day it is scheduled to begin. Even if the hearing in your case does begin at the time or even on the scheduled day and is the first hearing that day, you may not be the first witness, and even if you are scheduled to be the first witness, you may not begin to testify until long after the hearing has started.

After a hearing in which you are scheduled to appear does begin, you may be asked to remain outside of the courtroom until you are called to testify so that your testimony will not be influenced by the testimony of others or the arguments of the attorneys.

You will be called to testify either by one of the attorneys or by a court officer, like the **courtroom clerk** or the **bailiff**. When you are called, you will come forward and be sworn in by the clerk, bailiff or sometimes by the judge. Whoever swears you in, you will be asked to raise your right hand and then asked whether you swear or affirm to "tell the truth, the whole truth, and nothing but the truth." You simply respond, "I do." You will be directed where to go to be sworn and where to be seated after you are sworn. There usually is a special seat for those testifying on the **witness stand**.

The attorney who requested your appearance will question you first.[1] This questioning is called **direct examination**. Direct examination usually begins with the attorney asking your name and your address or place of work. Typically, he or she will also ask some preliminary questions that elicit information about your professional experience and your educational background.

If you are going to be testifying as an expert witness, the questions about your experience and background will be more extensive and probing. To qualify as an expert witness, you must show that you have training, experience, and knowledge of a matter that an ordinary person would not have.

After finishing this questioning, the attorney may move to have you qualified as an expert witness. The opposing attorney may question you further on your qualifications before the judge rules on the motion. The judge may also question you on

your qualifications before ruling on the motion. This questioning to determine if an expert witness is qualified is called *voir dire* (as is the questioning of a child witness to determine if the child is competent or the questioning of a juror to determine if the juror is qualified).

After the preliminary background questions and any *voir dire,* you will be asked a series of questions on direct examination that are designed to elicit information about the case. If you are an expert witness, you may also be asked to provide an opinion on an aspect of the case. Questions on direct examination are supposed to be nondirective or nonleading but are not supposed to call for a long, narrative answer. Typically, questions on direct examination will be questions like: "Did you go to the child's home?", "Who was there?" or "How was the child dressed?", rather than questions like "The child was dirty, wasn't she?" or "What did you see at the child's home?" Typical questions to an expert might be: "Do you think the respondent can take care of himself?" or "In your opinion, would the child benefit from a more structured environment?" Questions to an expert may be hypothetical, such as: "If this child had been beaten by his mother, in your opinion should he nevertheless remain with his mother?"

After the direct examination is finished, the attorney for the opposing party may question you. This questioning is called **cross examination**. During cross examination, the opposing attorney will typically ask questions intended to discredit (or **impeach**) your testimony during direct examination. Questions on cross examination may also be intended to discredit (or impeach) you. The latter type of

---

1. Throughout this discussion, it will be assumed that an attorney will be questioning you and that an attorney may be objecting to your testimony or the evidence you present. Of course, if the parties are not represented by attorneys, they may do the questioning and objecting themselves.

questions may go to your credibility, your biases, your motives to testify falsely or, if you are an expert, your qualifications and competence. On cross examination, you may be asked leading questions, such as: "Wasn't it dark in the corridor where you said you saw her hit the boy?", "You were drinking that day, weren't you?", "Didn't you only interview her for fifteen minutes?" or "You don't have any African-American friends, do you?"

Following cross examination, there may be **redirect examination**, that is, follow up questions by the attorney who conducted the direct examination. Redirect examination attempts to rehabilitate you and your testimony.

During questioning, the attorneys for either side may **object** to a question or to a response. The judge will then decide whether or not the question should be allowed or the testimony admitted, that is, whether the objection will be **sustained** or **overruled**. Without an objection, improper questions will normally be allowed and inadmissible testimony will usually be admitted. Most judges will only stop improper questions and declare testimony inadmissible on their own in rare or exceptional cases.

Disputes about admissibility are generally resolved outside of the presence of the jury, and perhaps also outside the presence of the witness. There may be a whispered conference at the bench, the jury or witnesses may be asked to leave the court, or the attorneys and judge may go to the judge's office, usually known as the judge's **chambers.** Sometimes, a judge reviews disputed evidence, particularly evidence claimed to be confidential, or a witness is questioned in chambers or *in camera. In camera* testimony is usually not included

in the record and *in camera* review of evidence is normally off the record.

Following questions by the attorneys, there may be questioning by any guardian *ad litem.* Some judges like to ask questions of witnesses at this point. Even though they may ask witnesses questions at any time, most judges do not do any questioning of witnesses.

When all questioning is finished, the judge will ask you to step down. You may leave unless the judge instructs you differently. In most cases, you will not be recalled for further testimony. However, you are subject to recall at any time until the hearing is concluded. If you are recalled, it simply means an attorney wants to ask you more questions.

Preparing to Testify. There are several steps you can follow in preparing to testify that will make the experience less stressful and that are important to your effectiveness in your role as a witness. Some of these steps may, and should, be taken well in advance of the hearing. Others will be taken right before you take the stand in the courtroom.

You may first learn that your presence will be required at a hearing when you are served with a subpoena, but you may know that your presence at a hearing is necessary or expected before you get any subpoena. If this is the case, you may want to ask the attorney who will call you to obtain a subpoena. A subpoena can be important to your continuing work with your client. In many cases, you will be providing information that may, from the client's perspective, be damaging to the client. This is clearly the case in juvenile court actions or in hearings involving probation violations or commitments to mental hospitals. And, yet, you may have to or want to continue to work with the client after the hearing ends. If you testify in response to a subpoena, you can honestly say that you did not choose to testify; you were forced to testify. It lessens the sense that you willingly took sides against the client. A subpoena may also be necessary to show to your employer or to obtain compensation for going to court and testifying.

A subpoena may require you to bring certain documents to the court as well as to appear to testify. Subpoenas that require documents are usually called **subpoenas *duces tecum***. Sometimes, you do not have to appear in response to a subpoena *duces tecum*; your obligation may be satisfied if you merely provide the documents. This may not be clear from the subpoena itself. Thus, you should find out your obligation from the attorney who sent you the subpoena.

If you receive a subpoena for documents or for testimony, unless you are very sure of the law concerning confidentiality, it is wise to consult with an attorney before turning over the documents or testifying. If the confidentiality of the information you are asked to provide is protected by law, certain legal actions can be taken to prevent its release.

You need to take several other steps in preparation for the hearing. First, if you have not written a court report, you should prepare notes for use while testifying. Second, you should read and reread the case record, your personal notes, and any reports you have written. Third, you should consult with the attorney who has requested that you appear regarding the questions he or she is likely to ask and the questions you can expect from the other side during cross examination. A role

play of your testimony with the attorney would be most helpful. Fourth, you should visit the courtroom where the hearing will be held if you have not appeared there before. Finally, you should verify the date, time, and place of the hearing.

Reading and rereading your material related to the case is particularly important. While you may believe you have the information firmly in mind, you may have been involved with many other cases and people. The particular details of this case may easily escape your recall, especially under the stress of actually testifying. You can be sure that the attorneys have carefully read all your documents. As they listen to your testimony, they will compare what you say with what you submitted earlier. They will note discrepancies, and they may use discrepancies to try to discredit you.

If you are testifying as an expert witness, you should prepare a current résumé or vita to show your qualifications to render an expert opinion. You should review your qualifications with the attorney who is calling you. Courts are increasingly recognizing social workers as expert witnesses, but being recognized as an expert is not assured. You must do your homework and be prepared to convince the judge that you are qualified to provide information and opinions of value to the court. In addition, you should familiarize yourself with the leading treatises and articles on the subject on which you are testifying. You may be questioned on the consistency of your opinion with those of established experts as found in these sources.

There are several steps to take and points to remember on the day of the hearing. Some of these points may seem simplistic. But they are important and often forgotten and thus need to be made.

First, dress conservatively. A conservative appearance is part of successful role performance. Judges and juries expect professionals to appear and to act professional. If professionals do not meet these expectations, their credibility and persuasiveness is diminished.

Second, you should check with the attorney who subpoenaed you to make sure that the hearing is going on as scheduled. Hearings are often postponed, that is, **continued** or **adjourned**, and cases are often settled after the witnesses have been subpoenaed. Attorneys may forget to notify the witnesses that their appearance is no longer required. There are few things more annoying than preparing for a court appearance and going to court only to be told your appearance is unnecessary. Indeed, it is best to check with the attorney before you start to prepare intensely and again a day or two before the hearing as well as on the day of the hearing, if possible. Postponements and settlements often come at the last minute.

Third, review your notes and reports. You do not want to memorize testimony, and you do not want your testimony to sound rehearsed. But you do want to be as prepared and knowledgeable as possible for questioning and you want everything fresh in your mind on the day of the hearing.

Fourth, be on time. As has been stated, the time on a subpoena is usually the time a hearing is scheduled to begin and you probably will not be testifying at this time. While it is annoying to be kept waiting, especially when faced with other work that needs to be done, and tempting to show up late, you should never assume that you will have to wait and therefore appear late. If you are not in court when you are called, you risk delaying the proceedings and irritating the judge, at best, and an arrest warrant or contempt citation, at worst.

Finding out from the attorney who subpoenaed you when you are realistically expected to testify and obtaining the attorney's permission to appear at this time rather than at the time stated on the subpoena may be possible. Alternatively, if your office is close to the courthouse, arranging to be on call may be possible. But unless you make alternative arrangements, you should appear at the time stated in the subpoena.

Fifth, while you are in the courthouse waiting to appear, do not discuss the case with anyone and do not show anyone your reports or notes. Act professionally even while you are waiting. There are always many people in the halls of the courthouse. Anyone you see might be a judge, a member of the jury, another witness, a party to a case, or an attorney in the case in which you are appearing. Improper comments or behavior can diminish your credibility and, under some circumstances, provide grounds for dismissal of the case.

As you are waiting to testify—and preparing to testify—you should remember that being a witness is simply another role a social worker plays. Like other roles, it is a demanding role, and it requires specific skills. But if you have prepared well, performing this role successfully is no more difficult than performing any other role.

Points to Remember While Testifying. In general, as you are testifying, you should remember that not only you but also the attorneys are playing certain roles and following certain rules. It is the role of the attorney who asked you to testify to get certain information from you. You should answer only the questions this attorney asks. If you volunteer information instead of answering these questions, you infringe on the attorney's right and responsibility to develop the case by asking you questions. The opposing attorney's role is to challenge your testimony or you. You should remember that the process is adversarial and you should not be defensive or hurt when this occurs. The attacks are not personal but are part of your and the attorney's roles. Your role is to provide information that is persuasive and credible. To perform this role, you should be polite and courteous and address the court as "your honor." You should also be serious and dignified and speak clearly and distinctly, without using jargon. And, even though you are playing a role, it is best to be yourself as much as possible and to be straightforward.

More specifically, you should always answer the question you are asked and only that question. You should not try to provide information you think is more important than the information you are being asked to provide; you should not try to determine the "real" meaning of the question and answer based on your determination; and you should not evade a hard question. Being evasive makes you less credible.

If an attorney objects to a question another attorney has asked you, do not answer the question immediately. Instead, wait for the judge to rule on the objection. If the objection is sustained, you need not answer the question. You only must answer if the objection is overruled. If there has been a long argument about the objection, by the time the court has overruled the objection, you may be unsure of the question. You should ask the attorney to repeat the question before you attempt to answer it.

Sometimes, you may be troubled by a question, particularly a question on cross examination, to which there is no immediate objection. If you pause before answering or somehow indicate you have a problem with the question, an attorney may object to it. If there is no objection, but you would find answering the question difficult, explaining your difficulty is better than attempting to answer.

A question with several parts is objectionable as a **compound question**, but if there is no objection to such a question, you should separate out the parts carefully and answer each part separately.

You are not expected to know and understand everything. If you do not understand a question, say you do not understand it and ask for clarification before you answer. If you do not know the answer to a question, say you do not know. Attempts to guess the meaning of a question or to guess an answer will only cause trouble for you.

If you realize after one question that you have answered a previous question incorrectly, you should correct your error as soon as possible.

Always think before you respond. There is no advantage to rushing out an answer.

Be aware of double negatives, particularly when responding to leading questions on cross examination. If you are asked: "Isn't it true that you didn't see her?" think whether a response of "yes" means you did or did not see her.

Your testimony will be more effective and credible if you answer with facts as much as possible—even if you are testifying as an expert witness. Do not state conclusions or give your opinion unless you are asked to do so. Your testimony will be more effective if you use simple, clear English instead of jargon or buzz words. You do not impress anyone if you use big words, particularly if you use the words incorrectly or mispronounce them. Say: "Mrs. Brown spoke in a low monotone, gave one word or very brief answers and kept her head lowered when I spoke to her," instead of saying: "Mrs. Brown was suffering from severe depression when I conducted my examination." Be as exact as possible. Say: "I spoke to her five times," not "several times."

If appropriate, admit your sympathies and beliefs honestly on direct examination. This will look better than if they are brought out on cross examination. Remember, the goal of the attorney who cross examines you is to discredit you and your testimony.

Attorneys may use a variety of tactics to discredit witnesses and witnesses' testimony during cross examination. They may use leading questions that require a yes or no answer when no such simple answer is possible or when it would be misleading. They may be condescending, attacking, or overly friendly. They may ask repetitious questions in an attempt to make you answer inconsistently or they may badger you. They may reverse your words. And they may question you about your personal beliefs and your personal life to show possible bias, prejudice, or motive to lie. For example, in a child custody case involving a gay father, you may be asked your sexual orientation, if you believe in the Bible, or if you know anyone who died of AIDS.

The important point to remember when faced with such tactics is that this is part of the system and not something that is happening to just you. Your best defense is to remain alert, calm, and professional. Resist being lulled into a false sense of security when an attorney seems overly friendly and resist becoming defensive or hostile when an attorney seems to be attacking you. Ask the court for permission to explain if a yes or no answer seems incomplete or misleading. Remember that the attorney who asked you to testify can and may object to inappropriate questioning, but only if you give him or her an opportunity to do so. In the absence of a sustained objection to a question, answer as well as you can. Also remember that the attorney who called you to testify can rehabilitate your testimony and give you a chance to explain on redirect examination. This will probably make you feel better and be more relaxed. It should also make you avoid attempts to explain instead of responding to questions during cross examination. Such attempts generally make witnesses look as if they are squirming.

This discussion of cross examination should not make you reluctant to ever be a witness. Rigorous cross examination is rare and cross examination that attacks the witness personally is even rarer. The discussion is included, not because you are likely to encounter such tactics on cross examination, but because you should be prepared if you ever do encounter them.

Learning from Experience

Your performance in court can, like all aspects of your professional performance, be improved. You should not just sit back after a hearing is over and heave a sigh of relief—at least if you want to improve your performance the next time you go to court. Instead, if possible, you should ask the attorneys who were involved and the judge to critique your petition, your court report, or your testimony. Many attorneys and judges are quite willing to offer suggestions about how you presented information. In addition, they may be willing to clarify legal points that were made that you might not have understood.

You may also find it useful to read a transcript of your testimony or to listen to a tape recording of it if either is available. In doing so, you will be able to identify patterns of speech and manners of responding to questions that you were unaware of and that you might want to correct.

Protecting Confidentiality

Much that has been said in this chapter involves releasing information about clients. Social workers must be sensitive to the consequences to clients of disclosing information about them and must be aware of legal and professional requirements to maintain confidentiality. In working with the courts, social workers must consider how they can fulfill the competing demands to disclose information and to keep information confidential.

Confidentiality will be considered more fully in chapter 18, but several points must be made here in relation to appearing in court. First, you must be knowledgeable about the law regarding confidentiality. Second, you should record only information that is essential and factual and should disclose only information that you are required to disclose. Third, you should inform the client that you are recording information and that you may be required to disclose some of it. Last, you should consult with your supervisor and, in some cases, with an attorney before you disclose any information.

4

Locating and Using the Law

Assume you have been asked to conduct an investigation and prepare an evaluation for a case in court where child custody and visitation are being contested by parents who are divorcing. Before you begin, you would want to know your powers and responsibilities, for example: What can and should you do in conducting the investigation and reporting your findings? What information should your evaluation contain? Who can and should you interview? What reports can you obtain? In other words, you would want to know the law on the subject.

This chapter attempts to tell you how to find and decipher the law that you may need to do your job. It describes the books in which you will find the law and offers suggestions for reading and understanding the law when you find it. It tells you what various references to the law mean and how they can lead you to the law. It describes the books and computer tools you can use to find the law. Finally, using a request to do a child custody investigation as an example and Colorado law to illustrate, this chapter suggests a procedure you could use to answer your questions.[1]

COMPUTERIZED RESEARCH

In the past twenty years, the computer has had a major impact on the law and legal research. While the law is still being published in the books described later in this chapter, much of the law is also being published on CD-ROM or is available through the Internet or computer services dedicated to legal work. It is likely that, in the future, many of the books described in this chapter will be replaced by computer media or will be revised to make them more accessible to computer users. At the least, it can be expected that official publications of statutes and regulations will be in both computer media and books.

Because much of the law has been included in CD-ROMs or in computerized data bases maintained by private companies, computerized legal research has become common for attorneys. However, computerized research can be expensive and you may not have access to it as a social worker. One must have the CD-ROM equipment and a full set of CD-ROMs or must subscribe to one of the private data base or legal research services. Using such a private service can cost hundreds of dollars for a relatively short research session on top of a large monthly subscription fee. Many law school libraries offer free use of a private computerized legal research service to law students or to attorneys, but you may not be given access or you may not be near any law school library.

Even if you have access to computerized legal research, you must understand the current system of books and know what law is in what books. At this time, the computerized data bases are simply providing the law in a computer media, but in the format of the books and as found in the books. The law is still identified and referred to in its book form.

Thus, using and understanding the current system of books we describe in this chapter is still necessary for you. You

---

1. The Colorado law on child custody investigations will also be used as an example throughout this chapter, but you should know that this chapter does not necessarily use the current law. Using the current law to illustrate legal research sources and techniques is not necessary, but the current law would be necessary if you had really been asked to do a child custody investigation.

should be aware of the possibility of computerized legal research and you might be able to take advantage of it, but computerized research is only an option for some of you, and all of you need to understand the traditional method of locating the law.

PRIMARY SOURCES OF THE LAW

Statutes

In the federal system and in most States, there are three kinds of books containing statutes: books of session laws, codified statutes, and annotated codified statutes. Books of **session laws** contain all the statutes in a jurisdiction printed exactly as they were enacted and in the order in which they were enacted. Books of **codified statutes** contain statutes grouped according to subject matter; all statutes may not be included in the codified statutes. Books of **annotated codified statutes** contain the codified statutes supplemented with references to court opinions interpreting the statutes and other legal literature.

Session Laws. Legislatures rarely enact a single statute (i.e., a simple statement of a single rule). Rather, they enact a whole legislative scheme that includes many rules in a group of many different statutes. A group of statutes enacted at one time and making up such a scheme is often called an **act** or a **code.**[2] An act begins as a bill. All the

---

2.   This book will use the term *act* to refer both to an individual statute and to a group of statutes passed at one time. A *code* is always a group of statutes, but the whole group is not necessarily enacted in its entirety at one time as part of one legislative scheme.

statutes making up the act will be found in one bill, but each will be individually numbered as separate sections of the bill. Each section may have further subdivisions which will be separately numbered. There may also be groupings of proposed statutes within a bill. These groupings may be designated as **titles, articles,** or **chapters** and numbered individually.

In most but not all jurisdictions, when a bill is introduced in the legislature, it is assigned a number reflecting the chamber in which it has been introduced and when it was introduced. For example, the 90th bill introduced in the California senate might be called "SB 90." After a bill is passed, it may be assigned another number reflecting when it was passed. Any section, title, chapter, or article numbers used by the legislature in the bill are retained in the new number. For example, after a bill relating to the education of disabled children was passed by Congress, it was assigned the number "P.L. 94–142," meaning it was the 142d public law passed by the 94th Congress, and after a law requiring the police to report all domestic assaults was enacted by the Michigan legislature, it was assigned the number "P.A. 1978, No. 319, #1," meaning it was the first of a group of statutes that were part of the 319th public act passed by the Michigan legislature in 1978.

After being enacted, acts will be placed in the books of session laws in chronological order. The books of session laws in many States are called "Laws of [Name of State]" or "Statutes of [Name of State]." The books of session laws of the federal government are called the **United States Statutes at Large,** abbreviated Stat.

After being published in the books of session laws, acts may be referred to by a number reflecting the act's location in these books. For example, P.L. 94–142, the federal act relating to education of disabled children, is the 773d law in volume 89 of the United States Statutes at Large and, as such, can be referred to as "89 Stat. 773." Again, any section, title, article, chapter, or other numbers used by the legislature in its bill will usually be retained. Thus, section 1 of Colorado House Bill No. 1105, relating to child custody investigations, which was enacted in 1988, remained section 1 when the act was placed in chapter 105 of the 1988 volume of the Laws of Colorado on page 639, and can be referred to as "88 Colo. L., § 1, p. 639."[3]

All proposed changes to existing acts are also initially introduced as bills. As with other bills, these bills are assigned numbers reflecting the order in which they were introduced. If passed, as with other passed bills, they may be assigned public act numbers reflecting the order in which they were passed. The enacted changes are then compiled in the session laws, as are other acts, chronologically rather than with the acts they are changing. Thus, in 1938 when Massachusetts enacted an act that forbade discrimination against people using Seeing Eye dogs, it was the 155th act placed in the session laws for 1938 and is referred to as "1938 Mass. Acts 155, § 5." When the law was amended in 1978 to include hearing dogs, the amendment was placed in the session laws for 1978, not 1938, as the 458th law, not the 155th, and is referred to as "1978 Mass. Acts 458, § 2."

Session laws, public laws, and even bills that have been introduced into the legislature may be available through the

Internet in some States and for the federal government.

Codified Statutes. As you might guess, finding the current law on a given subject would be very difficult if you could only locate statutes in the session laws. All the statutes on the subject would be scattered depending on when they were enacted. Even if you located a statute in the session laws, you would not know if changes had been made to it by the legislature at a later date or, indeed, if it had been repealed. All of the changes to statutes, including their repeals, would also be scattered.

Because of this difficulty with chronological compilations of statutes, most jurisdictions organize their statutes into subject matter groupings and publish books containing the most current version of each statute (i.e., with all amendments up to the time of publication) within an appropriate subject matter grouping. Since the process of organizing statutes into subject matter groupings is called **codifying**, the books are called **codified statutes**. Often, they are referred to as **revised statutes**.

You will usually use the codified statutes rather than the session laws. To understand why, think about the request that you conduct an investigation in a child custody case in Colorado and your desire to know the relevant law before you begin. You do not need to know that a statute on such investigations was passed by the Colorado legislature in 1971 and what this statute says. What you need to know is the current law. This law may be the 1971 statute, but, in fact, the 1971 statute was amended in 1979, 1983, 1988, and 1993. You can find the 1971 statute, as it has been amended, in one place in the codified statutes. The most recent Col-

---

3. The symbol § is used as a substitute for the word *section.*

orado codified statutes would contain the latest version of the law in the section reserved for law on child custody. Moreover, many related laws that could be useful to you would be compiled close by.

When statutes are codified, they are referred to by still another number that reflects their location in their subject matter grouping. These numbers may not correspond with the section numbers used by the legislature when it adopted or amended a law. That is, section 23 of an act adopting a law may be section 65–2048 of the codified statutes and section 9 of an act amending section 65–2048 of the codified statutes would be put with section 65–2048. For example, the 1971 Colorado statute on child custody investigations was passed as section 1 of an act, but was codified at section 14–10–127 of the Colorado codified statutes. Section 14–10–127 was amended in 1988 in section 1 of an act and the new language was just made part of section 14–10–127.

The codified United States statutes are published in the **United States Code** (U.S.C.). The U.S.C. is divided into titles that represent groupings of statutes on certain subjects and that are arranged alphabetically by subject and then numbered to reflect this alphabetical order. For example, one title is "agriculture" (Title 7); all statutes dealing with agriculture are placed in this title. This title comes before the title on "education" (Title 20), which comes before the title on "public health and welfare" (Title 42). A title is not the equivalent of a book or bound volume; one title may be in more than one volume and several titles may be in one book.

What statutes fall into what titles in the U.S.C. may not be readily apparent. Guess that P.L. 94–142, the federal act relating to

education of handicapped children, is in Title 20 (the title on education) may be easy, but would you guess that the laws forbidding discrimination in housing and in employment are both found in Title 42, the title on public health and welfare? And, knowing that Title 42 is the title on public health and welfare, you might guess that it includes the Social Security Act, but would you guess that many laws relating to subsidized housing are found in Title 12, the title on banks and banking (because they address the financing of subsidized housing projects)? Fortunately, the U.S.C. has a complete topic index. By using the index, you can find the location of specific statutes.

Most State statutes are also codified. The names of the books of codified statutes differ from State to State. Some States call their codified statutes "Revised Statutes of (Name of State)" or simply "Codes of (Name of State)." Some States have no official codification, but one or more private publishers have codified the statutes and the books are referred to by the publisher's name. Thus, in New York, there are codified statutes referred to as **McKinney's.**

Subject matter groupings may be called "chapters" rather than "titles." Some States do not number the subject matter groupings and only refer to them by name, such as the Texas Family Code or the California Penal Code. Some States do not name the subject matter groupings and only refer to them by number. Individual statutes within each numbered grouping are then identified by using the number followed by a hyphen, colon, or period and the number within the grouping (e.g., 14–121, 17:05, 17.30). Fortunately, like the federal codified statutes, State codified statutes are fully indexed.

Hardbound volumes of federal and State codified statutes cannot be republished each time there is a revision in the law. The revisions are published in supplements to the bound volumes. Often these supplements are inserted in a pocket in the back of a bound volume and are called **pocket parts**. You should always check the supplements or the pocket parts of codified statutes to ensure that you are referring to or relying on current law. Similarly, you should make sure that you are using the most recently published complete set of the statutes. While most libraries will have current materials, finding sets that are several years out of date in an agency's bookshelves is not unusual.

Codified statutes for many States are now available on CD-ROM and are included in private computer data bases. Computerized data bases are kept up to date, while CD-ROMs may be updated as frequently as monthly or as infrequently as annually. You must make sure that any CD-ROM you use is current.

Annotated Codified Statutes. As discussed in chapter 1, the law on a given subject may encompass, not only applicable statutes, but also the statutes as they have been interpreted by the courts and, in some instances, as they have been expanded through regulations. In order to fully understand the law, you must know these decisions and regulations. You can find references to court decisions interpreting statutes and sometimes to regulations expanding upon statutes in books of **annotated codified statutes** published by private companies.

Annotated codified statutes set forth all the statutes of a given jurisdiction, in the same order as that used by any official codifications. Following each statute, they also set forth brief excerpts from or synopses of all authoritative court decisions interpreting the statute. In addition, they may set forth references to journal articles and other literature on a statute and to regulations interpreting a statute. They may also provide a brief legislative history, telling you all revisions to a bill, and giving you citations to session laws.

The two annotated versions of the United States Code are the **United States Code Annotated**, abbreviated as U.S.C.A., and the **United States Code Service**, abbreviated as U.S.C.S. They are published by two different private publishing houses. Various private publishing companies publish State annotated codified statutes. Because they are published by commercial publishing houses for private purposes, annotated books of statutes are unofficial versions of the statutes (unless, as is the case in some States, an annotated version of the codified statutes is designated as the official codified version). This means that the books are not "the law" but merely republications of the law along with editorial comments and edited bits and pieces of the law. Nevertheless, most attorneys use only the annotated codified statutes.

Like the codified statutes, annotated statutes are fully indexed. Also, like the codified statutes, hardbound volumes are not republished each time there is a change in the statutes or a new court opinion interpreting a statute. Instead, as with codified statutes, publishers print pocket parts and supplements. You must check the supplements and pocket parts to assure that you are relying on current law. Finally, like the codified statutes, the annotated codified statutes may be found on CD-ROM or through private computer legal research services.

Regulations

Federal regulations and regulations in many States are published at least twice during the process of promulgation. They are published first as they are proposed and later as they are adopted.

Both proposed and final federal regulations are published in the **Federal Register**, abbreviated as Fed. Reg., in roughly chronological order. The Federal Register is published every day except weekends and holidays and also contains other matters, such as reports of actions of the executive branch.

Federal regulations and regulations in some States are codified after they are adopted. Codified regulations are similar to the codified statutes. That is, the regulations are organized into subject matter groupings, not published chronologically, and are fully indexed by topic.

Codified federal regulations are published in the **Code of Federal Regulations**, abbreviated as C.F.R. The C.F.R. subject matter groupings, known as *titles,* roughly correspond to the titles of the United States Code. The C.F.R. is republished annually, but, because regulations may change frequently, it is necessary to refer to an index of updates known as **C.F.R. Sections Affected**, which refers you to the Federal Register.

The C.F.R. and some State's codified regulations are available on CD-ROM and through private computer services. Additionally, some federal and State agencies now post proposed and final regulations on the Internet.

Court Opinions

Court opinions are published in books called **reporters**. *Official* reporters are published by the courts themselves or by commercial publishing houses under contract to the government. *Unofficial* reporters are published by commercial publishing houses solely for private purposes. The text of an opinion should be the same whether published in an official or an unofficial reporter.

Federal district court and court of appeals opinions are published in official reporters by a private publishing company. There are two different sets of reporters for district court opinions, the **Federal Supplement**, abbreviated as F.Supp. and the **Federal Rules Decisions**, abbreviated as F.R.D. Court of appeals opinions are published in only one reporter called the **Federal Reporter**.

Supreme Court opinions are found in an official reporter published by the Court, the **United States Reports**, abbreviated as U.S., and two unofficial reporters published by two different private companies, **United States Supreme Court Reports, Lawyer's Edition**, abbreviated as L.Ed. and **Supreme Court Reporter**, abbreviated as S.Ct. Supreme Court opinions are also published weekly by a private company in a loose-leaf service called **United States Law Week**, abbreviated U.S.L.W. Law Week also contains important recent court decisions by lower courts and recently enacted statutes of importance.

State *trial* court opinions are rarely published in reporters but *appellate* court opinions are generally printed in official reporters. These official reporters (which may be published by private companies but be designated as official reporters) have different names in different States. There may be one reporter for cases from the court of last resort and another for intermediate appellate court cases. The official reporter for opinions from a State supreme court is typically abbreviated solely by an abbreviation of the State's name (e.g., Ill.), while the reporter for intermediate appellate court opinions is typically abbreviated by using the same abbreviation for the State followed by App. (e.g., Ill.App.).

There may also be an unofficial reporter for a State's appellate court opinions, and most State appellate court opinions are also included in an unofficial national reporter system published by West Publishing Company. You will probably have to use this system if you want to find a case from another State and you do not have access to computerized legal research. Only large law libraries have the official or unofficial reporters from States other than where they are located but many law libraries have West's national reporters.

West's national reporter system divides the country into regions, with each region having its own reporter. In fact, West calls its system a regional reporter system. These regions may seem somewhat arbitrary and may make more sense historically or impressionistically than geographically. That is, the North Eastern Reporter (N.E.) contains cases from, among other States, New York, Massachusetts, Illinois, and Ohio, while cases from Pennsylvania, New Jersey, Maine and a number of other States are in the Atlantic Reporter (A.). Texas and Tennessee cases are included in the South Western Reporter (S.W.), while Kansas and Oklahoma cases are in the Pacific Reporter (P.).

Selected appellate court opinions from each State are published in the State's re-gional reporter. Usually, all opinions from the State's supreme court are included in the regional reporter but some or all intermediate appellate court opinions may not be included. New York's and California's intermediate appellate opinions are included in their own reporters, but not in the regional reporters. Some States designate the West regional reporter for their State as their official reporter.

In addition to West's regional reporters and the official and unofficial reporters for federal and State cases, private companies or special interest associations may publish reporters with cases and other items on a given topic. For example, there is a reporter for unemployment insurance cases and several different reporters with employment cases. Some of these reporters are national, some cover only one State or region. Most of these reporters also contain significant trial court or administrative decisions and proposed or newly enacted statutes and regulations.

Like statutes and regulations, federal and most State appellate court opinions are available on CD-ROM and through private computer data services. Additionally, some courts are releasing their newly-issued decisions on the Internet.

UNDERSTANDING AND USING LEGAL CITATIONS

All laws have citations. The citation is used to identify, refer to (i.e., **cite**), and locate a law. It provides information about a law, including, and most important, the law's location. A citation is like the name and address of a law. For some laws, the citation is the only name of a law. For all laws, the citation tells you in what set of books and where in the set you can find a law. Like a name and address, a citation follows a certain format and uses certain abbreviations or symbols.

If you are unfamiliar with the format of legal citations and do not recognize the abbreviations or symbols, deciphering a citation and locating a law can be confusing and difficult. However, once you start using legal citations and begin to recognize the most common formats and many of the abbreviations and symbols, you should not find understanding and using citations difficult. The following discussion on citations to statutes, regulations, and court opinions should also make understanding and using citations easier for you.[4]

It is important to stress that you must understand and use citations even if you are doing legal research on a computer. The easiest way for you to locate and retrieve a law while doing computer research may be to use the law's citation; your computer research results will probably give you the citation for any laws you locate through a topical search. And, if you want to tell someone about a law you find or make a reference to the law in any written materials, you will have to use its citation, that is, cite to it in proper form.

---

4. There are also sources you can turn to for help with citations. *A Uniform System of Citation* published by the Harvard Law Review Association (often referred to as *The Bluebook* for the color of its cover) is the most widely used and authoritative guide to citation forms and abbreviations for legal material, but it is quite detailed and difficult to use. There are other competing guides available, some of which may be simpler for you, and some States have their own guides, like the *California Style Manual*. Many books of laws have an introductory page giving the citation form and abbreviations for the laws in the book, which may be a helpful resource for you.

The first step to understanding citations is to learn the basic format. While citations for some laws do not follow this format and there are several variations of it, the basic format for citations to statutes, regulations, and court opinions is: *title or volume number* of the book in which the law is found; followed by the *name of the set* of books, generally *abbreviated*; and followed by the *page, paragraph*, or *section number* where the law is found in the book.

For example, an important federal statute, which was first enacted as part of the United States Civil Rights Act of 1871, allows individuals to sue for certain violations of their civil rights. This statute is now found in Title 42 of the United States Code at section 1983. As we have already mentioned, the abbreviation for the United States Code is U.S.C. and $\S$ is a symbol for section (and, indeed, is called the section sign). Thus, the citation to this statute is: 42 U.S.C. $\S$ 1983 (or you can spell out the word *section* or abbreviate it as sec.). Whenever one is referring to this statute in legal writing, it should be cited this way. Moreover, section 1983 is the name that is commonly used for this law. Thus, you might hear a lawyer say something like "my client has a section 1983 claim against the police."

We will give more examples and explanations of the format for citations to federal and State statutes, regulations, and court opinions in the next section.

Statutes

As you should be able to tell from the previous example, the basic citation format is the style that is used in citations to *federal* statutes. In other words, the citation to a *federal statute* is: the *title number* of the United States Code where the statute is found; followed by *U.S.C.* (or U.S.C.A. or U.S.C.S.); followed by the *section sign* and the statute's *section number* in the United States Code, as in "42 U.S.C. § 1983." You could also cite to federal statutes using their public law numbers or their session law location, but you will only see such citations occasionally and you would probably never need to use such citations. Such a citation is most often used when a statute's legislative history is being discussed and knowing when a law was passed or what it looked like in an earlier form is important. The most useful and used citation is to the codified statutes, either annotated or unannotated. Thus, while one could cite to 42 U.S.C. § 1983 by using the public law number it was assigned after it was enacted as part of the Civil Rights Act of 1871 or by using its location in the session laws for the Congress in session in 1871, in most legal writing, you will only see: 42 U.S.C. § 1983.

The format for citations to *State* statutes varies from State to State. For example, the citation to the Colorado statute on background investigations in child custody cases is: section 14–10–127, C.R.S., and an Oklahoma statute on the consideration of a child's preference in custody matters is cited: Okla. Stat., tit. 12, § 1277.1. These two different citation formats, however, have a lot in common with the basic format. Both include the elements of the basic format but in a different order; both use the abbreviation for the codified statutes (called revised statutes in Colorado and several other States, abbreviated *R.* in Colorado, and *Rev.* in other

States); both indicate the title or chapter number (*14* in Colorado and *12* in Oklahoma); and both indicate the paragraph or section number (*127* and *1277.1*)

Sometimes, the term *et seq.*, which means "and following," is used in a citation to a statute to cite to the beginning of a long act with many sections. For example, the federal Individual with Disabilities Education Act could be cited as 20 U.S.C. § 1401 *et seq.*, meaning the act begins at section 1401 and continues in further sections.

Regulations

A citation to a proposed or promulgated federal regulation in the Federal Register follows the basic format for legal citations. That is, the number of the *volume* in which the regulation appears is stated first; followed by the abbreviation for the Federal Register as Fed. Reg.; followed by the *page* in the volume where the regulation begins. There is also one variation to the basic format. Because the Federal Register is published daily, the day of publication should be set forth in parentheses at the end of the citation. For example, the citation to a proposed regulation on substance abuse confidentiality that was published in the August 25, 1987, issue of volume 48 of the Federal Register beginning at page 38,767 is: 48 Fed. Reg. 38767 (August 25, 1987).

A promulgated federal regulation must be cited to the Federal Register until it is published in the Code of Federal Regulations (C.F.R.), the codified version of the federal regulations. After it is published in C.F.R., it should be cited to C.F.R., not the Federal Register, following the basic format for citations to the United States Code. That is, a regulation found at section 200 of Title 38 of the Code of Federal Regulations would be cited as: 38 C.F.R. § 200.

Citation format varies for State regulation. Also, many States do not have codified regulations or publications like the Federal Register that publish all proposed regulations, promulgated regulations, or both. There may be no official way to locate or cite to regulations. If a State does have codified regulations, the citation format is generally the same as for the State's statutes.

Court Opinions

General Rules. Citations identify the location of court opinions in one or more reporters. All citations to opinions in reporters, whether federal or State, official or unofficial, follow the same format. This format, which is a variation of the basic format, is: *case name*; followed by a *comma*; the *volume number of the reporter* in which the case is found; the *abbreviation of the reporter*; the *page* on which the case begins; and, finally, in parenthesis, the *year the case was decided.* For example, the citation for the case *Pacheco v. Pacheco,* which relates to child custody investigations that was decided by the Colorado Court of Appeals in 1976 and that begins on page 181 in volume 38 of the reporter for the Colorado Court of Appeals (Colo.App.) opinions is: *Pacheco v. Pacheco,* 38 Colo.App.181 (1976).

As in the previous example, the name of a case used in a citation is always put in italics or underlined.[5] The name in a citation may be different from the name found in court documents and at the beginning

---

5. This book will always use italics.

of a published opinion. The name used in legal citations is an abbreviated version of the full official name; it usually only contains the name of one party on each side and does not include titles, designations, or descriptions of the parties (such as "Director of the Department of Protective Services, being sued in her official capacity" or "Jane Doe, a minor, through her guardian *ad litem*"). Use of the full, unabbreviated name in a citation is improper.

Also, the name of a case is usually two names separated by a *v.* standing for *versus.* The first name is usually the name of one of the plaintiffs or appellants, while the second is the name of one of the defendants or appellees. If the party is a person, generally only his or her last name will be used. Sometimes, pseudonyms or first names will be used to protect confidentiality, particularly of juveniles. An abbreviated name may be used if the party is not a person. Sometimes, the name of a case has a different form. You may see something like *In re Smith, Matter of Smith,* or *State ex rel. Jones v. Smith.* There are technical reasons for such names that do not reflect the importance of the case, and may not even reflect the nature of the case.

Although the format of a citation to a case is always the same, additional information may have to be added to some citations.

First, if the court that decided the case cannot be determined from the name of the reporter, the abbreviated name of the court must be included in the parentheses with the date. For example, Colorado no longer publishes its own official reporter but designates West's Pacific Reporter as its official reporter. *Pacheco* also appeared in volume 554 of the second series of the Pacific Reporter on page 97; now, it would only appear in the Pacific Reporter and would be cited: *Pacheco v. Pacheco*, 554 P.2d 97 (Colo.App. 1976). *Colo.App.* has to be included in the citation because otherwise one would not know whether the case was decided by the Colorado Court of Appeals or the Colorado Supreme Court or even that it was a case from Colorado.

Second, if a case appears in more than one reporter, you might have to or want to include references to more than one of these reporters. Cases should always be cited to the official reporter but can also be cited to any unofficial reporters. If you are citing to a State court case from another State, you should always use the West regional reporter cite in addition to the official reporter cite. This is because only the largest libraries have the official reporters for out-of-state cases, but many law libraries have the regional reporters. If you are citing to more than one reporter, the citations would all be together, before the date, separated by commas, with the official reporter first. For example, a complete citation to *Pacheco* by someone outside of Colorado would be: *Pacheco v. Pacheco*, 38 Colo.App. 181, 554 P.2d 97 (1976).

Third, if you are making a reference to or quoting from a particular page in an opinion, the citation should include this page following the page at which the opinion begins (separated by a comma). For example, if you were quoting from page 185 of the *Pacheco* opinion, your citation would be: *Pacheco v. Pacheco*, 38 Colo.App.181, 185, 554 P.2d 97 (1976).[6]

You do not need to use the full citation

each subsequent time you cite to a case. You can do an abbreviated citation and put the word **supra** after the name (or even an abbreviated version of the name).

Federal Trial Courts. A federal trial court opinion for a case called *Jones v. Smith* could have a citation: *Jones v. Smith*, 425 F.Supp. 916 (S.D.N.Y. 1978) or *Jones v. Smith*, 83 F.R.D. 264 (D.Wyo. 1980). The first citation tells you the case is in volume 425 of the Federal Supplement beginning at page 916. It also tells you which district court decided the case (the district court for the Southern District of New York, that is, New York City) and when (1978). The second citation tells you the case is in volume 83 of the Federal Rules Decisions at page 264 and that the case was decided in 1980 by the district court for Wyoming. You must always identify which federal district court issued the opinion in a citation to F.R.D. or F.Supp. because this information cannot be determined from the mere citation to these reporters.

Federal Appellate Courts. A federal Court of Appeals opinion called *Jones v. Smith* could have a citation like: *Jones v. Smith*, 52 F.3d 92 (2d Cir. 1981). This citation tells you the opinion can be found in volume 527 of the third series of the Federal Reporter at page 92 and that the case was decided by a panel from the Second Circuit in 1981. The circuit in Federal Reporter citations must always be identified because the circuit cannot be determined from the citation to the Federal Reporter.

United States Supreme Court. The preferred citation to a Supreme Court decision is to the official reporter. A decision may additionally be cited to one or both of the

---

6. Because of this books' method of quoting from or excerpting opinions (see the discussion of this method in the introduction), no page numbers for quotations or excerpts will be given in case citations in this book.

unofficial reporters. The citation to the official reporter should always be first. Because the official reporter comes out more slowly than the unofficial reporters and because the unofficial reporters come out more slowly than *Law Week,* it is often necessary to put the official reporter first with blanks for the volume and page number, and then to give the citation to the unofficial reporter or *Law Week.* Since only decisions of the Supreme Court are published in the United States Reports (U.S.), the Lawyer's Edition (L.Ed.), or the Supreme Court Reporter (S.Ct.), there is no need to identify the court. However, the name of the court should be included in a citation to Law Week since decisions of several courts are included in this publication.

A citation to a Supreme Court case may look like this: *Jones v. Smith,* 325 U.S. 892, 71 S.Ct. 12, 31 L.Ed.2d 643 (1965). If the decision is recent, the citation may look like this: *Jones v. Smith,* _____ U.S. _____, 117 S.Ct. 983 (1997) or *Jones v. Smith,* 62 U.S.L.W. 3526 (U.S. November 10, 1997).

UNDERSTANDING AND USING ANNOTATED CODIFIED STATUTES

We return to our example of a request that you do a child custody investigation to help you understand and use annotated codified statutes. We will be using Appendices 4–1 to 4–4, which are copies of Colorado statutes related to such investigations.[7]

---

7. As has been noted, these statutes are not necessarily the current law. Moreover, for instructional purposes, the copied pages come from statute books for different years.

Section 14–10–127 of the Colorado Revised Statutes is the Colorado statute dealing specifically with child custody investigations. It is one section of the Colorado act dealing with divorce (known in Colorado as dissolution of marriage). This act is called the Uniform Dissolution of Marriage Act because it is derived from a model act drafted by legal scholars and proposed for uniform adoption by the States. It is found in the portion of the codified statutes dealing with "domestic matters." The statutes in this portion of the codified statutes all begin with number *14* because this is the fourteenth subject matter grouping of the Colorado codified statutes. You can see much of this from Appendix 4–1, which shows you what section 14–10–127 looked like in the bound volume of the annotated codified statutes on domestic matters in use in 1987. Appendix 4–1 was copied from pages 394 and 395 of this volume.

Section 14–10–127 was enacted in its present form in 1971. It can be found in the sessions laws of Colorado for 1971 at page 530. You can see this from the abbreviations after the word *source* below the statute on the first page of Appendix 4–1. Section 14–10–127 replaced a similar law that was enacted in 1963 and codified in the Colorado Revised Statutes at section 46–1–27. You can see this from the same place and from the *annotator's note* further down the page.

In the Colorado annotated codified statutes, as with most other State or federal annotated statutes, any legislative history or comments on a statute are set forth after the statute followed by excerpts from or summaries of cases that have interpreted the statute. You can find such excerpts or summaries for section 14–10–127 at the bottom of the first page of Appendix 4–1 and continuing on the second page.

As has been stated, Appendix 4–1 was copied from the bound volume of the Colorado annotated statutes on domestic matters in use in 1987. However, because this bound volume was published many years before 1987, Appendix 4–1 would not necessarily show you the version of section 14–10–127 current in 1987 or the cases interpreting the section through 1987. You need to look in the pocket part.

Appendix 4–2 is a copy of pages 274 and 275 of the 1987 pocket part to this bound volume. These pages provide information on section 14–10–127 as of 1987. The *source* information on page 275 shows you that section 14–10–127 was amended three times after the publication of the bound volume, in 1976, 1979, and 1983, and that these amendments can be found, respectively, at pages 529, 646, and 649 of the session laws for these years. You could look at these session laws or compare the text of the versions of section 14–10–127 in the bound volume and the pocket part to find out what each of these amendments did, but all you really need to know is the current law. This current law, incorporating all of the amendments as of 1987, is what you see in Appendix 4–2, but this would not necessarily be the current law after 1988.

Appendix 4–3 is a copy of pages 72 through 74 of the pocket part of the annotated statutes relating to domestic matters for 1995. By this time, a new bound volume had been published which showed the revisions of section 14–10–127 and the cases interpreting section 14–10–127 through the date of publication. Thus, the 1995 pocket part only needed to show the revisions from this date to 1995.

You can see from Appendix 4–3 that the text of section 14–10–127 was substantially changed sometime between 1987 to 1995. The *source* information tells you that the *entire section* was amended in 1988 and that the amendment can be found in section 1 of chapter 105 of the 1988 sessions laws beginning on page 639. Appendix 4–4, which duplicates the pages of the 1988 sessions laws containing this amendment, shows you exactly how section 14–10–127 was changed by this amendment. However, the text of section 14–10–127 in Appendix 4–4 is not exactly the same as the text in Appendix 4–3. This is because, according to the source information in Appendix 4–3, section 14–10–127 was also amended in 1993 and 1994. The text in the pocket part incorporates these two changes. By comparing Appendix 4–4 with Appendix 4–3, you can see the changes made to section 14–10–127 in 1993 and 1994 and can also see the differences in form and information between the session laws and the annotated codified statutes. You should see that the annotated codified statutes not only provide you with the current version of the law but also provide you much more useful information. You probably will never need to use the session laws but you may often need to use the annotated codified statutes if you are involved with the law in your practice.

UNDERSTANDING AND USING PUBLISHED COURT OPINIONS

When you read a court opinion in a reporter, you will see many things in addition to the text of the opinion. To help you understand, read, and use all the parts of the opinion, the complete version of the opinion in *Pacheco v. Pacheco,* 38 Colo.App. 181, 554 P.2d 97 (1976), as copied from the Pacific Reporter, is presented in Appendix 4–5. You should refer to this opinion, which interprets section 14–10–127 of the Colorado Revised Statutes, it read before the 1988 amendment, as the parts of an opinion are discussed below.[8]

Identifying Information

When you look at a published court opinion in a reporter, the first thing you will usually see is the full official case name with all the parties and their capacity in the case. As explained earlier, this full name is not used in citations to or references to the case. The name used in citations is found, not at the beginning of a case in a reporter, but on the top of alternating pages of the opinion in a reporter or in boldface, capitalized letters in the name at the beginning of a case, or both.

Below the name, you will generally see numbers that are the court docket numbers. These numbers, like bill numbers or public act numbers, are chronological numbers used by the courts where the cases have been heard. They are of no importance except if you want to communi-

cate with the court that decided a case to obtain the file.

Next, you would generally see the official name of the court issuing the opinion and below this court's name, some dates. Only the date of the decision is important and generally only the year.

Syllabus and Headnotes

After the dates, you will sometimes see a summary of the case. This summary, often called a **syllabus**, is most helpful, but it is not an official statement of law, even in an official reporter. It may be written by a court official and approved by the court, but even then it is only a summary. It cannot be referred to as the law.

Next, in official or unofficial reporters printed by West Publishing Company, you will see excerpts from the case headed by a sequential number, a topic, a symbol representing a key, and another number, the key number. These excerpts, known as **headnotes** or **keynotes,** are inserted in West's annotated statutes if they relate to a statute. You can see several excerpts from *Pacheco* in the annotations to section 14–10–127, C.R.S., in the 1987 pocket part pages reproduced in Appendix 4–2. These excerpts are also entered in alphabetical topical order using the key numbers in books published by West called **digests**. As we shall see, digests can be used to find cases discussing a given topic.[9]

Like the case summary or syllabus, headnotes are not statements of law. They

---

8. The parts of an opinion discussed below are the ones you will usually find in the federal reporters, including the official and unofficial reporters for the Supreme Court, in West Publishing Company's regional reporters, and in most official and unofficial reporters for State court opinions. Computer media usually contain these parts, but topical reporters may not include all of these parts or may include one or more of these parts in a different place or order.

---

9. You might find similar headnotes in reporters printed by other private publishing companies that are used in their books of annotated statutes or digests.

are merely research tools. By skimming the topics and excerpts, you may determine if a case addresses a topic of interest, and you can locate a topic of interest in a lengthy case by finding an excerpt on the topic and looking for the number of the excerpt in brackets in the body of the opinion. You can also find other cases on subjects of interest to you in a case by noting the topic and key number used for the subject and looking in the appropriate digest under the topic and number. Thus, if you want to find cases in addition to *Pacheco* dealing with the exclusion of testimony about disciplining a child (headnote 9), you could look in a West digest under "parent and child," keynote 2(21). Appendix 4–6 shows you this headnote reproduced under the heading "parent and child" at keynote 2(21) in the West digest for the Pacific Reporter as of 1987. As you can see, there are excerpts from other cases in the Pacific Reporter addressing this topic, including another case from Colorado.

Because of their usefulness as a research tool, headnotes are usually included in CD-ROM and private computer data services compilations of court opinions, particularly those of West Publishing Company.

The Opinion or Opinions

Since several appellate justices generally hear and decide each case and since judges may and do disagree, there may be more than one opinion in a case. A **majority opinion** is an opinion written by one justice, which at least a majority of the justices hearing the case have joined. A majority opinion decides the case and may make law. When a majority of the justices do not agree on one opinion, there is a **plurality opinion**, the opinion that is joined in by the most justices. The plurality opinion decides the case, but may have little impact on the law. A **dissenting opinion** is an opinion written by a justice who disagrees with the result reached by the majority or plurality. Other justices may join in a dissenting opinion. There may be more than one dissenting opinion in a case if different justices disagree with the majority or plurality for different reasons. A **concurring opinion** is an opinion written by a justice who agrees with the result reached by the majority or plurality but who may not endorse their reasoning or who may want to stress certain points. Other justices may join in a concurring opinion. There may be more than one concurring opinion. Dissenting and concurring opinions neither make law nor have any effect on the result of the case.

To illustrate, the Supreme Court has nine justices. A case could have five or six justices joining a majority opinion and three joining a dissenting opinion for a total of two opinions. There could also be a case with five justices joining a majority opinion, one writing a concurring opinion, two joining one dissent and one writing her own dissent for a total of four opinions. Or there could be a case with three justices joining a plurality opinion, two concurring with the plurality, one other concurring but for different reasons than the others who concurred and three separate dissenting opinions, for a total of six opinions in one case. Because the justices may concur in part and dissent in part, and may join in other opinions and also write their own opinions, the number of opinions could theoretically exceed nine.[10]

The majority or plurality opinion would be reported first. Any concurring opinions would follow the majority or plurality opinion and any dissenting opinions would follow any concurring opinions. The name of the justice who wrote the opinion is put at the beginning of each opinion. The justices joining a majority or plurality opinion are put at the end of the opinion, while the justices joining concurring or dissenting opinions are put at the beginning of the opinion after the name of the author of the opinion.

After the headnotes, directly before the first or only opinion, you will find the names of the lawyers for the parties, and the names of the judge or judges who heard the case.

Reading a Majority or Plurality Opinion

Reading a majority or plurality opinion is not easy, but these opinions generally follow a certain pattern and once one understands the pattern, one can read and understand most cases. The essential elements found in most majority or plurality opinions are reviewed in the following sections.[11]

Procedural History. The procedural history of a case is a history of the court actions, rulings, and legal maneuvers in the case from the time the case was filed until it reached the court writing the opinion. The procedural history tells you who started the case, where and how it was started, the relief that was sought, the legal theories of both sides, any significant pre-trial motions and the rulings on them, whether there was a trial, whether there was a jury, any significant motions made during the trial and the rulings on them, who won, who appealed, the actions or rulings that are the subject of the appeal, and the decisions of any lower appellate courts that heard the case.

Most procedural history is not important to social workers, but, at a minimum, to really understand a case one should

---

10. To illustsrate with two actual cases of interest to social workers, in *Regents of the University of California v. Bakke*, 438 U.S. 265 (1978), a case dealing with affirmative action in university admissions, Justice Powell wrote the plurality opinion; Justice Brennan wrote an opinion concurring in part and dissenting in part joined by Justices White, Marshall, and Blackman; Justices White, Marshall, and Blackman also wrote separate opinions; and Justice Stevens wrote a sixth opinion, concurring in part and dissenting in part, in which Justices Burger, Stewart, and Rehnquist joined. And in *United States v. Dixon*, 509 U.S. 688 (1993), considering whether a man could be prosecuted both for violating a domestic violence order by assaulting his wife and for assaulting his wife. Justice Scalia wrote one plurality opinion on certain parts of the decision in which Justices Rehnquist, O'Conner, Kennedy, and Thomas joined and another plurality opinion in other parts of the decision in which Justice Kennedy joined; Chief Justice Rehnquist wrote a concurring and dissenting opinion in which Justice Stevens joined in part and Justice Souter joined as to another part; Justice Blackman wrote a concurring and dissenting opinion; and Justice Souter wrote a sixth concurring and dissenting opinion in which Stevens joined in part.

---

11. The pattern of opinions and the elements they contain may be more understandable to you if you **brief** each opinion you read. Briefing is the process by which one summarizes or outlines an opinion. (The term *brief* is also used to refer to a written argument presented by an attorney to a court.) Briefing is done differently by different people; there is no single preferred method. You should brief in a way that is comfortable for you. One style of briefing entails setting forth the following information about a case: citation, including name, date, and court; procedural history; facts; issues; holdings; reasoning; decision; and brief summaries of any dissenting or concurring opinions.

know the nature of the controversy and the relief or remedy sought (e.g., an action for monetary damages for medical malpractice; a suit challenging a commitment to a mental hospital and seeking a writ ordering the patient's release).

Facts. As has been noted, appellate courts do not decide facts, but the facts are nevertheless crucial to an appellate court opinion. Appellate courts examine the record and sift through the vast body of facts in the record to determine what facts are significant. The facts that are determined to be significant determine what law will be applied in deciding the case and how it will be applied. The facts that are determined to be significant will also determine the future precedential value of the case. These facts will be set forth in the statement of facts, which tells you the story of what happened before the case went to court.

Issues. An issue is a question of law that the court is deciding. There may be more than one issue in a case. Just as appellate courts sift through the facts to determine which facts are significant, they may sift through all the issues raised by the parties and determine which are worthy of in-depth consideration. Appellate courts may also restate an issue raised by the parties, framing it in broader or narrower terms. The way an issue is stated by a court may be crucial in determining what law to apply, how to apply it, and the future impact of the case.

Some or all of the issues resolved in an opinion may be procedural. These procedural issues are usually not important to social workers unless they relate to the social worker's roles in the hearing process.

Holdings. A **holding** is a statement of law made by the court which is the basis for the court's decision in a case. It is a statement of the court essential to resolving a case. Put another way, a holding is an answer to the question posed by an issue. It may be as narrow or as broad as an issue. Just as there may be more than one issue, there may be more than one holding. Holdings must be carefully distinguished from **dicta**, which are statements made by a court that are not essential to resolving the case or any issues in it.

Decision. The decision is what the court actually does in the case before it. The holding resolves the substantive legal questions, but it does not necessarily tell you what will happen to the parties or in the case. Will one party get an injunction or damages? Will someone be sent to prison or be released from a mental hospital? Will a case be dismissed? The decision can answer such questions. The decision of an appellate court will also affirm or reverse a lower court decision.[12]

Reasoning. The reasoning is the process by which the court resolves the issues and reaches its holdings and decisions. Understanding a court's reasoning is essential to understanding its opinion. Usually, the reasoning process is the common law process described in chapter 2.

---

12. The word *decision* is often used in legal writing to mean *opinion*. At times, people say "the court decided" when what they meant is "the court held." Strictly, however, the term *decision* should be used only to refer to the actions taken or directed by the court in the case while the term *holding* should be used only to refer to the resolution of the issues.

SECONDARY LEGAL SOURCES

The sources of the law that have been discussed to this point are what are termed **primary sources**, that is, they are the sources that present the law as it is written (sometimes along with other matters, as in the case of annotated codified statutes). There are also a number of **secondary sources** that do not themselves present the law but can be useful to understanding the law as well as locating the law. The following sections review the most common and helpful secondary sources along with suggestions for their use.

Legal Encyclopedias

Two legal encyclopedias that are comprehensive and national in scope are *American Jurisprudence* and *Corpus Juris.* Legal encyclopedias are also published for some States. The national and other encyclopedias provide an overview of the law on given topics, are organized alphabetically by topic, and are fully indexed. They are a useful resource when you are beginning a research project on an unfamiliar subject. The discussion may give you a basic understanding of the subject and give you an idea of where to look for the law. You can also use the citations in the discussions to find the law you need.

Similar to the legal encyclopedias is the *American Law Reports.* This publication presents court opinions of note, set forth in full, followed by articles that discuss the law related to the opinions in other jurisdictions. *American Law Reports* does not attempt to discuss all topics so it may have nothing to help you; it

is not arranged in any particular order so using the index is essential.

Treatises

There are numerous books or sets of books on selected legal topics. Some of these are difficult scholarly tomes not useful to social workers or practicing lawyers. Others are like encyclopedias, setting forth summaries of the law on a particular topic for practicing lawyers. Those designed primarily for law students are referred to as **hornbooks**, but they may also be used by practicing attorneys. Hornbooks and other treatises designed for practicing attorneys or students may be quite useful to social workers.

Legal Periodicals

Law reviews are topical or, more commonly, general interest legal periodicals published by law schools with editing and article selection done by law students. Almost every law school publishes at least one law review, so there are hundreds of different law reviews. Articles in the reviews are written by both legal scholars and law students. The articles typically discuss complex legal issues or survey, analyze, or critique the law on a given subject. The articles usually contain extensive references. They can be a valuable research tool, especially if you are writing a scholarly paper, but they are often too scholarly, legalistic, narrow, abstract, or detailed to be of use to social workers—or even practicing lawyers.

Just as there are journals like *Social Work* and *Child Welfare* published for social workers or those interested in social welfare, there are numerous topical or general interest journals published by private publishing houses or associations for lawyers or those interested in the law. Many of these legal journals publish articles written by practicing attorneys. Such articles are often practical and timely, and may therefore be more useful to social workers than articles written by legal scholars.[13] Bar journals, published by local, State, or national associations of lawyers, often known as bar associations, may be particularly helpful.

Law review and journal articles are indexed by title, author, and subject matter in the *Index to Legal Periodicals,* the *Current Law Index,* and the *Legal Resource Index.* All of these indexes are used just as *Social Work Research and Abstracts, Psychological Abstracts,* and other indexes to periodicals are used.

Practice Manuals

Practice manuals are books that summarize the law on given topics and provide procedural guidelines to follow in taking cases to court. They are written for attorneys, but they are usually at a fairly simple level and can help you understand legal proceedings in which you might be involved or how to complete legal forms.

Continuing Legal Education Series

Like practice manuals, continuing legal education books are written on various topics primarily for practicing lawyers. They are also generally at a fairly simple level. In States with continuing legal education requirements to retain bar membership or with active continuing legal education organizations, there are many such books available.

Loose-Leaf Services

There are several private companies and associations that publish loose-leaf books that compile cases, statutes and regulations on particular topics, like programs under the Social Security Act or family law. These loose-leaf books or series may have brief comments on the current law and may include court opinions of interest, many of which are not published elsewhere, and enacted and proposed statutes and regulations of interest. Loose-leaf series that publish court opinions are sometimes referred to as topical reporters. If an opinion is only published in a topical reporter, it will be cited to this reporter.

Loose-leaf services are kept in binders and are kept current by replacement of superseded pages and additions of new law. Because keeping loose-leaf services current is easy and because they contain laws not published elsewhere and proposed laws on a topic of interest, they can be most useful for research and for simply keeping abreast of developments.

Digests

Digests contain brief excerpts of one or two sentences from cases, arranged by topic. There is generally no text at all in a digest, and a topic may be very broad. Therefore, one often must wade through hundreds of excerpts to locate useful

---

13. It should be noted that some law school reviews are called journals, but the use of the term *journal* does not change their essential character. Some topical journals, such as the *Journal of Family Law,* are put out by law schools and are really law reviews.

cases. Nevertheless, digests can be helpful as a research tool.

Most digests are linked with a particular reporter series. For example, there are digests connected to each region of West Publishing Company's regional reporter system, to West's Supreme Court Reporter, and to its federal and many of its State reporters. A reprint of a digest page (for Pacific Reporter cases) relating to child custody investigations in Colorado is in Appendix 4–6.

Shephard's Citations

Shephard's Citations is a useful tool for finding cases that interpret a particular statute, or rely on a particular precedent, and for determining if a case has been overruled or distinguished. Different volumes of *Shephard's* cover specified statutes or case reporters. Each volume sets forth long lists of citations, without case names, courts, or dates, to all opinions citing a statute or case. Symbols tell you something about what the opinion did with the cited case (e.g., distinguished, followed, or overruled it) or what portion of the case it addressed. The lists of citations and symbols with no text can be intimidating, but any law librarian can help you use *Shephard's*.

Most computer data services have their own computerized versions of *Shephard's*.

CONDUCTING LEGAL RESEARCH

This section is written with you as a practitioner in mind. You may be a student at this time, and, if so, you might be required to write a paper that requires you to do legal research. You also can follow the steps presented in this section to complete such a paper, but, in addition, you will have access to a wide range of legal references and perhaps access to law school libraries with professional law librarians to assist you. When you are in practice, you are unlikely to have these luxuries. Moreover, when you are in practice, the questions you research are likely to be somewhat different than those you research as a student. They will typically arise in the course of your practice and relate to specific aspects of your practice. You will be less concerned with broad legal principles and issues and more concerned with what the law tells you to do in a particular case.

Steps in Legal Research

When faced with a legal question, how do you proceed? Of course you can always ask an attorney, but we are talking about how you can find and interpret information yourself.

The first step, and one that may seem so simple that it goes without saying, is to determine where you are likely to physically find the legal materials you will need. This step is easy if you are a student at a university with a law school and a law library, but it may not be so easy if you are far from any law schools or do not have access to a law school library. Where can you find legal materials outside of law school libraries? Even if you are not a student, you might have access to the general libraries at public colleges and universities. These libraries and many public libraries have state and federal statutes. If your legal research is not extensive, these sources may be sufficient. Most general college and university libraries and public libraries do not have the annotated statutes and case reporters, but these materials, at least for your State, should be available at a law library in your local courthouse. You should be able to gain access to this library as can any member of the public, but you should expect to get little help in using the collection and to do your work during normal business hours. Attorneys also have collections related to their own practices, and some might allow you access to their collections. Last, even without subscribing to a specialized legal computer data service, you should be able to find many laws through the Internet. And, many libraries, especially law school libraries, do subscribe to specialized legal computer data services and have terminals available to the public.

The second step in finding information is to determine whether the question relates primarily to federal or to State law. Since, as we have said, most laws important to social workers are State laws, it is safe to begin by searching State law. The major exceptions are questions related to federally administered benefit programs, immigration or naturalization, and services to Native Americans. Unless you have a question in these areas, begin with the assumption that the relevant law is State law. Move to federal law only if your search of State law is fruitless or takes you to federal law.

The third step is deciding what type of law you should look for first. Usually this will be statutes. Annotations to statutes will lead you to other types of law bearing on your problem. If you can find no relevant statutes, you will have to look for cases, regulations, and other types of law.

Assuming you have decided to begin with statutes but have no specific cita-

tions, the fourth step is to decide in what books of statutes to look. As has been stated, usually you should look in books of codified statutes, preferably annotated codified statutes.

Next you have to decide what terms to look for in the index to the books of statutes. You can expect the process of using the index to be somewhat frustrating because unfamiliar or legal terms may be used. For example, sections of the statutes referring to children might not be listed under the heading "children." Instead, they might be listed under "minors" or "infants." Also, an outdated term no longer used in common speech or in the law may be used in an index. For example, you may find statutes relating to children whose parents are not married in an index under "children born out of wedlock," "illegitimate children," or even "bastards." Looking at the table of contents of a title you think may contain the statutes you want may be easier for you to use than the index.

After you have located the applicable sections of the statutes, remember to also look in the pocket parts or supplements for the current law.

If you have looked in the annotated codified statutes, as you should have, you can easily identify relevant court opinions by using the annotations. The annotations might also suggest other helpful sources such as law review and encyclopedia articles.

The annotations often will not identify applicable regulations, so you must decide if there might be applicable regulations and, if so, search for them. For the most part, you can assume that if the statutes give any authority to a public agency, there will be regulations. You will then turn to the administrative code for the state or try to obtain information directly from the agency with authority. As with statutes, if you are faced with a book or set of books containing many regulations, you begin your search with the index or table of contents.

You might also consult a legal encyclopedia and other secondary sources. These sources can provide an overview of a topic and perhaps lead you to additional statutory, regulatory, and case references. Indeed, you might go to a secondary source first if you are unfamiliar with a topic or have general rather than specific questions about a broad topic. Secondary sources can also lead you to statutes and cases without using digests or annotated statutes and can give you an idea about what headings to look for in the indices and digests. For example, you may want to know about fathers' responsibility to support children born out of wedlock. You may not know that actions establishing that a man is the biological father of a child are called *paternity actions,* that the support obligation can only be imposed if paternity is established, and that the obligation is often imposed as part of a paternity action. You cannot find anything in the index to the statutes about fathers' responsibilities for support because the relevant statutes are all under the paternity heading. A secondary source might use the term *paternity* and lead you to look under this heading in the appropriate index. Of course, you might also have trouble using the indices to the secondary sources, but the tables of contents usually are arranged logically and are easy to use.

At this point, you will probably have obtained much of the information you need unless you need to conduct extensive research for some purpose, such as writing a paper for a class or making a presentation at a meeting. If this is the case, you can supplement your review of the statutes, cases, and regulations by consulting further secondary sources such as journals.

But assume you have located all the material you believe you need. In fact, your task has just begun. The challenge now is to understand the material you have located, determine what in the material is significant to you as a social worker, and identify any additional information you might need.

The statutes must be read carefully. They are written precisely, and there are big differences between a *shall* and a *may* and an *and* and an *or.* The rule is to read and then read again, trying to rephrase in common language.

As you read the excerpts of court opinions in the annotations, you need to decide to what extent the cases may apply to your problem as a social worker and therefore whether or not they are cases you should read carefully. While the holdings in some opinions might enlighten your practice, the holdings in many relate to legal points of no concern to social workers. They address problems for attorneys, not for social workers.

Finally you need to determine if you have all the information you need and if your understanding of what you have is accurate. As questions are answered, new questions should arise, and these questions should be pursued until you are sure you have adequate knowledge to guide your behavior. Then, you need to ask if your understanding is consistent with common sense and your experience. This is also the time to consult with colleagues and supervisors, and, if necessary, with attorneys.

An Illustration of Legal Research

To illustrate the process of conducting legal research, again assume you are a social worker in Colorado who has been asked to conduct a background investigation in a divorce case where child custody has been contested and you want to determine what is expected of you. What should you do?[14]

You correctly recognize that child custody investigations in conjunction with divorce are governed by State law, and probably statutes. Your search for information, thus, leads you to the index of the codified annotated statutes for Colorado. You look under the headings of *divorce* and *child custody* and find section 14–10–127, C.R.S., which deals with background investigations. You remember to check the pocket parts. If you did not, you would not discover that the section had been amended since the bound volume was published.

Carefully reading the current version of section 14–10–127 (as set forth in Appendix 4–2), you learn you may obtain information from professionals who have served the child in the past without obtaining the consent of the child's parents. You learn you can request the court to order professional assessments. You learn you must mail your report to counsel within ten days of the hearing on custody. And so on.

Looking at the annotations to the section in both the bound volume and the pocket part, you find some background information related to the section, and you learn that some published court opinions interpret the section. Carefully reading the annotations, you decide that *Pacheco v. Pacheco,* 38 Colo.App. 181, 554 P.2d 97 (1976) (in Appendix 4–5) is important to you. You would then read *Pacheco* because a mere excerpt is not the law and can be misleading. You might also want to check the digests for headnotes from *Pacheco* that seem particularly apt. A page of a digest is found in Appendix 4–6.

But what do section 14–10–127 and *Pacheco* not tell you? They do not tell you what to evaluate. Only by looking further do you find that section 14–10–124, C.R.S., tells you what the court should consider in deciding custody and, therefore, what you should evaluate. Section 14–10–127 also does not tell you that the court's request to you might have been made under the authority of section 14–10–126. This section allows the court to "seek the advice of professional personnel" but does not give this professional the specific authority given by section 14–10–127 and does not impose the same obligations as section 14–10–127. *Pacheco* and the annotations to section 14–10–127 do not tell you, moreover, if there are regulations governing the conduct of investigations by staff of public child welfare agencies, an important point if you are employed by such an agency. Your research may be far from complete at this point.

In summary, legal research demands specialized knowledge and skills. However, it requires knowledge and skills not unique to attorneys. The task of the social worker is to find and use legal information required to practice competently, consulting with attorneys as needed. Legal research, then, is simply one aspect of social work practice.

---

14. You should also assume that it is 1987 and should refer to the appendices that contain the law in Colorado on child custody investigations as of this year as we explain.

APPENDIX 4.1

14-10-127. Investigations and reports. (1) In all custody proceedings, the court shall, upon motion of either party or upon the court's own motion, order the court probation department or any county or district welfare department to investigate and file a written report concerning custodial arrangements for the child. Except as otherwise provided in this section, such report shall be considered confidential and shall not be available for public inspection unless by order of court. The cost of each investigation up to a maximum of fifty dollars may be assessed as part of the costs of the action or proceeding, and, upon receipt of such sum by the clerk of court, it shall be transmitted to the department or agency performing the investigation.

(2) In preparing his report concerning a child, the investigator may consult any person who may have information about the child and his potential custodial arrangements. Upon order of the court, the investigator may refer the child to professional personnel for diagnosis. The investigator may consult with and obtain information from medical, psychiatric, or other expert persons who have served the child in the past without obtaining the consent of the parent or the child's custodian; but the child's consent must be obtained if he has reached the age of sixteen unless the court finds that he lacks mental capacity to consent. If the requirements of subsection (3) of this section are fulfilled, the investigator's report may be received in evidence at the hearing.

(3) The court shall mail the investigator's report to counsel and to any party not represented by counsel at least ten days prior to the hearing. The investigator shall make available to counsel and to any party not represented by counsel the investigator's file of underlying data and reports, complete texts of diagnostic reports made to the investigator pursuant to the provisions of subsection (2) of this section, and the names and addresses of all persons whom the investigator has consulted. Any party to the proceeding may call the investigator and any person whom he has consulted for cross examination. No party may waive his right of cross-examination prior to the hearing.

Source: R & RE, L. 71, p. 530, § 1; C.R.S. 1963, § 46-1-27.

Am. Jur. See 24 Am. Jur.2d. Divorce and Separation, § 793.

C.J.S. See 27B C.J.S., Divorce, § 317(8).

Annotator's note. Since § 14-10-127 is similar to repealed § 46-1-5(7), C.R.S. 1963, relevant cases construing this provision have been included in the annotations to § 14-10-127.

The purpose of the legislation providing for court assistants in the capacity of investigators of domestic relations cases to assist the court in the transaction of the judicial business of said court was obviously to assist the court and not to replace it. The general assembly would have no power to substitute an investigator for a judge, and neither would such legislation authorize a trial court to deny to the parties any of the usual attributes of a fair trial in open court upon due notice. Anderson v. Anderson, 167 Colo. 88, 445 P.2d 397 (1968).

The act of the general assembly (§ 46-1-5(7), C.R.S. 1963), which purported to authorize the trial court to call upon the probation department for a report concerning "the ability of each party to serve the best interest of the child", and further directing that "Each report shall be considered by the court" could not be so construed as to deny due process which includes the right to be heard in open court and to have a determination of issues based upon competent evidence offered by persons who submit themselves to cross-examination. Anderson v. Anderson, 167 Colo. 88, 445 P.2d 397 (1968).

A probation officer, or other persons, who have been designated to investigate and report to the court in custody hearings matters involving the ability or fitness of parents to best serve the interests of their children, are subject to examination as wit-

Reprinted with the permission of the State of Colorado, Committee on Legal Services in accordance with Section 1-5-118, C.R.S.

nesses concerning matters contained in their reports. Saucerman v. Saucerman, 170 Colo. 318, 461 P.2d 18 (1969).

However, touching upon matters related to them in confidence, the trial court should preliminarily rule in each instance what matters are in fact confidential, and whether the public interest requires the confidence to be preserved, and no examination of the officer should be permitted with respect to such confidential matters. Saucerman v. Saucerman. 170 Colo. 318, 461 P.2d 18 (1969).

But, where the trial court received in evidence the investigative reports of welfare and health department employees in reference to conditions found in the respective homes of the two contestants, and in reference to the psychological effects living with the father or the mother might have on one of the children, and the record indicated that at one hearing after the reports were filed the individuals who made the reports were either in court or could have been made available to the parties for cross-examination, there was no unfairness nor a denial of due process. Aylor v. Aylor, 173 Colo. 294, 478 P.2d 302 (1970).

And in making an order changing the custody of children, the trial court is actually making the decision, though such order is based on the recommendations of a psychiatrist and welfare personnel whose reports constitute nothing more than recommendations. Aylor v. Aylor, 173 Colo. 294, 478 P.2d 302 (1970).

The reports simply furnish specific information of a specialized nature for aid and assistance to the trial court, but in the final analysis the judge makes the decision, and whatever recommendations may be made to the judge, be they by experts or counsel, they are merely recommendations and nothing more. Aylor v. Aylor, 173 Colo, 294, 478 P.2d 302 (1970).

Where objections and exceptions were filed to the report of the probation department, since it was a hearsay document, if the conclusions reached therein were objected to by either party, it would be necessary that competent evidence, upon which the conclusions were based, be presented in open court. Anderson v. Anderson, 167 Colo. 88, 445 P.2d 397 (1968).

And the trial court erred in relying upon the probation report where it afforded no opportunity for the husband to offer evidence in explanation thereof, or to disprove any conclusions based on hearsay that were contained therein. Anderson v. Anderson, 167 Colo. 88, 445 P.2d 397 (1968).

But, it was not prejudicial error for the trial court to have received in evidence the hearsay reports of the case worker of the welfare department in custody proceedings, since the nature of the "report" was such that the father could not possibly have been prejudiced by anything contained therein, and furthermore, it affirmatively appeared from the court's decree that it did not in any manner enter into the court's thinking to the prejudice of the father. Suzuki v. Suzuki, 162 Colo. 204, 425 P.2d 44 (1967).

14-10-128. Hearings. (1) Custody proceedings shall receive priority in being set for hearing.

(2) The court may tax as costs the payment of necessary travel and other expenses incurred by any person whose presence at the hearing the court deems necessary to determine the best interests of the child.

(3) The court without a jury shall determine questions of law and fact. If it finds that a public hearing may be detrimental to the child's best interests, the court may exclude the public from a custody hearing but may admit any person who has a direct and legitimate interest in the particular case or a legitimate educational or research interest in the work of the court.

(4) If the court finds it necessary in order to protect the child's welfare that the record of any interview, report, investigation, or testimony in a custody proceeding be kept secret, the court shall make an appropriate order sealing the record.

Source: R & RE, L. 71, p. 531, § 1; C.R.S. 1963, § 46-1-28.

C.J.S. See 27B C.J.S., Divorce. § 317(8).

APPENDIX 4.2

Temporary order is not "in any way res judicata" as to permanent order. In re Lawson, 44 Colo. App. 105, 608 P.2d 378 (1980).

Order granting temporary custody of children is not final for purposes of appeal. In re Henne, 620 P.2d 62 (Colo. App. 1980).

14-10-126. Interviews.

Law reviews. For article, "The Role of Children's Counsel in Contested Child Custody, Visitation and Support Cases", see 15 Colo. Law. 224 (1986).

Section does not mandate interviews. In re Rinow, 624 P.2d 365 (Colo. App. 1981).

Parent may not cross-examine child at interview. The father is not entitled, as a matter of law, to cross-examine the children at the time of the interview. In re Agner, 659 P.2d 53 (Colo. App. 1982).

Making record is for benefit of parties. Though the language of this section is mandatory in form, the obvious purpose of making a record is for the benefit of the parties. In re Armbeck, 33 Colo. App. 260, 518 P.2d 300 (1974).

Requirement for record of interview concerning child's preference not violated. Where the court conducted a 15 minute interview with the two minor children but did not inquire concerning their preference the requirement of this section for a record of an interview concerning the children's preference was not violated. In re Short, 675 P.2d 323 (Colo. App. 1983).

Requirement of making record may be waived. The requirement of making a record, i.e., a verbatim transcript, of the interview between the court and child may be waived either expressly or by implication. In re Armbeck 33 Colo. App. 260, 518 P.2d 300 (1974).

Waiver of the requirement of making a record by implication held sufficient. See In re Armbeck, 33 Colo. App. 260, 518 P.2d 300 (1974).

As to the standard of the common law with respect to interviews. See Rayer v. Rayer, 32 Colo. App. 400, 512 P.2d 637 (1973)

Applied in In re Schulke, 40 Colo. App. 473, 579 P.2d 90 (1978).

14-10-127. Evaluation and reports. (1) In all custody proceedings, the court shall, upon motion of either party, or may, upon its own motion, order the court probation department, any county or district social services department, or a licensed mental health professional to perform an evaluation and file a written report concerning custodial arrangements for the child, unless such motion by either party is made for the purpose of delaying the proceedings. Except as otherwise provided in this section, such report shall be considered confidential and shall not be available for public inspection unless by order of court. The cost of each probation department or social services department evaluation shall be based on an ability to pay and shall be assessed as part of the costs of the action or proceeding, and, upon receipt of such sum by the clerk of court, it shall be transmitted to the department or agency performing the evaluation. The court shall order an evaluation by an impartial licensed mental health professional selected by the court, upon motion of either party, only if the moving party agrees initially to pay all costs of such evaluation. The moving party shall, at the time of appointment of the evaluator, deposit a reasonable sum with the court to pay the cost of the evaluation. The court may order the reasonable charges of any evaluation and report to be assessed as costs between the parties.

(2) In preparing his report concerning a child, the evaluator may consult any person who may have information about the child and his potential custodial arrangements. Upon order of the court, the evaluator may refer the child to other professional personnel for diagnosis. The evaluator may consult with and obtain information from medical, psychiatric, or other expert persons who have served the child in the past without obtaining the consent of the parent or the child's custodian; but the child's consent must

be obtained if he has reached the age of sixteen unless the court finds that he lacks mental capacity to consent. If the requirements of subsection (3) of this section are fulfilled, the evaluator's report may be received in evidence at the hearing.

(3) The evaluator shall mail his report to counsel and to any party not represented by counsel at least ten days prior to the hearing. The evaluator shall make available to counsel and to any party not represented by counsel his file of underlying data and reports, complete texts of diagnostic reports made to the evaluator pursuant to the provisions of subsection (2) of this section, and the names and addresses of all persons whom the evaluator has consulted. Any party to the proceeding may call the evaluator and any person whom he has consulted for cross-examination. No party may waive his right of cross-examination prior to the hearing.

Source: (1) amended, L. 76, p. 529, § 1; (1) amended, L. 79, p. 646, § 1; amended, L. 83, p. 649, § 1.

Law reviews. For article, "Therapist Privilege in Custody Cases", see 15 Colo. Law. 47 (1986).

The purpose of the legislation providing for the preparation and filing of reports in custody proceedings is to make the information contained therein available to assist the court in determining what is in the best interest of the children concerned. Pacheco v. Pacheco, 38 Colo. App. 181, 554 P.2d 720 (1976).

Opportunity to test report's reliability and offer evidence exists. Because any party has the right to call for cross-examination of the investigator and any person he has consulted, and because the investigator's file is available to counsel, ample opportunity exists for a party to test the reliability of the report and to offer evidence in explanation of or to disprove any statements or conclusions based on hearsay. Pacheco v. Pacheco, 38 Colo. App. 181, 554 P.2d 720 (1976).

Compliance with the 10-day provisions of this section is not a condition precedent to the reception of the report. Pacheco v. Pacheco, 38 Colo. App. 181, 554 P.2d 720 (1976).

Effect of noncompliance. Noncompliance with the 10-day rule merely prohibits the court from proceeding with a hearing wherein the report can be considered absent consent of or waiver by the parties. Pacheco v. Pacheco, 38 Colo. App. 181, 554 P.2d 720 (1976).

Waiver of objections to admission of report. Unless a party notifies the court and the opposing party within 10 days after receipt of a copy of the report (or if a copy has not been received at least 10 days prior to the hearing day, then at or prior to the commencement of the hearing at which the report may be used) that he intends to object to the admission of the report on the grounds of noncompliance with the 10-day rule or the hearsay nature of the report, any such objections are waived. Pacheco v. Pacheco, 38 Colo. App. 181, 554 P.2d 720 (1976).

Where a copy of the report was received by counsel a reasonable time prior to the hearing and no objection was made thereto until after the commencement of the hearing, objections as to hearsay and the 10-day rule were waived. Pacheco v. Pacheco, 38 Colo. App. 181, 554 P.2d 720 (1976).

Effect of valid objection. If a valid objection is made within the period specified above, then, on motion of either party or of the court, the court shall grant a reasonable continuance of the custody hearing date in order that the parties may obtain appropriate testimony. Pacheco v. Pacheco, 38 Colo. App. 181, 554 P.2d 720 (1976).

Court did not improperly utilize an investigative report made by an officer of the juvenile probation department in arriving at its decision relative to custody, for while it is true that the investigative report was not formally offered and received in evidence, the report was made a part of the record and had been furnished previously to both parties, and although she did not choose to do so, the wife had the right to call and examine the author of the report. Rayer v. Rayer, 32 Colo. App. 400, 512 P.2d 637 (1973).

Communications disclosed pursuant to this section are not privileged under section 13-90-107 since the information was necessary to make an evaluation for the court, not to treat the person disclosing the information. Anderson v. Glismann, 577 F. Supp. 1506 (D. Colo. 1984).

Actions of a court-appointed expert are made under the authority of the state, but not on behalf of the state, and will not sustain a cause

APPENDIX 4.3

court limited the father to four days per four-week period where he previously had portions of eight days in any four week period and there was no evidence that the children would benefit by this reduction in visitation. This restriction was both contrary to the public policy of encouraging frequent visitation and to the evidence in the record. In re Lester, 791 P.2d 1244 (Colo. App. 1990).

    D.   Custody and Visitation.

Although the stability of the environment is a valid consideration in awarding custody, instability alone is not sufficient to justify a restriction on visitation. In re Jarman, 752 P.2d 1068 (Colo. App. 1988).

    Where evidence shows a lack of cooperation between the parties or between the therapists for the mother and the child, the general visitation order does not meet the purposes for which the visitation was intended and is in essence a nullity. In re Sepmeier, 782 P.2d 876 (Colo. App. 1989).

    Applied in In re Murphy, 834 P.2d 1287 (Colo. App. 1992).

14-10-126. Interviews.

Section does not mandate interviews. In accord with original. See In re Turek, 817 P.2d 615 (Colo. App. 1991).

14-10-127. Evaluation and reports. (1) (a) (I) In all custody proceedings, the court shall, upon motion of either party, or may, upon its own motion, order the court probation department, any county or district social services department, or a licensed mental health professional qualified pursuant to subsection (4) of this section to perform an evaluation and file a written report concerning custodial or parenting time arrangements, or both, for the child, unless such motion by either party is made for the purpose of delaying the proceedings. No later than January 1, 1990, any court or social services department personnel appointed by the court to do such evaluation shall be qualified pursuant to subsection (4) of this section. When a mental health professional performs the evaluation, the court shall appoint or approve the selection of the mental health professional. The moving party shall, at the time of the appointment of the evaluator, deposit a reasonable sum with the court to pay the cost of the evaluation. The court may order the reasonable charge for such evaluation and report to be assessed as costs between the parties. The court shall appoint another mental health professional to perform a supplemental evaluation at the initial expense of the moving party, unless, the court determines that any of the following applies, based on motion and supporting affidavits:

(A) Such motion is interposed for purposes of delay;

(B) A party objects, and the party who objects or the child has a physical or mental condition which would make it harmful for such party or the child to participate in the supplemental evaluation;

(C) The purpose of such motion is to harass or oppress the other party;

(D) The moving party has failed or refused to cooperate with the first evaluation; or

(E) The weight of the evidence other than the custody evaluation by the mental health professional demonstrates that a second evaluation would not be of benefit to the court in determining custody.

(II) Each party and the child shall cooperate in the supplemental evaluation. If the court finds that the supplemental evaluation was necessary and materially assisted the court, the court may order the costs of such supplemental evaluation to be assessed as costs between the parties. Except as otherwise provided in this section, such report shall be considered confidential and shall not be available for public inspection unless by order of court. The cost of each probation department or department of human services evaluation shall be based on an ability to pay and shall be assessed as part of the costs of the action or proceeding, and, upon receipt of such sum by the clerk of court, it shall be transmitted to the department or agency performing the evaluation.

(b) For the purposes of this section, a "licensed mental health professional" means an individual person licensed in a field of the healing arts with specific training in psychiatry, psychology, or a related field and the persons working under his supervision, whether or not those persons working under supervision are licensed.

(2) In preparing his report concerning a child, the evaluator may consult any person who may have information about the child and his potential custodial arrangements. Upon order of the court, the evaluator may refer the child to other professional personnel for diagnosis. The evaluator may consult with and obtain information from medical, mental health, educational, or other expert persons who have served the child in the past without obtaining the consent of the parent or the child's custodian; but the child's consent must be obtained if he has reached the age of fifteen unless the court finds that he lacks mental capacity to consent. If the requirements of subsections (3) to (7) of this section are fulfilled, the evaluator's report may be received in evidence at the hearing.

(3) The evaluator shall mail his report to the court and to counsel and to any party not represented by counsel at least twenty days prior to the hearing. The evaluator shall make available to counsel and to any party not represented by counsel his file of underlying data and reports, complete texts of diagnostic reports made to the evaluator pursuant to the provisions of subsections (2), (5), and (6) of this section, and the names and addresses of all persons whom the evaluator has consulted. Any party to the proceeding may call the evaluator and any person whom he has consulted for cross-examination. No party may waive his right of cross-examination prior to the hearing.

(4) A person shall not be allowed to testify regarding a custody or parenting time evaluation which the person has performed pursuant to this section unless the court finds that the person is qualified as competent, by training and experience, in the areas of:

(a) The effects of divorce and remarriage on children, adults, and families;

(b) Appropriate parenting techniques;

(c) Child development, including cognitive, personality, emotional, and psychological development;

(d) Child and adult psychopathology;

(e) Applicable clinical assessment techniques; and

(f) Applicable legal and ethical requirements of child custody evaluation.

(5) If evaluation is indicated in an area which is beyond the training or experience of the evaluator, the evaluator shall consult with a mental health professional qualified by training or experience in that area. Such areas may include, but are not limited to, domestic violence, child abuse, alcohol or substance abuse, or psychological testing.

(6) (a) A mental health professional may make specific recommendations when the mental health professional has interviewed and assessed all parties to the dispute, assessed the quality of the relationship, or the potential for establishing a quality relationship, between the child and each of the parties, and had access to pertinent information from outside sources.

(b) A mental health professional may make recommendations even though all parties and the child have not been evaluated by the same mental health professional in the following circumstances if the mental health professional states with particularity in his opinion the limitations of his findings and recommendations:

(I) Any of the parties reside outside Colorado and it would not be feasible for all parties and the child to be evaluated by the same mental health professional; or

(II) One party refuses or is unable to cooperate with the court-ordered evaluation; or

(III) The mental health professional is a member of a team of professionals which performed the child custody evaluation and is presenting recommendations of the team which has interviewed and assessed all parties to the dispute.

(7) (a) A written report of the evaluation shall be provided to the court and to the parties pursuant to subsection (3) of this section.

(b) The report of the evaluation shall include, but need not be limited to, the following information:

(I) A description of the procedures employed during the evaluation;

(II) A report of the data collected;

(III) A conclusion which explains how the resulting recommendations were reached from the data collected, with specific reference to criteria listed in section 14-10-124 (1.5), and, if applicable, to the criteria listed in sections 14-10-131 and 14-10-131.5, and their relationship to the results of the evaluation;

(IV) Recommendations concerning custody, parenting time, and other considerations; and

(V) An explanation of any limitations in the evaluations or any reservations regarding the resulting recommendations.

Source: L. 88: Entire section amended, p. 639, § 1, effective May 11, **L. 93:** IP(1)(a)(I), IP(4), and (7)(b)(IV) amended, p. 577, § 10, effective July 1, **L. 94:** (1)(a)(II) amended, p. 2645, § 108, effective July 1.

Cross references: (1) For the licensing of mental health professionals, see article 43 of title 12.

(2) For the legislative declaration contained in the act amending the introductory portions to subsections (1)(a)(I) and (4) and subsection (7)(b)(IV), see section 1 of chapter 165, Session Laws of Colorado 1993; for the legislative declaration contained in the act amending subsection (1)(a)(II), see section 1 of chapter 345, Session Laws of Colorado 1994.

Law reviews.
For article, "Helping a Client Handle a Child Custody Evaluation", see 16 Colo. Law. 1991 (1987). For article, "Custody Evaluations in Colorado", see 18 Colo. Law. 1523 (1989). For article, "Evaluating Child Custody Evaluations", see 22 Colo. Law. 2541 (1993).

Provisions of this section do not apply to custody determination in a dependency proceeding under the Children's Code. People in Interest of D.C., 851 P.2d 291 (Colo. App. 1993).

The language that "the court shall" order an evaluation or a supplemental evaluation is mandatory unless the express conditions apply, and a trial court must make specific findings to support its denial of any requested evaluation in order to insure effective and meaningful review. In re Sepmeier, 782 P.2d 876 (Colo. App. 1989).

"Custody proceedings" does not automatically include a motion to modify custody. The threshold requirements of § 14-10-132 must be met before a custody proceeding is established. In re Michie, 844 P.2d 1325 (Colo. App. 1992).

Denying petitioner's motion for custody evaluation based upon inability to pay was abuse of discretion by court. Hernandez v. District Ct., 814 P.2d 379 (Colo. 1991).

Applied in In re Kasten, 814 P.2d 11 (Colo. App. 1991).

14-10-128. Hearings.

Award for fees of eight witnesses without specific finding of their necessity held to be error in child custody hearing. Weber v. Wallace, 789 P.2d 427 (Colo. App. 1989).

14-10-129. Parenting time.

(1) A parent not granted custody of the child is entitled to reasonable parenting time rights unless the court finds, after a hearing, that parenting time by the parent would endanger the child's physical health or significantly impair the child's emotional development.

(2) The court may make or modify an order granting or denying parenting time rights whenever such order or modification would serve the best interests of the child;

APPENDIX 4.4

CHAPTER 105

DOMESTIC MATTERS

UNIFORM DISSOLUTION OF MARRIAGE ACT

HOUSE BILL NO. 1105. BY REPRESENTATIVES Fleming, Bowen, Dambman, P. Hernandez, Lawson, Neale, Reeser, Reeves, Tanner, Taylor-Little, Webb, and S. Williams; also SENATOR Schroeder.

AN ACT

CONCERNING CUSTODY PROCEEDINGS, AND, IN CONNECTION THEREWITH, ESTABLISHING STANDARDS FOR THE USE OF MENTAL HEALTH PROFESSIONALS.

Be it enacted by the General Assembly of the State of Colorado:

Section 1. 14-10-127, Colorado Revised Statutes, 1987 Repl. Vol., is amended to read:

14-10-127. Evaluation and reports. (1) (a) (I) In all custody proceedings, the court shall, upon motion of either party, or may, upon its own motion, order the court probation department, any county or district social services department, or a licensed mental health professional QUALIFIED PURSUANT TO SUBSECTION (4) OF THIS SECTION to perform an evaluation and file a written report concerning custodial OR VISITATION arrangements, OR BOTH, for the child, unless such motion by either party is made for the purpose of delaying the proceedings. NO LATER THAN JANUARY 1, 1990, ANY COURT OR SOCIAL SERVICES DEPARTMENT PERSONNEL APPOINTED BY THE COURT TO DO SUCH EVALUATION SHALL BE QUALIFIED PURSUANT TO SUBSECTION (4) OF THIS SECTION. WHEN A MENTAL HEALTH PROFESSIONAL PERFORMS THE EVALUATION, THE COURT SHALL APPOINT OR APPROVE THE SELECTION OF THE MENTAL HEALTH PROFESSIONAL. THE MOVING PARTY SHALL, AT THE TIME OF THE APPOINTMENT OF THE EVALUATOR, DEPOSIT A REASONABLE SUM WITH THE COURT TO PAY THE COST OF THE EVALUATION. THE COURT MAY ORDER THE REASONABLE CHARGE FOR SUCH EVALUATION AND REPORT TO BE ASSESSED AS COSTS BETWEEN THE PARTIES. THE COURT SHALL APPOINT ANOTHER MENTAL HEALTH PROFESSIONAL TO PERFORM A SUPPLEMENTAL EVALUATION AT THE INITIAL EXPENSE OF THE MOVING PARTY,

Capital letters indicate new material added to existing statutes; dashes through words indicate deletions from existing statutes and such material not part of act.

UNLESS THE COURT DETERMINES THAT ANY OF THE FOLLOWING APPLIES, BASED ON MOTION AND SUPPORTING AFFIDAVITS:

(A) SUCH MOTION IS INTERPOSED FOR PURPOSES OF DELAY;

(B) A PARTY OBJECTS, AND THE PARTY WHO OBJECTS OR THE CHILD HAS A PHYSICAL OR MENTAL CONDITION WHICH WOULD MAKE IT HARMFUL FOR SUCH PARTY OR THE CHILD TO PARTICIPATE IN THE SUPPLEMENTAL EVALUATION;

(C) THE PURPOSE OF SUCH MOTION IS TO HARASS OR OPPRESS THE OTHER PARTY;

(D) THE MOVING PARTY HAS FAILED OR REFUSED TO COOPERATE WITH THE FIRST EVALUATION; OR

(E) THE WEIGHT OF THE EVIDENCE OTHER THAN THE CUSTODY EVALUATION BY THE MENTAL HEALTH PROFESSIONAL DEMONSTRATES THAT A SECOND EVALUATION WOULD NOT BE OF BENEFIT TO THE COURT IN DETERMINING CUSTODY.

(II) EACH PARTY AND THE CHILD SHALL COOPERATE IN THE SUPPLEMENTAL EVALUATION. IF THE COURT FINDS THAT THE SUPPLEMENTAL EVALUATION WAS NECESSARY AND MATERIALLY ASSISTED THE COURT, THE COURT MAY ORDER THE COSTS OF SUCH SUPPLEMENTAL EVALUATION TO BE ASSESSED AS COSTS BETWEEN THE PARTIES. Except as otherwise provided in this section, such report shall be considered confidential and shall not be available for public inspection unless by order of court. The cost of each probation department or social services department evaluation shall be based on an ability to pay and shall be assessed as part of the costs of the action or proceeding, and, upon receipt of such sum by the clerk of the court, it shall be transmitted to the department or agency performing the evaluation. ~~The court shall order an evaluation by an impartial licensed mental health professional selected by the court, upon motion of either party, only if the moving party agrees initially to pay all costs of such evaluation. The moving party shall, at the time of appointment of the evaluator, deposit a reasonable sum with the court to pay the cost of the evaluation. The court may order the reasonable charges of any evaluation and report to be assessed as costs between the parties.~~

(b) FOR THE PURPOSES OF THIS SECTION, A "LICENSED MENTAL HEALTH PROFESSIONAL" MEANS AN INDIVIDUAL PERSON LICENSED IN A FIELD OF THE HEALING ARTS WITH SPECIFIC TRAINING IN PSYCHIATRY, PSYCHOLOGY, OR A RELATED FIELD AND THE PERSONS WORKING UNDER HIS SUPERVISION, WHETHER OR NOT THOSE PERSONS WORKING UNDER SUPERVISION ARE LICENSED.

(2) In preparing his report concerning a child, the evaluator may consult any person who may have information about the child and his potential custodial arrangements. Upon order of the court, the evaluator may refer the child to other professional personnel for diagnosis. The evaluator may consult with and obtain information from medical, ~~psychiatric,~~ MENTAL HEALTH, EDUCATIONAL, or other expert persons who have served the

child in the past without obtaining the consent of the parent or the child's custodian; but the child's consent must be obtained if he has reached the age of ~~sixteen~~ FIFTEEN unless the court finds that he lacks mental capacity to consent. If the requirements of ~~subsection~~ SUBSECTIONS (3) TO (7) of this section are fulfilled, the evaluator's report may be received in evidence at the hearing.

(3) The evaluator shall mail his report to THE COURT AND TO counsel and to any party not represented by counsel at least ~~ten~~ TWENTY days prior to the hearing. The evaluator shall make available to counsel and to any party not represented by counsel his file of underlying data and reports, complete texts of diagnostic reports made to the evaluator pursuant to the provisions of ~~subsection~~ SUBSECTIONS (2), (5), AND (6) of this section, and the names and addresses of all persons whom the evaluator has consulted. Any party to the proceeding may call the evaluator and any person whom he has consulted for cross-examination. No party may waive his right of cross-examination prior to the hearing.

(4) (a) A PERSON SHALL NOT BE ALLOWED TO TESTIFY REGARDING A CUSTODY OR VISITATION EVALUATION WHICH HE HAS PERFORMED PURSUANT TO THIS SECTION UNLESS THE COURT FINDS THAT HE IS QUALIFIED AS COMPETENT, BY TRAINING AND EXPERIENCE, IN THE AREAS OF:

(I) THE EFFECTS OF DIVORCE AND REMARRIAGE ON CHILDREN, ADULTS, AND FAMILIES;

(II) APPROPRIATE PARENTING TECHNIQUES;

(III) CHILD DEVELOPMENT, INCLUDING COGNITIVE, PERSONALITY, EMOTIONAL, AND PSYCHOLOGICAL DEVELOPMENT;

(IV) CHILD AND ADULT PSYCHOPATHOLOGY;

(V) APPLICABLE CLINICAL ASSESSMENT TECHNIQUES; AND

(VI) APPLICABLE LEGAL AND ETHICAL REQUIREMENTS OF CHILD CUSTODY EVALUATION.

(5) IF EVALUATION IS INDICATED IN AN AREA WHICH IS BEYOND THE TRAINING OR EXPERIENCE OF THE EVALUATOR, THE EVALUATOR SHALL CONSULT WITH A MENTAL HEALTH PROFESSIONAL QUALIFIED BY TRAINING OR EXPERIENCE IN THAT AREA. SUCH AREAS MAY INCLUDE, BUT ARE NOT LIMITED TO, DOMESTIC VIOLENCE, CHILD ABUSE, ALCOHOL OR SUBSTANCE ABUSE, OR PSYCHOLOGICAL TESTING.

(6) (a) A MENTAL HEALTH PROFESSIONAL MAY MAKE SPECIFIC RECOMMENDATIONS WHEN THE MENTAL HEALTH PROFESSIONAL HAS INTERVIEWED AND ASSESSED ALL PARTIES TO THE DISPUTE, ASSESSED THE QUALITY OF THE RELATIONSHIP, OR THE POTENTIAL FOR ESTABLISHING A QUALITY RELATIONSHIP, BETWEEN THE CHILD AND EACH OF THE PARTIES, AND HAD ACCESS TO PERTINENT INFORMATION FROM OUTSIDE SOURCES.

(b) A MENTAL HEALTH PROFESSIONAL MAY MAKE RECOMMENDA-TIONS EVEN THOUGH ALL PARTIES AND THE CHILD HAVE NOT BEEN EVALUATED BY THE SAME MENTAL HEALTH PROFESSIONAL IN THE FOLLOWING CIRCUMSTANCES IF THE MENTAL HEALTH PROFES-SIONAL STATES WITH PARTICULARITY IN HIS OPINION THE LIMITA-TIONS OF HIS FINDINGS AND RECOMMENDATIONS:

(I) ANY OF THE PARTIES RESIDE OUTSIDE COLORADO AND IT WOULD NOT BE FEASIBLE FOR ALL PARTIES AND THE CHILD TO BE EVALUATED BY THE SAME MENTAL HEALTH PROFESSIONAL; OR

(II) ONE PARTY REFUSES OR IS UNABLE TO COOPERATE WITH THE COURT-ORDERED EVALUATION; OR

(III) THE MENTAL HEALTH PROFESSIONAL IS A MEMBER OF A TEAM OF PROFESSIONALS WHICH PERFORMED THE CHILD CUS-TODY EVALUATION AND IS PRESENTING RECOMMENDATIONS OF THE TEAM WHICH HAS INTERVIEWED AND ASSESSED ALL PARTIES TO THE DISPUTE.

(7) (a) A WRITTEN REPORT OF THE EVALUATION SHALL BE PRO-VIDED TO THE COURT AND TO THE PARTIES PURSUANT TO SUBSEC-TION (3) OF THIS SECTION.

(b) THE REPORT OF THE EVALUATION SHALL INCLUDE, BUT NEED NOT BE LIMITED TO, THE FOLLOWING INFORMATION:

(I) A DESCRIPTION OF THE PROCEDURES EMPLOYED DURING THE EVALUATION;

(II) A REPORT OF THE DATA COLLECTED;

(III) A CONCLUSION WHICH EXPLAINS HOW THE RESULTING REC-OMMENDATIONS WERE REACHED FROM THE DATA COLLECTED, WITH SPECIFIC REFERENCE TO CRITERIA LISTED IN SECTION 14-10-124 (1.5), AND IF APPLICABLE, TO THE CRITERIA LISTED IN SECTIONS 14-10-131 AND 14-10-131.5, AND THEIR RELATIONSHIP TO THE RE-SULTS OF THE EVALUATION;

(IV) RECOMMENDATIONS CONCERNING CUSTODY, VISITATION, AND OTHER CONSIDERATIONS; AND

(V) AN EXPLANATION OF ANY LIMITATIONS IN THE EVALUATIONS OR ANY RESERVATIONS REGARDING THE RESULTING RECOMMEN-DATIONS.

Section 2. **Safety clause.** The general assembly hereby finds, determines, and declares that this act is necessary for the immediate preservation of the public peace, health, and safety.

Approved: May 11, 1988

Florence M. PACHECO, now known as
Florence M. Sellers, Plaintiff-
Appellee,

v.

Benjamin F. PACHECO, Defendant-
Appellant.

No. 75–799.

Colorado Court of Appeals,
Div. II.

Aug. 12, 1976.

Selected for Official Publication.

Father appealed from orders of the District Court, Jefferson County, George G. Priest, J., denying his motion for permanent change of custody of two children and granting wife's motions for increase in child support and for attorney fees. The Court of Appeals, VanCise, J., held that evidence regarding change of circumstances supported order increasing monthly child support; that trial court's order requiring father to contribute reasonable amount for mother's attorney fees was supported by the evidence; and that where copy of custody investigation report was received by father's counsel a reasonable time prior to custody hearing and no objection was made to report until after commencement of hearing, objections as to hearsay nature of report and the failure to provide father with report at least ten days prior to the hearing were waived.

Affirmed.

1. Parent and Child ⊂⊃ 3.3(8)

Court has continuing jurisdiction for purpose of later revisions of its orders pertaining to child support as changing circumstances may require. C.R.S. '63, 46–1–5(4).

2. Parent and Child ⊂⊃ 3.3(8)

If financial ability of father improves and needs of minor children increase, it is proper to make appropriate increases in amount of child support to be paid by father. C.R.S. '63, 46–1–5(4).

3. Parent and Child ⊂⊃ 3.3(8)

Evidence showing, inter alia, an increase in costs of needs of two children since 1970 support order requiring father to pay $50 per month per child and an increase in father's monthly take-home pay from $376 in 1970 to $516 supported trial court's order increasing child support by $35 per month per child. C.R.S. '63, 46–1–5(4).

4. Parent and Child ⊂⊃ 3.3(8)

Trial court's finding that mother who brought successful proceeding for increase in child support was entitled to have father contribute reasonable amount for her attorney fees was supported by evidence.

5. Infants ⊂⊃ 19.3(3)

Compliance with ten-day provision of statute requiring that court mail custody investigation report to counsel at least ten days prior to custody hearing is not a condition precedent to reception of report; noncompliance with ten-day rule merely prohibits court from proceeding with the hearing wherein report can be considered absent consent of or waiver by parties. C.R.S. '73, 14–10–127 (2,3).

6. Infants ⊂⊃ 19.3(1)

Purpose of legislation providing for preparation and filing of custody investigation report is to make information contained therein available to assist court in determining what is in best interests of children concerned. C.R.S. '73, 14–10–127.

7. Infants ⊂⊃ 19.3(3)

Trial ⊂⊃ 76

Unless a party notifies court and opposing party within ten days after receipt of copy of custody investigation report or if a copy has not been received at least ten days prior to custody hearing, at or prior to commencement of hearing at which report may be used that he intends to object to admission of report on grounds of noncompliance with ten-day rule of hearsay nature of report, any such objections are waived; if a valid objection on either of such grounds is made within the period specified, then, on motion of either party or court, court shall grant reasonable continuance of custody hearing date in order that parties may obtain appropriate testimony. C.R.S. '73, 14–10–127 (2, 3).

8. Trial ⚮ 76

Where copy of custody investigation report was received by father's counsel a reasonable time prior to custody hearing and no objection was made to report until after commencement of hearing, objections as to hearsay nature of report and the failure to provide father with report at least ten days prior to the custody hearing were waived and trial court could properly consider the report. C.R.S. '73, 14–10–127 (2, 3).

9. Parent and Child ⚮ 2(21)

Where objection to challenged testimony of witness as to disciplining of children was sustained, no offer of proof was made following objection and counsel, by other questions, was allowed to go into everything witness had observed concerning mother's treatment of children, no prejudicial error arose because of exclusion of such testimony at custody hearing.

10. Parent and Child ⚮ 2(18)

Evidence, in proceeding by father for change of custody, supported trial court's determination that it was in best interests of children that custody remain with mother.

11. Infants ⚮ 19.3(2, 7)

Determination of custody is matter left to discretion of trial judge and, absent an abuse of discretion, that determination will not be disturbed on appeal.

Betterberg & Stipech, Robert T. Bettenberg, Mark R. Shapiro, Denver, for plaintiff-appellee.

George G. Johnson, Jr., Denver, for defendant-appellant.

VANCISE, Judge.

Defendant, Benjamin F. Pacheco (the father), appeals from the orders denying his

motion for permanent change of custody and granting the motions for increase in child support and for attorney fees of plaintiff, Florence M. Sellers (the mother). We affirm.

In September 1970, custody of the two children of the parties was granted to the mother with prescribed visitation rights to the father, and the father was ordered to maintain medical insurance for the children and to pay $50 per month per child for support. In April 1975, the three motions above referred to were heard. The court denied the motion for change of custody, increased the child support from $50 to $85 per month per child, and ordered the father to pay $300 to the ex-wife's attorney.

I.

The father contends that the court abused its discretion in ordering increased child support payments and in requiring him to pay his ex-wife's attorney fees. No issue is made as to the reasonableness of the amount of the fee; the objection is to his being required to pay any fee.

[1, 2] The court has continuing jurisdiction for the purpose of such later revisions of its order pertaining to child support as changing circumstances may require. C.R.S. 1963, 46–1–5(4). And, if the financial ability of the father improves and the needs of the minor children increase, it is proper to make appropriate increases in the amount of child support. *Garrow v. Garrow,* 152 Colo. 480, 382. P.2d 809.

On supporting evidence, the court found that, at the time of the 1970 support order, the father's take-home pay was $376, and that, at the time of the 1975 hearing, his affidavit showed a net monthly take-home pay of $516.30 while an affidavit from his employer, admitted without objection, indicated that his net monthly income was in the $800 to $900 bracket. It further found that, at the time of the hearing, the mother was employed with a net monthly take-home pay of

$330, exclusive of child support payments. The evidence was that she was working in 1970, but the amount of her then earnings was not shown. Both parties testified that the costs of the needs of the children had increased since 1970.

[3] The change of circumstances being established, the court could modify support. A monthly increase of $35 per child, under the facts shown, is not unreasonable and is within the sound discretion of the trial court. Thus, its order will not be disturbed on review. *See Franco v. Franco,* 161 Colo. 507, 423 P.2d 327.

[4] Also, the court's finding that the mother was entitled to have the father contribute a reasonable amount for her attorney's fee is supported by the evidence. Hence, there is no abuse of discretion in the order entered.

II.

The father also contends that the court erred in denying his motion for permanent change of custody. He first claims error in the court's considering the custody investigation report prepared by the County Department of Social Services pursuant to court order.

This report is a summary of interviews by a social worker with the parties, their spouses, the two children involved, and with 15 other persons. The report concludes with the social worker's "impressions," but does not contain any specific recommendation or opinion. It is generally favorable to the mother and unfavorable to the father.

The report is dated April 18, 1975, and shows a copy going to each attorney. Counsel for the father received his copy April 23. No objections or exceptions to the report were made prior to or at the commencement of the April 28 hearing.

On cross-examination of the father, he was asked about a statement in the report allegedly made by him. The question was objected to on the ground of hearsay, and the document was objected to on the same ground. The court ruled:

"Well, you can't object to the document because you asked for it, and this is the one you received; but I will sustain the objection."

No further reference was made to the investigation report until the conclusion of the hearing. Its author was not called as a witness. At closing, the mother's attorney moved the admission of the report into evidence. The attorney for the father objected on the ground that the report had not been mailed to counsel "at least 10 days prior to the hearing" as prescribed by § 14–10–127(2) and (3), C.R.S.1973. To this, the court ruled that this objection should have been made at the beginning of the testimony, in which event the hearing would have been set over, and that it was now too late.

[5] Compliance with the 10-day provisions of the statute is not a condition precedent to the reception of the report. Noncompliance with the 10-day rule merely prohibits the court from proceeding with a hearing wherein the report can be considered absent consent of or waiver by the parties.

[6] The purpose of the legislation providing for the preparation and filing of these reports in custody proceedings, § 14–10–127, C.R.S.1973, is to make the information contained therein available to assist the court in determining what is in the best interests of the children concerned. *See Aylor v. Aylor,* 173 Colo. 294, 478 P.2d 302; *Anderson v. Anderson,* 167 Colo. 88, 445 P.2d 397. Because any party has the right to call for cross-examination the investigator and any person he has consulted, and because the investigator's file is available to counsel, ample opportunity exists for a party to test the reliability of the report and to offer evidence in explanation of or to disprove any statements or conclusions based on hearsay. *Cf. Anderson, supra.*

[7] In accordance with the intent and purpose of the statute, we hold that unless a party notifies the court and the opposing party within 10 days after receipt of a copy of the report [or if a copy has not been received at least 10 days prior to the hearing day, then at or prior to the commencement of the hearing at which the report may be used] that he intends to object to the admission of the report on the grounds of noncompliance with the 10-day rule or the hearsay nature of the report, any such objections are waived. If a valid objection on either of the above grounds is made within the period specified above, then, on motion of either party or of the court, the court shall grant a reasonable continuance of the custody hearing date in order that the parties may obtain appropriate testimony.

[8] Where, as here, a copy of the report was received by counsel a reasonable time prior to the hearing and no objection was made thereto until after the commencement of the hearing, objections as to hearsay and the 10-day rule were waived. *See In re Marriage of Armbeck,* 33 Colo. App. 260, 518 P.2d 300; *Rayer v Rayer,* 32 Colo. App. 400, 512 P.2d 637. Hence, no reversible error was committed in the court's considering the report.

[9] The father further contends that the court erroneously excluded certain testimony from the mother's present husband as to incidents showing her unfitness to have the children.

The challenged question was:

"[D]id we have a discussion about the disciplining of the children involved, the two Pacheco children?"

This was objected to as irrelevant, and the objection was sustained. No offer of proof was made following this objection, and, by other questions, counsel was allowed to go into everything the witness had observed concerning the mother's treatment of the children. There was no prejudicial error here.

[10, 11] The court made a determination that it was in the best interests of the chil-

dren that the custody remain with the mother. There was sufficient evidence to support that conclusion. Determination of custody being a matter left to the discretion of the trial judge, *Rayer v. Rayer, supra,* and there being no showing of an abuse of that discretion here, we will not disturb that determination.

Orders affirmed.

SILVERSTEIN, C. J., and SMITH, J., concur.

UNIVERSITY HILLS BEAUTY ACADEMY, INC., a Colorado Corporation, Plaintiff-Appellant and Cross-Appellee,

v.

The MOUNTAIN STATES TELEPHONE AND TELEGRAPH COMPANY, a Colorado corporation, Defendant-Appellee and Cross-Appellant.

No. 75–668.

Colorado Court of Appeals,
Div. II.

Aug. 19, 1976.

Selected for Official Publication.

Suit was instituted for loss of business profits and expenses in mitigating damages allegedly resulting from negligent omission of a listing in a classified telephone directory. The District Court of the City and County of Denver, Joseph N. Lilly, J., entered judgment in favor of defendant, and plaintiff appealed. The Court of Appeals, VanCise, J., held that enforcement of limitation of liability clause in contract with reference to services to be rendered by telephone utility, with result that utility was not liable to customer for loss of business profits and expenses incurred in mitigating damages allegedly resulting from negligent omission of customer's listing in classified "yellow pages" of directory published by utility, was not so unreasonable as to be unconscionable, where there were other directories and publications in which

APPENDIX 4.6

For later cases see same Topic and Key Number in Pocket Part

Or.App. 1972. Under circumstances of case, although question of custody was close because of time mother had allowed father to have child, court would not disturb trial judge's order refusing to change custody of child from mother to father.

King v. King, 500 P.2d 267, 10 Or.App. 324.

Wash. 1972. When, on appeal by maternal grandmother and legal guardian of eight-year-old child from order terminating guardianship and restoring custody of child to her natural parents, the Supreme Court was uncertain whether disposition of trial court reflected view that welfare of child was paramount consideration or whether right of parents to custody was given improper weight, case would be remanded to enable trial court to review standards used in deciding case in light of rules enunciated by the Supreme Court.

In re Guardianship of Palmer, 503 P.2d 464, 81 Wash.2d 604.

Wash.App. 1972. Although rarely is an appellate court justified in making new determination of custody of children, since trial judge had disqualified himself from proceedings, many witnesses had testified in the lengthy trial and record clearly substantiated findings, custody of children would be awarded by the Court of Appeals to the mother subject to the six-weeks' visitation time in summer with the father as well as a visitation of every other weekend rather than providing, as trial court had, for the alternating of custody on an annual basis between the father and the mother.

Rickard v. Rickard, 503 P.2d 763, 7 Wash.App. 907.

Wyo. 1968. Supreme Court considered it appropriate in particular case to award mother an attorney's fee of $300 for his representation in the defense of her right to continued custody of children.

Rau v. Rau, 441 P.2d 320.

⬭ **2(21). — Scope of review in general; discretion; harmless error.**

Ariz. 1970. Granting of visitation rights is a matter in which court enjoys broad discretion, since trial judge is in most favorable position to determine what is best for children, and unless it clearly appears that trial judge has mistaken or ignored the evidence a reviewing court will not disturb his finding.

Armer v. Armer, 463 P.2d 818, 105 Ariz. 284.

Ariz. 1964. Reviewing court should not substitute its opinion as to which parent should have custody.

In re Clay, 393 P.2d 257, 96 Ariz. 160.

Colo. 1969. Denial of father's right to cross-examine probation officer who submitted report of home investigations of both parties in custody proceedings pursuant to stipulation between parties was not prejudicial where father objected only to letter written by medical doctor and such letter was stricken from report and doctor became witness and was examined by both parties. C.R.S. '63, 154–1–7(6).

Saucerman v. Saucerman, 461 P.2d 18, 170 Colo. 318.

Colo.App. 1976. Where objection to challenged testimony of witness as to disciplining of children was sustained, no offer of proof was made following objection and counsel, by other questions, was allowed to go into everything witness had observed concerning mother's treatment of children, no prejudicial error arose because of exclusion of such testimony at custody hearing.

Pacheco v. Pacheco, 554 P.2d 720, 38 Colo.App. 181.

Hawaii 1974. The supreme court will not set aside the findings of fact of the family court unless there is a definite and firm conviction that a mistake has been committed.

Turoff v. Turoff, 527 P.2d 1275, 56 Haw. 51.

Kan. 1978. Judgment of trial court on question of change of custody will not be disturbed on appeal without an affirmative showing of an abuse in exercise of discretion, inasmuch as trial court is in most advantageous position to judge how interests of children may best be served for while an appellate court has only printed page to consider, trial court has advantage of seeing witnesses and parties, observing their demeanor, and assessing character of parties and quality of their affection and feeling for children.

Simmons v. Simmons, 576 P.2d 589, 223 Kan. 639.

Kan. 1973. Paramount consideration in custody disputes between parents is always the welfare and best interests of the children and trial court is in the best position to judge whether those interests are being served; in the absence of an abuse of judicial discretion, its judgment will not be disturbed.

Moudy v. Moudy, 505 P.2d 764, 211 Kan. 213.

Kan. 1968. When issue of child custody is between parents the primary consideration of a court is the best interests and welfare of the children, and in absence of abuse of sound judicial discretion the trial court's judgment determining the issue will not be disturbed on appeal.

Greene v. Greene, 443 P.2d 263, 201 Kan. 701.

Mont. 1977. Where district judge conducting hearing on permanent custody mistakenly assumed that another district judge had

SECTION II

CONSTITUTIONAL
AND CRIMINAL LAW

INTRODUCTION TO SECTION II

In this section, we are going to look at two specific areas of the law, constitutional and criminal law. The discussion of constitutional law in chapter 5 is still general, however. This is because constitutional law is a general and broad area of the law. As we have learned, the Constitution provides the framework for the American legal system and governs all other federal and State law. Thus, the concepts and principles of constitutional law must be general enough to apply to each specific area of the law. These general concepts and principles, however, can answer specific questions like:

- Can a woman accused of murder be denied bail?
- Is a hearing required before a child can be removed from her parents?
- May a group home for developmentally disabled adults locate in any neighborhood?
- Does a man have a right to refuse life-saving treatment?

We will look at how general constitutional concepts and principles impact the specific areas of the law significant to social work practice when we look at those areas of the law. In other words, in later chapters of the book, we will try to apply

general constitutional concepts and principles to answer such specific questions. In chapter 5, we will explain some general constitutional concepts and principles, focusing on the two that are most important to social work practice: due process of law and equal protection of the laws.

The discussion in chapters 6 and 7 is far more specific. In these chapters, we will look at the criminal law, that is, the law defining what is a crime and establishing the criminal justice process. We will look at this law for both adults and youths.

Two sets of laws in all of the States and in the federal system address crime: one set for adults and one set for some or all minors. The former set, which is generally found in a criminal code or penal code, identifies certain conduct as criminal (i.e., identifies and defines crimes) and establishes the procedures to be followed when adults are charged with committing the identified crimes and the actions that can be taken if it is determined that the adults have committed the crimes. The latter set, which is generally found in a juvenile court act, establishes the procedures to be followed when youths under a certain age (which may be younger than the age of majority) are charged with committing certain crimes (as identified and defined in the criminal code or in the juvenile court act) and identifies the actions that can be taken if it is determined that the youths have committed the crimes.

Although both sets of laws may address the same criminal behavior, they create separate criminal justice systems that operate differently. In particular, juveniles who fall within the jurisdiction of a juvenile court act are tried in special juvenile courts, apart from adults. The differences in the two separate criminal justice systems stem from the different legal doctrines on which they are based.

The criminal justice system for adults is based on the **police power** which gives the state the right to protect society against public wrongs, to preserve law and order and to foster morality. The juvenile court acts, by way of contrast, are based on the ***parens patriae* authority,** under which the state, literally as a parent, has the obligation and the power to protect individuals who are unable to protect themselves. Such people include not only children but also adults with severe mental or physical disabilities.

The first law creating a juvenile court and removing youthful offenders from the adult criminal courts was enacted in Illinois in 1899, in part as a result of the efforts of Jane Addams and other social workers. This juvenile court and the others that were eventually created in all other States (and to a limited extent in the federal system) were designed to address the needs of youth who had violated criminal laws (called delinquents) and also youth in need of protection because of parental abuse, neglect, or absence. They were intended to be *civil,* not criminal, courts and to *protect and treat,* not punish, delinquents and other youth in need of intervention. To best serve children's interests, the proceedings were designed to be flexible, informal and non-adversarial. Social workers played a far greater role than lawyers.

Juvenile law and juvenile court acts have changed significantly since 1899, especially in the way they respond to delinquents. This change has occurred because of a recognition that the informality and flexibility of the juvenile courts often sacrificed juveniles' rights and because of the outcry against the serious crimes being committed by juveniles and concerns for public safety. Today, delinquency actions in juvenile courts are much like criminal prosecutions of adults and more and more juveniles are being prosecuted as adults in the criminal courts. The role of lawyers in juvenile courts has increased significantly.

Although juvenile courts have changed and lawyers' roles in juvenile court proceedings have grown, social workers still have important roles to play related to delinquency. Social worker's also have important roles to play related to adult crime. These roles and the system in which they are performed will be examined in chapters 6 on adult crime and 7 on delinquency.

5

Basic Constitutional Concepts and Principles for the Social Worker

Because the Constitution shapes every area of the law, you must understand basic constitutional concepts and principles in order to understand the law relevant to social worker practice. This chapter is intended to provide this understanding. To that end, the chapter provides an overview of the Constitution and reviews some basic constitutional concepts and principles, focusing on the two principles most significant to social work practice: due process of law and equal protection of the laws. While other constitutional guarantees, like freedom of speech and religion, may be more important to you in your daily life than due process and equal protection, no constitutional principles are more important to your practice than due process and equal protection. Moreover, as you shall see, due process and equal protection have been important in securing rights for persons who historically have suffered from disadvantages and have turned to social workers for assistance.

The chapter concludes by looking at remedies that can be employed when there has been a violation of due process, equal protection, or other constitutional guarantees.

AN OVERVIEW OF THE CONSTITUTION

As has been stated, the Constitution provides the framework for the American legal system and is the supreme law of the land. The Constitution establishes the federal government and creates the American system of federalism by giving the federal government certain powers and reserving certain powers in the States. It also limits the powers of both the federal government and the States by establishing certain rights in the people that neither the federal government nor the States can infringe. And, because the Constitution is the supreme law of the land, all law—whether federal or State, or whether legislation, regulation, or court opinion—must be consistent with it.

Despite the Constitution's enormous importance, it is relatively short, containing only seven articles and twenty-six amendments. It is far shorter than most State constitutions and many federal or State statutes. You should read the entire Constitution to learn what is and what is not included in it and to become familiar with its key provisions. A brief overview of the Constitution is set forth below to make reading it a little easier for you.

The first three articles of the Constitution establish the three branches of the federal government.

Article I establishes the chief lawmaking branch, the legislative branch. It establishes Congress and sets forth the basic rules for the election of its members and for its operation. Section 8 sets forth the powers of Congress and, thus, of the federal government. Sections 9 and 10 distinguish the powers of the federal and State governments, respectively. Pursuant to these sections, the federal government may only exercise those powers granted to it by the Constitution, while the States may exercise all powers except those which they are prohibited from exercising by the Constitution.[1]

---

1. To make this division of powers absolutely clear, the Tenth Amendment to the Constitution provides: "The powers not delegated to the United States by the Constitution, nor prohibited by it to the States, are reserved to the States respectively, or to the people."

Section 8 of Article I, which gives Congress the power to "provide for the general welfare," is the source of all federal social welfare legislation—that is, legislation protecting workers, children, or others in need of government protection and creating social welfare programs that provide financial assistance or services to the sick, the poor, the disabled, the old, or others in need of government help. Thus, section 8 is of great significance to social workers. It is also of great significance to social workers that the States are not restricted from exercising the power to provide for the general welfare and, indeed, until well into the twentieth century, the courts narrowly construed the federal government's power to enact social legislation without ever questioning the States' powers.

Article II establishes the executive branch. It creates the offices of President and Vice-president, sets forth the method of their election, and enumerates the President's powers and duties.

Article III establishes the judicial branch. It creates the Supreme Court and authorizes Congress to establish inferior courts (which the first Congress did immediately). It also defines the jurisdiction of the Supreme Court and any other federal courts and establishes some procedural protections in these courts.

The remaining four articles contain several miscellaneous provisions. The most important provisions for social workers are the "full, faith and credit" clause in Article IV, which address the relations among the States, and the so-called "Supremacy Clause" in Article VI, which makes the Constitution and the laws of the federal government "the Supreme Law of the Land."

The first ten amendments to the Constitution, known as the **Bill of Rights**, were adopted immediately after the Constitution was ratified to ensure that the newly created federal government would not assume too much power over the States and their residents. The Bill of Rights establishes twenty-seven rights that are guaranteed or protected from government invasion, including:

- the First Amendment's guarantee of freedom of speech and religion and the right to assemble and petition the government;
- the Fourth Amendment's protection against unreasonable searches and seizures;
- the Fifth Amendment's protection against double jeopardy and self-incrimination and the guarantee that no property can be taken without "just compensation" and that "no person" can be "deprived of life, liberty or property without due process of law;"
- the Sixth Amendment's right to a speedy and public trial and to confront witnesses in criminal cases;
- the Seventh Amendment's right to a jury in certain civil cases;
- the Eighth Amendment's protection against excessive fines or bail and "cruel and unusual" punishment.

Because the Bill of Rights was designed to limit the power of the federal government, not of the States, it was initially interpreted to apply only to the federal government. Thus, the States could ignore its proscriptions and could infringe upon the rights it guarantees without having their actions declared unconstitutional. This limitation on the scope of the Bill of

Rights did not change until the adoption of the Thirteenth, Fourteenth, and Fifteenth Amendments after the Civil War. These amendments, which are specifically addressed to the States, were designed to prohibit slavery and give civil rights to the newly freed slaves. The Fourteenth Amendment, which has become the most important amendment, provides that no State can "deny to any person within its jurisdiction the *equal protection of the laws*" or "deprive any person of life, liberty, or property without *due process of law.*"[2]

The latter provision, known as the **due process clause** was gradually recognized as requiring the States to comply with most of the provisions in the Bill of Rights. In case after case, the Supreme Court ruled that a State's denial of a right guaranteed by the Bill of Rights was not consistent with due process and, thus, violated the Fourteenth Amendment. Put differently, the Supreme Court has gradually **incorporated** the Bill of Rights into the due process clause and, thus, applied it to the States.

The due process clause of the Fourteenth Amendment, along with the identical due process clause in the Fifth Amendment has also been used to require certain procedural protections before the government may deprive a person of certain property interests or certain rights and to require fundamental fairness and reasonableness in government actions. In other words, the due process clauses have served the important function of establishing rights which are not expressly in-

cluded in the Bill of Rights, the Civil War amendments, or elsewhere in the Constitution.

The Fourteenth Amendment's guarantee of equal protection of the laws, known as the **equal protection clause**, has also served an important function. This clause has been used to prevent unreasonable and discriminatory classifications by the States and by the federal government. While this clause only applies to the States and there is no equivalent clause applying to the federal government in the Fifth Amendment or elsewhere in the Constitution, the Supreme Court has incorporated the equal protection clause of the Fourteenth Amendment into the due process clause of the Fifth Amendment, and, thus, applies it to the federal government.

We will look closer at the due process and equal protection clauses in the Fourteenth Amendment later in this chapter. Other clauses in this amendment and other amendments to the Constitution are less important to you as a social worker, although some, like the Nineteenth Amendment giving women the right to vote or the Sixteenth Amendment establishing the income tax, may be important to you personally.

THE REQUIREMENT OF STATE ACTION

The Constitution regulates and applies to actions by the *government,* not by *private individuals.* Thus, it only protects rights from infringement by the federal or State governments. Put differently, there must be **state action**, which may be loosely defined as some kind of participa-

---

2.   The term *State* in the Fourteenth Amendment, as the term *State* in this book, should be understood to include local governments within a State.

tion or involvement of a government or a government official in an act or course of conduct, in order for there to be a violation of the Constitution. If there has been no state action, an invasion of a right guaranteed by the Constitution may violate a statute, but it would not violate the Constitution—no matter how unreasonable, unfair, or serious the invasion. As was stated in the *Civil Rights Cases,* 109 U.S. 3 (1883): "Individual invasion of individual rights is not the subject of the . . . [Constitution]."

To illustrate the requirement of state action, suppose you bought a car on the installment plan. The due process clauses of the Fifth and Fourteenth Amendments provide that you cannot be deprived of property without due process of law. As we shall see, this language has been interpreted to require that, in many circumstances, you must be given notice and an opportunity to be heard before your property can be taken away. If you miss several payments on your car however, the dealer that sold the car to you may go to your house and repossess the car without providing you prior notice or an opportunity to be heard. The dealer's action in repossessing your car may or may not be legal under State law, but it would most likely be considered constitutional. This is because if the dealer just came and got your car, without any assistance from or involvement of the government, there would have been no state action and if there has been no state action, there can be no violation of the due process guarantee. The due process clause of the Fourteenth Amendment does not require *private individuals* to give you due process before depriving you of property; it only requires *governments* to give you

due process before taking away your property.

Now suppose that a statute in the State where you bought your car provides that, before repossessing a car, an automobile dealer must go to court and get a court order for repossession and further provides that only the sheriff can actually go out and seize the car pursuant to the repossession order. Given this statute, it would most likely be considered unconstitutional for the dealer to obtain a repossession order for your car or for the sheriff to seize it without giving you prior notice and an opportunity to be heard. The involvement of the court and the sheriff in the repossession means that there is state action and, thus, that there must be due process accorded to you before your car is taken.

Determining if there has been enough governmental involvement in a private action to make the due process clause or other constitutional provisions applicable is often not easy. For example, if a State statute expressly authorizes automobile dealers to repossess cars theselves without court orders or the assistance of a sheriff, some would argue that the enactment of the statute is sufficient state action to trigger due process guarantees or that if a dealer repossessed a car on the authority of such a statute, sometimes referred to as acting **under color of law**, the dealer's action would be state action and the repossession must comply with due process guarantees. Most courts would reject these arguments, however.

In *Burton v. Wilmington Parking Authority,* 365 U.S. 715 (1961), the Supreme Court addressed the state action requirement in the context of the equal protection guarantee. The Court stated:

[P]rivate conduct abridging individual rights does no violence to the Equal Protection Clause unless to some significant extent the State in any of its manifestations has been found to have become involved in it. [But] . . . to fashion and apply a precise formula for recognition of state responsibility under the Equal Protection Clause is an impossible task which this Court has never attempted. Only by sifting facts and weighing circumstances can the nonobvious involvement of the State in private conduct be attributed its true significance.[3]

The Court then held that a privately owned and operated restaurant, located in a parking building that was constructed, owned, and operated by a city, could not refuse to serve African Americans. The interdependence of the restaurant and the city parking authority:

together with the obvious fact that the restaurant is operated as an integral part of a public building devoted to a public parking service, indicates that degree of state participation and involvement in discriminatory action which it was the design of the Fourteenth Amendment to condemn. It is irony amounting to grave injustice that in one part of a single building, erected and maintained with public funds by an agency of the State to serve a public purpose, all persons have equal rights, while in another portion, also serving the public, a Negro is a second-class citizen, offensive because of his race, without rights and unentitled to service . . .

In *Blum v. Yaretsky*, 457 U.S. 991 (1982), however, the Supreme Court found that there was insufficient participation and involvement by the government in the decisions of private nursing homes to discharge or transfer patients to different lev-

els of homes for there to be state action and a requirement of due process before a discharge or transfer. The Court so found even though the patients were all receiving government Medicaid benefits and the decisions were all made because of and based on State rules governing eligibility for and the amount of such benefits.

THE LEAST RESTRICTIVE ALTERNATIVE

One guiding principle in constitutional interpretation is the notion that whenever the government does something that may impact or restrict the exercise of a constitutional right, it should act in the least intrusive manner possible. This is known as the principle of the **least restrictive alternative**.

No right, even a basic constitutional right like freedom of speech, is absolute. The government may restrict the exercise of a right in certain situations, such as where speech may pose a clear and present danger of violence. But a restriction on the exercise of a basic constitutional right should be as precise as possible and no more restrictive than needed to accomplish the government's objective. If there are less drastic means or less restrictive alternatives available, government action infringing on a fundamental right must be declared unconstitutional. Thus, in *Shelton v. Tucker*, 364 U.S. 479 (1960), the court held unconstitutional an Arkansas statute requiring teachers to reveal all organizations with which they were or had been affiliated as a means of assessing their qualification to teach. The court reasoned that "the statute's comprehensive

---

3. See the discussion in the introduction to this book on the method used to excerpt or quote court opinions.

interference with associational freedom goes far beyond what might be justified in the exercise of the State's legitimate inquiry into the fitness and competence of its teachers," and that the statute's "unlimited and indiscriminate sweep" brought it within the ban of a long series of cases holding that:

> even though the governmental purpose be legitimate and substantial, that purpose cannot be pursued by means that broadly stifle fundamental personal liberties when the end can be more narrowly achieved. The breadth of legislative abridgment must be viewed in the light of less drastic means for achieving the same purpose.

Similarly, in *Dunn v. Blumstein,* 405 U.S. 330 (1972), the Supreme Court invalidated a requirement that one must have resided in a State for one year before one could vote, stating:

> It is not enough for the State to show that durational residence requirements further a very substantial state interest. In pursuing that important interest, the State cannot chose means that unnecessarily burden or restrict constitutionally protected activity. Statutes affecting constitutional rights must be drawn with precision, and must be tailored to serve their legitimate objectives. And if there are other reasonable ways to achieve those goals with a lesser burden on constitutionally protected activity, a State may not choose the way of greater interference. If it acts at all, it must choose less drastic means.

OVERBREADTH AND VAGUENESS

Closely related to the principle of the least restrictive alternative are the concepts of **overbreadth** and **vagueness**. Any law impinging on a basic right or freedom, particularly on First Amendment rights, must be narrowly drawn to address only a specific problem. As the Supreme Court stated in *NAACP v. Button,* 371 U.S. 415 (1963): "Precision of regulation must be the touchstone in an area . . . closely touching our most precious freedoms." If a law impacting on fundamental rights sweeps too broadly, it must be declared unconstitutional as overbroad.

A law impacting First Amendment or other fundamental rights must also be declared unconstitutional if it is too vague. When laws that impact constitutional rights are vague and unclear, there is a real danger that government officials will interpret them in a way that is overbroad and, thus, violate the principle of the least restrictive alternative. Vague laws are also dangerous because they permit the unbridled exercise of official discretion and because they deprive people of notice of what is expected of them and the ability to conform their conduct to the requirements of the law. This failure to give notice can constitute a violation of due process. For these reasons, in *People v. Beruman,* 638 P.2d 789 (Colo. 1982), a case involving a child welfare worker who was convicted of the crime of "official misconduct" for failing to respond to a report of suspected child abuse, the Colorado Supreme Court declared a portion of the law establishing the crime of official misconduct unconstitutionally vague. The Court stated:

> A statute is unconstitutionally vague if persons of common intelligence must guess at its meaning. Penal statutes and regulations must be clearly understandable and reasonably specific so that the defendant may be sufficiently apprised of the crime with which he stands charged. This affords the defendant due process notice . . . Fundamental fairness requires that no lesser standard be applied.

The language used to describe the proscribed conduct [in the statute in question here]—"refrains from performing a duty . . . clearly inherent in the nature of his office"—provides no readily ascertainable standards by which one's conduct may be measured. The legislature has failed to define that phrase, and it is totally without parameters for the determination of guilt or innocence, thus allowing the exercise of unbridled discretion by the police, judge, and jury. The vagueness present in the statutory language impermissibly infringes the constitutional safeguard of fundamental fairness and due process, and creates a danger of arbitrary enforcement.

The concepts of overbreadth and vagueness, like the principle of the least restrictive alternative, arise most often in the context of First Amendment freedoms, but, as we shall see, and as can be seen from *Beruman,* they also arise in many contexts of importance to social workers. For example, removing a child from her home because of parental neglect may violate the principle of the least restrictive alternative; there may be less drastic means than a guardianship to address the problem posed by a frail elderly person; a statute setting forth who may be involuntarily committed for treatment may be overbroad; and a statute defining elder abuse may be vague.

DUE PROCESS OF THE LAW

The due process clauses of the Fifth and Fourteenth Amendments provide that no one may be deprived of "life, liberty or property" without "due process of law," but these terms are nowhere defined. The courts, however, have broadly

interpreted these terms to require reasonableness and fundamental fairness, both procedurally and substantively, before one may be deprived of important interests or basic rights and freedoms. This broad interpretation of the due process clauses has allowed them to serve as the source of various protections against government interference and various procedural and substantive rights that are not included in the more specific provisions of the Bill of Rights, the Civil War amendments or other portions of the Constitution. In other words, the courts may use the due process clauses to fashion standards of fairness not tied to any specific language in the Constitution.

Thus, the courts have used the due process clauses when problems have arisen that are not addressed by the Constitution or when technological advances must be considered. For example, whether or not a State could be required to pay for blood tests in an action determining the father of a child was analyzed in light of due process. The due process clauses have also been used to recognize society's evolving view of what is fair or just. For example, although for many years children were taken away from parents alleged to be unfit with few procedural protections and little concern for the parents, growing recognition that families should be free from excessive government intervention led to a series of due process rulings making the process fairer and the standards employed in determining unfitness clearer.

Sometimes, the due process clauses have been used to extend the principle underlying a specific constitutional guarantee to an analogous situation. For example, the Sixth Amendment provides for a right to counsel in criminal cases, but there is no mention in the Constitution of a right to counsel in civil cases. The concept of due process has been used to fill this gap and to require counsel in certain civil cases that may have serious consequences for the individual, like an action seeking to involuntarily commit a person to a mental hospital. Sometimes, the due process clauses are used to create an entirely new right or procedural protection. For example, the concept of due process has been used to recognize adults' right to use contraception or juveniles' right to a hearing before being removed from their homes for extended periods.

We shall see how the due process clauses have been used to establish substantive rights and procedural protections not expressly guaranteed or required by the Constitution throughout this book. However, even though the clauses have been widely used, they cannot be used as widely as some would want and have not been used as widely as some would believe.

The due process clauses can only be invoked to protect "life, liberty or property" from government actions or laws. There can be no violation of due process unless there is a deprivation of a **protectible interest** in "life," "liberty," or "property." Determining whether or not there has been such a deprivation is the first step in determining if there has been a violation of due process, but determining whether there has been a deprivation of a protectible interest in "liberty" or "property."

The term *liberty* in the due process clauses has not been and probably cannot be defined with exactness, but the Supreme Court has recognized that its scope is not:

limited by the precise terms of the specific guarantees elsewhere provided in the Constitution. This "liberty" is not a series of isolated points pricked out in terms of [these specific guarantees]. It is a rational continuum which, broadly speaking, includes a freedom from all substantial arbitrary impositions and purposeless restraints . . .[4]

For example, in *Meyer v. Nebraska,* 262 U.S. 390 (1923), the Supreme Court decided that the term *liberty* in the due process clauses includes the freedom to study or teach whatever one wants and, thus, that a State law enacted during World War I that forbade the teaching of German violated the Fourteenth Amendment by depriving students and teachers of liberty without due process. The Court stated:

While this court has not attempted to define with exactness the [term] liberty . . . [in the due process clauses], the term has received much consideration, and some of the included things have been definitely stated. Without doubt, it denotes not merely freedom from bodily restraint, but also the right of the individual to contract, to engage in any of the common occupations of life, to acquire useful knowledge, to marry, to establish a home and bring up children, to worship God according to the dictates of his own conscience, and, generally, to enjoy those privileges long recognized . . . as essential to the orderly pursuit of happiness by free men.

More recently, in *Planned Parenthood of Southeastern Pennsylvania v. Casey,* 505 U.S. 833 (1993), the Supreme Court concluded that the term *liberty* includes a woman's choice to terminate a pregnancy. The plurality opinion recognizes that there are "profound moral and spiritual implications of terminating a pregnancy," and that:

---

4. *Poe v. Ullman,* 367 U.S. 497 (1961) (Harlan dissent).

[s]ome of us as individuals find abortion offensive to our most basic principles of morality, but that cannot control our decision. Our obligation is to define the liberty of all, not to mandate our own moral code. The underlying constitutional issue is whether the State can resolve these philosophical questions in such a definitive way that a woman lacks all choice in the matter . . .

Our law affords constitutional protection to personal decisions relating to marriage, procreation, contraception, family relationships, child rearing, and education. [These] matters, involving the most intimate and personal choices a person may make in a lifetime, choices central to personal dignity and autonomy, are central to the liberty protected by the Fourteenth Amendment. At the heart of liberty is the right to define one's own concept of existence . . . and of the mystery of human life.

The term *property* in the due process clauses has come to mean, not only tangible property, like money, bonds, livestock, land, or furniture, but also intangible property interests or privileges that are granted by the government. For example, in *Goss v. Lopez,* 419 U.S. 565 (1975), the Supreme Court held that an interest in a public education was a property interest so that a temporary suspension from a public high school without a hearing violated due process. The Court rejected an argument that:

because there is no constitutional right to an education at public expense, the Due Process Clause does not protect against expulsions from the public school system. Protected interests in property are normally not created by the Constitution. Rather, they are created and their dimensions are defined by an independent source such as state statutes or rules entitling the citizen to certain benefits. Accordingly, a state employee who under state law . . . has a legitimate claim of entitlement to continued employment absent sufficient cause for discharge may demand the procedural protections of due process. So may welfare recipients who have statutory rights to welfare as long as they maintain the specified qualifications. [T]he limitations of the Due Process Clause [have been applied] to governmental decisions to revoke parole, although a parolee has no constitutional right to that status. In like vein . . . the procedural protections of the Due Process Clause were triggered by official cancellation of a prisoner's good-time credits accumulated under state law, although those benefits were not mandated by the Constitution.

Here, on the basis of state law, [the students] plainly had legitimate claims of entitlement to a public education. Ohio [law] direct[s] local authorities to provide a free education to all residents between five and 21 years of age, and a compulsory-attendance law requires attendance for a school year of not less than 32 weeks. Having chosen to extend the right to an education to [youth] generally, . . . Ohio is constrained to recognize a student's legitimate entitlement to a public education as a property interest which is protected by the Due Process Clause and which may not be taken away for misconduct without adherence to the minimum procedures required by that Clause.[5]

As these example demonstrate, the courts have found many interests to be encompassed by the terms *liberty* and *property* in the due process clauses. However, the courts have been unwilling to

---

5. In *Goss,* the Court also recognized that a temporary suspension from school could be a deprivation of liberty in that a "person's good name, reputation, honor, or integrity [are] at stake . . . " The Court stated: "School authorities here suspended [the students] from school for periods of up to 10 days based on charges of misconduct. If sustained and recorded, those charges could seriously damage the students' standing with their fellow pupils and their teachers as well as interfere with later opportunities for higher education and employment. It is apparent that the claimed right of the State to determine unilaterally and without process whether that misconduct has occurred . . . collides with the requirements of the Constitution."

find every claimed deprivation of liberty or property by the government to be a deprivation of a protectible interest. For example, courts have concluded that individuals do not have protectible property interests in obtaining licenses to practice their professions (although they may have a protectible interest in keeping their licenses once they have obtained them) or in keeping their jobs as public employees (unless they have been clearly given contractural rights to a permanent position). Without a deprivation of a protectible interest, there can be no violation of due process.

Moreover, as has been stated, finding a deprivation of a protectible interest by a government law or action is only the first stop in deciding if there has been a violation of the due process. The second, and perhaps more important step, is to determine *whether* and *how* the deprivation may occur consistently with the Constitution.

The due process clauses guarantee, not that one cannot be deprived of life, liberty, or property by the government, but that one cannot be deprived of life, liberty, or property by the government *without* due process. This means one can be deprived of life, liberty, or property *with* due process, broadly defined as reasonable and with fundamental fairness. Put differently, government actions depriving individuals of interests protected by the due process clauses are not forbidden but are required to be reasonable and fundamentally fair and to be done in a reasonable and fundamentally fair manner.

The requirement that all government actions depriving individuals of protectible interests be reasonable and fundamentally fair, or in other words, have a constitutionally acceptable justification, is known as

the guarantee of **substantive due process**, while the requirement that governments use reasonable and fundamentally fair procedures before depriving individuals of a protectible interest is known as the guarantee of **procedural due process**.

We will look at substantive and procedural due process in depth later in the chapter, but you should keep in mind that deciding whether there has been a violation of a guarantee of substantive or procedural due process (or to predict whether or not a court will decide there has been a violation) is often not easy. As stated in *Lassiter v. Department of Social Services,* 452 U.S. 18 (1981), in which the Supreme Court decided that a woman was not denied due process when she was denied appointed counsel in a hearing to terminate her parental rights, the term *due process:*

> expresses the requirement of fundamental fairness, a requirement whose meaning can be as opaque as its importance is lofty. Applying the Due Process Clause is therefore an uncertain enterprise which must discover what fundamental fairness consists of in a particular situation by first considering any relevant precedents and then by assessing the several interests at stake.

You should also keep in mind that, in order for there to be a violation of either substantive or procedural due process there must be state action. As stated in *DeShaney v. Winnebago County Dept. of Social Services,* 489 U.S. 189 (1989), in which the Supreme Court decided social workers employed by a public agency did not violate due process guarantees by failing to remove a child from an abusing parent:

> [N]othing in the language of the Due Process Clause itself requires the State to protect the life, liberty and property of its citizens against

invasion by private actors. The Clause is phrased as a limitation on the State's power to act, not as a guarantee of certain minimal levels of safety and security. It forbids the State itself to deprive individuals of life, liberty, or property without due process of law, but its language cannot fairly be extended to impose an affirmative obligation on the State to ensure that those interests do not come to harm through other means. Like its counterpart in the Fifth Amendment, the Due Process Clause of the Fourteenth Amendment was intended to prevent the government from abusing [its] power, or employing it as an instrument of oppression. Its purpose was to protect the people from the State, not to ensure that the State protected them from each other.

Substantive Due Process

The Supreme Court's early approach to substantive due process is typified by the case of *Lochner v. New York,* 198 U.S. 45 (1905). In *Lochner,* the Court struck down a statute that made it unlawful for an employee to work more than a sixty-hour week as an unconstitutional interference with the "freedom of the master and employee to contract with each other in relation to their employment."

The *Lochner* approach was repudiated in the 1930s. The Court's new approach was almost the opposite of the old. Under the new approach, no law was to be struck down as a denial of due process unless the law was manifestly arbitrary and capricious. That is, no law could be invalidated on substantive due process grounds if there was any rational basis for its enactment.

This approach to substantive due process was, in turn, partially repudiated in the 1960s when the Court decided that laws which infringed fundamental rights, even those not explicitly guaranteed by

the Constitution, should be invalidated as violations of due process unless they served a substantial state interest. *Griswold v. Connecticut,* 381 U.S. 479 (1965), was the forerunner of this new approach to substantive due process. In *Griswold,* a doctor and the head of the Connecticut Planned Parenthood League were arrested because they gave birth control advice to married persons in violation of a Connecticut law that made using, giving information on, or providing contraceptive devices a crime. The Court decided that the Connecticut law intruded unnecessarily upon the right of marital privacy without substantial justification and held that the law, and thus the arrests, were invalid as a violation of due process. The Court stated:

> We do not sit as a super-legislature to determine the wisdom, need, and propriety of laws that touch economic problems, business affairs, or social conditions. This law, however, operates directly on an intimate relation of husband and wife and their physician's role in one aspect of that relation.
>
> [Our previous] cases suggest that specific guarantees in the Bill of Rights have penumbras, formed by emanations from those guarantees that help give them life and substance. Various guarantees create zones of privacy. The present case . . . concerns a relationship lying within the zone of privacy created by several fundamental constitutional guarantees. And it concerns a law which, in forbidding the use of contraceptives rather than regulating their manufacture or sale, seeks to achieve its goals by means having a maximum destructive impact upon that relationship. Such a law cannot stand . . .

Moore v. City of East Cleveland, 431 U.S. 494 (1977), is another example of this approach to substantive due process. An East Cleveland housing ordinance limited occupancy of a single dwelling unit to members of a single "family," defined in the ordinance as a nuclear family. Mrs. Moore, who lived in her East Cleveland home with her son, his son, and another grandson who came to live with her and his uncle, and cousin after his mother's death, was convicted of violating the ordinance because her household was not a family within the narrow definition in the ordinance. In reversing her conviction, the Court stated:

> East Cleveland . . . has chosen to regulate the occupancy of its housing by slicing deeply into the family itself. This is no mere incidental result of the ordinance. On its face it selects certain categories of relatives who may live together and declares that others may not. In particular, it makes a crime of a grandmother's choice to live with her grandson in circumstances like those presented here.
>
> When a city undertakes such intrusive regulation of the family, . . . the usual judicial deference to the legislature is inappropriate. This Court has long recognized that freedom of personal choice in matters of marriage and family life is one of the liberties protected by the Due Process Clause of the Fourteenth Amendment. A host of cases have consistently acknowledged a private realm of family life which the state cannot enter. Of course, the family is not beyond regulation. But when the government intrudes on choices concerning family living arrangements, this Court must examine carefully the importance of the governmental interests advanced and the extent to which they are served by the challenged regulation.
>
> [This Court has stated:]
>
> "Due process has not been reduced to any formula; its content cannot be determined by reference to any code. The best that can be said is that through the course of this Court's decisions it has represented the balance which our Nation, built upon postulates of respect for the liberty of the individual, has

> struck between that liberty and the demands of organized society. * * * No formula could serve as a substitute, in this area, for judgment and restraint.
>
> "[T]he full scope of the liberty guaranteed by the Due Process Clause cannot be found in or limited by the precise terms of the specific guarantees elsewhere provided in the Constitution. This 'liberty' is not a series of isolated points pricked out in terms of * * * the freedom of speech, press, and religion; the right to keep and bear arms; * * * and so on. It is a rational continuum which, broadly speaking, includes a freedom from all substantial arbitrary impositions and purposeless restraints, . . . and which also recognizes, what a reasonable and sensitive judgment must, that certain interests require particularly careful scrutiny of the state needs asserted to justify their abridgment."

Substantive due process has at times been a treacherous field for this Court. There are risks when the judicial branch gives enhanced protection to certain substantive liberties without the guidance of the more specific provisions of the Bill of Rights. As the history of the era [when this Court freely invalidated laws in the name of substantive due process] demonstrates, there is reason for concern lest the only limits to such judicial intervention become the predilections of those who happen at the time to be Members of this Court. That history counsels caution and restraint. But it does not counsel abandonment, nor does it require what the city urges here: cutting off any protection of family rights at the first convenient, if arbitrary boundary—the boundary of the nuclear family.

Appropriate limits on substantive due process come not from drawing arbitrary lines but rather from careful respect for the teachings of history [and], solid recognition of the basic values that underlie our society. Our decisions establish that the Constitution protects the sanctity of the family precisely because the institution of the family is deeply rooted in this Nation's history and tradition. It is through the family that we inculcate and pass down many of our most cherished values, moral and cultural.

Ours is by no means a tradition limited to respect for the bonds uniting the members of the nuclear family. The tradition of uncles, aunts, cousins, and especially grandparents sharing a household along with parents and children has roots equally venerable and equally deserving of constitutional recognition. Over the years millions of our citizens have grown up in just such an environment, and most, surely, have profited from it. Even if conditions of modern society have brought about a decline in extended family households, they have not erased the accumulated wisdom of civilization, gained over the centuries and honored throughout our history, that supports a larger conception of the family. Out of choice, necessity, or a sense of family responsibility, it has been common for close relatives to draw together and participate in the duties and the satisfactions of a common home. Especially in times of adversity, such as the death of a spouse or economic need, the broader family has tended to come together for mutual sustenance and to maintain or rebuild a secure home life. This is apparently what happened here.

Whether or not such a household is established because of personal tragedy, the choice of relatives in this degree of kinship to live together may not lightly be denied by the State. [T]he Constitution prevents East Cleveland from standardizing its children—and its adults—by forcing all to live in certain narrowly defined family patterns.

This sweeping view of the substantive due process guarantee has been sharply curtailed in recent years. The Supreme Court has recently found deprivations of unquestionably protectible interests consistent with the Constitution if the deprivations were considered necessary to accomplish a legitimate purpose and no more extensive than necessary to accomplish this purpose. For example, in *Reno v. Flores,* 507 U.S. 292 (1993), the Supreme

Court determined that alien juveniles who were suspected of being deportable could constitutionally be held in a "government-operated or government-selected child care institution" pending a deportation hearing if there was no parent, close relative or legal guardian to whom they could be released. While the Court recognized that "these children have a constitutionally protected interest in freedom from institutional confinement," the Court concluded:

> Where a juvenile has no available parent, close relative, or legal guardian, where the government does not intend to punish the child, and where the conditions of governmental custody are decent and humane, such custody surely does not violate the Constitution. It is rationally connected to a governmental interest in preserving and promoting the welfare of the child and is not punitive since it is not excessive in relation to that valid purpose.

Procedural Due Process

In order to pass constitutional muster, a government action that may deprive someone of life, liberty or property not only must be fair but also must be undertaken in a way that is fair. In other words, a government action that infringes upon a protectible interest must comport with both substantive and procedural due process. For example, even if the Supreme Court decided in *Moore v. City of East Cleveland, supra,* 431 U.S. 494, that the zoning ordinance was fair in its substance, the Court might not have upheld the ordinance's constitutionality if it permitted the police to go into peoples' homes and forcibly evict the illegal occupants without any sort of notice or hearing.

Thus, whenever a government action challenged on due process grounds is determined by a court to fall within the constitutional guarantee of due process because the action may cause a deprivation of a protectible interest, in addition to determining if the action is consistent with due process, the court may have to determine what procedures should be followed by the government in carrying out the action. For example, in *Reno v. Flores, supra,* 507 U.S. 292, the Supreme Court not only considered (and rejected) an argument that a juvenile alien could not be held in a child care institution pending a deportation hearing but also considered (and rejected) an argument that there had to be a hearing on the best interests of the juvenile before placement in the institution.

As was stated by the Supreme Court in *Morrisey v. Brewer,* 408 U.S. 471 (1972): "Once it is determined that due process applies, the question remains what process is due." This question is resolved through a balancing process.

The seriousness of a deprivation is not relevant in determining if the due process clause applies. As was stated in *Goss v. Lopez, supra,* 419 U.S. 565:

> [I]n determining whether due process requirements apply in the first place, we must look not to the weight but to the nature of the interest at stake. The Court's view has been that as long as a property deprivation is not *de minimis* [that is, so minor as to be insignificant], its gravity is irrelevant to the question whether account must be taken of the Due Process Clause.

By way of contrast, the seriousness of a deprivation and the importance of a protectible interest may be crucial in determining what process is due. They are factors to be balanced with the government's interest in an inexpensive and speedy process. As was also stated in *Goss,* which, as you should recall, considered the constitutionality of a ten-day suspension from school without a hearing:

> [T]he length and consequent severity of a deprivation . . . [is a] factor to weigh in determining the appropriate form of hearing, [although it] is not decisive of the basic right to a hearing of some kind.
>
> [T]he interpretation and application of the Due Process Clause are intensely practical matters and . . . [t]he very nature of due process negates any concept of inflexible procedures universally applicable to every imaginable situation. There are certain bench marks to guide us, however. [We have said that] "[m]any controversies have raged about the cryptic and abstract words of the Due Process Clause but there can be no doubt that at a minimum they require that deprivation of life, liberty or property by adjudication be preceded by notice and opportunity for hearing appropriate to the nature of the case." It also appears from our cases that the timing and content of the notice and the nature of the hearing will depend on appropriate accommodation of the competing interests involved.

In determining what process is due, that is, in balancing the competing interests, a court must determine if any required procedures must occur *before* any deprivation or if it is sufficient if they occur *after* a temporary period of deprivation. *Goldberg v. Kelly,* 397 U.S. 254 (1970), which dealt with the termination of welfare benefits to families with children, is an important case addressing this question. It also addresses the question of the nature of the hearing to be afforded. While you read the excerpts, note not only the points of law but also the compassion showed towards people who are very poor:

The extent to which procedural due process must be afforded the recipient [of welfare benefits] is influenced by the extent to which he may be condemned to suffer grievous loss, and depends upon whether the recipient's interest in avoiding that loss outweighs the governmental interest in summary adjudication. Accordingly, as we [have] said . . . "consideration of what procedures due process may require under any given set of circumstances must begin with a determination of the precise nature of the government function involved as well as of the private interest that has been affected by governmental action."

It is true, of course, that some governmental benefits may be administratively terminated without affording the recipient a pre-termination evidentiary hearing. But . . . when welfare is discontinued, only a pre-termination evidentiary hearing provides the recipient with procedural due process. For qualified recipients, welfare provides the means to obtain essential food, clothing, housing, and medical care. Thus the crucial factor in this context—a factor not present in the case of the blacklisted government contractor, the discharged government employee, the taxpayer denied a tax exemption, or virtually anyone else whose governmental entitlements are ended—is that termination of aid pending resolution of a controversy over eligibility may deprive an eligible recipient of the very means by which to live while he waits. Since he lacks independent resources, his situation becomes immediately desperate. His need to concentrate upon finding the means for daily subsistence, in turn, adversely affects his ability to seek redress from the welfare bureaucracy.

Moreover, important governmental interests are promoted by affording recipients a pre-termination evidentiary hearing. From its founding the Nation's basic commitment has been to foster the dignity and well-being of all persons within its borders. We have come to recognize that forces not within the control of the poor contribute to their poverty. This perception, against the background of our traditions, has significantly influenced the development of the contemporary public assistance system. Welfare, by meeting the basic demands of subsistence, can help bring within the reach of the poor the same opportunities that are available to others to participate meaningfully in the life of the community. At the same time, welfare guards against the societal malaise that may flow from a widespread sense of unjustified frustration and insecurity. Public assistance, then, is not mere charity, but a means to "promote the general Welfare, and secure the Blessings of Liberty to ourselves and our Posterity." The same governmental interests that counsel the provision of welfare, counsel as well its uninterrupted provision to those eligible to receive it; **pretermination evidentiary hearings are indispensable to that end.**

[T]he interest of the eligible recipient in uninterrupted receipt of public assistance, coupled with the State's interest that his payments not be erroneously terminated, clearly outweighs the State's competing concern to prevent any increase in its fiscal and administrative burdens. [H]owever, . . . **the pre-termination hearing need not take the form of a judicial or quasi-judicial trial.** We recognize . . . that both welfare authorities and recipients have an interest in relatively speedy resolution of questions of eligibility, that they are used to dealing with one another informally, and that some welfare departments have very burdensome caseloads. These considerations justify the limitation of the pre-termination hearing to minimum procedural safeguards, adapted to the particular characteristics of welfare recipients, and to the limited nature of the controversies to be resolved.

The fundamental requisite of due process of law is the opportunity to be heard. The hearing must be at a meaningful time and in a meaningful manner. In the present context these principles require that a recipient have timely and adequate notice detailing the reasons for a proposed termination, and an effective opportunity to defend by confronting any adverse witnesses and by presenting his own arguments and evidence orally.

The opportunity to be heard must be tailored to the capacities and circumstances of those who are to be heard. It is not enough that a welfare recipient may present his position to the decision maker in writing or second-hand through his caseworker. Written submissions are an unrealistic option for most recipients, who lack the educational attainment necessary to write effectively and who cannot obtain professional assistance. Moreover, written submissions do not afford the flexibility of oral presentations; they do not permit the recipient to mold his argument to the issues the decision maker appears to regard as important. Particularly where credibility and veracity are at issue, as they must be in many termination proceedings, written submissions are a wholly unsatisfactory basis for decision. **Therefore a recipient must be allowed to state his position orally. Informal procedures will suffice; in this context due process does not require a particular order of proof or mode of offering evidence. Welfare recipients must [also] be given an opportunity to confront and cross-examine the witnesses relied on by the department.**

The right to be heard would be, in many cases, of little avail if it did not comprehend the right to be heard by counsel. We do not say that counsel must be provided at the pretermination hearing, but only that the recipient must be allowed to retain an attorney if he so desires. Counsel can help delineate the issues, present the factual contentions in an orderly manner, conduct cross-examination, and generally safeguard the interests of the recipient. We do not anticipate that this assistance will unduly prolong or otherwise encumber the hearing.

Finally, the decision maker's conclusion as to a recipient's eligibility must rest solely on the legal rules and evidence adduced at the hearing. To demonstrate compliance with this elementary requirement, the decision maker should state the reasons for his determination and indicate the evidence he relied on, though his statement need not amount to a full opinion or even formal findings of fact and conclusions of law. **And, of course, an impartial decision maker is essential.**

to students under the due process clauses. In *Goss v. Lopez, supra,* the Court stated:

At the very minimum, . . . students facing suspension and the consequent interference with a protected property interest must be given some kind of notice and afforded some kind of hearing. We do not believe that school authorities must be totally free from notice and hearing requirements if their schools are to operate with acceptable efficiency. Students facing temporary suspension have interests qualifying for protection of the Due Process Clause, and **due process requires, in connection with a suspension of 10 days or less, that the student be given oral or written notice of the charges against him and, if he denies them, an explanation of the evidence the authorities have and an opportunity to present his side of the story.**

We stop short of construing the Due Process Clause to require, countrywide, that hearings in connection with short suspensions must afford the student the opportunity to secure counsel, to confront and cross-examine witnesses supporting the charge, or to call his own witnesses to verify his version of the incident. Brief disciplinary suspensions are almost countless. To impose in each such case even truncated trial-type procedures might well overwhelm administrative facilities in many places and, by diverting resources, cost more than it would save in educational effectiveness.

We should also make it clear that we have addressed ourselves solely to the short suspension, not exceeding 10 days. Longer suspensions or expulsions for the remainder of the school term, or permanently, may require more formal procedures. Nor do we put aside the possibility that in unusual situations, although involving only a short suspension, something more than the rudimentary procedures will be required.

Because a termination of welfare differs from a short school suspension, both in its seriousness and its nature, far fewer procedural protections must be afforded

In *Mathews v. Eldridge,* 424 U.S. 319 (1976), the Supreme Court determined that an evidentiary hearing was not required before the termination of social security disability payments. The difference between the types of financial assistance programs involved in *Mathews* and *Goldberg v. Kelly* lead to the difference in the due process requirement. The Court stated:

> [I]n Goldberg . . . the Court held that due process requires an evidentiary hearing prior to a temporary deprivation. It was emphasized there that welfare assistance is given to persons on the very margin of subsistence . . . Eligibility for disability benefits, in contrast, is not based upon financial need. Indeed, it is wholly unrelated to the worker's income or support from many other sources, such as earnings of other family members, workmen's compensation awards, tort claims awards, savings, private insurance, public or private pensions, veterans' benefits, food stamps, public assistance, or the many other important programs, both public and private, which contain provisions for disability payments affecting a substantial portion of the work force . . . .
>
> [Typically, it takes more than a year from the time of the cut off of Social Security disability benefits to a decision after an evidentiary hearing.] In view of the torpidity of [the] administrative review process, and the typically modest resources of the family unit of the physically disabled worker, the hardship imposed upon the erroneously terminated disability recipient may be significant. Still, the disabled worker's need is likely to be less than that of a welfare recipient. In addition to the possibility of access to private resources, other forms of government assistance will become available where the termination of disability benefits places a worker or his family below the subsistence level. In view of these potential sources of temporary income, there is less reason here than in *Goldberg* to depart from the ordinary principle, established by our decisions, that something less than an evidentiary hearing is sufficient prior to adverse administrative action.

Mathews is of great importance, not only because it expresses a new and less supportive attitude towards the imposition of due process safeguards in social welfare programs, but also because it enunciated the test to be used by courts in determining what process is due to individuals deprived of a protectible interest. This balancing test, which is still used today and which we will see used in many due process cases in later chapters, was expressed in the following language:

> [Our] decisions underscore the truism that [d]ue process, unlike some legal rules, is not a technical conception with a fixed content unrelated to time, place and circumstances. [D]ue process is flexible and calls for such procedural protections as the particular situation demands. Accordingly, resolution of the issue whether . . . procedures . . . are constitutionally sufficient requires analysis of the governmental and private interests that are affected. More precisely, **our prior decisions indicate that identification of the specific dictates of due process generally requires consideration of three distinct factors: First, the private interest that will be affected by the official action; second, the risk of an erroneous deprivation of such interest through the procedures used, and the probable value, if any, of additional or substitute procedural safeguards; and finally, the government's interest, including the function involved and the fiscal and administrative burdens that the additional or substitute procedural requirement would entail.**
>
> Financial cost alone is not a controlling weight in determining whether due process requires a particular procedural safeguard prior to some administrative decision. But the government's interest, and hence that of the public, in conserving scarce fiscal and administrative resources is a factor that must be weighed. At some point the benefit of an additional safeguard to the individual affected by the administrative action and to society in terms of increased assurance that the action is just, may be outweighed by the cost.
>
> But more is implicated in [procedural due process] cases than *ad hoc* weighing of fiscal and administrative burdens against the inter-

ests of a particular category of claimants. The ultimate balance involves a determination as to when, under our constitutional system, judicial-type procedures must be imposed . . . to assure fairness. The judicial model of an evidentiary hearing is neither a required, nor even the most effective, method of decision-making in all circumstances. The essence of due process is the requirement that a person in jeopardy of serious loss [be given] notice of the case against him and opportunity to meet it. All that is necessary is that the procedures be tailored, in light of the decision to be made, to the capacities and circumstances of those who are to be heard, to insure that they are given a meaningful opportunity to present their case.

EQUAL PROTECTION OF THE LAWS

The equal protection clause of the Fourteenth Amendment guarantees all persons equality under the law, but the guarantee is not considered absolute. Despite the clause's unqualified language, the courts have not required that the States or the federal government treat all persons exactly alike. Rather, they have held that governments may recognize and act upon certain differences that exist between classes of individuals without violating the guarantee of equal protection. Legislation that accords some people a benefit or that requires some people to bear a burden, while other people, because of some factual difference in their situations, neither receive the benefit nor bear the burden, may be upheld as consistent with the equal protection clause. How can this be?

Legislation generally involves drawing distinctions. Governments continually draw distinctions that discriminate against certain people as part of their normal func-

tioning. Put differently, the right to legislate implies the right to classify. But classification, by its very nature, gives some classes of people special burdens or benefits not given to other classes. If all distinctions drawn by the government and all classifications made by the government were considered to be unconstitutional violations of the equal protection guarantee, governments would be virtually paralyzed. As stated in a classic study of equal protection:

> Here, then, is a paradox: The equal protection of the laws is a pledge of the protection of equal laws. But laws may classify. And the very idea of classification is that of inequality. In tackling this paradox the [Supreme] Court has neither abandoned the demand for equality nor denied the legislative right to classify. It has taken a middle course. It has resolved the contradictory demands of legislative specialization and constitutional generality by a doctrine of **reasonable classification**.[6]

In accordance with the doctrine of reasonable classification, classifications made by governments are presumed to be constitutional. Even if a distinction drawn by a government causes it to discriminate among classes of people, the distinction will not be considered an unconstitutional denial of equal protection unless the distinction is unreasonable or, to use the courts' terms, is "without any rational basis," or is "wholly arbitrary and capricious." If a government has a reason to discriminate among its people and if those who are discriminated against fall into reasonably drawn categories, based on rational factual circumstances, the gov-

---

6.   Tussman and ten Broek, *The Equal Protection of the Laws,* 37 Cal. L. Rev. 341 (1949).

ernment will be permitted to discriminate, as *Dandridge v. Williams,* 397 U.S. 471 (1970), illustrates. *Dandridge* involved a challenge to a Maryland law setting a maximum welfare grant for a family regardless of its size. The law discriminated against large families, which would receive less benefits per member than smaller families. The Court stated:

> In the area of economics and social welfare, a State does not violate the Equal Protection Clause merely because the classifications made by its laws are imperfect. If the classification has some reasonable basis, it does not offend the Constitution simply because the classification is not made with mathematical nicety or because in practice it results in some inequality. The problems of government are practical ones and may justify, if they do not require, rough accommodations . . . A statutory discrimination will not be set aside if any state of facts reasonably may be conceived to justify it.
>
> Under [the] long-established meaning of the Equal Protection Clause, it is clear that the Maryland maximum grant regulation is constitutionally valid. [A] solid foundation for the regulation can be found in the State's legitimate interest in encouraging employment and in avoiding discrimination between welfare families and the families of the working poor. By combining a limit on the recipient's grant with permission to retain money earned, without reduction in the amount of the grant, Maryland provides an incentive to seek gainful employment. And by keying [a family's maximum welfare grant] to the minimum wage a steadily employed head of a household receives, the State maintains some semblance of an equitable balance between families on welfare and those supported by an employed breadwinner. It is true that in some [welfare] families there may be no person who is employable . . . [and that in small families which receive grants equal to their needs] the employment incentive is absent. But the Equal Protection Clause does not require that a State must choose between attacking every

aspect of a problem or not attacking the problem at all. It is enough that the State's action be rationally based and free from invidious discrimination. The regulation before us meets that test.

> We do not decide today that the Maryland regulation is wise, that it best fulfills the relevant social and economic objectives that Maryland might ideally espouse, or that a more just and humane system could not be devised. Conflicting claims of morality and intelligence are raised by opponents and proponents of almost every measure, certainly including the one before us. But the intractable economic, social, and even philosophical problems presented by public welfare assistance programs are not the business of this Court. The Constitution may impose certain procedural safeguards upon systems of welfare administration. But the Constitution does not empower this Court to second-guess state officials charged with the difficult responsibility of allocating limited public welfare funds among the myriad of potential recipients.

The doctrine of reasonable classification enunciated in *Dandridge* has its limits. All classifications made by governments are not upheld by the courts just because they are reasonable and all distinctions drawn by governments that have a rational basis are not considered consistent with the equal protection clause. Certain classifications are considered *suspect.* These classifications must meet a higher standard than mere reasonableness to pass constitutional muster. And certain distinctions may affect the exercise of *fundamental rights.* The courts will require more than mere reasonableness before these distinctions can be sustained.

For many years, the Supreme Court used a two-tier test when it was determining if a legislative classification violated the equal protection clause. Classifications that were considered inherently suspect or that impinged on the exercise of *basic* or fundamental rights were subjected to **strict judicial scrutiny**; such classifications could pass constitutional muster only if they served *compelling state interests.* All other classifications were simply required to be reasonable; they would be sustained if they had any rational basis. In other words, depending on the nature of the classification or on its effect, its constitutionality would be tested using either strict judicial scrutiny or the doctrine of reasonable classification.

San Antonio School District v. Rodriguez, 411 U.S. 1 (1973), illustrates the Court's use of the two-tier test. In *San Antonio,* members of poor families, who lived in school districts with many poor people and thus low property tax bases, challenged Texas's reliance on local property taxes to finance public schools. They claimed that such reliance denied them equal protection in that the public schools in their districts had less money and were thus inferior to public schools in districts with richer residents. The Supreme Court stated, however, that no suspect classification was established and that education was not a fundamental right and, thus, concluded:

> [T]his is not a case in which the challenged state action must be subjected to the searching judicial scrutiny reserved for laws that create suspect classifications or impinge upon constitutionally protected rights. A century of Supreme Court adjudication under the Equal Protection Clause affirmatively supports the application of the traditional standard of review, which requires only that the State's system be shown to bear some rational relationship to legitimate state purposes . . .

Finding that the Texas system of school finance "reflects what many educators for a half century have thought was an enlightened approach to a problem for which there is no perfect solution" and being "unwilling to assume for ourselves a level of wisdom superior to that of legislators, scholars, and educational authorities in 50 States, especially where the alternatives proposed are only recently conceived and nowhere yet tested," the Court concluded that the system "rationally furthers a legitimate state purpose or interest," and upheld it as constitutional.

In a concurring opinion, Justice Stewart noted:

> Unlike other provisions of the Constitution, the Equal Protection Clause confers no substantive rights and creates no substantive liberties. The function of the Equal Protection Clause, rather, is simply to measure the validity of classifications created by state laws. There is hardly a law on the books that does not affect some people differently from others. But the basic concern of the Equal Protection Clause is with state legislation whose purpose or effect is to create discrete and objectively identifiable classes. And with respect to such legislation, it has long been settled that the Equal Protection Clause is offended only by laws that are invidiously discriminatory—only by classifications that are wholly arbitrary or capricious. This settled principle of constitutional law was compendiously stated . . . in the following words:
>
> > "Although no precise formula has been developed, the Court has held that the Fourteenth Amendment permits the States a wide scope of discretion in enacting laws which affect some groups of citizens differently than others. The constitutional safeguard is offended only if the classification rests on grounds wholly irrelevant to the achievement of the State's objective. State legislatures are presumed to have acted within their constitutional power despite the fact that, in practice, their

laws result in some inequality. A statutory discrimination will not be set aside if any state of facts reasonably may be conceived to justify it."

This doctrine is no more than a specific application of one of the first principles of constitutional adjudication—the basic presumption of the constitutional validity of a duly enacted state or federal law. Under the Equal Protection Clause, this presumption of constitutional validity disappears when a State has enacted legislation whose purpose or effect is to create classes based upon criteria that, in a constitutional sense, are inherently "suspect." Because of the historic purpose of the Fourteenth Amendment, the prime example of such a "suspect" classification is one that is based upon race. But there are other classifications that, at least in some settings, are also "suspect"—for example, those based upon national origin, alienage, indigency, or illegitimacy.[7]

In a dissenting opinion, Justice Marshall urged the Court to abandon the two-tier test and adopt a balancing test akin to the test used in substantive due process cases. Voicing his "disagreement with the Court's rigidified approach to equal protection analysis," he stated:

> The Court apparently seeks to establish today that equal protection cases fall into one of two neat categories which dictate the appropriate standard of review—strict scrutiny or mere rationality. [It would be far better to adopt the]

sort of reasoned approach to equal protection analysis for which I previously argued—that is, an approach in which concentration[is] placed upon the character of the classification in question, the relative importance to individuals in the class discriminated against of the governmental benefits that they do not receive, and the asserted state interests in support of the classification. The majority suggests . . . that a variable standard of review would give this Court the appearance of a "superlegislature." I cannot agree. Such an approach seems to me a part of the guarantees of our Constitution and of the historic experiences with oppression of and discrimination against discrete, powerless minorities which underlie that document.

The Supreme Court has never adopted such balancing test but, in *Plyler v. Doe,* 457 U.S. 202 (1982), which dealt with the exclusion of illegal alien children from public schools, and in subsequent cases, the Court has apparently recognized a middle level of review between strict scrutiny and any rational basis. Certain classifications, like those based on alienage or illegitimacy, are considered quasi-suspect. These classifications are subjected to **intermediate scrutiny** and can be sustained only if they serve substantial state interests. Put differently, as the Court explained in *Metro Broadcasting, Inc. v. FCC,* 497 U.S. 547 (1990), **quasi-suspect classifications** must serve "important" (but not necessarily compelling) governmental objectives and must be "substantially" (not just conceivably) related to achievement of those objectives.

In addition, in *Plyler,* the Supreme Court implied that intermediate scrutiny should be used when considering discriminations that impinge important, although not fundamental or constitutional, interests, like education. The Court stated:

---

7. Justice Stewart also recognized that "a state law that impinges upon a substantive right or liberty created or conferred by the Constitution is, of course, presumptively invalid" and that to the extent the "law's purpose or effect is to create . . . classifications," the law could be invalidated as "invidiously discriminating against an identifiable class in violation of the Equal Protection Clause" even if it was supported by a rational basis. However, Justice Stewart thought that "more basically, such a law would be invalid simply because it abridged" a fundamental right without a compelling reason.

The Equal Protection Clause directs that all persons similarly circumstanced shall be treated alike. But so too, [t]he Constitution does not require things which are different in fact or opinion to be treated in law as though they were the same. The initial discretion to determine what is "different" and what is "the same" resides in the legislatures of the States. A legislature must have substantial latitude to establish classifications that roughly approximate the nature of the problem perceived, that accommodate competing concerns both public and private, and that account for limitations on the practical ability of the State to remedy every ill. In applying the Equal Protection Clause to most forms of state action, we thus seek only the assurance that the classification at issue bears some fair relationship to a legitimate public purpose.

But we would not be faithful to our obligations under the Fourteenth Amendment if we applied so deferential a standard to every classification. The Equal Protection Clause was intended as a restriction on state legislative action inconsistent with elemental constitutional premises. Thus we have treated as presumptively invidious those classifications that disadvantage a "suspect class," or that impinge upon the exercise of a "fundamental right." With respect to such classifications, it is appropriate to enforce the mandate of equal protection by requiring the State to demonstrate that its classification has been precisely tailored to serve a compelling governmental interest. In addition, we have recognized that certain forms of legislative classification, while not facially invidious, nonetheless give rise to recurring constitutional difficulties; in these limited circumstances we have sought the assurance that the classification reflects a reasoned judgment consistent with the ideal of equal protection by inquiring whether it may fairly be viewed as furthering a substantial interest of the State.

It should now be obvious to you that in order to determine whether a law or government action violates the guarantee of equal protection, it is necessary, first, to determine whether the law or action discriminates against an inherently suspect or quasi-suspect class or impinges the exercise of a fundamental or important right. If an inherently suspect class or a fundamental right is involved, the law or action will be subjected to strict scrutiny. If a quasi-suspect or important right is involved, the law or action will be subjected to intermediate scrutiny. If the classification is not suspect and no fundamental or important right is involved, the law or action need only be rationally related to a legitimate government purpose.

Determining the test to be used is a crucial first step in equal protection analysis. In practice, virtually all classifications that have been subjected to strict judicial scrutiny (because they were considered inherently suspect or impinged on a right considered basic) have been declared unconstitutional, while virtually all classifications required only to have a rational basis have been declared constitutional. It has been, in other words, all but impossible for a court to find a compelling state interest to justify an inherently suspect classification or a discrimination impinging on a fundamental right and it has been relatively easy for the courts to find a rational basis to justify a nonsuspect classification or a discrimination that did not affect a basic right.

Because it is crucial that you know which test is to be used in an equal protection analysis, we will now look at the test that has been applied to classifications of importance to social workers. As we look at these classifications, you should keep in mind the following description from *Plyler v. Doe, supra,* of the "several formulations" that explain the Supreme Court's "treatment of certain classifications as suspect."

Some classifications are more likely than others to reflect deep-seated prejudice rather than legislative rationality in pursuit of some legitimate objective. Legislation predicated on such prejudice is easily recognized as incompatible with the constitutional understanding that each person is to be judged individually and is entitled to equal justice under the law. Classifications treated as suspect tend to be irrelevant to any proper legislative goal. Finally, certain groups, indeed largely the same groups, have historically been relegated to such a position of political powerlessness as to command extraordinary protection from the majoritarian political process. The experience of our Nation has shown that prejudice may manifest itself in the treatment of some groups. Our response to that experience is reflected in the Equal Protection Clause of the Fourteenth Amendment. Legislation imposing special disabilities upon groups disfavored by virtue of circumstances beyond their control suggests the kind of "class or caste" treatment that the Fourteenth Amendment was designed to abolish.

Classifications

Race and National Origin. Classifications based on race or national origin are considered inherently suspect and thus subject to strict judicial scrutiny. Such classifications may be upheld only if they are "shown to be necessary to the accomplishment of some permissible state objective, independent of the racial discrimination which it was the object of the Fourteenth Amendment to eliminate." *Loving v. Virginia,* 388 U.S. 1 (1967). The permissible state objective must, moreover, be compelling. This standard of review for classifications based on race or national origin is so stringent that the Supreme Court has only upheld one classification based on race or national origin: the internment of the Japanese during World War II. In a much criticized opinion, *Korematsu v. United States,* 323 U.S. 214 (1944), the Court held the internment was justified for compelling national security reasons.

Just because legislation or another form of state action has a *disproportionate impact* on certain racial groups, however, it may not be considered a violation of equal protection. Thus, in *Washington v. Davis,* 426 U.S. 229 (1976), the Supreme Court made clear that it did "not embrace the proposition that a law or other official act, without regard to whether it reflects a racially discriminatory purpose, is unconstitutional solely because it has a racially disproportionate impact." However, the Court also made clear that:

This is not to say that the necessary discriminatory racial purpose must be express or appear on the face of the statute, or that a law's disproportionate impact is irrelevant in cases involving Constitution-based claims of racial discrimination. A statute, otherwise neutral on its face, must not be applied so as invidiously to discriminate on the basis of race. It is also clear from the cases dealing with racial discrimination in the selection of juries that the systematic exclusion of Negroes is itself such an unequal application of the law . . . as to show intentional discrimination.

Necessarily, an invidious discriminatory purpose may often be inferred from the totality of the relevant facts, including the fact, if it is true, that the law bears more heavily on one race than another. It is also not infrequently true that the discriminatory impact . . . may for all practical purposes demonstrate unconstitutionality because . . . the discrimination is very difficult to explain on nonracial grounds. Nevertheless, we have not held that a law, neutral on its face and serving ends otherwise within the power of government to pursue, is invalid under the Equal Protection Clause simply because it may affect a greater proportion of one race than of another. Disproportionate impact is not irrelevant, but it is not the sole touchstone of an invidious racial discrimination forbidden by the Constitution. Standing alone, it does not trigger the rule that racial classifications are to be subjected to the strictest scrutiny and are justifiable only by the weightiest of considerations.[8]

The Supreme Court has had a difficult time grappling with one problem in the area of discrimination on the basis of race or national origin: the constitutionality of affirmative action plans, which discriminate *in favor* of members of minority groups who have been discriminated against in the past. The following excerpts from *Adarand Constructors, Inc. v. Pena,* 515 U.S. 200 (1995), which concerned the constitutionality of a federal program providing financial incentives to government contractors who hired minority subcontractors, document this struggle. After discussing the Court's historical review of "classifications burdening groups that have suffered discrimination in our society," the plurality opinion traced the history of the Court's consideration of classifications to benefit such groups, that is, its review of affirmative action:

In 1978, the Court confronted the question whether race-based governmental action designed to benefit [groups that have suffered discrimination] should also be subject to the most rigid scrutiny. *Regents of Univ. of California v. Bakke,* 438 U.S. 265, involved an equal protection challenge to a state-run medical school's practice of reserving a number of spaces in its entering class for minority students. The petitioners argued that strict scrutiny should apply only to classifications that disadvantage discrete and insular minorities. *Bakke* did not produce an opinion for the Court [in other words, there was no majority opinion and, in fact, there were six opinions], but [the plurality opinion of two justices] rejected the argument. [This opinion stated] that "[t]he guarantee of equal protection cannot mean one thing when applied to one individual and something else when applied to a person of another color" [and] concluded that "[r]acial and ethnic distinctions of any sort are inherently suspect and thus call for the most exacting judicial examination." On the other hand, four Justices in *Bakke* would have applied a less stringent standard of review to racial classifications designed to further remedial purposes, and four Justices thought the case should be decided on statutory grounds.

Two years after *Bakke,* the Court faced another challenge to remedial race-based action . . . In *Fullilove v. Klutznick,* 448 U.S. 448 (1980), the Court upheld Congress' inclusion of a 10% set-aside for minority-owned businesses in the Public Works Employment Act of 1977. As in *Bakke,* there was no opinion for the Court [and there were five different opinions]. [Three justices joining in the plurality opinion] observed that "[a]ny preference based on racial or ethnic criteria must necessarily receive a most searching examination to make sure that it does not conflict with constitutional guarantees." That opinion, however, d[id] not adopt, either expressly or implicitly, the formulas of analysis articulated in such cases as [*Bakke*]. It employed instead a two-part test which asked, first, whether the **objectives** of th[e] legislation are within the power of Congress, and second, whether the limited use of racial and ethnic criteria, in the context presented, is a constitutionally permissible **means** for achieving the congressional objectives. It then upheld the program under that test . . .

In *Wygant v. Jackson Board of Ed.,* 476 U.S. 267 (1986), the Court considered a Fourteenth Amendment challenge to another form of remedial racial classification. The issue in

---

8. You should note, however, that disproportionate impact may be enough to establish a claim under a statute forbidding discrimination, like Title VII of the Civil Rights Act of 1964, 42 U.S.C. § 2000e, which prohibits discrimination in employment by certain employers.

Wygant was whether a school board could adopt race-based preferences in determining which teachers to lay off, [The] plurality opinion observed that "the level of scrutiny does not change merely because the challenged classification operates against a group that historically has not been subject to governmental discrimination," and stated the two-part inquiry as "whether the layoff provision is supported by a compelling state purpose and whether the means chosen to accomplish that purpose are narrowly tailored." In other words, [as stated in a concurring opinion] "racial classifications of any sort must be subjected to strict scrutiny." The plurality then concluded that the school board's interest in providing minority role models for its minority students, as an attempt to alleviate the effects of societal discrimination, was not a compelling interest that could justify the use of a racial classification. Four Justices dissented, three of whom again argued for intermediate scrutiny of remedial race-based government action.

The Court's failure to produce a majority opinion in *Bakke, Fullilove,* and *Wygant* left unresolved the proper analysis for remedial race-based governmental action. The Court resolved the issue, at least in part, in 1989. *Richmond v. J.A. Croson Co.,* 488 U.S. 469 (1989), concerned a city's determination that 30% of its contracting work should go to minority-owned businesses. A majority of the Court in *Croson* held that the standard of review under the Equal Protection Clause is not dependent on the race of those burdened or benefited by a particular classification, and that the single standard of review for racial classifications should be strict scrutiny. [However, a majority did not agree on the validity of the city's determination although a plurality agreed that the city had not acted with a "strong basis in evidence for its conclusion that remedial action was necessary," and that the "program is not narrowly tailored to remedy the effects of prior discrimination"].

With *Croson,* the Court finally agreed that the Fourteenth Amendment requires strict scrutiny of all race-based action by state and local governments. But *Croson* [did not concern the federal government and it and earlier cases did not resolve all questions in relation

to affirmative action]. Despite lingering uncertainty in the details, however, the Court's cases through *Croson* had established three general propositions with respect to governmental racial classifications. First, **skepticism**: [a]ny preference based on racial or ethnic criteria must necessarily receive a most searching examination. Second, **consistency**: the standard of review under the Equal Protection Clause is not dependent on the race of those burdened or benefited by a particular classification. And third, **congruence**: [e]qual protection analysis in the Fifth Amendment area is the same as that under the Fourteenth Amendment. Taken together, these three propositions lead to the conclusion that any person, of whatever race, has the right to demand that any governmental actor subject to the Constitution justify any racial classification subjecting that person to unequal treatment under the strictest judicial scrutiny.

A year later, however, the Court took a surprising turn. *Metro Broadcasting, Inc. v. FCC,* 497 U.S. 547 (1990), involved a Fifth Amendment challenge to two race-based policies of the Federal Communications Commission. In *Metro Broadcasting,* the Court repudiated the long-held notion that it would be unthinkable that the same Constitution would impose a lesser duty on the Federal Government than it does on a State to afford equal protection of the laws. It did so by holding that "benign" federal racial classifications need only satisfy intermediate scrutiny, even though *Croson* had recently concluded that such classifications enacted by a State must satisfy strict scrutiny. "[B]enign" federal racial classifications, the Court said—even if those measures are not "remedial" in the sense of being designed to compensate victims of past governmental or societal discrimination—are constitutionally permissible to the extent that they serve **important** governmental objectives within the power of Congress and are **substantially related** to achievement of those objectives. Applying this test, the Court . . . upheld the policies.

By adopting intermediate scrutiny as the standard of review for congressionally mandated "benign" racial classifications, *Metro Broadcasting* . . . turned its back on *Croson*'s explanation of why strict scrutiny of all governmental racial classifications is essential . . . [and undermined the three propositions enunciated in *Croson* and earlier cases:] congruence between the standards applicable to federal and state racial classifications, . . . skepticism of all racial classifications, and consistency of treatment irrespective of the race of the burdened or benefited group. *Metro Broadcasting* was thus a significant departure from much of what had come before it.

The three propositions undermined by *Metro Broadcasting* all derive from the basic principle that the Fifth and Fourteenth Amendments to the Constitution protect **persons**, not **groups**. It follows from that principle that all governmental action based on race—a group classification long recognized as in most circumstances irrelevant and therefore prohibited—should be subjected to detailed judicial inquiry to ensure that the personal right to equal protection of the laws has not been infringed. These ideas have long been central to this Court's understanding of equal protection, and holding "benign" state and federal racial classifications to different standards does not square with them. [A] free people whose institutions are founded upon the doctrine of equality, should tolerate no retreat from the principle that government may treat people differently because of their race only for the most compelling reasons. Accordingly, **we hold today that all racial classifications, imposed by whatever federal, state, or local governmental actor, must be analyzed by a reviewing court under strict scrutiny. In other words, such classifications are constitutional only if they are narrowly tailored measures that further compelling governmental interests.** To the extent that *Metro Broadcasting* is inconsistent with that holding, it is overruled.

This overruling of a decision from just five years before, however, came in an opinion of only three justices. *Adarand,* moreover, was decided in a vote of five to four with a total of six opinions, one plurality, two concurring, and three dissenting.

Clearly, the constitutional questions related to affirmative action have not yet been definitively answered and the debate over affirmative action is likely to continue.

Gender. For many years, the Supreme Court refused to consider classifications based on gender suspect, but, in *Frontiero v. Richardson,* 411 U.S.677 (1973), the Court declared that such classifications were, indeed, suspect. *Frontiero* addressed the treatment of women in the military. Servicemen were entitled to claim their spouses as dependents for the purposes of obtaining increased quarters allowances and medical and dental benefits without regard to whether their wives were in fact dependent upon them for any part of their support. Servicewoman, on the other hand, could not claim their spouses as dependents unless their husbands were in fact dependent upon them for over one-half their support. The Court stated:

There can be no doubt that our Nation has had a long and unfortunate history of sex discrimination. Traditionally, such discrimination was rationalized by an attitude of romantic paternalism which, in practical effect, put women, not on a pedestal, but in a cage. Indeed, this paternalistic attitude became so firmly rooted in our national consciousness that, 100 years ago, a distinguished Member of this Court was able to proclaim:

"Man is, or should be, women's protector and defender. The natural and proper timidity and delicacy which belongs to the female sex evidently unfits it for many of the occupations of civil life. The constitution of the family organization, which is founded in the divine ordinance, as well as in the nature of things, indicates the domestic sphere as that which properly belongs to the domain and functions of womanhood. The harmony, not to say identity, of interests and views which belong, or should belong, to the family institution is repugnant to the idea of a woman adopting a distinct and independent career from that of her husband . . . . The paramount destiny and mission of woman are to fulfill the noble and benign offices of wife and mother. This is the law of the Creator."

As a result of notions such as these, our statute books gradually became laden with gross, stereotyped distinctions between the sexes and, indeed, throughout much of the 19th century the position of women in our society was, in many respects, comparable to that of blacks under the pre-Civil War slave codes. Neither slaves nor women could hold office, serve on juries, or bring suit in their own names, and married women traditionally were denied the legal capacity to hold or convey property or to serve as legal guardians of their own children. And although blacks were guaranteed the right to vote in 1870, women were denied even that right—which is itself preservative of other basic civil and political rights—until adoption of the Nineteenth Amendment half a century later.

It is true, of course, that the position of women in America has improved markedly in recent decades. Nevertheless, it can hardly be doubted that, in part because of the high visibility of the sex characteristic, women still face pervasive, although at times more subtle, discrimination in our educational institutions, in the job market and, perhaps most conspicuously, in the political arena. Moreover, since sex, like race and national origin, is an immutable characteristic determined solely by the accident of birth, the imposition of special disabilities upon the members of a particular sex because of their sex would seem to violate the basic concept of our system that legal burdens should bear some relationship to individual responsibility . . . . And what differentiates sex from such non-suspect statuses as intelligence or physical disability, and aligns it with the recognized suspect criteria, is that the sex characteristic frequently bears no relation to ability to perform or contribute to society. As a result, statutory distinctions between the sexes often have the effect of invidiously relegating the entire class of females to inferior legal status without regard to the actual capabilities of its individual members.

Later cases seemed to retreat from this position, however. For example, in *Kahn v. Shevin,* 416 U.S. 351 (1974), the Court upheld a property tax exemption plan for widows, but not for widowers, stating: "Gender has never been rejected as an impermissible classification in all instances." It could well be, however, that the Court's refusal to invalidate the tax exemption for widows in *Kahn* was due to its view that, like affirmative action plans designed to remedy the effects of past discrimination on the basis of race, remedial efforts designed to remedy the effects of past discrimination on the basis of gender may be constitutional. In several cases, the Court has specifically held that ameliorative efforts that discriminate against men in order to remedy past discrimination against women are constitutional.

While cases like *Kahn* may have backed down from the Court's prior position that discrimination on the basis of gender is inherently suspect, there can be no question that gender is considered a quasi-suspect basis for a classification.

It has frequently been claimed that discrimination on the basis of pregnancy is sex-based discrimination. In *Geduldig v. Aiello,* 417 U.S. 484 (1974), however, the Court upheld the exclusion of pregnancy from the disabilities covered by California's public disability insurance system, stating: "We cannot agree that the exclusion of this disability from coverage amounts to invidious discrimination under the Equal Protection Clause." The Court reasoned that:

The California insurance program does not exclude anyone from benefit eligibility because of gender but merely removes one physical condition—pregnancy—from the list of compensable disabilities. While it is true that only women can become pregnant it does not follow that every legislative classification concerning pregnancy is a sex-based classification ... The program divides potential recipients into two groups—pregnant women and nonpregnant persons. While the first group is exclusively female, the second includes members of both sexes.[9]

---

9. Congress apparently did not agree with the Court that discrimination on the basis of pregnancy is not sex-based discrimination. Soon after *Geduldig,* Congress amended Title VII of the Civil Rights Act of 1964, 42 U.S.C. § 2000e, the law forbidding sex-based discrimination in employment, to provide that discrimination on the basis of pregnancy is sex-based discrimination and, thus, prohibited. In *California Savings and Loan Association v. Guerra,* 479 U.S. 272 (1987), the Supreme Court held that this provision in Title VII, while seeming "to mandate treating pregnant employees the same as other employees," does not prohibit discrimination in favor of pregnant women and upheld a provision in Title VII giving pregnant women maternity leave. The Court reasoned that unlike "the protective labor legislation prevalent earlier in this century" that had the effect of keeping women out of the workplace, maternity leave "promotes equal employment opportunity" by allowing "women, as well as men, to have families without losing their jobs."

Interestingly, in *Bray v. Alexandria Women's Health Clinic,* 506 U.S. 263 (1993), the Supreme Court held that a conspiracy to obstruct an abortion clinic was not sex-based invidious discrimination against women. The Court stated: "Some activities may be such an irrational object of disfavor that, if they are targeted, and if they also happen to be engaged in exclusively or predominantly by a particular class of people, an intent to disfavor that class can readily be presumed. A tax on wearing yarmulkes is a tax on Jews. But opposition to voluntary abortion cannot possibly be considered such an irrational surrogate for opposition to (or paternalism towards) women. Whatever one thinks of abortion, it cannot be denied that there are common and respectable reasons for opposing it, other than hatred of or condescension toward (or indeed any view at all concerning women as a class) as is evident from the fact that men and women are on both sides of the issue ... "

Sexual Orientation. In *Baehr v. Lewin* 852 P.2d 44 (HA 1993), the Hawaii Supreme Court held that a Hawaii statute prohibiting the issuance of marriage licenses to same-sex couples established a sex-based classification in violation of the Hawaii constitution and must be subject to a strict scrutiny test. While deciding that there is no fundamental right to a same-sex marriage, in remanding the case, the Court stated that the statute must be held unconstitutional unless "the State of Hawaii can show that (a) the statute's sex-based classification is justified by compelling state interests and (b) the statute is narrowly drawn to avoid abridgement of the applicant couples' constitutional rights." After remand, the statute was declared unconstitutional.

How the United States Supreme Court might rule in such a case is unclear. While in *Bowers v. Hardwick,* 478 U.S. 186 (1986), the Court upheld the constitutionality of a statute making homosexual relations between consenting adults a crime, the Court held in *Romer v. Evans,* ___ U.S. ___, 116 S. Ct. 1620 (1996), that an initiative measure amending the Colorado constitution that prohibited "all legislative, executive or judicial action at any level of state or local government designed to protect ... a class we shall refer to as homosexual persons or gays and lesbians" violated the equal protection clause. The majority opinion in *Romer* reasoned "that the Constitution neither knows nor tolerates classes among citizens" and requires a "commitment to the law's neutrality where the rights of persons are at stake." Because the initiative measure (known as "Amendment 2") deprived homosexuals, but not other classes, of the right to seek redress from discrimination they have suffered, it was not neutral. The opinion states:

> Homosexuals, by state decree, are put in a solitary class with respect to transactions and relations in both the private and governmental spheres. The amendment withdraws from homosexuals, but no others, specific legal protection from the injuries caused by discrimination, and it forbids reinstatement of these laws and policies.
>
> [W]e cannot accept the view that Amendment 2's prohibition on specific legal protections does no more than deprive homosexuals of special rights. To the contrary, the amendment imposes a special disability upon those persons alone. Homosexuals are forbidden the safeguards that others enjoy or may seek without constraint. They can obtain specific protection against discrimination only by enlisting the citizenry of Colorado to amend the state constitution or perhaps, in the State's view, by trying to pass helpful laws of general applicability. This is so no matter how local or discrete the harm, no matter how public and widespread the injury. We find nothing special in the protections Amendment 2 withholds. These are protections taken for granted by most people either because they already have them or do not need them; these are protections against exclusion from an almost limitless number of transactions and endeavors that constitute ordinary civic life in a free society.
>
> The Fourteenth Amendment's promise that no person shall be denied the equal protection of the laws must co-exist with the practical necessity that most legislation classifies for one purpose or another, with resulting disadvantage to various groups or persons. We have attempted to reconcile the principle with the reality by stating that, if a law neither burdens a fundamental right nor targets a suspect class, we will uphold the legislative classification so long as it bears a rational relation to some legitimate end. Amendment 2 fails, indeed defies, even this conventional inquiry. First, the amendment has the peculiar property of imposing a broad and undifferentiated disability on a single named group, an exceptional and, as we shall explain, invalid form of legislation. Second,

> its sheer breadth is so discontinuous with the reasons offered for it that the amendment seems inexplicable by anything but animus toward the class that it affects; it lacks a rational relationship to legitimate state interests.
>
> Taking the first point, even in the ordinary equal protection case calling for the most deferential of standards, we insist on knowing the relation between the classification adopted and the object to be attained. The search for the link between classification and objective gives substance to the Equal Protection Clause; it provides guidance and discipline for the legislature, which is entitled to know what sorts of laws it can pass; and it marks the limits of our own authority. In the ordinary case, a law will be sustained if it can be said to advance a legitimate government interest, even if the law seems unwise or works to the disadvantage of a particular group, or if the rationale for it seems tenuous. By requiring that the classification bear a rational relationship to an independent and legitimate legislative end, we ensure that classifications are not drawn for the purpose of disadvantaging the group burdened by the law.
>
> Amendment 2 confounds this normal process of judicial review. It is at once too narrow and too broad. It identifies persons by a single trait and then denies them protection across the board. A law declaring that in general it shall be more difficult for one group of citizens than for all others to seek aid from the government is itself a denial of equal protection of the laws in the most literal sense. The guaranty of equal protection of the laws is a pledge of the protection of equal laws.
>
> A second and related point is that laws of the kind now before us raise the inevitable inference that the disadvantage imposed is born of animosity toward the class of persons affected. [I]f the constitutional conception of equal protection of the laws means anything, it must at the very least mean that a bare . . . desire to harm a politically unpopular group cannot constitute a legitimate governmental interest. Even laws enacted for broad and ambitious purposes often can be explained by reference to legitimate public policies which justify the incidental disadvantages they impose on certain persons. Amendment 2, how-

ever, in making a general announcement that gays and lesbians shall not have any particular protections from the law, inflicts on them immediate, continuing, and real injuries that outrun and belie any legitimate justifications that may be claimed for it.

We cannot say that Amendment 2 is directed to any identifiable legitimate purpose or discrete objective. It is a status-based enactment divorced from any factual context from which we could discern a relationship to legitimate state interests; it is a classification of persons undertaken for its own sake, something the Equal Protection Clause does not permit.

We must conclude that Amendment 2 classifies homosexuals not to further a proper legislative end but to make them unequal to everyone else. This Colorado cannot do. A State cannot so deem a class of persons a stranger to its laws. Amendment 2 violates the Equal Protection Clause . . .

In so holding, however, the Supreme Court did not hold, and has never held, that discrimination on the basis of sexual orientation is a suspect or quasi-suspect classification.

Age. In *Massachusetts Bd. of Retirement v. Murgia,* 427 U.S. 307 (1976), the Court held that classifications based on age are neither suspect nor quasi-suspect and thus sustained a law mandating the retirement of all Massachusetts State Police officers at the age of fifty, regardless of their physical or mental health. The Court stated:

[T]he class of uniformed state police officers over 50 [does not] constitute a suspect class for purposes of equal protection analysis. [We have] observed that a suspect class is one saddled with such disabilities, or subjected to such a history of purposeful unequal treatment, or relegated to such a position of political powerlessness as to command extraordinary protection from the majoritarian political process. While the treatment of the aged in this Nation has not been wholly free of discrimination,

such persons, unlike, say, those who have been discriminated against on the basis of race or national origin, have not experienced a history of purposeful unequal treatment or been subjected to unique disabilities on the basis of stereotyped characteristics not truly indicative of their abilities.

[The compulsory retirement law] cannot be said to discriminate only against the elderly. Rather, it draws the line at a certain age in middle life. But even old age does not define a discrete and insular group in need of extraordinary protection from the majoritarian political process. Instead, it marks a stage that each of us will reach if we live out our normal span.

We do not make light of the substantial economic and psychological effects premature and compulsory retirement can have on an individual; nor do we denigrate the ability of elderly citizens to continue to contribute to society. The problems of retirement have been well documented and are beyond serious dispute. But [w]e do not decide today that the [Massachusetts statute] is wise, that it best fulfills the relevant social and economic objectives that [Massachusetts] might ideally espouse, or that a more just and humane system could not be devised. We decide only that the system enacted by the Massachusetts Legislature does not deny [healthy police officers over age 50] equal protection of the laws.[10]

Discrimination against young people may also pass constitutional muster. For example, in *Dallas v. Stranglin,* 409 U.S. 19 (1989), the Supreme Court held that a Dallas ordinance, which restricted teenagers' admission to certain dance halls, was valid since age was not a suspect classification and there was a rational relationship between the age restriction and Dallas's interest in promoting the welfare of young people.

---

10. The Court reiterated that age is not a suspect classification when it upheld the mandatory retirement of judges at the age of seventy in *Gregory v. Ashcroft,* 501 U.S. 452 (1991).

Legitimacy. For a time, classifications based on illegitimacy apparently were considered inherently suspect. In several opinions, however, the Court retreated from this position. For example, in *Mathews v. Lucas,* 427 U.S. 495 (1976), dealing with the right of illegitimate children to receive their father's social security benefits, the Court stated:

> [I]rrationality in some classifications [relating to illegitimacy] does not in itself demonstrate that other, possibly rational, distinctions made in part on the basis of legitimacy are inherently untenable. Moreover, while the law has long placed the illegitimate child in an inferior position relative to the legitimate in certain circumstances, perhaps in part because the roots of discrimination rest in the conduct of the parents rather than the child, and perhaps in part because illegitimacy does not carry an obvious badge, as race and sex do, this discrimination against illegitimates has never approached the severity or pervasiveness of the historic legal and political discrimination against women and Negroes. We therefore adhere to our earlier view that discrimination between individuals on the basis of their legitimacy does not command extraordinary protection from the majoritarian political process.

It would be fair to say that the Court seesawed on this subject, but that classifications based on legitimacy now would undoubtedly be considered quasi-suspect and, thus, subject to intermediate scrutiny.

Alienage. As with classifications based on legitimacy, classifications based on alienage seemed to be suspect, but the Court was not totally clear on this point. *Plyler v. Doe, supra,* 457 U.S. 202, made clear, however, that classifications based on *illegal* alienage were not suspect. The Court stated:

> We reject the claim that illegal aliens are a suspect class. No case in which we have attempted to define a suspect class, has addressed the status of persons unlawfully in our country. Unlike most of the classifications that we have recognized as suspect, entry into this class, by virtue of entry into this country, is the product of voluntary action. Indeed, entry into the class is itself a crime. In addition, it could hardly be suggested that undocumented status is a constitutional irrelevancy. With respect to the actions of the Federal Government, alienage classifications may be intimately related to the conduct of foreign policy, to the federal prerogative to control access to the United States, and to the plenary federal power to determine who has sufficiently manifested his allegiance to become a citizen of the Nation.

The children of illegal aliens, however, were held to fall into a quasi-suspect class. The Court stated:

> Persuasive arguments support the view that a State may withhold its beneficence from those whose very presence within the United States is the product of their own unlawful conduct. These arguments do not apply with the same force to classifications imposing disabilities on the minor children of such illegal entrants. At the least, those who elect to enter our territory by stealth and in violation of our law should be prepared to bear the consequences, including, but not limited to, deportation. But the children of those illegal entrants are not comparably situated. Their parents have the ability to conform their conduct to societal norms, and presumably the ability to remove themselves from the State's jurisdiction; but the children who are plaintiffs in these cases can affect neither their parents' conduct nor their own status. Even if the State found it expedient to control the conduct of adults by acting against their children, legislation directing the onus of a parent's misconduct against his children does not comport with fundamental conceptions of justice. [V]isiting . . . condemnation on the head of an infant is illogical and unjust. Moreover, imposing disabilities on the . . . child is

contrary to the basic concept of our system that legal burdens should bear some relationship to individual responsibility or wrongdoing. Obviously, no child is responsible for his birth and penalizing the . . . child is an ineffectual—as well as unjust—way of deterring the parent."

Wealth. The case of *San Antonio Independent School District v. Rodriguez, supra,* 411 U.S. 1, seemed to indicate that classifications based on wealth are not inherently suspect. However, the Court described the class discriminated against by the Texas system of school finance, not as a class of poor parents, but as a

> large, diverse, and amorphous class, unified only by the common factor of residence in districts that happen to have less taxable wealth than other districts. [This class has] none of the traditional indicia of suspectness: the class is not saddled with such disabilities, or subjected to such a history of purposeful unequal treatment, or relegated to such a position of political powerlessness as to command extraordinary protection from the majoritarian political process.

A different type of classification based solely on wealth could be considered at least quasi-suspect.

Mental Retardation. In *City of Cleburne, Tex. v. Cleburne Living Center,* 473 U.S. 432 (1985), which involved a zoning ordinance that had been interpreted to prevent a group home for the mentally retarded from locating in a residential neighborhood, the Supreme Court ruled that classifications based on such a mental disability are neither suspect nor quasi-suspect. The Court stated:

> The lesson of [our cases] is that where individuals in the group affected by a law have distinguishing characteristics relevant to in-

terests the state has the authority to implement, the courts have been very reluctant, as they should be in our federal system and with our respect for the separation of powers, to closely scrutinize legislative choices as to whether, how, and to what extent those interests should be pursued. In such cases, the Equal Protection Clause requires only a rational means to serve a legitimate end. Against this background, we conclude for several reasons that . . . mental retardation [is not] a quasi-suspect classification calling for a more exacting standard of judicial review than is normally accorded economic and social legislation.

First, it is undeniable . . . that those who are mentally retarded have a reduced ability to cope with and function in the everyday world. Nor are they all cut from the same pattern: as the testimony in this record indicates, they range from those whose disability is not immediately evident to those who must be constantly cared for. They are thus different, immutably so, in relevant respects, and the states' interest in dealing with and providing for them is plainly a legitimate one.

Second, the distinctive legislative response, both national and state, to the plight of those who are mentally retarded demonstrates not only that they have unique problems, but also that the lawmakers have been addressing their difficulties in a manner that belies a continuing antipathy or prejudice and a corresponding need for more intrusive oversight by the judiciary. Thus, the federal government has not only outlawed discrimination against the mentally retarded in federally funded programs, but it has also provided the retarded with the right to receive appropriate treatment, services, and habilitation in a setting that is least restrictive of [their] personal liberty. In addition, the government has conditioned federal education funds on a State's assurance that retarded children will enjoy an education that, to the maximum extent appropriate, is integrated with that of non-mentally retarded children. The government has also facilitated the hiring of the mentally retarded into the federal civil service by exempting them from the requirement of competitive examination. Such legislation thus singling out the retarded for special treatment reflects the real and undeniable differences between the retarded and others. That a civilized and decent society expects and approves such legislation indicates that governmental consideration of those differences in the vast majority of situations is not only legitimate but desirable.

Third, the legislative response, which could hardly have occurred and survived without public support, negates any claim that the mentally retarded are politically powerless in the sense that they have no ability to attract the attention of the lawmakers. Any minority can be said to be powerless to assert direct control over the legislature, but if that were a criterion for higher level scrutiny by the courts, much economic and social legislation would now be suspect.

Fourth, if the large and amorphous class of the mentally retarded were deemed quasi-suspect . . . it would be difficult to find a principled way to distinguish a variety of other groups who have perhaps immutable disabilities setting them off from others, who cannot themselves mandate the desired legislative responses, and who can claim some degree of prejudice from at least part of the public at large. One need mention in this respect only the aging, the disabled, the mentally ill, and the infirm. We are reluctant to set out on that course, and we decline to do so.

Despite refusing to find mental retardation to be a suspect or quasi-suspect class, the Court held that the zoning ordinance was unconstitutional as applied. In so holding, the Court seemed to use a somewhat heightened scrutiny. However, in *Heller v. Doe,* 509 U.S. 312 (1993), the Court repeated that mental disability was not a suspect or quasi-suspect classification and upheld a law discriminating between the mentally ill and the mentally retarded in the procedures for involuntary commitments using the simple rational basis test.

Protected Rights

As has been stated, the courts may use heightened scrutiny to determine if a law or action comports with equal protection not only when a suspect or quasi-suspect classification is involved, but also when a fundamental or important right is implicated.

To determine "whether a class-based denial of a particular right is deserving of strict scrutiny," that is, whether the right is a basic or fundamental right, "we look to the Constitution to see if the right infringed has its source, explicitly or implicitly, therein." *Plyler v. Doe, supra,* 457 U.S. 202. As this quotation from *Plyler* makes clear, the right need not be explicitly set forth in the Constitution, but may be implied from it, like the right to marital privacy discussed in *Griswold v. Connecticut, supra,* 381 U.S. 479. To give a further example, in *Shapiro v. Thompson,* 394 U.S. 618 (1969), several States' one-year residency requirements before one could receive welfare, which were challenged as denials of equal protection, were subjected to strict scrutiny because the requirements, in creating "two classes of needy resident families indistinguishable from each other except that one is composed of residents who have resided a year or more, and the second of residents who have resided less than a year, in the jurisdiction," impinged on the *right to travel.* Although the Constitution nowhere recognizes such a right, the Court stated:

This Court long ago recognized that the nature of our Federal Union and our constitutional concepts of personal liberty unite to require that all citizens be free to travel throughout the length and breadth of our land uninhibited by statutes, rules, or regulations which unreasonably burden or restrict this movement. We have no occasion to ascribe the source of this right to a particular constitutional provision.

If rights are not explicitly or implicitly found in the constitution, they will not be considered fundamental rights—no matter how important they are—and classifications that impinge on the exercise of these rights will not, for this reason, be subject to strict scrutiny. Thus, many government actions and laws impinging on important, but not fundamental rights and interests (such as the interest in the means to support one's children, the right to employment, and the interest in living where one chooses) may be sustained merely if they are rationally related to a legitimate government purpose. Some rights and interests are so important, however, that laws or government actions that impinge on them may be subjected to heightened scrutiny. Thus, in *Plyler v. Doe, supra,* 457 U.S. 202, the Court subjected a law that impinged on the right to a public education to intermediate scrutiny. The Court stated:

> Public education is not a "right" granted to individuals by the Constitution. But neither is it merely some governmental "benefit" indistinguishable from other forms of social welfare legislation. Both the importance of education in maintaining our basic institutions, and the lasting impact of its deprivation on the life of the child, mark the distinction. The American people have always regarded education and [the] acquisition of knowledge as matters of supreme importance. We have recognized the public schools as a most vital civic institution for the preservation of a democratic system of government, and as the primary vehicle for transmitting the values on which our society rests. [A]s . . . pointed out early in our history, . . . some degree of education is necessary to prepare citizens to participate effectively and intelligently in our open political system if we are to preserve freedom and independence. And these historic perceptions of the public schools as inculcating fundamental values necessary to the maintenance of a democratic political system have been confirmed by the observations of social scientists. In addition, education provides the basic tools by which individuals might lead economically productive lives to the benefit of us all. In sum, education has a fundamental role in maintaining the fabric of our society. We cannot ignore the significant social costs borne by our Nation when select groups are denied the means to absorb the values and skills upon which our social order rests.

REMEDIES FOR VIOLATIONS OF CONSTITUTIONAL RIGHTS

Individuals who believe their constitutional rights have been violated can seek redress in the courts. This section reviews major federal and State statutes that can be invoked to seek such redress or to provide remedies for violations of constitutional and civil rights. Discrimination on the basis of race, gender, or other characteristics may also be prohibited by municipal ordinance, executive orders, administrative regulations, civil service rules, or agency policy. If this is the case, remedies will also be available at these levels which may be used instead of or in addition to federal and State statutory remedies we discuss.

Federal Remedies

In the 1960s, significant numbers of the poor, minorities, and members of oppressed groups (such as prisoners and mental patients) began using the courts to assert their constitutional rights and to challenge laws that discriminated against or otherwise injured them. Most of the cases were brought in federal courts because it was generally believed that federal courts were more receptive to the needs of the disadvantaged and to their constitutional arguments than State courts. The cases were also brought in federal courts because most of them were against State officials or sought to invalidate State laws and it was believed that federal judges were more likely to rule against State officials or invalidate State laws than were State judges.

The primary vehicle used to assert constitutional claims against State officials and to challenge State laws in federal courts was a cluster of civil rights laws known as the **Civil Rights Acts**, which were enacted after the Civil War to provide rights to the newly freed slaves. These Acts, now found at 42 U.S.C. sections 1981 through 1985, had virtually lain dormant from the Reconstruction Era until civil rights advocates and social reformers of the 1960s recognized their usefulness. Section 1983, which allows an individual to sue whenever he or she is deprived of "rights, privileges or immunities secured by the Constitution and laws of the United States" by a person acting "under color of any statute, ordinance, regulation, custom, or usage of any State," is particularly useful.

The language in section 1983 sweeps broadly; its only significant limitation is the requirement that the defendant was acting under **color of law** when depriving the plaintiff of his or her rights. The color of law requirement is usually interpreted as the equivalent of the state action re-

quirement, but in some cases it is interpreted as requiring no more than that the defendant acted with the knowledge of and pursuant to State law.

Although section 1983 reaches only state action, the Fourteenth Amendment gives Congress the power to legislate against discriminatory private action. Thus, all federal civil rights laws do not require state action and no state action is required under other sections of the Civil Rights Acts. For example, section 1981 prohibits all discrimination in housing, private, or public, and section 1982, prohibits all discrimination in contracts. These sections are not as useful as section 1983, however, in that their scope is limited to specific types of discrimination while section 1983 goes to any violation of any federal civil right—whether constitutional or statutory.

The list of rights that are within the purview of section 1983 is a lengthy one. Every right protected explicitly or implicitly by the Constitution can be the subject of a suit under section 1983 as can any unconstitutional discrimination. Further, the statutory language in section 1983 allows suits for violations of the Constitution "and laws" of the United States. One may, thus, rely on a federal statute as the source of an asserted right in addition to the Constitution. The sweep of section 1983 is so great that nearly every constitutional case or Supreme Court case excerpted in this book was brought under it, whether or not that is stated in the excerpts. Indeed, its sweep is so great it has been used repeatedly to bring what are essentially malpractice actions against social workers who work for public agencies.

Under section 1983 and other sections of the Civil Rights Acts, a successful litigant may usually obtain an injunction, a declaratory judgment, or monetary damages. Cases may be brought as class actions. The members of the class in some civil rights suits, like those challenging the operation of statutory benefit provisions, can number in the millions. Having hundreds or even thousands of class members would not be unusual. Many of the cases excerpted in this book are class actions, again whether or not that is stated in the excerpts.

The extensive use of the Civil Rights Acts, particularly section 1983, to assert constitutional and statutory rights, which began in the 1960s, greatly expanded in the 1970s. In the 1980s and 1990s, however, the Supreme Court began issuing several rulings that restrict access to the federal courts and that sharply curtail federal judicial remedies, including the use of section 1983. Additionally, the Supreme Court has somewhat curtailed the class action device. As a result, many feel that the federal civil rights litigation boom of the 1960s and 1970s has ended.

In addition to the Civil Rights Acts, there are other routes to raise denials of constitutional and federal rights in federal courts. For example, numerous civil rights statutes directed at discrimination in such matters as voting, education, employment, housing, and public accommodations were enacted in the 1960s. Of these statutes (codified in scattered sections of Titles 18, 20, 25, 28, and 42 of the United States Code), Title VII of the Civil Rights Act of 1964, 42 U.S.C. § 2000e, which is the law dealing with discrimination in employment, is perhaps the most important and most used.

Title VII, like most of the federal civil rights laws of the 1960s, deals with dis-

crimination on the basis of race, religion, national origin, or sex. Newer civil rights laws deal with discrimination on other grounds. For example, the Americans with Disabilities Act of 1990, 42 U.S.C. § 12101 *et seq.,* prohibits discrimination on the basis of disability, and 29 U.S.C. § 621, prohibits discrimination in employment on the basis of age.

Title VII, also like many of the other federal civil rights laws of the 1960s, creates an administrative agency to consider claims of discrimination and requires exhaustion of administrative remedies before one may sue.

Title VII, again like many of the other federal civil rights laws of the 1960s, is specifically directed at private discrimination. That is, no state action is required although small private employers or businesses, with no connection to interstate commerce may not be covered. By way of contrast, some of the newer civil rights laws may be directed only at government entities or at recipients of federal funds. For example, 29 U.S.C. § 6101 *et seq.,* prohibits discrimination on the basis of age by federally assisted programs.

In addition to Title VII, section 1983 and other laws specifically protecting civil rights and prohibiting discrimination, the Administrative Procedure Act, 5 U.S.C. § 551 *et seq.,* which allows the federal courts to review actions taken by a federal agency, may be used to challenge federal administrative agency actions in violation of civil rights. The APA applies to every agency unless expressly excepted, but review under the APA is limited to determining whether the offending agency action was "arbitrary, capricious, or an abuse of discretion."

The federal courts may also **imply a**

remedy from a general statute which does not specifically authorize private actions or from the Constitution itself. For example, in *Bivens v. Six Unknown Named Agents of the Federal Bureau of Narcotics,* 403 U.S. 388 (1971), federal agents had allegedly violated the Fourth Amendment prohibition on unreasonable searches and seizures. The Supreme Court concluded that the Fourth Amendment expresses policies so basic that a private remedy for damages is implied. The implication of remedies has allowed private actions under several federal statutes in several significant areas, such as relocation benefits, public housing, and food stamps. Remedies have not been implied under all federal statutes, however.

Where there is no adequate judicial remedy for the violation of a constitutional right or where a right is not clearly based on the Constitution or found in any federal statute, the poor, minorities, and other disadvantaged groups must seek relief, not from the courts, but from the Congress and administrative agencies. Many civil rights laws and other laws that create specific rights or that protect specific groups, like the Americans with Disabilities Act of 1990, are in large part the result of active lobbying by the disadvantaged and their allies.

State Remedies

The poor, minorities, and members of oppressed groups have also asserted their rights in State courts. Many States have civil rights laws that authorize suits in State court when State constitutional rights have been violated. In addition, State courts can hear cases brought under 42 U.S.C. § 1983. Further, many States have laws like the federal Administrative Procedure Act, which allows an individual to sue a State agency that has violated one's rights, and many State courts imply private remedies from State laws creating State social welfare programs. Finally, many States have special laws according individuals special rights and privileges or giving them special opportunities for lawsuits. For example, Rhode Island has a law forbidding discrimination against the disabled that gives disabled persons who are the victims of prohibited discrimination the ability to go to State court to obtain "equitable relief, compensatory and/or punitive damages, or such other relief as the court deems appropriate." R.I. Gen. Laws, § 42-87-4.

As the federal courts became more conservative in the 1980s and 1990s, there was more focus on State courts to protect the rights of the disadvantaged. Moreover, because, as has been stated, lobbying is often easier and more fruitful at the State level than at the federal level, there has been greater focus on getting State laws to protect the constitutional rights of minorities and the disadvantaged. As a result, many States have civil rights commissions or agencies with far-reaching power to investigate complaints and take action in behalf of individuals suffering discrimination. Going to court may, thus, not be necessary to protect one's civil rights.

6

Prosecution and Punishment of Adult Offenders

Social workers may play a variety of roles in the criminal justice system and may be involved in many stages of the criminal justice process. They may regularly work with clients referred by a criminal justice agency or they may be employed by a criminal justice agency, performing evaluative functions or providing service to clients for the agency. They may work behind the scenes or they may be witnesses in criminal hearings, particularly those involving children or mentally disabled defendants. They may also make recommendations that can be a major factor in determining what will happen to a criminal defendant.

Social workers who are not regularly connected with the criminal justice system may intervene in the criminal justice process to prevent further processing of clients or to help clients achieve favorable outcomes. Moreover, social workers may counsel clients who are going through the process, may work with victims of crime by helping them go through the process and cope with the trauma, and may counsel the families of those who are going through or have gone through the system. The families of criminal defendants and those serving time in jail or prison are often forgotten by the other participants in the criminal justice process.

Despite the potential range of the social worker's involvement in the criminal justice system, you may never be active participants in the process. Nevertheless, you should understand the criminal law and the criminal justice process for at least two reasons.

First, criminal prosecution imposes severe psychological and financial stress on the person being prosecuted as well as on the person's family. As has been noted, many of you, while not working in the criminal justice system, will work with individuals and families affected by criminal prosecution. By understanding the process, you can better appreciate your clients' situations and offer appropriate services.

Second, the criminal justice system is often used as a model when courts are attempting to determine the rights of an individual in another sort of proceeding in which you might be involved. A court may decide that a juvenile charged with being delinquent, persons who are being involuntarily committed to mental hospitals, parents whose children are being taken away, or many others who come before the courts are entitled to some or all of the rights accorded to criminal defendants. You should, thus, be familiar with these rights.

This chapter will review the basic principles of **substantive criminal law**, that is, the law defining and classifying criminal conduct, and of **procedural criminal law**, that is, the law establishing how criminal conduct will be prosecuted and punished. This chapter will then describe the criminal justice process, looking closely at the roles of social workers and the rights of the accused at each stage in that process. The chapter concludes by looking at the rights of those who have been imprisoned and the process for erasing convictions.

AN OVERVIEW OF CRIMINAL LAW

Criminal laws may be found at the federal, State, and local levels. There is a federal criminal justice system that enforces federal substantive criminal laws in accordance with federal procedural criminal laws; each State has a criminal justice system that enforces the State's substantive criminal laws in accordance with the State's procedural criminal laws; and many States have local criminal justice systems that enforce local substantive criminal laws in accordance with State or local procedural criminal laws.

Federal substantive criminal laws deal mainly with activities on federal property (e.g., post offices), with behavior that affects the national interest (e.g., treason), or with interstate or international actions (e.g., taking a kidnap victim across state lines or bringing narcotics into the country). In other words, federal substantive criminal laws deal with uniquely federal problems. Because such problems are limited in number, there are not many federal substantive criminal laws.

Local substantive criminal laws enacted by cities, counties, and other local governments generally deal with uniquely local problems (e.g., leash laws or noise limits). Again, because such problems are limited in number, there are not many local criminal laws.

Most substantive criminal laws are found at the State level. These laws generally encompass all of the behavior you might think of as criminal and may encompass problems that are also local or federal. That is, there may be an overlap between State and federal or local substantive criminal laws—and among State, federal, and local criminal laws. The possession or sale of narcotics, for example, may violate the criminal law of all three levels of government.

When there is an overlap, there may be questions as to which criminal justice system will handle the case. The federal criminal justice system is not considered to be "superior" to the State systems and will not automatically handle the case.

Instead, the federal and State criminal justice systems are considered to be parallel systems and decisions will be made as to which system will handle a given case based on principles of **comity**, that is, cooperation and courtesy. In some States, local criminal justice systems have the same relationship to the State system as the State system has to the federal system, that is, they are parallel systems, but, in most States, the local criminal justice systems are inferior to the State system. Nevertheless, it may be decided that a local criminal justice system should handle a case.

Federal criminal law, except for the criminal law found in the Constitution, is also not considered superior to State criminal law. But the Constitution contains a number of provisions that have direct bearing on the criminal law. Indeed, the Bill of Rights establishes the basic procedural protections found in the criminal law. Thus, the federal Constitution is extremely important in criminal law. State constitutions may also contain the basic procedural protections found in the Bill of Rights and other protections. Thus, they too are extremely important in criminal law.

Most criminal law is found in *legislation* enacted by Congress, State legislatures, and local legislative bodies. This is because it is believed that legislation provides the best notice to the populace of what behavior is criminal and how criminal behavior will be prosecuted and punished. It is further believed that elected representatives best express the majority's will on this important subject.

Because most criminal law is State law, most criminal law is found in State statutes. These statutes may be contained in a special criminal code, but statutes creating crimes may usually also be found in other codes and laws. For example, a juvenile code may contain a statute making a social worker's failure to report child abuse a crime.

Criminal law may also be found in regulations promulgated by federal, State, and local administrative agencies. Violating a regulation may be a crime that may be processed through the appropriate criminal justice system or by the administrative agency itself. For example, a violation of a federal regulation dealing with toxic waste disposal may be handled by the federal Environmental Protection Agency or may be prosecuted in a federal court.

Finally, criminal law may also be found in court decisions. Although most of the common law establishing which behavior is criminal has been replaced by statutes, and although courts may not create common law crimes in many States, courts may interpret statutes and regulations creating crimes, and procedural criminal law may, in large part, be common law.

BASIC PRINCIPLES AND CONCEPTS OF SUBSTANTIVE CRIMINAL LAW

What Is a Crime?

You, like most people, probably have an idea what behavior constitutes a crime. Legally, however, only conduct that is in violation of a law and that can result in prosecution and punishment by the government is a crime. Without a law forbidding a certain act, it is not a crime to commit the act—no matter how offensive you may consider the commission or omission. And unless a law authorizes

prosecution by the government and prescribes punishment for certain conduct, the prescribed conduct is not criminal—even if it is a violation of the law. Conduct may have severe consequences for the perpetrator, but these consequences will not include an accusation of criminal behavior and a criminal conviction—unless there is a law against the conduct and this law authorizes prosecution and punishment by a government.

To illustrate, suppose you are injured by a man who was driving while under the influence of prescription drugs. You may be able to sue him for damages, but he can only be charged with a crime if it is against the law to drive while under the influence of prescription drugs and if the law provides that one may be prosecuted and punished by the government for driving while under the influence of prescription drugs. A law providing only that it is against the law to drive while under the influence of prescription drugs and authorizing civil suits for damages for violating the law is not enough to make driving while under the influence of prescription drugs criminal. And even a law authorizing the government to take action against those who drive while under the influence of prescription drugs by, for example, suspending their driver's licenses, may not be enough to make a violation of the law a crime. Suspension of a driver's license may be sought in a civil suit and may not be considered punishment.

Sometimes, certain behavior can give rise to both civil and criminal suits. Even if driving while under the influence of prescription drugs is a crime and even if the government is criminally prosecuting a man who injured you while driving under the influence of prescription drugs, you would not be precluded from suing him. One government agency would not be precluded from bringing a civil suit to suspend his driver's license just because another government agency is criminally prosecuting him. It would not be considered double punishment if he was sent to jail and was forced to pay you damages or had his license suspended because neither paying compensatory damages nor losing one's license may be considered "punishment."

Societies differ in how they determine what behavior should be made criminal. In America, as we have said, by and large only elected representatives (or those to whom they have specifically delegated the authority) determine what behavior should be made criminal. When these elected representatives believe that certain behavior is wrong, that private efforts to control it are insufficient, and that the full authority of the government should be put behind the control effort, they will make the behavior criminal. But to be made criminal, behavior should not just be a private wrong. It should be considered a public wrong, that is, it should be viewed as harmful, not just to those who may be injured by it, but to the social order or to society as a whole. Indeed, certain behavior that may actually not injure anyone—except, perhaps, those who engage in the behavior—like prostitution, not wearing a seat belt, or gambling, may be made criminal because legislators consider the behavior as harming society as a whole.

There is substantial debate as to whether some or all crimes without victims, called **victimless crimes**, should exist and whether or not the government should, in effect, legislate morality. Attacks on such crimes as denials of substantive due process and invasions of the right to privacy, however, have generally been unsuccessful. For example, in *Bowers v. Hardwick,* 478 U.S. 186 (1987), the Supreme Court rejected a due process challenge to a law making sodomy between consenting adults a crime, stating: "The law . . . is constantly based on notions of morality, and if all laws representing essentially moral choices are to be invalidated under the Due Process Clause, the courts will be very busy indeed."

Elements of a Crime

All statutory definitions of crime, at a minimum, must set forth the *conduct* which is illegal, the *state of mind* one must have at the time of the conduct, and the *circumstances* which make the conduct illegal. These are known as the **elements of a crime**.

Criminal Conduct. There must be a specific act in order for there to be a crime.[1] Bad thoughts or being a bad person is not enough. In a case involving this principle,

---

1. Certain failures to act may be criminal. For example, it may be a crime for a social worker to fail to report suspected child abuse or for a parent to fail to provide medical care for a child. For simplicity, however, this text will discuss criminal conduct as if it consisted only of acts, not of omissions, unless the context requires otherwise.

It may also be criminal conduct to attempt to commit a criminal act, to assist in the commission of a criminal act (often referred to as **aiding and abetting**), or to help avoid prosecution for a criminal act (often referred to as being an accessory to a crime). Aiding and abetting a crime or attempting to commit a crime may be included within the definition of particular crimes or may be established as separate crimes. Similarly, conspiring with others to commit a crime may be a crime itself. For simplicity, this text will discuss crimes and criminal conduct as including attempts, aiding and abetting, being an accessory, and conspiracy.

Robinson v. California, 370 U.S. 660 (1962), the Supreme Court declared a California law making it a crime for a person "to be addicted to the use of narcotics" unconstitutional. The Court so held since the California law did not forbid specific antisocial conduct, but rather made a status, being addicted, illegal. The criminal act is often referred to as the ***actus reus.***

A Criminal State of Mind. To convict someone of a crime, it must be shown not only that he or she committed the illegal act but also that he or she did so in a state of mind appropriate for the imputation of responsibility. This state of mind is known as the ***mens rea***.

The *mens rea* of most crimes used to be a criminal or guilty intent. One had to intend to commit a crime or have an actual consciousness of guilt in order to be found guilty of most crimes. This requirement has now been abandoned for most crimes. One may now be found guilty of committing most crimes even if one did not intend to commit the crime or any other crime; it is enough if one intended to commit the act which is a crime. For a few crimes, it may even be enough if one did not intend to commit an act but acted recklessly or negligently.

Although the *mens rea* requirement may range from intent to commit the specific crime to negligent commission of an act, it is always necessary that the illegal act be voluntary and intentional. The intentional and voluntary quality of the illegal behavior is what makes it punishable. Even in those few cases where negligence or recklessness is a sufficient *mens rea,* one must still voluntarily intend to do what was done (e.g., reckless or careless driving).

How the *mens rea* requirement can differ for different crimes is illustrated by statutes involving **homicide**, that is, the killing of another person. If the killer deliberately with premeditation intended to kill the victim, a homicide may be considered a first degree murder; if there was an intent to kill, but no premeditation or deliberation, a homicide may be considered a second degree murder; if there was no intent to kill but there was an intent to harm the victim or another person, a homicide may be considered voluntary manslaughter; if a homicide was the result of an act performed recklessly, with no intent to kill or harm anyone, it may be considered involuntary manslaughter; and if a homicide was solely the result of negligence, there may be no crime. The different categories of homicide created by the different *mens rea* requirements may have different penalties. For example, murder may carry a sentence of death or a long minimum term in prison; voluntary manslaughter may carry a maximum sentence in prison that is less than the minimum sentence for murder; involuntary manslaughter may carry an even shorter maximum sentence; and reckless homicide may carry a still shorter maximum.

A **motive**, that is, a reason to commit a crime, is different than an intent to commit a crime, but a motive may be circumstantial evidence of an intent.

The Attendant Circumstances. Although there may have been criminal conduct and a criminal state of mind, there may not have been a crime unless certain circumstances accompanied the intent and the conduct or the conduct had a certain result. For example, although a woman may have intended to assault a man and did, in fact, assault him, she would not have committed the crime of "assault with a deadly weapon" unless she used something considered a deadly weapon and there could not be assault with intent to kill if the assault could not have had this result. The circumstances and result may also affect the degree of and punishment for a crime. For example, theft of something worth more than $500 could be grand theft, usually punishable by imprisonment of more than a year, while theft of something worth less than $500 could only be petty theft, usually punishable by imprisonment for a maximum of six months.

Classification of Crimes

Crimes are generally classified as either **felonies** or **misdemeanors**. Felonies are the more serious offenses. Most States distinguish between felonies and misdemeanors in terms of length or place of punishment. Usually a felony may be punished by incarceration for a year or more in a State prison, while the maximum punishment for a misdemeanor is a year in a local jail.

Some States also have **petty offenses** or **infractions**, which are minor crimes, like traffic offenses or violations of local laws, such as curfews. The prosecution process may be quite abbreviated and there may be few procedural protections for these minor crimes.

Defenses to Criminal Charges

A person who engages in criminal conduct with a required *mens rea* under the attendant circumstances may not be guilty of a crime if he or she has a **defense** to the crime. Defenses are of two types: they may justify or excuse a criminal act or they may make the act not criminal because they negate an element of the crime. Some defenses that may be important to social workers are explained below.

Self-Defense. A person who is in immediate danger of being harmed by another person's unlawful use of force is generally allowed to use force to ward off the attack. The law will specify when and how force may be used to defend oneself or when, in other words, one may claim self-defense. The law in most States will also specify when a person may use force to defend others from attack, to protect property, or to prevent the commission of a crime, or when, in other words, one may claim a defense related to self-defense. Generally, one may use only the minimum level of force that is reasonably necessary to prevent harm. Reasonableness may be assessed *subjectively*, that is, from the point of view of the accused, or *objectively*, that is, by considering what a reasonable person would do in the circumstances. Distinctions are often made between *deadly* and *nondeadly* force. A person generally has the right to use deadly force to defend oneself but not to defend others or to defend property and only if this amount of force is necessary to prevent severe bodily harm or death. Some States require those who can do so to retreat rather than to use deadly force.

Often the defense of self-defense, and the related defenses like defense of property or defense of others, are confused with the defenses of necessity or duress. These rarely used—and rarely successful—defenses excuse conduct when it was compelled by the circumstances or by a threat of grave harm.

Intoxication. The law generally does not relieve an individual of responsibility for crimes committed while voluntarily intoxicated, but involuntary intoxication (such as when a person has been tricked into consuming a substance, not knowing that it might result in intoxication) is generally a defense. Voluntary intoxication may operate as a defense, however, if the intoxication is such that it negates a required *mens rea*. For example, voluntary intoxication may be a defense to a charge of theft if the crime of theft requires a specific intent to steal and if a woman's intoxication was such that she could not form this intent. Further, in some circumstances, voluntary intoxication may be considered to reduce the seriousness of a charge or the punishment upon conviction.

Insanity. There has been considerable debate on the defense of insanity and no consensus on who should be entitled to claim a defense of insanity, how insanity should be defined, or even whether insanity should be a defense at all. Different jurisdictions have come to different conclusions on these questions. Basically all have allowed the insanity defense, but they have used different variations of one of four basic tests of legal insanity or have adopted a combination of two or more of the tests.

The traditional test, known as the ***M'Naghten* Rule**, is derived from an 1843 English case in which the House of Lords ruled that a criminal defendant is legally insane and not criminally responsible if: "at the time of the committing of the act, the party accused was laboring under

such a defect of reason, from disease of the mind, as not to know the nature and quality of the act he was doing, or if he did know it that he did not know he was doing what was wrong."

The *M'Naghten* Rule, often referred to as the "right-from-wrong test," has been used in some form by most States, but it has been criticized as not conforming with modern psychiatric concepts and for failing to recognize different degrees of insanity. It has also been argued that individuals who may be able to distinguish right from wrong may be unable to control their behavior because of their insanity. These individuals, it is argued, should be excused from criminal responsibility, but the *M'Naghten* Rule does not excuse them.

Some States have dealt with the last of these arguments by supplementing the *M'Naghten* Rule with the **Irresistible Impulse Test**. This test excuses one from responsibility where one is powerless to control one's behavior or where, in other words, an uncontrollable impulse compels one to commit the crime—even when one knows it is wrong to do so.

A few States have used the ***Durham* Rule**, so-called because it was adopted in the District of Columbia in the case of *Durham v. United States,* 214 F.2d. 863 (D.C. Cir. 1954). In *Durham,* the court stated that an accused is not criminally responsible "if an unlawful act is the product of mental disease or mental defect."

The *Durham* Rule was seen as too broad, however, and, in 1972, even the District of Columbia abandoned it in favor of a modified version of a test from the Model Penal Code, a criminal code drafted by law professors and other experts that was proposed for adoption by the States. This test, known as the **Sub-**

stantial Capacity Test, is now used in some form in most States. It provides that a person is not responsible for criminal conduct if: "at the time of such conduct as a result of mental disease or defect he lacks substantial capacity either to appreciate the criminality of his conduct or to conform his conduct to the requirements of law."

The Substantial Capacity Test is essentially a combination, modification, and broadening of the *M'Naghten* Rule and the Irresistible Impulse Test. Of great importance, the test does not require that a defendant be completely unable to distinguish right from wrong or completely unable to control his or her behavior; the defendant need only lack "substantial capacity" to do so.

Whatever the test, legal insanity is generally established through the testimony of expert witnesses, usually psychiatrists, who testify on the defendant's mental state at the time of the crime. Although the jury, or the judge if the case is tried without a jury, must ultimately decide if the defendant met the jurisdiction's test for legal insanity, the decision usually depends on the credence given to the psychiatric testimony. This testimony is necessarily based, at least to some extent, on guess-work since the psychiatric experts may first see the defendant a long time after the crime and since they have to reconstruct the events surrounding the crime. Moreover, psychiatry is hardly an exact science and psychiatrists can and do differ in diagnoses. Thus, in cases where the insanity defense is asserted, there is often a battle of the experts.

If the insanity defense is successfully asserted, defendants are found "not guilty by reason of insanity." This means they are cleared of all criminal charges, but, as we will see, they may be committed to an institution or required to undergo treatment under the civil law.

There is often public outcry against the insanity defense when a notorious defendant is found not guilty by reason of insanity, but there are, in fact, few successful assertions of the insanity defense. Nevertheless, some believe that this defense should be abolished, arguing, erroneously, that it is used to free dangerous people. Others emphasize that most criminals are somewhat unbalanced or that psychiatry is too far from an exact science to be relied on in making important decisions like guilt or innocence. Still others argue that the wealthy are able to pay for the testimony of psychiatrists in support of their defense, while the poor cannot.

Because of the arguments against the insanity defense, some States have replaced or augmented the "not guilty by reason of insanity" verdict with the "guilty but mentally ill" verdict or a similar verdict. Such verdicts generally mean that defendants can be held responsible for their conduct but will be treated or might be held in special facilities, such as a prison hospital or secure mental health facility.

The "not guilty by reason of insanity" verdict must be distinguished from the determination that an accused is **incompetent** or **unfit** to stand trial. Such a determination does not mean that a defendant is freed of criminal responsibility; it means only that a trial to determine criminal responsibility cannot be held because the defendant cannot understand the nature of the proceedings or participate in his or her own defense. The insanity verdict resolves the criminal action, while the unfitness determination only postpones it until such time as the defendant is competent to stand trial.[2] With the insanity defense, courts are concerned with a defendant's mental state at the time of commission of the crime, while with the competency determination, courts are concerned with the defendant's mental state at the time of trial. Decisions on insanity are made at the conclusion of a trial by a judge or jury, while decisions on competency are made before trial after a hearing on a pretrial motion by a judge.

There are, however, similarities between a not guilty by reason of insanity verdict and a determination of unfitness to stand trial. Most important, psychiatric experts are crucial to both decisions and, like those found not guilty by reason of insanity, those found unfit to stand trial may be released under the criminal law but may be held under the civil law if they pose a danger to themselves or others.

BASIC PRINCIPLES AND CONCEPTS OF PROCEDURAL CRIMINAL LAW

As we have stated, procedural criminal law is that part of the criminal law which establishes the process for prosecuting and punishing those accused and convicted of crimes. If the substantive criminal law is the "what," procedural criminal law is the "how."

Procedural criminal law attempts to balance the rights of persons accused of

committing crimes against society's need for safety and order. The balancing occurs through safeguards that historically have shaped our adversarial system and accusatorial process. In addition, the balancing has occurred through Supreme Court interpretation of constitutional requirements, particularly the Fourteenth Amendment's guarantee of due process.

Burden and Standard of Proof

The American legal system, as we have said, is an adversary system that uses an accusatorial process. This is particularly true in the area of criminal law. In a criminal case, the opposing parties are the **prosecution**, the State, federal, or local government entity which initiates and pursues criminal cases, and the **defendant**, the person who is accused of committing a crime by the prosecution.

As we have also said, the adversary system is only fair if each party has the capacity to present its case and if the parties' capacities are roughly equal. In the usual criminal case, however, the defendants may not have the capacity to present their cases because of poverty or another reason. And even when the defendants have the capacity, the prosecution may have so many resources it can simply overpower them. Thus, the criminal justice system has long been subject to various safeguards designed to ensure that the prosecution will not win a case simply because it has more money, more lawyers, and the investigative power of the government at its disposal and to ensure that defendants will not lose simply because they have no money, no lawyer, or no ability to investigate. The most im-

---

2. State law may provide, however, that if the defendant does not regain competency within a certain period of time or is determined to be unable to ever regain competency, charges must be dismissed.

portant safeguards are the requirements that the prosecution carry the burden of proof and that it establish proof beyond a reasonable doubt.

The accusation is viewed as no more than a statement of the belief of the accuser. It may not be assumed that the allegations are true simply because the government is prosecuting the case. Indeed, the accused is presumed to be innocent, a presumption that can only be rebutted by proof of guilt beyond a reasonable doubt.

Although the prosecution has the burden of proof, it is not required to prove the absence of all defenses. Some defenses are considered affirmative defenses that must be raised by defendants. Defendants need not always prove affirmative defenses, however. It is enough if they raise a reasonable doubt as to their guilt with their defenses. For example, insanity is generally considered an affirmative defense. Thus, the prosecution does not have to prove that defendants were sane at the time of the crime. But, to prevail with this defense, defendants do not have to prove they were insane. Rather, they merely must raise a reasonable doubt as to their sanity.

Due Process

Besides the presumption of innocence and the requirement of proof beyond a reasonable doubt, there are many other protections built into the criminal justice system to remedy the imbalance between the parties to a criminal case and to ensure that the innocent are not convicted. Many of these protections are found in the Bill of Rights. While the Bill of Rights only applies to the federal government, as was discussed in chapter 5, the Supreme Court has used the due process clause in the Fourteenth Amendment to incorporate most of these specific guarantees to the States. For example, through the process of incorporation, the Fourth Amendment's prohibition against unlawful search and seizure, the Fifth Amendment's privilege against self-incrimination, and the Sixth Amendment's guarantee of a jury trial and its right to counsel have been made applicable to the States. These and other specific constitutional rights made applicable to the States through the due process clause will be discussed more fully below.

Many other safeguards are not specifically required by the Bill of Rights, but have been derived from the due process clause. For example, in *Ake v. Oklahoma,* 470 U.S. 68 (1985), the due process clause was held to require that a State provide some indigent defendants with the assistance of psychiatrists if their sanity is likely to be an issue in their trials. We review *Ake* at some length because, in addition to demonstrating the use of the due process clause to ensure fairness in the criminal justice process, it may help you understand incompetency, the insanity defense, and the role of psychiatric expert witnesses in a criminal trial.

Ake was charged with murdering a husband and wife and wounding their two children. His behavior in jail and in court was so bizarre that the court ordered a psychiatric examination to assess whether Ake was competent to stand trial. The psychiatrist diagnosed Ake as a probable paranoid schizophrenic and recommended a further, prolonged psychiatric evaluation. The court committed Ake to a mental hospital for this further examination.

After Ake had been at the hospital a few weeks, a hospital psychiatrist reported to the court that Ake was not competent to stand trial. The court then held a competency hearing. It found Ake to be incompetent to stand trial, and ordered him committed to a mental hospital. Six weeks later, the same psychiatrist informed the court that Ake, who was heavily medicated, had become competent to stand trial. The criminal proceedings against him were then renewed.

Ake's attorney immediately informed the court that Ake wanted to raise an insanity defense and moved the court to appoint a psychiatrist to examine Ake as to his insanity at the time of the crime. Although Ake had been committed soon after the murders with which he was charged and had spent three months at the hospital, no inquiry had ever been made into his sanity at the time of the offense. As an indigent, Ake could not afford to pay for a psychiatrist. The court denied the motion.

Ake was tried for two counts of murder. His sole defense was insanity. Nevertheless:

> there was no expert testimony for either side on Ake's sanity at the time of the offense. The jurors were [told] that . . . Ake was to be presumed sane at the time of the crime unless **he** presented evidence sufficient to raise a reasonable doubt about his sanity at that time. If he raised such a doubt in their minds, the jurors were informed, the burden of proof shifted to the State to prove sanity beyond a reasonable doubt.

The jury rejected Ake's insanity defense, found him guilty on all counts, and sentenced him to death. The Supreme Court reversed the conviction, stating:

> This Court has long recognized that when a State brings its judicial power to bear on an

indigent defendant in a criminal proceeding, it must take steps to assure that the defendant has a fair opportunity to present his defense. This elementary principle, grounded in significant part on the Fourteenth Amendment's due process guarantee of fundamental fairness, derives from the belief that justice cannot be equal where, simply as a result of his poverty, a defendant is denied the opportunity to participate meaningfully in a judicial proceeding in which his liberty is at stake. Meaningful access to justice has been the consistent theme of [our] cases. We recognized long ago that mere access to the courthouse doors does not by itself assure a proper functioning of the adversary process, and that a criminal trial is fundamentally unfair if the State proceeds against an indigent defendant without making certain that he has access to the raw materials integral to the building of an effective defense. Thus, while the Court has not held that a State must purchase for the indigent defendant all the assistance that his wealthier counterpart might buy, it has often reaffirmed that fundamental fairness entitles indigent defendants to an adequate opportunity to present their claims fairly within the adversary system.

In this case we must decide whether, and under what conditions, the participation of a psychiatrist is important enough to preparation of a defense to require the State to provide an indigent defendant with access to competent psychiatric assistance in preparing the defense. Three factors [derived from *Mathews v. Eldridge,* 424 U.S. 319 (1976), discussed in chapter 5] are relevant to this determination. The first is the private interest that will be affected by the action of the State. The second is the governmental interest that will be affected if the safeguard is to be provided. The third is the probable value of the additional or substitute procedural safeguards that are sought, and the risk of an erroneous deprivation of the affected interest if those safeguards are not provided.

After noting the defendant's "obvious" and "uniquely compelling" interest in the accuracy of a criminal proceeding in which life and liberty are at stake and the

State's insubstantial interest in denying a defendant the ability to establish a defense to a criminal charge, the Court discussed the "pivotal role that psychiatry has come to play in criminal proceedings." The Court stated:

[T]he assistance of a psychiatrist may well be crucial to the defendant's ability to marshal his defense. [P]sychiatrists gather facts, both through professional examination, interviews, and elsewhere, that they will share with the judge or jury; they analyze the information gathered and from it draw plausible conclusions about the defendant's mental condition, and about the effects of any disorder on behavior; and they offer opinions about how the defendant's mental condition might have affected his behavior at the time in question. They know the probative questions to ask of the opposing party's psychiatrists and how to interpret their answers. Unlike lay witnesses, who can merely describe symptoms they believe might be relevant to the defendant's mental state, psychiatrists can identify the elusive and often deceptive symptoms of insanity, and tell the jury why their observations are relevant. Further, where permitted by evidentiary rules, psychiatrists can translate a medical diagnosis into language that will assist the trier of fact, and therefore offer evidence in a form that has meaning for the task at hand. Through this process of investigation, interpretation and testimony, psychiatrists ideally assist lay jurors, who generally have no training in psychiatric matters, to make a sensible and educated determination about the mental condition of the defendant at the time of the offense.

Psychiatry is not, however, an exact science, and psychiatrists disagree widely and frequently on what constitutes mental illness, on the appropriate diagnosis to be attached to given behavior and symptoms, on cure and treatment, and on likelihood of future dangerousness. Perhaps because there often is no single, accurate psychiatric conclusion on legal insanity in a given case, juries remain the primary factfinders on this issue, and they

must resolve differences in opinion within the psychiatric profession on the basis of the evidence offered by each party. When jurors make this determination about issues that inevitably are complex and foreign, the testimony of psychiatrists can be crucial and a virtual necessity if an insanity plea is to have any chance of success. By organizing a defendant's mental history, examination results and behavior, and other information, interpreting it in light of their expertise, and then laying out their investigative and analytic process to the jury, the psychiatrists for each party enable the jury to make its most accurate determination of the truth on the issue before them.

The foregoing leads inexorably to the conclusion that, without the assistance of a psychiatrist to conduct a professional examination on issues relevant to the defense, to help determine whether the insanity defense is viable, to present testimony, and to assist in preparing the cross-examination of a State's psychiatric witnesses, the risk of an inaccurate resolution of sanity issues is extremely high. With such assistance, the defendant is fairly able to present at least enough information to the jury, in a meaningful manner, as to permit it to make a sensible determination.

We therefore hold that when a defendant demonstrates to the trial judge that his sanity at the time of the offense is to be a significant factor at trial, the State must, at a minimum, assure the defendant access to a competent psychiatrist who will conduct an appropriate examination and assist in evaluation, preparation, and presentation of the defense.

This is not to say, of course, that the indigent defendant has a constitutional right to choose a psychiatrist of his personal liking or to receive funds to hire his own. Our concern is that the indigent defendant have access to a competent psychiatrist for the purpose we have discussed, and . . . we leave to the State the decision on how to implement this right.

The wide use of the due process clause to establish procedural protections in the criminal justice system from the 1960s to the 1980s slowed in the 1990s. In fact, in *Medina v. California,* 505 U.S. 437 (1992), while the Supreme Court observed that "fundamental fairness" remains the touchstone for due process rulings involving criminal procedure, the Court stressed that it has defined and should define those actions:

> that violate fundamental fairness very narrowly based on the recognition that beyond the specific guarantees enumerated in the Bill of Rights, the Due Process Clause has limited operation. The Bill of Rights speaks in explicit terms to many aspects of criminal procedure, and the expansion of those constitutional guarantees under the open-ended rubric of the Due Process Clause invites undue interference with both considered legislative judgment and the careful balance that the Constitution strikes between liberty and order.[3]

Screening and Diversion

Because those accused of crimes may be deprived of liberty—even though they are presumed innocent and may ultimately be found innocent—and because enduring a criminal prosecution is a great hardship even if one is not held in custody, many constitutional safeguards and statutory protections have been built into the early stages of the criminal justice process. Some of these safeguards and protections are designed to ensure that persons accused of crimes are not unduly deprived of liberty or made to suffer unduly as they move through the stages of the criminal justice process, while others are designed to move some persons accused of crimes entirely out of the criminal justice system. In other words, there are many screening devices

built into the various stages of the criminal justice process. As cases move through the process, they may have to be reviewed by a court and the prosecution may have to meet progressively higher burdens of proof to justify holding the accused in custody or moving the case to the next stage.

In *Gerstein v. Pugh,* 420 U.S. 103 (1975), the Supreme Court mandated such a screening device as a constitutional requirement. It held that, when a person is held in custody solely on the basis of a prosecutor's charge, the Constitution "requires a judicial determination of **probable cause** [i.e., some likelihood the accused is guilty] as a prerequisite to extended restraint of liberty following arrest." The method of making this judicial determination was left up to the States, but the Court specifically stated that an informal, nonadversary hearing would be constitutionally sufficient.

The Supreme Court has never held that the Constitution requires an evidentiary hearing or a finding of probable cause before an accused may be forced to go to trial if the accused is not held in custody. Indeed, in *Albright v. Oliver,* 510 U.S. 266 (1994), a divided Court rejected a claim that initiation of a prosecution without probable cause violated substantive due process. However, most States require review by a grand jury or an evidentiary hearing in front of a judge before a trial for a felony.

Screening devices, such as the hearing required in *Gerstein* or the requirement of grand jury review, remove some of those who are accused of crimes from the criminal justice process because the prosecution has insufficient evidence to proceed. Others are removed from the process, not because there is insufficient evidence, but because it is decided that prosecution is

---

3. The Court also expressly rejected the use of the *Mathews v. Eldridge* balancing process that was used in *Ake.*

inappropriate or that there are better ways to handle a case. In other words, a decision is made to **divert** them from the process.

Diversion can take place at a number of points in the process and can be a purely discretionary decision or may be required by a specific diversion law or program. It can be formal or informal. Informal diversion occurs whenever an official decides not to pursue a case whatever the reason for the decision. Formal diversion may occur in two different ways: 1) no arrest or formal charge may be made for a crime in exchange for the accused participating in some sort of formal diversion program; or 2) a trial on a formal charge is delayed on certain conditions. In the latter case, if the defendant satisfies the conditions, the charges will be dropped. Formal diversion may be purely discretionary or be required or suggested by a diversion law or program.

To illustrate the difference between discretionary and mandatory diversion and how formal and informal diversion may operate, consider a police officer who sees a highly intoxicated man walking down a street late at night. She may decide not to arrest him even though public intoxication is a crime in her State. This is discretionary and informal diversion. Alternatively, she may be required by a State statute to take him to a detoxification center rather than arresting him. This is mandatory diversion. In the absence of such a statute, she may decide to arrest him, but the prosecutor may exercise her discretion and informally divert him by choosing not to file any charges against him. Alternatively, the prosecutor may bring charges against him, but before trial, the judge may send the man to an alcohol abuse program, telling him the trial will be stayed and the charges will be dropped if the man participates in the program and is not arrested again for a year. The judge's actions may be purely discretionary, or may be required by law for this kind of case or this kind of defendant, in which case this would be considered mandatory and formal diversion.

THE CRIMINAL JUSTICE PROCESS FOR ADULT OFFENDERS

The criminal justice process for adults is described in the following sections and pictured in diagram 6.1, but this process is only an approximation of the process you may actually encounter. From the initial arrest to the final sentencing, a criminal case passes through numerous stages and numerous constitutional and statutory rights come into play. These stages and rights may vary from jurisdiction to jurisdiction and, even within jurisdictions, each court may have its own procedures. To complicate matters further, the stages and rights may vary within a jurisdiction or a court according to the severity of the offense. For example, a jury trial might not be allowed for petty offenses and the appointment of counsel might not be mandated for certain misdemeanors. Moreover, within a jurisdiction or a court, the stages do not necessarily occur in a set order in each case. For example, a defendant may be formally charged with an offense before she is arrested or she may be arrested and then formally charged. Finally, the criminal justice process is not a straight and narrow route with offenders steadily moving along until they have been convicted and served their sentences. The process is filled with numerous detours, roadblocks and escape hatches. At each

Diagram 6.1

THE CRIMINAL JUSTICE PROCESS

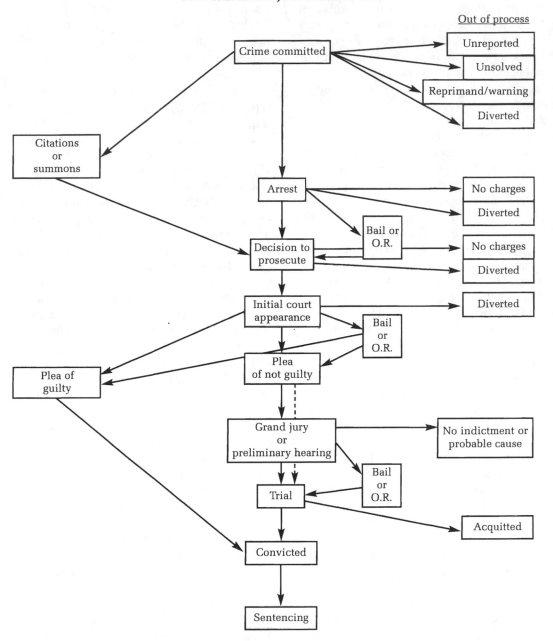

stage, officials may or must decide whether to advance a case to the next stage, reroute it, or terminate it and, as we have noted, various screening and diversion methods may operate to remove some from the process. Thus, not all defendants that begin the process complete it.

Nevertheless, there are similarities in the process everywhere and certain procedures and rights are constitutionally mandated in all jurisdictions. We shall focus on these similarities and mandates in our discussion of the stages of the process. As we review the stages of the process, it might be helpful for you to refer to diagram 6.1.

Investigation

Some of the procedural protections in the Constitution relate to the methods that law enforcement officers may use to investigate and solve crimes.[4] The Fourth Amendment provides several of these protections. It establishes a right to be free of "unreasonable searches and seizures" and requires that "**warrants**," that is, documents issued by judicial officers that authorize searches, arrests, or other law enforcement activities, be issued only with "**probable cause**."

The importance of the Fourth Amendment in protecting privacy is unquestioned, but its application has caused a number of problems and is subject to continuous debate. For example, warrants require *probable cause* but what does this mean? Further, searches and seizures without a warrant are not prohibited; only those that are *unreasonable* are prohibited, but what should be

considered unreasonable? Also, when the police search illegally, what should be done as a sanction? In particular, what should be done with evidence that is illegally obtained? Should offenders be let free because a vital piece of evidence was seized unreasonably without a warrant?

There is no clear definition of probable cause in the Fourth Amendment, but a working definition has emerged from the many cases on the subject. **Probable cause** to search is defined in terms of facts and circumstances that would lead a reasonable person to conclude that crucial evidence would be uncovered.

The Supreme Court has tried on numerous occasions to define what is meant by *reasonable* in the context of the search-and-seizure provisions of the Fourth Amendment. No clear definition has emerged but, in deciding each case, the Court has attempted to balance the needs of law enforcement with the right to privacy. The Court has required the police to obtain a search warrant before conducting a search if it is reasonably possible to do so. However, many searches without warrants are considered reasonable, such as searches of persons at the time of their arrests or searches of cars that may be easily moved.

Since 1914, federal courts have been required to exclude illegally seized evidence from criminal trials. Since 1961, the Supreme Court has required that such evidence also be excluded from criminal trials in State courts. This requirement, known as the **exclusionary rule**, is based on the argument that the government must not profit from illegally seized evidence and on the idea that the rule will deter the police from searching in violation of the Fourth Amendment. Many are opposed to the exclusionary rule, however, arguing

---

4. Henceforth, for simplicity, the term *police* will be used for all law enforcement officers.

that it has not been effective in deterring police misconduct and that it exacts a high price from society, that is, the release of the guilty. The Supreme Court has responded to such criticism by narrowing both the protections of the Fourth Amendment and the scope of the exclusionary rule, but the rule has not been eliminated.

A long-standing question of great importance to social workers is whether and how the Fourth Amendment applies to searches conducted by government agents other than the police for purposes other than criminal investigations, such as a home visit undertaken by a social worker employed by a public child protection agency to determine the conditions in a child's home.[5]

The courts have determined if warrants are required for such searches, often referred to as **administrative searches**, on a case by case basis. For example, in *Wyman v. James,* 400 U.S. 309 (1971), the Supreme Court held that a warrantless search to determine eligibility for welfare was constitutional, but made clear that all administrative searches conducted without a warrant, including some searches conducted to determine welfare eligibility, such as "midnight raids" to find men in welfare mothers' homes, would not necessarily be constitutional. The Court reiterated that "the specific content and

incidents of [the Fourth Amendment right to privacy] must be shaped by the context in which it is asserted."

If it is decided that the Fourth Amendment applies to a particular administrative search, it still must be determined if the search violated the Fourth Amendment and if so, if evidence uncovered as a result of the search should be subject to the exclusionary rule. The courts have not yet resolved whether such evidence should be excluded from all criminal proceedings or from noncriminal proceedings, such as juvenile hearings to determine if parental rights should be terminated.

Like the Fourth Amendment, the Fifth Amendment provides for an important procedural protection during the investigative stage of the criminal justice process. It provides that: "No person shall be compelled in a criminal case to be a witness against himself." Because of this guarantee, known as the guarantee against **self-incrimination**, criminal defendants may not be compelled to testify and witnesses in any type of proceedings may refuse to answer questions that would incriminate themselves (i.e., they can "take the Fifth"). This guarantee also protects those suspected of a crime from unfair interrogations and unwarranted confessions before any charges are made or after charges are made but before any court proceedings.

Historically, the admissibility of confessions into evidence hinged on their being voluntary rather than coerced. In the cases of *Escobedo v. Illinois,* 364 U.S. 478 (1964), and *Miranda v. Arizona,* 384 U.S. 436 (1966), the Supreme Court added that confessions obtained without notifying suspects of their right against self-incrimination could not be admitted into evidence. *Miranda* gave rise to the now fa-

---

5. Like other constitutional protections, the Fourth Amendment would not apply to a search by a private person unless there was some involvement by the state in the search, that is, state action. For example, the Fourth Amendment would probably not apply to a search by a social worker in private practice doing an investigation of the conditions of a child's home for a parent involved in a custody dispute but it might apply if the social worker had been asked to do the investigation for a court, as under the Colorado statute discussed in chapter 4.

miliar **Miranda warnings**: "You have a right to remain silent. Anything you say can be held against you in a court of law. You have a right to have a lawyer present. If you cannot afford a lawyer, one will be appointed to represent you." These warnings are routinely given to suspects by the police before they are questioned. If the *Miranda* warnings are not given or if suspects assert their rights after being given the warnings and the assertions of rights are ignored by the police, anything said by the suspects is subject to the exclusionary rule. The exclusionary rule in this context is intended to deter police from unfair and unreasonable interrogations.

The *Miranda* warnings include a notification of the right to have a lawyer present during the interrogation process and the right to have a lawyer appointed if the accused cannot afford one. The Supreme Court has emphasized this aspect of *Miranda* and has stated that *Miranda* is based, not only on the Fifth Amendment right against self-incrimination, but also on the Sixth Amendment right to counsel. The courts have, thus, concluded that requests to speak to someone other than a lawyer, such as a therapist, do not necessarily prevent the use in court of confessions taken after the requests have been made and ignored.

The courts have also concluded that *Miranda* may not apply if an individual is questioned by someone other than the police or is not in custody. For example, in *Minnesota v. Murphy*, 465 U.S. 420 (1984), without any *Miranda* warnings, a probation officer questioned a probationee about a rape and murder he had admitted to his drug counselor. The Court refused to exclude his confession to the probation officer, stating:

To dissipate the overbearing compulsion . . . caused by isolation of a suspect in police custody, the *Miranda* Court required the exclusion of incriminating statements obtained during custodial interrogation unless the suspect fails to claim the Fifth Amendment privilege after being suitably warned of his right to remain silent and of the consequences of his failure to assert it. We have consistently held, however, that this extraordinary safeguard does not apply outside the context of the inherently coercive custodial interrogations for which it was designed.

Thus, social workers employed by public agencies are probably not constitutionally required to give *Miranda* warnings even if they are questioning individuals about activities that might lead to criminal prosecutions, such as possession of illegal drugs or criminal child abuse. However, some kind of warning might be required by State law or might be advisable to ensure that any admission would not be excluded from evidence in a criminal or noncriminal proceeding.

Arrest and Booking

The criminal justice process typically begins with the arrest of a suspect by the police. The fact that a suspect to a crime is identified as a result of police criminal investigative techniques does not necessarily mean that an arrest will be made, however. As has been stated, the police may cite suspects and release them upon their promises to appear in court (i.e., give them **tickets, citations**, or **summons**) instead of arresting them, or may formally or informally divert suspects from the criminal justice process before any arrest.

Police diversion can take several forms. For example, a suspect may be released after a referral to a social services agency or upon a promise that the suspect will participate in a treatment program. To give another example, a suspect may not be arrested but may be involuntarily transported to a designated diversion center, such as a detoxification unit of a local hospital, or a suspect may be brought or referred to a formal screening or diversion program.

The range of programs or activities to which the police may divert offenders is extensive, as is the range of offenders who may be diverted. Social workers may be involved with all the different kinds of programs, activities, and offenders. In addition, many large police departments have special units, often employing social workers or using them as consultants, which work on certain kinds of cases, like domestic disputes or child abuse, or with certain kinds of people, like persons with mental disabilities or alcoholics. A police officer may refer a diversion decision to such a unit before or immediately after an arrest.[6]

Generally arrests are made by a police officer in the field without a warrant or a formal charge, but sometimes arrests are based on a warrant that authorizes or orders the police to take a person into custody as a suspect or to respond to a formal charge. Where there is a warrant, a police officer may have no discretion to divert.

Because arrests are considered "seizures" within the Fourth Amendment's protection from unreasonable searches and seizures, objections may be made to arrests without warrants or with warrants claimed to be improperly issued. As with searches and search warrants, the courts have struggled to make clear when an arrest warrant may be issued and when the police may arrest someone without a warrant consistent with the Fourth Amendment. Basically, arrest warrants, like search warrants, require probable cause and the police may arrest without a warrant when they have probable cause to believe a crime has been committed. Some States, by statute, under their common law, or pursuant to their constitutions, require more than probable cause to arrest for misdemeanors as opposed to felonies. These States may require that misdemeanors be committed in an officer's presence for a warrantless arrest to be legal.

There is no clear remedy when an arrest violates the Fourth Amendment. Confessions taken after unlawful arrests and evidence seized incident to such arrests may be excluded from evidence, but suspects may not be released from custody and freed of all charges simply because of the unlawfulness of their arrests.

A person who is arrested is taken to a police station for processing. Before going to the police station or before processing, a person may generally be searched. The processing generally consists of taking personal data and, where required, pho-

---

6.   These special units may perform other roles for the police. Much of the police role has nothing to do with crime fighting. Much police time is spent performing social service and order maintenance functions, such as aiding the elderly with health problems, dealing with potential suicides, or resolving domestic disputes. Social workers in special police units can assist in the police service role.

Social workers can also assist the police in this role and other roles outside of special units, as staff social workers or on a referral basis. Social workers can train the police in crisis intervention techniques or other social work skills. They can also make the police aware of community resources for assisting with behavior and social problems. Without this awareness, the police may respond in ways that are familiar to them. Since they are familiar with the arrest, they may use that tool even when other responses may be more appropriate.

tographing and fingerprinting. The word *booking* is often used to describe what is done to arrested persons, although booking is actually an entry in an arrest record and a minor part of the processing.

After processing, a person is either kept in custody, released on bail, or released on a promise to appear. A release without posting of bail is often called a release on one's **own recognizance** or O.R. The nature of the alleged offense determines whether and how one is released. In many jurisdictions, the police must release a suspect who posts bail in an amount set in a schedule of bail amounts for different offenses. In most jurisdictions, the police can make a discretionary decision to release less serious offenders without bail but with a promise to appear. Social workers may help the police make decisions about releasing suspects, including through formal O.R. programs.

After an arrest and processing, it is unlikely that informal police diversion will occur, but some big police departments have special units that screen cases for diversion after booking and, in some jurisdictions, referrals may or must be made to formal diversion programs after booking.

Charge

If there was no arrest warrant or formal charge before an arrest, the police cannot continue detaining a suspect indefinitely after processing has been completed. There must be a formal charge or warrant to justify continued detention. Booking for a particular offense is not the equivalent of such a charge.

Some jurisdictions provide that a suspect cannot be held for more than a set amount of time, like seventy-two hours, without a formal charge but others trust police discretion. No specific constitutional limitations on the amount of time a suspect can be held without a formal charge have ever been set.

Often, the police make formal charges for minor crimes, like traffic offenses, without making an arrest, as when a traffic ticket is issued and a suspect is released. If there has been an arrest, in some jurisdictions, the police may make a formal charge, but usually the police can only make a formal charge if the crime is a minor one. In most jurisdictions, if a crime is a serious one, the police are required to get a formal charge from the prosecuting attorney to continue holding the suspect.

Prosecutors have wide discretion in deciding whether and what criminal charges should be filed. A major consideration in making this decision is the strength of the evidence, but other factors may also play a role. The appropriateness of diversion for treatment, for example, may be considered. If there is a formal diversion law or program in a jurisdiction, the prosecutor's discretion to divert may be somewhat limited. Even where there are formal diversion programs, however, the prosecutor may usually decide which cases will be referred to the program.

Among the persons who may assist prosecutors in the exercise of their discretion at this stage of the criminal justice process are social workers who may be asked to evaluate the rehabilitation potential of a suspect or to make a recommendation on a diversion. Social workers may also work in the formal diversion programs that screen the accused at this stage.

In some jurisdictions and in the federal system, the prosecutor cannot make the formal charges in most or all felony cases. Rather, a **grand jury**, that is, a group of citizens selected to investigate crimes and make criminal charges, must make the charges. In other jurisdictions, prosecutors can make charges themselves or can elect to have a grand jury make them. This is because the Fifth Amendment requirement of a grand jury for "a capital, or otherwise infamous crime" has not been incorporated into the due process clause of the Fourteenth Amendment and, thus, has not been applied to the States.

If a grand jury makes a charge, it is generally called an **indictment**. A prosecutor's charge may also be called an indictment, but commonly is called a **complaint**. Other terms, like **information** are also used for prosecutors' or police charges. Sometimes, in serious cases, an information of the prosecutor or the police must be approved by a court after a hearing to determine if there is sufficient evidence to formally charge the accused. Such a hearing is usually a more effective screening device than a grand jury.

In some jurisdictions, the victim or complaining witness must sign, join in, or otherwise agree to a complaint. Sometimes, social workers counsel victims who are reluctant to sign complaints, such as in domestic violence cases.

Initial Appearance

A person who has been arrested and **detained** (i.e., kept in custody) must be brought before a judge without unnecessary delay for an initial appearance. Even with formal charges, suspects may not be detained for an indefinite period of time without bringing them before a court. However, the length of time that suspects can be held without appearing before a court has never been definitely established. As with detention before a formal charge, State statutes may set forth the length of time one may be held before being brought before a judge, but no specific time has ever been required constitutionally.

The initial appearance may have different names depending on the charge and the jurisdiction. It is commonly called an **arraignment**. Defendants who have not been detained and even those who have not been arrested but have been cited to court will also have arraignments. The arraignment is usually the accused's first encounter with the court for an alleged offense.

At this initial appearance, defendants are given formal notice of the charges, advised of their rights, and asked to enter a plea to the charges. In some jurisdictions, however, a formal felony charge may not be made and a plea may not be entered at the initial appearance.

A plea may be *guilty, not guilty, not guilty by reason of insanity,* or **nolo contendere**. This last plea means the defendant will not contest the charge but does not admit it. A plea of guilty or *nolo contendere* waives the defendant's right to a trial.

It is quite common for petty offense and misdemeanor defendants to plead guilty at the initial appearance and to be sentenced immediately. Thus, the initial appearance may be their only courtroom encounter.

Bail

Bail is frequently set at the initial appearance. Although, as has been noted, in some jurisdictions there are bail schedules that permit the police to set and take bail before any appearance in court, usually bail schedules cannot be used for more serious crimes and often the bail amounts on the schedules are quite high. Moreover, bail schedules are not binding on judges. Thus, even in jurisdictions with bail schedules, defendants who are arrested and detained seek to have bail set at the initial appearance (or to be released without bail).

The Eighth Amendment prohibits "excessive" bail. While it would seem that this means that bail must be granted to all defendants, the Eighth Amendment has been interpreted not to give a right to bail but only to prohibit excessive bail if bail is granted. Many States do not allow bail for serious charges, such as murder, or for charges carrying long sentences. Moreover, the amount that is considered excessive has never been defined so that bail can be set in such a high amount that it realistically cannot be paid.

It is generally agreed that the purpose of bail is to ensure that those who have been released from custody while they are awaiting trial will appear at their trials. There are those who believe that bail should be set at a high amount or should be denied to keep dangerous defendants in custody and, thus, prevent them from committing other crimes. Despite the presumption of innocence, the constitutionality of this practice, known as **preventive detention**, was upheld in *United States v. Salerno,* 481 U.S. 739, (1987).

The most common form of bail is a cash bond. For felony defendants, bail may be set at amounts that range from $1,000 to over $500,000. Because most defendants do not have that much money, they hire a bail bondsman who, in return for a 10 to 15 percent nonrefundable fee, will post bond. Some States and the federal courts permit the defendant to post the bondsman's usual percentage with the court. This eliminates the unfairness of a nonrefundable fee. Whether posting actual bail or paying a bondsman's fee, payments generally must be in cash. Sometimes, courts will accept some other form of security, like a deed on a house.

A judge may also be willing to release defendants without bail simply on their promise to return to court, that is, on their own recognizance. Defendants may be released on O.R. even for serious offenses if they are viewed as unlikely to flee because they have strong ties to the community or are supporting a family. A court may require a report from a court officer, who is sometimes a social worker, before agreeing to O.R. for serious offenses.

Defendants who cannot pay the bail or the bond fees or who do not qualify for release on recognizance must await trial in jail. Many defendants are detained for long periods in overcrowded jails awaiting trial. To address this problem, several jurisdictions have established recognizance or bail projects, sometimes employing social workers, to help courts obtain information that can enable them to release more defendants on recognizance or to make better bail decisions. As has been stated, even without a formal project, court service workers, who may be trained social workers, often help courts in the recognizance or bail decision.

Securing a Defense Attorney

The Sixth Amendment guarantees criminal defendants the right to assistance of counsel. In *Gideon v. Wainwright*, 372 U.S. 335 (1963), the Court interpreted this guarantee to mean that felony defendants not only are entitled to have an attorney present at their trials but also are entitled to have one appointed to represent them if they cannot afford to pay a lawyer. After *Gideon*, the Supreme Court extended the right to appointment of counsel for felony defendants to all stages of the criminal justice process it considered "critical," including the investigation stage. Moreover, the Court has held that defendants charged with misdemeanors with a possible penalty of jail time are also entitled to appointment of counsel. State statutes in many States provide for further rights to appointment of counsel.

Most criminal defendants cannot afford to hire a lawyer. To illustrate, in 1992, 80 percent of defendants charged with felonies in the country's seventy-five largest counties relied on a court-appointed attorney for legal representation, and in 1991, approximately 75 percent of State prison inmates and 50 percent of federal prison inmates reported they had court-appointed attorneys.[7]

While the Supreme Court has mandated appointment of counsel for defendants accused of felonies and many misdemeanors, it has not specified how courts are to provide the required representation. As a result, different jurisdictions have developed different approaches, but most have used one or a combination of three approaches: **public defender, assigned counsel**, and **contract attorney**. Public defender programs are publicly funded private law firms or, more, commonly, public agencies with salaried staff attorneys who represent all criminal defendants requiring court-appointed attorneys in a particular jurisdiction. Assigned counsel systems involve the appointment by the courts of attorneys in private practice from a list of available attorneys on an as needed basis. With contract attorney systems, courts contract with private attorneys, law firms or bar associations to provide services for a specified dollar amount for a specified time. Public defender programs are the most common approach for urban areas.

Social workers can and do perform many functions as part of the defense team, particularly in public defender offices. For example, as has been noted, social workers may gather information to justify defendants' release on recognizance or can help with plea bargaining by arranging for sentencing alternatives. Social workers may also help defense attorneys interview and prepare witnesses and defendants for the ordeal of trial and may interpret sentencing reports for attorneys or offer sentencing alternatives to courts after convictions. Because of these and other roles as part of the defense team, social workers have been employed in public defender offices for over seventy years and their employment in such offices has been recommended by several commissions.

Preliminary Hearing

The **preliminary hearing**, known as a **preliminary examination** or a **probable cause hearing** in some States, is a screen-

---

7. Smity S.K. & DeFrances, C.J., "Indigent Defense," *Bureau of Justice Statistics Selected Findings* (NCJ–158909) (U.S. Government Printing Office 1996).

ing device designed to protect defendants against unwarranted prosecutions. At the preliminary hearing, a judge will evaluate the strength of the evidence against the accused and determine if there is sufficient evidence to bring the defendant to trial.

As has been stated, a preliminary or probable cause hearing is only constitutionally required when the defendant is kept in custody, but many States require such hearings by statute for all felony cases whether or not the defendant is in custody. Generally, there are no preliminary hearings statutorily required in misdemeanor cases and defendants accused of misdemeanors are usually not kept in custody so that a hearing is not constitutionally required.

Sometimes, the grand jury is used as a substitute for a preliminary hearing, but, because an accused does not have an opportunity to be heard before a grand jury, a preliminary hearing may be required even where there is a grand jury indictment.[8]

Plea Bargaining

Whatever the initial plea, the great majority of criminal defendants ultimately plead guilty. Not all of these pleas are the result of a deal or a bargain with the prosecutor, but many are. And even when a case has gone to trial, it is likely that plea bargaining occurred—albeit unsuccessfully.

Plea bargaining is pervasive. While many question its propriety, it has been recognized and accepted by the courts as a basic part of the criminal justice system. For example, see *Bordenkircher v. Hayes,* 434 U.S. 357 (1987); and *United States v. Mezzanatto,* 513 U.S. 196 (1995).

Plea bargaining is conducted differently in different jurisdictions and the participants may vary. Some judges are active participants; others may refuse to take part. The nature of the bargain also varies widely. In some instances, the defendant pleads guilty to a less serious charge than the one initially charged (e.g., simple robbery rather than armed robbery) or to one or more of the counts in return for a dismissal of others, but there is no agreement as to a sentence. In another type of plea bargain, the defendant admits guilt to the crime as charged or to another crime in return for a specific sentence.

Social workers sometimes assist defense attorneys with plea bargaining by arranging for alternative sentences for defendants, such as treatment in a residential drug abuse center. These alternative sentences can be offered to the prosecution.

Trial

The Sixth Amendment guarantees criminal defendants a "speedy" and "public" trial. The word *speedy,* however, has never been defined. Moreover, the Supreme Court has recognized that the defendant's interest in a speedy trial may be in conflict with other interests of society as well as with other interests of the defendant. It has, thus, not established rigid time requirements for trials but rather has adopted a balancing test designed to give judges guidance in determining when the right to a speedy trial has been violated. State statutes may,

---

8. As has been stated, the Fifth Amendment's requirement of a grand jury has not been incorporated into the due process clause and, thus, does not apply to the States.

however, set the maximum time period between a charge or arrest and a trial for all crimes, for certain types of crimes, or when the defendant is in custody.

The right to a public trial is based on the assumption that if justice is done in the open, courts will act according to the law. The press may also assert the public's right to know what is happening in the courts. As with the matter of speed, however, the Supreme Court has recognized that there may be circumstances when the need for a public trial has to be balanced against other interests. For example, in trials for sex crimes, particularly when the victim is a minor, courts have temporarily barred the public to spare embarrassment to the parties involved and to make witnesses more comfortable.

The Sixth Amendment also guarantees a right to an "impartial jury" in all criminal cases. Nevertheless, in some criminal cases, there is no right to a jury. Just as the Eighth Amendment's prohibition on excessive bail does not guarantee release on bail, the Sixth Amendment's right to an impartial jury does not guarantee a defendant a jury—only an impartial jury if there is a jury. The Supreme Court has, however, ruled that defendants who are charged with serious offenses with a possible sentence of more than six months in jail are entitled to a jury. In other rulings, the Supreme Court has said that the size of the jury is left up to the State and that unanimous verdicts are not required in any criminal trial. State laws generally specify when a criminal defendant has a right to be tried by a jury, the size of the jury, and whether a jury verdict must be unanimous—of course, within constitutional guidelines.

The requirement that juries be impartial usually means that jurors must be representative of the community. Various methods are used to select juries to ensure such representativeness. Also, the Supreme Court has forbidden the systematic exclusion of jurors based on race or gender, stating in *J.E.B. v. Alabama ex rel.* T.B., 511 U.S. 127 (1994), that "discrimination in jury selection, whether based on race or gender, causes harm to the litigants, the community, and the individual jurors who are wrongfully excluded from participation in the judicial process." However, the Court implied that discrimination on other grounds could be acceptable.

Whether or not there is a jury, the rules of evidence and of procedure of a jurisdiction control the conduct of a trial. The rules of evidence may be stricter in criminal trials to protect the rights of the accused. For example, hearsay may be more restricted in criminal trials than in civil trials because of the constitutional right to confront one's accusers.[9]

If there has been a jury trial, at the conclusion of the presentation of evidence and any argument, the judge will instruct the jurors on the applicable law and the jurors will retire to deliberate in secret. As in a civil case, the jury's decision is known as a **verdict**. If its verdict is guilty or if the judge decides the defendant is guilty in a bench trial, the judge enters a judgment of **conviction**.[10] If the jury's or judge's verdict is not guilty, there will be a judgment of acquittal.

---

9. However, in criminal prosecutions for child abuse, hearsay rules may be relaxed and social counselors may often testify as to what a child has said to them.

10. There will also be a judgment of conviction entered where there has been a plea of guilty or *nolo contendere*.

The **double jeopardy** guarantee in the Fifth Amendment means that a person charged with a criminal act can be subjected to only one trial for that act in the same jurisdiction. Thus, if a criminal defendant is acquitted rather than convicted, the prosecution may not retry the defendant and may not appeal. But the prohibition against double jeopardy may not always rule out successive prosecutions for an illegal act that violates the law in two jurisdictions or that constitutes two distinct offenses. Furthermore, the double jeopardy guarantee does not rule out a civil and a criminal trial for the same act. Thus, in the Rodney King case, the officers could be tried in federal court after they were acquitted in State court and O.J. Simpson could be tried civilly for wrongful death after his acquittal of murder charges.

Sentencing

If a defendant is found guilty or has pleaded guilty with no agreement as to the sentence, the question of the appropriate sentence arises. A criminal sentence can serve for different purposes: deterence, that is, the imposition of the sentence might deter others from committing a similar crime; retribution; punishing one for an offense; protection of society by isolating or removing offenders; and rehabilitation, that is, assisting offenders to reform. The appropriate sentence may depend on which purposes are paramount. The only constitutional stricture at this point is the Eighth Amendment prohibition of "cruel and unusual punishment." Because social workers may play a significant role in discretionary sentencing decisions and in working with defendants after they have

sentenced, it is important for you to understand the sentencing process.

In a few States, primarily in the South, the jury may decide on the sentence, but, usually, except for the imposition of the death penalty, sentencing is left up to the judge. Judges traditionally had considerable discretion in sentencing, but, beginning in the 1980s, there has been a movement to lessen or eliminate this judicial discretion, particularly for serious offenses or repeat offenders. Nevertheless, for most crimes in most jurisdictions, the law only specifies a minimum or maximum sentence and a court may turn to a social service professional for advice in sentencing.

The traditional sentencing options, whether chosen by a judge in his or her discretion or set forth in a law as a mandate or a maximum, include:

- *Probation.* A specific period of supervision is required, but the defendant is not held in custody. The supervision may range from minimal to extensive and may be combined with a requirement of counseling or treatment.

- *Suspended sentence.* A specific time in custody is required, but the imposition of the sentence is suspended if the defendant fulfills certain conditions (e.g., drug treatment) or, more commonly, does not have further problems with the law.

- *Fine.* The defendant must pay a certain amount of money to the court or into a special fund.

- *Community service.* The defendant is required to perform a certain number of hours of work for the benefit of the community.

- *Restitution.* The defendant must pay compensation to the victim of the crime.
- *Split sentence.* A short time in custody is combined with an extended period of probation.
- *Work release or periodic imprisonment.* The defendant is sentenced to serve time in jail but only on weekends or only at night so that he or she may work or look for work.
- *Imprisonment or incarceration.* The defendant is sentenced to serve a term in jail or prison.
- *Capital punishment.* The defendant is sentenced to death.

Frequently, more than one of these options are chosen or mandated. That is, they are used in combination. For example, a common sentence for a serious misdemeanor would be probation, a suspended sentence, and a. fine. A short jail sentence is also often combined with a long period of probation or a long suspended sentence.

Some courts have experimented with alternative sentences beyond these traditional sentencing options, such as chemical castration for sex offenders or bumper stickers or apologies in newspapers for drunk drivers; some legislatures have required or allowed such alternative sentences; and some social agencies have developed pilot programs to propose alternative sentences to judges. Certain alternative sentences, however, may be argued to violate the Eighth Amendment prohibition on cruel and unusual punishment.

It should be noted that **jails** and **prisons** are differentiated in criminal justice terminology. Jails are local institutions used to detain all those who are awaiting their initial court appearance, trial, or sentencing. Jails are also used to incarcerate those who have been convicted of misdemeanors and occasionally felonies. Prisons, on the other hand, are State or federal institutions used only to incarcerate those who have been convicted of felonies. Usually, jail sentences cannot exceed one year while prison sentences are for at least one year. Because of the short time generally spent in jails and because of the combination of serious offenders awaiting trial and minor offenders serving short sentences, jails, unlike prisons, rarely have organized rehabilitation or training programs.

You should also note that **probation** is different from **parole**. In some jurisdictions, inmates may be released or paroled from jail or prison after they have served a certain minimum term or a certain portion of the term to which they have been sentenced. Parole decisions may be made by jail or prison officials or special parole agencies. Usually, those who are paroled must have a period of supervision in the community much like probation except it occurs after being incarcerated. The period of supervision is usually for the remainder of the term.

If there is no parole in a jurisdiction, there usually is a system of **good-time**. With a good-time system, inmates get credit for time served without problems or disciplinary actions. When a one day good-time credit is given for each day served without problems, the usual formula, inmates with clean records will be released after serving one half of their sentences.

In some jurisdictions, **mandatory** sentencing laws require judges to give defendants convicted of certain crimes specific sentences prescribed by law. For example, those convicted of drunk driving may have to serve a jail sentence, while prison may be mandatory for certain serious crimes or if certain circumstances exist (e.g., the defendant used a gun when committing the crime or the defendant committed a third felony). Under **determinate** sentencing laws, also called mandatory sentencing laws in some jurisdictions, a judge may or may not have discretion to decide whether or not to imprison defendants, but if the judge decides to imprison a defendant, the judge has little discretion and must sentence the defendant to a term set by the legislature or within a narrow range set by the legislature. If there are aggravating or mitigating circumstances, the judge may raise or lower the sentence, but only according to a fixed formula. The federal system now uses such a determinate. sentencing system under which judges are required to follow strict **sentencing guidelines**. By way of contrast, with **indeterminate** or **discretionary** sentencing laws, whether or not a judge has discretion to decide if certain defendants should be imprisoned, the judge has discretion in setting the length of the jail or prison term within a broad range, above any minimum, or below any maximum set by the legislature.[11]

Whether or not sentencing to jail or prison is mandatory, and whether the length of the sentence is determinate or indeterminate, parole authorities may have discretion to parole sentenced defendants.

There has been substantial debate over which is the best type of sentencing law. The trend, however, is toward mandatory and determinate sentencing for the most serious crimes, if not for all felonies. Further, several States have enacted "three strike" laws making a life sentence mandatory for a third serious offense or "truth in sentencing" laws requiring that criminals serve a substantial portion (such as at least 85 percent of their sentence).

There has also been considerable debate on the death penalty. Those who oppose it have used the Eighth Amendment's prohibition against cruel and unusual punishment as a vehicle to challenge it. In *Furman v. Georgia,* 408 U.S. 238 (1972), the Supreme Court ruled that the death penalty, because it was so "capriciously" administered, was cruel and unusual "in the same way that being struck by lightning is cruel and unusual."

After *Furman,* many States passed laws designed to maintain the death penalty by removing the arbitrary aspects of the proceedings. Some of these laws were invalidated, but many have been upheld. The Supreme Court has now made clear that capital punishment is permissible as long as there are standards to guide the judge's or jury's discretion and procedures to ensure against arbitrary and discriminatory imposition of the death sentence. The Court also made clear in *Penry v. Lynaugh,* 492 U.S. 302 (1989), that executing a mentally retarded defendant who was competent to stand trial is permissible and further made clear in *Stanford v. Kentucky,* 492 U.S. 361 (1989), that executing a minor defendant is permissible.

---

11. It should be noted that in some jurisdictions sentencing is called determinate, whether or not judges have discretion in setting prison terms if sentences are for a fixed term (e.g., seven years), while in some jurisdictions sentencing is called indeterminate, again whether or not judges have discretion, if sentences are for a range (e.g., three to fifteen years).

While capital punishment is still prohibited or rare in many States, from 1976 to 1994, 257 persons were executed in twenty-four States, primarily in Texas and four other States in the South.[12]

Increasingly, victims of crimes are being given the right to address the court at the time of sentencing, including in capital cases. While it had been argued that victims' statements would impermissibly prejudice a jury, particularly in capital cases, in *Payne v. Tennessee,* 501 U.S. 808 (1991), the Supreme Court allowed such statements, holding that if the defendant is allowed to present mitigating factors, a jury should be allowed to consider the impact of the defendant's actions on the victim's family in order to "assess meaningfully the defendant's moral culpability and blameworthiness."

When a judge has discretion in sentencing—and even when a judge has little or no discretion—a judge may ask or be required to ask for a presentence report prepared by a probation officer or court service worker. To the extent that a sentence is intended to serve the goal of rehabilitation or to keep dangerous defendants out of the community, a judge may have little expertise or training to make the sentencing decision. Further, the judge knows relatively little about defendants except for what was revealed in any hearings. Judges may not have defendants' official criminal records or may have records that are inaccurate or incomplete. The presentence report provides the necessary information to make a good

sentencing decision. At a minimum, the presentence report will contain the defendant's criminal record, a brief social history, and a description of the defendant's present employment and living situation, but the range and nature of the information received by a judge can vary widely, as is made clear by 18 U.S.C., § 3661, which provides: "No limitation shall be placed on the information concerning the background, character and conduct of a person convicted of an offense which a court of the United States may receive and consider for the purpose of imposing an appropriate sentence."

The form of presentence reports and the weight given to them by a judge also vary from jurisdiction to jurisdiction and from court to court. The educational qualifications of those who prepare presentence reports similarly varies, but often they are prepared by trained social workers.

The collection, interpretation, and presentation of information about the defendant in the presentence report is a major social service role in the criminal justice process, but the role of the social worker in corrections is also important. Social workers may work in prisons, jails, in alternative sentencing settings, or in treatment programs for convicted offenders. Social workers may provide counseling or treatment in these settings or may perform evaluative functions, such as determining whether offenders who are sentenced to prison should be sent to maximum or minimum security institutions or when they should be paroled. Social workers are also employed to do planning for inmates after their release and may work as probation or parole officers, supervising them after their release.

---

12. Stephan, J.J. & Snell, T.L. "Capital Punishment 1994," *Bureau of Justice Statistics Bulletin* (NCJ-158023) (Washington, D.C.: U.S. Government Printing Office 1996)

THE RIGHTS OF PRISONERS

For many years, no rights of prisoners were established.[13] In a series of cases beginning in the 1970s, however, the Supreme Court ruled that conviction of a crime and incarceration should not lead to a forfeiture of all constitutional rights, and that prisoners should keep those rights that were not inconsistent with their status as prisoners or with legitimate correctional objectives. See *Bell v. Procunier,* 417 U.S. 817 (1974), *Bell v. Wolfish,* 441 U.S. 520 (1979). Following the Supreme Court's lead, the courts provided prisoners with a wide variety of substantive and procedural rights. For example, prisoners were given rights to practice their religion and to communicate with outsiders pursuant to the First Amendment and were given freedom from undue restraint and excessive use of seclusion pursuant to the due process clause. Further, the courts repeatedly found that the conditions in or practices of a prison or prison system were such that confinement in the prison or the system constituted cruel and unusual punishment in violation of the Eighth Amendment. For example, in *Estelle v. Gamble,* 429 U.S. 97 (1977), the Supreme Court held that a prison's deliberate indifference to serious medical needs of prisoners is an "unnecessary and wanton infliction of pain" proscribed by the Eighth Amendment. Prison overcrowding, which threatened personal security and deprived inmates of rights to privacy through such mechanisms as double-celling, was frequently condemned and the courts required prisons to provide inmates with basic necessities and humane conditions. Indeed, during the 1970s, the courts found more than one hundred correctional institutions to have unconstitutional conditions of confinement and subjected them to sweeping orders related to the conditions of confinement and inmates' rights.

Prisoners' rights were always limited by the need to maintain order in the prisons and by a recognition that prisoners were, after all, convicted criminals who were being subjected to punishment. Nevertheless, the conditions of confinement for prisoners greatly improved in the 1970s because of the courts' intervention. This intervention, however, was limited in the 1980s by a series of cases in which the Supreme Court restricted the use of 42 U.S.C. § 1983 to challenge prison conditions or denied prisoners due process protections. For example, see *Parratt v. Taylor,* 451 U.S. 527 (1983); *Hudson v. Palmer,* 468 U.S. 517 (1984); and *Daniels v. Williams,* 474 U.S. 327 (1986).

The new approach of the Supreme Court towards prisoners' rights is typified by *Hudson v. Palmer,* in which the Court held that prisoners have no Fourth Amendment right to privacy in their cells and that their cells can be searched and their private property seized without regard to Fourth Amendment guarantees. The Court stated:

> We have repeatedly held that prisons are not beyond the reach of the Constitution. No

---

13. Hereafter, for convenience, the term *prisoner* will be used to refer to convicted criminals in any type of correctional institution and the term *prison* will be used to refer to all types of correctional facilities, including jails. You should note that, because of the presumption of innocence, the rights of those accused of crimes who are imprisoned while awaiting their trials may be greater than the rights of those who are imprisoned after conviction. These greater rights will not be discussed.

"iron curtain" separates one from another. Like others, prisoners have the constitutional right to petition the government for redress of their grievances, which includes a reasonable right of access to the courts. Prisoners must be provided reasonable opportunities to exercise their religious freedom guaranteed under the First Amendment. Similarly, they retain those First Amendment rights of speech not inconsistent with [their] status as . . . prisoner[s] or with the legitimate penological objectives of the corrections system. They enjoy the protection of due process. And the Eighth Amendment ensures that they will not be subject to "cruel and unusual punishments." The continuing guarantee of these substantial rights to prison inmates is testimony to a belief that the way a society treats those who have transgressed against it is evidence of the essential character of that society.

However, while persons imprisoned for crime enjoy many protections of the Constitution, it is also clear that imprisonment carries with it the circumscription or loss of many significant rights. These constraints on inmates, and in some cases the complete withdrawal of certain rights, are justified by the considerations underlying our penal system. The curtailment of certain rights is necessary, as a practical matter, to accommodate a myriad of institutional needs and objectives of prison facilities, chief among which is internal security. Of course, these restrictions or retractions also serve, incidentally, as reminders that under our system of justice, deterrence and retribution are factors in addition to correction.

Prisons, by definition, are places of involuntary confinement of persons who have a demonstrated proclivity for antisocial criminal, and often violent, conduct. Inmates have necessarily shown a lapse in ability to control and conform their behavior to the legitimate standards of society by the normal impulses of self-restraint; they have shown an inability to regulate their conduct in a way that reflects either a respect for law or an appreciation of the rights of others. Within this volatile community, prison administrators are to take all necessary steps to ensure the safety of not only the prison staffs and administrative personnel, but also visitors . . . [and] the inmates themselves.

A right of privacy in traditional Fourth Amendment terms is fundamentally incompatible with the close and continual surveillance of inmates and their cells required to ensure institutional security and internal order. We are satisfied that society would insist that the prisoner's expectation of privacy always yield to what must be considered the paramount interest in institutional security. We believe that it is accepted by our society that [l]oss of freedom of choice and privacy are inherent incidents of confinement.

There has not, however, been the complete retreat from protection of prisoners' rights in the 1990s that many feared. For example, in *Hudson v. McMillan,* 503 U.S. 1 (1992), the Supreme Court held that the use of excessive force against a prisoner could violate the Eighth Amendment even if the prisoner did not suffer serious injury, and in *Helling v. McKinney,* 509 U.S. 25 (1993), the Court held that a prisoner's claim that a prison violated the Eighth Amendment by subjecting him to high levels of second-hand smoke could state a claim under 42 U.S.C. § 1983 if the prisoner could establish "deliberate indifference" by prison officials to his health. Quoting a case holding social workers liable for failing to protect a child who had been removed from his home because of parental abuse, the Court stated:

When the State takes a person into its custody and holds him there against his will, the Constitution imposes upon it a corresponding duty to assume some responsibility for his safety and general well-being. . . . The rationale for this principle is simple enough: when the State by the affirmative exercise of its power so restrains an individual's liberty that it renders him unable to care for himself, and at the same time fails to provide for his basic human needs—e.g., food, clothing, shelter, medical care, and reasonable safety—it transgresses the substantive limits on state action set by the Eighth Amendment.

In *Farmer v. Brennan,* 511 U.S. 825 (1993), the Supreme Court again recognized prisoners' rights to personal safety and reinstated the case of a diagnosed transsexual who claimed he was subjected to rapes and beatings when incarcerated with other males. The Court, however, held that prison officials cannot be found liable under the Eighth Amendment simply for denying an inmate humane conditions of confinement. Deliberate indifference was necessary and such indifference cannot be tested objectively. The official must: "[know] of and [disregard] an excessive risk to inmate health or safety; the official must both be aware of facts from which the inference could be drawn that a substantial risk of serious harm exists, and he must also draw the inference." This is a difficult standard for an inmate to meet.

CLEARING CRIMINAL RECORDS

A person who has been convicted of a crime, particularly of a felony, may lose various civil rights, like the right to vote or hold public office. Also a conviction, or even an arrest, may affect a person's ability to get employment, to get credit, or to get other benefits or privileges you may take for granted. For these reasons, social workers' clients who have been convicted of crimes, or even those who have been arrested but not convicted, may seek to have their records cleared.

A **pardon** will clear the record but is generally a purely discretionary act by the chief executive officer of the jurisdiction where the crime was committed, and is difficult to obtain. Further, there may be no procedures established to get a pardon.

There may be clear procedures established to obtain an **expungement**, that is, an erasure, of a criminal record, but one may only obtain expungement if one meets the criteria set forth in an expungement law. These criteria may severely limit the opportunity for expungement.

Records may be **sealed**, that is, closed to the public, but if one's record is sealed rather than expunged, one must admit convictions and arrests when asked in most circumstances and convictions may be brought up in subsequent cases. Further, the criteria for sealing records may also be stringent.

One should have no record of a conviction if one has been diverted but the record of the arrest may remain. If diversion occurs formally pursuant to a statute, often the record of the arrest is expunged or sealed.

7

Adjudication and Treatment of Juvenile Offenders

This chapter reviews the juvenile justice process for youthful offenders, comparing and contrasting it to the criminal justice process for adult offenders. Despite increasing seriousness and violence of juvenile crime and punitiveness towards juvenile offenders, society seems reluctant to totally abandon the idea of special juvenile courts and the rehabilitative ideal of the juvenile court movement. Thus, the need for evaluation and treatment of youthful offenders continues and social workers continue to play vital roles in the juvenile justice system.

Many social workers choose to work with youthful offenders. These social workers perform evaluation and treatment functions in probation offices, youth correctional systems, private and public social service agencies that serve youth, and even in private practice. Perhaps, as important, many social workers choose to work with children who have been abused or neglected. These social workers often find they are working, not only in the child welfare system, but also in the juvenile justice system for two primary reasons. First, many youths who are in the custody of public child welfare agencies because of neglect or abuse commit criminal offenses and, thus, are involved in delinquency actions. Second, many judges place delinquents in the care of public child welfare agencies or place them in child care and treatment facilities rather than correctional facilities because they believe the possibility for rehabilitation is higher when a youth is in a program geared towards child protection rather than correction.

JUVENILE COURT ACTS

Since Illinois enacted a statute establishing special courts for youths charged with committing crimes in 1899, all of the States have enacted similar statutes and have expanded the scope of the statutes to address not only children whose behavior is criminal or troublesome but also children whose parents or guardians cannot or will not care for them. In other words, these State statutes are designed both to protect society from youthful crime and to protect youth in need of intervention.[1]

The names of the State statutes that establish either special courts or special procedures to hear cases involving children differ from State to State, but many are simply called **juvenile court acts**. This book will use this term. The names and structure of the special courts or procedures also vary from State to State. For example, in New York, family courts operate as juvenile courts; in California, any higher level trial court may sit as a juvenile court; in Illinois, special departments of the general trial courts employ special procedures for cases under the Illinois ju-

---

1. You should note that when we refer to the *State* in this chapter, unlike elsewhere in this book, we are not including local governments within the State. This is because there is virtually no law relating to youthful offenders or the protection of children at the local level. Indeed, the vast body of the law is at the State level. There are some federal laws designed to assist the States when they act to protect children or address juvenile crime and there are also some federal laws on the procedures to follow in the federal courts when a juvenile has violated a federal criminal statute. There are, however, no federal laws that would allow other children in need of intervention to be brought before federal courts and the treatment and protection of children is not undertaken by the federal government.

venile court act; and in Michigan, there is a juvenile division of the probate court. However, in these and other States there are usually specially appointed court officers, who may or may not be called judges, who handle juvenile cases on a full or part time basis. This book will refer to all special courts for youth or all courts employing special procedures for cases involving youth as **juvenile courts**.

In addition to the differences in the names and structure of juvenile courts from State to State, there are differences in terminology and details of juvenile court acts. Nevertheless, all juvenile courts and juvenile court acts are essentially similar. All of the acts authorize the State to intervene in the family in three instances: 1) when a child has committed a crime; 2) when a child has been neglected or abused; and 3) when a child has no parent able to care for him or her. The juvenile courts have jurisdiction over all cases in which it is asserted that a youth falls into one of these categories. In addition, some juvenile court acts allow juvenile court intervention when a child's behavior is thought to be dangerous or injurious to his or her own welfare (e.g., if the child is a habitual truant). In some States, this behavior is merged with category one, while in others it is merged with category two.

States differ in the labels they assign to the categories, the precise definitions of the categories, and the age limits for children within each category. Most commonly, children who fall into the first category are called **delinquents**. This book will use this term.

We will look at the processes established by the juvenile court acts for delinquents in this chapter and at the processes for children falling into the latter two categories in chapters 8 and 9.

WHO IS DELINQUENT?

The juvenile court acts in the various States typically define a delinquent as a minor who has violated any federal, State, or local criminal law. The acts in all the States further specify that the juvenile courts have the **exclusive jurisdiction** to determine if a minor is a delinquent, that is, if a minor has committed a criminal offense. In other words, only juvenile courts, not regular criminal courts, can try minors for criminal conduct. There are, however, exceptions to this exclusive jurisdiction.

First, many States establish a maximum age for juvenile court jurisdiction on the basis of delinquency that is less than eighteen years of age, the age of legal majority. For example, the maximum age is fifteen in New York. Thus, sixteen- and seventeen-year-old juveniles who are alleged to have committed crimes in New York will be tried as adults.

Second, the juvenile court acts all provide that certain juveniles who are within the age for exclusive juvenile court jurisdiction may or must be prosecuted as adults. To illustrate, the juvenile court act in Illinois provides that no minor who was under the age of seventeen at the time of committing an alleged offense may be prosecuted under the criminal laws *except* in certain specific circumstances set forth in the act. For example:

- *Any* juvenile *may* be prosecuted as an adult for an alleged *traffic* violation.

- A juvenile court *may* enter an order permitting prosecution as an adult for the violation of a State criminal law if a juvenile is *thirteen years or older* and the court has determined that "it is *not in the best interests* of the minor or of the public" to try the minor under the juvenile court act.

- A juvenile court *must* enter an order permitting prosecution as an adult if a juvenile is *fifteen years or older* and is alleged to have committed a forcible felony and if the court finds that the juvenile has previously been adjudicated delinquent for commission of a gang-related felony.

- If a juvenile is *fifteen years or older* and is charged with certain serious crimes, such as murder, aggravated sexual assault or robbery armed with a gun, or with certain drug offenses on school grounds or in public housing, the juvenile *must* be charged as an adult. 705 ILCS § 405/5-4.

As you can see from these examples, in Illinois prosecution as an adult might be mandatory or discretionary and might or might not require a determination by the juvenile court depending on the situation and the age of the juvenile. Prosecution as an adult occurs for minor offenses because it is not considered necessary to invoke the jurisdiction of the juvenile court and it occurs for certain very serious offenses because it is not considered appropriate to invoke the jurisdiction of the juvenile court.

As in Illinois, typically, juvenile court acts provide that juveniles can be tried in either juvenile or adult court for minor offenses. In addition to traffic violations, minor offenses may include violations of city or county ordinances, like curfew laws, or even violations of certain State criminal statutes, like those relating to graffiti or shoplifting. Generally, a delinquency action will not be pursued unless the juvenile has offended several times or the particular conduct is considered particularly serious.

Also as in Illinois, all juvenile court acts provide that a juvenile court may transfer a delinquency case to adult court, or, in other words, **waive** its exclusive jurisdiction over the case, when, because of the seriousness of the crime, it would not be in the best interests of the juvenile or society to remain in juvenile court or because the juvenile is not seen as amenable to special treatment in the juvenile court. This situation must be distinguished from the situation where juveniles under the maximum age for delinquency in a jurisdiction are automatically prosecuted as adults for certain serious crimes, as is also done in Illinois. In the case of waiver, the juvenile court has jurisdiction but makes a discretionary decision that the case is not appropriate for juvenile court action and releases its authority, while in the case of automatic prosecution as an adult, because of the statutory definition of delinquency, the juvenile court never has jurisdiction. In the former situation, a case begins by initiating a delinquency action in the juvenile court. In the latter situation, a case begins by filing a criminal complaint in the adult court. This is often called **direct filing**. Because of its importance, we will look at waiver in greater depth below.

Before looking at waiver, you should note that, as has been stated, some States include within the category of delinquents those juveniles whose behavior, even if it is not criminal, is troublesome or may be injurious to themselves or others. For example, California places within the jurisdiction of the juvenile court any minor who is a habitual truant or "who persistently or habitually refuses to obey the reasonable and proper orders or directions of his or her parents, guardian, or custodian, or who is beyond the control of that person, or who . . . [has] violated any ordinance of any city or county of this state establishing a curfew based solely on age." Cal. Welfare & Institutions Code § 601.

This group of minors, who may be referred to as **predelinquents** or **status offenders**, are processed like delinquents but may not be housed in the same facilities with delinquents.

WAIVER TO ADULT COURT

In *Kent v. United States*, 383 U.S. 541 (1966), the Supreme Court recognized the serious consequences of waiver to adult court and set forth the due process requirements before a delinquency case may be waived. Kent concerned a sixteen year old, charged with housebreaking, robbery, and rape, who had been waived to adult court by the juvenile court judge.[2] Kent contended that waiver was invalid because, among other things, no hearing was held, no findings were made by the judge, and the judge stated no reasons for the waiver. The

Court agreed that the waiver was invalid, stating:

> The provision of the Juvenile Court Act governing waiver . . . reads as follows: "If a child sixteen years of age or older is charged with an offense which would amount to a felony in the case of an adult, or any child charged with an offense which if committed by an adult is punishable by death or life imprisonment, the judge may, after full investigation, waive jurisdiction and order such child held for trial under the regular procedure of the court which would have jurisdiction of such offense if committed by an adult." [T]he statute contemplates that the Juvenile Court should have considerable latitude within which to determine whether it should retain jurisdiction over a child or—subject to the statutory delimitation—should waive jurisdiction. But this latitude is not complete. At the outset, it assumes procedural regularity sufficient in the particular circumstances to satisfy the basic requirements of due process and fairness, as well as compliance with the statutory requirement of a full investigation. The statute . . . does not confer upon the Juvenile Court a license for arbitrary procedure. The statute does not permit the Juvenile Court to determine in isolation and without the participation or any representation of the child the critically important question whether a child will be deprived of the special protections and provisions of the Juvenile Court Act. It does not authorize the Juvenile Court . . . without any hearing or statement or reasons, to decide . . . that the child will be taken from [a juvenile facility] and transferred to jail along with adults, and that he will be exposed to the possibility of a death sentence instead of treatment for a maximum, in Kent's case, of five years, until he is 21.

The theory of the District's Juvenile Court Act, like that of other jurisdictions, is rooted in social welfare philosophy rather than in the *corpus juris* [that is, literally, the body of the law]. Its proceedings are designated as civil rather than criminal. The Juvenile Court is theoretically engaged in determining the needs of the child and of society rather than adjudicating criminal conduct. The objectives are to

---

2.   The offenses occurred in the District of Columbia, which has its own juvenile court act and its own court system separate from other federal courts.

provide measures of guidance and rehabilitation for the child and protection for society, not to fix criminal responsibility, guilt, and punishment. The State is *parens patriae* rather than prosecuting attorney and judge. But the admonition to function in a parental relationship is not an invitation to procedural arbitrariness.

It is clear beyond dispute that the waiver of jurisdiction is a critically important action determining vitally important statutory rights of the juvenile. The statutory scheme makes this plain. The Juvenile Court is vested with original and exclusive jurisdiction of the child. This jurisdiction confers special rights and immunities. He is, as specified by the statute, shielded from publicity. He may be confined, but with rare exceptions he may not be jailed along with adults. He may be detained, but only until he is 21 years of age. The court is admonished by the statute to give preference to retaining the child in the custody of his parents unless his welfare and the safety and protection of the public can not be adequately safeguarded without . . . removal. The child is protected against consequences of adult conviction such as the loss of civil rights, the use of adjudication against him in subsequent proceedings, and disqualification for public employment.·

The net, therefore, is that petitioner—then a boy of 16—was by statute entitled to certain procedures and benefits as a consequence of his statutory right to the exclusive jurisdiction of the Juvenile Court. In these circumstances, considering particularly that decision as to waiver of jurisdiction and transfer of the matter to the [adult] Court was potentially as important to petitioner as the difference between five years' confinement and a death sentence, **we conclude that, as a condition to a valid waiver order, petitioner was entitled to a hearing, including access by his counsel to the social records and probation or similar reports which presumably are considered by the court, and to a statement of reasons for the Juvenile Court's decision.** We believe that this result is required by the statute read in the context of constitutional principles relating to due process and the assistance of counsel.

As a further protection for juveniles whose waiver is sought, the Supreme Court ruled in *Breed v. Jones,* 421 U.S. 519 (1975), that transferring a juvenile to adult court for prosecution after an adjudication of delinquency violates the Fifth Amendment protection against double jeopardy.

Despite these constitutional barriers to waiver and the preference for juvenile court treatment, as expressed in *Kent,* more and more juveniles are being tried in adult court. This is due not only to more waivers but also to revisions in the juvenile court acts of many States lowering the age at which the juvenile court has jurisdiction over minors and providing for automatic prosecution as adults for certain minors committing certain serious crimes. Both actions are in response to the fact that juveniles can and do commit very serious crimes; to the view that the juvenile court, as a court under the **parens patriae authority**, not the police power, is not an appropriate place to deal with such crimes; and to increased emphasis on public safety.

The increasing provisions for automatic prosecution of certain minors as adults without any hearing do not violate the due process guarantees set forth in *Kent.* As stated by the Illinois Supreme Court in *People v. J.S.,* 103 Ill.2d.395, 469 N.E.2d 1090 (1984), *Kent* imposed due process protections to limit the discretion of the judge, but the Illinois's automatic prosecution law does "not leave room for disparity in treatment between individuals within its proscription. All 15- and 16-year-olds who have committed the enumerated offenses . . . are to be prosecuted in the adult criminal court system. There is no discretionary decision to be made by the juvenile court, and therefore we do not believe that . . . *Kent* is dispositive . . . ."

You should note that, while the discussion of waiver up to this point assumes that a juvenile would not wish to be prosecuted as an adult, the juvenile court acts in some States allow the juvenile to request waiver, and some of these acts further provide that if a request is made, the court must grant it.

Why would a juvenile ask to be tried as an adult? First, a juvenile who is tried as an adult for serious crimes has a constitutional right to trial by jury. As we will see, a juvenile who is tried in the juvenile court does not have a constitutional right to a jury. Second, although it is generally the rule that a juvenile tried in adult court, if convicted, will have a criminal record and will be sentenced as if he or she were an adult, it is possible that a sentence imposed after conviction as an adult might be less severe than a disposition following adjudication as a delinquent. For example, a fourteen-year-old girl convicted of vandalism as an adult is likely to be placed on probation and ordered to clean up and repair the damage or to make restitution. Any sentence would be served quickly, and the girl would then be free of the court's jurisdiction. However, if she were found to be delinquent on the basis of the vandalism, she might be removed from the custody of her parents and committed to a correctional institution for several years. She could remain under the jurisdiction of the court until she was eighteen years old, or even older in some States.

For serious crimes, it is unlikely that sentencing as an adult would be less severe or onerous. However, in most States, juveniles convicted as adults will not be held in the same facilities as adults. Instead, they will be held in juvenile facilities or special facilities for young offenders until they have reached the age of majority or older. And, although *Kent* observed that a juvenile tried in adult court under District of Columbia law at the time could be subjected to the death penalty, it is not necessarily true that the death penalty may be imposed on a juvenile.

In *Thompson v. Oklahoma,* 487 U.S. 815 (1988), the Supreme Court held in a plurality opinion that the death penalty could not constitutionally be imposed on a juvenile who was fifteen years old at the time of the crime. The Court observed that only eighteen State legislatures had established a minimum age for the death penalty, but all of these legislatures "require that the defendant have attained the age of at least 16 at the time of the capital offense." It further observed that prosecutors have been reluctant to ask for the death penalty in cases involving juveniles under age sixteen and that juries have been reluctant to impose it, a fact that led the Court "to the unambiguous conclusion that the imposition of the death penalty on a 15-year-old offender is now generally abhorrent to the conscience of the community." The Court stated:

> Although the judgments of legislatures, juries, and prosecutors weigh heavily in the balance, it is for us ultimately to judge whether the Eighth Amendment permits imposition of the death penalty on [the juvenile before us] who committed a heinous murder when he was only 15 years old. In making that judgment, we first ask whether the juvenile's culpability should be measured by the same standard as that of an adult, and then consider whether the application of the death penalty to this class of offenders measurably contributes to the social purposes that are served by the death penalty.

The Court has already endorsed the proposition that less culpability should attach to a crime by a juvenile than to a comparable crime committed by an adult. The basis for this conclusion is too obvious to require extended explanation. Inexperience, less education, and less intelligence make the teenager less able to evaluate the consequences of his or her conduct while at the same time he or she is much more apt to be motivated by mere emotion or peer pressure than is an adult. The reasons why juveniles are not trusted with the privileges and responsibilities of an adult also explain why their irresponsible conduct is not as morally reprehensible as that of an adult.

[In *Gregg v. Georgia,* 428 U.S. 153 (1976), we said:] "The death penalty is said to serve two principal social purposes: retribution and deterrence of capital crimes by prospective offenders." [W]e concluded that as "an expression of society's moral outrage at particularly offensive conduct," retribution was not "inconsistent with our respect for the dignity of men." Given the lesser culpability of the juvenile offender, the teenager's capacity for growth, and society's fiduciary obligations to its children, this conclusion is simply inapplicable to the execution of a 15-year-old offender.

For such a young offender, the deterrence rationale is equally unacceptable. With respect to those under 16 years of age, it is obvious that the potential deterrent value of the death sentence is insignificant for two reasons. The likelihood that the teenage offender has made the kind of cost-benefit analysis that attaches any weight to the possibility of execution is so remote as to be virtually nonexistent. And, even if one posits such a cold-blooded calculation by a 15-year-old, it is fanciful to believe that he would be deterred by the knowledge that a small number of persons his age have been executed in the 20th century. In short, we are not persuaded that the imposition of the death penalty for offenses committed by persons under 16 years of age has made, or can be expected to make, any measurable contribution to the goals that capital punishment is intended to achieve.

A year later, however, in *Stanford v. Kentucky,* 492 U.S. 361 (1989), a different plurality upheld the death penalty for two juveniles who were sixteen and seventeen years old at the time of the crime, stating: "We discern neither a historical nor a modern societal consensus forbidding the imposition of capital punishment on any person who murders at sixteen or seventeen years of age. Accordingly, we conclude that such punishment does not offend the Eighth Amendment's prohibition against cruel and unusual punishment."

Nevertheless, the Supreme Court made clear in *Johnson v. Texas,* 509 U.S. 350 (1993), that youth must be considered by a jury or judge in deciding whether or not to impose the death penalty, even in the case of a nineteen year old. The Court stated:

> There is no dispute that a defendant's youth is a relevant mitigating circumstance that must be within the effective reach of a capital sentencing jury if a death sentence is to meet the requirements [of our cases]. Our cases recognize that youth is more than a chronological fact. It is a time and condition of life when a person may be most susceptible to influence and to psychological damage. A lack of maturity and an underdeveloped sense of responsibility are found in youth more often than in adults and are more understandable among the young. These qualities often result in impetuous and ill-considered actions and decisions. A sentencer in a capital case must be allowed to consider the mitigating qualities of youth in the course of its deliberations over the appropriate sentence.[3]

---

3. However, see *McCollum v. North Carolina,* 512 U.S. 1254 (1994), in which the Supreme Court refused to take a case allowing the death penalty to be imposed on a youth who was nineteen at the time of the crime and who "is mentally retarded[,] . . . has an IQ between 60 and 69, and the mental age of a 9-year-old."

THE JUVENILE JUSTICE PROCESS

The juvenile court process in cases of delinquency is outlined in diagram 7.1. You should refer to this diagram as you read the following section. You should also refer to diagram 6.1, setting forth the criminal justice process, and compare the two processes.

As with the discussion of the criminal justice process, juvenile court processes may vary from jurisdiction to jurisdiction and from case to case. In fact, there may be more differences between the generalized process we describe and the actual process for a particular case for juvenile offenders than for adult offenders because with juvenile offenders there are more screening devices, and discretionary diversion decisions are far more likely.

Taking a Juvenile into Custody

If it is thought that a juvenile has committed a criminal act that could make him or her a delinquent, his or her first encounter with the juvenile justice system will probably be with a police or other law enforcement officer in the field.[4] In some States, a police officer may not be authorized to make a decision concerning a juvenile except to re-

lease him or her with no action taken or to take him or her into custody where a decision on further action will be made by a special juvenile or probation officer. In most States, however, an officer in the field can additionally release a juvenile suspected of committing a crime on a promise to appear before a special juvenile or probation officer who is authorized to make a decision on how to proceed.

Even if a decision is made to take a juvenile into custody, whether for further processing by the officer in the field or for referral to a special officer, the juvenile is not considered to have been "arrested." Because juvenile court proceedings are considered to be civil and because, at least in theory, society does not wish to stigmatize juvenile offenders, it is said that the police merely take juveniles "into custody" or "detain" them. This use of special terminology is important to the juvenile offender, who, as an adult, can honestly assert, "I have no arrest record."

Juveniles who are taken into custody are entitled to full *Miranda* rights, including the right to remain silent and to have an attorney present during questioning. These rights may not fully protect juveniles, as explained in a dissenting opinion in *Fare v. Michael C.,* 442 U.S. 707 (1979). In *Fare,* the Supreme Court refused to consider a juvenile's request to talk to his probation officer during a police interrogation as an assertion of *Miranda* rights which would stop an interrogation as would a request for a lawyer. The dissenting opinion points out the serious problems with this decision.

> In *Miranda,* this Court sought to ensure that the inherently coercive pressures of custodial

---

4. Hereafter, this discussion relates only to juveniles who would be within the exclusive jurisdiction of the juvenile court absent a decision to waive jurisdiction or who would be in either the jurisdiction of the juvenile or adult courts for minor offenses. In other words, this discussion does not address the process for juveniles who must be tried in adult court because of their age and their alleged offense.

Diagram 7.1

The Juvenile Justice Process

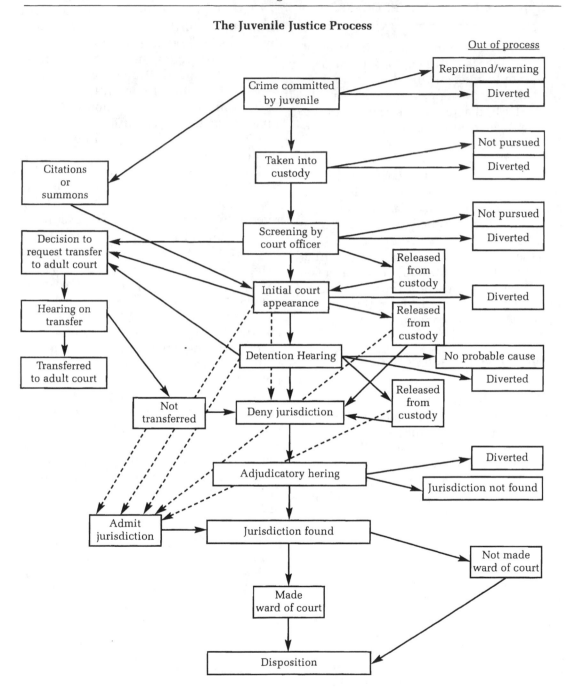

interrogation would not vitiate a suspect's privilege against self-incrimination. Noting that these pressures can operate very quickly to overbear the will of one merely made aware of his privilege, the Court held:

> "If [a suspect in custody] indicates in any manner, at any time prior to or during questioning, that he wishes to remain silent, the interrogation must cease. At this point he has shown that he intends to exercise his Fifth Amendment privilege; any statement taken after the person invokes his privilege cannot be other than the product of compulsion, subtle or otherwise. If the individual states that he wants an attorney, the interrogation must cease until an attorney is present."

As this Court has consistently recognized, the coerciveness of the custodial setting is of heightened concern where, as here, a juvenile is under investigation. [For example, this Court recognized in one case] that because a 15½ year old minor was particularly susceptible to overbearing interrogation tactics, the voluntariness of his confession could not be judged by the more exacting standards of maturity [and this Court observed in another case] that a 14-year-old suspect could not be compared with an adult in full possession of his senses and knowledgeable of the consequences of his admissions.

It is therefore critical . . . that we construe *Miranda*'s prophylactic requirements broadly to accomplish their intended purpose—dispel[ling] the compulsion inherent in custodial surroundings. To effectuate this purpose, the Court must ensure that the protective device of legal counsel be readily available, and that any intimation of a desire to preclude questioning be scrupulously honored. Thus, I believe *Miranda* requires that interrogation cease whenever a juvenile requests an adult who is obligated to represent his interests. Such a request, in my judgment, constitutes both an attempt to obtain advice and a general invocation of the right to silence. For, it is fatuous to assume that a minor in custody will be in a position to call an attorney for assis-

tance, or that he will trust the police to obtain a lawyer for him. A juvenile in these circumstances will likely turn to his parents, or another adult responsible for his welfare, as the only means of securing legal counsel. Moreover, a request for such adult assistance is surely inconsistent with a present desire to speak freely. Requiring a strict verbal formula to invoke the protections of *Miranda* would protect the knowledgeable accused from stationhouse coercion while abandoning the young person who knows no more than to ask for the . . . person he trusts.

The Decision to Detain

If juveniles are taken into custody, just as they are not "arrested," they are not "booked." Rather, **intake** or the equivalent is done. Again, the use of special terminology stems from a desire to protect juveniles. After intake is completed, essentially three options are available: 1) juveniles may be released to their parents or legal guardians without any referral to the juvenile court; 2) juveniles may be released but their cases may be referred to the juvenile court; or 3) juveniles may be detained.[5] If juveniles are detained, their cases must be referred to the juvenile court.

The decision as to which option may have to be made by a special youth police officer, not the officer who took a juvenile into custody. In addition or alternatively, a probation officer, who may be a trained social worker, may or must make these decisions. For example, in Illinois, a specially designated youth officer must first see a juvenile who has been taken into custody, and if the juvenile is not to be immediately released, a probation officer

---

5. Hereafter, in this chapter the term *parents* will be used to refer to both parents and legal guardians.

must screen the case. In many jurisdictions, the whole intake process occurs, not at a police station (except perhaps for the initial stages) or a jail, but at a juvenile hall or special youth detention center.

Whoever makes the decision, a decision to detain a juvenile may be based on the likelihood that the juvenile would commit further delinquent acts. In *Schall v. Martin,* 467 U.S. 253 (1984), in effect, the Supreme Court said that alleged delinquents may be held in preventive detention. Because the opinion reveals much about the philosophy and operation of the juvenile courts and the applicability of due process guarantees to juvenile courts, a portion of the opinion is excerpted:

> There is no doubt that the Due Process Clause is applicable in juvenile proceedings. The problem, we have stressed, is to ascertain the precise impact of the due process requirement upon such proceedings. We have held that certain basic constitutional protections enjoyed by adults accused of crimes also apply to juveniles. But the Constitution does not mandate elimination of all differences in the treatment of juveniles. The State has a *parens patriae* interest in preserving and promoting the welfare of the child, which makes a juvenile proceeding fundamentally different from an adult criminal trial. We have tried, therefore, to strike a balance—to respect the informality and flexibility that characterize juvenile proceedings, and yet to ensure that such proceedings comport with the fundamental fairness demanded by the Due Process Clause.
>
> The [New York] statutory provision at issue in this case, permits a brief pretrial detention based on a finding of a serious risk that an arrested juvenile may commit a crime before his [trial]. [This] [p]reventive detention . . . is purportedly designed to protect the child and society from the potential consequences of his criminal acts. When making any detention decision, the . . . judge is specifically directed to consider the needs and best interests of the

> juvenile as well as the need for the protection of the community. As an initial matter, therefore, we must decide whether, in the context of the juvenile system, the combined interest in protecting both the community and the juvenile himself from the consequences of future criminal conduct is sufficient to justify such detention.
>
> The legitimate and compelling state interest in protecting the community from crime cannot be doubted. We have stressed before that crime prevention is a weighty social objective, and this interest persists undiluted in the juvenile context. The harm suffered by the victim of a crime is not dependent upon the age of the perpetrator. And the harm to society generally may even be greater in this context given the high rate of recidivism among juveniles.
>
> The juvenile's countervailing interest in freedom from institutional restraints, even for the brief time involved here, is undoubtedly substantial as well. But that interest must be qualified by the recognition that juveniles, unlike adults, are always in some form of custody. Children, by definition, are not assumed to have the capacity to take care of themselves. They are assumed to be subject to the control of their parents, and if parental control falters, the State must play its part as *parens patriae.* In this respect, the juvenile's liberty interest may, in appropriate circumstances, be subordinated to the State's *parens patriae* interest in preserving and promoting the welfare of the child.
>
> [I]n upholding the statute at issue here, [the court below] stressed at some length the desirability of protecting the juvenile from his own folly. Society has a legitimate interest in protecting a juvenile from the consequences of his criminal activity—both from potential physical injury which may be suffered when a victim fights back or a policeman attempts to make an arrest and from the downward spiral of criminal activity into which peer pressure may lead the child.
>
> The substantiality and legitimacy of the state interests underlying this statute are confirmed by the wide-spread use and judicial acceptance of preventive detention for juveniles. Every State . . . permits preventive de-

tention of juveniles accused of crime. A number of model juvenile justice acts also contain provisions permitting preventive detention. And the courts of eight States, including the [highest New York appellate court,] have upheld their statutes with specific reference to protecting the juvenile and the community from harmful pretrial conduct, including pretrial crime.

The fact that a practice is followed by a large number of States is not conclusive in a decision as to whether that practice accords with due process, but it is plainly worth considering in determining whether the practice offends some principle of justice so rooted in the traditions and conscience of our people as to be ranked as fundamental. In light of the uniform legislative judgment that pretrial detention of juveniles properly promotes the interests both of society and the juvenile, we conclude that the practice serves a legitimate regulatory purpose compatible with the fundamental fairness demanded by the Due Process Clause in juvenile proceedings.

You should note that under the New York statute in question in *Schall,* if juveniles were detained at their initial appearances and denied the charges against them, they were entitled to a judicial hearing within three days. At this hearing, to justify continued detention, a judge had to determine both that there was probable cause to believe the juvenile committed the crime alleged and that there was a continued need to detain the juvenile. Moreover, detained juveniles were entitled to a final hearing within a short time—seventeen days from the initial appearance for serious offenses and six days for less serious offenses. It could well be that the Court would not have upheld a statute allowing preventive detention for a more extended period and without a judicial hearing. The Court stated that "in some circumstances detention of a juvenile would not pass constitutional muster."

Many States have more stringent time limits than those approved in *Schall* and require immediate judicial hearings to determine probable cause and the need for continued detention. Although the Court did not say so in *Schall,* such judicial hearings, typically known as **detention hearings**, are probably constitutionally required.

Generally, the decision to detain, whether made by a police or probation officer or by a judge after a detention hearing, is based not so much on the offense charged but on other considerations, such as the willingness and ability of the parents to supervise the juvenile and the juvenile's attitude and history. Many States' juvenile court acts list factors to consider when deciding whether or not to release a juvenile. The acts may provide that preference should be given to releasing a juvenile.

Juveniles have no constitutional right to release on bail—unless they are being tried as adults—but a few States do give them a right to release on bail, for all crimes or for certain crimes.

Where to detain juveniles has posed a problem for many years. It is alien to the philosophy and special nature of the juvenile courts to detain juveniles in jails with adults, many of whom are awaiting trial for crimes like murder and rape, but many jurisdictions have done precisely that. To remedy this, the federal Juvenile Justice and Delinquency Prevention Act, 42 U.S.C. § 5601 *et seq.,* mandated as early as 1974, that in order to receive federal funds for delinquency prevention, a State must, among other things, provide that "no juvenile shall be detained or confined in any jail or lockup for adults" and, indeed, that "juveniles alleged to be or found to be delinquent . . . shall not be detained or confined in any institution in which they have regular contact with adult persons incarcerated because they have been convicted of a crime or are awaiting trial on criminal charges." § 5633 (13) & (14).

Exceptions were and continue to be allowed to the latter mandate in areas with a low population density and for juveniles accused of serious crimes against persons when no existing alternative placement is available. Moreover, many States are out of compliance with the federal law, and there is nothing under federal law to prohibit detention of alleged delinquents in the same facility in which adjudicated delinquents are held. Further, there is nothing requiring that a facility for delinquents be home-like. Indeed, the dissent in *Schall* pointed out the prison-like nature of the detention center in New York where the named plaintiffs in the case were held.

The Decision to Pursue a Case

Juvenile court action is initiated through the filing of a petition. The petition presents information about a juvenile and alleges that a juvenile falls under the jurisdiction of the court for specified reasons. This point is illustrated by the statutory requirements in New York (found in section 311.1 of the Family Court Act), which provides:

1. A petition originating a juvenile delinquency proceeding is a written accusation . . .
2. A petition shall charge at least one crime . . .
3. A petition must contain:
   (a) the name of the family court in which it is filed;
   (b) the title of the action;

(c) the fact that the respondent [i.e., the alleged delinquent] is a person under sixteen years of age at the time of the alleged act or acts;
(d) a separate accusation or count addressed to each crime charged . . . ;
(e) the precise crime or crimes charged;
(f) & (g) [the date and place of each crime charged];
(h) a plain and concise statement in each count which . . . asserts facts supporting every element of the crime charged and the respondent's commission of thereof with sufficient precision to clearly apprise the respondent of the conduct which is the subject of the accusation;
(i) the name or names, if known of other persons who are charged as co-respondents in the family court or as adults in a criminal court proceeding . . . ;
(j) a statement that the respondent requires supervision, treatment or confinement . . . .

The petition will typically be entitled "*In re* (the child's name)" or "In the Matter of (the child's name)."

The decision to file a delinquency petition may be made by the police, a probation officer, or by a prosecuting attorney. The petition usually is prepared and filed by a prosecuting attorney if serious crimes are alleged or if the juvenile is being detained and therefore must have a detention hearing.

Often a decision is made to divert a juvenile from the juvenile court system instead of filing a petition. Many juvenile court acts urge diversion as an alternative to pursuing a case in juvenile court. Also, as discussed earlier, often a decision is made to seek a transfer of a case to adult court instead of pursuing the case in juvenile court. In some States, like Colorado, when certain crimes are alleged to have been committed, a prosecutor has discretion to decide whether to prosecute the case in adult court or pursue it in juvenile court, but in most States, if a case involving a juvenile does not have to be filed in adult court, it is within the exclusive jurisdiction of the juvenile court and a prosecutor must move a juvenile court to waive its exclusive jurisdiction.

The Adjudication of Delinquency

Juvenile courts technically do not decide whether a youth is guilty or innocent of committing a crime. Rather, they determine if they have *jurisdiction* over a juvenile because the juvenile has committed a crime within the scope of the juvenile court act. In other words, juvenile courts **adjudicate** whether the juveniles are delinquent. This occurs at a hearing usually called, not surprisingly, the **jurisdictional hearing,** or the **adjudicatory hearing**. Some States call the hearing a **fact-finding hearing** because its purpose is to determine if the allegation that the juvenile committed a crime is supported by the evidence.

Depending on the jurisdiction and the offense, a juvenile may have had several hearings before any adjudicatory hearing. In addition to any detention hearing, there may be one or more hearings to inform a juvenile of the nature of the charge, the possible outcomes of the delinquency action, and his or her rights related to the action or to determine if the juvenile needs or wants appointment of counsel and wants to admit the commission of the crime (i.e., waive adjudication). Such hearings are equivalent to arraignments for adults. As with adults, there may also be hearings on various pre-trial motions, including a juvenile's motion to suppress evidence or a prosecutor's motion for

waiver of jurisdiction. And, where a juvenile's mental or physical health is in question, there may be hearings concerning referral for evaluation and treatment.

As has been suggested, a child may admit commission of the offense charged and waive the adjudicatory hearing. Such waivers are very common. If a hearing is not waived, it must comport with due process. In the landmark case *In re Gault,* 387 U.S. 1 (1967), the Supreme Court set forth many of the elements of due process essential to a fair jurisdictional hearing. The facts of this case were not untypical at the time.

Gerald Gault, a fifteen year old from Arizona, had been taken into custody after he allegedly made lewd remarks to a neighbor in a telephone call. He was on probation at the time. Gerald's parents were not notified that their son had, in effect, been arrested, they were not served with a copy of the petition alleging delinquency, and the petition itself did not include specific notice of the charges. Gerald had several appearances before the juvenile court judge, but no formal hearing was ever held, the complaining witness was not present at any appearance, no transcript or recording of the appearances was ever made, and Gerald was not represented by counsel. Gerald nevertheless was found to be delinquent and was committed to the State Industrial School until he reached the age of majority. Gerald sought release through a writ of habeas corpus since no appeal of his adjudication and commitment was allowed under Arizona law. He challenged the proceedings that led to his commitment as a violation of due process.

The Supreme Court agreed that Gault's due process rights had been violated. Excerpts from the Court's opinion, which is perhaps the most important Supreme Court opinion relating to the rights of juveniles, follow. These excerpts illustrate the history and theory of the juvenile court movement and later criticism of it.

The Juvenile Court movement began in this country at the end of the last century. From the juvenile court statute adopted in Illinois in 1899, the system has spread to every State in the Union, the District of Columbia, and Puerto Rico. The early reformers were appalled by adult procedures and penalties, and by the fact that children could be given long prison sentences and mixed in jails with hardened criminals. They were profoundly convinced that society's duty to the child could not be confined by the concept of justice alone. They believed that society's role was not to ascertain whether the child was guilty or innocent, but "What is he, how has he become what he is, and what had best be done in his interest and in the interest of the state to save him from a downward career." The child—essentially good, as they saw it—was to be made to feel that he is the object of [the state's] care and solicitude, not that he was under arrest or on trial. The rules of criminal procedure were therefore altogether inapplicable. The apparent rigidities, technicalities, and harshness which they observed in both substantive and procedural criminal law were therefore to be discarded. The idea of crime and punishment was to be abandoned. The child was to be "treated" and "rehabilitated" and the procedures, from apprehension through institutionalization, were to be "clinical" rather than punitive.

These results were to be achieved, without coming to conceptual and constitutional grief, by insisting that the proceedings were not adversary, but that the state was proceeding as *parens patriae*. The Latin phrase proved to be a great help to those who sought to rationalize the exclusion of juveniles from the constitutional scheme; but its meaning is murky and its historic credentials are of dubious relevance. [T]here is no trace of the doctrine in the history of criminal jurisprudence. At common law, children under seven were considered incapable of possessing criminal intent. Beyond that age, they were subjected to arrest, trial, and in theory to punishment like adult offenders. In these old days, the state was not deemed to have authority to accord them fewer procedural rights than adults.

The right of the state, as *parens patriae*, to deny to the child procedural rights available to his elders was elaborated by the assertion that a child, unlike an adult, has a right not to liberty but to custody. He can be made to attorn to his parents, to go to school, etc. If his parents default in effectively performing their custodial functions—that is, if the child is delinquent—the state may intervene. In doing so, it does not deprive the child of any rights, because he has none. It merely provides the custody to which the child is entitled. On this basis, proceedings involving juveniles were described as "civil" not "criminal" and therefore not subject to the requirements which restrict the state when it seeks to deprive a person of his liberty.

Accordingly, the highest motives and most enlightened impulses led to a peculiar system for juveniles, unknown to our law in any comparable context. The constitutional and theoretical basis for this peculiar system is—to say the least—debatable. And in practice . . . the results have not been entirely satisfactory. Juvenile Court history has again demonstrated that unbridled discretion, however benevolently motivated, is frequently a poor substitute for principle and procedure. The absence of substantive standards has not necessarily meant that children receive careful, compassionate, individualized treatment. The absence of procedural rules based upon constitutional principle has not always produced fair, efficient, and effective procedures. Departures from established principles of due process have frequently resulted not in enlightened procedure, but in arbitrariness.

Due process of law is the primary and indispensable foundation of individual freedom. It is the basic and essential term in the social compact which defines the rights of the individual and delimits the powers which the state may exercise. As Mr. Justice Frankfurter has said: "The history of American freedom is, in no small measure, the history of procedure." But, in addition, the procedural rules which have been fashioned from the generality of due process are our best instruments for the distillation and evaluation of essential facts from the conflicting welter of data that life and our adversary methods present. It is these instruments of due process which enhance the possibility that truth will emerge from the confrontation of opposing versions and conflicting data. Procedure is to law what scientific method is to science.

It is claimed that juveniles obtain benefits from the special procedures applicable to them which more than offset the disadvantages of denial of the substance of normal due process. As we shall discuss, the observance of due process standards, intelligently and not ruthlessly administered, will not compel the States to abandon or displace any of the substantive benefits of the juvenile process. But it is important, we think, that the claimed benefits of the juvenile process should be candidly appraised. Neither sentiment nor folklore should cause us to shut our eyes, for example, to such startling findings as that reported in an exceptionally reliable study . . . [that found, among other things, that 66% of the 16- and 17-year-old juveniles referred to the juvenile court had been before the court previously and that 56% of those held in a detention center were repeaters].

Certainly, these figures and the high crime rates among juveniles . . . could not lead us to conclude that the absence of constitutional protections reduces crime, or that the juvenile system, functioning free of constitutional inhibitions as it has largely done, is effective to reduce crime or rehabilitate offenders. We do not mean by this to denigrate the juvenile court process or to suggest that there are not aspects of the juvenile system relating to offenders which are valuable. But the features of the juvenile system which its proponents have asserted are of unique benefit will not be impaired by constitutional domestication. For example, the commendable principles relating to the processing and treatment of juveniles separately from adults are in no way involved or affected by the procedural issues under discussion. Further, we are told that

one of the important benefits of the special juvenile court procedures is that they avoid classifying the juvenile as a "criminal." The juvenile offender is now classified as a "delinquent." There is, of course, no reason why this should not continue. It is disconcerting, however, that this term has come to involve only slightly less stigma than the term criminal applied to adults. It is also emphasized that in practically all jurisdictions, statutes provide that an adjudication of the child as a delinquent shall not operate as a civil disability or disqualify him for civil service appointment. There is no reason why the application of due process requirements should interfere with such provisions.

Beyond this, it is frequently said that juveniles are protected by the process from disclosure of their deviational behavior. [T]he summary procedures of Juvenile Courts are sometimes defended by a statement that it is the law's policy "to hide youthful errors from the full gaze of the public and bury them in the graveyard of the forgotten past." This claim of secrecy, however, is more rhetoric than reality. [And] . . . there is no reason why, consistently with due process, a State cannot continue if it deems it appropriate, to provide and to improve provision for the confidentiality of records of police contacts and court action relating to juveniles.

Further, it is urged that the juvenile benefits from informal proceedings in the court. The early conception of the Juvenile Court proceeding was one in which a fatherly judge touched the heart and conscience of the erring youth by talking over his problems, by paternal advice and admonition, and in which, in extreme situations, benevolent and wise institutions of the State provided guidance and help to save him from a downward career. Then, as now, goodwill and compassion were admirably prevalent. But recent studies have, with surprising unanimity, entered sharp dissent as to the validity of this gentle conception. They suggest that the appearance as well as the actuality of fairness, impartiality and orderliness—in short, the essentials of due process—may be a more impressive and more therapeutic attitude so far as the juvenile is concerned. For example, in a recent study, . . .

[it is observed] that when the procedural laxness of the *parens patriae* attitude is followed by stern disciplining, the contrast may have an adverse effect upon the child, who feels that he has been deceived or enticed. [The study] conclude[s] as follows: "Unless appropriate due process of law is followed, even the juvenile who has violated the law may not feel that he is being fairly treated and may therefore resist the rehabilitative efforts of court personnel." Of course, it is not suggested that juvenile court judges should fail appropriately to take account, in their demeanor and conduct, of the emotional and psychological attitude of the juveniles with whom they are confronted. While due process requirements will, in some instances, introduce a degree of order and regularity to Juvenile Court proceedings to determine delinquency, and in contested cases will introduce some elements of the adversary system, nothing will require that the conception of the kindly juvenile judge be replaced by its opposite.

Ultimately, however, we confront the reality of that portion of the Juvenile Court process with which we deal in this case. A boy is charged with misconduct. The boy is committed to an institution where he may be restrained of liberty for years. It is of no constitutional consequence—and of limited practical meaning—that the institution to which he is committed is called an Industrial School. The fact of the matter is that, however euphemistic the title, . . . an industrial school for juveniles is an institution of confinement in which the child is incarcerated for a greater or lesser time. His world becomes a building with whitewashed walls, regimented routine and institutional hours. . . . Instead of mother and father and sisters and brothers and friends and classmates, his world is peopled by guards, custodians, state employees, and delinquents confined with him for anything from waywardness to rape and homicide.

In view of this, it would be extraordinary if our Constitution did not require the procedural regularity and the exercise of care implied in the phrase due process. Under our Constitution, the condition of being a boy does not justify a kangaroo court. The traditional ideas of Juvenile Court procedure, in-

deed, contemplated that time would be available and care would be used to establish precisely what the juvenile did and why he did it—was it a prank of adolescence or a brutal act threatening serious consequences to himself or society unless corrected? Under traditional notions, one would assume that in a case like that of Gerald Gault, where the juvenile appears to have a home, a working mother and father, and an older brother, the Juvenile Judge would have made a careful inquiry and judgment as to the possibility that the boy could be disciplined and dealt with at home, despite his previous transgressions. [But, in this case,] . . . the points to which the judge directed his attention were little different from those that would be involved in determining any charge of violation of a penal statute. The essential difference between Gerald's case and a normal criminal case is that safeguards available to adults were discarded in Gerald's case. The summary procedure as well as the long commitment was possible because Gerald was 15 years of age instead of over 18. So wide a gulf between the State's treatment of the adult and of the child requires a bridge sturdier than mere verbiage, and reasons more persuasive than cliche can provide. As . . . [has been observed by two sociologists:] "The rhetoric of the juvenile court movement has developed without any necessarily close correspondence to the realities of court and institutional routines."

The Court went on to conclude that in juvenile court proceedings to adjudicate delinquency, due process requires at a minimum:

- **"[N]otice which would be deemed constitutionally adequate in a civil or criminal proceeding** . . . [Due Process] does not allow a hearing to be held in which a youth's freedom and his parents' right to his custody are at stake without giving them timely notice, in advance of the hearing, of the specific issues that they must meet."

- "[T]he child and his parents must be notified of the child's **right to be represented by counsel** retained by them, or if they are unable to afford counsel, that **counsel will be appointed to represent the child.**"
- "[T]he constitutional **privilege against self-incrimination** is applicable in the case of juveniles as it is with respect to adults."
- "[A]bsent a valid confession, a determination of delinquency and an order of commitment to a state institution cannot be sustained in the absence of sworn testimony subjected to the **opportunity for cross-examination** in accordance with our law and constitutional requirements."

In a later decision, *In re Winship*, 397 U.S. 358 (1970), the Supreme Court added *proof beyond a reasonable doubt* to these essential elements of due process established by *Gault*. The Court stated:

> The constitutional safeguard of proof beyond a reasonable doubt is as much required during the adjudicatory stage of a delinquency proceeding as are those constitutional safeguards applied in *Gault*—notice of charges, right to counsel, the rights of confrontation and examination, and the privilege against self-incrimination. [W]here a 12-year-old child is charged with an act of stealing which renders him liable to confinement for as long as six years, then, as a matter of due process . . . the case against him must be proved beyond a reasonable doubt.

Taken together, *Gault* and *Winship* gave juveniles accused of committing a crime all the basic rights at trial accorded to adults accused of committing a crime except one—trial by jury. The Supreme Court later held in *McKeiver v. Pennsylva-nia*, 403 U.S. 441 (1971), that trial by jury was not a "constitutional requirement" for juveniles. The Court offered a number of reasons for its conclusion, among them that trial by jury was disallowed by either statute or court opinion in the majority of the States and a number of model juvenile court acts had not provided for trial by jury. But as the following excerpts from *McKeiver* illustrate, the Court perhaps was simply unwilling to abandon the belief in the wisdom of less formal proceedings that underlies the juvenile court philosophy:

> There is a possibility, at least, that the jury trial, if required as a matter of constitutional precept, will remake the juvenile proceeding into a fully adversary process and will put an effective end to what has been the idealistic prospect of an intimate, informal protective proceeding.
>
> The juvenile concept held high promise. We are reluctant to say that, despite disappointments of grave dimensions, it still does not hold promise, and we are particularly reluctant to say . . . that the system cannot accomplish its rehabilitative goals. So much depends on the availability of resources, on the interest and commitment of the public, on willingness to learn, and on understanding as to cause and effect and cure. In this field, as in so many others, one perhaps learns best by doing. We are reluctant to disallow the States to experiment further and to seek in new and different ways the elusive answers to the problems of the young, and we feel that we would be impeding that experimentation by imposing the jury trial. The States, indeed, must go forward. If, in its wisdom, any State feels the jury trial is desirable in all cases, or in certain cases, there appears to be no impediment to its installing a system embracing that feature. That, however, is the State's privilege and not its obligation.
>
> Finally, the arguments advanced by the juveniles here . . . equate the juvenile proceed-

ing—or at least the adjudicative phase of it—with the criminal trial. [In seeking to equate the two types of proceedings, they] . . . ignore, it seems to us, every aspect of fairness, of concern, of sympathy, and of paternal attention that the juvenile court system contemplates. If the formalities of the criminal adjudicative process are to be superimposed upon the juvenile court system, there is little need for its separate existence. Perhaps that ultimate disillusionment will come one day, but for the moment we are disinclined to give impetus to it.

If the judge determines at the conclusion of the adjudicatory hearing, after hearing all the evidence, that the juvenile did not commit any crime, the judge will dismiss the petition. If the judge determines, however, that the juvenile did commit the crime or crimes charged, the judge will enter a finding of delinquency and assume jurisdiction. The judge may then determine the appropriate intervention in behalf of the juvenile, but, generally, this determination will be made at a later hearing, usually known as a **dispositional hearing.**

Before a dispositional hearing, at the adjudicatory hearing, the judge may be able to arrange some form of diversion. For example, the judge may be able to delay a finding of delinquency and ultimately dismiss the petition if the juvenile abides by certain conditions that the judge imposes, such as that the juvenile commit no more illegal acts, attend school regularly, and participate in counseling. If the judge learns that the juvenile has violated these conditions, the judge can resume the hearing.

Disposition

The dispositional alternatives available to the court following an adjudication of delinquency are generally defined by State statutes. The commonly available dispositions are court supervision, probation, commitment to a child welfare agency, and commitment to a correctional agency. The choice of disposition reflects both the offense and the juvenile's characteristics and is usually not made until an investigation of the juvenile and the juvenile's potential for rehabilitation has been completed, generally by a probation officer or other court officer.

Court supervision, probation, and commitment to a child welfare agency may occur with or without an order removing the child from his or her home. Court supervision and probation are similar in that in both cases, the juvenile must comply with certain orders of the court. For example, the juvenile may be ordered to make restitution, go to school, work part-time, attend counseling sessions, be home by nine P.M. every night, and so on. The difference is that a juvenile who is on probation must report regularly to a probation officer while a juvenile who is under court supervision, is not required to report to a probation officer or anyone else. If the juvenile is ordered to be removed from the home and committed to a child welfare agency or to a correctional agency, usually the agency will assess the juvenile and itself determine the proper placement for the juvenile, consistent with any orders made or restrictions imposed by the court. Some courts, however, make specific placement decisions themselves.

A juvenile who has been adjudicated a delinquent may or may not be made a **ward of the court,** a term used in most States to describe the continuing authority of the court over the juvenile. If the juvenile is made a ward of the court, certain rights and responsibilities may be removed from the juvenile's parents and vested with the court. The court will, in turn, typically delegate these rights and responsibilities to the probation office, a child welfare agency, or a correctional agency as part of its disposition. The court will often give the agency **custody** of the juvenile—that is, the responsibility for the juvenile's daily care—and **guardianship** over the juvenile—that is, the right and responsibility to make legal decisions for the juvenile.

You should note that even if custody and guardianship of a juvenile are given to an agency, the juvenile may remain at home with his or her parents. And, while foster care is usually associated with neglected or abused minors, delinquents may also be placed with foster parents.

Whatever the disposition of a juvenile adjudicated delinquent, if he or she is made a ward of the court, the court will retain jurisdiction over him or her and may modify its disposition at any time. Often, it will retain jurisdiction until the juvenile reaches majority or possibly older. During the period it retains jurisdiction, the agency to which the court delegated authority will report periodically to the court.

The retention of jurisdiction and the ability to modify a disposition are major ways in which the juvenile court differs from the adult criminal court. When adults are sentenced, the sentencing court loses jurisdiction of the case and has no continuing authority to modify orders. Even if a defendant is sentenced to probation or if the sentence is suspended, the court may only intervene if the defendant violates specific conditions of probation or of the suspension of the sentence. If this occurs, the court may only revoke probation or impose the suspended sentence.

The public, judges and legislators have expressed frustration with the juvenile court's treatment of serious juvenile offenders and the response has been increasing prosecution of juveniles in adult courts. The public, judges, and legislators have grown increasingly frustrated with "revolving door" adjudication and disposition of youthful offenders by juvenile courts and with what is perceived as lack of parental concern for and control over youth. The response to this frustration had been statutory changes to increase dispositional alternatives in some States and to limit them in others. For example, changes have been made that require judges to order a youth incarcerated in an institution after adjudication for certain violent offenses or after a specified number of offenses. Moreover, changes have been made in the laws to hold parents responsible for their children's behavior by, for example, ordering them to pay restitution or to attend parenting classes as part of their children's dispositions.

Social workers play a role throughout the juvenile court process, but their greatest role may be in relation to dispositions. Social workers, thus, have had and will continue to have a great role in the continuing debate over the proper treatment and disposition of youthful offenders.

SECTION III

THE CHILD,
THE FAMILY, AND
THE LAW

INTRODUCTION TO SECTION III

In this section, we turn to an area of the law of great importance to social workers: the law related to families and children. While the law related to children is sometimes seen as separate from the law related to the family, these two areas of the law are naturally intertwined. In our legal system, it is the family that is primarily responsible for raising children, and the family is given legal recognition because of this responsibility. When a family breaks down or fails to perform responsibly, the legal system may step in to protect and provide for the children—with the assistance of a social worker.

Our legal system has always had a special relationship with the family. On the one hand, the family is recognized as an institution that is protected from government intervention by the Constitution and parents are recognized as having a constitutional right to raise their children as they wish. As the Supreme Court stated in *Smith v. OFFER*, 431 U.S. 816 (1977): "[T]he freedom of personal choice in matters of . . . family life is one of the liberties protected by the Due Process Clause of the Fourteenth Amendment. There does exist a private realm of family life which the state cannot enter, and that has been afforded both substantive and procedural protection."

Indeed, "the liberty interest in family privacy" was recognized in *OFFER*, not only as stemming from the Constitution, but also as having its source "in intrinsic human rights, as they have been understood in this Nation's history and tradition."

However, on the other hand, as the Supreme Court stated in *Prince v. Commonwealth of Massachusetts*, 321 U.S. 158 (1944), the family "is not beyond regulation in the public interest," and "the state has a wide range of power for limiting parental freedom and authority in things affecting the child's welfare." In other words, while the state must recognize the integrity of the family and not infringe upon its privacy, the state will act to protect the interests of children and other family members.

Moreover, the state may itself define the family. The Court explained in *OFFER* that: "the usual understanding of family implies biological relationships . . . [b]ut biological relationships are not the exclusive determination of the existence of a family. The basic foundation of the family in our society, the marriage relationship, is, of course, not a matter of blood relation." Marriage is, instead, a relationship that is legally defined and recognized. And, as the Court further explained in *OFFER*, adoption is a legal action that is "recognized as the legal equivalent of biological parenthood."

Also, in certain instances such as when there has been severe child abuse, the parental relationship created by blood may be denied legal recognition. That is, the legal relationship between biological parent and child may be severed and biological parents may be denied the rights that normally flow from parenthood.

You learned in section II that the state may intervene in the family under the authority of a juvenile court act in instances of juvenile delinquency. You will learn in this section that the state may also intervene in the family under the authority of a variety of laws where there is a need to protect children or other vulnerable family members, such as older homemakers without a source of income or abused elderly parents. The laws that allow state intervention include the juvenile court acts, the laws relating to marriage, and laws enacted to address domestic violence. You will learn about these laws and the laws that define or regulate the family in this section.

In chapter 8, we will look at the actions initiated by the State to protect children. These actions are often taken under the authority of juvenile court acts as part of the juvenile court process, but they may also be taken under the authority of other laws designed to protect children. Because many social workers practice in the area of child protection, and because social workers play a large part in the juvenile court process established by juvenile court acts, this chapter covers many of the different laws designed to protect children by focusing on juvenile court acts and the juvenile court process. In the course of this discussion, we will identify the various roles of the social worker and the rights

of the different participants in the juvenile court process.

In chapter 9, we will look at one action taken to protect children: adoption. Children may be without parents for a variety of reasons. Sometimes, the juvenile courts determine that it would be in the best interest of children who have come before the court to terminate their legal relationship with their parents permanently. Sometimes, parents terminate their legal relationships with their children voluntarily without coming before the juvenile courts. Sometimes, parents die or abandon their children. Whatever the reason a child is without parents, a court may establish a new parent-child relationship through the process of adoption. In some States, in some or all cases, this process occurs in the juvenile courts under juvenile court acts. In most States, and in most cases, the adoption process occurs under separate laws in regular trial courts. Wherever and however it occurs, social workers play a variety of important roles in the adoption process. In chapter 9, we will examine the adoption process and the various roles of the social worker in the process. We will further look at the rights of the different participants in the process and consider the issues related to what may be the ultimate intervention into the family relationship: the termination of parental rights to free a child for adoption.

In chapter 10, we turn to another way the law creates and terminates a familial relationship, that is, through the institution of marriage and the recognition of divorce and other mechanisms to terminate a marriage. We will first look at how the law defines marriage, regulates the marriage relationship, and protects (or fails to protect) the parties to a marriage. We will then look to the law on the termination of marriage and to the rights and obligations of the parties that survive the end of a marriage.

While social workers should be familiar with the laws on marriage and termination of marriage and while some social workers may play active roles in parts of the termination process, social workers generally only have an indirect counseling role in relation to marriage and termination of marriage—except where children are involved. If there are minor children of a marriage, the issues of child custody and support may arise and social workers have several direct and crucial roles to play. The issues of child custody and support may also arise—may be of even greater importance to social workers—where there are children outside of a legally-recognized marriage. We will discuss the law related to these issues and the social worker's roles related to this law in chapter 11.

Another family law issue of particular importance to social workers is the problem of domestic violence, that is, one member of a family or household assaulting or otherwise abusing another member. Because social workers have several crucial roles to play in relation to domestic violence cases, it is important that social workers be familiar with the law designed to prevent domestic violence and to protect victims of the violence. These laws are reviewed in chapter 12.

No discussion of the law related to youth and families would be complete without a discussion of the law related to education. While the family has the primary responsibility for raising children, the state has assumed a large responsibility for educating children. In chapter 13, will look at legal issues related to education, reviewing those areas of greatest importance to social workers: school attendance, discipline in the schools, and special education services for disabled children. These areas are important to social workers because they frequently work with children who present troublesome behavior or who are disabled. Because social workers have a particular concern about persons who have historically suffered discrimination under the law, chapter 13 will also review legal prohibitions against discrimination in public primary and secondary education.

With the exception of the laws related to public education, the laws related to children and families we will be discussing in this section are almost exclusively found at the State (not including the local) level. As with juvenile delinquency, there are virtually no laws at the local level related to protection, adoption, custody and support of children, to the marriage relationship, or to domestic violence. Also as with juvenile delinquency, there are some federal laws related to these subjects designed to help the States perform their responsibilities, but the federal law in these areas is very limited and the federal courts only entertain cases dealing with these subjects when a State law or practice is challenged as a violation of the Constitution or of federal civil rights laws.

The laws related to public education are found at all three levels: local, State, and federal. Moreover, the laws at the State level may be the least important. In this country, public education is primarily the responsibility of local governments, either specialized school districts or cities and counties.

Protection of Children

The Supreme Court has repeatedly affirmed that parents have a broad authority over their children, which they may generally assert without interference from the government. A series of decisions established the right of parents in the care, custody, and management of their children. The following excerpt from *Parham v. J.R.*, 442 U.S. 584 (1979), which affirmed the right of the parents to admit their children to mental institutions, even against the children's wishes, illustrates how firmly rooted these traditions are:

> Our jurisprudence historically has reflected Western civilization concepts of the family as a unit with broad parental authority over minor children. Our cases have consistently followed that course; our constitutional system long ago rejected any notion that a child is "the mere creature of the state" and, on the contrary, asserted that parents generally "have the right, coupled with the high duty, to recognize and prepare [their children] for additional obligations." The law's concept of the family rests on a presumption that parents possess what a child lacks in maturity, experience, and capacity for judgment required for making life's difficult decisions. More important, historically it has recognized that natural bonds of affection lead parents to act in the best interests of their children.

Although the family has long been protected from government intervention, it has also been recognized that the State, under the doctrine of *parens patriae*, can intervene in the family to protect children from abuse and neglect that threatens their well being. As the Court went on to say in *Parham*: "[W]e have recognized that a state is not without constitutional control over parental discretion in dealing with children when their physical or mental health is jeopardized."

The State can also intervene under its *parens patriae* authority when *dependent* children have no parents to care for them, or when children behave in a manner that is not criminal but may be injurious to their welfare.

The federal government and the States have paid increasing attention to the plight of abused or neglected children. The response has been passage of a number of federal and State laws to identify children who have been abused or neglected and to provide services to them. This chapter will review these federal and State laws and other laws significant to social workers.

BASIC PRINCIPLES AND CONCEPTS OF CHILD ABUSE, NEGLECT, AND DEPENDENCY LAW

What Are Child Abuse, Neglect, and Dependency?

Definitions of abuse and neglect are usually found in juvenile or family court acts, criminal codes, or laws mandating or encouraging reporting suspected instances of child abuse or neglect (called reporting laws). Definitions of dependency are usually found in juvenile or family court acts or in adoption acts. Statutory definitions of abuse, neglect, and dependency may differ from definitions used in the professional literature and in common usage.

Abuse concerns acts of commission by the parent or other responsible adult, whereas **neglect** concerns acts of omission. **Dependency**, on the other hand, can be thought of as "no fault" neglect; the parent cannot care for the child properly because of severe disability or absence.

Definitions of abuse and neglect found in State statutes are similar. The Federal Child Abuse Prevention and Treatment Act of 1974 (CAPTA), 42 U.S.C. § 5101, *et seq.*, requires States to have definitions in reporting statutes that are "in accordance" with the definitions in the federal act. 45 C.F.R. § 1340.14. The federal act defines **child abuse** as "physical or mental injury, sexual abuse or exploitation, negligent treatment, or abuse or neglect of a child under the age of eighteen, or the age specified by the child protection law of the state" and defines **negligent treatment** or **maltreatment** as "failure to provide adequate food, clothing, shelter, or medical care." 45 C.F.R. § 1340.2.

State statutes have added other provisions to their definitions of child abuse. For example, the statutes in California allow the juvenile court to assume jurisdiction when, due to the parents' conduct, the minor is suffering serious emotional damage, evidenced by severe anxiety, depression, withdrawal, or aggressive behavior toward self or others. Cal. Welf. and Inst. Code § 300(c). The statutes in Illinois define as abused "any newborn infant whose blood or urine contains any amount of a controlled substance as defined in . . . the Illinois Controlled Substances Act . . . or metabolites of such substances" unless the presence is the result of medical treatment of the mother or infant. § 705 ILCS § 405/2-3(1)(c).

Parent spanking may not constitute child abuse. Indeed, State statutes may allow parents to use reasonable corporal punishment on their children. If the child is seriously injured, however, or if the discipline is excessive, courts will not hesitate to find abuse. Such was the case in *State v. Crouser*, 911 P.2d 725 (Hawaii 1996), where the Supreme Court of Hawaii upheld a criminal child abuse conviction based on the mother's boyfriend, Crouser, infliction of corporal punishment on the mother's fourteen-year-old daughter. The daughter was a special education student required to bring home a daily progress report signed by her teachers. One day the daughter forgot to bring home the signed report so she filled out a blank report herself and forged the teacher's signature. Excerpts of the opinion show what happened:

Crouser somehow learned that Minor had made changes to the report and went to Minor's room, where she was doing her homework. Minor testified that Crouser called her a liar and hit her across both sides of her face, knocking her to the floor. As she was trying to get up, Crouser grabbed her and threw her face down on the bed. According to Minor's testimony, Crouser put his knee on Minor's back, pulled her pants and underwear down to her knees, and started "whacking" her bare buttocks. When Crouser left the room, Minor pulled up her underwear and pants, but Crouser returned with a plastic bat and closed the door. He again pulled down Minor's pants and underwear and struck her with the bat on the buttocks, arm, thighs, and torso until the bat broke. Minor could not remember the number of times that she had been struck, but testified that the incident lasted approximately thirty minutes . . . Minor testified that her bottom hurt for a couple of weeks after the incident. She also testified that, while in school on the day following the incident, she could not sit on the hard student chairs, that one of her teachers let her use the padded teacher's chair, and that, in her other classes, she just stood.

On the day following the incident, May 29, 1993, Minor was sent by a teacher to the office of the school health aide, Shirley Yamaguchi, because she complained of being unable to sit down. Yamaguchi observed that

Minor waddled stiffly as though she was in extreme pain, was very emotional, and was unable to sit at the desk, where she customarily talked with students. Minor told Yamaguchi that she got a spanking from her "stepfather," because of her grades. Yamaguchi called the school counselor, Diane McCary, into the office, and Yamaguchi and McCary observed that Minor's buttocks were bruised and colored a deep reddish-purple. They also observed bruising to Minor's arm, thigh and torso, which Minor explained had occurred when she was moving around to try to block the blows from the bat. Yamaguchi testified that, of the approximately eighty to one hundred children who had come to her attention for discipline injuries, Minor's was the worst case she had seen. She further testified that, when Minor began describing what happened to her, she cried uncontrollably, "a deep sobbing hurt kind of cry like a cry that's been held in for a while." At trial, McCary similarly testified.

Marilyn Hagoes, the unit supervisor of the crisis intake and investigation unit of Child Protective Services . . . testified that she interviewed Crouser on May 27, 1993. She showed Crouser the photographs of Minor and asked him how the bruising got there. According to Hagoes, Crouser told her that he "worked [Minor's] butt," explaining that he hit her about twenty-five times on the buttocks, mostly with his hand and some with a plastic bat. Crouser also advised Hagoes that he wanted to make it hard for her to sit down, but when asked about the bruising to Minor's arm, torso, and leg, Crouser stated that those bruised were self-inflicted. Hagoes also testified that, in her ten years of experience, she had never seen such extensive bruising in a parental discipline case and that she considered the discipline excessive and not reasonably related to the purpose of safeguarding or promoting the welfare of a minor, including the punishment of misconduct.

Perhaps the most controversial aspects of neglect relate to parents deciding to withold medical care from their children.

Parents have the right and the responsibility to make decisions regarding the medical care of their children, and physicians generally cannot treat a minor without the consent of a parent. Thus, some question whether it should be considered neglect when a parent refuses to consent to life-saving surgery for a child with severe and multiple birth defects, without or against the advice of physicians. Similarly, some question whether it is neglect when a parent chooses to treat a child with a nontraditional, not generally acceptable treatment when the child's physicians recommend a different, more generally acceptable course of treatment. Others question whether neglect occurs when a parent refuses to consent to surgery or another course of treatment because it is not consistent with the parent's religious beliefs.

State statutes have provided answers to some of these questions. For example, a Colorado statute allows parents to treat their children with prayer instead of medical treatment. It provides: "No child who in lieu of medical treatment is under treatment solely by spiritual means through prayer in accordance with a recognized method of religious healing shall, for that reason alone, be considered to have been neglected or dependent within the purview of this article." § 19-3-102, C.R.S.

The federal government has allowed States to come up with their own answers about parents' religious beliefs. Federal regulations provide:

Nothing in this part should be construed as requiring or prohibiting a finding of negligent treatment or maltreatment when a parent practicing his or her religious beliefs does not, for that reason alone, provide medical treatment for a child; provided, however, that if such a finding is prohibited, the prohibition shall not limit the administrative or judicial authority or the state to ensure that medical services are provided to the child when his health requires it. 45 C.F.R. § 1340.2(d)(2)(ii).

The federal government, however, has not given States such freedom in relation to parents' witholding medical treatment from critically ill newborns. Following several highly publicized cases in the early 1980s, federal regulations of the Department of Health and Human Services (DHHS) were amended to provide that the withholding of medical care from infants born with severe physical or mental impairments violated section 504 of the Rehabilitation Act of 1973 which states: "No otherwise qualified handicapped individual . . . shall, solely by reason of his handicap, be excluded from participation in, be denied the benefits of, or be subjected to discrimination under any program or activity receiving federal financial assistance." 29 U.S.C. § 794. Hospitals that were not in compliance with these regulations risked losing federal funds. The regulations, however, were struck down by the Supreme Court in *Bowen v. American Hospital Association*, 476 U.S. 610 (1986). The court held that DHHS in issuing the regulations exceeded the authority given to it by Congress.

The federal government responded to *Bowen* by providing in the CAPTA that States, to receive federal funds, define, *medical neglect* in their statutes as "the withholding of medically indicated treatment from a disabled infant with a life-threatening condition." 45 C.F.R. § 1340.15(b)(1). Such withholding, in turn, was defined as

the failure to respond to the infant's life-threatening conditions by providing treatment (in-

cluding appropriate nutrition, hydration, and medication) which, in the treating physician's (or physicians') reasonable medical judgment, will be most likely to be effective in ameliorating or correcting all such conditions, except that the term does not include the failure to provide treatment (other than appropriate nutrition, hydration, or medication) to an infant when, in the treating physician's (or physicians') reasonable medical judgment any of the following circumstances apply:

(i.) The infant is chronically and irreversibly comatose;
(ii.) The provision of such treatment would merely prolong dying, not be effective in ameliorating or correcting all of the infant's life-threatening conditions, or otherwise be futile in terms of the survival of the infant; or
(iii.) The provision of such treatment would be virtually futile in terms of the survival of the infant the treatment itself under such circumstances would be inhumane. 45 C.F.R. § 1340.15(b)(2).

A **dependent child** is usually defined as a child who has been deprived of parental support or care without fault on the part of the parent. Children may be defined as dependent when their parents are deceased, hospitalized, incarcerated, or cannot care for them because of mental illness, developmental disability, or addiction to alcohol or other drugs, or when their parents no longer wish to care for them. This is illustrated in the Illinois definition:

Those who are dependent include any minor under the age of 18 years:

(a) who is without a parent, guardian or legal custodian;
(b) who is without proper care because of the physical or mental disability of his parent, guardian, or custodian; or
(c) who is without proper medical or other remedial care recognized under state law or

other care necessary for his or her well being through no fault, neglect or lack of concern by his parents, guardian or custodian. . . ; or
(d) who has a parent, guardian or legal custodian who, with good cause, wishes to be relieved of . . . parental rights and responsibilities . . . 705 ILCS § 405/2-4.

Although definitions of child abuse and neglect may differ slightly by State, professional ethical standards require the social worker "to have basic knowledge of the indicators of child abuse and neglect," and to "obtain knowledge of the state's child abuse and neglect laws and procedures." Standards #37 and #38, NASW Standards for Social Work Practice in Child Protection, National Association of Social Workers (1981).

Mandatory Reporting

State reporting statutes require social workers and a number of other professionals to file a report when there is reasonable cause to believe that child abuse or neglect has occurred. Known as **reporting acts**, these statutes have three primary purposes: 1) to encourage identification of children at risk; 2) to designate an agency to receive and investigate reports of suspected abuse and neglect of children; and 3) to offer, where appropriate, protective services to children. Also, these acts typically specify procedures to be followed in filing and investigating the reports. In some States, reporting acts also allow certain professionals such as physicians, police officers and designated social workers to take immediate protective custody of children in emergencies—that is, to temporarily remove children from the custody of their parents without a court

order when necessary to protect children from serious harm.

Reporting acts encourage reporting in several ways. First, they may offer anonymity to the person who reports. Second, they may grant persons who report in good faith immunity from civil and criminal liability. Third, they may contain language that makes reporting an exception to confidentiality laws. Finally, reporting acts may provide that the failure to report is a crime, constitutes grounds for license suspension or revocation, and that failing to report can give rise to civil liability.

Even if the acts do not provide for civil liability, courts have recognized personal liability for civil damages for the harm to a child caused by the failure to report the abuse or neglect. Liability is premised on the duty imposed by reporting statutes to both recognize abuse and make an immediate report to local authorities to prevent further injury to the child. In the landmark case, *Landeros v. Flood*, 123 Cal.Rptr. 713, 551 P.2d 389 (1976), an emergency room physician was sued under a theory of medical malpractice because he did not diagnose or even recognize that an infant's injuries were caused by child abuse and thus did not report the injuries to the local authorities. Excerpts of the opinion indicate what happened to the young child in this case:

On repeated occasions during the first year of [the infant's] life she was severely beaten by her mother and the latter's common law husband, one Reyes. On April 26, 1971, when plaintiff was 11 months old, her mother took her to the San Jose Hospital for examination, diagnosis, and treatment. The attending physician was defendant [Dr.] Flood . . . At the time [the infant] was suffering from a comminuted spiral fracture of the right tibia and fibula, which gave the appearance of having been caused by a twisting force. [Her] mother had no explanation for this injury. [The infant] also had bruises over her entire back, together with superficial abrasions on other parts of her body. In addition, she had a nondepressed linear fracture of the skull, which was then in the process of healing. [She] demonstrated fear and apprehension when approached. Inasmuch as all [her] injuries gave the appearance of having been intentionally inflicted by other persons, she exhibited the medical condition known as the battered child syndrome.

The trial court dismissed the case, ruling that the physician could not have foreseen that the child would suffer further permanent physical injuries, including the probable loss of or amputation of her left hand. After reviewing literature of what constitutes battered child syndrome, the California Supreme Court reversed, holding that the facts established a cause of action. They decided that a prudent physician who had properly diagnosed battered child syndrome would have foreseen the likelihood of further serious injury. Thus, the child (who was the plaintiff in the case) was entitled to prove by expert testimony that Dr. Flood should reasonably have foreseen that her caretakers were likely to resume their physical abuse and inflict further injuries on her and should have made a child abuse report to the authorities rather than returning her to her mother.

Courts have also recognized liability for civil damages against agencies whose staff failed to recognize abuse and failed to make an immediate report to local authorities to prevent further injuries to a child. For instance, in *Doe v. New York City Dept. of Social Services*, 649 F.2d 134 (1981), *cert. denied*, 464 U.S. 864 (1983),

a child (through an adult guardian) sued a private child placement agency and local social services agency under a civil rights statute, 42 U.S.C. § 1983, for various forms of child abuse—including forcible withdrawal from school, rape, and severe beatings—she suffered at the hand of her foster father. The child alleged that the child placement agency supervised her foster care but did not report her situation to the local authorities as a suspected case of child abuse, and that this failure to report led to the continuation of her mistreatment in the home. The following excerpts of this case indicate what happened:

> Anna was born in April, 1961 and, when she was two years old, was placed in foster care along with her sister Evelyn, in the legal custody of the New York City Commissioner of Welfare. The Commissioner arranged for . . . Catholic Home Bureau to supervise the care of Anna and her sister, beginning January 5, 1964, and pursuant to this duty, the Bureau placed both girls in the home of Frank and Josephine Senerchia, whom it had investigated and certified on September 30, 1963.
>
> The Senerchias had come well recommended by the parish priest, physician, neighbors, friends and Frank Senerchia's employer. As part of its investigation and decision to certify the home, the Bureau prepared a report, which described Senerchia, a New York City policeman, as "a pleasant man, quite ordinary in achievements." Frank Senerchia expressed the view that corporal punishment was sometimes good for children but did not believe that spanking "should be the one and only course of parents."
>
> Anna and her foster sisters testified that starting when she was about ten years of age, she was regularly and frequently beaten and sexually abused by Senerchia. [Anna] testified that he beat her with his hands and belt all over her body, threw her down the stairs, and on one occasion lacerated her with a hunting knife, that he confined her to her

room for days at a time, and ultimately forced her to have intercourse and oral sexual relations with him.

[Anna] contends that the agency's failure to discover the abuse to which she had been subjected for some six years before defendant acknowledged that something was wrong was due, at least in part, to its failure to make a thorough periodic investigation of her circumstances and to comply with its statutory duties.

[Anna] maintains that as she grew older, visits to the home by the agency's case workers declined in frequency, so that between 1968 and 1972, for example, there were periods, once two and a half years and once fourteen months, when no one from the agency visited the Senerchia home, whereas the previous and usual pattern had been four or five home visits a year. [The Bureau] maintains that additional contacts outside the home compensated for any shortage of visits.

Although one case worker had expressed suspicion in 1967 that Senerchia might have "severe emotional problems," most Bureau personnel continued to give the home a favorable rating in spite of nagging suspicions that the father was excessively involved with intimate details of the girls' personal hygiene, and after 1973 had become increasingly resistant to the agency's supervision.

In early January, 1975, the Bureau received its first clear tangible evidence of things going awry with Anna when she was removed from school by her father without the agency's knowledge or consent.

On January 7, the agency, after discovering that Anna had been removed from school, questioned Senerchia and was told that Anna had been engaged extensively in group sex with the other children at school, that this had gone on since the first grade, and had included full sexual intercourse, even between first-graders. Senerchia claimed that Anna had told him she would be forced to resume sexual activities when she returned to school, and for that reason he was enrolling Anna in a parochial school.

Anna remained out of school throughout January and continuing through June, 1975. On February 18, 1975, at a conference with Senerchia and Anna, the agency informed

them that to get a special class placement Anna would need to see a psychiatrist and for this purpose an appointment was made with Dr. Lois Bellinger deAlvarado. On March 19, Anna met with Dr. deAlvarado, an expert in child abuse, who based on Anna's responses and the other information she had received, concluded that Anna was sexually involved with her foster father and should be immediately removed from the foster home.

The Bureau responded by holding an administrative review on April 10, 1975. Present were agency administrative personnel and the caseworker. It was decided that Senerchia's "involvement with Anna should be further investigated." However, no action appears to have been taken other than to have Dr. deAlvarado revise her report, deleting the references to sexual involvement with Senerchia.

In July of 1977, Senerchia told the agency that he was planning to divorce his wife to marry his pregnant seventeen-year-old girlfriend. This news concerned agency personnel but nothing was done until a month later when Josephine Senerchia, on learning of her husband's plans for divorce, made her disclosure to Bureau officials.

Anna sued on two separate theories of liability. First, the failure to report was a "cause" of Anna's continuing injury since reporting would have led to an investigation that might have discovered and stopped the abuse. Second, the failure to report despite statutory instructions to do so was evidence of "an overall posture of deliberate indifference toward Anna's welfare." Money damages in the amount of $250,000 against the Bureau were later affirmed on appeal in *Doe v. New York City Dept. of Social Services*, 709 F.2d 782 (1983).

State laws now require that agencies who serve children conduct background checks of all prospective employees. States also have **central registries** that list people determined to have been perpetrators of child abuse. Often, social workers employed at local social services departments decide whether a person's name should be listed on a State's central registry.

THE CHILD ABUSE, NEGLECT, AND DEPENDENCY PROCESS

Cases involving minors who are alleged to be abused, neglected, or dependent generally will proceed through a set of hearings similar to those cases involving an alleged juvenile delinquent; however, there are some significant differences. A first difference between the two processes is that cases of abuse, neglect, or dependency are usually brought to the attention of the court not by the police, but by a social services agency. In most cases, the child will have been the subject of an abuse or neglect report, and, in many cases, the child will be in temporary protective custody at the time a court action is initiated. If the child is in custody, the court will be asked to allow the social services agency to retain custody pending an adjudication. In some cases, the child has remained at home while the agency works with the parents to improve the child's care; this may also be known as family preservation and will be discussed in more detail later in this chapter. Most juvenile court and reporting acts express an intent to keep children in their homes whenever possible.

The Parties in the Process

Child abuse cases involve a number of professionals. A simple case may have several attorneys, expert witnesses, or community volunteers all working from diverse perspectives. The social worker's role in the process is critical; however, it is also important for the social worker to respect the unique roles the other parties play to understand how the legal process may be used to protect children and provide appropriate services.

The parents or family members asked to respond to a charge of abuse or neglect may be called **respondent** and may have an **attorney** represent their wishes and interests in the case. The court may apoint this attorney if the parents are indigent. There may be other people required to appear if they are somehow associated with the child or if they will be involved in the treatment plan. A **guardian *ad litem*** (GAL) (literally guardian "for the lawsuit") is appointed to represent the child's best interests. It is important to realize that the GAL, although an attorney, does not necessarily represent the wishes of the child and so does not function in the way that an attorney normally does. Instead of or in additon to a GAL, a **Court Appointed Special Advocate** (CASA) may be appointed as a volunteer to speak on behalf of the best interests of the child. The CASA functions in much the same way as a GAL. Generally, the CASA is not an attorney. Some States also provide for an appointment of an attorney to represent the wishes of a child. Also there will likely be a social worker from the local social services agency. This social worker may be called the **petitioner**, that is, the social worker is the one asking the court to intervene and protect the child. The social worker may have been the intake worker who received the initial child abuse complaint or may be assigned to manage the case as the ongoing worker. Generally, a **district attorney**, a **county attorney**, or a **city attorney**, who is responsible for prosecuting the child abuse complaint, will represent the social worker. The agency that is looking after the child may send *agency representatives* to be present at various hearings. In addition, there may be a *therapist* if the child or parent has been evaluated or is receiving some type of treatment. If a *foster parent* or *relative* of the child has temporary custody or an interest in the case they may also be included. Finally, a *police officer* may be involved, especially if the parent is also being charged with a crime associated with abuse or neglect. Many of these people have a unique contribution to the case and may assist the social worker in both assessing the case and providing an effective treatment plan or permanency plan for the family and child.

The parent may impede the case if he or she has pending criminal charges stemming from the abuse incident.[1] The parent's attorney, for example, may advise the parent not to speak with anyone about the case—especially the social worker. Otherwise, the court in the criminal case may rule that the parent, by talking, has waived the Fifth Amendment privilege against self-incrimination. This creates a dilemma for the social worker who has to speak to the parent to learn what happened to set up an appropriate treatment plan. In response to this dilemma, States have enacted statutes that afford the parent a privilege preventing a prosecutor

from introducing the parent's statements to the social worker in the criminal case. States have afforded prosecutors a hearing before this privilege may be asserted to allow the prosecutor in the criminal case an opportunity to object to the privilege being used.

The Temporary Custody Hearing

When court action is initiated, the agency may ask for authority either to take custody of the child or to order certain conditions on the parents with the intent of allowing the child to remain in the home. If the child is in custody, or if the agency believes the child should be taken into custody, there will be a **temporary custody hearing**. These hearings have different names in different States; however, the function is basically the same—to address the question of the need for custody. This hearing is the equivalent of a detention hearing for juvenile delinquents, except that the advisement given by the court is to the parents in a civil case instead of to the child in a quasi-criminal case. Essentially, the court decides if there is **probable cause** or reason to believe the child is abused, neglected, or dependent, as alleged in the petition, and if the child should remain in custody or be taken into custody. As is true of detention hearings for delinquents, temporary custody hearings are often brief. The issues that must be decided, however, are quite significant.

An important question at this early stage in the proceedings is whether "reasonable efforts" were made to prevent the child's placement out of the home. The "reasonable efforts" requirement is based upon federal law. Under Title IV-E of the

---

1. The term *parent* will from this point on refer to the mother, father, or both parents. *Parent* may also refer to a legal guardian who is assuming the role of a mother or father.

Social Security Act, a State may claim federal funds for foster care and adoption assistance in a case. To receive these funds a court must make a determination that "reasonable efforts" were made "to prevent or eliminate the need for removal of the child from his home." 42 U.S.C. §§ 671(a)(15) and 672(a)(1). This "reasonable efforts" requirement, however, was weakened by the Supreme Court's holding in *Suter v. Artist M.*, 503 U.S. 347 (1992), in which the Court determined that the "reasonable efforts" requirement was not enforceable.

Out of Congressional concern that social services agencies were encouraged to return children to homes where they would be in danger, the federal government in 1997 passed the Adoption and Safe Families Act (ASFA) to declare that notwithstanding the "reasonable efforts" requirement, "the child's health and safety" were the paramount concern. 42 U.S.C. § 671(a)(15)(A).[2] Three specific exceptions, therefore, exist where "reasonable efforts" determinations are not required:

> (i) the parent has subjected the child to aggravated circumstances (as defined in state law, which definition may include but need not be limited to abandonment, torture, chronic abuse, and sexual abuse);
> (ii) the parent has—
>
> (I) committed murder (which would have been an offense under section 1111(a) of title 18, United States Code, if the offense had occurred in the special maritime or territorial jurisdiction of the United States) of another child of the parent;
> (II) committed voluntary manslaughter (which would have been an offense under section 1112(a) of title 18, if the offense had

occurred in the special maritime or territorial jurisdiction of the United States) of another child of the parent;

> (III) aided or abetted, attempted, conspired, or solicited to commit such a murder or such a voluntary manslaughter; or
> (IV) committed a felony assault that results in serious bodily injury to the child or another child of the parent; or
>
> (iii) the parental rights of the parent to a sibling have been terminated involuntarily. 42 U.S.C. § 671 (a)(15)(A).

At this early stage in the proceedings, the social services agency is also responsible for developing a "case plan" for each child to assure that the child is in the most family-like, least restrictive setting available. 42 U.S.C. § 675(1)8. The case plan must specify either what care is being provided to "improve the conditions in the parents' home or "indicate the permanent placement of the child" when it appears that the child will not return home. 42 U.S.C. § 675(1)(B). The social services agency may also, at this stage in the proceedings, make "reasonable efforts to place a child for adoption or with a legal guardian concurrently" if the "reasonable efforts" requirement to reunite child and family is not possible. 42 U.S.C. § 671(a)(15)(F). This is not an easy task, given the newness of the proceedings and the difficulties identifying the issues that led to the abuse or neglect.

The Pre-trial Conference

The next stage in the process is the **pre-trial conference**, which is an informal hearing that affords the parties an opportunity to settle the case or determine whether the case is ready for trial.

---

2. B. Grimm, "Adoption and Safe Families Act Brings Big Changes in Child Welfare," *Youth Law News*, Vol. XVIII, No. 6 (1997), p. 2.

Most cases settle at this stage in the proceedings. If the case does not settle, civil procedural rules may require the parties to determine what witnesses will be called to testify and what issues will be resolved at trial. The social worker must have a clear understanding of the family treatment needs and of the permanent plan for the child before any settlement can be reached. State statutes may allow less serious cases to remain at the pre-trial conference stage as **deferred adjudications** or **informal adjustments**. This may mean that if the parent cooperates with a treatment plan he or she will not have to admit to the child abuse complaint.

The Adjudicatory Hearing

The **adjudicatory hearing** is a trial that determines whether the child is abused or neglected. There is a significant difference between delinquency cases and dependency and neglect cases at this stage in the process. A delinquency case determines whether the child offender is guilty of a crime and, because the case may involve punishment or incarceration of some kind, requires the highest legal evidentiary burden—**beyond a reasonable doubt** (reasonable certainty). In contrast, the noncriminal adjudication of a parent's abuse, neglect or dependency, does not determine guilt or innocence, but is a determination of the status of the child, to see if the State may continue to offer protective services and treatment to the child and family. The burden of proof here is thus based upon the most lenient legal burden—the **preponderance of the evidence** standard.

The Dispositional Hearing

At the **dispositional hearing** the court will decide what should happen to the child if an adjudication of abuse, neglect, or dependency has occurred. If the child is removed from home, the agency or the court may order placement with relatives, in foster care, or in an institution. Whichever placement is chosen, attempts will usually be made to improve parental functioning so that the child can return home. Generally, the court will approve a formal case plan that will reunite the child and the family upon completion of specific goals to rehabilitate the family situation.

The Review Hearing

Review hearings are required under federal and State law. Their purpose is to determine if the child is safe and in an appropriate placement, if there has been compliance with the case plan, and to project a likely date the child may be returned home or placed for adoption. 42 U.S.C. § 675(5)(B). Review hearings must be held at least once every six months under federal law, but some State laws require more frequent review hearings.

The Permanency Hearing

To encourage adoptions and support of children in foster care, the federal government passed the Adoption Assistance and Child Welfare Act of 1980 (AACWA). If a child was removed from the home, this Act required the social services agency to hold a **permanency hearing** within eighteen months of the child being removed from the home. This hearing was to "determine the future status of the child" including options of returning the child to the parent, continuing the child in foster care, placing the child for adoption or, because of special needs, continuing the child in long-term foster care. 42 U.S.C. § 675(5)(c). In 1997, the ASFA significantly changed the permanency hearing requirements, requiring a hearing to approve a "permanency plan" within twelve months of the child being removed from the home. This hearing considers the options of returning the child to the parent, placing the child for adoption by terminating parental rights, referring the child for legal guardianship, placing the child "in another planned permanent living arrangement," or if a child has attained age of sixteen, assisting the child to make the transition from foster care to independent living." 42 U.S.C. § 675(5)(c).

Consistent with its preference for the child being placed in the most family-like setting in the case of a child who is not to return home, the ASFA requires a preference for placement with another family member. 42 U.S.C. § 675(5)(E). The child's placement may also be with a legal guardian, defined as "a judicially created relationship between child and caretaker. This relationship is intended to be permanent and self-sustaining as evidenced by the transfer to the caretaker of the following parental rights with respect to the child: protection, education, care and control of the person, custody of the person, and decision making. The term 'legal guardian' means the caretaker in such a relationship." 42 U.S.C. § 675(7).

The ASFA also includes use of the Federal Parent Locator Service to help social workers identify a person "who has or may have parental rights with respect to a child." 42 U.S.C. § 653(a)(2)(A)(iv). The Federal Parent Locator Service was originally created to identify people not current in child support payments. 42 U.S.C. § 653 (1).

The Termination of Parental Rights Hearing

Reuniting the child and parents may not be possible. The ASFA requires a State to terminate parental rights

> in the case of a child who has been in foster care under the responsibility of the State for 15 of the most recent 22 months, or, if a court of competent jurisdiction has determined a child to be an abandoned infant (as defined under State law) or has made a determination that the parent has committed murder of another child of the parent, committed voluntary manslaughter of another child of the parent, aided or abetted, attempted, conspired, or solicited to commit such a murder or such a voluntary manslaughter, or committed a felony assault that has resulted in serious bodily injury to the child or to another child of the parent . . .
>
> In such cases the State shall file a petition to terminate the parental rights of the child's parents (or, if such a petition has been filed by another party, seek to be joined as a party to the petition), and, concurrently, to identify, recruit, process, and approve a qualified family for an adoption. 42 U.S.C. § 675(5)(E).

The ASFA contains three exceptions to the termination of parental rights requirement:

> (i) at the option of the State, the child is being cared for by a relative;

(ii) a State agency has documented in the case plan (which shall be available for court review) a compelling reason for determining that filing such a petition would not be in the best interests of the child; or

(iii) the State has not provided to the family of the child, consistent with the time period in the State case plan, such services as the State deems necessary for the safe return of the child to the child's home, if reasonable efforts of the type described [elsewhere in ASFA] are required to be made with respect to the child. 42 U.S.C. § 675(5)(E).

When a State seeks to intervene and legally terminate the fundamental rights of parents in the care, custody, and management of their children, the Supreme Court has required a heightened burden of proof by at least clear and convincing evidence. For example, see *Santosky v. Kramer*, 455 U.S. 745 (1982), which is discussed in more detail in chapter 9. In cases involving Native American Children, the Indian Child Welfare Act (ICWA) requires at termination hearings proof beyond a reasonable doubt. 25 U.S.C. § 1912.

The Social Worker's Unique Role

Social workers are an integral and essential part of the juvenile court process for abused, neglected, and dependent children. Social workers investigate complaints involving abused, neglected, and dependent children, take such children into custody, file petitions requesting juvenile court action, assist attorneys in gathering evidence, testify as expert witnesses, recommend dispositional alternatives for children found to be within the jurisdiction of the courts, develop treatment plans and reports for the court on the status of children, and provide treatment and services for children and their parents under the direction of the court. In much of their work with children who come before the juvenile court, social workers are agents of the court.

Frequently, social workers participate in **multidisciplinary staffings** in child protection cases. These staffings may involve local professionals from a number of disciplines, such as psychologists, teachers, medical doctors, guardians *ad litem*, attorneys for the parent, therapists, or probation officers. Discussion at these staffings may indicate the need for additional evaluations or family interventions.

When social workers intervene in the family to protect children, they have a tremendous amount of discretion. The occasional lack of procedural protections for children and parents require the exercise of sound professional judgment on the part of the social worker; courts have tended to trust that social workers will use such judgment. Most, if not all, of the orders made by juvenile court judges reflect, in significant part, the recommendations of social workers.

RIGHTS AND DUTIES OF THE PARTIES IN THE PROCESS

The process of investigating reports of abuse and neglect and the juvenile court process in abuse and neglect cases raise many constitutional questions related to the rights of children and the rights and responsibilities of parents, substitute caregivers, and the State.

The State authority to intervene in a family to investigate reports of abuse and neglect, to interview third parties such as teachers, neighbors, and physicians regarding reports, or to make unannounced visits to the homes of subjects of reports has been challenged as violative of the parental right to privacy, privilege against self-incrimination, right to counsel, and freedom from unreasonable searches, all of which are protected by the Fourth, Fifth, and Fourteenth Amendments to the Constitution. The constitutional challenges, however, have largely been unsuccessful. Courts have consistently held that States should have broad authority to investigate to determine the need of protection for children. These challenges will be discussed in the next section.

Obviously, children victims of abuse experience considerable trauma by testifying in open court. To protect these children from such trauma, States have enacted evidentiary rules and statutes that allow the children's hearsay statements made to a social worker, for example, to be introduced into evidence by the social worker. The right to introduce these statements will also be discussed in the next section.

Reasonable Search

The Supreme Court in *Wyman v. James*, 400 U.S. 309 (1971), considered whether a requirement that welfare recipients and applicants allow home visits by caseworkers violated the reasonable search requirement of the Fourth Amendment. The Court defined the purpose of the home visit as the welfare of the dependent child and held that the visit did not offend the Fourth Amendment, explaining: "There is no more worthy object

of the public's concern [than a child]. The dependent child's needs are paramount, and only with hesitancy would we relegate those needs, in the scale of comparative values, to a position secondary to what the mother claims as her rights."

Privilege Against Self-Incrimination

The Supreme Court in *Baltimore City Department of Social Services v. Bouknight*, 493 U.S. 549 (1990), determined that the Fifth Amendment privilege against self-incrimination may not be used to circumvent a court's order directing a parent to turn a child over to authorities. Based on evidence that Jacqueline Bouknight had abused her infant son, Maurice, the Baltimore City Department of Social Services obtained a juvenile court order removing him from her custody. That order was later modified to return custody of Maurice to his mother subject to extensive conditions and further court orders. After Ms. Bouknight violated the conditions, the court granted the Department's petition to remove Maurice from her custody, held her in civil contempt when she failed to produce the child as ordered, and further ordered her imprisoned until she either produced Maurice or revealed his exact whereabouts. The court expressed concern that Maurice was endangered or perhaps dead.

Ms. Bouknight subsequently claimed that the contempt order violated her Fifth Amendment guarantee against self-incrimination. The Supreme Court disagreed, stating:

The Court has on several occasions recognized that the Fifth Amendment privilege may not be invoked to resist compliance with a regulatory regime constructed to effect the

State's public purposes unrelated to the enforcement of its criminal laws.

Even when criminal conduct may exist, the court may properly request production and return of the child, and enforce that request through exercise of the contempt power, for reasons related entirely to the child's well-being and through measures unrelated to criminal law enforcement or investigation.

Ms. Bouknight remained in prison on the contempt charge for over seven years. Maurice was never found.

Hearsay Evidence

Generally, rules of evidence that govern hearings and trials require that a witness testify under oath and have personal knowledge of the matter he or she is testifying about. The proponent presents this witness's testimony as **direct evidence** to support the case. The opponent is then allowed to challenge the truthfulness of this witness's testimony through **cross-examination**. The person conducting the cross-examination may use leading questions (questions that when asked suggest the answer) to reveal, for example, the witness's motive for lying or to show the witness did not see what happened. The purpose of cross-examination allows the judge or the jury to assess the truthfulness of the statement by observing the witness's demeanor.

During child abuse investigations or in a treatment setting, social workers frequently come across situations where a child victim of abuse makes statements incriminating the perpetrator. Statutes and court rules have been enacted that allow these incriminating hearsay statements into evidence through the testimony of the

social worker who heard the child, for example, without also subjecting the child victim to the trauma of testifying.[3] The court, however, must generally hold a separate hearing to determine that the circumstances surrounding the child's utterance of the statements indicate the statements are truthful and reliable without the need for cross-examination. See *Idaho v. Wright*, 497 U.S. 805 (1990). In other words, the court must determine that cross-examination would not reveal any new information about the truthfulness of the hearsay statement. Thus, when trying to find out the truth about what happened to the child victim, social workers: 1) should not ask leading questions of the child (that suggest the answer); 2) should accurately record (not summarize) the child's exact statements; 3) should ask clarifying questions if necessary; 4) should accurately document (not summarize or give an opinion about) the mood and appearance of the child; and 5) if possible, have another person also listen to the interview to independently corroborate (confirm) the accuracy of the social worker's records.

When testifying, social workers may also want to offer opinion evidence as expert witnesses to corroborate the child's hearsay statement. The social worker may be qualified to testify as an expert but, to do so, would have to first show the judge he or she has the skill, experience, training, education, or relevant knowledge, of the matter. It is important, however, that the social worker understand

---

3.   The child's hearsay statements may also be admissible through the testimony of other people who heard the child, such as pediatricians, police officers, or parents.

that an opinion may not be permissible if it goes to the issue of whether the child was telling the truth—the judge or jury must decide that issue. It would generally be appropriate, however, for a qualified social worker to offer expert opinion evidence that the child was behaving in a way that indicated he or she had experienced trauma, such as abuse. The opinion, for example, may state that the child was behaving in a manner consistent with posttraumatic stress disorder (PTSD).

The use of anatomically correct dolls can also result in objections—especially if the social worker has not received training in this area. Such dolls, if improperly used, can be suggestive and result in a judge denying admission of the child's hearsay statement.

Right to Counsel

At the temporary custody hearings, adjudicatory hearings, and dispositional hearings, the parent may be entitled to appointed counsel by statute or case law, but the Supreme Court held in *Lassiter v. Department of Social Services*, 452 U.S. 18 (1981), that, while it may be wise to provide counsel in proceedings to permanently terminate parental rights, there is no constitutional right to appointed counsel in such proceedings. This undoubtedly means that there is no constitutional right to appointed counsel in hearings on abuse, neglect, and dependency.

Most States offer counsel, GAL or a CASA volunteer for the child. Appointment of a GAL or CASA is a requirement for receiving federal funds under CAPTA. 42 U.S.C. § 5106a(b)(2); 45 C.F.R. § 1340.14.

Rights of Parents

It has been asserted that children should not be removed from the home without providing parents notice and an opportunity to be heard. The potential harm to the child in abuse and neglect situations, however, has led courts to sustain placement of children in protective custody without a prior hearing or even without prior notice as long as there will be notice and a prompt opportunity to be heard after the removal and there are clear standards to guide official discretion in making the removals. Likewise, as we have seen, there are federal and State statutes that require reasonable efforts be made to reunify a child and parent whenever possible. 42 U.S.C. §§ 671 (a)(15) and 672 (a)(1).

Rights of Foster Parents

The rights of foster parents in the process has been the subject of much debate. The majority of children who are removed from their homes because of abuse, neglect, or dependency are placed by agencies with foster parents. The relationship between the agency and the foster parent is contractual: foster parents provide childcare under the direction of the agency and are reimbursed by the agency for the costs of the care they provide. Foster care, in theory, offers temporary, time-limited care to children until they can return home, be placed with relatives, or be placed for adoption. Many children, however, spend long periods of time in foster care, often with the same foster parents, creating a strong psychological tie between the child and the foster parents.

Given the ties that develop, there is a question as to what rights foster parents should have regarding children in their care. Moreover, how can the rights of foster parents, if any, be balanced against the rights of a child's biological parents and of the child? These questions were addressed by the Supreme Court in *Smith v. Organization of Foster Families for Equality and Reform (OFFER)*, 431 U.S. 816 (1977), an action arising in New York on behalf of a class of foster parents. Each foster parent named as a plaintiff in the case had been a foster parent to a child for a substantial length of time, in some cases, beginning when the child was an infant. In each case, an agency proposed to remove the child from the foster home, either to return the child to his or her parents or to place the child in a different home or an institution. The foster parents objected to the removal of their foster children and claimed that, like biological or adoptive parents, they were entitled to a due process hearing before a foster child could be taken from them. The Court held that foster parents were not entitled to the same rights as biological or adoptive parents and that New York's procedures governing the removal of foster children from foster homes, which provided foster parents notice, an opportunity for conferences, and in some cases, administrative hearings or even judicial review of proposals to remove children, were constitutionally sufficient.

The ASFA provides no more protections to foster families than the Court in *Smith*. It requires that foster parents be:

> provided with notice of, and an opportunity to be heard in, any review or hearing to be held with respect to the child, except that

> this subparagraph shall not be construed to require that any foster parent, preadoptive parent, or relative providing care for the child be made a party to such a review or hearing solely on the basis of such notice and opportunity to be heard. 42 U.S.C. § 675(4)(G).

Agency Protection of Children

Given the many statutes related to child protection, it might appear that children are well protected. This protection, however, has been limited by the Supreme Court in *DeShaney v. Winnebago County Department of Social Services*, 489 U.S. 189 (1989). In that case the Court held that the duty of the county social services agency to protect a child from his father's repeated abuse did not exist where the State did not take the child into custody. Excerpts from the opinion follow:

> The facts of this case are undeniably tragic. Petitioner Joshua DeShaney was born in 1979. In 1980, a Wyoming court granted his parents a divorce and awarded custody of Joshua to his father, Randy DeShaney. The father shortly thereafter moved to Neenah, a city located in Winnebago County, Wisconsin, taking the infant Joshua with him. There he entered into a second marriage, which also ended in divorce.
>
> The Winnebago County authorities first learned that Joshua DeShaney might be a victim of child abuse in January 1982, when his father's second wife complained to the police, at the time of their divorce, that he had previously hit the boy causing marks and [was] a prime case for child abuse. The Winnebago County Department of Social Services (DSS) interviewed the father, but he denied the accusations, and DSS did not pursue them further. In January 1983, Joshua was admitted to a local hospital with multiple bruises and abrasions. The examining physician suspected child abuse and notified DSS, which immediately obtained an order from a Wis-

consin juvenile court placing Joshua in the temporary custody of the hospital. Three days later, the county convened an ad hoc "Child Protection Team"—a pediatrician, a psychologist, a police detective, the county's lawyer, several DSS caseworkers, and various hospital personnel—to consider Joshua's situation. At this meeting, the Team decided that there was insufficient evidence of child abuse to retain Joshua in the custody of the court. The Team did, however, decide to recommend several measures to protect Joshua, including enrolling him in a preschool program, providing his father with certain counseling services, and encouraging his father's girlfriend to move out of the home. Randy DeShaney entered into a voluntary agreement with DSS in which he promised to cooperate with them in accomplishing these goals.

Based on the recommendation of the Child Protection Team, the juvenile court dismissed the child protection case and returned Joshua to the custody of his father. A month later, emergency room personnel called the DSS caseworker handling Joshua's case to report that he had once again been treated for suspicious injuries. The caseworker concluded that there was no basis for action. For the next six months, the caseworker made monthly visits to the DeShaney home, during which she observed a number of suspicious injuries on Joshua's head; she also noticed that he had not been enrolled in school, and that the girlfriend had not moved out. The caseworker dutifully recorded these incidents in her files, along with her continuing suspicions that someone in the DeShaney household was physically abusing Joshua, but she did nothing more. In November 1983, the emergency room notified DSS that Joshua had been treated once again for injuries that they believed to be caused by child abuse. On the caseworker's next two visits to the DeShaney home, she was told that Joshua was too ill to see her. Still DSS took no action.

In March 1984, Randy DeShaney beat 4-year-old Joshua so severely that he fell into a life-threatening coma. Emergency brain surgery revealed a series of hemorrhages caused by traumatic injuries to the head inflicted over a long period of time. Joshua did

not die, but he suffered brain damage so severe that he is expected to spend the rest of his life confined to an institution for the profoundly retarded. Randy DeShaney was subsequently tried and convicted of child abuse.

Joshua and his mother brought this action under 42 U.S.C. § 1983 . . . against respondents Winnebago County, DSS, and various individual employees of DSS. The complaint alleged that respondents had deprived Joshua of his liberty without due process of law, in violation of his rights under the Fourteenth Amendment, by failing to intervene to protect him against a risk of violence at this father's hands, of which they knew or should have known.

After reviewing the scope of the due process clause as conferring, "no affirmative right to governmental aid, even where such aid may be necessary to secure life, liberty, or property interests" the Supreme Court denied relief to Joshua and his mother. The Court reasoned that Joshua's injuries were inflicted by his father when Joshua was in the custody of his father. The Court held that:

> While the State may have been aware of the dangers that Joshua faced in the free world, it played no part in their creation, nor did it do anything to render him any more vulnerable to them. That the State once took temporary custody of Joshua does not alter the analysis, for when it returned him to his father's custody, it placed him in no worse position than that in which he would have been had it not acted at all; the State does not become the permanent guarantor of an individual's safety by having once offered him shelter. Under these circumstances, the State had no constitutional duty to protect Joshua.

Judges and lawyers, like other humans, are moved by natural sympathy in a case like this to find a way for Joshua and his mother to receive adequate compensation for the grievous harm inflicted upon them. But before yielding to that impulse, it is well to remember once again that the harm was inflicted not by the State of Wisconsin, but by Joshua's father. The most that can be said of the state functionaries in this case is that they stood by and did nothing when suspicious circumstances dictated a more active role for them. In defense of them, it must also be said that had they moved too soon to take custody of the son away from the father, they would likely have been met with charges of improperly intruding into the parent-child relationship, charges based on the same Due Process Clause that forms the basis for the present charge of failure to provide adequate protection.

The *DeShaney* Court was sharply divided. In dissent, Justice William Brennan wrote:

My disagreement with the Court arises from its failure to see that inaction can be every bit as abusive of power as action, that oppression can result when a State undertakes a vital duty and then ignores it. Today's opinion construes the Due Process Clause to permit a State to displace private sources of protection and then, at the critical moment, to shrug its shoulders and turn away from the harm that it has promised to prevent. Because I cannot agree that our Constitution is indifferent to such indifference, I respectfully dissent.

Justice Blackmun added in a separate dissent:

Poor Joshua! Victim of repeated attacks by an irresponsible, bullying, cowardly, and intemperate father, and abandoned by respondents who placed him in a dangerous predicament and who knew or learned what was going on, and yet did essentially nothing except, as the Court revealingly observes, "dutifully recorded these incidents in [their] files." It is a sad commentary upon American life, and constitutional principles—so full of late of patriotic fervor and proud proclamations of "liberty and justice for all"—that this child, Joshua DeShaney, now is assigned to live out the remainder of his life profoundly retarded.

Although under the rationale of *DeShaney*, States have no constitutional obligation to protect children not in their custody, the opinion also suggests that States do have such an obligation to children in foster care. This was the conclusion of the case *Norfleet v. Arkansas Department of Human Services*, 989 F.2d 289 (8th Cir. 1993), which held that child welfare employees are not immune from damages brought by children mistreated while in foster care. In denying defendants' claim of qualified immunity in response to a suit brought under 42 U.S.C. § 1983, the Court reviewed the reasoning of *DeShaney* and stated, "Had the State by the affirmative exercise of its power removed Joshua from free society and placed him in a foster home operated by its agents, we might have a situation sufficiently analogous to incarceration or institutionalization to give rise to an affirmative duty to protect." *Norfleet* cited opinions from other circuits holding that the State had a duty to protect children in foster care.

CHILD WELFARE SERVICES FOR THE ABUSED AND NEGLECTED CHILD

Prevention Efforts

Research over the past twenty-five years has shown child maltreatment to be linked to many social problems such as domestic violence, substance abuse, criminal behavior, teen pregnancy, unemployment, and homelessness. Thus, child abuse and neglect result in a significant cost to society, financially as well as in human lives.[4]

In the late 1970s, a policy initiative of the National Committee to Prevent Child Abuse, an advocacy organization based in Chicago, was launched to advance prevention efforts at the State level by creating Children's Trust and Prevention Funds. The idea of Children's Trust Funds originated with the late Dr. Ray Helfer, a pediatrician nationally recognized in the field of child abuse. Dr. Helfer proposed designating a specific funding source and establishing a mechanism to promote a public-private partnership for prevention at the State level. In 1980, Kansas became the first State to pass a law creating a Children's Trust Fund. Today, all fifty States, and the District of Columbia and Puerto Rico have established Children's Trust or Prevention Funds through legislation.

Trust or Prevention Funds are administered through various board structures and receive funding from a variety of sources, including voluntary income tax check-off contributions; surcharges or fees on marriage; birth, death, or divorce certificates; interest; federal grants; foundations; and corporate or private contributions. The Federal Child Abuse Prevention and Treatment Act (CAPTA), 42 U.S.C. § 5101, *et seq.*, has provided funding to States to establish and maintain child abuse and neglect prevention and family-based support services through the Challenge, Prevention, and most recently, the Community-Based Family Resource and Support Grants.

Funds from State Children Trust or Prevention Funds are allocated for many creative and innovative prevention activities. Funding is primarily provided to community-based organizations for a broad range of prevention strategies, all designed to assist and support families and individuals in developing or maintaining positive parenting skills and relationship behaviors with the goal to reduce the risk of child abuse and neglect. Other activities supported by trust funds include direct funding for primary and secondary prevention services, that is, early intervention strategies specifically designed to prevent abuse and neglect before it occurs.

Prevention efforts also occur through other State and local government agencies, such as health and social services, and are supported by foundations, service clubs, businesses, private individuals, and philanthropic organizations. To effectively address prevention and ameliorate child maltreatment, the commitment of every citizen, community organization, government agency, corporation, business, and faith community is needed to support and strengthen families.

Services to Children and Families

Legislation both gives State social services agencies the responsibility for providing services to children who have been abused or neglected and authorizes public moneys to support these services. State statutes typically define what services will be provided and by whom and specify who is eligible to receive services. In addition, they generally grant agencies

---

4. *Child Maltreatment in Colorado: The Value of Prevention and the Cost of Failure to Prevent*, A Cost of Failure Analysis Commissioned by the Colorado Children's Trust Fund, 1995.

the authority to promulgate regulations as necessary to carry out their duties. In the ASFA, the federal government has authorized "time-limited family reunification services." These services are provided to a child who has been placed out of the home to "include individual, group, and family counseling, substance abuse treatment services, mental health services, assistance to address domestic violence, temporary child care and transportation services." 42 U.S.C. § 6292(7).

Managed Care

The increasing costs associated with managing the care of children in out-of-home placements has resulted in many public sector agencies contracting with private sector agencies for the provision of services. States now use some form of managed care for Medicaid recipients, particularly those who receive behavioral health care. It is important for the social worker, however, whose child or family is receiving services under a managed care program to serve as an advocate, to ensure that children and families are receiving necessary and appropriate services from the managed care agencies. Managed care concepts will be more fully explored in chapter 14.

Family Preservation

The disruption to the family and costs associated with placing children out of the home has led federal and State governments to enact family preservation programs. Washington was one of the first States to initiate a family preservation program. The act that created Washington's family preservation services provides as follows:

> The legislature believes that protecting the health and safety of children is paramount. The legislature recognizes that the number of children entering out-of-home care is increasing . . . Reasonable efforts by the department to shorten out-of-home placement or avoid it altogether should be a major focus of the child welfare system . . .
>
> Within available funds, the legislature directs the department to focus child welfare services on protecting the child, strengthening families and, to the extent possible, providing necessary services in the family setting, while drawing upon the strengths of the family. The legislature intends services be locally based and offered as early as possible to avoid disruption to the family; out-of-home placement of the child; and entry into the dependency system. The legislature also intends that these services be used for those families whose children are returning to the home from out-of-home care. Wash. Rev. Code § 74.14C.005(1).

On the federal level, the Social Security Act was amended in 1993 to provide financial assistance for family preservation services "designed to improve parenting skills by reinforcing parents' confidence in their strengths, and helping them to identify where improvement is needed and to obtain assistance in improving those skills with respect to matters such as child development, family budgeting, coping with stress, health, and nutrition." 42 U.S.C. § 6292(a)(1). Social workers do family preservation work at mental health agencies, private family preservation agencies, or at local social services departments.

Kinship Care

Kinship care involves placing children whose parents are unable to care for them with relatives. These relatives may provide temporary care, may be certified as an approved foster home, or may assume legal guardianship, or custody of the child. States may provide subsidies to the guardians for care of children who would otherwise be in foster care. An example of these guardianship laws is found in Nebraska Rev. Stat. § 43(a)84.02:

> The Department of Social Services may make payments as needed on behalf of a child who has been a ward of the department after the appointment of a guardian for the child. Such payments to the guardian may include maintenance costs, medical and surgical expenses, and other costs incidental to the care of the child. All such payments shall terminate on or before the childs' nineteenth birthday. The child under guardianship shall be a child for whom the guardianship would not be possible without the financial aid provided under this section.

SPECIAL CIRCUMSTANCES IN CHILD ABUSE, NEGLECT, AND DEPENDENCY LAW

The Disabled Family Member

The disabled parent or child presents unique challenges to the social worker charged with reasonable efforts to prevent out-of-home placement. The parent, for example, may have a disability that interferes with their ability to parent; this disability may have been the contributing cause of the abuse or neglect case being filed. The Americans with Disabilities Act (ADA) may require the social worker to provide reasonable accommodations to a willing family member who would oth-

erwise qualify for services. The ADA provides: "Subject to the provisions of this subchapter, no qualified individual with a disability shall, by reason of such disability, be excluded from participation in or be denied the benefits of the services, programs, or activities of a public entity, or be subjected to discrimination by any such entity." 42 U.S.C. § 12132. Based on the ADA, government agencies must "administer services, programs, and activities in the most integrated settings appropriate to the needs of qualified individuals with disabilities." 28 C.F.R. § 35.130(d). Thus, courts have held that social service agencies must provide appropriate services to disabled persons notwithstanding an agency's claim that it could not do so because there was a long waiting list. For example, in *Helen L. v. Didario*, 46 F. 3d 325 (3d Cir. 1995), the Court stated "The fact that it is more convenient, either administratively or fiscally, to provide services in a segregated manner, does not constitute a valid justification for separate or different services under title II of the ADA."

The Native American Child

The social worker's role in the placement of Native American children and adoption by white parents has been the subject of much debate and controversy. Arguments were made that social workers were overlooking cultural differences, were ignorant of Native American child-rearing practices, and were placing Native American children in foster care or in adoptive homes at significantly greater rates than non-Native American children. A report to the House of Representatives prior to the passage of the Indian Child Welfare Act (ICWA) stated, for example:

> In judging the fitness of a particular family, many social workers, ignorant of Indian cultural values and social norms, make decisions that are wholly inappropriate in the context of Indian family life and so they frequently discover neglect or abandonment where none exists.
>
> For example, the dynamics of Indian extended families are largely misunderstood. An Indian child may have scores of, perhaps more than a hundred, relatives who are counted as close, responsible members of the family. Many social workers, untutored in the ways of Indian family life or assuming them to be socially irresponsible, consider leaving the child with persons outside the nuclear family as neglect and thus as grounds for terminating parental rights.
>
> Indian child-rearing practices are also misinterpreted in evaluating a child's behavior and parental concern. It may appear that the child is running wild and that the parents do not care. What is labeled "permissiveness" may often, in fact, simply be a different but effective way of disciplining children. 1978 U.S. Code Cong. And Adm. News, p. 7532.

In response to such criticisms, the federal government passed the ICWA, which provides a number of specific jurisdictional and procedural requirements and presumptions for any child the court "knows or has reason to know" is a Native American child. Requirements under ICWA include:

(a) Notice; time for commencement of proceedings; additional time for preparation
In any involuntary proceeding in a State court, where the court knows or has reason to know that an Indian child is involved, the party seeking the foster care placement of, or termination of parental rights to, an Indian child shall notify the parent or Indian custodian and the Indian child's tribe, by registered mail with return receipt requested, of the pending proceedings and of their right of intervention.

(b) Appointment of counsel
In any case in which the court determines indigency, the parent or Indian custodian shall have the right to court-appointed counsel in any removal, placement, or termination proceeding. The court may, in its discretion, appoint counsel for the child upon a finding that such appointment is in the best interest of the child.

(c) Examination of reports or other documents
Each party to a foster care placement or termination of parental rights proceeding under State law involving an Indian child shall have the right to examine all reports or other documents filed with the court upon which any decision with respect to such action may be based.

(d) Remedial services and rehabilitative programs; preventive measures
Any party seeking to effect a foster care placement of, or termination of parental rights to, an Indian child under State law shall satisfy the court that active efforts have been made to provide remedial services and rehabilitative programs designed to prevent the breakup of the Indian family and that these efforts have proved unsuccessful.

(e) Foster care placement orders; evidence; determination of damage to child
No foster care placement may be ordered in such proceeding in the absence of a determination, supported by clear and convincing evidence, including testimony of qualified expert witnesses, that the continued custody of the child by the parent or Indian custodian is likely to result in serious emotional or physical damage to the child.

(f) Parental rights termination orders; evidence; determination of damage to child
No termination of parental rights may be ordered in such proceeding in the absence of a determination, supported by evidence beyond a reasonable doubt, including testimony of qualified expert witnesses, that the continued custody of the child by the parent or Indian custodian is likely to result in serious emotional or physical damage to the child. 25 U.S.C. § 1912.

The requirements under ICWA thus require social workers to immediately notify the tribe of any Native American child who is alleged to be abused or neglected. Otherwise, the tribe may later intervene and undo whatever has occurred to that point, including adoption proceedings.

Protection from Domestic Violence

Legislation enacted in response to the problem of domestic violence, which will be discussed in detail in chapter 12, generally is used to allow courts to enter orders in cases when one parent has abused another parent. This use of the legislation may provide protection to children by mandating arrest and prosecution of the abuser. Under the authority of domestic violence laws, the court may order the abuser to leave the home or to participate in counseling.

Punishing Criminal Behavior

Criminal laws may authorize the State to prosecute and punish adults who abuse or neglect children. Child abuse or neglect may be a distinct crime; the defendant in such cases may be prosecuted criminally at the same time there is a civil child protection case. Criminal charges may protect children victims through restraining orders that may prohibit contact with the victim. Subsequent conviction may protect children victims by requiring the perpetrator to comply with terms and conditions of probation or by incarcerating the perpetrator.

Status Offenders

Juvenile courts have been able to assume jurisdiction over minors whose behavior is injurious to their own welfare and beyond the control of the parent. These minors are frequently termed **status offenders**, suggesting that they have not committed crimes but have a certain status, such as incorrigibility, or that they have committed offenses that are crimes only by virtue of the status of being a minor, such as truancy or curfew violations. Although the term *status offender* is commonly used, it is not a label that accurately describes either the behavior or the way in which the juvenile court intervenes. Nor is it a term that is found in definitions in most juvenile court acts. Minors who have been termed *status offender* are better thought of as youth who are troubled and who present troublesome behavior in the eyes of their parents, in other adults in authority, or both.

States differ in the statutory labels assigned to these minors. Common terms are **minor, children**, or **persons in need of supervision** (MINS, CHINS, or PINS), and **child in need of protection and services** (CHIPS). Some States recognize that troubled and troublesome behavior in children reflects dysfunction in the family and provides for a **family in need of supervision** (FINS).

States also differ in what behavior invokes juvenile court intervention. Statutes generally include behavior such as repeated runaways or include children who are otherwise beyond the control of their parents, chronically truant, or drug or alcohol dependent. States may include such vague bases for intervention as "incorrigibility," "dissolute behavior," and "promiscuity."

As we noted in chapter 7, some States include some or all status offenders as delinquents in their juvenile court acts. Other States, however, characterize status offenders as abused or neglected children.

Some States have been placing restrictions on the assumption of juvenile court jurisdiction unless there is evidence of abuse or neglect. In addition, agencies have become increasingly unwilling to assume custody or guardianship of such minors. The reluctance of State intervention reflects a preference for use of community-based voluntary services, a desire to avoid stigmatizing children, a recognition that traditional child welfare services have not, and perhaps cannot, serve such children effectively, and a recognition that such services are very costly. Notwithstanding this reluctance, juvenile courts may order social services agencies assume custody of status offenders.

9

Adoption

Adoption is a legal process through which a new legal parent-child relationship is created. While both children and adults may be adopted, adoption of adults rarely occurs, and when it does, it rarely involves social workers. This chapter will only address the law and legal issues concerning adoption of children.

Adoption of children involves two stages, both of which are governed by State law. One process, which may not occur in all cases, dissolves any existing legal relationship between a living parent and his or her child. The other process, which does occur in all cases, creates a new legal parent-child relationship. The dissolution of an existing legal parent-child relationship may or may not involve court action although, to be effective, the dissolution should be recognized by a court. The creation of a new legal parent-child relationship always involves court action.

Adoption may be arranged in several ways. The form of adoption that is perhaps most familiar is what might be termed **traditional agency adoption**. In such an adoption, prospective adoptive parents apply to an adoption agency and are evaluated for their suitability. Generally, this evaluation is done by social workers. If the prospective parents are approved for adoption and a suitable child becomes available, the agency places the child with them. A court later approves of the adoption.

Closely related to traditional agency adoption is *adoption by foster parents*—a form of adoption that is occurring more and more frequently. Adoption by foster parents is similar to traditional adoption in that an adoption is arranged and approved by an agency, and a court simply approves the adoption.

There are two types of foster parent adoptions. In the first type, the parents apply to provide foster care, and a child is placed with them for temporary care. The child later becomes eligible for adoption, and the child's foster parents wish to adopt the child. Adoption by the foster parents is determined to be the best plan for the child.

The other type of foster parent adoption is sometimes termed **legal risk** or **foster-adopt adoption**. The foster parents from the outset agree to provide foster care for a child who the agency believes will ultimately be free for adoption. It is understood that if the child becomes eligible, the foster parents will adopt the child, subject to court approval.

Another form of adoption is termed **private adoption**. A private adoption is arranged between a child's birth parents and the adoptive parents, typically with the assistance of an intermediary, generally a physician or an attorney. Social workers may be asked by a court to evaluate the suitability of the adoptive parents, but will not be involved in arranging the adoption, at least not as employees of an agency.

States forbid paying a parent for a child—often called **black market adoption**—but States may allow adoptive parents to reimburse a mother's expenses in bearing a child. This is often referred to as **grey market adoption** because the reimbursement may be tantamount to payment. Because grey market adoptions are frowned upon, some States forbid or very carefully regulate private adoptions.

The most common form of adoption is *adoption by relatives*. In this form of adoption, a relative, often a step-parent, adopts the child. Social workers usually are not involved in stepparent adoptions in any way unless State statute or local practice requires an investigation of the stepparent. Depending on state law, social workers may be involved when another relative, such as a grandparent, seeks to adopt the child. Such situations often occur when a child has been found by a court to be abused, neglected, or dependent and is in the custody of an agency.

THE ADOPTION PROCESS

Dissolution of an Existing Legal Parent-Child Relationship

Before a new parent-child relationship can be created, any existing parent-child relationship must be dissolved. This is true for agency, private, and relative adoptions. An existing relationship can be dissolved in one of two ways: voluntary relinquishment or involuntary termination of parental rights.

Voluntary Relinquishment. A parent may voluntarily relinquish or surrender the right to raise and care for the child. Relinquishment for the purposes of adoption generally occurs by consent or surrender.

A parent may **consent** to the adoption of his or her child by another person. Consents are typically used when the adoptive parent or parents are known to the birth parent or have been identified. In most private adoptions, the child's birth parents consent to their child's adoption by the prospective adoptive parents. In many adoptions by a stepfather, the child's birth father consents to the adoption of the child by the stepfather.

A **surrender** is similar to a consent in that a parent voluntarily agrees to the adoption of his or her child. It is different, however, because the specific adoptive parents are not identified. A surrender grants an agency the authority to choose adoptive parents and to approve of the child's adoption by the adoptive parents. Essentially, the parents surrender to the agency their authority concerning their child's adoption. Unless agency policy states differently, the birth parent who surrenders a child to an agency has no right to select the adoptive parent or to approve or disapprove of the adoption.

State statutes generally require that both consents and surrenders be in writing. Social workers frequently are involved in consents and surrenders, meaning that the parent signs the required forms in the presence of the social worker. Attorneys and judges are also often involved in consents and surrenders.

Once parents have signed a consent or a surrender, they have no further legal rights regarding their child. Typically, State statutes provide that consents and surrenders are final and are irrevocable—either immediately or after a brief period of time. To protect birth parents' rights, some States have liberalized the provisions for revocation of consents and surrenders to make them revocable for a long time after they are executed, often as long as six months. This approach can cause serious problems for adopted children and adoptive parents.

Consents and surrenders can be revoked if they are given either under duress or fraud. Thus, State statutes include provisions designed to assure that consents and surrenders are given knowingly and voluntarily. For example, the statutes may provide that a mother cannot surrender her child or consent to her child's adoption before or within a specified period after the child is born. The statutes may require the parent to indicate in writing or in open court that the consent or surrender was given knowingly and voluntarily. Moreover, special provisions, such as appointing a guardian *ad litem*, may be made for parents who are minors or who are mentally disabled.

The consequences to a child and adoptive parents when consent is not clearly given are enormous. Consider the Florida case that denied an adoption of a child, and placed that child back with her mother, even though the child had been in the custody of the prospective adoptive parents for well over a year. In *In re Adoption of Baby Girl C*, 511 So. 2d 345 (Fla.App. 2 Dist. 1987), the court found that the natural mother's consent had been effectively revoked because it had been given under great personal pressure—she feared being arrested and jailed because of statements made by a detective to her. In fact, she was jailed. The court concluded that she had given consent under duress. The judgement included the following findings:

> The Mother . . . is a woman of limited intelligence. According to the psychological testimony, she has an I.Q. of approximately 83. Her state of mind at the time of this incident was such that she would have unusual difficulty making a rational decision under stress. The testimony which the Court accepts as true is that she would have "locked" her position and would have refused to rationally consider available alternatives.

The court concluded:

> the natural mother . . . did not mislead appellants and was not the proximate cause of their

pain. She withdrew her consent about a week after it had been given and before appellants took custody of, and developed their love for, the child . . . [t]he record indicates that [the appellants] took custody of the child knowing, as did [social services], that the natural mother's consent to the adoption had been withdrawn. As the trial court said in its order denying appellants' motion for post judgement relief, "[social services] took it upon themselves to interpret the law [as to whether the natural mother could effectively withdraw her consent about a week later] and give the . . . [appellants] the 'choice' of trying to live with an adverse ruling." Appellants took that choice and are now suffering the consequences. They are suffering deeply but not through the fault of the natural mother. This sad state of affairs is not injustice or manifest injustice requiring that we now depart from the law of the case and take the child from the natural mother. We certainly understand appellants' feelings of enormous loss. But, again, that loss evidently resulted after appellants' own decision, when or about the time they took custody of the child, to try, if there were ultimately an adverse ruling against them as there has been, to live with that ruling. Also, there should be no ignoring the enormous loss which would surely occur to a natural mother if her child were taken away from her.

Obviously, social workers must exercise extreme caution as they take consents and surrenders. Social workers are obligated to explore the emotional, social, and legal consequences of the decision with a parent who is considering giving up a child for adoption. In addition, although it may not be required by statute, it is good practice not to allow parents to execute consents or surrenders immediately after they have decided to give up the child. Moreover, it is good practice to encourage, and perhaps insist, that the parents discuss the decision with an attorney or a trusted professional who is not involved in the decision. The parent should sign the relinquishment before a judge who has, at least for the record, fully informed the parent of the legal consequences of the action and obtained assurances that it is being done voluntarily. States may also require the relinquishing parent to undergo counseling in this regard, prior to formalizing the relinquishment process.

Termination of Parental Rights. A legal parent-child relationship can be dissolved involuntarily through a court action, commonly called **termination of parental rights**. Courts may terminate parental rights when: 1) a parent is unwilling or unable to consent to his or her child's adoption or to surrender the child for adoption; 2) there is sufficient evidence that the parent is an unfit parent as defined by State law; and 3) termination is in the best interests of the child.

Occasionally, courts will also terminate parental rights after a child's parents have either surrendered or consented to their child's adoption. This reinforces the validity of the surrenders or consents and protects the subsequent adoption from later attack.

The words used in termination statutes varies from State to State. Statutes in some States speak specifically of termination of parental rights, while statutes in other States allow a "waiver" of the requirement that a parent consent to the adoption of his or her child if there is sufficient evidence of parental unfitness and adoption is in the best interests of the child. Whatever words are used, a termination means a total and final end to all parental rights and responsibilities. Stated differently, it causes a complete severance of the legal parent-child relationship, with the probable exception of the child's right to inheritance pending an adoption.

Grounds for Termination. Termination of parental rights actions typically are taken in behalf of children who have been adjudicated abused, neglected, or dependent and who have been removed from the custody of their parents. The actions are often initiated by the social workers who have been providing services to the children and their parents with the goal of returning the child home. The actions are initiated only when it becomes apparent that reunification is impossible.

As we saw in the previous chapter, the Adoption and Safe Families Act of 1997 (ASFA) requires a State to terminate parental rights,

> in the case of a child who has been in foster care under the responsibility of the State for 15 of the most recent 22 months . . . [or] the parent has committed murder of another child of the parent, committed voluntary manslaughter of another child of the parent, aided or abetted, attempted, conspired, or solicited to commit such a murder or such a voluntary manslaughter, or committed a felony assault that has resulted in serious bodily injury to the child or to another child of the parent.

Other grounds for termination, all of which relate to the unfitness of the parent, will also be specified in State statutes. Typical grounds include: depravity or immorality; mental disability; abandonment; extreme or repeated abuse or neglect; failure to make reasonable efforts to correct the conditions that were the basis for removing a child from the parent's custody; failure to make reasonable progress toward the return of a child who has been removed from the parent's custody; and failure to visit, meaningfully communicate with, or plan for the future of a child who is in foster care.

The various grounds for termination related to unfitness raise somewhat different legal and practical questions. Many of these grounds may be unconstitutionally vague and overbroad. Unlike a mere finding of abuse or neglect in a proceeding under a juvenile court act, however, a termination means a final and complete deprivation of parental rights. Consequently, courts may be more willing to find grounds for termination unconstitutionally vague and overbroad, whereas they are unwilling to find definitions of neglect and abuse unconstitutionally vague and overbroad. For example, in *Alsager v. Iowa*, 406 F.Supp. 10 (S.D. Iowa 1975), the Alsagers argued that an Iowa statute that provided the basis for terminating their parental rights for five of their six children was unconstitutionally vague. The statute allowed termination when parents: "have substantially and continuously or repeatedly refused to give the child necessary parental care and protection" or "are unfit by reason of conduct found by the court likely to be detrimental to the physical or mental health or morals of the child."

The court agreed that these statutory grounds for termination were unconstitutionally vague, stating:

> The standards of "necessary parental care and protection," and of "[parental] conduct . . . detrimental to the physical or mental health or morals of the child," are susceptible to multifarious interpretations which prevent the ordinary person from knowing what is and is not prohibited. An examination of these phrases will not inform an ordinary person as to what conduct is required or must be avoided in

order to prevent parental termination. For instance, a parent might follow a rigid scheme of "discipline-instilling" corporal punishment believing himself in full compliance with the law, only to learn of his folly at a termination proceeding . . .

> The second danger present in a vague statute is the impermissible delegation of discretion from the state legislature to the state law enforcement body . . . The termination of the parent-child relationship in any given case may thus turn upon which state officials are involved in the case, rather than upon explicit standards reflecting legislative intent. This danger is especially grave in the highly subjective context of determining an approved mode of child rearing. The Court finds these standards unconstitutionally vague in that they are permeated with the "dangers of arbitrary and discriminatory application."

> The third danger present in a vague statute is the risk that the exercise of constitutional rights will be inhibited . . . Wary of what conduct is required and what conduct must be avoided to prevent termination, parents might fail to exercise their rights freely and fully. The risk that parents will be forced to steer far wider of "the unlawful zone" than is constitutionally necessary is not justified when the state is capable of enacting less ambiguous termination standards.

> This Court is not indifferent to the difficulties confronting the State of Iowa when attempting to regulate parental conduct vis-à-vis the child. Nevertheless, Due Process requires the state to clearly identify and define the evil from which the child needs protection and to specify what parental conduct so contributes to that evil that the state is justified in terminating the parent-child relationship.

Historically, courts have also been reluctant to terminate parental rights on the basis of abandonment. Some courts hold that as long as the parent shows some interest in the child, the child is not abandoned. Parents who occasionally visited their children in foster care or who sent birthday gifts but had little meaningful contact with their children have been found not to have abandoned them.

The terms *extreme* or *repeated* abuse or neglect as a basis for termination presents a different set of problems. Once a child has been removed from a parent's care, there is or should be little opportunity for the parent to continue to abuse or neglect the child; at this point, the child is under the protection of a child welfare agency. Since children in foster care will usually visit their parents, abuse or neglect can and does occur during visits. If the caseworker, however, suspects abuse or neglect during visits, the visits will be restricted or supervised, thus preventing extreme or repeated abuse or neglect.

Because of the inherent problems in using grounds related to character, abandonment, or extreme or repeated abuse or neglect, States have shifted to an emphasis on parental behavior while children are in foster care. Termination statutes have been amended to allow termination when parents fail to maintain contact with or plan for their children who are in foster care or when parents do not make reasonable efforts to correct the conditions that were the basis for the child originally being removed from their custody. Where statutes provide such grounds, they usually require the agency having custody or guardianship of the child to make diligent efforts to encourage contact between parents and children and to help the parents correct the conditions that resulted in the child being removed.

While a finding of unfitness is usually required before parental rights can be terminated, in a few cases, it has been argued that a termination should occur solely because it is in the best interest of a child. Usually, in these cases, a parent has

had no or limited contact with a child, through no fault of the parent's or for reasons unrelated to the parent relationship with the child, and the child has formed strong emotional bonds with a nonparent who wishes to adopt the child. Although the parent is not unfit, it is argued that the parent's rights should be terminated and the nonparent allowed to adopt the child. In a few such cases around the country, courts have terminated parental rights, but their rulings have been questioned.

Social workers should remember that most children who are removed from the custody of their parents will be returned to the custody of their parents. While the child is in foster care, the agency will, or at least should, given federal and State statutory provisions, work with the parent to correct the conditions that necessitated removal. This work, as well as efforts to terminate parental rights if reunification is impossible, will be facilitated by written case plans specifying the responsibilities of parents and caseworkers. The case plans can direct intervention and can also implicitly define "reasonable efforts" and "reasonable contact," common phrases in the statutes setting forth grounds for termination of parental rights. Documentation that parents failed to make reasonable efforts or maintain reasonable contact as defined in case plans can be introduced as evidence in termination proceedings.

Procedural Protections. There are procedural protections that must be followed when terminating parental rights. These protections, many of which are mandated by the Constitution, are specified in State statutes, which are part of a State's juvenile court act or part of a separate law dealing specifically with adoption. Wherever located, the statutes provide for notice to the parent and for a full evidentiary hearing before parental rights are terminated.

State statutes generally provide that children who are the subject of termination proceedings will have guardians *ad litem* appointed for them, and that indigent parents will have appointed counsel. Appointment of counsel, however, is not constitutionally required. The Supreme Court held in *Lassiter v. Department of Social Services*, 452 U.S. 18 (1981), that the Fourteenth Amendment requirement of due process is not violated by leaving the decision whether to appoint counsel to the trial court's discretion. The Court, however, noted:

> A wise public policy . . . may require that higher standards be adopted than those minimally tolerable under the Constitution. Informed opinion has clearly come to hold that an indigent parent is entitled to the assistance of appointed counsel not only in parental termination proceedings, but also in dependency and neglect proceedings as well. Most significantly, 33 States and the District of Columbia provide statutorily for the appointment of counsel in termination cases. The Court's opinion today in no way implies that the standards increasingly urged by informed public opinion and now widely followed by the States are other than enlightened and wise.

The Supreme Court has since increased the procedural protections in termination. proceedings. For example, less than a year after *Lassiter*, the Supreme Court, in *Santosky v. Kramer*, 455 U.S. 745 (1982), addressed the standard of proof in termination proceedings. The Court held that due process required a specific procedural protection in termination proceedings: proof by at least clear and convincing evidence. The decision was 5-4. Justice Blackmun, who sharply dissented from the majority in

Lassiter, wrote the opinion for the Court in *Santosky*, a portion of which is excerpted below.

> In *Lassiter*, to be sure, the Court held that fundamental fairness may be maintained in parental rights termination proceedings even when some procedures are mandated only on a case-by-case basis, rather than through rules of general application. But this Court never has approved case-by-case determination of the proper *standard of proof* for a given proceeding. Standards of proof, like other "[p]rocedural due process rules[,] are shaped by the risk of error inherent in the truth-finding process as applied to the *generality of cases*, not the rare exceptions." Since the litigants and the factfinder must know at the outset of a given proceeding how the risk of error will be allocated, the standard of proof necessarily must be calibrated in advance. Retrospective case-by-case review cannot preserve fundamental fairness when a class of proceedings is governed by a constitutionally defective evidentiary standard.
>
> In parental rights termination proceedings, the private interest affected is commanding; the risk of error from using a preponderance standard is substantial; and the countervailing governmental interest favoring that standard is comparatively slight . . . use of a "fair preponderance of the evidence" standard in such proceedings is inconsistent with due process.

The Supreme Court in *M.L.B v. S.L.J.*, 519 U.S. 102, (1996), extended the procedural protections afforded parents beyond *Lassiter* and held that the State cannot deprive a parent of an appeal of a decision terminating parental rights just because the parent cannot afford to pay for preparation of the record.

Creation of a New Legal Parent-Child Relationship

The prospective adoptive parent or parents file an adoption petition, which initiates adoption proceedings. This petition typically presents information about the prospective adoptive parents, the child to be adopted, the relationship between the child and the prospective adoptive parents, and the child's legal status. If the adoption is an agency adoption, the petition will also include information about the agency. If the child's birth parents have not consented to the adoption, surrendered the child to an agency, or had their parental rights terminated, the petition will also present information about them and seek to terminate their rights.

If the adoption does not involve a related child, the court will appoint an agency or an individual to investigate the prospective adoptive parents soon after the petition is filed. In some jurisdictions, an investigation will also be ordered even if the adoption is of a related child. If the child is being placed through an agency, staff in that agency will complete the investigation; usually it will have been completed before the petition was filed. Upon completion of the investigation, the social worker involved will file a report of the investigation with the court.

In most cases there will be two court hearings related to the adoption. The first, which is usually called an interim hearing, occurs soon after the petition is filed. The primary purpose of the hearing is to assure that the consents, surrenders, or termination orders are valid.[1] This hearing is particularly important in private adoptions of unrelated children where there is less assurance of the validity of consents or surrenders than there is when an agency has been involved with the parent or when the adoption is by a relative. If parental rights have not been terminated, the court may terminate rights at this point. The court may also appoint a guardian *ad litem* to represent the best interests of the child. All these steps are necessary to protect the adoptive parent-child relationship from later attack. The custody of a child pending the adoption may also be considered at an interim hearing.

At some later point, after the report of the investigation is filed with the court, a final hearing will be held. The judge will hear evidence regarding the prospective adoptive parents and their relationship with the child. If the judge has not done so at an interim hearing, the judge will rule on the validity of the consents, surrenders, or termination orders. If satisfied that the child is legally free to be adopted and that the proposed adoption is in the best interests of the child, the judge will enter an order of adoption. This order is final, subject to appeal.

The order of adoption creates a legal relationship between the adoptive parent and child identical to the legal relationship between a child and a birth parent. The adoptive parent has all of the rights and responsibilities of a birth parent. The adoptive legal relationship, like the relationship between a child and birth parents, can be ended only through consent, surrender or termination of parental rights. The State has the same authority to intervene as with birth parents.

Following the adoption, a new birth certificate will be issued for the child. The

---

1. You should note that when the term *consent* is used in this chapter, it refers to a consent to adopt a child by the child's parent or by an agency acting under the authority of a surrender or a termination order. The consent of the child to be adopted may also be required. The statutes in most States specify an age beyond which a child's consent to the adoption is required.

new certificate will list the child's new name if different from the name given by his or her birth parents, and it will list the adoptive parents' names as parents and the age they were at the time the child was born. The original birth certificate will be sealed. While provisions vary from State to State, the statutes in most States also allow the judge to seal all court records related to an adoption.

If procedures involved in the adoption process are not strictly followed, the consequences can be disastrous to the child and to the prospective adoptive parents. Consider the highly publicized and emotionally laden case, *In re Baby Girl Clausen*, 442 Mich. 648, 502 N.W.2d 649 (1993). Excerpts from this case show what happened:

> On February 8, 1991, Cara Clausen gave birth to a baby girl in Iowa. Proceedings in Iowa have established that defendant Daniel Schmidt is the child's father. On February 10, 1991, Clausen signed a release of custody form, relinquishing her parental rights to the child. Clausen, who was unmarried at the time of the birth, [she and Daniel Schmidt married in April 1992] had named Scott Seefeldt as the father. On February 14, 1991, he executed a release of custody form.
>
> On February 25, 1991, petitioners Roberta and Jan DeBoer, who are Michigan residents, filed a petition for adoption of the child in juvenile court in Iowa. A hearing was held the same day, at which the parental rights of Cara Clausen and Seefeldt were terminated, and petitioners were granted custody of the child during the pendency of the proceeding. The DeBoers returned to Michigan with the child, and she has lived with them in Michigan continuously since then.
>
> However, the prospective adoption never took place. On March 6, 1991, nine days after the filing of the adoption petition, Cara Clausen filed a motion in the Iowa Juvenile Court to revoke her release of custody. In an

affidavit accompanying the request, Clausen stated that she had lied when she named Seefeldt as the father of the child, and that the child's father actually was Daniel Schmidt. Schmidt filed an affidavit of paternity on March 12, 1991 and on March 27, 1991, he filed a petition in the Iowa district court, seeking to intervene in the adoption proceeding initiated by the DeBoers.

The district court in Iowa conducted a bench trial and concluded that the De-Boer's position to adopt the child must be denied. The case was appealed and, on remand from the Iowa Supreme Court, the district court ordered the DeBoers to appear on December 3, 1992, with the child. The DeBoers did not appear at the hearing so the court entered an order on December 3, 1992, terminating the DeBoers' rights as temporary guardians and custodians of the child. The court found that "Mr. And Mrs. Deboer have no legal right or claim to the physical custody of this child. They are acting outside any legal claim to physical control and possession of this child." The DeBoers then filed a petition in Michigan asking the district court there to assume jurisdiction. The petition requested that the court enjoin enforcement of the Iowa custody order and find that it was not enforceable, or, in the alternative, to modify it to give custody to the DeBoers. On December 3, 1992, the Michigan Court entered an *ex parte* temporary restraining order, which directed that the child remain in the custody of the DeBoers, and ordered Schmidt not to remove the child from Michigan.

The Michigan Court of Appeals reversed the trial court, concluding that that court lacked jurisdiction and the DeBoers lacked standing to bring the action. Following the Court of Appeals decision the

DeBoers filed a complaint for "child custody, declaratory relief, and injunctive relief" in the Michigan District Court. More than *two years* had elapsed since Baby Girl Clausen was placed with the DeBoers. The plaintiff was described as "Jessica DeBoer (a/k/a Baby Girl Clausen), by her next friend, Peter Darrow." Mr. Darrow, who was a Michigan attorney, was appointed by the court as guardian *ad litem* for the child. The District Court directed the De-Boers and Schmidts to appear at a hearing on April 22 and the Court ordered that pending that hearing, "the minor child's residence and status quo shall be maintained." On April 22, after hearing argument by counsel for the Schmidts and the DeBoers, the district court entered another order "continuing status quo."

On April 27, 1993, the Schmidts filed an application for leave to appeal. After conducting an extensive legal analysis, the Michigan Supreme Court rejected the arguments presented by the DeBoers. The court held,

> The United States Supreme Court cases on which the DeBoers rely do not establish that they have a federal constitutional right to seek custody of the child . . . as the Iowa district court noted after reviewing these United States Supreme Court cases: "It is therefore now clearly established that an unwed father who has not had a custodial relationship with a child nevertheless has a constitutionally protected interest in establishing that relationship."
>
> And, as the Iowa Supreme Court concluded: "We agree with the district court that abandonment was not established by clear and convincing evidence. In fact, virtually all of the evidence regarding Daniel's intent regarding this baby suggests just the opposite: Daniel did everything he could reasonably do to assert his parental rights, beginning even before he actually knew that he was the father."

We direct the [district] Court to enter an order enforcing the custody orders entered by the Iowa courts. In consultation with counsel for the Schmidts and the DeBoers, the [district] court shall promptly establish a plan for the transfer of custody, with the parties directed to cooperate in the transfer with the goal of easing the child's transition into the Schmidt home. The [district] court shall monitor and enforce the transfer process, employing all necessary resources of the court, and shall notify the clerk of this Court 21 days following the release of this opinion of the arrangements for transfer of custody. The actual transfer shall take place within 10 days thereafter.

To a perhaps unprecedented degree among the matters that reach this Court, these cases have been litigated through fervent emotional appeals, with counsel and the adult parties pleading that their only interests are to do what is best for the child, who is herself blameless for this protracted litigation and the grief that it has caused. However, the clearly applicable legal principles require that the Iowa judgement be enforced and that the child be placed in the custody of her natural parents. It is now time for the adults to move beyond saying that their only concern is the welfare of the child and to put those words into action by assuring that the transfer of custody is accomplished promptly with minimum disruption of the life of the child.

In response to the publicity surrounding this case and others like it, States have amended adoption statutes to provide that the best interests of the child is paramount in any adoption revocation proceeding.

SPECIAL CIRCUMSTANCES IN ADOPTION LAW

The popular image of agency adoption is of a woman who had desperately wanted to be a mother cradling a smiling infant while her husband looks down adoringly. The infant has been surrendered by his or her young, unmarried mother who loved the child but recognized other parents could offer her child more than she could. To be sure, this image fits reality in some cases. As stated earlier, however, agency adoptions increasingly involve children who have entered foster care because they were abused or neglected and who cannot return home. Many of these children are of minority race or ethnicity or are of sibling groups who should be adopted together. Creating permanent nurturing homes that are responsive to the special needs of such children is often challenging to the social worker.

Transracial Adoption

A practice that has raised significant controversy over time is the adoption of children by parents of a different race. While the term *transracial adoption* is racially neutral, in reality it has meant the adoption of black or Native American children by white parents.

The National Association of Black Social Workers has argued forcefully that adoption of black or mixed race children by white parents is not in the best interest of the child. The position of the Association has been widely accepted, and, either by policy or in practice, transracial adoption is discouraged. Similarly, representatives of tribes have argued that placing Native American children with non-Native American adoptive parents was not the best interests of either the child or the child's tribe. This will be discussed in more detail in the next section.

An important case related to transracial adoption is *Drummond v. Fulton County Department of Family and Children's Services*, 563 F.2d 1200 (5th Cir. 1977); *cert. den'd.* 437 U.S. 910 (1978). The Drummonds brought the case after their application for the adoption of a mixed race child in their care was denied by the placing agency. The Drummonds were white, and their application was denied in part because of their race and their racial attitudes. The Court of Appeals held that since the denial was not totally or automatically based on race, it did not violate equal protection, noting the following factors:

First, consideration of race in the child placement process suggests no racial slur or stigma in connection with any race. It is a natural thing for children to be raised by parents of their same ethnic background.

Second, no case has been cited to the Court suggesting that it is impermissible to consider race in adoption placement. The only cases which have addressed this problem indicate that, while the automatic use of race is barred, the use of race as one of the factors in making the ultimate decision is legitimate.

Third, the professional literature on the subject of transracial child placement stresses the importance of considering the racial attitudes of potential parents. The constitutional strictures against racial discrimination are not mandates to ignore the accumulated experience of unbiased professionals. A couple has no right to adopt a child it is not equipped to rear, and according to the professional literature race bears directly on that inquiry. From the child's perspective, the consideration of race is simply another facet of finding him the best possible home. Rather than eliminating certain categories of homes from consideration it avoids the potentially tragic possibility of placing a child in a home with parents who will not be able to cope with the child's problems.

Fourth, in the analogous inquiry over the permissibility of considering the religion of would-be adoptive parents, numerous courts have found no constitutional infirmity. Those cases make the same distinction as this Court makes in the racial context. So long as religion is not an automatic factor, its consideration as one of a number of factors is unobjectionable.

Finally, adoption agencies quite frequently try to place a child where he can most easily become a normal family member. The duplication of his natural biological environment is part of that program . . . This Court does not have the professional expertise to assess the wisdom of [this practice], but it is our province to conclude, as we do today, that the use of race [in duplicating the biological environment] is not unconstitutional.

The federal government, concerned that race played too much of a role in adoption decision, passed the Multiethnic Placement Act of 1994. This Act was intended to reduce the number of children in foster care. The Act however, allowed race to be a factor in placing children for adoptions. It simply stated that children were not to be placed for adoption solely on the basis of race, color, or national origin of the adoptive or foster parent or the child involved. 42 U.S.C. § 5115(a). Two years later, the federal government repealed the Multiethnic Placement Act.[2] Federal law now provides that race may no longer be used to deny any adoption.

[N]either the State nor any other entity in the State that receives funds from the Federal Government and is involved in adoption or foster care placements may—

(A) deny to any person the opportunity to become an adoptive or a foster parent, on the basis of the race, color, or national origin of the person, or of the child, involved; or

(B) delay or deny the placement of a child for adoption or into foster care, on the basis of the race, color, or national origin of the adoptive or foster parent, or the child, involved. 42 U.S.C. § 671(a)(18).

The Native American Child

The Indian Child Welfare Act (ICWA), discussed in the previous chapter, grants tribal courts exclusive jurisdiction over adoption proceedings concerning Native American children—even if a social worker may not think that a child should be returned to the tribe.

The adoption of Native American children by white parents was addressed by the Supreme Court in *Mississippi Band of Choctaw Indians v. Holyfield*, 490 U.S. 30 (1988), which answered the question of whether the State court had jurisdiction to order an adoption of Native American children after their parents executed consents to their adoption. The specific question in this case was whether twin babies born off the reservation were domiciled there within the meaning of ICWA.

The children's parents, who were not married, were both enrolled members of the Choctaw Tribe and lived on the reservation. The children were born some two hundred miles from the reservation on December 29, 1985, and their parents executed consents to their adoption in a county court on January 10, 1986. Six days later the Holyfields, who were non-Indian, filed a petition to adopt in the same court, and twelve days later the court issued a final decree of adoption—despite its apparent awareness of the ICWA. Two months later the Tribe moved in the same court to vacate the adoption on the grounds that the ICWA gave the

2. P.L. 104-188, Title I, § 1808(d), Aug. 20, 1996, 110 stat. 1904.

tribal court exclusive jurisdiction. The court ruled against the Tribe concluding the Tribe never obtained jurisdiction based on the facts that the twins' mother purposely arranged that the children be born off-reservation and be adopted by the Holyfields. The Supreme Court of Mississippi agreed with the trial court in light of the facts that the children never lived on the reservation and that their mother intended they be adopted by the Holyfields.

The U.S. Supreme Court reversed, holding that although the ICWA does not define "domicile," Congress clearly intended a uniform federal law of domicile and did not consider it to be a matter of State law. It further stated that in the absence of a statutory definition, the ordinary meaning of "domicile" for minors who are illegitimate is the domicile of their mother.

> It is undisputed in this case that the domicile of the mother (as well as the father) has been, at all relevant times, on the Choctaw Reservation. Thus, it is clear that at their birth the twin babies were also domiciled on the reservation, even though they themselves had never been there. The statement of the Supreme Court of Mississippi that "[a]t no point in time can it be said the twins . . . were domiciled within the territory set aside for the reservation," may be a correct statement of that State's law of domicile, but it is inconsistent with generally accepted doctrine in this country and cannot be what Congress had in mind when it used the term in the ICWA.
>
> Tribal jurisdiction under § 1911(a) was not meant to be defeated by the actions of individual members of the tribe, for Congress was concerned not solely about the interests of the Indian children and families, but also about the impact on the tribes themselves of the large numbers of Indian children adopted by non-Indians. [As the ICWA provides:] "[T]here is no resource that is more vital to the continued existence and integrity of Indian tribes than their children."

> In addition, it is clear that Congress' concern over the placement of Indian children in non-Indian homes was based in part on evidence of the detrimental impact on the children themselves of such placements outside their culture. Congress determined to subject such placements to the ICWA's jurisdictional and other provisions, even in cases where the parents consented to an adoption, because of concerns going beyond the wishes of individual parents.
>
> The appellees in this case argue strenuously that the twins' mother went to great lengths to give birth off the reservation so that the Holyfields could adopt her children. But that was precisely part of Congress' concern. Permitting individual members of the tribe to avoid tribal exclusive jurisdiction by the simple expedient of giving birth off the reservation would to a large extent, nullify the purpose the ICWA was intended to accomplish.

The Court concluded with some observations and, in a sense, warnings that are well to remember in an area of law as important as adoption.

> We are not unaware that over three years have passed since the twin babies were born and placed in the Holyfield home, and that a court deciding their fate today is not writing on a blank slate in the same way it would have in January 1986. Three years' development of family ties cannot be undone, and a separation at this point would doubtless cause considerable pain.
>
> Whatever feelings we might have as to where the twins should live, however, it is not for us to decide that question. We have been asked to decide the legal questions of *who* should make the custody determination concerning these children—not what the outcome of that determination should be. The law places that decision in the hands of the Choctaw tribal court. Had the mandate of the ICWA been followed in 1986, of course, much potential anguish might have been avoided, and in any case the law cannot be applied so as automatically to "reward those who obtain custody, whether lawfully or otherwise, and maintain it during any ensuing (and protracted) litigation." It is

not ours to say whether the trauma that might result from removing these children from their adoptive family should outweigh the interest of the Tribe . . . and perhaps the children themselves—in having them raised as part of the Choctaw community. Rather, "we must defer to the experience, wisdom, and compassion of the [Choctaw] trial courts to fashion an appropriate remedy."

Children with Special Needs

Children of all ages who have special needs present unique challenges to the social worker. These children may be the most time-consuming in a social worker's caseload. Physical disabilities, illnesses such as AIDS, or mental disabilities may make these children unwanted by a prospective adoptive family. Other factors, such as ethnic background or the need to keep siblings together, may also limit opportunities for adoption.

To encourage adoption of children with special needs, the federal government passed the Adoption Assistance and Chlid Welfare Act of 1980 (AACWA), which provides federal assistance for States (under the Social Security Act) to offer subsidized adoption assistance to adoptive parents of children with special needs. The subsidies may assist the parents in meeting the costs of caring for a child or may provide medical assistance. The ASFA requires that States, as a condition of federal funding for their adoption assistance program, provide health insurance coverage to special needs children who "cannot be placed with an adoptive parent or parents without medical assistance because such child has special needs for medical, mental health, or rehabilitative care." 42 U.S.C. § 671(a)(21).

Parents who adopt children with special needs have later tried to revoke these adoptions after learning significant additional background information about the adoptive child. In one of the first significant cases to recognize a claim of "wrongful adoption," *Burr v. Board of County Com'rs Stark Cnty.*, 23 Ohio St.3d 69, 491 N.E 2d 1101 (1986), the social workers had misrepresented information provided in the adoption papers. Excerpts from this case indicate what happened:

[The parents] contacted the adoption division of the Stark County Welfare Department in 1964 expressing their desire to adopt a child. Betty Burr is partially disabled, having earlier lost a leg to polio, and the Burrs expressed an interest in adopting a male child up to six months old.

Nevertheless, a few days later an employee of [the county social services department] telephoned the Burrs and told them a seventeen-month-old boy was available for adoption. At appellants' suggestion, the Burrs met the county caseworker, Schaub, in order to be introduced to the child. During this meeting Schaub told the Burrs the infant was borne by an eighteen-year-old unwed mother, that the mother was living with her parents, that the mother was trying to take care of the child and trying to work during the day, that the grandparents were mean to the child, that the mother was going to Texas for better employment, and that she had surrendered the child to appellants for adoption. Russell Burr testified that Schaub represented to them that the child ". . . was a nice big, healthy, baby boy" who had been born at the Massillon City Hospital. The Burrs decided to proceed with the adoption. Soon thereafter, the child, Patrick, became a member of appellees' family.

The Burrs testified that during the ensuing years Patrick suffered from a myriad of physical and mental problems. Physical twitching, speech impediment, poor motor skills, and learning disabilities were among Patrick's more apparent problems. During primary school, the Burrs were advised that Patrick was not like other children. He was classified as E.M.R. (educable, mentally retarded) and attended special education classes.

[B]y high school, Patrick was observed to also suffer from hallucinations. He was thereafter admitted to several hospitals for diagnosis and treatment. Eventually, Patrick was diagnosed as suffering from Huntington's Disease, a genetically inherited disease which destroys the central nervous system. Movement disorders, delusions and intellectual deterioration are all associated with the disease. The average life expectancy after onset if the disease begins during childhood is 8.5 years. During the course of Patrick's treatment, the Burrs obtained a court order opening the sealed records concerning his background prior to adoption.

From these records the Burrs first learned in 1982 that the representations made to them by the county case worker in 1964 were all false. These previously sealed records revealed that Patrick's mother was actually a thirty-one-year old mental patient at the Massillon State Hospital. Patrick had not been born at Massillon City Hospital, but rather was delivered at the state mental institution. The father's identity was unknown, but he was presumed to also have been a mental patient. Patrick's biological mother shared his low intellectual level and also had a speech impediment. She was diagnosed as having a "mild mental deficiency, idiopathic, with psychotic reactions" and was described as "bovine." The "mean" grandparents, the trip to Texas, voluntary placement, and seemingly all other information regarding Patrick other than his age and sex were fabrications. In fact, prior to adoption, he had been placed in two foster homes.

The records also showed that Patrick suffered a fever at birth, and was known by appellants to be developing slowly. A series of psychological assessments was conducted by appellants prior to adoption, some of which indicated that the boy was functioning at a lower intellectual level than his chronological age. The reports opined that future assessments of the child should be conducted for evidence of deviant social and emotional development.

Damages in the amount of $125,000 were affirmed on appeal.

States have defined by statute what information must be disclosed about an adoptive child's health or background.[3]

Adoption by a Gay or Lesbian Couple

State adoption statutes generally do not include sexual orientation in defining who is eligible to adopt. Instead, courts determine on a case-by-case analysis whether an adoption by someone who is gay or lesbian is in the best interests of the child to be adopted. In the case, *In re Adoption of Charles B*, 50 Ohio St. 3d 88, 552 N.E. 2d 884 (1990), eight-year-old Charles was less adoptable than other children because he suffered from leukemia, had a low I.Q., a speech disorder, and possibly suffered from fetal alcohol syndrome. A professional relationship between Charles and Mr. B., his counselor, eventually developed into a close personal relationship such that Mr. B. became the consistent and caring person in Charles' life. Mr. B. decided to adopt Charles and the court appointed a guardian *ad litem* to represent Charles. The local Department of Human Services (DHS), on the day before the scheduled adoption hearing, withheld its consent to the adoption because Mr. B. was a homosexual. Despite the position of DHS, the trial court awarded an interlocutory (nonfinal) order of adoption. The Ohio Court of Appeals reversed, concluding as a matter of law that homosexuals are not eligible to adopt. The Supreme Court of Ohio reversed the Court of Appeals, concluding that it was in Charles'

---

3. See Madelyn DeWoody, *Adoption and Disclosure: A Review of the Law.* Child Welfare League of America: Washington, DC, 1993), p. 16.

best interests to be adopted by Mr. B. The Court reasoned:

> The polestar by which courts in Ohio, and courts around the country, have been guided is the best interest of the child to be adopted. This standard is applied in every adoption case and the case before us can be no different.
>
> The record discloses that Charles, although still a young boy, already has endured many emotional as well as physical hardships. Charles has had a neglected and abused childhood. His natural parents signed a voluntary permanent surrender of him. He has been in the permanent custody of appellee since April 1985. Although [DHS] originally attempted to place Charles and his two sisters with one family, this plan was abandoned after [DHS] determined that individual placements would be better for Charles and his siblings.
>
> The agency then developed a list of requirements for the family adopting Charles. These requirements were: a family of two parents with older siblings, at least one of which would be male; a family with a child-centered life style; a couple with definite parenting experience, preferably with adoption experience; parents with proven ability in dealing with behavior disorder issues; a family that is open to counseling; and a family that demonstrates an ability to deal with leaning disabilities, speech problems and medical problems. A tall order, indeed.
>
> In 1985, Charles was registered as an individual child available for adoption. In early 1987, Mr. B. indicated to appellee his general interest in adopting a child, and Charles in particular. A supervisor of [DHS's] Family Services Unit indicated that if Mr. B. had a home study completed, he would be given consideration to adopt Charles if no other final decision had been made prior to that time.
>
> Several potential families were chosen by appellee for Charles. None of these potential adoptive families proved successful for Charles. In May 1987, appellee located a two-parent family for Charles. [DHS] prepared both the family and Charles for eventual placement. Charles met the family in August 1987 but after several weeks, the family demonstrated, according to appellee, a "lack

> of commitment to adopting Charlie." Appellee, on October 1, 1987, decided not to place Charles with this family.
>
> Witnesses called by Mr. B. at the hearing testified that Mr. B. has the necessary qualifications to be a good parent for Charles. The guardian stated that Mr. B. and Charles have developed a close relationship and that Charles would like to make his home with Mr. B. The guardian further stated that Mr. B. would have the support of his immediate family with sufficient female role models. The guardian concluded his report with a recommendation that the adoption be approved.
>
> Dr. Shannon, a licensed psychologist, testified as a professional and, in addition, stated that he was acquainted with Mr. B. and found his reputation to be beyond reproach. Dr. Blubaugh, also a licensed psychologist, testified that in her counseling role she had observed a bonding develop between Charles and Mr. B. She testified that it was in Charles's best interest to be adopted by Mr. B. especially given the special needs of Charles . . .
>
> Upon review of the record now before us, we determine that the trial court did not abuse its discretion in granting the petition for adoption. "The term 'abuse of discretion' connotes more than an error of law or of judgement; it implies that the court's attitude is unreasonable, arbitrary, or unconscionable." There is no evidence in this record that the trial court's attitude was unreasonable, arbitrary or unconscionable. Accordingly, we find that the trial court did not abuse its discretion when it placed Charles with Mr. B. for adoption.

The justice who dissented in the case stated, in part:

> I respectfully dissent from the majority decision. However, I do not agree with the court of appeals wherein it found as a matter of law a homosexual is ineligible to adopt a minor. Existing Ohio law is very clear that a homosexual is not as a matter of law barred from adopting a child . . . When deciding whether to grant or deny a petition for adoption, a court must consider all relevant factors before determining what is in the child's best interest. The fact

that the party seeking to become an adoptive parent is a homosexual should not, in and of itself, be determinative. However, neither can it be ignored. When a homosexual seeks to adopt a minor, a trial court must have before it sufficient evidence to show that the prospective parent's homosexuality will not have an adverse effect on the minor. The prospective parent must present evidence demonstrating that his or her homosexuality will not harm the child. Likewise, the party opposing the adoption by the homosexual must also submit evidence establishing not only that the homosexuality of the adopting parent had or will have an effect on the child, but also that the effect is or will be harmful.

Other jurisdictions, when confronted with a parents' homosexuality in a child custody or visitation context, with a similar situation to the one before us have used a "nexus test" or an affirmative showing of harm to the child caused by the parent's sexual orientation . . . Based on the facts of this case there does exist a nexus between the homosexuality of Mr. B. and the adoption of Charles . . . which could adversely affect the child and thus would not be in the best interest of the child.

While I agree that homosexuality is just one factor to be considered by the court in adoption proceedings, it should be weighed along with all other factors and the ultimate decision must be based upon the best interest of the child. I also agree that a nexus must be found to exist between the sexual preference of the father and the adoption, which could have an adverse effect on the child. In this case that nexus was well established by Dr. Frederick B. Ruymann, M.D., Director, Hematology Division; Professor, Department of Pediatrics, Children's Hospital, the Ohio State University, wherein he stated in a letter to the court dated April 13, 1988 that adoption of Charlie by a homosexual ". . . would, with our present knowledge place Charles at increased risk for exposure to HIV infection, i.e. infection with the AIDS virus." Charles has an altered immune system. The AIDS virus attacks the immune system further destroying it.

Mr. B. was aware of this problem and was tested, proving to be HIV negative. However, we must remember that adoption is not just for

today but forever. Mr. B. falls within a high-risk population for AIDS. Why place a child whose immune system has already been altered in such an environment? It was best stated by Kathleen Handley, Administrator of Social Services for the Licking County Department of Human Services, at the hearing that "[o]ur feeling is that professionally it would be an adoption risk to place a child in a setting where there is no practiced precedent to give us support. We do not view this as a child that needs experimentation. He has too many other issues that he has to conquer in his life."

Charlie thus far in his life has had many problems and there is nothing more that anyone would want for him than to be placed in a loving permanent home. But due to Charlie's many medical problems, a homosexual environment is not in his long-term best interest. I sincerely regret that the record in this case was not better developed by the appellee during trial. This was a difficult decision for the trial court to make and the manner in which it was tried on the part of the appellee made it even more difficult for the court. However, we are dealing with the life of an eight-year-old boy; therefore, the paramount concern is the well-being of this child. Because Charlie's immune system has been dramatically altered due to treatment for leukemia, in the long term, this adoption simply is not in his best interest. Therefore, I find that the trial court abused its discretion in granting the petition for adoption.

Access to Adoption and Birth Records

A child's birth certificate is typically amended following an adoption and, under the authority of State statutes, the original birth certificate and the court records related to the adoption are typically sealed. Once sealed, the original birth certificate and the records generally can be opened only by court order upon a showing of "good cause" for opening them.

Because records are sealed and may be opened only upon a showing of good cause, adoptees that want information about their birth family often cannot get it. Two cases, one from Illinois and one from New York, illustrate the response of courts to constitutional challenges in this area. At the same time, the Supreme Court declined to hear the two cases, *In re Roger B.*, 84 Ill.2d 323, 418 N.E.2d 751 (1981), and *Linda F. M. v. Department of Health of the City of New York*, 52 N.Y. 2d 236, 418 N.E.2d 1302 (1981), *appeals dismissed*, 454 U.S. 806 (1981).

In *Roger B.*, the adoptee contended that the Illinois statute providing for sealing of adoption records, among other claims, deprived him of a fundamental right "to know his own identity." The Illinois Supreme Court disagreed, stating:

> We have found no case holding that the right of an adoptee to determine his genealogical origin is explicitly or implicitly guaranteed by the Constitution . . . Although information regarding one's background, heritage, and heredity is important to one's identity, it does not fall within any heretofore delineated zone of privacy implicitly protected within the Bill of Rights. We believe the adoptee does not have a fundamental right to examine his adoption records.
>
> Confidentiality is needed to protect the right to privacy of the natural parent. The natural parents, having determined it is in the best interest of themselves and the chld, have placed the child for adoption. This process is done not merely with the expectation of anonymity, but also with the statutory assurance that his or her identity as the child's parent will be shielded from public disclosure. Quite conceivably, the natural parents have established a new family unit with the expectation of confidentiality concerning the adoption that occurred several years earlier . . .
>
> Confidentiality also must be promoted to protect the right of the adopting parents. The adopting parents have taken into their home a child whom they will regard as their own and whom they will love, support, and raise as an

integral part of the family unit. They should be given the opportunity to create a stable family relationship free from unnecessary intrusion. The [statute] creates a situation in which the emotional attachments are directed toward the relationship with the new parents. The adoptive parents need and deserve the child's loyalty as they grow older, and particularly in their later years.

> Upon reaching maturity, the adoptee often develops a countervailing interest that is in direct conflict with the other parties, particularly the natural parents. The adoptee wishes to determine his natural identity, while the privacy interest of the natural parents remains, perhaps stronger than ever. The [statute] recognizes that the right of privacy is not absolute. It allows the court to evaluate the needs of the adoptee as well as the nature of the relationships and choices made by all parties concerned. The statute, by providing for release of adoption records only upon issuance of a court order, does no more than allow the court to balance the interests of all the parties and make a determination based on the facts and circumstances of each individual case.

Linda F. M. also focused on the reasons for confidentiality in denying an adoptee's claim of "good cause" to discover her identity. The court stated:

> [C]onfidentiality serves several purposes. It shields the adopted child from possibly disturbing facts surrounding his or her birth and parentage, it permits the adoptive parents to develop a close relationship with the child free from interference or distraction, and it provides the natural parents with an anonymity that they may consider vital.
>
> A natural parent understandably can feel deep effects when the records of an adoption are opened years after the child was surrendered for adoption. Although the sudden reappearance of the child may often be a source of great pleasure to the natural parent, in other cases it may be a destructive intrusion into the life that the parent has built in the years since the adoption. It may be the source of much discomfort. In some cases, it

may even open the way for the child or others to blackmail the natural parents by threatening to disclose embarrassing circumstances surrounding the birth.

Petitioner . . . summarized her reasons for wanting access to her records as a desire "[t]o know who I am. I feel cut off from the rest of humanity. I was given birth in the same way as everyone else, but everyone else can send away $3 and get a copy of their birth certificate. I want to know who I am. The only person in the world who looks like me is my son. I have no ancestry. Nothing." A desire to learn about one's ancestry should not be belittled. When balanced against the interests of other parties to the adoption process, however, it cannot alone constitute good cause [to breach confidentiality.] This is not to say that concrete psychological problems, if found by the court to be specifically connected to the lack of knowledge about ancestry, would never constitute good cause. By its very nature, good cause admits of no universal, black letter definition. Whether it exists, and the extent of disclosure that is appropriate, must remain for the courts to decide on the facts of each case. Nevertheless, mere desire to learn the identity of one's natural parents cannot alone constitute good cause, or the requirement of [confidentiality] would become a nullity.

In contrast to the courts, legislatures in States may allow adoptees access to records. Access is granted in several ways: 1) States may allow access to court adoption records or birth certificates on the adoptee's demand; 2) States may allow release of either identifying or non-identifying information about birth parents to the adoptee or the adoptive parents—with the consent of the birth parents or without any requirement of such content; and 3) States may create registries and intermediary systems designed both to help adult adoptees locate birth parents and to facilitate exchange of information.

Often, statutes mandating confidentiality generally apply to birth and court records, not to agency records. Many agencies do seal records, making them unavailable to adoptees, but there may be nothing in the law to prevent agencies from sharing information. Many agencies, in recognition of the value of sharing information, have developed various forms of what is termed "open adoption." Open adoption may involve birth and adoptive parents meeting each other prior to the adoption and continuing to have contact after the adoption, either directly or by exchanging information through the agency. Many private adoptions are open adoptions, often chosen by a birth parent desiring continued contact with the adopted child.

The Rights of Unmarried Fathers

A large proportion of children available for adoption have birth fathers who are not married to their birth mothers and who have not been providing for them physically or financially. Questions surrounding present and potential rights of such fathers have caused substantial debate among lawyers and social workers.

The question of unmarried fathers' rights often arises when unmarried mothers have surrendered their children or consented to their adoption by a stepfather without notifying or obtaining the natural father's consent or surrender. The Supreme Court has wrestled with the question of rights of unmarried fathers in a series of cases.

In *Lehr v. Robertson*, 463 U.S. 248 (1983), the child in question, Jessica, was born out of wedlock. Jessica's mother, Lorraine, and Lehr, had lived together for several years before Jessica's birth, and Lorraine always acknowledged Lehr was the father of her unborn child. Lehr visited Jessica and Lorraine every day in the hospital after Jessica was born, but when they were discharged from the hospital, Lorraine hid herself and Jessica from Lehr. Eight months after Jessica was born, Lorraine married Robertson, and when Jessica was two, Robertson sought to adopt her. Although the trial court was aware that Lehr had been seeking Jessica and had filed a court action to establish his rights to Jessica, the court approved Robertson's petition to adopt Jessica without providing Lehr notice of the adoption and an opportunity to be heard. The Supreme Court upheld the court's action, which was in accordance with the New York statutory scheme providing that a man who files with New York's "putative father registry" demonstrates his intent to claim paternity of a child born out of wedlock and is therefore entitled to receive notice of any proceeding to adopt that child. Although Lehr claimed to be Jessica's natural father, he had not entered his name in the registry. The Supreme Court held:

> The significance of the biological connection is that it offers the natural father an opportunity that no other male possesses to develop a relationship with his offspring. If he grasps that opportunity and accepts some measure of responsibility for the child's future, he may enjoy the blessings of the parent-child relationship and make uniquely valuable contributions to the child's development. If he fails to do so, the Federal Constitution will not automatically compel a state to listen to his opinion of where the child's best interest lie.

Since *Lehr*, courts have protected the rights of fathers who have complied with statutory requirements related to paternity and child support and who have promptly asserted their interests in their children.

Frequently, the location of an unmarried father may be unknown, or the mother may be unwilling to provide information to the father. The latter was the case *In re Petition of John Doe*, 159 Ill. 2d 347, 638 N.E. 2d 181 (1994). The mother's failure to inform a child's natural father of her decision to consent to an adoption may result in tragic consequences to the child.

> John and Jane Doe filed a petition to adopt a newborn baby boy. The baby's biological mother, Daniella Janikova, executed a consent to have the baby adopted four days after his birth without informing his biological father, Otakar Kirchnor, to whom she was not yet married.
>
> The mother told the father that the baby had died and he did not find out otherwise until 57 days after the birth. The trial court ruled that the father's consent was unnecessary because he did not show sufficient interest in the child during the first 30 days of the child's life . . .
>
> Otakar and Daniella began living together in the fall of 1989, and Daniella became pregnant in June of 1990. For the first eight months of her pregnancy, Otakar provided for all of her expenses.
>
> In late January 1991, Otakar went to his native Czechoslovakia to attend to his gravely ill grandmother for two weeks. During this time, Daniella received a phone call from Otakar's aunt saying that Otakar had resumed a former romantic relationship with another woman.
>
> Because of this unsettling news, Daniella left their shared apartment, refused to talk with Otakar on his return, and gave birth to the child at a different hospital than where they had originally planned. She gave her consent to the adoption of the child by the Does, telling them and their attorney that she knew who the father was but would not furnish his name. Daniella and her uncle warded

off Otakar's persistent inquiries about the child by telling him that the child had died shortly after birth.

Otakar found out that the child was alive and had been placed for adoption 57 days after the child was born. He then began the instant proceedings by filing an appearance contesting the Does' adoption of his son . . . [T]he trial court ruled that Otakar was an unfit parent because he had not shown a reasonable degree of interest in the child within the first 30 days of his life. Therefore, the father's consent was unnecessary.

The finding that the father had not shown a reasonable degree of interest in the child is not supported by the evidence. In fact, he made various attempts to locate the child, all of which were either frustrated or blocked by the actions of the mother. Further, the mother was aided by the attorney for the adoptive parents, who failed to make any effort to ascertain the name or address of the father despite the fact that the mother indicated she knew who he was. Under the circumstances, the father had no opportunity to discharge any familial duty.

In the opinion below, the appellate court, wholly missing the threshold issue in this case, dwelt on the best interests of the child. Since, however, the father's parental interest was improperly terminated, there was no occasion to reach the fact of the child's best interests. That point should never have been reached and need never have been discussed.

Unfortunately, over three years have elapsed since the birth of the baby who is the subject of these proceedings. To the extent that it is relevant to assign fault in this case, the fault here lies initially with the mother, who fraudulently tried to deprive the father of his rights, and secondly, with the adoptive parents and their attorney, who proceeded with the adoption when they knew that a real father was out there who had been denied knowledge of his baby's existence. When the father entered his appearance in the adoption proceedings 57 days after the baby's birth and demanded his rights as a father, the petitioners should have relinquished the baby at that time. It was their decision to prolong this litigation through a lengthy, and ultimately fruitless, appeal.

The adoption laws of Illinois are neither complex nor difficult to apply. Those laws intentionally place the burden of proof on the adoptive parents in establishing both the relinquishment and/or unfitness of the natural parents and, [their own fitness and right to adopt]. In addition, Illinois law requires a good-faith effort to notify the natural parents of the adoption proceedings. These laws are designed to protect natural parents in their preemptive rights to their own children wholly apart from any consideration of the so-called best interests of the child. If it were otherwise, few parents would be secure in the custody of their own children. If best interests of the child were a sufficient qualification to determine child custody, anyone with superior income, intelligence, education, etc., might challenge and deprive the parents of their right to their own children. The law is otherwise and was not complied with in this case.

In cases where the location of the father may be unknown, notice to the father may be by publication in a newspaper or by other means. Such notice may be constitutionally sufficient. State statutes will specify which fathers must be notified and how.

The Question of Best Interests

As has been noted, State statutes generally provide that parental rights can be terminated only when a court finds that a parent is unfit and that a termination is in the child's best interests. But when is termination in a child's best interests?

Both a surrender and a termination leave a child without a legal parent. While the child and the parent may maintain an emotional attachment and may even continue to see each other, they have no legal relationship and no enforceable rights to contact. Moreover, a surrender or a termination ends the legal relationship between a child and his or her siblings and other relatives to whom there may be strong attachments.

Termination is often justified on the basis that it will ultimately provide a child with a stable life in a caring family and that this stability outweighs any losses the child might suffer. But some children may not be easily adopted. As we have seen, these include children of color, children with disabilities, children diagnosed as HIV-positive, and children who should be adopted with siblings. And, as demonstrated in the following excerpts from *Alsager v. Iowa, supra,* stability may by no means be assured after a termination. After noting that the Alsagers were "affectionate parents, of below average but by no means inadequate intelligence, who lost their children through application of the loose standards, if any, contained within" the Iowa law, and that it was never established that the children faced "actual or imminent harm" if they remained with their parents, the court stated:

> If anything has been made clear throughout these proceedings, it is that the area of predicting what will be in the best future interests of the child is a delicate one. Through the benefit of the hindsight, this Court can today see no apparent benefit to the 1970 termination. [D]uring the interim from 1969 to 1974, [four] Alsager children . . . between them experienced some 15 separate foster home

placements, and eight juvenile home placements. The uncertainty of post-termination life is further depicted by the fact that when the case was first argued. . . , [the] experts recommended that even if the termination proceedings were ruled unconstitutional, two of the children should be permanently placed in their present foster homes. Some months later [at another hearing] the situation had changed in that the two "well-adjusted" boys had apparently rejected their foster homes and were being considered for probationary placements with their parents.

> Termination has thus failed to provide the Alsager children with either stable or improved lives. Based on their parents' capabilities, the Court cannot say that separation has benefited the children in any discernible way. In the eyes of [some] experts, they have been harmed. One lesson emerges clearly from this sad testament. Termination is a drastic, final step which, when inappropriately employed, can be fraught with danger.

The fact that a termination or surrender can leave a child with no parent and can end other significant relationships suggests the need for the social workers who are involved, and who are often in the position of arguing for termination, to exercise extreme caution. They should have something to offer the child through adoption before they move to terminate. They also must do whatever they can to assure that termination does not end contact with people who are important to the child.

Marriage

In legal terms, marriage is a contractual relationship. The parties to the contract, the husband and wife, agree to certain obligations towards one another, for example, to support one another. The marriage contract, however, is a special kind of contract in that entering into the contract creates a new legal status for the parties. After marrying, one is something new in the eyes of the law and the eyes of others—a married person. Having the status of a married person means having certain rights, privileges and obligations not afforded to nonmarried persons, such as the right to have sexual intercourse with one's spouse legally, the privilege of receiving insurance benefits on one's spouse's account, and the obligation to support one's spouse. Of great importance, marriage may also affect the legal status of a couple's children. Children conceived or born while their birth parents were married to one another are considered **legitimate**, while children whose birth parents were not married at the time of their conception or birth may be considered **illegitimate**.[1]

We will examine legitimacy in chapter 11. In this chapter, we will look at marriage, termination of marriage, and the consequences of getting married and terminating a marriage. Understanding these matters is necessary for social workers because social workers may advise their clients about getting married or terminating their marriages. Social workers may also help their clients cope with the decisions to terminate their marriages and, more and more, may play an active role in

the termination process, not only as advisors or counselors, but also as mediators.

GETTING MARRIED

There are certain legal prerequisites to entering into the marriage contract. These prerequisites, which are both substantive and procedural, vary in certain respects from State to State but are essentially the same. All have similar purposes. They were established primarily to protect the public health, to assure that the parties have the legal capacity to understand and assume the obligations of marriage, and to provide an official record that a marriage has, in fact, occurred.

Substantive Prerequisites

The Parties Must Have Capacity. Generally, in order to marry, the parties must have the legal capacity to enter into a marriage contract and be legally competent to do so. That is, they must be of a certain age and have the requisite mental capacity to form a contract.

The age at which persons can marry without parental consent is eighteen years old in almost all of the States. The statutes in many States allow marriage at an earlier age in certain circumstances such as if the woman is pregnant or has given birth, if the couple's parents or guardians consent, or if a court approves. Traditionally, women were permitted to marry at an earlier age than men, but such gender-based distinctions are now generally considered unconstitutional.

Some States have specific restrictions limiting marriage by persons who are

---

1.   This term, which replaced the stigmatizing term *bastard*, has been replaced in much legal writing by the less stigmatizing term *children born out of wedlock*.

mentally ill or mentally disabled in addition to the general requirement that one must have the mental capacity to enter into a contract.

The Parties Must Be Unrelated. All States prohibit certain blood relatives from marrying one another, but the specific relatives who are forbidden to intermarry differ from State to State. Relatives by adoption or marriage are also generally forbidden to intermarry. This prohibition has been declared invalid in at least one State. See *Israel v. Allen*, 185 Colo. 263, 577 P.2d 762 (1978), which allowed an adopted brother and sister to marry.

The Parties Must Be of Different Sexes. The statutes in many States specify that marriage is a union between a man and a woman. In the remaining States, the statutes do not explicitly so provide but the courts have unanimously interpreted the statutes to implictly so provide when faced with a request to enter into a same-sex marriage. For example, in *Singer v. Hara*, 11 Wash.App. 247, 522 P.2d 1187 (1974), the court stated that, although the Washington statutes did not explicitly say so, "it is apparent from a plain reading of our marriage statutes that the legislature has not authorized same-sex marriages." To give another example, in *Rutgers Council of AAUP Chapters v. Rutgers University*, 298 N.J.Super. 442, 689 A.2d 828 (App.Div. 1997), the court observed that while "[n]o specific language in New Jersey's marriage statutes prohibits same-sex marriages," it is a

> fundamental premise that a lawful marriage requires the performance of a ceremonial marriage of two persons of the opposite sex, a male and a female. Despite winds of change,

> this understanding of a valid marriage is almost universal. . . . In the matrimonial field the heterosexual union is usually regarded as the only one entitled to legal recognition and public sanction. There is not the slightest doubt that New Jersey follows the overwhelming authority. The historic assumption in the application of common law and statutory strictures relating to marriages is that only persons who can become "man and wife" have the capacity to enter marriage. The pertinent statutes relating to marriages and married persons do not contain any explicit references to a requirement that marriage must be between a man and a woman. Nevertheless that statutory condition must be extrapolated. It is so strongly and firmly implied from a full reading of the statutes that a different legislative intent, one which would sanction a marriage between persons of the same sex, cannot be fathomed.

One court even refused to allow a transsexual man who underwent a sex change operation to marry another man because the transexual was still genetically a man. See *In re Ladrach*, 32 Ohio Misc.2d 6, 513 N.E.2d 828 (Prob. Ct. 1987); but see, *M.T. v. J.T.*, 140 N.J.Super. 77, 355 A.2d 204 (App.Div. 1976), recognizing a marriage between a man and a woman who had been born a male but who, through surgery and hormonal therapy, became a female

There have been several constitutional challenges to the implicit or explicit requirement that marriage must be between a man and a woman. With the exception of courts in Hawaii, all courts have rejected such challenges. For example, in *Baker v. Nelson*, 291 Minn. 310, 191 N.W.2d 185 (1971), appeal dismissed, 409 U.S. 810 (1972), the court reasoned that it did not violate due process or equal protection to deny two men the fundamental right to marry because the historic view of marriage, "as a union of man and woman, uniquely involving the procreation and rearing of children within a family," was more deeply founded than the concept of same-sex marriage and served societal interests; in *Singer v. Hara, supra,* 522 P.2d 1187, the court held that a refusal to let two men marry does not deny gays equal protection because gays do not constitute a suspect class and because the men were "not being denied entry into the marriage relationship because of their sex; rather, they are being denied entry into the marriage relationship because of the recognized definition of that relationship as one which may be entered into only by two persons who are members of the opposite sex"; in *Dean v. District of Columbia,* 653 A.2d 307 (D.C. App.1995), the court concluded that same-sex marriage was not a fundamental right protected by the due process or equal protection clauses because that kind of relationship was not deeply rooted in this country's history and tradition; and in *Storrs v. Holcomb,* 168 Misc.2d 898, 645 N.Y.S.2d 286 (Sup.Ct.1996), the court held that limiting marriage to opposite sex couples served a valid public purpose and did not constitute invidious or irrational discrimination.

In *Baehr v. Lewin,* 74 Haw. 530, 852 P.2d 44 (1993), the Hawaii Supreme Court agreed that same-sex couples had no fundamental right to marry, holding that the "right to same-sex marriages is [not] so rooted in the traditions and collective conscience of [society] that failure to recognize it would violate the fundamental principles of liberty and justice that lie at the base of our civil and political institutions." However, the court concluded that denying a marriage license to two men could violate the equal protection clause in the Hawaii Constitution. This clause, which is broader than the equal protection clause in the Fourteenth Amendment to the United States Constitution, provides that "[n]o person shall . . . be denied the equal protection of the laws, nor be denied the enjoyment of the person's civil rights or be discriminated against in the exercise thereof because of race, religion, sex, or ancestry." The court found the marriage statute established a sex-based classification and that the matter had to be remanded to the trial court to determine, using a "strict scrutiny" standard, if there was a compelling justification for this classification. On remand, the trial court concluded that the State failed to bear its burden of justifying this sex-based classification and enjoined the State from denying marriage licenses solely because the applicants were of the same sex. *Baehr v. Miike,* 65 U.S.L.W. 2399 (HA Cir.Ct.1996).

As of 1998, no appellate court in Hawaii and no court in any other State has similarly concluded and no legislature has recognized same sex marriages. Indeed, in response to the Hawaii Supreme Court's decision in *Baehr,* the Hawaii legislature explicitly defined marriage as a union between a man and a woman.

Some steps have been taken to recognize gay and lesbian unions and to give the partners in these unions some of the legal status of married persons. For example, some public and private employers give certain gay or lesbian partners insurance benefits that are given to legal spouses. And, as stated in *Storrs v. Holcomb, supra,* 645 N.Y.S.2d 286: "Conceivably, a new consensus may emerge which the legislatures of the several states will see fit to recognize. Future legislation, perhaps, will authorize civil contracts in which same sex life partners will enjoy [rights and privileges such as the] social insurance benefits now becoming available from private and public employers." But, in the absence of such legislation, as was stated in *Shahar v. Bowers*, 70 F.3d 1218 (11th Cir. 1995), "[a]lmost unanimously American cases have held that same-sex couples are not constitutionally entitled to attain the legal and civil status of marriage." For example, see *Adams v. Howerton*, 673 F.2d 1036 (9th Cir. 1982), refusing to recognize a homosexual, who was "married" in a religious ceremony to a United States citizen, as a "spouse" entitled to immigrate to the United States under immigration laws; *In the Matter of Cooper*, 187 A.D.2d 128, 592 N.Y.S.2d 797 (App.Div. Sup. Ct. 1993) and *Stewart v. Schwartz Brothers-Jeffer Memorial Chapel, Inc.*, 159 Misc.2d 884, 606 N.Y.S.2d 965 (Sup. Ct. 1993), refusing to recognize a gay partner as a "surviving spouse" entitled, respectively, to inheritance rights or to determine the nature of funeral and burial services for a deceased partner; *Ross v. Denver Dep't of Health and Hospitals*, 883 P.2d 516 (Colo. App. Ct. 1994), refusing to recognize a same sex partner as "immediate family" entitled to sick leave to take care of an ailing partner; and *Rutgers Council of AAUP Chapters v. Rutgers University, supra*, 689 A.2d 828, refusing to order a public university to provide same-sex domestic partners the same insurance benefits as spouses.

The Parties Must Not Already Be Married.

All States require that both parties to a marriage be unmarried and make **bigamy**, that is, getting married to one person while still being legally married to another, a crime. This requirement and the crime of bigamy have been challenged as violating freedom of religion in that certain religions allow or even advocate **polygamy**, that is, marriage of either spouse more than one mate at one time. Over one hundred years ago, in the case of *Reynolds v. United States*, 98 U.S. 145 (1878), the Court rejected such a challenge by a Mormon, stating that: "it is within the legitimate scope of the power of every civil government to determine whether polygamy or monogamy shall be the law of social life under its dominion."

The Parties Must Be Free of Certain Diseases or Disabilities.

Early statutes forbade marriage by "insane" persons, "alcoholics," or "epileptics." Most modern statutes have eliminated these prohibitions except to the extent that they relate to capacity to contract. Early statutes also forbade marriage by persons with certain venereal disease. Testing for certain venereal diseases is still required in some States, but the prohibition on marriage by those with certain venereal diseases has been eased. A Utah statute prohibiting marriage by persons with certain venereal diseases and HIV was held unconstitutional in *T. E. P. v. Leavitt*, 840 F.Supp. 110 (D. Utah 1993).

Limits on Substantive Prerequisites.

The States' authority to establish substantive prerequisites to marriage is not unlimited. As we have seen, if the substantive prerequisites unreasonably interfere with the right to marry or disproportionately burden certain classes of people, the prerequisites may violate the due process or equal protection clauses. This point is illustrated by *Zablocki v. Redhail*, 434 U.S. 374 (1978), in which the Court struck down a Wisconsin statute making marriage difficult or impossible for certain poor people as violative of equal protection. The statute provided that no one who was obligated to support any children could marry unless he or she submitted proof that the children "are not then and are not likely thereafter to become public charges." However, as we have seen, the prohibition on same-sex marriage has been upheld by every court except the Hawaii courts under the Hawaii Constitution.

Procedural Perequisites

Blood Tests. The States generally require blood tests for certain venereal diseases as a condition of obtaining a marriage license, but the number of States requiring such tests has been declining. A few of the States that still require blood tests have added HIV testing. Positive results can bar marriage but, more commonly, the parties are simply told the results and advised of the dangers involved. A few States also require blood tests for other conditions such as sickle cell anemia, rubella immunity, tuberculosis, or Rh compatibility. With such tests, positive results do not bar marriage, but warnings will be given.

Licenses. All the States require the parties to obtain a marriage license. Licenses are required to give States control over who marries and to maintain statistics. Obtaining a marriage license does not mean that the parties are married; the license merely give the parties the authority to marry.

Most States require a couple to wait a period of time after applying for or obtaining a marriage license before they can be married. This waiting period is intended as a "cooling off" period or a time to "think it over." It is also designed to prevent marriage under the influence of alcohol or drugs.

Solemnization. All the States require some kind of formal ceremony in order for a marriage to be valid. The ceremony solemnizes the event and impresses its seriousness on the participants. It also serves as proof that the marriage occurred.

Depending on State law, the marriage ceremony may be performed by members of the clergy, judges, or certain public officials, like city clerks or mayors. The formal requirements of the ceremony depend on State law.

COMMON LAW MARRIAGE AND COHABITATION

If there has been no marriage license issued and no solemnization, in most States there is no marriage. A few States, however, recognize **common law marriage**, sometimes called **informal marriage**. Generally, a common law marriage occurs when the parties agree to be married, live together and hold themselves out as husband and wife, and have met the substantive prerequisites for a marriage, but have not met the procedural prerequisites. If a State recognizes common law marriage, a couple who meet the requirements are considered married for all intents and purposes. In other words, they must divorce if they wish to terminate their relationship, they are entitled to all the rights, privileges and benefits of married persons, and they owe to each other all the rights and obligations of married persons. The children of their union would be considered legitimate. Thus, in *White v. State Farm Mutual Automobile Insurance Company*, 907 F.Supp. 1012 (E.D.Tex. 1995), a woman was recognized as the "surviving spouse" of a man killed in an accident and was held to be entitled to insurance benefits under his policy because they met the requirements for a common law marriage under Texas law, even though she had been separated from him for three years. The court stated; "There is no 'common-law divorce' in Texas and the mere passage of time and ceasing of cohabitation will not serve to terminate a common law marriage once it is in existence."

If a State does not recognize common law marriage, it still may impose some or all of the rights and obligations of marriage on the partners to a common law union. In the famous case of *Marvin v. Marvin*, 18 Cal.3d 660, 557 P.2d 106 (1977), involving the actor Lee Marvin and Michelle Marvin who lived with him for several years, the California Supreme Court did not recognize common law marriage but held that an alleged oral agreement between Lee and Michelle could be recognized and enforced if it were proven to exist. She claimed they had agreed to treat his property as marital property and to impose an obligation of support on him, like a husband's obligation of support, in consideration of her ceasing to work outside the home and performing wifelike duties. The court reasoned that:

> Although the past decisions hover over the issue in the somewhat wispy form of the figures of a Chagall painting, we can abstract from those decisions a clear and simple rule.

> The fact that a man and woman live together without marriage, and engage in a sexual relationship, does not in itself invalidate agreements between them relating to their earnings, property, or expenses. Neither is such an agreement invalid merely because the parties may have contemplated the creation or continuation of a nonmarital relationship when they entered into it. Agreements between nonmarital partners fail only to the extent that they rest upon a consideration of meretricious sexual services.

> [W]e base our opinion on the principle that adults who voluntarily live together and engage in sexual relations are nonetheless as competent as any other persons to contract respecting their earnings and property rights. Of course, they cannot lawfully contract to pay for the performance of sexual services, for such a contract is, in essence, an agreement for prostitution and unlawful for that reason. But they may agree to pool their earnings and to hold all property acquired during the relationship in accord with the law governing community property; conversely they may agree that each partner's earnings and the property acquired from those earnings remains the separate property of the earning partner. So long as the agreement does not rest upon illicit meretricious consideration, the parties may order their economic affairs as they choose, and no policy precludes the courts from enforcing such agreements.

The court also held that Michelle could be entitled to a share of defendant's property under a theory of implied contract. Under this theory, even if there is no express contract, if the conduct of the parties is such as to give rise to an implied agreement, the courts will enforce the agreement as if it were an express contract. The court rejected all arguments that recognizing explicit or implied agreements to divide property made in nonmarital relationships would undermine marriage or foster immorality. It stated:

Although we recognize the well-established public policy to foster and promote the institution of marriage, perpetuation of judicial rules which result in an inequitable distribution of property accumulated during a nonmarital relationship is neither a just nor an effective way of carrying out that policy. [T]he prevalence of nonmarital relationships in modern society and the social acceptance of them, marks this as a time when our courts should by no means apply the doctrine of the unlawfulness of the so-called meretricious relationship to the [division of property.] As we have explained, the nonenforceability of agreements expressly providing for meretricious conduct rested upon the fact that such conduct, as the word suggests, pertained to and encompassed prostitution. To equate the nonmarital relationship of today to such a subject matter is to do violence to an accepted and wholly different practice.

We are aware that many young couples live together without the solemnization of marriage, in order to make sure that they can successfully later undertake marriage. This trial period, preliminary to marriage, serves as some assurance that the marriage will not subsequently end in dissolution to the harm of both parties. We are aware, as we have stated, of the pervasiveness of nonmarital relationships in other situations. The mores of the society have indeed changed so radically in regard to cohabitation that we cannot impose a standard based on alleged moral considerations that have apparently been so widely abandoned by so many.

The court made clear, however, that in removing the judicial barriers to division of the property of partners in a nonmarital relationship:

We do not seek to resurrect the doctrine of common law marriage, which was abolished in California by statute in 1895. Thus, we do not hold that plaintiff and defendant were 'married,' nor do we extend to plaintiff the rights which the [law] grants . . . spouses; we hold only that she has the same rights to enforce contracts and to assert her equitable in-

terest in property acquired through her effort as does any other unmarried person.[2]

Courts in California and other States have followed *Marvin* and have granted property rights to nonmarital partners using the *Marvin* express or implied contract theory or other theories.[3] Minnesota has recognized nonmarital property rights by statute. Interestingly, the Minnesota statutes provide that a contract between "co-habitants" establishing rights to property will be enforced by a court only if it is in writing; if there is no written contract between the parties: "the courts of this state are without jurisdiction to hear and shall dismiss as contrary to public policy any claim by an individual if the claim is based on the fact that the individuals lived together in contemplation of sexual relations and out of wedlock within or without this state." Minn. Stat. §§ 513.075; 513.076.

In *Hewitt v. Hewitt*, 77 Ill.2d 49, 394 N.E. 2d 1204 (1979), the Illinois Supreme Court was not willing to recognize a contract between the parties to a nonmarital relationship and said no marital rights and obligations should arise from such a rela-

---

2. It should be noted that the court in *Marvin* only held that implied or explicit contracts could be recognized and enforced; it did not hold that Michelle proved such a contract existed. On remand of the case, no implied or explicit contract for Lee to support Michelle after they ceased living together was found to exist.

3. For example, see *Pickens v. Pickens*, 490 So. 2d 872 (Miss. 1986), which used a trust theory; *Kenkenon v. Hue*, 207 Neb. 698, 301 N.W. 2d 77 (1981); *Kozlowski v. Kozlowski*, 80 N.J. 378, 403 A.2d 902 (1979); and *Morone v. Morone*, N.Y. 2d 481, 407 N.E. 2d 438 (1980), which recognized claims of express contracts; and *Beal v. Beal*, 282 Or. 115, 577 P.2d 507 (1978); *Caroll v. Lee*, 148 Ariz. 10, 712 P.2d 923 (1979), and *Watts v. Watts*, 137 Wis. 2d 506, 405 N.W.2d 303 (1987), which recognized implied contracts or other equitable remedies.

tionship on any theory. This was so even though, unlike in *Marvin*, the partners had a long-time relationship since their college days, had three children, and everyone believed they were married. The court stated:

> [W]e believe ... [t]he issue of unmarried cohabitants' mutual property rights ... cannot appropriately be characterized solely in terms of contract law, nor is it limited to considerations of equity or fairness as between the parties to such relationships. There are major public policy questions involved in determining whether, under what circumstances, and to what extent it is desirable to accord some type of legal status to claims arising from such relationships. Of substantially greater importance than the rights of the immediate parties is the impact of such recognition upon our society and the institution of marriage. Will the fact that legal rights closely resembling those arising from conventional marriages can be acquired by those who deliberately choose to enter into what have heretofore been commonly referred to as "illicit" or "meretricious" relationships encourage formation of such relationships and weaken marriage as the foundation of our family-based society? And ... what of the children born of such relationships? What are their support and inheritance rights and by what standards are custody questions resolved? What of the sociological and psychological effects upon them of that type of environment? Does not the recognition of legally enforceable property and custody rights emanating from nonmarital cohabitation in practical effect equate with the legalization of common law marriage at least in the circumstances of this case? And, in summary, have the increasing numbers of unmarried cohabitants and changing mores of our society reached the point at which the general welfare of the citizens of this State is best served by a return to something resembling the judicially created common law marriage our legislature outlawed in 1905?

The court felt that these questions had been answered long ago when the Illinois legislature outlawed common law marriage and the courts ruled that "an agreement in consideration of future illicit cohabitation ... is void." The court was unwilling to abandon this rule despite the "changes in societal norms and attitudes." The Court stated:

> It is urged that social mores have changed radically in recent years, rendering this principle of law archaic. It is said that because there are so many unmarried cohabitants today the courts must confer a legal status on such relationships. If this is to be the result, however, it would seem more candid to acknowledge the return of varying forms of common law marriage than to continue displaying the naivete we believe involved in the assertion that there are involved in these relationships contracts separate and independent from the sexual activity, and the assumption that those contracts would have been entered into or would continue without that activity.
>
> [Moreover, e]ven if we were to assume some modification of the rule of illegality is appropriate, we return to the fundamental question earlier alluded to: If resolution of this issue rests ultimately on grounds of public policy, by what body should that policy be determined? *Marvin*, viewing the issue as governed solely by contract law, found judicial policy-making appropriate. In our view, however, the situation alleged here was not the kind of arm's length bargain envisioned by traditional contract principles, but an intimate arrangement of a fundamentally different kind. The issue, realistically, is whether it is appropriate for this court to grant a legal status to a private arrangement substituting for the institution of marriage sanctioned by the State. The question whether change is needed in the law governing the rights of parties in this delicate area of marriage-like relationships involves evaluations of sociological data and alternatives we believe best suited to the superior investigative and fact-finding facilities of the legislative branch in the exercise of its traditional authority to declare public policy in the domestic relations field. That belief is reinforced by the fact that

judicial recognition of mutual property rights between unmarried cohabitants would, in our opinion, clearly violate the policy of our . . . [new marriage act, which was enacted soon after] *Marvin* was decided and received wide publicity. [This act, which nowhere mentions nonmarital contracts, but which continues to outlaw common law marriage] constitute[s] a recent and unmistakable legislative judgment disfavoring the grant of mutual property rights to knowingly unmarried cohabitants. Even if we disagreed with the wisdom of that judgment, it is not for us to overturn or erode it.

The recognition of agreements made by those who live in nonmarital sexual relationships to share property and to assume some of the rights and obligations of marriage is of some importance to gays and lesbians, who, as we have seen, are not allowed to marry their same-sex lovers. Courts have recognized the agreements of same-sex domestic partners, even when they do not recognize same-sex marriage. See *Whatten v. Dillingham*, 202 Cal. App.3d. 447, 248 Cal.Rptr. 405 (1988). As an alternative, some gays and lesbians have attempted to adopt their partners, hoping that adoption could provide legal recognition for a longstanding relationship. In *Matter of Adoption of Robert Paul P.*, 63 N.Y. 2d, 471 N.E.2d 424 (1984), however, a man was not permitted to adopt his male lover. The court stated: "Adoption is not a means of obtaining a legal status for a non-marital sexual relationship—whether homosexual or heterosexual. Such would be a 'cynical distortion of the function of adoption.' Nor is it a procedure by which to legitimize an emotional attachment, however sincere, but wholly devoid of the filial relationship that is fundamental to the concept of adoption."

The situation where there is cohabitation without a marriage license and solemnization or recognition as a common law marriage must be contrasted with the situation where there has been a marriage license issued and a solemnization of the marriage or all the requirements for legally recognized common law marriage have been met and one or both of the parties have a good faith belief that the marriage is valid, but the marriage is, in fact, invalid. In the latter situation, the States may recognize marital rights and obligations of the parties. It may make a difference if the marriage is *void*, that is, prohibited or impossible for some reason, or *voidable*, that is, merely technically invalid, but a party with a good faith belief in the validity of a solemnized marriage is generally recognized as a **putative spouse**, entitled to all the rights and privileges of a married person as long as the invalidity of the marriage is not due to his or her fault. Thus, a man who marries a woman believing in good faith that her prior marriage has been terminated by divorce would generally be considered a putative spouse entitled to all the rights of a spouse even if the woman's divorce was not final at the time of the marriage, but the woman might not be recognized as a putative spouse even if she believed in good faith that her divorce was final.

Putative spouses are generally entitled to all the rights of a real or legal spouse, but they would not be given these rights if to do so would adversely affect a legal spouse. Thus, for example, if a man were a bigamist, both his putative spouse and his legal, that is, his first spouse should be entitled to widow's social security benefits upon his death, but the putative spouse would not be entitled to full inheritance rights of two-thirds of her husband's property because granting her full inheritance rights would deny the first spouse her full inheritance rights. Both wives cannot have two-thirds of the husband's property.

INTERSTATE RECOGNITION OF MARRIAGES

Article IV, Section 1 of the Constitution provides that "Full Faith and Credit shall be given in each State to the Public Acts, Records and judicial Proceedings of every other State." Pursuant to this clause, known as the **Full Faith and Credit Clause**, a marriage that is valid in the State in which it was entered into, even a common law marriage, must be recognized as valid in all other States. However, a State need not recognize as valid a marriage entered into in another State solely to evade the requirements of the State where the parties to the marriage reside. For example, if State A allows marriages between first cousins, while State B forbids such marriages, and if John and Mary are first cousins who live in State B and who were married in State A, State B would recognize their marriage, but not if they went to State A to get married solely to avoid State B's requirements.

In fear of Hawaii's ruling on same-sex marriage, there have been efforts in Congress to except same-sex marriage from the Full Faith and Credit Clause.

PROPERTY RELATIONSHIPS DURING MARRIAGE

There are two different systems for determining the property rights between a husband and wife during the marriage: the **common law system**, also known as the **separate property system**, and the **community property system**.

As of 1990, forty-one States plus the District of Columbia used the common law system. Under this system, unless a couple decides to hold property acquired during a marriage jointly, property acquired during a marriage by one spouse remains that spouse's separate property; the other spouse has no right to or interest in that property during the marriage. The other States (Arizona, California, Idaho, Louisiana, Nevada, New Mexico, Texas, Washington and Wisconsin) used the community property system (although Wisconsin's system is called a **marital property system** not a community property system). Under this system, each spouse is deemed to have a one-half interest in all property acquired during marriage except property inherited or received by one spouse as a gift.

There are variations in the community property systems from State to State. For example, who controls the community property differs from State to State as does the status of income earned during marriage from property acquired before marriage. There are also variations in the separate property systems from State to State. For example, whether one spouse must pay the other's debts and which debts differs from State to State.

Many consider the community property system to be fairer to the wife, who generally earns less than the husband or who may earn nothing at all. Under the separate property system, the wife may own little or no property. Further, because she has no right to her husband's earnings and a creditor cannot necessarily collect her debts from her husband, she may not be able to obtain credit in her own name.

Under the community property system, by way of contrast, the wife has a right to one-half of her husband's earnings and a creditor can collect from this one-half share. Thus, she may obtain credit in her own name whether or not she earns any money.

The Equal Credit Opportunity Act, 15 U.S.C. § 1691, has somewhat eased the problem of a woman obtaining credit in separate property States. The Act prohibits discrimination by creditors on the basis of sex or marital status. It also permits a woman to use as a credit reference jointly used credit cards. However, under the Act, creditors can inquire into marital status. Further, the Act provides: "[c]onsideration or application of State property laws directly or indirectly affecting creditworthiness shall not constitute discrimination . . ." and that "each party to the marriage shall be solely responsible for the debt [separately] contracted." § 1691d.

Whether a State uses a community or separate property system, it probably requires spouses to support one another. However, courts may not be willing to intervene into the marriage relationship to enforce the duty of support. This point is illustrated by *McGuire v. McGuire*, 157 Neb. 226, 59 N.W.2d 336 (1953), an extreme case which nevertheless expresses the current view in most States today. *McGuire* held that a sixty-six-year-old woman who was in failing health was not entitled to court-ordered support payments from her husband although he had substantial assets and income and although he had given her no money for three or four years with the result that she was living in a state of considerable deprivation. She was provided with food but was not provided with any new clothing during this time except a coat. The furnishings and furnace in the home were very old, the newest appliance in the kitchen was a wood burning stove, the house had no bathroom or inside toilet, and water came from a well. The couple had one very old car. The court stated:

> The living standards of a family are a matter of concern to the household, and not for the courts to determine, even though the husband's attitude toward his wife, according to his wealth and circumstances, leaves little to be said in his behalf. As long as the home is maintained and the parties are living as husband and wife it may be said that the husband is legally supporting his wife and the purpose of the marriage relation is being carried out.

Even if a State uses a separate property system to allocate property *during* marriage, one spouse may have a right to a share of the other spouse's property *after* the marriage ends because of death or divorce. For example, a spouse may inherit a set share, like one-third or one-half, of a deceased spouse's property whether or not there is a will and even if a will does not provide for inheritance of this share. And one spouse may have a right to division of the property acquired during marriage following a divorce. How much may be inherited regardless of a will or when there is no will varies from State to State and, as we shall see, how the property will be divided and how much each spouse will receive after a divorce also differs from State to State.

AGREEMENTS CONCERNING PROPERTY RELATIONSHIPS

The parties to a marriage may enter into agreements to create their own property relationships during their marriage or after it ends. Such agreements, which are called **prenuptial contracts** or **antenuptial contracts** when they are entered into before marriage and **postnuptial contracts** when they are entered into during marriage, may be recognized and enforced by the courts. States differ, however, on the requirements for valid nuptial contracts and on the subjects they may cover. Postnuptial contracts are less commonly recognized than prenuptial ones. Typically, to be recognized, the contracts must be in writing and be entered into knowingly and voluntarily with full knowledge of the other party's assets and income. Generally, the contracts may not alter certain obligations, such as the obligation to support one another. Also, contracts that set forth what may happen if the couple divorces have not been recognized on the theory that before they even marry, couples should not be contemplating divorce.

Nuptial contracts may address aspects of the marital relationship in addition to property relationships, such as the responsibility for housework and the religion of any children of the marriage. While the courts may not be willing to enforce such provisions, believing that courts should not intervene in certain sensitive areas despite a contract, setting forth expectations and obligations in writing may avoid later misunderstanding and conflict.

People who are living together without marriage might be well-advised to write contracts related to property rights and other aspects of their relationships. Written contracts are far more likely to be recognized and enforced by the courts than tacit agreements. Written contracts may not, however, resolve inheritance rights. If people who are living together, particularly gays and lesbians whose relationship may not be acknowledged or accepted by relatives, wish their partners to inherit their property, it is necessary that they execute a proper will. Moreover, written contracts establishing a marital-like distribution of property or relationship cannot confer the status of marriage upon the partners. As long as the parties to the contract are not married, without the benefit of a law recognizing their relationship for a particular purpose, they may not be allowed, for example, to be included in their partner's insurance coverage as dependents, to file a joint income tax return, to file a law suit for the wrongful death of their partner, to collect a pension or social security benefits on their partner's account, or to claim a partner's rent-controlled apartment upon a partner's death.

While social workers are not permitted or qualified to advise clients on the legal requirements for or consequences of agreements related to marriage, social workers may advise clients to consult an attorney about an agreement or discuss the psychological and social aspects of such agreements.

TERMINATION OF MARRIAGE

Divorce

All States have laws specifically prescribing how one may terminate a marriage through divorce. All such laws are premised on the principle that the State should uphold the stability of marriage and should protect all the parties involved in a marriage. Thus, traditionally, one could get a divorce only if there were specific legal grounds for divorce such as desertion, adultery, or conviction of a felony. Now, all the States have some kind of so-called **"no-fault" divorce**, which permits the parties to obtain a divorce if the marriage has "irretrievably broken down," if the parties "mutually agree" to divorce, or if the parties have "irreconcilable differences."[4] This does not mean, however, that a divorce is available simply at the will of one party or that it is simple to terminate a marriage. In all States, a divorce may only be granted at the conclusion of a court proceeding and if the parties have met certain procedural and substantive requirements. Moreover, in a desire to preserve the family and lower divorce rates, some States are cutting back on no-fault divorce.

A divorce, called a **dissolution of marriage** in many States, is the legal termination of a valid marriage. A judgment of divorce not only terminates a marriage. It also may resolve the rights and obligations of the parties stemming from the marriage. Specifically, it may divide the property acquired during the marriage, order spousal and child support payments, and determine child custody and visitation. These rights and obligations resolved in a divorce judgment are sometimes referred to as **ancillary matters.**

Annulment

While a divorce is the termination of a *valid* marriage, an **annulment** is the termination of an *invalid* one. A statute usually sets forth a few specific grounds for an annulment, all of which go to the validity of the marriage. An annulment cannot be obtained unless one or more of these grounds exist. Typical annulment statutes provide that a marriage may be terminated by an annulment if, and only if: 1) the marriage was not valid at the time of solemnization (e.g., the wife's previous marriage was not yet finally terminated; the husband was under age); 2) the marriage is prohibited (e.g., the husband and wife are uncle and niece; the wife had a venereal disease); 3) the marriage has not been consummated (i.e., the parties have not had sexual relations); or 4) consent to the marriage was obtained through fraud. The last ground has generally been interpreted to require fraud about an essential element of the marriage or that was essential to obtaining consent. Mere boasting or a false inducement to obtaining consent may not be considered fraud. Thus, lying about one's income may not be the kind of fraud that constitutes a ground for annulment, but lying about one's sexual impotence may be.

The legal grounds for an annulment may differ from the grounds recognized for an annulment by a religion. Moreover, an annulment granted by a court may not be recognized by a religion and an annulment granted by a religious body would generally have no legal effect.

The consequences of a legal annulment differ from State to State. Generally, the children of an annulled marriage will be considered legitimate. The rights and entitlement of parties to annulled marriages may be equal to that of divorced spouses, may be equal to that of divorced spouses only where they are putative spouses, or

---

4. Generally, the previous fault standards may additionally or alternatively be able to be asserted as the basis for a divorce. Whether or not they can be or are specifically asserted, they may affect the resolution of matters related to a divorce, such as distribution of property or child custody.

may depend on the entitlement in question. For example, a woman whose marriage was annulled may be entitled to alimony if, and only if, she were a putative spouse, but she may not be entitled to her husband's retirement benefits even if she were a putative spouse. The consequences of an annulment and the rights and entitlements of the parties may also depend on the grounds for the annulment and whether a marriage was void or voidable. Whether a spouse in an annulled marriage is entitled to benefits of a divorced spouse, including federal benefits like social security or veterans' benefits, usually depends on the spouse's State law status.

Separation

Sometimes, the parties to a marriage may not be eligible for an annulment and may not want to divorce for religious or other reasons, but may want to live apart and cease all marital relations. If they separate without any judicial action, there may be no legal consequences to their separation. All rights, obligations, entitlements, and incidents of marriage will probably be unaffected by the separation except that, if the parties have physically separated, the courts generally feel free to intervene in the marriage to enforce the support obligation. If, however, the parties go to court for a judicial decree of separation, that is, a **legal separation**, depending on State law, all or some of the rights, obligations, entitlements, and incidents of marriage will probably be affected. In most States, the parties will be treated exactly like divorced people with one essential difference—they are not free to marry again. The tax consequences, including the federal tax consequences, of a separation depend on State law.

The Divorce Process

We shall discuss only the divorce process, but the process may be similar for an annulment or a legal separation.

A party to a marriage who wants a divorce must file a petition for a divorce in a State court. Several States, including New York, have special courts, called Family Courts or Domestic Relations Courts, which hear all divorce cases and other matters related to families. Most States simply hear divorces in their trial courts of general jurisdiction or in special departments of these courts. If there are two levels of trial courts in a State, usually only the higher level court is a court of general jurisdiction that can grant a divorce.

The party who is seeking the divorce must generally have been a resident of the State where the divorce is filed for a certain period of time, such as six months. In *Sosna v. Iowa*, 419 U.S. 393 (1975), the Court upheld a one-year residency requirement to file for a divorce. Usually, a court in a State in which only one spouse resides has jurisdiction to grant a divorce, but the other spouse may have to be in the State to be served. See *Burnham J. Superior Court of California*, 495 U.S. 604 (1990). Moreover, a court in a State where only one party resides may not have jurisdiction to make certain ancillary orders related to property in the divorce judgment. If it proceeds to make such orders without jurisdiction, its orders are void and need not be recognized in another State despite the command of the Full Faith and Credit Clause of the Constitution. Thus, if one spouse deserts and moves to another State, unless the deserted spouse can seek an order in the deserting spouse's State, the deserted spouse may never get certain orders on ancillary matters.

In *Boddie v. Connecticut*, 401 U.S. 371 (1971), the Court ruled that Connecticut's fee to file a petition for a divorce that indigents could not afford to pay was an impermissible barrier to divorce in violation of due process. Thus, any filing fee for a petition for divorce must be waived if a petitioner is indigent.

The petition may be a simple form that the party who seeks a divorce can complete without the assistance of an attorney. Generally, however, people seeking divorces need attorneys to assist them, particularly if there is substantial property or the ancillary matters are complex or hotly contested.

A person's inability to afford a lawyer to assist in filing the necessary papers and obtaining a divorce may appear to be a substantial barrier to divorce like the high filing fee found to violate due process in *Boddie v. Connecticut*, but several courts have held that there is no right to the appointment of a lawyer in a divorce case. State law generally provides, however, that one party to a divorce may be required to pay the other party's attorney's fees at the conclusion of a divorce. Thus, an attorney may be willing to accept a divorce case for a party who has no funds on the contingency that the other party will be ordered to pay all fees.

A divorce petition, like other petitions, must be served on the respondent. When the respondent's whereabouts are unknown, publication of a notice in a newspaper may be sufficient service.

Because publication is often the method of service, because respondents may not be able to afford a lawyer, and because divorces are often not contested, respondents may not answer divorce petitions, that is, they may **default**. They are then not entitled to further notice or an opportunity to contest the contents of the petition.

In an effort to prevent divorce, most States require the parties to a divorce to wait a period of time, often several months, from the time a divorce petition is filed until a judgment can be granted. Such waiting periods are designed to prevent hasty divorces. Also, in an effort to prevent divorce, some States require divorcing couples to have counseling, often called **divorce conciliation**, aimed at reconciling them. Some States only require such counseling in certain circumstances, as when the couple has children or when the marriage has been of long duration. Other States have laws giving a judge discretion to order conciliation in an appropriate case.

Divorce conciliation, whether it is mandatory or ordered by a court in its discretion, may be done by special court employees, who may be social workers, or by private social workers who work under contract with the court. Couples may also go to counselors of their choice or be referred to independent counselors by the court. The counseling may be free of charge, may be paid for by the court, or may be paid for by the parties.

In contrast to divorce conciliation, **divorce mediation** assumes that a couple's divorce will occur, and rather than trying to help them reconcile, it helps them reach a fair agreement, through the use of a neutral mediator, on the ancillary matters related to their divorce. Since the 1970s, more than half of the States have adopted laws authorizing courts to order mediation or mandating mediation be ordered in some or all divorce cases. Typically, issues related to children are referred for court-ordered mediation.

Even without a law authorizing or mandating court-ordered mediation and even without a court order for mediation, the parties to a divorce may choose to mediate rather than litigate their differences. Such private mediation is becoming increasingly popular as a cheaper and more effective method of obtaining satisfactory results for both parties to a divorce.

Social workers can and often do act as divorce mediators, sometimes acting in tandem with a lawyer. Indeed, the California mediation law, the first mandatory mediation law in the country, provides that the "minimum qualifications required" for court-ordered mediators (or counselors in court-supervised conciliation programs) include a "master's degree in psychology, social work, marriage, family and child counseling, or other behavioral science substantially related to marriage and family interpersonal relationships." Cal. Family Code, §§ 1815, 3164.

While all ancillary matters associated with divorce may be mediated and while social workers may mediate on any subject, social workers generally do not have the professional expertise to address property distribution and other financial arrangements, especially when the couple has substantial assets and income. Thus, social workers most often mediate child custody and visitation agreements and related child (and possibly spousal) support arrangements.

Whether or not there has been a formal effort to arrange a settlement of ancillary matters through divorce mediation, divorcing couples, like other litigants, often settle certain ancillary matters without a trial. In divorce cases, as in most other types of litigation, settlement is the norm. Unlike in most other types of litigation, however, in divorce cases, a judge may not always honor the parties' settlement. If a judge believes that a settlement (or mediated agreement) is not in the best interests of a party or does not protect the party's interests, the judge may refuse to recognize it.

In addition to acting as mediators, social workers often assist clients in negotiating divorce settlements, addressing the psychological issues, which lawyers are often ill-equipped to address.

Even when there has been a settlement agreement or a divorce is uncontested, most States require a hearing before a divorce judgment can be granted. The hearing is designed to ensure that the divorce is fair to all parties. In some States, the parties must speak to an officer of the court, who may be a social worker, before the final hearing. This officer of the court provides a recommendation on certain ancillary matters, particularly those related to children, to the court. In other States, any final hearing is before a special magistrate or referee who is not officially a judge. This referee or magistrate makes a recommendation to the judge who ultimately decides the case.

After a contested or uncontested final hearing, the court generally grants a divorce and resolves all ancillary matters in one judgment. This judgment is final insofar as it grants a divorce, but some ancillary matters resolved in the judgment may be modified if the circumstances of the parties change.

In some States, in some cases, because there may be substantial delays in resolving the ancillary matters, as a matter of court practice or pursuant to statute, courts may grant a judgment of divorce and then consider the ancillary matters. This process is known as **bifurcating a divorce**. Also, because of the substantial delays in obtaining a divorce judgment, either party may have obtained a temporary order for property division and child custody and support before judgment. Such temporary orders, which may be referred to as *pendente lite* or **interlocutory orders**, can be sought at any time before judgment, including at the time of filing a petition. Orders *pendente lite* generally are modifiable at any time before the judgment and only remain in effect until the judgment. The judgment generally supercedes all orders *pendente lite*.

Social workers may help those involved in the divorce process throughout the process and after the process has been completed. People contemplating a divorce frequently need counseling to help them make a wise decision. People who have decided on a divorce frequently need counseling to help them cope with the process. As has been noted, they also frequently need the help of social workers to negotiate settlements of the ancillary matters. Social workers may be particularly helpful when it comes to arranging workable child custody and visitation agreements. After a divorce, people need help adjusting to their new status, coping with the guilt and ambivalent feelings they may have, and living with any child custody and visitation orders, among other things. Throughout and after the process, social workers may help the children involved in a divorce adjust to the divorce and to any child custody arrangements.

PROPERTY RELATIONSHIPS AFTER TERMINATION OF MARRIAGE

Alimony

At the termination of marriage, one spouse may be required to pay an amount, known as **maintenance**, **support**, or **alimony**, to the other spouse: 1) for a set period; 2) until a certain event occurs, such as the remarriage of the spouse receiving alimony or the retirement of the spouse paying alimony; or 3) indefinitely. Alimony may be paid monthly, yearly, or in a lump sum. Until the Supreme Court ruled in *Orr v. Orr*, 440 U.S. 268 (1979), that the practice was an unconstitutional denial of equal protection, in some States, men were required to pay alimony to women, but there was no reciprocal obligation on women to pay alimony to men. Despite the gender-neutral alimony laws compelled by *Orr*, however, it is the rare case where a woman is ordered to pay alimony to a man. Thus, and for convenience, the discussion of alimony in this chapter will ignore the possibility that an ex-wife could be ordered to pay alimony to her ex-husband. Of course, everything that is said about the award of alimony to a woman would apply with equal force to the award of alimony to a man.

Many argue that the greater equality between men and women which we have today and the ever increasing opportunities for women's employment mean that alimony should never be granted to the wife. While there undoubtedly are cases where an award of alimony would be unnecessary and unjust, alimony is necessary in some cases. As was said in *In re*

Marriage of Brantner, 67 Cal.App. 3d 416, 136 Cal.Rptr. 635 (1977):

> A marriage license is not a ticket to a perpetual pension and, as women approach equality in the job market, the burden on the husband will be lessened. . . . However, in those cases in which it is the decision of the parties that the woman becomes the homemaker, the marriage is of substantial duration and at separation the wife is to all intents and purposes unemployable, the husband simply has to face up to the fact that his support responsibilities are going to be of extended duration—perhaps for life. This has nothing to do with feminism, sexism, male chauvinism, or any other trendy social ideology. It is ordinary common sense, basic decency and simple justice.

A belief in the equality of women and of their opportunity for employment, however, has led to a decrease in awards of alimony and a decrease in the amount awarded. Not only is alimony no longer routinely awarded, in fact, it is rarely granted. Where it is awarded, it is often in a low amount, representing a small percentage of the husband's income. Even this low amount often is not paid.

Whether alimony should be awarded as a matter of course, in certain circumstances, or never is a question that may trouble courts and legislatures for years to come. And even if it is finally decided that alimony should be awarded in certain kinds of cases, troubling questions will remain, such as: How much alimony should be awarded? Should alimony be awarded based on the husband's income or the wife's needs? Should alimony be in an amount calculated to keep the wife's standard of living equivalent to that during marriage or only in an amount calculated to meet basic needs? Should it make a difference whether or not there are children and

who has custody of them? Does the duration of the marriage make a difference? Does the "fault" of the wife (such as her committing adultery) make any difference?

An alimony order is generally modifiable or terminable. A judgment may provide when alimony is to be terminated or modified (e.g., when the wife remarries; if the husband retires; in seven years), but even if nothing is said about modification or termination in the decree, an alimony order will usually be modifiable or terminable, after a motion and hearing, if circumstances have changed. The modifiability and terminability of alimony payments also raise many questions, such as: Should alimony be lowered if the husband assumes new responsibilities by remarrying or fathering more children? May the husband quit his job without regard for his ex-wife's needs? What should happen if the wife begins living with a man but does not marry him to avoid losing her alimony?[5]

The answers to these and the many other questions posed by alimony may be resolved by legislatures as a matter of social policy or by courts on a case-by-case basis.

Property Division

A decree terminating a marriage generally divides the property acquired by the

---

5. Some States and some divorce judgments resolve this question by providing for the termination of alimony when the wife lives with another in a marriage-like relationship. However, in the case of *Gajovski v. Gajovski*, 81 Ohio App.3d 11, 610 N.E.2d 431 (1991), the court held that the wife's living with another woman in a lesbian relationship was not "concubinage," which would terminate alimony because lesbians could not marry and concubinage must be a marriage-like relationship.

couple during the marriage. In all the separate property jurisdictions and in half the community property States, the courts, in accordance with case law or with statutory mandates, will distribute the property equitably. This means the property will be distributed as fairly as possible in light of such considerations as who acquired the property; the contribution of the party who did not actually acquire the property to the acquisition of the property and to the household; and the needs of the parties.

Equitable distribution is not the same as *equal* distribution, the system used in half of the community property States. Indeed, only a few of the equitable distribution jurisdictions presume that an equitable distribution is an equal distribution; and most specifically do not equate equity with equality. Rather, the bulk of the property is generally allocated to the major wage-earner, who is usually the husband.

Some excerpts from the majority and concurring opinions in *LaRue v. LaRue*, 304 S.E. 2d 312 (W.Va. 1983), may help you to understand the concept of equitable distribution of property and some of the issues that arise when equitable, or equal, distribution is attempted. In *LaRue*, an appeal from a divorce judgment, the West Virginia Supreme Court reversed the trial court's refusal to equitably distribute the property acquired during the LaRue's thirty-year marriage. The *LaRue* marriage was "a traditional one in the sense that Mr. LaRue exclusively handled the family's financial affairs and Mrs. LaRue was mainly a homemaker." Mrs. LaRue only worked in the first years of their marriage. "Mr. LaRue encouraged his spouse to be a housewife and home-maker, and accordingly she raised two children, cared for the house and the comfort of her family, and entertained her husband's business associates." In the judgment, Mrs. LaRue was awarded alimony and an allowance for health insurance, but, except for some items of personal property, she was awarded none of the property acquired during the marriage, all of which was in Mr. LaRue's name only. The majority opinion in the West Virginia Supreme Court stated:

The concept of equitable distribution of marital property has achieved an almost universal acceptance in the divorce laws of the various states. It originated when courts applied their equitable powers to secure equitable rights for one spouse in property titled or held by the other spouse based on the claim that a resulting or constructive trust should be impressed on the property. The basis for such a claim was that the spouse seeking an interest in the property had made a substantial economic contribution toward the acquisition of the property. Consequently, under the principles of unjust enrichment, it would be unfair to permit the spouse with title or possession to keep the entire interest. [The general rule is:]

"Where a wife has made a material contribution to the husband's acquisition of property during coverture [marriage], she acquires a special equity in the property so accumulated which equity entitles her, on divorce, to an award in satisfaction thereof; and it is not a necessary prerequisite that the wife show that she has contributed by funds or efforts to the acquiring of the specific property awarded to her, but division may be had even though the wife has not contributed funds or efforts to the acquisition of the specific property awarded to her."

Judicial decisions involving these equitable principles have more recently been supplemented and enhanced by various forms of legislative enactments. A . . . common statute which a majority of [the separate property] states have enacted, permits the court upon the dissolution of a marriage to make an equitable distribution of the marital property based upon a detailed list of factors. [Another] category of statutes, used in a few states, is more general and provides that an equitable distribution of property may be made by the court without specifying any guidelines. Finally, in those few jurisdictions that have no specific statute on equitable distribution, the courts have continued to evolve their concepts of equitable distribution with a broad interpretation of traditional equity principles. We are in this category. Thus, it would appear that in virtually every state either by way of express statute or through court interpretation, some mechanism exists to permit a court in granting a final divorce to provide the wife with some distribution for her homemaker and economic contributions.

In determining an appropriate amount for equitable distribution where there have been economic contributions made [other than homemaker services], it is necessary to consider the respective economic contributions made by both parties during the marriage as weighed against the net assets that are available at the time of the divorce. The term "net assets" does not include assets acquired by a party prior to the marriage, or obtained during the marriage by way of inheritance or gifts from third parties. In computing the value of any net asset, the indebtedness owed against such asset should ordinarily be deducted from its fair market value. In an appropriate case, the court in calculating the amount of equitable distribution arising from economic contributions may take into account the value of gifts made to the spouse seeking equitable contribution by the other spouse.

Homemaker services . . . present a more complex problem than economic contributions. In the traditional view of marriage, the husband's obligation was to support his wife and she in turn rendered domestic or homemaker services. The theory of alimony is based upon the husband's legal obligation to support his wife, and thus upon the dissolution of a marriage where she was not at fault, the wife is entitled to alimony. Thus, to some

extent, it may be argued that homemaker services were the consideration for the husband's traditional obligation to support his wife. There is, however, an increasing recognition that homemaker services cannot be viewed as a mere adjunct to the husband's duty of support. [They may, instead, be viewed as a contribution to the marriage, which can be recognized in the distribution of property.]

[As a contribution to the marriage,] . . . homemaker services is not to be measured by some mechanical formula, but instead rests on a showing that the homemaker has contributed to the economic well-being of the family unit through the performance of the myriad of household and child-rearing tasks which make up the term "homemaker services." In valuing this service, the length of the marriage is an important factor and consideration should be given to the quality of the services. Some consideration should also be given to the age, health, and skills of the homemaker as well as the amount of independent assets possessed. [Further], we believe that fault is a factor to consider when valuing homemaker services even though it is not a factor where economic contributions have been made. The reason for considering fault is that, historically, homemaker services were the wife's marital contribution upon which rested the husband's countervailing support obligation and his duty to pay alimony if the marriage was dissolved without fault on the wife's part. We do not suggest that fault on the wife's part is an absolute bar to her receiving some equitable distribution for homemaker services. [W]e do not foreclose the trial court from giving some equitable distribution for homemaker services even where traditional fault grounds exist, where an otherwise compelling case for equitable distribution for homemaker services can be shown.

Just as in the economic contribution area, a court may consider the value of any gifts given to the homemaker spouse during the marriage by the other spouse. The value of homemaker services must also be considered in relation to the net assets available at the time of the divorce and in light of the alimony award.

Applying these principles of equitable distribution to the facts of the present case, . . . Mrs. LaRue was entitled to some equitable distribution on both theories. First, during the early years of her marriage, she had contributed her earnings. . . . This economic contribution must be considered, but its value will have to be determined based on a comparison of the contributions made by Mr. LaRue as weighed against the net assets at the time of the divorce. Second, Mrs. LaRue's homemaker services, which were contributed over a considerable period of time, also entitle her to some equitable consideration. Again, her contributions must be calculated against the net marital assets.

The concurring opinion stated:

A marriage is, as the majority has stated, to some degree an economic partnership. Both partners contribute services that have a recognizable value to the household. In most marriages a surplus is generated by the parties' forbearance from immediate consumption of the marital income. This marital surplus is commonly invested in a dwelling, and in insurance and other investments to assure the protection of the partners from penury should sudden and unforeseen events, or the quiet onslaught of age, diminish the family earnings. It does no violence to [West Virginia law], I believe, to recognize that contributions of a party to his or her marriage give rise to a property right to a proportionate share of that marital surplus.

My enthusiasm for today's holding arises largely from my understanding of the economic plight of women in America. Simply put, women are poorer than men. The mean wage for women who work full time is 59 percent of the equivalent mean wage for men. Among single men and women who are not living with relatives, the poverty rate for men is 18.1 percent; the rate for women is 27.7 percent. Once a man and woman are married, if both are working full time, the woman's wage on average amounts to only 34.7 percent of the family earnings. When a marriage has ended, the situation becomes bleaker; 10.3

percent of male single parents fall below the poverty line (a total of 205,000); 34.6 percent of single women with children, or a total of 3.4 million such women, fall below the poverty line. In fact, divorced women with children now make up a new class of the poverty-stricken. By contrast, the poverty rate for families headed by a married couple is only 6.8 percent.

Among the factors leading to [these statistics] two are prominent. The first is that court-ordered awards . . . are frequently not paid. The second [is] that divorced women often do not have access to that part of the marital surplus invested in pensions or insurance. . . .

Among divorced or currently separated women, 14.3 percent were entitled to alimony or maintenance as of the spring of 1979. The alimony or maintenance award amounted to over 25 percent of the mean income of those women who actually received it. However, of those women entitled to receive alimony or maintenance payments in 1978, 28.4 percent did not receive the full amount due them, and 30.5 percent received nothing at all.

Our growing experience with the financial position of divorced women leads me to the conclusion, confirmed by this statistical data, that West Virginia's current scheme for allocating marital property acquired through joint efforts is inadequate to protect women . . . from unfair results. Since the statute [on distribution of property] does not by its terms foreclose us from developing equitable doctrines that will provide greater financial security upon divorce, it is incumbent upon us to do so.

This Court's holding today opens a wide field of opportunity to the [trial] courts, whose options previously were by and large limited to alimony and child support. It is my hope that the courts . . . will creatively avail themselves of the opportunities that equitable distribution presents. Unfortunately, there are many problems which are beyond the capacity of courts to solve. Courts can only distribute wealth, they cannot create any. The economies of scale that prevail in joint households are irretrievably lost when a married couple separates. Pensions adequate to support two retired people living together may not be adequate to support the two retired people living separately. Similarly, when an active head of a household becomes disabled, he may still be able to support a joint household with insurance proceeds, but may no longer be able to meet his alimony . . . obligations.

However, there is a second problem which courts may successfully address, which comes to mind because of some of the peculiar forms the marital surplus is likely to assume. The "savings" of the average American family no longer take the form of cash on hand in a savings account in the local bank. Rather, the "savings" are invested in the family home, plowed back into ongoing business ventures, or used to buy institutional insurance and pension programs. These forms of "savings" are often tied to the family wage-earner personally, or held in the name of the partner who is responsible for taking care of the financial affairs of the family. The advent of societal institutions selling financial protection in a pension/insurance package has transformed the nature of America's wealth from present capital to future interest. To the extent that these various forms of savings represent investments rather than assets—and some are investments under very strict terms—they present a new challenge to courts attempting to effect among divorcing parties a fair financial reconciliation. With a little effort and imagination, courts can see that divorcing parties, who own an apple orchard for instance, leave the courthouse with apples for life rather than a truckload each of applewood kindling.

We must be aware, for instance, of the importance of the family home in terms both of its emotional and financial value. I am concerned that the dominant financial value of the family home will cause inequities, and even forced sale, as a result of our adoption of equitable distribution. My concern is particularly aroused when I contemplate minor children, who are the innocent victims of their parents' inability to maintain the marriage. Our courts should bend over backward to maintain minor children with a custodial parent in the family home when appropriate.

This can be accomplished under traditional child support and alimony doctrines.

Pension rights and insurance plans present a particularly challenging opportunity for . . . creative solution. Investment in pensions and insurance is probably the largest slice of the investment pie. In addition to social security are myriad company, union, and public employee pensions. These programs are generally tied to the wage-earner in a family, and would therefore seem to be an asset ripe for redistribution under a court's equitable powers. However, pension rights present one of the most complex problems in equitable distribution cases [as do problems with] . . . private insurance. Many middle income people have whole life insurance policies but their cash surrender values are negligible until people have reached comfortable middle age. A husband whose insurance policy is paid for with marital assets may on termination of the marriage eliminate the former wife's beneficiary status. . . . Where alimony is not a charge on a former husband's estate the wife may then be left with nothing upon his death. Although the present cash surrender value of the policy may be negligible, its value as insurance [particularly if the husband is in poor health] may be substantial.

As can be seen from *LaRue*, the distribution of property after a divorce, whether it be an equitable or an equal distribution, poses many questions. Some of the questions are similar to the questions posed by alimony, such as: Should fault matter? Does it make any difference who was awarded custody of the children? Does the amount of the wife's or husband's separate income and property make any difference? Other questions are unique to property distribution. Two of these unique questions warrant further discussion.

First, what should happen to the wife's and children's health insurance coverage if, as is often the case, the wife and children have been included in a group plan through the husband's job? Can they remain on the plan as long as the husband remains on the plan? Should it make any difference if the husband or the employer pays for dependents' insurance coverage? Should it make a difference if the husband remarries and acquires new dependents? If the wife is required to obtain new health insurance because she and the children cannot be included on her husband's policy, what happens if she or the children have pre-existing conditions that the new insurance company will not cover? Many States have adopted laws that address some of these questions. Some of these laws require insurance companies to continue divorced spouses and children in group plans upon payment of the group rate premium. Other States routinely make orders that the husband continue providing insurance coverage for the wife and children as part of alimony or child support orders instead of as part of property distribution.

Second, what should be done with pensions? Should the wife get a share of a husband's pension, which will be paid upon his retirement many years in the future? Does it make any difference if the pension is the major asset of the husband and that the family sacrificed in the present because of the promise of a future pension, as is often the case with military families? In *McCarty v. McCarty*, 435 U.S 210 (1981), the Court held that a federal military pension could not be divided by a State divorce court based on its view of federal versus State authority, but Congress has now provided that a State divorce court may make certain orders related to a military pension and the military can pay a portion of a pension directly to an ex-wife. See 10 U.S.C § 1408.

Pensions provided by private employers are probably the most common type of pension. Most such pensions are regulated by a federal law, the Employee's Retirement Income Security Act, 29 U.S.C. § 1001, *et seq.*, known as ERISA. The Supreme Court also held that a State court could not make an order dividing a pension regulated by ERISA, again because of the relation between federal and State law, and again Congress reversed the Supreme Court. However, only certain qualified domestic relations orders can allocate pensions covered by ERISA and only in certain circumstances. See 29 U.S.C. § 1056(d).

Despite Congress' actions, other problems arise with respect to pensions. Courts may be unwilling or unable to divide pensions that will be paid in the future. They may be willing or able to order the payment of future dependents' benefits to former spouses, but the wage earner may be able to opt for pension plans that pay the wage earner a higher amount in return for eliminating dependents' benefits. Some statutes prevent married persons from so electing without notice to or the consent of a spouse or a former spouse. However, special pension benefits for dependents may be in a small amount on the assumption that they supplement the wage earner's pension, an assumption that is not valid when the spouses are living apart.

One other problem in the area of property distribution must be discussed. Typically, divorcing American couples have little property; it is their income (or their earning capacity) that determines their standard of living. When couples divorce young, the husband's future earning capacity may not yet be realized. He may have just obtained a professional degree or just begun a professional practice or a business. Should a wife get an equitable share of her husband's professional degree or license if she supported him while he obtained it? Can a wife somehow claim a portion of future earnings if she contributed to the foundation of such earnings? The States are split on this. Some States consider a professional license or degree to be an "asset" that can be distributed on divorce through a variety of methods (such as determining its present value and reflecting that value in the distribution of the couple's other assets). Other States have expressly rejected this idea, but some of these States and a few other States may allow or require courts to consider a pro-

fessional degree or license in setting alimony. For example, an Illinois statute requires that courts consider in setting alimony a spouse's "contributions . . . to the education, training, career or career potential, or license of the other spouse," 750 ILCS § 5/504, while a California statute provides for "reimbursement" for "contibutions to education or training of a party that substantially enhances the earning capacity of the party." Cal. Family Code, § 2641.

As with the questions that arise in the area of alimony, some of the questions that arise in the area of distribution of property may be answered by legislatures as a matter of policy or by courts on a case-by-case basis.

Custody and Support of Children

Whenever a marriage is terminated or a husband and wife legally separate, the courts must determine who will be awarded custody of any children of the marriage, what rights a noncustodial parent may have to make decisions for or visit a child, and what amounts a parent may have to pay in child support. Courts may also have to resolve these issues when the parents of a child never married or when nonparents seek custody of or rights to visit a child.

Whether or not the parents of a child have been married, social workers perform a very important direct role in child custody and visitation determinations and an equally important, but indirect, counseling role in relation to such determinations. Social workers also perform an important, although generally indirect role, in relation to child support determinations, particularly where the parents have never married.

Because of the importance of the social worker's role, this chapter will look at the laws and issues related to child custody, visitation, and support in some depth. Except in regard to the determination of parentage, these laws and issues are generally the same for married and unmarried parents.

CHILD CUSTODY AND VISITATION

Standards Used in Awarding Custody

Until well into the nineteenth century, the father was routinely awarded custody of his children after divorce. The children were considered his "property"; he

had a right to their "services." Moreover, women's limited civil rights meant men were the logical choice as legal guardians of children.

As society became more urban, it was recognized that fathers generally worked away from the home and were not responsible for child care and child rearing and that mothers were the parents who were home with the children and who had primary responsibility for their care. Moreover, the fact that the mother was generally the more nurturing and caring parent, particularly for young children, began to be considered important. The courts adopted the **tender years presumption** under which the mother was presumed to be the "natural" parent of a child of "tender" years and was awarded custody unless she was shown to be unfit.

In the 1920s, the idea took hold that child custody decisions after divorce should be based, not on the father's interests in his "property" or on the alleged "natural" relationship between mother and child, but rather on the **best interests of the child**. Nevertheless, mothers still were routinely awarded custody. The courts continued to use the tender years presumption, presuming that, absent a showing of unfitness, it was in the best interest of a child, particularly a young child, to be raised by his or her mother.

The idea that custody awards, whether after divorce or otherwise, should be based on the best interests of the child is now part of the law in every State typically in a statute. The continued use of the tender years presumption, however, has been called into question by the increased equality of men and women and the increased use of the equal protection clause to challenge laws fostering or per-petuating sexual inequality. Most States have officially abandoned the presumption by statute or court decision. Nevertheless, in a dispute between the parents, it is still likely that child custody will be awarded to the mother for several reasons. First, judges may still assume, even though the assumption is unstated, that child rearing is a woman's role and that, absent a showing of unfitness, it is in the best interests of young children that they be placed in the custody of their mothers. Second, many jurisdictions follow the **primary caretaker rule**, which requires that, other things being equal, a child's primary caretaker in the past should be given his or her custody in the future. Because mothers are generally children's primary caretakers, mothers are generally given custody under this rule. Further, fathers may not seek custody particularily when there has been no marriage, and divorcing mothers may agree to settlements giving up alimony or giving them a disadvantageous property division if they are given custody.

Whatever the likelihood that the mother will be awarded custody of her children, as has been stated, typically, a statute mandates the use of the best interests standard. Sometimes, the statute sets forth the factors that should be considered by a judge in deciding what is in a child's best interests. This is the case with the **Uniform Marriage and Divorce Act** (UMDA), a model act, which has been adopted in whole or in part, with or without modifications, by several States. Section 402 of the UMDA provides:

> The court shall determine custody in accordance with the best interest of the child. The court shall consider all relevant factors including:
>
> (1) The wishes of the child's parent or parents as to his custody;
> (2) The wishes of the child as to his custodian;
> (3) The interaction and interrelationship of the child with his parent or parents, his siblings, and any other person who may significantly affect the child's best interest;
> (4) The child's adjustment to his home, school, and community; and
> (5) The mental and physical health of all individuals involved.

Sometimes, a custody statute sets forth no factors and it is solely up to the judge to decide what factors to consider. Usually, even if there is a list of relevant factors in a statute, as in the UMDA, a judge may still consider other factors. Sometimes, factors that may not be considered, like the sex or morality of a custodian, are listed in a statute. For example, Section 402 of the UMDA also provides that: "The court shall not consider conduct of a proposed custodian that does not affect his relationship to the child."

Many factors could conceivably come into play in making child custody determinations. Sometimes, courts make these determinations based on factors that are neither included in statutes nor relevant to the best interests of the child, such as a parent's professional status. Basing child custody determinations on such factors would be contrary to law. Sometimes, the factors that a judge considers may be relevant to a child's best interests, but consideration of the factors is nevertheless erroneous as a violation of constitutional rights or as contrary to public policy. For example, as we shall see, custody determinations based on a parent's interracial marriage or disability have been held, respectively, to violate equal protection and to be contrary to proper respect for and consideration of the rights and dignity of the disabled.

Child custody orders are usually accompanied by orders granting visitation to noncustodial parents, but visitation may be denied if a court believes visitation would not be in a child's best interests. Factors that lead to a denial of custody may equally lead to a denial of visitation. Further, the more acrimonious a divorce, the more difficult and potentially disruptive visitation may be. Nevertheless, a complete denial of all visitation would be extreme and unusual. Far more commonly, visitation may be curtailed, conditions may be imposed on any visitation (e.g., all visits must occur in a certain location), or visitation may be supervised, often by a social worker.

The best interest standard and the factors related to it are used not only in making initial custody and visitation determinations but also when a parent seeks to change an initial custody or visitation determination. Child custody orders and accompanying visitation orders are generally modifiable for changed circumstances. But, the modifiability of child custody orders is usually limited because of the belief that a child needs the stability of one parent and because it is believed that uprooting a child from a parent with whom he or she has lived for many years, even if the parent may no longer be the "best" parent for the child, can cause lasting harm to a child. Statutes and court decisions in most States provide that a child custody order may not be changed unless the circumstances have changed substantially since the initial custody order and unless the

changed circumstances will have a substantial, identifiable adverse effect on the child.

The Use of Experts

Making an initial determination of custody and visitation or deciding when custody or visitation should be changed is not easy. It is particularly difficult for a judge whose training and experience have probably not provided any expertise in the area. Moreover, judges must make custody determinations in adversary hearings where mud-slinging and recriminations rather than dispassionate truth seeking are the norm. Thus, many judges ask social workers and other mental health professionals to provide them with assistance in child custody matters.

Referring a child custody dispute to a social worker or another mental health professional may be authorized by a statute, such as the Colorado statute used as an example of legal research techniques in chapter 4, or may be a discretionary act of a judge, done without benefit of a statute. Whichever is the case, it is often done. And because social workers are generally recognized as experts in child custody, the parties themselves may hire social workers to appear as their expert witnesses.

Even with a complete social work report or several expert witnesses, determining child custody and visitation may still not be an easy matter for a judge. There may be conflicting recommendations made by the experts on each side, and reports of court social workers or the testimony of experts may not be persuasive or credible. For example, in *Pact v.*

Pact, 70 Misc.2d 100, 332 N.Y.S.2d 940 (1972), several psychiatric and social worker expert witnesses expressed conflicting views on a mother's request to terminate the father's visitation of their two girls and a father's request to transfer custody of both girls to him. The court stated: "Starting with King Solomon's famous decision in the first recorded custody case and down through the ages, experienced jurists will unreservedly agree that child custody proceedings are the most trying, vexatious, and complex of all legal proceedings."

A lengthy excerpt from *Pact* is set forth because it reveals some of the factors considered by judges in making child custody determinations. You should note that this is a trial, not an appellate, court decision. New York is one of the few States that publishes such decisions.

> Custody is perhaps the most critical phase in the growing pains of a child's life and should not provide an arena where parents will engage in an unenviable contest of undermining the child's love for the other parent. The cardinal rule of custody law is now well established that the court must be governed above all by a concern for the best interests or welfare of the child. In all cases there shall be no *prima facie* right to the custody of the child in either parent, and [custody shall be awarded] as justice requires, having regard to the circumstances of the case and of the respective parties and to the best interests of the child. **Questions of custody are generally for the court in its discretion, but that discretion is not an absolute or uncontrolled one. Discretion should encompass a full and incisive review of the facts adduced including the social, spiritual, psychological and economic conditions prevailing at the alternative environments. To guide the Court in cases of this kind psychiatrists, psychologists and trained social workers should be consulted and their findings given serious consideration.**

To avoid the pitfall of balancing the rights of either parent in total disregard of the best interests and welfare of the children the Court [in this case] did reach out for guidance of the psychiatric, psychological and social work professions and seriously considered their reports and conclusions yet always mindful that the ultimate decision must be made by the Court.

In transferring custody from one parent to another, the Court must be aware of the child's need for stability in the home in the early years of his developing personality and through his formative years. Psychiatrists maintain that stability is practically the principal element in raising children. A child can handle almost everything better than he can handle instability. Shuttling children between parents is therefore not to be looked upon with favor if stability is an important ingredient in the development of a child. The overriding consideration of the child's welfare dictates that a continual shifting back and forth of custody should be avoided whenever possible. Yet we cannot deny that time does bring about changes in a person's lifetime and more so during his infancy and formative years. A child's needs are in a constant state of dynamic alteration. They change with age and in response to daily experiences. Plans for children must keep these changes in mind. If a child's needs change as time goes along then courts of law must be ever alert to the fact that orders of custody must likewise be flexible and courts should not hesitate to modify custody where the exigencies of the case so demand.

While an award of custody is always subject to modification or change if conditions or the requirements of the children so warrant, the change of circumstances or requirements must be material and should be used sparingly and under extraordinary circumstances.

If the balancing of equities between parents was the determinative factor in deciding child custody cases [Mr. Pact's] application for change of custody would be denied since Mrs. Pact is doing her utmost to adequately care for the children even in the face of opposition from the children and their father. But . . . a custody hearing should not be relegated to a contest between parents bent on victory for each other at the expense of the welfare and future happiness of their children. [Mr. Pact] readily admits to encouraging the children to rebel against their mother but he attributes his action solely to his sympathy for their strong and unwavering desire to live with him. He joins them in pleading for their custody.

In the absence of any grave disability such as the unfitness of a parent a child's preference will be given paramount consideration if it further appears that her best interests, welfare, and development will be improved by awarding custody to the preferred parent. The Court . . . interrogate[d] the children as to their experience in the mother's home and elicit[ed] their wishes as to the place in which they would prefer to live. The expressed wishes of a child, provided it is of sufficient age and understanding, as to the parent in whose custody it desires to be placed is a factor taken into consideration by the court in determining the child's custody as between contesting parents. However, the weight to be given the preference is within the discretion of the trial court and may be disregarded altogether. It is not, in the final analysis, controlling and will not bar the court from making a contrary determination in the best interest of the child. . . . Any other policy would be practically to abandon the jurisdiction of the Court and make the child the sole judge of his own best interests and welfare. [W]here the stated preference is deemed to have been inspired by pressure or brain washing, it will not be given any weight.

After carefully reviewing all of the evidence adduced including the findings of the psychiatrists and the social workers, the Court is now firmly convinced of Debra's strong and unyielding desire to reside with her father even absent the incidents of his encouragement and inducement. The desire to live with her father has increased rather than diminished during the past year as evidenced by her constant refusal to accommodate her mother and the two attempts of absconding from her home. She does not appear to be motivated toward making any type of adjustment in regard to her mother psychotherapy

notwithstanding. The prevailing opinion of the psychiatrists and social workers who examined the parties and the children is that the older child would not be affected psychologically if she was permitted to reside with her father. Even . . . [the] psychiatric social worker who was most critical in his evaluation of [the father] indicated that the child is extremely dependent on her father. The Law Guardian, [a guardian *ad litem*] who represented the children during the hearing, indicated that she too believes that the sisters should be separated although she looked askance at the thought of Debra being awarded to [the father.]

Under all the circumstances the Court finds that as to Debra there exists a clear showing of a substantial change of circumstances to justify modification of the existing order of custody. There does not seem any justification . . . [however, for changing the custody of her sister Allison and] disrupting her home stability at this time. Division of the siblings between the parties seems to furnish the only sensible answer to their continued welfare. If at all possible, it is assumed that children should be reared together, rather than partitioned off, unless there is a clear necessity that separate custody be awarded due to the circumstances of the parties. From all of the evidence adduced the Court believes that Allison's best interest would be served if she remained with her mother and free from the manipulative acts of both her sister and her father.

Unlike the Court in *Pact*, sometimes courts pay no attention to social work experts and erroneously decide custody cases based on their own biases and prejudices. For example, in *Pikula v. Pikula*, 349 N.W.2d 322 (Minn. App. 1984), an appellate court reversed a divorce judgment awarding custody of the couple's two children, aged three and four, to the father, because the trial court ignored the experts and the statutory factors, and decided custody based on irrelevant factors. The appellate court stated:

A court ordered custody evaluation, involving at least three social workers, recommended that custody of both daughters remain with the mother and that she undergo counseling, not to overcome any deficit in her ability to parent, but rather as recognition that the role of the single parent is extremely demanding. Witnesses testifying at trial disputed the abilities of each parent. Both parties claimed the best interests of the two children lay with their having legal custody with visitation to the other.

Little reference was made by the trial court to the factors found in [the custody statute]. Instead, the court emphasized the desirability of the father's extended family. The custody evaluation, virtually ignored by the court, noted that appellant-mother, as the primary care giver and person most able to provide a loving environment, was the most functional parent. The custody study contained a clear statement of preference for appellant as custodian. **The court dismissed the expert opinions of three social workers on the ground that only the court had the benefit of all the evidence.**

The court chose not to examine the mental and physical health of the parents, . . . gave no weight to testimony that respondent-father is chemically dependent, habitually untruthful, is extremely dependent upon his parents, has poor control of his temper and is unable to give the children's welfare priority over his own desires. The court noted that respondent's environment is improving, but ignored all evidence of appellant's growing maturity and gains made in counselling. The court apparently placed great importance on the continuation of religious training for the children. Despite appellant's plans to continue raising her daughters in the Catholic faith, the court concluded that [the custody statute] required contact with the respondent and significant other persons to raise the children "in their religion, creed and culture." No reference was made to the ability of either party to give the children love and affection.

Both parties are imperfect parents. However, the trial court noted only the father's good points and the mother's problems. The trial court, for all practical purposes, disregarded the custody evaluation. The court indicated it was better qualified than the social workers to evaluate the complete facts.

A trial court ruling on child custody has broad discretion. However, because this record . . . fails to support the findings, this court is obligated to apply the [custody] statute and grant custody to the mother.

Sometimes, courts do pay attention to social work reports when they should not. For example, in *Goodman v. Goodman*, 180 Neb. 83, 141 N.W.2d 445 (1966), the Nebraska Supreme Court criticized a trial court for deciding a custody case in reliance on an inadequate and biased social worker's report. The mother in the case, who had raised the children as Catholic, had been found unfit three years earlier, and custody had been awarded to the father. The mother now sought to have custody returned to her, primarily because the father was raising the children as Jewish. A social worker made a report for the judge recommending that the children be returned to the mother and stating, among other things, that the children would be emotionally damaged by having two religions. Primarily on the basis of this report, the court changed custody back to the mother. The Nebraska Supreme Court reversed, stating:

[I]t is quite obvious that a social worker, largely on information submitted by the children and the [mother] in one interview, expressed fear of emotional damage to the children. The testimony of public school teachers, of . . . the children, the Rabbi, and virtually every other witness was to the contrary, and the social worker herself found the children to be "relatively well adjusted for their age." The social worker's opinion was that the absence of a "mother figure" in the home of the [father] made it unstable. No reference is made to the absence of a "father figure" if custody be changed. She termed the [father's] housekeeper a "servant figure," but did not even meet the [maternal grandmother] who was going to care for the children while the mother worked, nor did she visit her home where the [mother] intended to leave them for such care.

Hearsay, opinion, gossip, bias, prejudice, and the hopes and fears of social workers should not be the basis for a change of custody. Findings of fact must rest on a preponderance of evidence, the verity of which has been carefully and legally tested. The relationship of parent and child should not be severed or disturbed unless the facts justify it.

Fritschler v. Fritschler, 60 Wis.2d 283, 208 N.W.2d 336 (1973), sums up this discussion of the role of social work experts in custody cases. The divorce decree in the case granted custody of the two children, then aged three and four, to their mother. When their mother moved from Wisconsin to Colorado, however, custody was awarded to the father and the mother appealed.

The main issue on appeal is whether the lower court abused its discretion in not allowing Mrs. Fritschler to have custody of the children except in Wisconsin. It is claimed the trial court disregarded the recommendations of three family specialists [from Colorado] who had recommended in effect that Mrs. Fritschler should have custody of the children in Colorado. The trial court considered [the letters and reports that were submitted into evidence] and commented thereon to the effect that it was not very helpful to a determination of the issue presented.

This court has held social workers' reports are not binding upon a trial court which may determine the weight to be given to the reports of social workers. It has recommended the use of social workers as a helpful tool in determining the best interests of the child. But neither the use of such witnesses nor the acceptance of their recommendations is mandatory. If it were, the social

workers would be performing the function of a judge on the bench rather than that of a witness. [W]e can find no abuse of discretion in its failure to accept or give more weight to the social workers' reports . . .

The Appointment of a Guardian *Ad Litem*

Because a child's preference may be considered in child custody proceedings, as many cases and statutes provide, and because custody proceedings are focused on the child, many courts provide an opportunity for a child to be heard, in their discretion or pursuant to a statute. Courts may interview a child in chambers or appoint a counsel or a guardian *ad litem* for a child. The guardian *ad litem* may be a social worker, but he or she usually is a lawyer.

In *Provencal v. Provencal*, 122 N.H. 793, 451 A. 2d 374 (1982), the court stated that a guardian *ad litem* "represents the interests of the child and is treated as a full party to all proceedings. The guardian *ad litem* serves primarily as an advocate for the best interests of the child. Nevertheless, the guardian *ad litem* should also assist the court and the parties in reaching a prompt and fair determination, while minimizing the acrimony during this process."

One issue raised in *Provencal* was the confidentiality of the guardian *ad litem*'s report. The court stated:

Although we recognize that confidentiality brings anonymity to individuals who might otherwise be reluctant to provide information to a guardian *ad litem*, we find that the parental interest in disclosure outweighs the need for anonymity. However, because the guardian *ad litem* serves [in some respects] as an attorney for his ward, the attorney-client evidentiary privilege will apply to all communications between the guardian and the child. References in the report to these communications should remain confidential, and . . . [t]he court should determine the circumstances under which [they] will be made available to the parties.

Permissible and Impermissible Factors to Consider

The following pages review some of the factors that a court may or may not be permitted to consider in deciding a child custody case.

Who Is the Child's Primary Caretaker? As was stated earlier, in the absence of a showing of unfitness, many courts will award custody to a child's primary caretaker. Some courts have elevated the inclination to award custody to a child's primary caretaker to a presumption. In *Garska v. McCoy*, 278 S.E.2d 357 (W.Va. 1981), the rationale for so doing was the fear that otherwise the child could suffer economically. The court stated:

> The loss of children is a terrifying specter to concerned and loving parents; however, it is particularly terrifying to the primary caretaker parent who, by virtue of the caretaking function, was closest to the child before the divorce or other proceedings were initiated. Since the parent who is not the primary caretaker is usually in the superior financial position, the subsequent welfare of the child depends to a substantial degree upon the level of support payments which are awarded in the course of a divorce. Our experience instructs us that uncertainty about the outcome of custody disputes leads to the irresistible temptation to trade the custody of the child in return for lower alimony and child support payments. Since trial court judges generally approve consensual agreements on child support, underlying economic data which bear upon the equity of settlements are seldom investigated at the time an order is entered. [T]he one enormously important function of legal rules is to inspire rational and equitable settlements in cases which never reach adversary status in court.

The court then concluded that a rule creating a presumption in favor of primary caretakers would tend to make primary caretakers less likely to fear loss of custody and thus less likely to give up property and support in return for custody.

The primary caretaker presumption may be so strong that it overcomes other factors. For example, in *Rhodes v. Rhodes*, 192 W.Va 14, 449 S.E.2d 75 (1994), both parents had taken care of the children during their marriage, but after their divorce the children had lived with the mother in Germany, where she had a job, and spent summers with their father. The father petitioned for custody and the trial court awarded him custody on the ground that it was inappropriate for children to be raised by only one parent in a foreign country. The appellate court reversed on the ground that the mother was the primary caretaker based on her performance of several duties for the majority of the children's lives, including "preparation of meals, grooming, medical care, discipline, and education." The court stated: "It is the parent who has assumed these childrearing duties who is to be awarded custody. Only if neither parent is entitled to the primary caretaker presumption does the court endeavor to determine which placement would be in the best interest of the child."

In most States, however, "the primary caretaker factor is not a presumptive rule but only one of many considerations to be evaluated by the trial court in making its finding as to the best interest of the child." *Wolf v. Wolf*, 474 N.W.2d 257 (N.D. 1991). See also, *In re Maxwell*, 8 Ohio App.3d 302, 456 N.E.2d 1218 (1982), holding that, although the Ohio custody statute precluded courts from adopting the primary caretaker presumption, Ohio courts should give "strong consideration" to the primary caretaker factor and that ignoring this factor "ignores the benefits likely to flow to the child from maintaining day to day contact with the parent on whom the child has depended for satisfying his basic physical and psychological needs."

Morality of a Parent. The States are split on whether the morality or sexual misconduct of a parent is relevant to a custody determination. Some courts consider the sexual misconduct of a parent and his or her immoral activities as directly bearing on the best interests of a child. Others like the court in *Dunlap v. Dunlap*, 475 N.E.2d 723 (Ind. App. 1985), assert:

> In order to deprive a parent of the custody of a child because of sexual misconduct, the misconduct must be shown to have an adverse effect upon the welfare of the child. Although it is a factor to be considered, evidence of sexual misconduct alone is insufficient to deny a parent the custody of a child. Without some evidence that the [misconduct] is in some way detrimental to the welfare of . . . [the child, a custody award] based solely upon [misconduct] is improper.

In some States, a consideration of morality is mandated by statute while in other States, as in the UMDA, a statute precludes consideration of "conduct of a present or proposed custodian that does not affect his relationship to the child."

Wealth. If courts gave great weight to the financial resources of the parties in awarding custody, fathers would receive most custody awards and mothers who had only been homemakers would rarely receive custody. Thus, many argue that financial considerations should never come into play or should not outweigh the primary caretaker rule.

The dissenting opinion in *Fritschler v. Fritschler, supra*, in which custody of children was changed from the mother to the father because the mother wished to move with them from Wisconsin to Colorado, points out, in vivid language, what can happen when wealth and professional status are factors in child custody decisions:

> [O]nly proper and relevant factors are to be considered in determining what custody placement order would best serve the welfare and well-being of the children involved. The financial income, the professional status and the community standing of the two ex-spouses are not such proper factors. Here the trial court obviously gave heavy weight to such income, such status and such standing. In its memorandum opinion, the trial court stated: "[the] children should be able to enjoy and bask in the delights of their father's reputation as a competent and leading attorney . . ." Earlier in the same opinion, the trial court added to status and standing as an attorney, the matter of the substantial income earned in his profession by the father, stating: "[t]he Defendant is a very successful attorney—is well respected in the community as evidenced by his substantial income over a long period of time. . . ."
>
> Wherever the father is a successful attorney and the mother is a full-time homemaker, giving weight to these considerations puts a butcher's thumb on the scales. Of course, the barrister father will have a greater income, professional status and standing in the community than the mother who stayed home to raise the children. By such scales, so

weighted, [a successful lawyer] would be assured custody of children should lawyer-husband and homemaker-wife go separate ways. The best interests of a child are not to be determined by a comparison of income tax returns or resort to [professional directories and résumés]. Success, status or [professional] standing does not make one a preferred custodian of minor children. One's law school diploma and license to practice law, or the financial success or community prestige one attains in this profession are not relevant or proper foundation stones for a change of custody order.

In a further twist on the consideration of wealth, in *Buchard v. Garay*, 42 Cal. 3d 531, 724 P.2d 486 (1986), the trial court awarded custody to the father of a two-and-a-half-year-old child, who had lived exclusively with his mother since birth, because of the father's better economic circumstances and because the mother worked and had to place the child in day care. The California Supreme Court reversed, stating:

> [I]n an era when over 50 percent of mothers and almost 80 percent of divorced mothers work, the courts must not presume that a working mother is a less satisfactory parent or less fully committed to the care of her child. A custody determination must be based upon a true assessment of the emotional bonds between parent and child . . . [and reflect] a factual determination of how best to provide continuity of attention, nurturing, and care. It cannot be based on an assumption, unsupported by scientific evidence, that a working mother cannot provide such care—an assumption particularly unfair when, as here, the mother has in fact been the primary caregiver.

Sexual Preference of a Parent. The States are also split on the question of the impact of the sexual preference of a parent. Some courts consider homosexuality immoral and would deny custody to a gay or lesbian parent on that ground. Others would consider it as having an adverse impact on children. Thus, in *Jacobson v. Jacobson*, 314 N.W.2d 78 (N.D. 1981), a lesbian mother was denied custody. The court stated:

> It is not inconceivable that one day our society will accept homosexuality as "normal." Certainly it is more accepted today than it was only a few years ago. We are not prepared to conclude, however, that it is not a significant factor to be considered in determining custody of children, at least in the context of the facts of this particular case. Because the trial court has determined that both parents are "fit, willing and able" to assume custody of the children we believe the homosexuality of [the mother] is the overriding factor. [D]espite the fact that the trial court determined the relationship [between the mother and her lover] . . . to be a "positive one," it is a relationship which, under the existing state of the law, never can be a legal relationship. Furthermore, we cannot lightly dismiss the fact that living in the same house with their mother and her lover may well cause the children to "suffer from the slings and arrows of a disapproving society" to a much greater extent than would an arrangement wherein the children were placed in the custody of their father with visitation rights in the mother.
>
> We . . . cannot determine whether or not the fact the custodial parent is homosexual or bisexual will result in an increased likelihood that the children will become homosexual or bisexual. However, that issue does not control our conclusion. Rather, we believe that because of the mores of today's society, because [the mother] is engaged in a homosexual relationship in the home in which she resides with the children, and because of the lack of legal recognition of the status of a homosexual relationship, the best interests of the children will be better served by placing custody of the children with [the father].

By way of contrast, based on near unanimous psychiatric testimony that a lesbian lifestyle, in and of itself, would not have adverse affect on a child, the court in *Doe v. Doe*, 16 Mass.App. 499, 452 N.E.2d 293 (1983), permitted a lesbian mother, who was living with her lover, to share joint custody of her ten-year-old son. And, in *M.A.B. v. R.B.*, 134 Misc.2d 317, 510 N.Y.S.2d 960 (1986), custody was awarded to a gay father although the twelve-year old son expressed his strong embarrassment over his father's homosexuality and his strong desire to remain with his mother. The court found that the father was a "caring, worthy father. His homosexuality is not flaunted and has no deleterious effect on his twelve-year old son. [I]t is impermissible as a matter of law to decide the question of custody on the basis of the father's sexual orientation. The guiding consideration must be [the son's] best interest. At this time, [the son's] needs can best be met by his father."

The question of the relevance of the sexual preference of a parent has been complicated by the AIDS epidemic. The courts are split on whether AIDS is a basis to deny custody or visitation. For example, in *Stewart v. Stewart*, 521 N.E.2d 956 (Ind. App. 1987), the court held that it was improper to deny a father visitation solely because he had AIDS, and in *Steven L. v. Dawn J.*, 561 N.Y.S.2d 322 (N.Y. Fam.Ct. 1990), the court held that a positive HIV test was not a grounds to change custody from the mother. However, in *H.J.B. v. P.W.*, 628 So.2d 753 (Ala.App. 1993), the appellate court affirmed a trial court's order changing a girl's custody from a gay father (who had been given custody of his daughter after the mother's second husband was accused of molesting the girl) back to the mother

(who had divorced her second husband) partially because it was revealed that the gay father was HIV-positive. The appellate court stated:

> [W]hile neither of these parents can be considered a paradigm of parenthood, nevertheless, from the evidence in the record, the trial court could have easily concluded that the father's present health and lifestyle, coupled with the living arrangements he has provided for the daughter . . . , when considered with the actions of the mother to improve her situation . . . , resulted in a change of circumstances sufficient to warrant a change of custody, and that such a change would materially promote the best interests of the daughter.

Handicap of a Parent. Despite laws forbidding discrimination against the disabled, the physical condition of a parent may be considered in making a custody award. In *Carney v. Carney*, 24 Cal.3d 725, 598 P.2d 36 (1979), however, a change of custody based solely on the custodial parent's disability was reversed. Because *Carney* is the leading case on the subject and because the court's language is instructive, the following pages review it in some detail.

The father in *Carney* (William) took custody of his two young boys when he and the mother separated after four years of marriage and he moved with the boys to California. Four years later, he was injured in an accident and rendered a quadriplegic. He spent a year in a hospital, but his sons remained in the care of the woman with whom he had been living and saw him regularly. After William's release from the hospital, when he finally sought a divorce in order to marry the woman with whom he had been living and by whom he had a daughter, the mother of the boys sought custody. Although the mother had never visited the boys or contributed to their support from the time they had moved to California and although her sole contact with them had consisted of some telephone calls and a few letters and packages, she was awarded custody based on William's disability. The California Supreme Court reversed the custody award, stating:

> In this case . . . we are called upon to resolve an apparent conflict between two strong public policies: the requirement that a custody award serve the best interests of the child, and the moral and legal obligation of society to respect the civil rights of its physically handicapped members, including their right not to be deprived of their children because of their disability. As will appear, we hold that upon a realistic appraisal of the present day capabilities of the physically handicapped, these policies can both be accommodated. The trial court herein failed to make such an appraisal, and instead premised its ruling on outdated stereotypes of both the parental role and the ability of the handicapped to fill that role. Such stereotypes have no place in our law.
>
> [We do not rule] that the health or physical condition of the parents may not be taken into account in determining whose custody would best serve the child's interests. [H]owever, this factor is ordinarily of minor importance; and whenever it is raised . . . it is essential that the court weigh the matter with an informed and open mind. In particular, if a person has a physical handicap, it is impermissible for the court simply to rely on that condition as *prima facie* evidence of the person's unfitness as a parent or of probable detriment to the child; rather, in all cases the court must view the handicapped person as an individual and the family as a whole. To achieve this, the court should inquire into the person's actual and potential physical capabilities, learn how he or she has adapted to the disability and manages its problems, consider how the other members of the household have adjusted thereto, and take into account the special contributions the person may make to the family

> despite or even because of the handicap. Weighing these and all other relevant factors together, the court should then carefully determine whether the parent's condition will in fact have a substantial and lasting adverse effect on the best interests of the child. The record shows the contrary occurred in the case at bar.

The Supreme Court rejected the trial court's apparent belief that there could be no "normal relationship" between William and his sons unless he engaged in "vigorous sporting activities" with them. The Court stated that this was an example of "conventional sex- stereotypical thinking" and "wholly apart from its outdated presumption of proper gender roles, also stereotypes William as a person deemed forever unable to be a good parent simply because he is physically handicapped. Like most stereotypes, this is both false and demeaning."

The Court observed that:

> [C]hildren are more adaptable than the court gives them credit for; if one path to their enjoyment of physical activities is closed, they will soon find another. In addition, it is erroneous to presume that a parent in a wheelchair cannot share to a meaningful degree in the physical activities of his child, should both desire it. Although William cannot actually play on his children's baseball team, he may nevertheless be able to take them to the game, participate as a fan, a coach, or even an umpire and treat them to ice cream on the way home. Nor is this companionship limited to athletic events: such a parent is no less capable of accompanying his children to theaters or libraries, shops or restaurants, schools or churches, afternoon picnics or long vacation trips.

"On a deeper level," the Court observed that the stereotype that disabled parents cannot be effective parents fails to reach the heart of the parent-child relationship. Contemporary psychology confirms what wise families have perhaps always known that the essence of parenting is not to be found in the harried rounds of daily carpooling endemic to modern suburban life, or even in the doggedly dutiful acts of "togetherness" committed every weekend by well-meaning fathers and mothers across America. Rather, its essence lies in the ethical, emotional, and intellectual guidance the parent gives to the child throughout his formative years, and often beyond. Even if it were true, as the court herein asserted, that William cannot do "anything" for his sons except "talk to them and teach them, be a tutor," that would not only be "enough," contrary to the court's conclusion, it would be the most valuable service a parent can render. Yet his capacity to do so is entirely unrelated to his physical prowess: however limited his bodily strength may be, a handicapped parent is a whole person to the child who needs his affection, sympathy, and wisdom to deal with the problems of growing up. Indeed, in such matters his handicap may well be an asset: few can pass through the crucible of a severe physical disability without learning enduring lessons in patience and tolerance.

Both the state and federal governments now pursue the commendable goal of total integration of handicapped persons into the mainstream of society . . . : the Legislature declares that "It is the policy of this state to encourage and enable disabled persons to participate fully in the social and economic life of the state . . ." Thus far these efforts have focused primarily on such critical areas as employment, housing, education, transportation, and public access. No less important to this policy is the integration of the handicapped into the responsibilities and satisfactions of family life, [the] cornerstone of our social system. Yet as more and more physically disabled persons marry and bear or adopt children or, as in the case at bar, previously nonhandicapped parents become disabled through accident or illness, custody disputes similar to that now before us may well recur. In discharging their admittedly difficult duty in such proceedings, the trial courts must avoid impairing or defeating the foregoing public policy. [W]e are confident of their ability to do so.

Race. In *Palmore v. Sidoti*, 466 U.S. 429 (1984), the Supreme Court held that race was an invalid consideration in a custody case. In that case, when the parents divorced, the mother was awarded custody of their three-year-old daughter. The mother, father, and daughter were white. Approximately eighteen months later, the father sought custody of the daughter on the ground that the mother married an African-American. Although the Florida trial court found both parents fit, it awarded custody to the father stating that "despite the strides that have been made in bettering relations between the races in this country, it is inevitable that [the child] will, if allowed to remain in her present situation . . . suffer from the social stigmatization that is sure to come." The Supreme Court reversed, stating:

A core purpose of the Fourteenth Amendment was to do away with all governmentally-imposed discrimination based on race. Classifying persons according to their race is more likely to reflect racial prejudice than legitimate public concerns; the race, not the person, dictates the category. Such classifications are subject to the most exacting scrutiny; to pass constitutional muster, they must be justified by a compelling governmental interest and must be necessary . . . to the accomplishment of its legitimate purpose. The State, of course, has a duty of the highest order to protect the interests of minor children, particularly those of tender years. In common with most states, Florida law mandates that custody determinations be made in the best interests of the children involved. The goal of granting custody based on the best interests of the child is indisputably a substantial governmental interest for purposes of the Equal Protection Clause.

It would ignore reality to suggest that racial and ethnic prejudices do not exist or that all manifestations of those prejudices have been eliminated. There is a risk that a child living with a step-parent of a different race may be subject to a variety of pressures and stresses not present if the child were living with parents of the same racial or ethnic origin. The question, however, is whether the reality of private biases and the possible injury they might inflict are permissible considerations for removal of an infant child from the custody of its natural mother. We have little difficulty concluding that they are not. The Constitution cannot control such prejudices but neither can it tolerate them. Private biases may be outside the reach of the law, but the law cannot, directly or indirectly, give them effect. The effects of racial prejudice, however real, cannot justify a racial classification removing an infant child from the custody of its natural mother found to be an appropriate person to have such custody.

Religion. The religion, or lack of religion, of a parent may be considered by a court in making a custody determination. However, the First Amendment to the Constitution, "flatly prohibits a trial court from ever evaluating the merits of religious doctrine or defining the contents of that doctrine." *Pater v. Pater*, 588 N.E.2d 794 (Ohio 1992). In other words, the courts must "preserve an attitude of impartiality between religions" and must not deny custody because of a parent's religious beliefs, particularly "where there is no showing that the religious beliefs . . . seriously threaten the health or well-being of the child." *Goodman v. Goodman, supra.*

Joint Custody

Because an award of custody to one parent may not be wholly satisfactory and because contested child custody cases may be difficult for all concerned, **joint custody**, also called **shared responsibility** or **divided custody** may be ordered. The reasons for joint custody and how it works are explained well in *Beck v. Beck*, 86 N.J. 480, 432 A.2d 63 (1981):

In recent years the concept of joint custody has become topical, due largely to the perceived inadequacies of sole custody awards and in recognition of the modern trend toward shared parenting in marriage. Sole custody tends both to isolate children from the noncustodial parent and to place heavy financial and emotional burdens on the sole caretaker, usually the mother . . . Moreover, because of the absolute nature of sole custody determinations, in which one parent "wins" and the other "loses," the children are likely to become the subject of bitter custody contests and post-decree tension. The upshot is that the best interests of the child are disserved by many aspects of sole custody.

Joint custody attempts to solve some of the problems of sole custody by providing the child with access to both parents and granting parents equal rights and responsibilities regarding their children. At the root of the joint custody arrangement is the assumption that children in a unified family setting develop attachments to both parents and the severance of either of these attachments is contrary to the child's best interest.

Properly analyzed, joint custody is comprised of two elements, legal custody and physical custody. Under a joint custody arrangement, legal custody, the legal authority and responsibility for making "major" decisions regarding the child's welfare, is shared at all times by both parents. Physical custody, the logistical arrangement whereby the parents share the companionship of the child and are responsible for "minor" day-to-day decisions, may be alternated in accordance with the needs of the parties and the children. Through its legal custody component joint custody seeks to maintain these attachments by permitting both parents to remain decision-makers in the lives of their children. Alternating physical custody enables the children to share with both parents the intimate day-to-day contact necessary to strengthen a true parent-child relationship.

Most States authorize joint custody as an option, many States have a preference for joint custody in all or some circumstances, and some States have a presumption in favor of joint custody.

An authorization of joint custody, a preference for it, or a presumption in favor of it may be found in statutes or may come from a court decision like *Beck v. Beck, supra.* A statutory preference or presumption for joint custody may be limited to certain circumstances, such as where the parents are willing to cooperate and live near each other. There may also be a statutory presumption against joint custody or a preference for sole custody in certain circumstances, such as where there has been spousal abuse. Indeed, after the initial enthusiasm for joint custody in the 1980s, there has been some retreat from it and at least one State (Vermont) has a presumption against joint custody in all circumstances.

As you saw from *Beck v. Beck, supra,* joint custody is of two types: legal and physical. Generally, a parent with sole custody is able to make all major decisions concerning a child, such as the religion of the child, the type of education and the need for medical care. With joint legal custody, however, decision making would be shared. Less common is joint physical custody where the children actually live with both parents, moving back and forth on a daily, weekly, or monthly basis. Because of the disruption of frequent moves, joint physical custody orders are rare or may resemble sole custody orders with liberal visitation. Also, statutes or court opinions favoring joint custody may actually only favor joint legal custody. For example, in *Beck v. Beck, supra,* which expressed a preference for joint custody, the court stated:

> The physical custody element of a joint custody award requires examination of practical considerations such as the financial status of the parents, the proximity of their respective homes, the demands of parental employment, and the age and number of the children. Joint physical custody necessarily places an additional financial burden on the family. Although exact duplication of facilities and furnishings is not necessary, the trial court should insure that the children can be adequately cared for in two homes. The geographical proximity of the two homes is an important factor to the extent that it impinges on school arrangements, the children's access to relatives and friends (including visitation by the noncustodial parent), and the ease of travel between the two homes. If joint custody is feasible except for one or more of these practical considerations, the court should consider awarding legal custody to both parents with physical custody to only one and liberal visitation rights to the other. Such an award will preserve the decision-making role of both parents and should approximate, to the extent practicable, the shared companionship of the child and non-custodial parent that is provided in joint physical custody.

Florida's shared responsibility law is really a law providing for joint legal custody, but it permits the parties to share decisions on the physical residence of a child. The law provides:

> In ordering shared parental responsibility, the court may consider the expressed desires of the parents and may grant to one party the ultimate responsibility over specific aspects of the child's welfare or may divide those aspects between the parties based on the best in-

terests of the child. [A]reas of responsibility may include primary physical residence, education, medical and dental care, and any other responsibilities which the court finds unique to a particular family. Laws of Florida, § 61.13(2)(b)2a.

Many people are opposed to joint custody. As stated in *Beck v. Beck, supra*:

Joint custody . . . is not without its critics. The objections most frequently voiced include contentions that such an arrangement creates instability for children, causes loyalty conflicts, makes maintaining parental authority difficult, and aggravates the already stressful divorce situation by requiring interaction between hostile ex-spouses. Although these same problems are already present in sole custody situations, some courts have used these objections either to reject or strictly limit the use of joint custody.

A serious problem with joint custody is the restrictions it imposes on a parent's ability to relocate. If a parent who shares joint custody of a child moves out of State or even to a distant place in the same State, joint custody would probably be impossible.

This problem also arises in sole custody arrangements in relation to visitation. A distant move with a child may deprive the other parent of visitation. Yet, the movement of a custodial parent should not be unduly restricted. Sometimes, there are good reasons for relocating. Thus, some States provide by statute that a parent with sole custody of a child may move out of State or out of the area but, generally only with court permission. Whether or not there is such a statute, many custody orders provide that a parent with custody may only move with court approval. And even if there is no such provision in an order or

a statute, a noncustodial parent with visitation rights may always go to court to oppose a move by the custodial parent. Courts do not lightly approve of a custodial parent's desire to move. As stated in *Fritschler v. Fritschler, supra*, in which a custodial mother was not permitted to move from Wisconsin to Colorado with the children: "[O]ne having custody of a child is not free to move about the country disregarding state lines, as that person would be if she did not have custody. The parent's responsibility to the child and its interests and the rights of the other parent qualify and limit the right and liberty to move about freely—that is one of the burdens of having custody of minor children."

Restrictions on a custodial parent's right to move have further been held not to violate the constitutional right to travel. See *Rowsey v. Rowsey*, 329 S.E.2d 57 (Va. 1985).

Relying in part on the expertise of social workers, the California Supreme Court expressed a different attitude towards a parent's move in *In re Marriage of Burgess*, 13 Cal.4th 25, 913 P.2d 473 (1996). In upholding a trial court order allowing a custodial mother to move forty miles away from the father, the Court held:

[I]n an initial judicial custody determination based on the "best interest" of minor children, a parent seeking to relocate does not bear a burden of establishing that the move is "necessary" as a condition of custody. Similarly, after a judicial custody order is in place, a custodial parent seeking to relocate bears no burden of establishing that it is "necessary" to do so. Instead, he or she has the right to change the residence of the child, subject to the power of the court to restrain a removal that would prejudice the rights or welfare of the child.

The Court so held although California Family Code section 3020 provides:

The Legislature finds and declares that it is the public policy of this state to assure minor children frequent and continuing contact with both parents after the parents have separated or dissolved their marriage, and to encourage parents to share the rights and responsibilities of child rearing in order to effect this policy, except where the contact would not be in the best interest of the child . . .

The Court observed that the Family Code does not "constrain the trial court's broad discretion to determine, in light of all the circumstances, what custody arrangement serves the 'best interest' of minor children." It further observed that the Family Code "specifically refrains from establishing a preference or presumption in favor of any arrangement for custody and visitation" and that it does not "purport to define" what is meant by "frequent and continuous contact" or "specify a preference for any particular form of contact." Thus, a court should not unnecessarily interfere with a custodial parent's "presumptive right" to change the residence of a minor child in order to preserve its own notion of "frequent and continuous contact."

The Court went on to observe:

[O]urs is an increasingly mobile society. [It has been pointed out] that approximately one American in five changes residences each year. Economic necessity and remarriage account for the bulk of relocations. Because of the ordinary needs for both parents after a marital dissolution to secure or retain employment, pursue educational or career opportunities, or reside in the same location as a new spouse or other family or friends, it is unrealistic to assume that divorced parents will permanently remain in the same location after dissolution or to exert pressure on them to do so. It would also undermine the interest in minimizing costly litigation over custody and require the trial courts to "micromanage" family decisionmaking by second-guessing reasons for everyday decisions about career and family.

More fundamentally, the "necessity" of relocating frequently has little, if any, substantive bearing on the suitability of a parent to retain the role of a custodial parent. A parent who has been the primary caretaker for minor children is ordinarily no less capable of maintaining the responsibilities and obligations of parenting simply by virtue of a reasonable decision to change his or her geographical location.

At the same time, we recognize that bright line rules in this area are inappropriate: each case must be evaluated on its own unique facts. Although the interests of a minor child in the continuity and permanency of custodial placement with the primary caretaker will most often prevail, the trial court, in assessing "prejudice" to the child's welfare as a result of relocating even a distance of 40 or 50 miles, may take into consideration the nature of the child's existing contact with both parents . . . and the child's age, community ties, and health and educational needs. Where appropriate, it must also take into account the preferences of the child.

On this last point, the Court noted:

Professor Judith S. Wallerstein [a professor at the School of Social Welfare at the University of California at Berkeley] who has published extensively on issues concerning children after divorce, observes that for "reasonably mature adolescents, i.e., those who are well adjusted and performing on course in their education and social relationships . . . stability may not lie with either parent, but may have its source in a circle of friends or particular sports or academic activities within a school or community." She suggests that "[t]hese adolescents should be given the choice . . . as to whether they wish to move with the moving parent."

Finally, the Court observed that, while a trial court may approve a move of a custodial parent and disapprove a change in custody:

> [T]he trial court has broad discretion to modify orders concerning contact and visitation to minimize the minor children's loss of contact and visitation with the noncustodial parent in the event of a move, *e.g.*, by increasing the amount of visitation with the noncustodial parent during vacations from school, allocating transportation expenses to the custodial parent, or requiring the custodial parent to provide transportation of the children to the noncustodial parent's home. Indeed, such modifications of orders regarding contact and visitation may obviate the need for costly and time-consuming litigation to change custody, which may itself be detrimental to the welfare of minor children because of the uncertainty, stress, and even ill-will that such litigation tends to generate. Similarly, a noncustodial parent's relocation far enough away to preclude the exercise of existing visitation rights can be ground for modifying a visitation order to allow for a different schedule for contact with the minor children, *e.g.*, longer, but less frequent, visitation periods.

Interstate Custody Issues

As has been stated, a court in a State where only one spouse resides may not have jurisdiction to resolve certain ancillary matters related to a divorce, but a State where only one parent lives with a child, may have jurisdiction to award custody of the child. This is because a court has jurisdiction over a resident child—even if it does not have jurisdiction over both the child's parents.

The ability of a court to make a child custody order when only the child and one parent are residents of the State can cause problems when a parent takes a child from one State to another State to evade an order awarding custody of the child to the other parent. Because child custody orders are generally modifiable, a court in the State where a child has been brought does not have to recognize the child custody order of the State from which the child has been taken pursuant to the Full Faith and Credit Clause of the Constitution or can recognize the order, but exercise its authority to modify it. Either way, a court is likely to rule in favor of the in-state parent and is unlikely to return a child to an out-of-state parent—even if the in-state parent has brought the child to the State in violation of a valid custody order.

Further problems could arise when a parent takes a child from one State to another to avoid a valid child custody order. The court in the State from which the child has been taken may still have jurisdiction to enforce its child custody order, but how is a parent who lives in one State going to enforce an order in another State? What should happen if parents do not have the financial ability to take their cases to the State where their children now reside? And what should happen if two States make conflicting orders on child custody and both orders were within the courts' jurisdiction?

To resolve some of these problems, all the States have adopted the Uniform Child Custody Jurisdiction Act (UCCJA). The UCCJA enables a parent in one State to initiate a child custody action and enforce a child custody award when the child lives in another State without going to the State where the child lives. The UCCJA also limits a court's jurisdiction to modify another State's custody orders or make their own orders. The Parental

Kidnapping Prevention Act, 28 U.S.C. § 1738A, enacted by Congress in 1980, is another attempt to resolve these problems. It provides that a court in one State must recognize a child custody order of another State if the court which made the order had jurisdiction to do so and goes further than the UCCJA in limiting courts' jurisdiction to modify another State's child custody orders or to make their own orders when there has been an order in another State. Most important, the federal Act provides that a parent's interstate movement to avoid child custody orders falls under federal kidnapping and interstate flight criminal statutes and may be investigated by the FBI and prosecuted in federal court. However, the Supreme Court has ruled that the Act does not give federal courts jurisdiction to consider interstate custody disputes. *Thompson v. Thompson*, 484 U.S. 174 (1988).

Nonparents' Rights to Custody and Visitation

Because of increased agitation for grandparents' rights to visit their grandchildren after a divorce or the death of a parent, all of the States now afford grandparents some visitation rights or privileges by statute. Some States even give grandparents' visitation rights after a stepparent or other adoption severs their biological relationship with the child, provided that visitation is not contrary to the child's best interests.

There has been agitation for and concern for stepparents' rights and for rights of same-sex partners who are not the birth or adopted parents of children they have raised with their partners. The trend is still small, but stepparents are beginning to get visitation in negotiated settlements and in divorce decrees, and a few States have statutes giving stepparents' rights to visitation. Same-sex partners have fared less well. For example, in *Matter of Alison D. v. Virginia M.*, 569 N.Y.S.2d 586, 572 N.E.2d 27 (N.Y. 1991), the highest appellate court in New York held that a woman had no right even to seek visitation with the biological child of her former lesbian partner despite the following facts set forth by the court.

> Petitioner Alison D. and respondent Virginia M. established a relationship in September 1977 and began living together in March 1978. In March 1980, they decided to have a child and agreed that respondent would be artificially inseminated. Together, they planned for the conception and birth of the child and agreed to share jointly all rights and responsibilities of child-rearing. In July 1981, respondent gave birth to a baby boy, A.D.M., who was given petitioner's last name as his middle name and respondent's last name became his last name. Petitioner shared in all birthing expenses and, after A.D.M.'s birth, continued to provide for his support. During A.D.M.'s first two years, petitioner and respondent jointly cared for and made decisions regarding the child.

When the relationship between Alison and Virginia terminated, Alison continued to visit A.D.M. but when he turned six, she was denied further visitation. She sought visitation rights under a statute providing for such rights for a "parent" (New York Domestic Relations Law, section 70), the courts held she was not a "parent" and, thus, not entitled to seek visitation rights. The Court of Appeals stated:

> Petitioner concedes that she is not the child's "parent"; that is, she is not the biological mother of the child nor is she a legal parent by

virtue of an adoption. Rather she claims to have acted as a *"de facto"* parent . . . Therefore, she claims she has standing to seek visitation rights. These claims, however, are insufficient under section 70. Traditionally, in this State it is the child's mother and father who, assuming fitness, have the right to the care and custody of their child, even in situations where the nonparent has exercised some control over the child with the parents' consent. To allow the courts to award visitation—a limited form of custody—to a third person would necessarily impair the parents' right to custody and control. Petitioner concedes that respondent is a fit parent. Therefore she has no right to petition the court to displace the choice made by this fit parent in deciding what is in the child's best interests.

Where the Legislature deemed it appropriate, it gave other categories of persons standing to seek visitation and it gave the courts the power to determine whether an award of visitation would be in the child's best interests [citing laws providing for visitation by siblings and grandparents]. We decline petitioner's invitation to read the term parent in section 70 to include categories of nonparents who have developed a relationship with a child or who have had prior relationships with a child's parents and who wish to continue visitation with the child. While one may dispute in an individual case whether it would be beneficial to a child to have continued contact with a nonparent, the Legislature did not in section 70 give such nonparent the opportunity to compel a fit parent to allow them to do so.

The dissenting opinion strongly objected to the majority's decision, stating:

The Court's decision, fixing biology as the key to visitation rights, has impact far beyond this particular controversy, one that may affect a wide spectrum of relationships—including those of longtime heterosexual stepparents, "common-law" and nonheterosexual partners such as involved here, and even participants in scientific reproduction procedures. Estimates that more than 15.5 million children do not live with two biological parents, and that as many as 8 to 10 million children are born into families with a gay or lesbian parent, suggest just how widespread the impact may be. But the impact of today's decision falls hardest on the children of those relationships, limiting their opportunity to maintain bonds that may be crucial to their development. The majority's retreat from the courts' proper role . . . to take the children's interests into account [in visitation petitions] compels this dissent.

[A] strong parent-child relationship . . . apparently existed between A.D.M. and Alison D. during the first six years of the child's life. While acknowledging that relationship, the Court nonetheless proclaims powerlessness to consider the child's interest at all, because the word "parent" in the statute imposes an absolute barrier to Alison D.'s petition for visitation. That same conclusion would follow . . . were the coparenting relationship one of 10 or more years, and irrespective of how close or deep the emotional ties might be between petitioner and child, or how devastating isolation might be to the child. I cannot agree that such a result is mandated by section 70, or any other law.

Apart from imposing upon itself an unnecessarily restrictive definition of "parent," and apart from turning its back on a tradition of reading of section 70 so as to promote the welfare of the children, in accord with the *parens patriae* power, the Court also overlooks the significant distinction between visitation and custody proceedings. While both are of special concern to the State, custody and visitation are significantly different. Custody disputes implicate a parent's right to rear a child—with the child's corresponding right to be raised by a parent. Infringement of that right must be based on the fitness—more precisely the lack of fitness—of the custodial parent. Visitation rights also implicate a right of the custodial parent, but it is the right to choose with whom the child associates. Any burden on the exercise of that right must be based on the child's overriding need to maintain a particular relationship. Logically, the fitness concern present in custody disputes is irrelevant in visitation petitions, where continuing contact with the child rather than severing of a parental tie is in issue.

Of course, there must be some limitation on who can petition for visitation. [Section 70] specifies that the person must be the child's "parent," and the law additionally recognizes certain rights of biological and legal parents. Arguments that every dedicated caretaker could sue for visitation if the term "parent" were broadened, or that such action would necessarily effect sweeping change throughout the law, overlook and misportray the Court's role in defining otherwise undefined statutory terms to effect particular statutory purposes, and to do so narrowly, for those purposes only.

[As in a Pennsylvania case, the person seeking visitation rights should be required to] demonstrate actual assumption of the parental role and discharge of parental responsibilities. It should be required that the relationship with the child came into being with the consent of the biological or legal parent, and that the petitioner at least have had joint custody of the child for a significant period of time. Other factors likely should be added to constitute a test that protects all relevant interests . . . It is not my intention to spell out a definition but only to point out that it is surely within our competence to do so. It is indeed regrettable that we decline to exercise that authority in this visitation matter, given the explicit statutory objectives, the courts' power, and the fact that all consideration of the child's interest is, for the future, otherwise absolutely foreclosed.

Unlike New York law, a few State statutes give visitation rights to de facto parents like Alison D. For example, Oregon Rev.Stat.Ann. § 109.119[1] gives the right to seek visitation or other right of custody to any person "who has established emotional ties creating a child-parent relationship with a child," expressly including a step or foster parent.

While nonparents like grandparents, stepparents, or even same-sex partners are increasingly being given *visitation* rights, there is still a strong preference for bio-

logical or adoptive parents over nonparents in *custody* disputes. However, in rare cases, particularly where a child has been living with a nonparent for a substantial period, courts may be unwilling to remove the child from the nonparent's home and return the child to the parent—even where the parent is not found unfit.

CHILD SUPPORT

Children are entitled to financial support from their parents unless and until the parents' rights are terminated. An order denying a parent custody of a child does not relieve the parent of the obligation to support the child. Indeed, sole custody awards often impose a child support obligation on the noncustodial parent.

In *Gomez v. Perez*, 409 U.S. 535 (1973), the Supreme Court held that **children born out of wedlock** (i.e., with unmarried parents) are entitled to the same support from their parents as children born in wedlock (i.e., with married parents). However, it may not be known who is the father of a child born out of wedlock. A support obligation cannot be imposed on a man merely because the mother says he is the father of a child born out of wedlock. Either a man must acknowledge that he is the father of a child or it must be legally established that he is the father. In other words, **paternity** must be acknowledged or established.

By way of contrast, if a child is born during wedlock, the mother's husband is presumed to be the father of the child. In the past, the husband could not rebut this presumption. It now may be rebutted in most States, at least in some circumstances. But, in the absence of a statute permitting a husband to rebut the presumption of paternity or satisfactory rebuttal evidence, the support obligation can be imposed on the husband—and cannot be imposed on any other man.

The legal action to establish that a certain man is or is not the legal father of a child on whom a support obligation can be imposed is known as a **paternity action**. Because establishing paternity is necessary before a support obligation can be imposed on a father and because child support is most commonly collected from fathers, we will review paternity actions before discussing child support.

The Establishment of Paternity

Paternity actions, like all other domestic relations actions, are authorized and controlled by State law. The laws differ from State to State, but there are basic similarities in all the laws. Moreover, about half of the States have adopted the Uniform Parentage Act (UPA) or a variation of it. Among other things, the UPA establishes a procedure for determining paternity.[1]

Under the UPA and the law in many States, paternity petitions may be filed by the mother in the name of the child, by the mother in her own name, or by the child in his or her own name. The UPA and some States also permit the father to bring a paternity action to establish his rights to

a child or to establish nonpaternity. A maternity action in which it is established that a woman is or is not the mother of a child is also theoretically possible.

A major legal issue related to paternity actions has been how long after the child's birth can they be brought or, in other words, what is the statute of limitations for paternity actions? A **statute of limitations** establishes how long after an event a suit concerning the event may be brought. Generally, statutes of limitations may be **tolled**. This means time will not run during a certain period. Tolling may occur for a variety of reasons, such as inability to bring a suit because one is in prison or is abroad in the military. Minority, a legal disability that prevents one from suing, generally tolls a statute of limitations.

In *Mills v. Habluetzel*, 465 U.S. 91 (1982), *Pickett v. Brown*, 462 U.S.1 (1983), and *Clark v. Jeter*, 486 U.S. 456 (1988), the Supreme Court struck down, respectively, one-year, two-year, and six-year statutes of limitations for paternity actions, with no tolling allowed for minority, on the grounds that the statutes unconstitutionally discriminated against illegitimate children and "did not provide them with an adequate opportunity to obtain paternal support." The Court has never stated the permissible outer limits for paternity action statutes of limitations, but the UPA provides for tolling for minority (in effect, an eighteen-year plus statute of limitations) and an eighteen-year statute is now the norm. This is because a minimum eighteen-year statute of limitations is required by federal law as a condition of receiving federal welfare funds. We will discuss this federal law, known as the IV-D Program later in this chapter.

Because a paternity action may result in

---

1. The UPA also eliminates any distinction between legitimate and illegitimate children. It provides in Section 2: "The parent and child relationship extends equally to every child and to every parent, regardless of the marital status of the parents." Further, the UPA presumes, not only that the husband of the mother is the father, but also that a man who lives with the mother at the time of birth and supports a child is the father.

the imposition of a long and substantial burden of support on a man and may have other serious repercussions, including for a child, many procedural protections for the defendant have been included in the UPA and in other State statutes. The courts, including the Supreme Court, have also mandated procedural protections for the defendant as a matter of due process.

The Supreme Court has not considered whether the alleged father is entitled to the appointment of an attorney if he cannot afford to retain one, but courts in several States have held that the appointment of a counsel is constitutionally required in all cases or if the action is brought by a welfare department. Courts in several States have held otherwise, but many State statutes and the UPA require appointment of counsel for the alleged father in all cases.

In *Little v. Streater*, 452 U.S. 1 (1981), the Supreme Court held that a defendant in a paternity action brought by the State for a mother on welfare who cannot afford to pay for blood tests has a constitutional right to have the blood tests paid for by the State, but in *Rivera v. Minnich*, 483 U.S. 574 (1987), the Court held that the preponderance of evidence standard is constitutionally sufficient in a paternity case. However, many States require clear and convincing evidence for a judgment of paternity.

No Supreme Court case has addressed the issue of a right to a jury trial, but, again, many States give the alleged father a right to a jury trial by statute. The UPA does not allow a jury trial, and because the standard of proof is not specified, it is a mere preponderance of the evidence.

If paternity is established, the UPA permits a court to impose a specific support obligation as part of the paternity action. Most State statutes similarly provide.

The Federal Title IV-D Program

Paternity actions are often brought by welfare authorities because no support obligation can be imposed on a father unless paternity is established and because it is believed that children should be supported by their parents rather than the State. Further, the Title IV-D program established by Title IV-D of the Social Security Act, 42 U.S.C. §§ 651-669b, as amended by Personal Responsibility and Work Opportunity Reconciliation Act of 1996, Pub.L. 104-193, 110 Stat. 2105, provides that to qualify for federal welfare funds, a State must establish a comprehensive program to collect child support for children who receive welfare. These programs must include systems to establish paternity, locate absent parents, obtain support orders, and collect support payments. Mandated systems include a Child Support Registry; centralized Child Support Collection and Distribution Service; and a Parent Locating Service.

California Welfare and Institutions Code sections 11478.5 and 11478.8 are examples of the kind of statutes States must enact to comply with Title IV-D. Section 11478.5 establishes a

California Parent Locator Service and Central Registry which shall collect and disseminate all of the following, with respect to any parent, putative parent, spouse, or former spouse:

(1) The full and true name of the parent together with any known aliases.
(2) Date and place of birth.
(3) Physical description.

(4) Social security number.

(5) Employment history and earnings.

(6) Military status and Veterans Administration or military service serial number.

(7) Last known address, telephone number, and date thereof.

(8) Driver's license number, driving record, and vehicle registration information.

(9) Criminal, licensing, and applicant records and information.

(10)(A) Any additional location, asset, and income information . . . that may be of assistance in locating the parent, putative parent, abducting, concealing, or detaining parent, spouse, or former spouse, in establishing a parent and child relationship, in enforcing the child support liability of the absent parent, or enforcing the spousal support liability of the spouse or former spouse . . .

Section 11478.5 further requires and allows the California Parent Locator Service and Central Registry, despite privacy and confidentiality laws, to obtain information from federal and State tax authorities (including the "Assets, Credits, Deductions, Exemptions, Identity, Liabilities, Nature, source, and amount of Income, Net worth, Payments, Receipts, Address, and Social security number" listed on any taxpayer's income tax return) and from public utilities and cable television corporations (including "the full name, address, telephone number, date of birth, employer name and address, and social security number of customers of the public utility or the cable television corporation to the extent that this information is stored within the computer data base of the public utility or the cable television corporation"). Subds. (b) & (c).

Further, information must be provided by employers. Section 11478.8 provides:

(a) Upon receipt of a written request from a district attorney enforcing the obligation of parents to support their children . . . or from an agency of another state enforcing support obligations pursuant to Section 654 of Title 42 of the United States Code, every employer . . . and every labor organization shall cooperate with and provide relevant employment and income information which they have in their possession to the district attorney or other requesting agency for the purpose of establishing, modifying, or enforcing the support obligation. No employer or labor organization shall incur any liability for providing this information to the district attorney or other requesting agency.

Relevant employment and income information shall include, but not be limited to, all of the following:

(1) Whether a named person has or has not been employed by an employer or whether a named person has or has not been employed to the knowledge of the labor organization.

(2) The full name of the employee or member or the first and middle initial and last name of the employee or member.

(3) The employee's or member's last known residence address.

(4) The employee's or member's date of birth.

(5) The employee's or member's social security number.

(6) The dates of employment.

(7) All earnings paid to the employee or member and reported as W-2 compensation in the prior tax year and the employee's or member's current basic rate of pay.

(8) Other earnings . . . paid to the employee or member.

(9) Whether dependent health insurance coverage is available to the employee through employment or membership in the labor organization.

(b) An employer or labor organization which fails to provide relevant employment information to the district attorney or other requesting agency within 30 days of receiving a request pursuant to subdivision (a) may be assessed a civil penalty of a maximum of one thousand dollars ($1,000), plus attorneys' fees and costs.

Further, States must enact laws designed to streamline paternity and child support actions and create mechanisms to collect overdue support. The federal government underwrites roughly two-thirds of the cost of the State's child support efforts, but the State's program must conform with numerous requirements included in Title IV-D and be approved by the federal IV-D agency.

A State must provide required child support services free of charge to welfare recipients and, when requested, for a nominal fee to children and custodial parents who are not receiving welfare. Welfare recipients must assign their child support rights to the State and fully cooperate with the State's efforts to establish paternity and obtain support payments. The State keeps most of the support payments it collects for welfare families but must distribute most of the payments to families once they leave welfare. Non-welfare recipients who request the State's aid are entitled to all of the funds collected.

Each State must establish a Title IV-D agency which, like the services it provides, must conform to federal requirements. For example, the agency must maintain required detailed records of all pending cases and must generate the various reports required by federal authorities, States must also set up computer systems that meet numerous federal specifications.

The federal government oversees State's compliance with Title IV-D requirements and can impose substantial penalties if a State does not comply or meet its child support collection obligations. However, in *Blessing v. Freestone*, ___ U.S. ___, 117 S.Ct. 1353 (1997), the Supreme Court held that welfare recipients could not sue the State of Arizona for failing to meet its child support collection obligations.

The Imposition and Collection of Child Support

Unlike alimony, child support is generally ordered in all cases where a noncustodial parent is before the court, but as with alimony, there is no unanimity as to how child support should be set. Many of the same questions that arise with alimony arise with child support. For example, should child support be based on the noncustodial parent's income or the child's needs? Other questions that are unique to child support also arise. For example, should the child support obligation of a noncustodial parent be reduced if a child is living with a wealthy stepparent even if the stepparent has no legal obligation to support the stepchild?

However these questions are answered, every study on the subject has concluded that child support is generally set at an amount that lowers children's standard of living after a divorce and that keeps many children born out of wedlock in poverty. Judges have generally had considerable discretion in setting child support awards and have felt that child support should not take a large percentage of a noncustodial parent's income. Moreover, as was stated in *Garska v. McCoy, supra*, 278 S.E.2d 357, divorcing mothers may bargain away child support in return for custody, and courts may approve their settlements without inquiry. Thus, noncustodial parents generally pay only a small amount of child support.

In an attempt to address this problem, many States established formulas or schedules for child support based on the parents' income. In 1984, the federal government, as part of the IV-D program, mandated that all States adopt such guidelines for child support awards. Because many judges ignored discretionary guidelines, however, in 1988, Congress said such guidelines must be mandatory and can be ignored only if a specific finding is made that using the guideline would impose an unfair burden in a particular case. States still have discretion, however, to decide how to set the guidelines (by use of percentages, schedules or formulas) and the minimum amount.

Even with mandatory guidelines for setting child support, questions will remain. For example, how long should child support continue? Should child support continue after a child reaches majority, while a child is continuing his or her education, in college, or beyond? Should it be continued indefinitely for a disabled child?

Like alimony awards, child support awards are modifiable. The modifiability of child support awards raises other questions. For example, how and when can child support be modified? Should a noncustodial parent be able to quit a job and thus reduce his or her ability to pay child support obligations? Should a noncustodial parent's child support obligation be reduced if he or she assumes new responsibilities by remarrying and having more children?

These and other questions may be answered by legislatures as a matter of policy or by courts on a case-by-case basis. However these questions are answered and whatever the amount of child support ordered, it is clear that many noncustodial parents, most of whom are fathers, have

failed and will fail to make court ordered child support payments.[2] Increasing attention has been paid to the failure of fathers to pay court-ordered child support. This attention has led to new mechanisms, many of which were created or required by the IV-D program, to enforce child support obligations. These mechanisms include: mandatory **wage garnishments**, that is, judicial orders that require an employer to withhold a certain percentage of an employee's wages or salary from his or her paycheck and to pay the withheld amount to the court; withholding of income tax refunds; reporting of child support arrearages to consumer credit agencies; reporting the names of delinquent fathers in newspapers; and placement of liens on delinquent fathers' property. This attention has also led to renewed interest in old enforcement mechanisms, like arrest and imprisonment of delinquent fathers for contempt of child support orders or for nonsupport, a crime in most jurisdictions.

Interstate Support Problems

As has been stated, child support is generally ordered when a noncustodial parent comes before a court, but many of the women living with children with an absent father are not awarded child support for their children. One reason for this is that many mothers do not know who is the father of their children or do not know the whereabouts of the father to

---

2. Because most noncustodial parents are fathers and because noncustodial mothers are rarely ordered to pay child support, for convenience, we will hereinafter discuss only fathers, but what is said about fathers could apply equally to mothers.

establish paternity. Another reason is that a court may not have jurisdiction to award child support if the noncustodial parent lives out of state and does not voluntarily appear before the court. A court also may not have jurisdiction to entertain a paternity action involving an out-of-state father.

In an attempt to collect child support from out-of-state absent fathers, all of the States have adopted the Uniform Reciprocal Enforcement of Support Act (URESA). URESA allows a parent with custody of a child to seek and enforce child support orders from a parent in another State without great difficulty or expense. Through URESA, a custodial parent may file an action for support in the State where he or she lives. The action will be transferred to the State where the noncustodial parent lives and will be pursued by a public attorney in that State.

URESA greatly assists with interstate collection and enforcement of child support, but it is still difficult to pursue a case from a distance. A poor mother may not be able to go to a distant State to testify in a case. A public official from one State may give low priority to a case from another State. Moreover, URESA like the Uniform Child Custody Jurisdiction Act, does not resolve the problem of a court's natural bias for its residents. Resident fathers may, thus, be favored over nonresident children. The federal Child Support Recovery Act of 1992, 18 U.S.C. § 228, addresses this problem by making failure to support a child in another State a federal crime.

Moreover, in 1994, President Clinton signed into law the Full Faith and Credit for Child Support Orders Act, 28 United States Code section 1738B (FFCCSOA), which requires that state courts give "full faith and credit" to child support orders issued by sister states. FFCCSOA requires that "[t]he appropriate authorities of each State . . . (1) shall enforce according to its terms a child support order made consistently with this section by a court of another State; and (2) shall not seek or make a modification of such an order" except under certain limited circumstances. "Child support" is defined to encompass "continuing support, or arrearages" and "a child support order" includes "a judgment, decree, or order of a court requiring the payment of child support," whether it is "a permanent or temporary order."

Domestic Violence and Abuse

Millions of women in America suffer from domestic violence each year. The problem arises within and outside of marriage. Women are assaulted and abused by their husbands or ex-husbands, their lovers or ex-lovers, or by other members of their families or households. Men are also assaulted by family or household members, but the problem is far more acute for women. Thus, when we look at the laws related to domestic violence in the first sections of this chapter, we shall focus on violence against women.

Both men and women who are elderly or who are mentally or physically disabled may suffer from domestic violence and abuse at the hands of family members and caretakers. We will look at the laws designed to protect these vulnerable men and women from violence and abuse in the last sections of this chapter.

Social workers play many important roles in relation to domestic violence and abuse of women, the elderly and the disabled. For example, social workers can be found working in shelters for battered women, helping women get court protection from their batterers, testifying in defense of women who have killed their batterers, counseling battered women or their batterers, working in adult protective services, and helping elderly clients find safe homes. All of these and other crucial roles social workers play in relation to domestic violence and abuse require an understanding of the laws discussed in this chapter.

WOMEN'S NEED FOR PROTECTION AGAINST DOMESTIC VIOLENCE

The problem of the domestic violence suffered by women was largely ignored until fairly recent times. By and large, domestic violence was a well-kept secret. Its extent and severity were unknown. And even if it was known that some men beat their wives, generally their behavior was excused. Husbands were believed to have a right to beat their wives just as parents are believed to have a right to physically discipline their children. Indeed, the expression "rule of thumb" was derived from an English rule, adopted widely in America, that a husband could discipline his wife with any reasonable instrument, including a rod no thicker than his thumb.

A few legal methods existed to combat domestic violence, but most were inadequate or totally ineffective. We will review the remedies against domestic violence available in the past and consider their inadequacies in order to put the present situation into perspective. Also many of the remedies, despite their inadequacies, are still used today.

In the past, criminal prosecutions could have been initiated against men who beat their wives or lovers. Domestic violence, in and of itself, may not have been a crime, but where a beating was not excused as proper disciplining of a wife, it could have constituted the crime of assault or battery. Victims of crimes, however, generally cannot initiate criminal prosecutions themselves. Thus, a woman could not herself initiate a criminal action against a man who beat her. Only the police could arrest the man who beat her, and only the prosecutor could bring criminal charges against him. But police officers were reluctant to arrest men who beat their wives or lovers, and prosecuting attorneys were reluctant to prosecute them. Thus, criminal prosecutions for domestic violence were few and far between. Only the most severe and egregious instances of domestic violence were prosecuted.

In some instances, the police or prosecutors were willing to pursue criminal actions against batterers, but the victims of the battering were reluctant to cooperate with them. There could have been several reasons for this reluctance.

First, a criminal prosecution could have left a woman quite vulnerable. A woman would not be protected against further violence if a man who beat her were released on bail while a prosecution was pending. Even if he were convicted, a woman would not be protected against further violence at his hands. Violence could occur when he was released after serving his sentence or if he did not serve time at all. Indeed, more serious violence could occur after a criminal prosecution as retaliation for the victim initiating the prosecution.

Second, a woman could have been prevented from taking action against a man who assaulted her by psychological forces and by social pressure. Pursuing a criminal action is often difficult; victims are sometimes made to feel guilt or responsibility for their situation. Both were particularly true for battered women in the male dominated courts. Moreover, social pressure, psychological forces, and the persuasiveness of husbands and lovers could operate to prevent a woman from taking action against a man who beat her, in addition to a quite natural fear of the criminal process.

Finally, homemakers with no possibility of employment might have reasonably refused to prosecute a man upon whom they were financially dependent, knowing they would be unable to support themselves and their children if the men who supported them were jailed.

Even if the police, the prosecutors, and the victims of domestic violence were willing to pursue a criminal prosecution, most States had laws that prevented many arrests and prosecutions. As has been noted, it was believed that a man had a right to beat his wife; a beating that would be considered a battery if the victim were a stranger might have been considered perfectly acceptable if the victim were one's wife. Moreover, no State considered forced sexual intercourse with one's wife a crime until quite recently. Further, even if an incident of domestic violence was considered to be a crime, it was likely to be considered a misdemeanor, and the police might not have been able to arrest the man. Laws in many States provided that misdemeanor arrests could not be made without warrants unless they occurred in the arresting officer's presence; getting a warrant was often cumbersome and difficult and could cause dangerous delays.

Thus, criminal prosecution was an inadequate answer to the problem of domestic violence. Another possible answer, a civil suit for assault or battery, was perhaps even more inadequate.

A person who has been beaten or assaulted may bring a civil action for damages against the person who did the beating or committed the assault. But until recently, many States prohibited law suits between spouses under a doctrine known as **interspousal immunity**. If there was no interspousal immunity, a woman still might not have been able to bring suit against her husband. In many States, married women did not have the right to bring suit in their own name without the consent of their husbands.

Although some women were not barred from bringing suits for assault and battery against the men who beat them, such suits would probably have been impossible to bring without a lawyer, would have been difficult and expensive, and could have taken years before they came to trial or were resolved. Moreover, women bringing such suits would have been provided with absolutely no protection from the men who beat them. All a woman could receive if she successfully pursued such a suit would be monetary damages for her past injuries.

Some States permitted women to obtain a **peace bill, peace bond, restraining order**, or an **injunction** against their husbands to prevent further violence. Again, a lawyer would probably be required to bring suit and the suit would be difficult, expensive, and slow. Moreover, the effectiveness of the orders was questionable; many considered them as worth little more than the paper on which they were written since the police would not assist in enforcing them and the only method of enforcement, a civil contempt action for violating a court order, was also difficult, slow, and expensive.

Wives could generally seek orders protecting them against further violence in conjunction with a divorce, but the procedure to obtain such orders was usually cumbersome, and the orders, like peace bills and other such civil orders, were often ineffective. Seeking a divorce was often impossible without a lawyer, and until the advent of no-fault divorce, specific grounds were required for a divorce. A husband's hitting a wife might not have been one of these grounds. Moreover, residency requirements for divorce actions and religious beliefs prevented some women from bringing divorce actions. Perhaps most important, many women wanted the violence to stop but did not want a divorce.

A woman could always leave her home to get away from the violence, but then she left herself vulnerable to a charge of desertion in a divorce action. If found to be a deserting spouse, she could be denied alimony and a share in her husband's property as the party considered "at fault" in the divorce. And if she left her home without her children, she could be denied their custody at the conclusion of any divorce action because of her so-called "abandonment."

MODERN DOMESTIC VIOLENCE LEGISLATION

In the 1960s and 1970s, the women's movement changed the public's view of the acceptability of wife beating. Moreover, it made the public aware that domestic violence was a serious and pervasive problem in this country, affecting women at all levels in society, and that the existing remedies to deal with domestic violence were inadequate. It became clear that these remedies had to be improved and that new remedies had to be fashioned—that there was a need for simple, fast procedures which were accessible to all women; for mechanisms, not only to protect women against violence, but also to provide them with necessary financial support while they took action against their batterers; and for ways to help women overcome the barriers to taking action against their batterers. In addition, there was recognition of the need to develop mechanisms to provide services to batterers, services that many of them were unwilling or reluctant to seek.

Beginning in the 1970s, every State enacted laws to address the problem of domestic violence. These laws differ from State to State. Some States just improved and expanded existing remedies, but slightly more than half of the States enacted laws that provided a new legal remedy for victims of domestic violence—a quick and easy procedure for them to obtain meaningful protection against violence. These laws also differ, but they all permit a court to issue an order, generally called a **protective order**, a **restraining order**, or an **order of protection**, enjoining a person from assaulting, harming, or even seeing a family or household member. All of the laws establish special procedures for obtaining an order and all of the laws permit issuance of an emergency order without notice to the batterer. Many of the laws also recognize, create, and/or fund special temporary shelters for victims of domestic violence, or address police response to domestic violence matters by requiring the police to make arrests.

Procedures for Obtaining a Protective Order

The procedure employed to obtain a protective order differs from State to State, but it is usually fairly uncomplicated. Generally, a petition is filed in the trial court that hears domestic relations matters. The petition may be quite simple in form. Often, it is only necessary to fill in the blanks in an approved court form. Handwritten petitions or forms may be acceptable. The intent is that a victim of domestic violence will be able to complete the petition or fill in the form without a lawyer. Some States instruct court personnel to help victims of domestic violence do the necessary paper work. For example, the

Minnesota Domestic Abuse Act provides: "The court shall provide simplified forms and clerical assistance to help with the writing and filing of a petition under this Section." Minn. Stat. § 518B.01, subd. 4(d).

The Washington Domestic Violence Prevention Act also provides that instructional brochures shall be made available to assist petitioners. Wash. Rev. Code § 26.50.035.

Employees of shelters for victims of domestic violence may help victims do the paper work necessary to file a petition. Such employees may be social workers but are probably not lawyers. Although, technically, assisting someone to file court papers may be viewed as practicing law without a license, in the context of domestic violence, it is rarely viewed this way. For example, the Washington law specifically provides that: "Any assistance or information provided by clerks [in filing petitions] . . . does not constitute the practice of law and clerks are not responsible for incorrect information contained in a petition." Wash. Rev. Code § 26.50.030(3).

Further, the laws may provide immunity for those who help victims of domestic violence in good faith. This immunity could extend to an action for practicing law without a license.

In most States, petitions for protective orders may be filed as independent actions or in connection with a divorce, annulment, or separation. Illinois so provides and additionally permits one to seek a protective order in certain criminal or delinquency matters or in any civil proceeding. 750 ILCS § 60/202.

A petition must generally allege specific acts of domestic violence. How much must be alleged and the nature of the domestic violence that must be alleged depend on the statutory definitions of domestic violence in the law and the requirements of the law. Washington requires that a petition "shall be accompanied by an affidavit made under oath stating the specific facts and circumstances from which relief is sought." Wash. Rev. Code § 26.50.030(1). The statute narrowly defines domestic violence to mean: "Physical harm, bodily injury, assault, or the infliction of fear of imminent physical harm, bodily injury or assault." *Id.* at § 26.50.010(1)(a).

By way of contrast, in Illinois, a petition merely has to allege "abuse," which is broadly defined as "physical abuse, harassment, intimidation of a dependent or interference with personal liberty or willful deprivation . . ." 750 ILCS § 60/103 (1). Each of these terms is, in turn, broadly defined. For example, *harassment* is defined as:

"knowing conduct which is not necessary to accomplish a purpose that is reasonable under the circumstances; would cause a reasonable person emotional distress; and does cause emotional distress to the petitioner. . . . [T]he following types of conduct shall be presumed to cause emotional distress:

(i) creating a disturbance at petitioner's place of employment, home or residence;
(ii) repeatedly telephoning petitioner's place of employment or school;
(iii) repeatedly following petitioner about in a public place or places;
(iv) repeatedly keeping petitioner under surveillance by remaining present outside his or her home, school, place of employment, vehicle or other place occupied by petitioner or by peering in petitioner's windows;
(v) improperly concealing a minor child from petitioner [or] threatening to improperly remove a child of petitioner's from the juris-

diction or from the physical care of a minor child . . . ; or
(vi) threatening physical force, confinement or restraint on one or more occasions." *Id.* at § 60/103 (7).

Filing fees for petitions for protective orders may be quite low or there may be no filing fees at all. For example, Washington eliminated all fees in 1995. Wash. Rev. Code § 26.50.040. Many States specifically provide that indigents need not pay a filing fee but may instead submit applications to file in forma pauperis.

Service requirements for petitions for protective orders may be simplified. Sheriffs or marshals may be required to do personal service for reduced fees or for no fees. Service by published notice may be authorized under certain circumstances. See Minn. Stat. § 518B.01, subd. 5(b).

Courts are usually authorized to issue emergency protective orders. These emergency orders may be issued **ex parte**, that is, without prior service on the respondent and without providing him an opportunity to be heard. The victim of domestic violence can simply file the necessary papers with the court and, without providing notice to the respondent, obtain an immediate hearing. At the conclusion of this hearing, the court can issue an immediate protective order. Some States only permit *ex parte* hearings under certain circumstances, such as when attempts to provide notice fail or when it is alleged that providing notice could cause serious injury. Illinois not only allows emergency *ex parte* orders, but also provides for issuance of such orders after regular hours or on holidays and weekends. 750 ILCS § 60/217.

The duration of emergency orders differs from State to State, but generally the duration is quite limited. In some States, they may only last for a few days. The relief that can be ordered in an *ex parte* order also differs from State to State; some States only allow limited relief in an *ex parte* order. Most States authorize *ex parte* orders requiring men to vacate their homes or stay away from their victims. Such orders have been challenged as violations of due process, but the courts have rejected such challenges on the ground that exigent circumstances justify restricting due process protections. See *Grist v. Grist*, 946 S.W.2d 780 (Mo. App. 1997).

Whether or not an *ex parte* order has been entered, generally the respondent must answer the petition in a short time and a hearing on the petition will be held soon after the petition is filed. At the hearing, evidence will be taken on the nature and extent of the violence. An order may be issued based solely on the victim's testimony, but the more other evidence of violence and the more credible it is, the more likely it is that the petitioner will obtain an order. Evidence like photographs of injuries or testimony of a doctor who treated the victim is most helpful. Testimony of a social worker employed by a shelter who saw the petitioner after she was injured and can describe the injury is also helpful. Testimony of a social worker on comments made by the petitioner while the social worker was counseling her would generally be inadmissible hearsay, could be barred by confidentiality rules, and would probably not be helpful.

The law may set forth the factors that may and may not be considered by a judge in determining whether or not to issue a protective order. In Illinois, among other things, a judge must consider:

the nature, frequency, severity, pattern and consequences of the respondent's past abuse of the petitioner or any family or household member . . . ; any unauthorized physical violence by respondent; . . . the likelihood or danger of future abuse . . . to petitioner or any member of petitioner's or respondent's family or household [and] . . . the danger that any minor child will be abused or neglected or improperly removed from the jurisdiction, improperly concealed within the State or improperly separated from the child's primary caretaker. 750 ILCS § 60/214.

A judge may not consider, among other things, evidence that:

Respondent has cause for any physical abuse, unless that cause satisfies the standards for justifiable use of force [in the Illinois Criminal Code];
Respondent was voluntarily intoxicated;
Petitioner acted [or did not act] in self-defense or defense of another . . . ; [and]
Petitioner left [or did not leave] the residence or household to avoid further abuse by respondent. *Id.* at § 60/214 (e).

If a protective order is issued, it can be of long duration, typically one year. The relief that can be included in the protective order varies from State to State. All States allow issuance of a protective order forbidding a respondent from assaulting, molesting, harassing, or harming the petitioner in any way. In most States, the respondent can also be required to move from the residence he shares with the petitioner and to stay away from the petitioner's place of work or other locations where he might encounter the petitioner. The protective order can include an order placing any children in the custody of the petitioner and requiring the respondent to pay support to the petitioner and the children. It may include an order requiring the respondent to compensate the petitioner for expenses incurred filing and pursuing the petition and related to any injuries. It may require the respondent to have counseling.

Special provisions may be made for service of the order on the respondent and execution of the order. In Minnesota, for example, "upon request of the petitioner, the court shall order the sheriff or constable to accompany the petitioner and assist in placing the petitioner in possession of the dwelling or residence, or otherwise assist in execution or service of the order of protection." Minn. Stat. § 518.B01, subd. 9.

Some States require the court to send a copy of the protective order to State law enforcement agencies or establish a procedure whereby the petitioner can file a copy with law enforcement agencies. Whether or not the order is provided to law enforcement, generally law enforcement officers are required to arrest those who violate an order. The arrest may be without a warrant with probable cause only.

In most States, a man who violates the order can be prosecuted criminally for assault or for criminal contempt. Contempt of a protective order may be established as a distinct crime or may be included in the general crime of contempt of a court order. A petitioner can also seek civil contempt against a respondent who violates a protective order. Civil contempt may result in jail in many States.

Problems with the Procedures

Domestic violence legislation establishing special procedures for obtaining a protective order has definitely been helpful, but the legislation has not solved all the problems of domestic violence. And, there are problems with many States' laws.

First, the laws may only be available to certain victims of domestic violence. A victim of domestic violence may not be able to get a protective order against someone who is not a relative by blood or marriage or who does not live in the same household. Thus, many women are unprotected against their lovers, particularly if they do not live with them, or against their ex-husbands. The Washington law had been narrow, but it now has been broadened to protect women from violence not only by husbands and men they live with, but also by former husbands, men they had lived with, men they have had a child with, and men they have or "have had a dating relationship" with, which is defined as a "social relationship of a romantic nature." Wash. Rev. Code § 26.50.010 (2) and (3). Many other States' laws are still too narrow.

Second, the definition of *domestic violence* in many of the laws may be too restrictive. Acts of harassment and non-physical abuse may not be included in the laws. Further, forced sexual intercourse with a wife may not be considered domestic violence.

Third, many victims of domestic violence who are unquestionably covered by their State's law may be unaware of the law and of the availability of protective orders. To address this problem, some laws provide that the police must inform the victims of domestic violence about the law or tell them about shelters where they can learn about the law whenever they respond to a domestic violence call. Further outreach may be necessary, however, particularly in areas where there are no or few shelters.

Fourth, even if the victims of domestic violence are aware of the laws, there may be psychological and social barriers to using the laws. To address this problem, some laws provide that the police should not only tell women about shelters but also should transport them to shelters or refer them to other social service agencies where they may be counseled.

Fifth, some victims of domestic violence may be aware of the laws and have no psychological or other opposition to the laws, but may believe obtaining a protective order is difficult and that the assistance of an attorney and the expenditure of substantial sums are necessary. Others may be intimidated by the mere thought of going to court. Thus, many women will not use the laws available to them, especially if they do not have help in doing so.

Sixth, while the domestic violence laws are generally intended to establish simple procedures that all victims of domestic violence can follow without the assistance of an attorney, in fact, this may not be the case. The laws are often far more complex than legislators realize and use words that nonlawyers may not understand. Victims of domestic violence who are uneducated may have great difficulties understanding and using the laws. It may be impossible for those victims who are illiterate or not English speaking to use the law. And despite provisions in some laws that court personnel are to assist the victims to complete the necessary papers, court personnel may not be helpful. Court staff may be too busy or too impatient to help the victims of domestic violence. Some are frankly hostile towards victims of domestic violence or towards anyone who tries to go to court without a lawyer to lead the way. The situation is usually worse in States where the law does not impose a duty on court personnel to help the victims. The combi-

nation of the intimidating nature of courts and the impatience or hostility of court personnel can keep many victims from pursuing their cases.

Seventh, judges may also be impatient with unrepresented litigants who do not do things "right." They may, indeed, be hostile towards victims of domestic violence. For example, in a Massachusetts case, a judge told a woman who came before him for a protective order that "she was wasting the court's time, that her fears of [her husband] were unfounded and that she should act more like an adult." He gave her a protective order but refused her request for police protection. A few months later, she was murdered by her husband.[1] A 1985 statewide study of the Massachusetts domestic violence legislation in response to this case and other complaints about judges concluded that the legal system's response to the domestic violence law was "noncompliance," and that "judges misapply or refuse to apply the law."[2]

Finally, if a protective order can be obtained, enforcing it or pursuing a violator for contempt may be difficult. A proceeding for civil contempt may be far more complex than a proceeding for a protective order. The police may not be willing to arrest violators of protective orders and prosecutors may not be willing to pursue criminal charges if the police do make arrests. Interestingly, Minnesota law specifically provides that a peace officer "shall arrest and take into custody a person whom the peace officer has probable cause to believe has violated an order," but also provides that "[a] peace officer is not liable . . .

---

1. "Judges in Massachusetts Criticized in Harrassment," *New York Times*, November 30, 1986.
2. *Id.*

for a failure to perform [this] duty." Minn. Stat. § 518.B01, subd. 14 (b) and (g).

All of these problems with the legislation creating special procedures to obtain a protective order underscore the importance of social services to battered women. Given the social isolation and fears of many women who are abused, obtaining the protection accorded by the law may be impossible in the absence of such services.

Other Protective Legislation and Remedies

Because of problems with the laws permitting women to use special procedures to obtain protective orders and because not all States have such laws, many battered women have to rely on the criminal justice system for relief. Most States have amended their criminal laws to provide that domestic violence is a crime or have made clear that domestic violence is included within the definition of other crimes, such as assault. While the situation has improved in the last twenty years, many States still do not consider forced sexual intercourse with a spouse a crime.[3] Moreover, in all States, it remains difficult to establish a rape by a man with whom a woman previously had voluntary sexual intercourse, by a man whom a woman was dating, or even by a man with whom a woman is acquainted. Many so-called **date rapes** or **acquaintance rapes** are rarely prosecuted and, when prosecuted, are rarely successful.

Even where it is clear that a crime has been committed, the police may be unwilling to make arrests for domestic violence—even in States where special domestic violence laws impose duties on law enforcement officers to arrest batterers or ease warrant requirements in cases of domestic violence. The Massachusetts study of domestic violence enforcement, referred to earlier, concluded that: "Police do not treat domestic violence as a crime."

To address this problem, the Illinois domestic violence law provides that law enforcement officers must investigate and make a written report on every "bona fide allegation" of domestic violence, which "shall include the victim's statements as to the frequency and severity of prior incidents of abuse . . . by the same family or household member and the number of prior calls for police assistance to prevent such further abuse." Ill. 750 ILCS § 60/303 (a). The Illinois law further provides that if an officer does not make an arrest, he or she must "inform the victim of abuse of the victim's right to request that a criminal proceeding be initiated, including specific times and places for meeting with [a prosecutor or other official] in accordance with local procedure." *Id.* at § 60/214 (b). Nevertheless, several years after this law was enacted, the supervisor of the Domestic Violence Court Advocacy Project in Chicago claimed it was not enforced and that the police almost never arrested alleged batterers or even responded to 911 calls.[4]

Similarly in Minnesota, although the domestic violence law had long provided

---

3. Even those States that consider spousal rape a crime, may limit the crime to spouses who are separated, are in the process of divorce, or are in situations where extreme force is employed.

4. Nancy Blodgett, "Violence in the Home," 73 A.B.A.J. 66, 68-69 (May 1, 1987).

that police were required to arrest batterers on probable cause, the police were not arresting batterers unless they witnessed the assault, according to the director of the Minnesota Program for Battered Women.[5]

In the past, some women were able to successfully sue the police for their failure to act. For example, in *Thurman v. City of Torrington*, 595 F.Supp. 1521 (D.Conn. 1984), a woman won $1.9 million after the police refused to arrest her husband for severe abuse, and in *Bartalone v. County of Berrien*, 643 F.Supp. 574 (W.D. Mich. 1986), the court stated that a police officer's failure to arrest a batterer may have violated a wife's right to equal protection if he failed to act "because she was a spouse seeking protection from an abusive husband." Such cases have not been very influential in changing laws and police practices. However, the United States Supreme Court's decision holding that child welfare workers could not be held liable for a civil rights violation for their failure to act to remove a child from an abusive home, *DeShaney v. Winnebago County Dept. of Social Services*, 489 U.S. 189 (1989), which was cited in chapter 5 and will be further discussed in chapter 19, now makes such cases unlikely to succeed. In order to succeed, a battered woman must demonstrate she had a "special relationship" with the police, requiring them to protect her as distinct from women in general. Thus, in *Semple v. City of Moundsville*, 963 F.Supp. 1416 (N.D. Va 1997), the court rejected a suit against the police brought by relatives of a woman murdered by her former boyfriend who had been a subject of a domestic violence protective order, citing *DeShaney*.

As with civil domestic violence legislation, enforcement has been and remains a major problem with the criminal laws protecting battered women. Moreover, the very laws designed to protect victims of domestic violence—that is, the laws enabling them to obtain protective orders—have been used to deny them access to the criminal justice system. The attitude of some police (and prosecutors and judges) is that women have a civil remedy and thus do not need a criminal remedy.[6]

Even if enforcement problems are solved, some women will not want to use the criminal justice system. As in the past, a criminal prosecution, particularly when no protective order is issued, can leave a woman quite vulnerable; psychological forces and social pressures can prevent a woman from seeking to prosecute her batterer; and a women who relies on her batterer for support for herself or her children may not wish to see him jailed.

Of course, wives who are abused can still seek protection against their husbands in divorce actions. But barriers to divorce remain and, as we have seen, the economic consequences of divorce for a woman may be severe. Moreover, a husband's abuse of a wife may not prevent his obtaining custody of the children.

All the difficulties entailed in civil suits for assault against batterers remain in the present day, although barriers to

---

5. *Id.* at 68

6. In fact, in *United States v. Dixon*, 509 U.S. 688 (1993), the Supreme Court concluded in a plurality opinion that a man who has been prosecuted for criminal contempt for violating a domestic violence protective order for assaulting his wife was unconstitutionally subjected to double jeopardy when he was later criminally prosecuted for assault. However, the Court concluded it did not violate double jeopardy to later prosecute him for assault with intent to kill or kidnapping.

such suits, such as interspousal immunity and a married woman's inability to sue in her own name, may have been removed. Similarly, all the problems with obtaining and enforcing peace bonds remain, although some problems have been addressed in modern laws.

Despite the publicity and attention given to domestic violence, particularly as a result of high profile cases like those involving O. J. Simpson, domestic violence may be ignored, trivialized, tolerated, or even condoned and many battered women are left without any practical legal remedy.

THE BATTERED WOMAN SYNDROME

Some women have taken matters into their own hands and killed their batterers. If these women are able to establish that they acted in self-defense, they are generally not charged with or convicted of murder. But, traditionally, the claim of self-defense is only available in a homicide case if the killer was in imminent danger of physical injury or death, and often women kill their batterers at a time when they are in no immediate danger of serious injury, such as when their batterers are asleep. Thus, the traditional claim of self-defense is not available to them.

In recent years, battered women for whom the traditional claim of self-defense is not available have been asserting a special kind of self-defense based on what is known as the **battered woman syndrome**. It is argued that some victims of repeated domestic violence develop this syndrome, which causes them to live in a constant state of fear of violence. It is further argued that if these women strike back and

kill their batterers, their actions are really done in self-defense—even if they are not done at the time of a battering episode—because the actions stem from this constant state of fear.

State v. Leidholm, 334 N.W.2d 811 (N.D. 1983), is one of the first cases accepting the battered woman syndrome as a form of self-defense. In *Leidholm*, the court stated:

[A] correct statement of the law of self-defense [in an instruction to the jury] is one in which the court directs the jury to assume the physical and psychological properties peculiar to the accused, viz., to place itself as best it can in the shoes of the accused, and then decide whether or not the particular circumstances surrounding the accused at the time he used force were sufficient to create in his mind a sincere and reasonable belief that the use of force was necessary to protect himself from imminent and unlawful harm.

[The] battered woman syndrome is not of itself a defense. . . . The existence of the syndrome in a marriage does not of itself establish the legal right of the wife to kill the husband, the evidence must still be considered in the context of self-defense. [But a jury may be instructed to consider the] battered woman syndrome and the psychological effects it produces in the battered spouse when deciding the issue of the existence and reasonableness of the accused's belief that force was necessary to protect herself from imminent harm.

Other courts have not accepted the battered woman syndrome as a form of self-defense or have refused to allow expert witnesses to testify on the battered woman syndrome. Without expert testimony, establishing self-defense may be impossible.

As was stated in chapter 3, in order for expert testimony to be admissible, the testimony must be on a subject beyond the knowledge of an ordinary person, be based on reliable and scientific data, and be helpful to the trier of fact. Some courts have been unwilling to accept expert testimony on the battered woman syndrome as meeting any or all of these criteria. Thus, in *Buhrle v. State*, 627 P.2d 1374 (Wyo. 1981), the trial court refused to allow Dr. Lenore Walker, the author of *The Battered Woman* (Harper & Row: New York, 1979) and a recognised expert on the syndrome who had testified in *Leidholm* and other cases, to testify in the murder case before it. The Supreme Court of Wyoming upheld the trial court, stating that "research in the battered woman syndrome is in its infancy" and that the "defendant failed to demonstrate to the trial court that the state of the art would permit a reasonable expert opinion" or that Dr. Walker's testimony would aid the jury. The Court stated, however, that it was neither denying "a battered woman syndrome and all its ramifications" nor "saying that this type of expert testimony is not admissible; we are merely holding that the state of the art was not adequately demonstrated to the court, and because of inadequate foundation the proposed opinions would not aid the jury."

Now that research in the battered woman syndrome has developed further, the existence of the syndrome and the admissibility of expert opinion on it is more likely to be accepted. Indeed, the California Supreme Court has accepted various definitions of the syndrome, including:

> a series of common characteristics that appear in women who are abused physically and psychologically over an extended period of time by the dominant male figure in their lives; a pattern of psychological symptoms that develop after somebody has lived in a battering relationship; [and] a pattern of responses and perceptions presumed to be characteristics of women who have been subjected to continuous physical abuse by their mate. *People v. Romero*, 8 Cal., 4th 728, 883 P.2d 388 (1994).

Even more important, the California Legislature has expressly provided for the admissibility of expert testimony on the syndrome. California Evidence Code section 1107 provides:

> (a) In a criminal action, expert testimony is admissible by either the prosecution or the defense regarding battered women's syndrome, including the physical, emotional or mental effects upon the beliefs, perceptions, or behavior of victims of domestic violence. . . .
> (b) The foundation shall be sufficient for the admission of this expert testimony if the proponent of the evidence establishes its relevancy and the proper qualifications of the expert witness. Expert opinion testimony on battered women's syndrome shall not be considered a new scientific technique whose reliability is unproven.

A similar rule exists in Florida as a result of *Rogers v. State*, 616 So.2d 1098 (Fla.App. 1993). In that case, in reversing a first degree murder conviction of a woman who had been physically abused by her father and three former boyfriends, the Court held that "expert testimony relating to the syndrome is henceforth admissible . . . without any necessity for a case-by-case determination that the scientific knowledge regarding the syndrome is sufficiently developed to permit a reasonable opinion to be given by an expert." In reaching this holding, the Court observed:

> The evidence below was that the battered woman's syndrome has now gained general acceptance in the relevant scientific community, i.e., the psychological community. The prosecution did not offer any of its own evidence to counter the testimony of [the defendant's expert Dr. Harry Krop]. On both direct examination and cross-examination, Dr. Krop testified that the battered woman's syndrome is recognized by the American Psychological Association and that he was unaware of any dis-

agreement regarding its acceptance. Although Dr. Krop stated that the data on the syndrome continues to be developed, he explained that in all medical and psychological fields, the search for new data is continual. And he reiterated that the battered woman's syndrome is accepted within a reasonable degree of psychological certainty within the psychological community. Furthermore, Dr. Krop testified that battered woman's syndrome is essentially diagnosable as post-traumatic stress disorder, which is commonly recognized by the mental health community. Florida cases have consistently recognized the admissibility of expert testimony on post-traumatic stress disorder as it relates to war veterans. We are also persuaded by the declarations of many other courts that the theory underlying the battered woman's syndrome has now gained general acceptance in the scientific community.[7] Equally compelling is the clear trend across the United States towards admissibility of expert testimony on battered woman's syndrome.[8] Numerous books and articles also indicate general acceptance.[9]

Despite the general acceptance of the battered women syndrome and the use of expert testimony to explain the syndrome, it is still necessary for a woman accused of murdering her batterer to establish not merely that she had the syndrome but that she acted in self-defense because of the syndrome. This can be seen in *State v. Thomas*, 77 Ohio St.3d 323, 673 N.E.2d 1339 (1997), in which the Ohio Supreme Court upheld a trial court's jury instructions in a case charging the defendant Teresa Thomas with killing her live-in lover Jerry Flowers.

Thomas had requested a jury instruction with a detailed definition of battered women syndrome and the statement that if the jury believed she had the syndrome and that her expert was qualified to testify about the syndrome, the jury should consider such testimony in determining whether she acted in self-defense. Instead, the trial court had instructed the jury that to establish the defense of self-defense, it had to be shown that Thomas, "had an honest belief that she was in imminent danger of death or great bodily harm and that her only means of escape from that danger was in the use of such force" and that if she "had reasonable ground and an honest belief that she was in imminent danger of death or great bodily harm and that the only means of escape from such danger was by killing [Flowers], then she was justified even though she was mistaken as to the existence of such danger." The trial court further instructed the jury:

---

7. Citing, *inter alia*, *Bechtel v. State*, 840 P.2d 1 (Okla. Crim.App. 1992); *State v. Koss*, 49 Ohio St.3d 213, 551 N.E.2d 970 (Ohio 1990); and *People v. Torres*, 128 Misc.2d 129, 488 N.Y.S.2d 358 (N.Y. Sup.Ct 1985).

8. Citing, *inter alia*, *McMaugh v. State*, 612 A.2d 725 (R.I. 1992); *State v. Burtzlaff*, 493 N.W.2d 1 (S.D. 1992); *People v. Wilson*, 194 Mich.App. 599, 487 N.W.2d 822 (1992); *People v. Yaklich*, 833 P.2d 758 (Colo. Ct.App. 1991); *State v. Williams*, 787 S.W.2d 308 (Mo. Ct.App. 1990); *State v. Hennum*, 441 N.W.2d 793 (Minn. 1989); *Fielder v. State*, 756 S.W.2d 309 (Tex. Crim.App. 1988); *State v. Hill*, 287 S.C. 398, 339 S.E.2d 121 (1986); *State v. Gallegos*, 104 N.M. 247, 719 P.2d 1268 (1986); *State v. Kelly*, 97 N.J. 178, 478 A.2d 364 (1984); *State v. Allery*, 101 Wash.2d 591, 682 P.2d 312 (1984); *People v. Minnis*, 118 Ill.App.3d 345, 455 N.E.2d 209 (1983); *Smith v. State*, 247 Ga. 612, 277 S.E.2d 678 (1981); *State v. Anaya*, 438 A.2d 892 (Me. 1981); *State v. Baker*, 120 N.H. 773, 424 A.2d 171 (1980); and *State v. Dozier*, 163 W.Va. 192, 255 S.E.2d 552 (W.Va. 1979).

9. Citing thirteen books and articles, including two by Dr. Lenore Walker.

In determining whether Teresa Thomas had reasonable grounds for an honest belief that she was in imminent danger, you must put yourselves in her position, with her characteristics, her knowledge or lack of knowledge, and under the circumstances and conditions that surrounded her at that time. You must consider the conduct of [Flowers] and determine if his acts and words caused her to reasonably and honestly believe that she was about to be killed or to receive great bodily harm. Testimony was offered concerning the battered woman syndrome, and that Teresa Thomas suffered from this syndrome. This testimony is offered to assist you in determining whether she acted out of an honest belief that she was in imminent danger of death or great bodily harm and that the force used by her was her only means of ending the danger. You may consider such testimony together with all the other evidence in determining whether she acted in self-defense.

In upholding this instruction, the Supreme Court noted that expert testimony on battered women syndrome was admissible in Ohio and that evidence of the syndrome may support a defense of self-defense, but the syndrome

does not establish a new defense or justification independent of the defense of self-defense. The trial court's instructions correctly emphasized to the jury that [it must use] a combined subjective and objective test. [T]he jury first must consider the defendant's situation objectively, that is, whether, considering all of the defendant's particular characteristics, knowledge, or lack of knowledge, circumstances, history, and conditions at the time of the attack, she reasonably believed she was in imminent danger. This standard is sometimes labeled the "reasonable battered woman standard." Then, if the objective standard is met, the jury must determine if, subjectively, this particular defendant had an honest belief that she was in imminent danger. This same two-prong standard is used in a number of states.[10] The jury instructions given by the trial court . . .

properly instructed the jury to consider all the circumstances when determining if [Thomas] had an objectively reasonable belief of imminent danger and whether she subjectively honestly believed she was in danger of imminent harm. [Her] requested instructions would attempt to more precisely define the battered woman syndrome and would require the jury to determine whether appellant was a battered woman in order to find that appellant believed she was in imminent danger. Adding these proposed instructions would therefore set up an entirely separate defense, rather than charge the jury to consider the syndrome when the jury determines appellant's state of mind regarding [a required] element of self-defense. This addition, therefore, would have been improper.

PROTECTION OF THE ELDERLY OR DISABLED

Protection Through Domestic Violence Legislation

Violence against an elderly or disabled member of a household would be covered by a State's domestic violence statute if the victim and the abuser are spouses. Further, depending on the definitions of domestic violence in a State's law, it may be covered when the victim and the abuser are not spouses but are living in the same household, as in the case of an elderly woman living with her daughter or a mentally impaired adult living with his parents. Paid caretakers living in a household may even be covered.

When violence against the elderly or the disabled is covered by domestic violence statutes, the victim can obtain orders of protection just as an abused woman can obtain an order of protection—with all, or

---

10. Citing many of the cases cited in *Rogers* and also citing *Robinson v. State*, 308 S.C. 74, 417 S.E.2d 88 (1992); *State v. Norman*, 324 N.C. 253, 378 S.E.2d 8 (1989); *Commonwealth v. Stonehouse*, 521 Pa. 41, 55 A.2d 772 (1989); *State v. Stewart*, 243 Kan. 639, 763 P.2d 572 (1988); and *State v. Leidolm, supra*, 334 N.W.2d 811 (N.D. 1983).

more, of the attendant difficulties. If it is difficult, practically and psychologically, for an adult woman to obtain a protective order, consider the practical and psychological difficulties for a person who is elderly and frail or mentally impaired.

Protection Through Criminal Laws

Violence or threat of violence against anyone is a crime in every State. Many States, moreover, either define violence against a person who is elderly or disabled as a more serious offense than violence against someone who is younger or able-bodied, or create separate criminal offenses for abuse of an elderly or disabled person. An example of the first approach was seen in Colorado where the statutes, after specifying sanctions for different types of assault against elderly or disabled persons, formerly stated:

> Elderly persons and handicapped persons are seldom as physically or emotionally equipped to protect themselves or aid in their own security as are their younger or more physically able counterparts in society. At the same time, they are far more susceptible than other groups to the adverse long-term effects of assault. The general assembly therefore finds that the penalty for the crime of assault on an elderly or handicapped person should be more severe than the penalty for assault on other members of society. § 18–3–209 C.R.S.

This statutory scheme, however, was repealed in 1995 after it was found to violate defendants' right to equal protection in *People v. Suazo*, 867 P.2d 161 (Colo.App. 1993).

An example of the second approach is found in California, which permits imprisonment for up to four years of any caretaker of an elderly or disabled adult who willfully permits the person's health to be injured or places the person in a situation that endangers the person's health. Cal. Penal Code § 368.

Protection Through Adult Protective Services Legislation

Just as in the case of child abuse and neglect, the States have come to recognize that criminal prosecution is usually an ineffective way to address the problem of abuse of elderly and disabled persons. Abuse of the elderly and disabled by caregivers typically evolves from the physical, emotional, and often financial stress of caring for a person who is dependent. As in the case of child abuse, the maltreatment occurs within a relationship that is conflicted but caring in many ways. To criminally prosecute the abuser in such situations will harm the family and put the victim at risk of institutionalization—outcomes that may ultimately be more detrimental to the victim than the abuse itself. In recognition of these facts, the majority of States have enacted adult protective services legislation designed to protect the elderly and persons who are mentally or physically disabled.

The definition of adult protective services varies widely from State to State. To illustrate, protective services in California are defined primarily in terms of the conditions that necessitate the need for societal intervention:

> "Adult protective services" means those preventive and remedial activities performed on behalf of elders and dependent adults who are unable to protect their own interests; harmed or threatened with harm; caused physical or

mental injury due to the action or inaction of another person or their own action due to ignorance, illiteracy, incompetence, mental limitation or poor health; lacking in adequate food, shelter, or clothing; exploited of their income and resources; or deprived of entitlement due them. Calif. Welf. and Inst. Code § 15610.

Other States, however, define the services in terms of social and other services that may be provided, or in terms of who will provide services or where they will be provided.

Similarly, the specific provisions of protective services legislation vary widely from State to State, but all the statutes have similar elements. The statutes define who is elderly or disabled for the purposes of providing services; define what constitutes abuse, neglect, or **exploitation**, which is a category of abuse unique to the elderly and disabled; require or encourage the reporting of suspected abuse, neglect, or exploitation to designated authorities; provide immunity from civil or criminal liability to those who report in good faith; outline procedures for investigating reports; and state the conditions under which services can be provided with and without the consent of a person found to be in need of services. As you can see, the provisions are much like those of the child abuse and neglect reporting statutes. As you can also see, the provisions typically offer broader protection than do domestic violence statutes and the criminal code in that they include neglect and exploitation.

In most States, the protective services legislation, including reporting laws, covers persons living alone or with relatives or friends as well as persons who live in nursing homes or other institutions.

Protection of vulnerable adults who are living in the community is complex, both legally and practically, and the statutes represent an attempt to balance the difficult problems involved in offering this protection. The legal issues revolve around privacy and liberty. While children are assumed to be incompetent and thus in need of the *parens patriae* protection of the State, adults are assumed to be competent and thus capable of making decisions on their own behalf. This is often not an issue in instances where a frail elderly person has been physically abused by a caregiver, but it is clearly an issue when a frail elderly person is living, apparently by his or her own choice, in a home that is unsanitary and unsafe. Such is the case with many elderly persons who want at all costs to continue living in their own homes. Should the State intervene against the individual's wishes in such cases, especially when the intervention might result in the individual being placed in a nursing home because no community services are available? This question relates to competency and guardianship, topics that will be discussed later in the text, but regardless of how this question is answered, social workers have important roles to play in developing appropriate law, providing services under the law, and acting as advocates and counselors of the elderly and disabled.

Protection in Nursing Homes

As has been stated, adult protective services legislation may cover elderly or disabled residents of nursing homes. Additionally, nursing home residents have been accorded certain rights by statutes and regulations. Many of these rights were first gained by patients in mental hospitals and institutions for the mentally disabled through court action. This is because while many mental health facilities are public, many nursing homes are private, and while many of those in mental health facilities have been committed involuntarily pursuant to a court order, most residents of nursing homes have admitted themselves voluntarily or have been admitted by their relatives without a court order. In other words, in contrast to the situation with many mental patients, there may have been no government involvement with a nursing home patient's confinement. Without government involvement, that is, without "state action," no rights may arise under the Fourteenth Amendment or other sections of the Constitution. For example, *Doyle v. Unicare Health Services, Inc., Aurora Center*, 399 F.Supp. 69 (N.D. Ill. 1975), *aff'd.* 541 F.2d 283, held that being subject to extensive federal regulation and receiving federal funds did not make an otherwise private nursing home subject to a suit for deprivation of civil rights under 42 U.S.C. § 1983. However, beginning in the seventies and eighties, numerous State statutes and regulations provided for the rights of nursing home residents similar to those afforded to mental patients in court decisions. Additionally, federal statutes and regulations provide for rights of nursing home residents whose care is paid for, wholly or partially, by federal funds. Nursing homes have to meet certain standards and provide certain rights to residents in order to qualify for Medicaid or Medicare reimbursement. The imposition of these standards and the provision of these rights also benefits the residents of the nursing

homes whose care is not reimbursed by Medicaid or Medicare, but these residents may bear the brunt of the cost of meeting the standards.

The rights provided to nursing home residents by federal regulations have long included:

1) the right to be fully informed of their health and medical condition and to participate in planning care and treatment;
2) the right to refuse treatment;
3) the right to exercise all rights as citizens and to submit complaints freely;
4) the right to privacy;
5) freedom from restraints except under certain conditions and with certain safeguards;
6) the right to be treated with consideration and respect and with recognition of their dignity and individuality; and
7) the freedom to communicate, associate, and meet privately with individuals of their own choice, to send and receive personal mail unopened, and to participate in social, religious, and community group activities.

Since 1987, Congress has also mandated that residents of nursing homes who receive Medicaid or Medicare, among other rights, have the right: 1) "to chose a personal attending physician;" 2) to notice of any change of room or roommate; 3) "to be free from physical or mental abuse, corporal punishment, involuntary seclusion and any physical or chemical restraints imposed for purposes of discipline or convenience;" and 4) to have grievances addressed promptly. 42 U.S.C. § 1396r *et seq.* The 1987 law further requires nursing homes to maintain or enhance "the quality of life of each resident" and requires annual comprehensive assessments of each resident's ability to perform such everyday tasks as bathing, dressing, eating, and walking. These assessments must be used to develop written plans of care for each resident, describing how the resident's medical, psychological, and social needs will be met. The law, moreover, set forth staffing requirements for nursing homes, including the requirement that any nursing home with more than 120 beds must employ at least one full-time social worker with a degree in social work or similar qualifications. Nursing home residents denied rights under this law may sue the homes under 42 U.S.C. § 1983. See *Talbot v. Lucy Corr Nursing Home*, 118 F.3d 215 (4th Cir. 1997).

Another federal statute, known as the Keys Amendment and found at 42 U.S.C. § 1382e, protects disabled residents of residential board and care facilities, personal care facilities and nursing homes who receive federal welfare benefits for the disabled. See also, 45 C.F.R. §§ 1397.1–1397.20 [implementing regulations]; and *Wolford v. Mackey*, 860 F.Supp. 1123 (S.D.W.Va. 1994), finding that West Virginia's regulation of these facilities and enforcement of these standards violated the Keys Amendment and State law.

In addition to the regulation of private nursing homes that stems from federal law, private nursing homes generally have to be licensed. State licensing laws may mandate certain rights of residents of nursing homes. Many States additionally or alternatively have statutes specifically providing for rights for nursing home residents akin to those in federal law or those afforded mental patients by court decisions.

See also Tex. Human Resources Code § 102.003; Colo. Rev. Stat. § 25–1–120; and Mich. Comp. Laws § 333.20201.

Contracts for private nursing home care may specify residents' rights, but few people are in a position to negotiate for their rights when entering into a contract for nursing home care. Thus, some States now regulate the content of nursing home contracts. See Cal. Health & Safety Code § 1599.60 *et seq.* Comprehensive consumer protection laws may also regulate the contents of such contracts. Patients who have been denied contractual rights may sue nursing homes for breach of contract in addition to claims for violation of statutory rights or tort claims for personal injuries. For example, *Petre v. Living Centers-East, Inc.*, 935 F.Supp. 808 (E.D.La. 1996), allowed a suit for damages brought by the administrator of the estate of a nursing home resident. The suit sought damages for breach of contract, tort, and violation of the rights of nursing home residents set forth in a Louisiana statute (La.Rev.Stat.Ann. § 40.2010.8). The suit claimed, among other things, that the ninety-year-old resident was not provided with suitable care, was verbally abused, and was not properly supervised. In denying the nursing home summary judgment, the court noted that section 40.2010.9 created a private right of action for damages and attorney's fees and that a 1995 amendment to section 40.2010.9 stated that the "remedies provided in this section are in addition to and cumulative with other legal and administrative remedies available to a resident."

A particular problem for nursing home residents is involuntary transfers or discharges. Such transfers or discharges may occur for several reasons. A nursing home may want to replace Medicaid recipients with patients using insurance that pays at a higher rate than Medicaid; a nursing home may have been decertified for Medicaid or Medicare reimbursement or lost its license; a nursing home may not want to keep a troublesome or difficult patient. Whatever reason for the transfer or discharge, it may be a traumatic experience for the resident. "Transfer trauma," as it has been called, may even lead to death of fragile patients. In *O'Bannon v. Town Court Nursing Center*, 447 U.S. 773 (1980), the Supreme Court assumed that transfer trauma exists but held that it did not amount to a deprivation of liberty that would entitle nursing home residents to a pretransfer hearing. Various federal and State statutes and regulations do exist, however, to protect nursing home residents against transfer trauma. For example, the 1987 federal statute restricts transfers and discharges and provides procedural protections before residents may be discharged or transferred, including a requirement that each State establish an administrative process for a resident to challenge a discharge or transfer. 42 U.S.C. § 1396r *et seq.*

13

Education of Children

345

Many social workers work with children, particularly those from groups who may suffer discrimination. Moreover, many social workers are employed by public elementary and secondary schools, particularly to work with disabled children and children whose behavior is troublesome. Therefore, it is important for social workers to understand the law related to discrimination in the schools, school attendance, discipline in the schools, and special education services for disabled children. This law will be reviewed in this chapter, focusing on the statutory and traditional role of school social workers.

It should be noted that, as was stated in the introduction to this section, public education is an area of the law where local law is significant, if not predominant, and where federal law may be quite significant to social workers. In all the States but Hawaii, public primary and secondary schools are created, financed, and operated by local government entities, which are typically independent school districts governed by elected school boards. State governments may provide some funds to local school districts, and State laws may regulate some aspects of the operation of the schools, but local financing (generally from property taxes) is usually primary, and local laws customarily control the day-to-day operation of the schools. The federal government provides limited funds to local school districts and has a limited say in the operation of the schools, except in relation to the education of disabled children. In this area of great importance to social workers, federal law governs.

DISCRIMINATION

Throughout our history, certain groups of children have been denied educational opportunities. Disabled children were excluded from the schools. Separate school systems for African American children existed under the authority of the law. Children were prevented from taking certain classes simply because they were boys or they were girls, and there were few opportunities for women to participate in athletics. While such discrimination is now prohibited by statute and through court interpretations of the equal protection clause of the Fourteenth Amendment, vestiges of discrimination remain and continue to affect children. Moreover, debate continues over exactly what violates equal protection in the context of education.

Race

The Supreme Court held in *Brown v. Board of Education*, 347 U.S. 483 (1954), that laws either requiring or permitting segregation by race in public schools violate the equal protection guarantee of the Fourteenth Amendment. In so holding, the Court overruled the "separate but equal" doctrine it had established in *Plessy v. Ferguson*, 163 U.S. 537 (1899), stating: "In the field of public education the doctrine of 'separate but equal' has no place. Separate educational facilities are inherently unequal." The Court reasoned: "To separate [children] from others of similar age and qualifications solely because of their race generates a feeling of inferiority as to their status in the community that may affect their hearts and minds in a way unlikely ever to be undone."

The Court decided what should be done to implement its decision in a second *Brown* decision, 349 U.S. 294 (1955), in which it stated:

> Full implementation of [desegregation] may require solution of varied local school problems. School authorities have the primary responsibility for elucidating, assessing, and solving these problems; courts will have to consider whether the action of the school authorities constitutes good faith implementation of the governing constitutional principles.
>
> In fashioning and effectuating the decrees, the courts will be guided by equitable principles. Traditionally, equity [special courts which operate under equitable principles and give special kinds of remedies or regular courts which so operate] has been characterized by a practical flexibility in shaping its remedies and by a facility for adjusting and reconciling public and private needs.
>
> While giving weight to [various] public and private considerations, the courts will require that the defendants make a prompt and a reasonable start toward full compliance with our [earlier] ruling. Once such a start has been made, the courts may find that additional time is necessary to carry out the ruling in an effective manner. The burden rests upon the defendants to establish that such time is necessary in the public interest and is consistent with good faith compliance at the earliest practicable date.

This decision was followed by a long line of federal court decisions ruling that schools were segregated in violation of *Brown* and that officials were not making sufficient efforts to desegregate. The decisions at first merely ordered compliance with *Brown* and later, when compliance did not occur, imposed desegregation plans, sometimes run by the courts. The federal government's commitment to de-

segregation, and then integration of the public schools, was later articulated in the Civil Rights Act of 1964, 42 U.S.C. § 2000, *et seq.* The Act includes provisions prohibiting federal assistance to schools that discriminate on the basis of race and providing funds to support the costs of integrating the schools and remedying the effects of past discrimination.

Despite these court decisions and the provisions in the Civil Rights Act of 1964, and although progress has been made, segregation in the public schools has not been eliminated and integration has not been achieved. There are several factors that account for this.

First, there has been resistance by school boards to integration, manifested not only in outright refusals to comply with court orders but also in the development of unrealistic or thwarted plans for integration, often calling for voluntary action that may not be forthcoming. Second, white parents have demonstrated their resistance to integration by removing their children from public schools or by moving from integrated communities. The public schools in some areas, particularly central cities, may now have entirely or mostly minority students, while schools in other areas, particularly suburbs, may be almost all white. As this suggests, a third reason it has been difficult to achieve integration in America is the system of community schools and the fact that many communities remain racially segregated. In other words, integration is difficult to achieve when there is **de facto segregation** (i.e., segregation resulting from housing patterns, not laws forbidding integration) rather than **de jure segregation** (i.e., segregation resulting from the law, not economic and geographic factors). Bussing has been the primary solution devised to deal with *de facto* segregation, but where entire school districts are predominantly composed of children of one race, integration can only be achieved if children are bussed across district lines. Plans that order such interdistrict bussing have been imposed by lower courts but have been struck down by the Supreme Court. Indeed, in *Missouri v. Jenkins*, 515 U.S. 70 (1995), the Court even questioned a plan designed to attract students from outside a school district to achieve integration.

Because of the pervasiveness of *de facto* segregation, voluntary action rather than court imposed plans may be necessary to achieve integration.

Wealth

In *San Antonio Independent School District v. Rodriguez*, 411 U.S. 1 (1973), discussed in chapter 5, the Supreme Court held that dependence on local property taxes to finance the schools, a dependence that results in less funds per child in poor school districts, was not an unconstitutional denial of equal protection. Some States and the federal government have sought to remedy discrimination on the basis of wealth by easing local school districts' dependence on local property taxes, but, as long as public education is financed primarily through local property taxes, there will be differences between districts in the financing, and therefore the quality, of education. And, because minority children are disproportionately poor and tend to live in poor districts, many will continue to receive an education inferior to that of white children.

Alienage

While discrimination on the basis of wealth may be constitutional, the Supreme Court ruled in *Plyler v. Doe*, 457 U.S. 202 (1982), also discussed in chapter 5, that to exclude alien children, including illegal alien children, from the schools violated the Fourteenth Amendment. This ruling remains controversial as does a related problem of language. Bilingual education for children who do not speak English as a native language has been urged and is funded by the federal government, but many question its wisdom and its constitutionality.

Sex

Discrimination on the basis of sex has occurred through restrictions on enrollment in certain classes and unequal access to participation in athletic programs. Title IX of the Education Amendments of 1972, 20 U.S.C. § 1681, forbids such discrimination by any school that receives federal funds, which means virtually all public elementary and secondary schools. In addition, many State constitutions and statutes prohibit discrimination in public education on the basis of gender. Nevertheless, single sex education is now being urged to solve problems in the schools. Some cases have held different varieties of single sex education in the public schools unconstitutional.

A subcategory of sex discrimination is discrimination on the basis of pregnancy. In the past, pregnant girls often were not allowed to attend school or were exempt from compulsory education laws. Presently, because of sex discrimination claims, pregnant girls generally may continue their education in school unless continuing is contraindicated by health. Moreover, if a pregnant student cannot attend school because of health, the school must generally provide a home education equivalent to that in the classroom.

Another subcategory of sex discrimination is sexual harassment. More and more courts are wrestling with the question whether certain acts of sexual harassment in the schools creates a "hostile environment" and whether such a hostile environment constitutes discrimination in violation of Title IX or the Constitution. The courts have answered differently depending on who is doing the harassment: school personnel or fellow students. In *Franklin v. Gwinnett County Public Schools*, 503 U.S. 60 (1992), the Supreme Court held that damages could be claimed under Title IX by a high school student who alleged sexual harassment by a coach-teacher, but in *Rowinsky v. Bryan Independent School District*, 80 F.3d 1006 (5th Cir. 1996), the United States Court of Appeals held that Title IX does not impose liability on a school district for peer sexual harassment absent allegations that the school district itself directly discriminated on the basis of sex. The school's knowledge of the harassment by fellow students and its failure to do anything about it may, however, be enough to impose liability. For example, in *Davis v. Monroe County Board of Education*, 74 F.3d 1186 (11th Cir. 1996), the court held that Title IX encompassed a claim by a fifth grader for damages due to a sexually hostile educational environment created by fellow students that the school knowingly failed to eliminate. Interestingly, in *Kinman v. Omaha Public School District*, 94 F.3d 463 (8th Cir. 1996), the plaintiff high school student alleged he had a homosexual relationsip with a teacher, the court held that sexual harassment between members of the same sex could be actionable and that the school district could be liable under Title IX if school officials were aware of the relationship and did not take steps to stop it, but also held that the district and the teacher would not be liable for creation of a hostile environment under 42 U.S.C. § 1983.

Disability

In *Pennsylvania Association for Retarded Children v. Pennsylvania*, 334 F.Supp. 1257 (E.D.Pa. 1971), and *Mills v. D.C. Board of Education*, 348 F.Supp. 866 (D.D.C. 1972), the district courts ruled that disabled children could not be excluded from the schools, essentially extending to disabled children the rights extended to African Americans in *Brown v. Board of Education*. These cases led to the enactment in 1975 of Public Law 94–142, 20 U.S.C. § 140, *et seq.*, now called the Individuals with Disabilities Education Act (IDEA). The IDEA, together with Section 504 of the Rehabilitation Act of 1973 (Section 504), 29 U.S.C. § 794, which forbids discrimination against the disabled by federally assisted entities, and the Americans with Disabilities Act of 1990 (ADA), 42 U.S.C. § 12101, *et seq.*, which has a more sweeping prohibition of discrimination against the disabled, enforce the goal of providing full educational opportunity for disabled children.

These statutes will be discussed in more detail later in the chapter, but you should note here that, to the extent children with AIDS are excluded from schools because of fear of contagion not because of symptoms that interfere with their ability to be educated, they may not be protected by the IDEA, which only covers disabilities that require special education services. However, they should be protected by Section 504 of the Rehabilitation Act and the ADA. This was made clear by *School Bd. of Nassau County, Fla. v. Arline*, 480 U.S. 273 (1987), which dealt with discrimination against a teacher on the basis of tuberculosis. The Supreme Court stated that Section 504 prohibits discrimination, not only against those who are impaired but also against those "regarded as impaired," and that this means the Act encompasses discrimination because of "public fear and misapprehension [of] contagiousness." The Court stated: "The Act is carefully structured to replace . . . reflexive reactions to actual or perceived handicaps with actions based on reasoned and medically sound judgments . . ." More recently, in *Bragdon v. Abbott*, ____ U.S. ___, 118 S.Ct. 2196 (1998), the Supreme Court ruled that AIDS was a disability covered by the ADA of a woman with AIDS who a dentist refused to treat.

ATTENDANCE

Either the constitution or statutes in all the States but Mississippi guarantee a free public education to all children through the twelfth grade. These provisions guaranteeing a free education are supported by statutes in all the States requiring children within certain ages to attend school, that is

compulsory attendance laws, and usually by statutes imposing civil and criminal penalties on parents who fail to educate their children in compliance with the law. These provisions may also be supported by laws that put failure to attend school within the jurisdiction of the juvenile court. For example, the Texas Constitution states: "A general diffusion of knowledge being essential to the preservation of the liberties and rights of the people, it shall be the duty of the Legislature of this State to establish and make suitable provision for the support and maintenance of an efficient system of public free schools." Tex. Const. art. VII, § 1.

The Texas statutes provide that, with limited exceptions, every child from seven to sixteen years old must attend school a certain minimum number of days per year and that it is a criminal offense for a parent or other person to contribute to a child's failure to attend school as required. Tex. Educ. Code Ann. §§ 25.085, 25.086. The statutes further include within the definition of a minor in need of supervision (MINS) under the juvenile law a child who is absent from school for extended periods. Tex. Fam. Code Ann. § 51.03(b)(2).

The ability of the State to require school attendance is not absolute. For example, in *Pierce v. Society of Sisters*, 268 U.S. 510 (1925), the Supreme Court held that a State could not compel attendance in public schools, thereby allowing parents to send their children to private schools. The Court later held in *Wisconsin v. Yoder*, 400 U.S. 205 (1972), that a State could not require Amish children to attend school until the age of sixteen when doing so conflicted with their parents' religious beliefs and when the parents provided continuing informal vocational instruction consistent with their beliefs. Further, courts have upheld a parent's right to teach a child at home, but a State may impose requirements on home schooling, such as requirements related to instructional hours, curriculum, or testing.

Where school attendance is required, the statutes in some States recognize that truancy may reflect social and educational problems. Thus, the statutes may require schools to offer services, such as services of a social worker, in an effort to correct truant behavior or may, as in Texas, address truancy under special provisions in the State's juvenile court act. Referrals for criminal and civil penalties are rare and usually only a last resort when other efforts fail.

DISCIPLINE

School authorities have an obligation to maintain discipline on school grounds and are typically given broad discretion in the administration of discipline. But some forms of discipline and the manner of administering discipline raise legal questions of interest to social workers.

Corporal Punishment

Corporal punishment is any physical striking or paddling of a child. In *Ingraham v. Wright*, 430 U.S. 662 (1977), the Supreme Court considered and rejected a challenge to corporal punishment in a public school. The Court ruled that corporal punishment did not violate the Eighth Amendment's prohibition on cruel and unusual punishment, holding that the Eighth Amendment was designed to protect only convicted criminals. The Court did rule that the use of corporal punishment is governed by the Fourteenth Amendment, stating: "It is fundamental that the state cannot hold and physically punish an individual except in accordance with due process of law. [W]here school authorities, acting under color of state law, deliberately decide to punish a child for misconduct by restraining the child and inflicting appreciable pain, we hold that Fourteenth Amendment liberty interests are implicated."

However, the Court was not willing to hold that the imposition of corporal punishment necessarily violates substantive due process guarantees in the Fourteenth Amendment. It noted that corporal punishment has long been used in this country and has been widely accepted by the courts.

The use of corporal punishment in this country as a means of disciplining school children dates back to the colonial period. [T]he practice continues to play a role in the public education of school children in most parts of the country. Professional and public opinion is sharply divided on the practice, and has been for more than a century. Yet we can discern no trend toward its elimination.

Although the early cases viewed the authority of the [schools to impose corporal punishment] as deriving from the parents, the concept of parental delegation has been replaced by the view—more consonant with compulsory education laws—that the State itself may impose such corporal punishment as is reasonably necessary for the maintenance of group discipline.

Some States have statutes that specifically authorized the use of corporal punishment in the schools. For example, a

South Dakota law gives school personnel—and school bus drivers—the authority "to use the physical force that is reasonable and necessary for supervisory control over the student." S.D. Codified Laws Ann. § 13-32-2.

Some States prohibit use of corporal punishment. For example, a statute in California provides: "No person employed by or engaged in a public school shall inflict, or cause to be inflicted corporal punishment upon a pupil. Every resolution, bylaw, rule, ordinance, or other act or authority permitting or authorizing the infliction of corporal punishment upon a pupil attending a public school is void and unenforceable." Cal. Educ. Code § 49001.

Other States have no statutes forbidding or authorizing the use of corporal punishment, but the courts have held that corporal punishment is allowed. For example, although the Indiana statutes on school discipline in effect in 1986 did not mention corporal punishment, *Cole ex rel. Cole v. Greenfield-Central Community Schools*, 657 F.Supp. 56 (S.D. Ind. 1986) held that school officials in Indiana have the power to use corporal punishment.[1] As the Supreme Court stated in *Ingraham*:

"Where the legislatures have not acted, the . . . courts have uniformly preserved the common-law rule permitting teachers to use reasonable force in disciplining children . . ."

The use of **unreasonable** or **excessive force**, however, may give rise to due process claims, as the Court made clear in *Ingraham*. Thus, the courts have allowed students who were badly hurt or had corporal punishment imposed for minor infractions to bring civil rights actions against their teachers or schools for damages. For example, in *Garcia v. Miera*, 817 F.2d 650 (10th Cir. 1987), *cert den'd.* 108 S. Ct. 1220, the court upheld a civil rights claim where a nine-year-old girl was beaten so hard she was permanently scarred; and in *P.B. v. Koeh*, 96 F.3d 1298 (9th Cir. 1996), the court held a school principal who choked, slapped, and punched students had no immunity from a civil rights suit under 42 U.S.C. § 1983. By way of contrast, in *Wallace v. Batavia School Dist. No. 101*, 68 F.3d 1010 (7th Cir. 1995), the court held that simply grabbing a student and escorting the student from the classroom was not a violation of § 1983.

Moreover, while reasonable corporal punishment may be constitutional, there may be limitations on its use, under local or State law, and certain procedural protections may be required before it may be imposed. In *Baker v. Owen*, 423 U.S. 907 (1975), the Supreme Court, without opinion, affirmed a lower court decision allowing schools to paddle students, even over parental objection, but requiring minimal notice and an opportunity for the student to be heard before the punishment could be administered. In *Ingraham*, however, the Court held

---

1. The Indiana statutes are still silent on corporal punishment but do provide:

"(a) Student supervision and the desirable behavior of students in carrying out school purposes is the responsibility of a school corporation and the students of a school corporation.

(b) In all matters relating to the discipline and conduct of students, school corporation personnel stand in the relation of parents and guardians to the students of the school corporation. Therefore, school corporation personnel have the right, subject to this chapter, to take any disciplinary action necessary to promote student conduct that conforms with an orderly and effective educational system." Ind. Code § 20–8.1–5.1–3.

that the Fourteenth Amendment procedural due process requirements were met even if no notice or hearing preceded the administration of corporal punishment because a child could sue school officials if the punishment was excessive.

Ingraham leaves school authorities with great freedom in use of corporal punishment, but there is nothing in the opinion to prevent States and local school boards from requiring procedural protections. Thus, certain protections, such as review by an administrator before a teacher can paddle a student, may be required by local or State law.

Exclusion from School

Students can be excluded from school through suspension or expulsion. If a child is suspended, he or she is not allowed to attend school for a short period of time, typically three to ten days. If a child is expelled, he or she is typically not allowed to attend school for the remainder of the school year or is permanently excluded from school. The student is not given credit for any work due during the period of suspension or expulsion. Some schools use in-school suspension in which children are required to continue attending school and receive credit for work done but do not attend their regular classes and may receive counseling or special supervision.

As we saw in chapter 5, the Supreme Court held in *Goss v. Lopez*, 419 U.S. 565 (1975), that if a State offers free public education to all children and requires all children within certain ages to attend school, it creates a property right protected by the Fourteenth Amendment.

Having created a protected right, a State cannot deprive a child of the right, even for a short period of time, without due process. A child, therefore, cannot be suspended or expelled unless certain protection is offered.

Goss gave students facing up to a ten-day suspension only a right to notice and a minimum right to be heard. Such students were not accorded a right to an evidentiary hearing with the right of confrontation, a right to counsel, or any of the rights we have come to expect when one is deprived of a significant interest. With a longer suspension or with an expulsion, given the traditional due process balancing test, however, one should expect more procedural protection. This protection is generally set forth in State statutes and regulations and in local school district laws. These State and local laws may also provide more procedural protections attendant to short suspensions than those required as a minimum by *Goss*.

Grounds for Punishment in the Schools

Given that corporal punishment and exclusion from school are governed by the Fourteenth Amendment, in addition to the question of what procedural protections must surround the administration of punishment by exclusion from school or corporal punishment, the question arises as to what constitutes reasonable grounds for such punishment.

The Supreme Court stated in *Tinker v. Des Moines School District*, 393 U.S. 503 (1968), that: "In our system, state-operated schools may not be enclaves of totalitarianism. School officials do not possess absolute authority over their students. Students in school as well as out of school are 'persons' under our Constitution. They are possessed of fundamental rights which the State must respect, just as they themselves must respect their obligations to the State."

Tinker concerned high school students who were suspended for wearing black arm bands in protest of American involvement in Vietnam. The Court held that the students' conduct was protected by the First and the Fourteenth Amendments because it constituted political speech, it was not disruptive and it did not impinge on the rights of others. Suspension for such conduct, therefore, was not justified. In *Bethel School District No. 403 v. Fraser*, 478 U.S. 675 (1986), however, the Supreme Court distinguished wearing an arm band from making a speech that was considered lewd and obscene by school officials. Although the speech was only lewd by innuendo and was given at a rally in support of a candidate for student office, and was thus clearly political, the Court held that it was not protected by the First Amendment and therefore was a legitimate ground for disciplinary action.

Given these seemingly contradictory cases, what conduct justifies punishment? There is no easy answer. It is only clear that the authority of school officials to maintain order and protect all students must be balanced against the rights of individual students and that, while students have certain constitutionally protected rights, they may exercise these rights only to the extent that they do not disrupt the educational process. It is also clear that the grounds for discipline may be left largely to the discretion of school authorities and that the courts will only reverse disciplinary decisions when school authorities have clearly abused their discretion.

The statutes in some States are not specific, providing only that local school authorities must maintain discipline and establish a policy on discipline. For example, an Illinois statute provides that teachers

> shall maintain discipline in the schools . . . In all matters relating to the discipline in and conduct of the schools . . . , they stand in the relation of parents and guardians to the pupils. [E]ach board must establish a policy on discipline, and the policy so established shall provide that a teacher . . . may use reasonable force to maintain safety [and] may remove a student from the classroom for disruptive behavior and shall include provisions which provide due process to students. 10 ILCS § 5/24-24.

There are no statutes on the subject in some States and punishment is left entirely to local school authorities. The statutes in some States may include a nonexclusive list of mandatory grounds for punishment, but may otherwise leave the grounds for punishment up to local school authorities. Alternatively, certain grounds for punishment may simply be suggested. A California statute takes a different approach. It provides that a student cannot be suspended or expelled except for certain specified grounds, like bringing a gun to school, injuring another person on school grounds, or smoking or drinking alcohol at school. Cal. Educ. Code § 48900. It further provides that, "[i]t is the intent of the Legislature that alternatives to suspension or expulsion be imposed against any student who is truant, tardy or otherwise absent from school activities." The difficult problem of punishment of disabled children is discussed at the end of the chapter.

Searches

Because of the need to maintain order in the schools, school authorities may have wider powers than law enforcement officials to question and search students for evidence of misbehavior. In *New Jersey v. T.L.O.*, 469 U.S. 325 (1985), the Court ruled that a search of a student's purse after she was caught smoking in the lavatory did not violate the Fourth Amendment. The Court stated that, while the Fourth Amendment applies to searches in schools,

> [i]t is evident that the school setting requires some easing of the restrictions to which searches by public authorities are ordinarily subject. The warrant requirement, in particular, is unsuited to the school environment: requiring a teacher to obtain a warrant before searching a child suspected of an infraction of school rules [or of the criminal law] would unduly interfere with the maintenance of the swift and informal disciplinary procedures needed in the schools. [Further,] the accommodation of the privacy interests of schoolchildren with the substantial need of teachers and administrators to maintain order in the schools does not require strict adherence to the requirement that searches be based on probable cause to believe that the subject of the search has violated or is violating the law. Rather, the legality of a search of a student should depend simply on the reasonableness, under all the circumstances, of the search.

Applying *T.L.O.*, in *Cornfield v. Consolidated High School Dist. No. 230*, 991 F.2d 1316 (7th Cir. 1993), the Court of Appeals upheld a strip search of a sixteen-year-old enrolled in a behavioral disorder program who was believed to be "crotching drugs" and in *Jenkins v. Talledega City Board of Education*, 115 F.3d 821 (11th Cir. 1997), the Court of Appeals held that a teacher

and school counselor had qualified immunity from liability for a strip search of two eight year olds to find $7 alleged to be stolen from a classmate.

Sometimes, searches of students are conducted not for purposes of discipline, but to determine if students have been abused by their parents or others. These searches may be conducted by social workers employed by the schools or child protective workers called to the schools. In several cases, the courts have held that students do not have a constitutional right to be free from questioning and examination of their bodies when school authorities, teachers or social workers have reasonable cause to believe the students have been abused and that school authorities, teachers and social workers have a qualified immunity from suits under 42 U.S.C. § 1983, challenging their actions. See, e.g., *Landstrom v. Jensen*, 892 F.2d 670 (7th Cir. 1988); *Tennenbaum v. Williams*, 862 F.Supp. 962 (E.D.N.Y. 1994). We will further discuss this issue in chapter 19.

EDUCATION OF DISABLED CHILDREN

As has been noted, after two courts ruled that disabled children had a right to an equal educational opportunity, Congress enacted the Individuals with Disabilities Education Act (IDEA), 20 U.S.C. § 1400, *et seq.*[2] The IDEA was substantially revised in 1997, by Public Law 105-17, based on the following Congressional

---

2. The IDEA was originally known as the Education of the Handicapped Act (EHA) and later as the Education for all Handicapped Children Act (EAHCA) and is referred to by either of these names in earlier cases.

findings and statement of purposes, which are set forth at 20 U.S.C. § 1400 (c) and (d):

Congress finds as follows:

(1) Disability is a natural part of the human experience and in no way diminishes the right of individuals to participate in or contribute to society. Improving educational results for children with disabilities is an essential element of our national policy of ensuring equality of opportunity, full participation, independent living, and economic self-sufficiency for individuals with disabilities.

(2) Before the date of the enactment of the Education for All Handicapped Children Act of 1975 (Public Law 94–142)—

(A) the special educational needs of children with disabilities were not being fully met;

(B) more than one-half of the children with disabilities in the United States did not receive appropriate educational services that would enable such children to have full equality of opportunity;

(C) 1,000,000 of the children with disabilities in the United States were excluded entirely from the public school system and did not go through the educational process with their peers;

(D) there were many children with disabilities throughout the United States participating in regular school programs whose disabilities prevented such children from having a successful educational experience because their disabilities were undetected; and

(E) because of the lack of adequate services within the public school system, families were often forced to find services outside the public school system, often at great distance from their residence and at their own expense.

(3) Since the enactment and implementation of the Education for All Handicapped Children Act of 1975, this chapter has been successful in ensuring children with disabilities and the families of such children access to a free appropriate public education and in improving educational results for children with disabilities.

(4) However, the implementation of this chapter has been impeded by low expectations, and an insufficient focus on applying replicable research on proven methods of teaching and learning for children with disabilities.

(5) Over 20 years of research and experience has demonstrated that the education of children with disabilities can be made more effective by—

(A) having high expectations for such children and ensuring their access in the general curriculum to the maximum extent possible;

(B) strengthening the role of parents and ensuring that families of such children have meaningful opportunities to participate in the education of their children at school and at home;

(C) coordinating this chapter with other local, educational service agency, State, and Federal school improvement efforts in order to ensure that such children benefit from such efforts and that special education can become a service for such children rather than a place where they are sent;

(D) providing appropriate special education and related services and aids and supports in the regular classroom to such children, whenever appropriate;

(E) supporting high-quality, intensive professional development for all personnel who work with such children in order to ensure that they have the skills and knowledge necessary to enable them—

(i) to meet developmental goals and, to the maximum extent possible, those challenging expectations that have been established for all children; and

(ii) to be prepared to lead productive, independent, adult lives, to the maximum extent possible;

(F) providing incentives for whole-school approaches and pre-referral intervention to reduce the need to label children as disabled in order to address their learning needs; and

(G) focusing resources on teaching and learning while reducing paperwork and requirements that do not assist in improving educational results.

(6) While States, local educational agencies, and educational service agencies are responsible for providing an education for all children with disabilities, it is in the national interest that the Federal Government have a role in assisting State and local efforts to educate children with disabilities in order to improve results for such children and to ensure equal protection of the law.

(7)(A) The Federal Government must be responsive to the growing needs of an increasingly more diverse society. A more equitable allocation if resources is essential for the Federal Government to meet its responsibility to provide an equal educational opportunity for all individuals.

(B) America's racial profile is rapidly changing. Between 1980 and 1990, the rate of increase in the population for white Americans was 6 percent, while the rate of increase for racial and ethnic minorities was much higher: 53 percent for Hispanics, 13.2 percent for African–Americans, and 107.8 percent for Asians.

(C) By the year 2000, this Nation will have 275,000,000 people, nearly one of every three of whom will be either African–American, Hispanic, Asian–American, or American Indian.

(D) Taken together as a group, minority children are comprising an ever larger percentage of public school students. Large-city school populations are overwhelmingly minority, for example: for fall 1993, the figure for Miami was 84 percent; Chicago, 89 percent; Philadelphia, 78 percent; Baltimore, 84 percent; Houston, 88 percent; and Los Angeles, 88 percent.

(E) Recruitment efforts within special education must focus on bringing larger numbers of minorities into the profession in order to provide appropriate practitioner knowledge, role models, and sufficient manpower to address the clearly changing demography of special education.

(F) The limited English proficient population is the fastest growing in our Nation, and the growth is occurring in many parts of our Nation. In the Nation's 2 largest school districts, limited English proficient students make up almost half of all students initially entering school at the kindergarten level. Studies have documented apparent discrepancies in the levels of referral and placement of limited English proficient children in special education. The Department of Education has found that services provided to limited English proficient students often do not respond primarily to the pupil's academic needs. These trends pose special challenges for special education in the referral, assessment, and services for our Nation's students from non-English language backgrounds.

(8)(A) Greater efforts are needed to prevent the intensification of problems connected with mislabeling and high dropout rates among minority children with disabilities.

(B) More minority children continue to be served in special education than would be expected from the percentage of minority students in the general school population.

(C) Poor African–American children are 2.3 times more likely to be identified by their teacher as having mental retardation than their white counterpart.

(D) Although African–Americans represent 16 percent of elementary and secondary enrollments, they constitute 21 percent of total enrollments in special education.

(E) The drop-out rate is 68 percent higher for minorities than for whites.

(F) More than 50 percent of minority students in large cities drop out of school.

(9)(A) The opportunity for full participation in awards for grants and contracts; boards of organizations receiving funds under this chapter; and peer review panels; and training of professionals in the area of special education by minority individuals, organizations, and historically black colleges and universities is essential if we are to obtain greater success in the education of minority children with disabilities.

(B) In 1993, of the 915,000 college and university professors, 4.9 percent were African–American and 2.4 percent were Hispanic. Of the 2,940,000 teachers, prekindergarten through high school, 6.8 percent were African–American and 4.1 percent were Hispanic.

(C) Students from minority groups comprise more than 50 percent of K–12 public school enrollment in seven States yet minority enrollment in teacher training programs is less than 15 percent in all but six States.

(D) As the number of African–American and Hispanic students in special education increases, the number of minority teachers and related service personnel produced in our colleges and universities continues to decrease.

(E) Ten years ago, 12 percent of the United States teaching force in public elementary and secondary schools were members of a minority group. Minorities comprised 21 percent of the national population at that time and were clearly underrepresented then among employed teachers. Today, the elementary and secondary teaching force is 13 percent minority, while one-third of the students in public schools are minority children.

(F) As recently as 1991, historically black colleges and universities enrolled 44 percent of the African–American teacher trainees in the Nation. However, in 1993, historically black colleges and universities received only 4 percent of the discretionary funds for special education and related services personnel training under this chapter.

(G) While African–American students constitute 28 percent of total enrollment in special education, only 11.2 percent of individuals enrolled in preservice training programs for special education are African–American.

(H) In 1986–87, of the degrees conferred in education at the B.A., M.A., and Ph.D. levels, only 6, 8, and 8 percent, respectively, were awarded to African–American or Hispanic students.

(10) Minorities and underserved persons are socially disadvantaged because of the lack of opportunities in training and educational programs, undergirded by the practices in the private sector that impede their full participation in the mainstream of society.

The purposes of this chapter are—

(1)(A) to ensure that all children with disabilities have available to them a free appropriate public education that emphasizes special education and related services designed to meet their unique needs and prepare them for employment and independent living;

(B) to ensure that the rights of children with disabilities and parents of such children are protected; and

(C) to assist States, localities, educational service agencies, and Federal agencies to provide for the education of all children with disabilities;

(2) to assist States in the implementation of a statewide, comprehensive, coordinated, multidisciplinary, interagency system of early intervention services for infants and toddlers with disabilities and their families;

(3) to ensure that educators and parents have the necessary tools to improve educational results for children with disabilities by supporting systemic-change activities; coordinated research and personnel preparation; coordinated technical assistance, dissemination, and support; and technology development and media services; and

(4) to assess, and ensure the effectiveness of, efforts to educate children with disabilities.

The 1997 revisions did not change the essential provisions of the IDEA. Basically, the IDEA provides and has always provided that a State wanting to receive federal financial assistance under the Act for schools in the State must submit a plan to the federal government for approval demonstrating that local school districts will provide disabled children with an "appropriate" education and "related services" at no cost to the parents in the "least restrictive" appropriate environment and in accordance with an "individualized education program" (IEP) prepared by appropriate professionals with parental input. The IDEA further establishes the procedures that school districts must follow in identifying disabled children and preparing an IEP and the procedures that parents may follow if they object to an IEP or to a school district's refusal to recognize a child as requiring an IEP. These latter procedures include informal conferences, formal administrative hearings and judicial review.

Because the IDEA has always required that qualified professionals prepare IEPs and states that disabled children are entitled to "related services," *expressly including social work and counseling,* most school districts now employ social workers. Because a major function of school social workers is working with disabled children and because many other social workers work with disabled children or their parents, we will review the IDEA and some of the many questions of interpretation it has raised and still raises in depth below.

While we focus on the IDEA because of its important procedural protections and administrative apparatus, Section 504 and the ADA also provide a vehicle to ensure that disabled children receive an equal educational opportunity and that schools accomodate to their needs. Section 504 provides that "[n]o otherwise

qualified individual with a disability in the United States . . . shall, solely by reason of her or his disability, be excluded from the participation in, be denied the benefit of, or be subjected to discrimination under any program or activity receiving Federal financial assistance." 29 U.S.C. § 794. The ADA similarly provides that "no qualified individual with a disability shall, by reason of such disability, be excluded from participation in or be denied the benefits of the services, programs, or activities of a public entity, or be subjected to discrimination by any such entity." 42 U.S.C. § 12132.

Parents may use Section 504 and the ADA to sue schools if they believe that their children have been discriminated against because of a disability or that the schools have not accomodated their children. However, parents must first follow the procedures in the IDEA, that is, exhaust the IDEA administrative remedies.[3]

The Definition of *Disability*

The first question posed by the IDEA is who is disabled. The IDEA defines disabled children as children with "mental retardation, hearing impairments (including deafness), speech or language impairments, visual impairments (including blindness), serious emotional disturbance . . . , orthopedic impairments, autism, traumatic brain injury, other health impairments or specific learning disabilities." 20 U.S.C. § 1401(a)(3)(A)(i).

---

3. See, e.g., *Babicz v. School B. of Broward County,* 135 F. 3d 1420 (11th Cir. 1998); *Neil F. v. Board of Educ. of Skokie School District 68,* 98 F.3d 989 (7th Cir. 1996); and *Hope v. Cortines,* 69 F.3d 687 (2d Cir. 1995).

But it is not enough simply to have one of these disabilities. A child must also "need" special education and related services "by reason thereof." *Id.* at (ii). In other words, the child's disability must interfere with learning or be an educational disability. Thus, as has been noted, a child with AIDS who has no symptoms of the disease which interfere with learning may not be considered disabled under the IDEA.

It is also not enough for a child to be educationally disabled solely because of social causes or cultural background. The definition of disability has been interpreted to require a physical or mental condition. However, social causes or cultural background could lead to such a condition, that is, a diagnosable educational disability.

The limited definition of *disability* in the IDEA should be contrasted with the broad definition in the ADA, which the Supreme Court observed in *Bragdon v. Abbott, supra*, was "drawn almost verbatim from the definition of 'handicapped individual' in [Section 504] and the definition of 'handicap' contained in the Fair Housing Amendments Act of 1988, 42 U.S.C. § 3602(h)(1)." The ADA defines *disability* as: "(A) a physical or mental impairment that substantially limits one or more of the major life activities of such individual; (B) a record of such an impairment; or (C) being regarded as having such impairment." § 12102(2).

In deciding that AIDS was a disability covered by the ADA in *Bragdon v. Abbott, supra*, the Supreme Court followed a three-step analysis.

> First, we consider whether respondent's HIV infection was a physical impairment. Second,

we identify the life activity upon which respondent relies (reproduction and child bearing) and determine whether it constitutes a major life activity under the ADA. Third, tying the two statutory phrases together, we ask whether the impairment substantially limited the major life activity. In construing the statute, we are informed by interpretations of parallel definitions in previous statutes and the views of various administrative agencies which have faced this interpretive question.

The Definition of *Appropriate*

Perhaps the most serious question posed by the IDEA is what is the "appropriate" education that must be provided to a disabled child. The Supreme Court answered this and other important questions in *Board of Education of the Hendrick Hudson Central School District v. Rowley*, 458 U.S. 176 (1982). Several excerpts from this case are included in the discussion below, but you may want to read the whole opinion, not only because of the questions it answers, but also because of its thorough discussion of the history and essential provisions of the previous version of IDEA.

As explained by the Supreme Court, the case

> arose in connection with the education of Amy Rowley, a deaf student. . . . Amy has minimal residual hearing and is an excellent lipreader. As required by the Act, an IEP was prepared for Amy during the fall of her first-grade year. The IEP provided that Amy should be educated in a regular classroom at [the school where she went to kindergarten], should continue to use the FM hearing aid [she was provided in kindergarten], and should receive instruction from a tutor for the deaf for one hour each day and from a speech therapist for three hours each week. The Row-

leys agreed with parts of the IEP, but insisted that Amy also be provided a qualified sign-language interpreter in all her academic classes in lieu of the assistance proposed in other parts of the IEP.

Amy's school had determined that an interpreter was not necessary and refused to provide one. Her parents pursued the administrative remedies set forth in the IDEA without success and then sued the school district. The federal district court found that Amy "performs better than the average child in her class and is advancing easily from grade to grade," but that she "understands considerably less of what goes on in class than she could if she were not deaf" and, thus, "is not learning as much, or performing as well academically, as she would without her handicap." According to the Supreme Court: "This disparity between Amy's achievement and her potential led the [district] court to decide that she was not receiving a 'free appropriate public education,' which the court defined as an opportunity to achieve [her] full potential commensurate with the opportunity provided to other children."

The Supreme Court disagreed with this definition of "free, appropriate public education," observing that:

> According to the definitions contained in the Act, a 'free appropriate public education' consists of educational instruction specially designed to meet the unique needs of the handicapped child, supported by such services as are necessary to permit the child 'to benefit' from the instruction. Almost as a checklist for adequacy under the Act, the definition also requires that such instruction and services be provided at public expense and under public supervision, meet the State's educational standards, approximate the grade levels used in the State's regular education, and comport with

the child's IEP. Thus, if personalized instruction is being provided with sufficient supportive services to permit the child to benefit from the instruction, and the other items on the definitional checklist are satisfied, the child is receiving a 'free appropriate public education' as defined by the Act."

The Court further observed that there was no requirement anywhere in the Act or in its legislative history "that States maximize the potential of handicapped children" or even to provide disabled children with an "equal educational opportunity." While the Court recognized that the legislative history of the Act spoke of the need for disabled children to be provided with "a basic floor of opportunity consistent with equal protection," the Court also observed that "neither the Act nor its history persuasively demonstrates that Congress thought that equal protection required anything more than equal access." On this point, the Court reasoned:

> The educational opportunities provided by our public school systems undoubtedly differ from student to student, depending upon a myriad of factors that might affect a particular student's ability to assimilate information presented in the classroom. The requirement that States provide equal educational opportunities would thus seem to present an entirely unworkable standard requiring impossible measurements and comparisons. Similarly, furnishing handicapped children with only such services as are available to nonhandicapped children would in all probability fall short of the statutory requirement of free appropriate public education; to require, on the other hand, the furnishing of every special service necessary to maximize each handicapped child's potential is, we think, further than Congress intended to go. Thus to speak in terms of equal services in one instance gives less than what is required by the Act and in another instance more. The theme of the Act is free appropriate public education, a

phrase which is too complex to be captured by the word equal whether one is speaking of opportunities or services.

Further, the Court noted that maximizing the potential of each disabled child commensurate with the opportunity provided nondisabled children might be a "desirable" goal, but "it is not the standard that Congress imposed upon States which receive funding under the Act. Rather, Congress sought primarily to identify and evaluate handicapped children, and to provide them with access to a free public education."

But, while Congress may have primarily intended that disabled children be provided with access to education, the Court also observed:

> Implicit in the congressional purpose of providing access to a free appropriate public education is the requirement that the education to which access is provided be sufficient to confer some educational benefit upon the handicapped child. It would do little good for Congress to spend millions of dollars in providing access to a public education only to have the handicapped child receive no benefit from that education. The statutory definition of free appropriate public education, in addition to requiring that States provide each child with specially designed instruction, expressly requires the provision of such . . . supportive services . . . as may be required to assist a handicapped child to benefit from special education. **We therefore conclude that the basic floor of opportunity provided by the Act consists of access to specialized instruction and related services which are individually designed to provide educational benefit to the handicapped child.**

In conclusion, the Court stated:

> When the language of the Act and its legislative history are considered together, the re-

quirements imposed by Congress become tolerably clear. Insofar as a State is required to provide a handicapped child with a free appropriate public education, we hold that it satisfies this requirement by providing **personalized instruction with sufficient support services to permit the child to benefit educationally from that instruction.** In addition, the IEP, and therefore the personalized instruction, should be formulated in accordance with the requirements of the Act and, if the child is being educated in the regular classrooms of the public education system, should be reasonably calculated to enable the child to achieve passing marks and advance from grade to grade.

You should note that the IDEA requires that the education provided to a disabled child not only must be "appropriate," but also must be "free." In other words, as the Court stated in *Rowley*, the required personalized instruction and supportive services must be provided "at public expense." This means that if the most appropriate education is in a private school, the school district must pay the tuition at the private school regardless of the parents' wealth. After all, public education is provided free regardless of wealth. Moreover, the Supreme Court held in *Burlington School Committee v. Department of Education*, 471 U.S. 359 (1985), that when parents pay for private special education they believe is necessary for their child while they are in the process of protesting an IEP that does not provide for this education, a court may order the school district to reimburse the parents if the court has determined that the IEP was wrong and the school district should have provided the private special education for the child. The Court stated:

> In a case where a court determines that a private placement desired by the parents was proper under the EAHCA and that an IEP call-

ing for placement in a public school was inappropriate, it seems clear beyond cavil that [the provision in the Act, allowing a court to order] appropriate relief would include a prospective injunction directing the school officials to develop and implement at public expense an IEP placing the child in a private school. If the administrative and judicial review under the Act could be completed in a matter of weeks, rather than years, it would be difficult to imagine a case in which such prospective injunctive relief would not be sufficient. As this case so vividly demonstrates, however, the review process is ponderous. [The Supreme Court decision was rendered six years after the child in question was placed in a private school by his parents. The six-year review process included numerous administrative hearings, numerous trial court hearings, including a four-day trial, and two Court of Appeals decisions.] A final judicial decision on the merits of an IEP will in most instances come a year or more after the school term covered by that IEP has passed. In the meantime, the parents who disagree with the proposed IEP are faced with a choice: go along with the IEP to the detriment of their child if it turns out to be inappropriate or pay for what they consider to be the appropriate placement. If they choose the latter course, which conscientious parents who have adequate means and who are reasonably confident of their assessment normally would, it would be an empty victory to have a court tell them several years later that they were right but that these expenditures could not in a proper case be reimbursed by the school officials. If that were the case, the child's right to a free appropriate public education, the parents' right to participate fully in developing a proper IEP, and all of the procedural safeguards [in the Act] would be less than complete. Because Congress undoubtedly did not intend this result, we are confident that by empowering the court to grant appropriate relief Congress meant to include retroactive reimbursement to parents as an available remedy in a proper case.

The Court was apparently correct. The IDEA now expressly provides for reimbursement if parents enroll their children

in private schools pending resolution of a dispute with a school district and "if the court or hearing officer finds that the [school district] has not made a free appropriate public education available to the child in a timely manner prior to that enrollment." 20 U.S.C. § 1412(a)(10)(c). However, reimbursement may not be for the full tuition if a court determines that the tuition is excessive or unreasonable. *Florence County School District Four v. Carter*, 510 U.S. 7 (1993).

The Definition of *Related Services*

As you saw, *Rowley* observed that, as part of a free appropriate education for disabled children, in addition to instructional services, schools are mandated to provide "related services," which the Court defined as individually designed supportive services necessary for a disabled child to achieve an educational benefit. The statutory definition also includes a nonexclusive list of such services. Specifically, the IDEA defines "related services" as:

> transportation, and such developmental, corrective and other supportive services (including speech-language pathology and audiology services, psychological services, physical and occupational therapy, recreation, including therapeutic recreation, social work services, counseling, orientation and mobility services, and medical services, except that such medical services shall be for diagnostic and evaluation purposes only) as may be required to assist a child with a disability to benefit from special education . . . 20 U.S.C. § 1401(a) (22).

Under this definition, it is clear that "social work services" must be provided if they are necessary for a disabled child to benefit from his or her education, but "medical services" need not be provided even if they are necessary for a child to attend school. Thus, it is important to answer the question what supportive services should be characterized as medical services. In *Irving v. Tatro*, 468 U.S. 883 (1984), the Supreme Court accepted the federal government's narrow definition of medical services and held that clear intermittent catheterization (CIC) was a related service that must be provided to Amber, an eight-year-old girl with spinal bifida, by her school. After observing that CIC was a simple procedure that could be done by anyone with a minimal amount of training (although Amber could not do it for herself) and that Amber could not stay in school unless CIC were done at least once during the school day, the Court concluded:

> CIC is a supportive servic[e] . . . required to assist a handicapped child to benefit from special education. It is clear on this record that, without having CIC services available during the school day, Amber cannot attend school and thereby benefit from special education. CIC services therefore fall squarely within the definition of a supportive service.
>
> [P]rovision of CIC is not a [medical service], which a school is required to provide only for purposes of diagnosis or evaluation. [T]he regulations of the Department of Education, which are entitled to deference . . . [,] define "related services" for handicapped children to include "school health services," which are defined in turn as "services provided by a qualified school nurse or other qualified person." "Medical services" are defined as "services provided by a licensed physician." This definition of "medical services" is a reasonable interpretation of congressional intent.
>
> Congress plainly required schools to hire various specially trained personnel to help handicapped children, such as "trained occu-

pational therapists, speech therapists, psychologists, social workers and other appropriately trained personnel." School nurses have long been a part of the educational system, and the Secretary could therefore reasonably conclude that school nursing services are not the sort of burden that Congress intended to exclude as a "medical service." By limiting the "medical services" exclusion to the services of a physician or hospital, both far more expensive, the Secretary has given a permissible construction to the provision.

> In [the school district's] view, CIC is a medical service, even though it may be provided by a nurse or trained layperson [because it may only be used] in accordance with a physician's prescription and under a physician's ultimate supervision. Aside from conflicting with the Secretary's reasonable interpretation of congressional intent, however, such a rule would be anomalous. Nurses in [Amber's] school district are authorized to dispense oral medications and administer emergency injections in accordance with a physician's prescription. This kind of service for nonhandicapped children is difficult to distinguish from the provision of CIC to the handicapped. It would be strange indeed if Congress, in attempting to extend special services to handicapped children, were unwilling to guarantee them services of a kind that are routinely provided to the nonhandicapped.

Psychiatric services performed by a physician rather than a psychologist or nonmedically trained psychotherapist and psychiatric hospitalization may, however, be considered medical services that do not have to be provided. See *Darlene L. v. Illinois State Board of Education*, 568 F.Supp. 1340 (N.D.Ill. 1983), holding that psychiatric hospitalization was a medical service that need not be provided, but see also, *Gary B. v. Cronin*, 542 F.Supp. 102 (N.D.Ill. 1980), holding that psychotherapy provided in a residential setting may be a related service that must be provided.

You should be aware that, just as a private education must be provided at no cost to parents if an IEP indicates the private education is necessary, any required related services must be provided at no cost. For example, Amy Rowley's school district would have had to pay the full cost of a sign language interpreter if the Supreme Court had held such an interpreter was required for her to benefit from her education. Moreover, a school district may be required to pay for supportive services for a student in a private school and, if so required, can pay for the services without violating the Establishment Clause of the Constitution even if the private school is religious. For example, *Zobrest v. Catalina Foothills School District*, 500 U.S. 1 (1993), held that a school district was required to pay for a sign language interpreter for a deaf student in a Catholic school.

The Setting for the Education of Disabled Children

Questions have arisen related to the setting for education of children with disabilities. The IDEA requires education in the **least restrictive environment**, which means that, as a condition of receiving federal funds, State plans must provide,

> to the maximum extent appropriate, children with disabilities, including children in public or private institutions or other care facilities, are educated with children who are not disabled and . . . special classes, separate schooling, or other removal of disabled children from the regular educational environment occurs only when the nature or severity of the disability is such that education in regular classes with the use of supplementary aids

and services cannot be achieved satisfactorily. 20 U.S.C. § 1412(a)(5).

Educating disabled children in regular classrooms is called **mainstreaming**. It has always been a major component of the IDEA, but it has always caused considerable controversy, both in theory and in practice, and its wisdom has been questioned.

Where mainstreaming is not appropriate, the IDEA provides that a placement is supposed to be as close as possible to a child's home. However, distant placements are often necessary. If a parent refuses a distant placement suggested in a proper IEP, should a school be relieved of all responsibility to provide a free appropriate education? If a distant placement is far cheaper than an equally appropriate local placement, which must be chosen?

There are other questions related to the cost of placements outside of the regular classroom. For example, if an appropriate private placement is very expensive, may a school district chose a less expensive but less appropriate placement?

Procedural Protections

The procedures that must be followed by school districts and the procedures available to parents to challenge school district actions are set forth in some detail in *Rowley*. Basically, local, state, and federal legislation and regulations all set forth procedures for developing an IEP and for making placements and providing services pursuant to it. All procedures established in regulations must be consistent with any authorizing statutes and with any regulations on a higher level. All procedures established in statutes must be consistent with any statutes and regulations at a higher level. All these procedures must be followed by school districts. As can be expected, construing all this legislation and these regulations and following all these procedures cause many problems for school districts. Nevertheless, *Rowley* stressed the importance of schools following the proper procedures. The Court stated:

> When the elaborate and highly specific procedural safeguards embodied in [the Act] are contrasted with the general and somewhat imprecise substantive admonitions contained in the Act, we think that the importance Congress attached to these procedural safeguards cannot be gainsaid. It seems to us no exaggeration to say that Congress placed every bit as much emphasis upon compliance with procedures giving parents and guardians a large measure of participation at every stage of the administrative process, as it did upon the measurement of the resulting IEP against a substantive standard. We think that the congressional emphasis upon full participation of concerned parties throughout the development of the IEP, as well as the requirements that state and local plans [for development of IEPs] be submitted to the [federal government] for approval, demonstrates the legislative conviction that adequate compliance with the procedures prescribed would in most cases assure much if not all of what Congress wished in the way of substantive content in an IEP.

Later, in *Burlington School Committee v. Dept. of Educ., supra*, the Court stressed the importance of the procedural safeguards accorded to parents. The Court stated that Congress recognized that school officials and parents would not always achieve consensus and that "in any disputes the school officials would have a natural advantage" and thus it "incorporated an elaborate set of what is labeled 'procedural safeguards' to insure the full participation of the parents and proper resolution of substantive disagreements." These procedural safeguards ensure that parents have a right: to notice; to participate in developing an IEP; to an administrative hearing to protest an IEP or the school's refusal to do an IEP; and to judicial review. Parents, however, do not have a right to any special burden of proof, to juries, or to appointed counsel (although they may retain counsel and may be awarded attorney's fees if they win in court).

Rowley answered the question of the role of courts in reviewing disputes over compliance with the IDEA. The Court noted:

> [T]he Act permits [a]ny party aggrieved by the findings and decision of the state administrative hearings to bring a civil action in . . . [a State or federal trial court.] The complaint, and therefore the civil action, may concern any matter relating to the identification, evaluation, or educational placement of the child, or the provision of a free appropriate public education to such child. In reviewing the complaint, the Act provides that a court shall receive the record of the [State] administrative proceedings, shall hear additional evidence at the request of a party, and, basing its decision on the preponderance of the evidence, shall grant such relief as the court determines is appropriate.

The Court further noted that, while the "parties disagree sharply over the meaning of these provisions," the statute as a whole makes clear that courts are not supposed to second-guess school officials or to consider questions of methodology or educational approaches. Rather, courts are merely supposed to ensure that all procedures are followed, that individualized attention is given to a child's needs, and that a child is given all that is required to realize an educational benefit. The Court reasoned:

[T]he provision that a reviewing court base its decision on the preponderance of the evidence is by no means an invitation to the courts to substitute their own notions of sound educational policy for those of the school authorities which they review. The very importance which Congress has attached to compliance with certain procedures in the preparation of an IEP would be frustrated if a court were permitted simply to set state decisions at nought. The fact that [the Act] requires that the reviewing court receive the records of the [state] administrative proceedings carries with it the implied requirement that due weight shall be given to these proceedings. And we find nothing in the Act to suggest that merely because Congress was rather sketchy in establishing substantive requirements, as opposed to procedural requirements, for the preparation of an IEP, it intended that reviewing courts should have a free hand to impose substantive standards of review which cannot be derived from the Act itself.

Therefore, a court's inquiry in suits brought under [the Act] is twofold. First, has the State complied with the procedures set forth in the Act? And second, is the individualized educational program developed through the Act's procedures reasonably calculated to enable the child to receive educational benefits? If these requirements are met, the State has complied with the obligations imposed by Congress and the courts can require no more.

In assuring that the requirements of the Act have been met, courts must be careful to avoid imposing their view of preferable educational methods upon the States. The primary responsibility for formulating the education to be accorded a handicapped child, and for choosing the educational method most suitable to the child's needs, was left by the Act to state and local educational agencies in cooperation with the parents or guardian of the child. The Act expressly charges States with the responsibility of "acquiring and disseminating to teachers and administrators of programs for handicapped children significant information derived from educational research, demonstration, and similar projects, and [of] adopting, where appropriate, promising educational practices and materials." In the face of such a clear statutory directive, it seems highly unlikely that Congress intended courts to overturn a State's choice of appropriate educational theories . . .

[In previous cases, we have stated] that courts lack the specialized knowledge and experience necessary to resolve persistent and difficult questions of educational policy. We think that Congress shared that view when it passed the Act. . . . Congress' intention was not that the Act displace the primacy of States in the field of education, but that States receive funds to assist them in extending their educational systems to the handicapped. Therefore, once a court determines that the requirements of the Act have been met, questions of methodology are for resolution by the States.

Entrusting a child's education to state and local agencies does not leave the child without protection. Congress sought to protect individual children by providing for parental involvement in the development of state plans and policies . . . and in the formulation of the child's individual educational program . . . As this very case demonstrates, parents and guardians will not lack ardor in seeking to ensure that handicapped children receive all of the benefits to which they are entitled by the Act.

Discipline

Finally, it has been questioned whether disabled students can be suspended or expelled because of troublesome behavior, and if so, under what circumstances.

The Supreme Court addressed these questions in *Honig v. Doe*, 484 U.S. 305 (1988). The two students in that case had been receiving special education services because they were considered emotionally disturbed. They were suspended from school indefinitely by their school district for violent and disruptive conduct related to their disabilities. The Court held that such indefinite suspensions were "changes of placement" under the IDEA and that if parents objected to the changes, the children could not be moved while the parents pursued their objections. It so ruled because of the so-called "stay-put" provision in the IDEA, which then provided and still provides that, during the pendency of any challenge to a school district decision, "unless the State or local educational agency and the parents or guardian otherwise agree, the child shall remain in the then current educational placement of such child." 20 U.S.C. § 1415(k).

The Court observed that the stay-put provision "does not leave educators hamstrung" and that consistently with the IDEA: 1) a school could suspend a child for up to ten days without the suspension being considered a change of placement; 2) a school was not precluded from using other "normal procedures for children who are endangering themselves or others," such as "the use of study carrels, timeouts, detentions, or the restriction of privileges"; and, 3) when a child was considered a danger, school officials could seek immediate injunctive relief in court without exhaust-

ing administrative remedies.[4] However, in adopting the stay-put provision,

> Congress very much meant to strip schools of the unilateral authority they had traditionally employed to exclude disabled students, particularly emotionally disturbed children, from school. In so doing, Congress did not leave school administrators powerless to deal with dangerous students; it did, however, deny school officials their former right to self-help, and directed that in the future the removal of disabled students could be accomplished only with the permission of parents or, as a last resort, the courts.

The ADA and Section 504 may impose further restrictions on discipline of disabled children. Disciplining children for behavior associated with their disability may be seen as a failure to accomodate the children and to provide an education in a nondiscriminatory fashion.

---

4. The IDEA now also allows a school to place a child in "an appropriate interim alternative educational setting for the same amount of time that a child without a disability would be subject to discipline, but not for more than forty-five days" if the child brought a weapon to school or possessed, used, sold or tried to sell drugs at school and if a "behavioral intervention plan" or "functional behavioral assessment" is prepared or a prior one modified, as necessary, to address "the behavior that resulted in the suspension."

SECTION IV

HEALTH AND
THE LAW

INTRODUCTION TO SECTION IV

In this section, we will look at the legal issues that arise in connection with the treatment and care of mentally ill, mentally and physically disabled, and physically ill adults and children. In other words, we will look at the law related to mental and physical health. Obviously, this law is important to the many social workers who work in hospitals or in institutions and agencies serving the ill and disabled, but it is also important to other social workers for several reasons.[1]

First, all social workers, wherever they may work, may be considered health care providers or part of a health care team. Indeed, social workers in private practice often seek to be characterized as mental health care providers so that their services may be covered by health insurance. As health care providers or as part of a health care system, social workers obviously must be aware of the law related to health.

Second, all social workers, whatever the nature of their practice, will have clients who face health problems or whose families face health problems. In fact, health problems are often the reason for initial or continuing contacts with social workers. Social workers may be the first or only professional to recognize the legal issues related to these health problems and the need for legal advice.

Third, the line is often blurred between the kind of social problems addressed by social workers and the health problems, particularly mental health problems, addressed by other health care providers. Social workers must be aware of the legal issues when their clients' problems cross or even approach this blurry line.

Finally, social workers can play many roles in relation to health care even if they do not consider themselves health care providers or do not work directly with health care providers. They may not be doing all they can do for their clients if they do not perform some of these roles; performing these roles may require an understanding of the legal issues related to health.

This section of the text will discuss the legal issues and the roles social workers may perform in relation to these legal issues. Specifically, chapter 14 discusses the law of importance to social workers

---

1. Before looking at these reasons, it should be noted that from this point forward in the book, the terms **mental disorders** and **mentally disabled** will be used interchangeably to include those who are mentally ill or who have developmental disabilities. The term **developmental disabilities** includes people with disabilities that manifest when they are in the developmental period of life; this term will be limited to include those who are mentally retarded. See 42 U.S.C. § 6001(5).

and the roles of social workers related to the treatment of the mentally disabled. Chapter 15 focuses on competency and guardianship of the mentally disabled, while chapter 16 addresses the care and treatment of the physically ill. In all three areas, one of social workers' roles, perhaps the most important role, is advising clients about their rights in relation to treatment and care for mental and physical illness and disability. Thus, the discussion focuses on these rights.

14

Commitment and Treatment of Persons with Mental Disabilities

This chapter will provide the social worker a broad understanding of constitutional parameters and laws that govern commitment and treatment of persons with mental disorders. State law governs commitment, but federal constitutional guarantees have played a large part in shaping commitment law. It is difficult to imagine a greater deprivation of liberties protected by the Fourteenth Amendment than either depriving an adult or child of his or her freedom through forced hospitalization, or compelling a person to undergo psychiatric treatment that could be mind-altering. Nevertheless, the State through its police powers and *parens patriae* authority, can deprive adults and children of liberties as long as the State complies with substantive and procedural due process guarantees. As we saw in chapter 8, *parens patriae* allows a State to intervene and protect those who cannot protect themselves, including minors and, as we shall see in this chapter, those with mental disorders. The police power allows a State to protect others from harm.

COMMITMENT AND TREATMENT OF THE MENTALLY ILL

Legal Requirements for Commitment

Commitment includes compulsory treatment, hospitalization, confinement, or other restriction of liberty based on a mental disability or temporary mental condition. A commitment can occur with or without court involvement depending on State law and the circumstances of the individual case. Many people assume commitment always involves court action and involuntary hospitalization. This assumption is false. In fact, individuals may be involuntarily hospitalized without a court hearing and may remain hospitalized for extended periods of time without court review; the commitment might be authorized by a mental health professional, not ordered by a judge. Individuals who are committed through court action might not be hospitalized. Instead, they might be ordered by the court to participate in an outpatient treatment program, or they might be placed by the court in the custody of relatives or other persons.

The standards used to determine who is subject to commitment for a mental illness are found in State statutes. The language differs considerably from State to State. Generally, however, a person may be committed only if he or she has a mental illness and, as a result of the illness is a danger to self or others or is so gravely disabled that the person is unable to care for himself or herself. In other words, two conditions must be satisfied for commitment: the presence of a mental illness and a danger due to the mental illness.

Terms typically used in the statutes such as *mental illness* or *mental disease* or *dangerous* are usually not defined or the definitions are stated in general terms. Nonetheless, these terms probably satisfy constitutional standards.

Moreover, State statutes may authorize mental health commitment for what is not commonly thought of as mental illness. In 1994, Kansas enacted the Sexually Violent Predator Act, which established procedures for the commitment of persons who are likely to engage "in predatory acts of sexual violence" due to a "mental abnormality" or a "personality disorder."

Kan. Stat. Ann. § 59-29a01, *et seq.* This Act was adopted because the legislature expressly found that the existing commitment statutes for the "mentally ill" would not cover persons with a "mental abnormality" and that such persons "generally have anti-social personality features which are unamenable to existing mental illness treatment modalities." § 59-29a01.

In *Kansas v. Hendricks,* 521 U.S. 346 (1997), the Supreme Court rejected a constitutional challenge to the Kansas Sexually Violent Predator Act, which authorized an involuntary civil commitment of an admitted pedophile with a long history of sexual molestation of children. This pedophile was scheduled for release from prison after serving a ten-year sentence for molesting two boys. The defendant in *Hendricks* argued that "mental illness" is a "prerequisite for civil commitment" and that "a 'mental abnormality' is *not* the equivalent of 'mental illness' because it is a term coined by the Kansas Legislature, rather than by the psychiatric community." The Court stated:

> [T]he term "mental illness" is devoid of any talismanic significance. Not only do psychiatrists disagree widely and frequently on what constitutes mental illness, but the Court itself has used a variety of expressions to describe the mental condition of those properly subject to civil confinement [including "emotionally disturbed," "incompentency," and "insanity"]. Indeed, we have never required State legislatures to adopt any particular nomenclature in drafting civil commitment statutes. Rather, we have traditionally left to legislatures the task of defining terms of a medical nature that have legal significance. As a consequence, the States have, over the years, developed numerous specialized terms to define mental health concepts. Often those definitions do not fit precisely with the definitions employed by the medical community. The legal definitions of "insanity" and "competency," for example, vary substantially from their psychiatric counterparts. Legal definitions, however, which must "take into account such issues as individual responsibility . . . and competency need not mirror those advanced by the medical profession."

The Court also addressed the issue of dangerousness, stating that the statute satisfied due process. It required a finding of future dangerousness, and linked that finding to the existence of a "mental abnormality" or "personality disorder" that made it difficult, if not impossible, for the person to control his dangerous behavior.

Twenty years earlier, in the landmark case *O'Connor v. Donaldson,* 422 U.S. 563 (1975), the Supreme Court addressed the "dangerousness" requirement in a civil commitment statute. *O'Connor* involved a challenge to the fifteen-year involuntary hospitalization of a man, Kenneth Donaldson, who was committed for "care, maintenance, and treatment" after having been found by a court on a petition of his father to be suffering from "paranoid schizophrenia." Despite Donaldson's many requests to be released over the years, the hospital staff refused to release him—although it had the power to do so. He was finally released after filing suit. The Supreme Court stated:

> The testimony at the trial demonstrated, without contradiction, that Donaldson had posed no danger to others during his long confinement, or indeed at any point in his life. There was no evidence that Donaldson had ever been suicidal or been thought likely to inflict injury upon himself . . . Donaldson could have earned his own living outside the hospital. He had done so for some 14 years before his commitment, and immediately upon his release he secured a responsible job . . . Furthermore,

Donaldson's frequent requests for release had been supported by responsible persons willing to provide him any care he might need on release.

The evidence showed that Donaldson's confinement was a simple regime of enforced custodial care, not a program designed to alleviate or cure his supposed illness. . . O'Connor [the hospital superintendent] described Donaldson's treatment as "milieu therapy." But witnesses from the hospital staff conceded that "milieu therapy" . . . was a euphemism for confinement in the "milieu" of a mental hospital. For substantial periods, Donaldson was simply kept in a large room that housed 60 patients, many of whom were under criminal commitment.

At the conclusion of the trial, the jury "found that Donaldson was neither dangerous to himself nor dangerous to others, and also found that, if mentally ill, Donaldson had not received treatment" and awarded him damages for the denial of his constitutional right to freedom. The Supreme Court agreed that Donaldson had been unconstitutionally confined. It stated:

> A finding of "mental illness" alone cannot justify a State's locking a person up against his will and keeping him indefinitely in simple custodial confinement. Assuming that that term can be given a reasonably precise content and that the "mentally ill" can be identified with reasonable accuracy, there is still no constitutional basis for confining such persons involuntarily if they are dangerous to no one and can live safely in freedom.
>
> May the State confine the mentally ill merely to ensure them a living standard superior to that they enjoy in the private community? That the State has a proper interest in providing care and assistance to the unfortunate goes without saying. But the mere presence of mental illness does not disqualify a person from preferring his home to the comforts of an institution. Moreover, while the State may arguably confine a person to save

him from harm, incarceration is rarely if ever a necessary condition for raising the living standards in those capable of surviving safely in freedom, on their own or with the help of family or friends.

> May the State fence in the harmless mentally ill solely to save its citizens from exposure to those whose ways are different? One might as well ask if the State, to avoid public unease, could incarcerate all who are physically unattractive or socially eccentric. Mere public intolerance or animosity cannot constitutionally justify the deprivation of a person's physical liberty.
>
> In short, a State cannot constitutionally confine without more a nondangerous individual who is capable of surviving safely in freedom by himself or with the help or willing and responsible family members or friends.

The phrase "without more" has been difficult to interpret. The Court specifically left open the constitutionality of committing a mentally ill but not dangerous person for treatment. Nevertheless, *O'Connor* has lead to the view expressed in *Hendricks* that commitment is allowed only when there is clear evidence that an individual is a danger to self or others. This, in turn, has led to questions concerning the ability of mental health practitioners to predict dangerousness and the ability and willingness of our society to address the needs of the nondangerous mentally ill through community-based services.

Determining whether someone is a danger to self or others under a State's commitment statute is an often-litigated point in commitment hearings and it is subject to varied professional opinions. The case *In re Matter of Boggs*, 136 Misc. 2d 1082, 522 N.Y.S. 2d 407, (1987), illustrates how a judge evaluated testimony from a number of professionals to determine whether a homeless woman in New

York City should be committed as a danger to self or others.

Billie Boggs was subject to involuntary confinement at Belleview Hospital in New York City. Prior to her confinement she called a sidewalk area on Second Avenue between 65th and 66th Streets her home. She received money by panhandling, which was used to purchase one meal a day comprised of a chicken cutlet, juice, milk, and ice cream. She kept warm next to an air vent that released hot air; the street was her bedroom, toilet, and living room. Selected excerpts reflect how the trial court decided whether Billie Boggs should be released from involuntary confinement.

Joyce Brown [Billie Boggs] comes from a middle class home in New Jersey and worked as a secretary for over ten years. However, in 1985 her sister found it necessary to take her to the East Orange General Hospital where she was placed in four point restraint and administered a massive dosage of Thorazine. Upon her release 15 days later on July 11, 1985, the discharge summary described her as "not psychotic" and "not dangerous." Sometime thereafter she came to New York.

Medical records from Metropolitan Hospital show Joyce Brown was brought by the Police to its emergency room in February, April, May, and September 1987. She was discharged each time as not dangerous.

The diagnosis of the hospital psychiatrists is that Joyce Brown suffers from schizophrenia paranoid type. They state she is delusional and suicidal, incapable of insight and incompetent to make decisions. Dr. Maeve Mahon, her treating physician, described her insight as "nil." In the judgment of the hospital psychiatrists she is incapable of caring for herself and should not be allowed to return to the street where her condition would deteriorate within days. They recommend continued hospitalization.

All [psychiatrists] cited her hostility, aggressiveness and abusive, obscene language as part of the basis for their diagnosis. One hospital psychiatrist, who had observed her on the street, testified she had on one occasion hurled at him a lunch he had offered her. These doctors fear her hostility may provoke others to cause her harm. None of the hospital doctors found any suicidal or homicidal ideation.

The diagnosis of the NYCLU psychiatrists is nearly at complete variance with that of the hospital psychiatrists . . . Dr. Gould discerned no delusional or psychotic behavior. He found her coherent, logical, and not tangential. He found her memory for recent and remote events good, her mood and affect appropriate, her abstract thinking good. He says she knows right from wrong. He saw no suicidal or homicidal ideation. He did find her judgment and insight "slightly impaired."

Regarding her objectionable toilet habits of urinating and defecating on the street, Dr. Gould said she [Joyce Brown] had no choice but to use the street since she was not allowed to enter the restroom of the neighborhood restaurant. To quote him, "It's not nice but it's not delusional."

When asked to predict whether Ms. Brown is likely to harm herself or others, all NYCLU psychiatrists answered in the negative. Dr. Gould, however, conceded that psychiatry is an uncertain science that yields no predictions of future behavior with certainty.

In short, the psychiatric experts do not agree. In fact, the doctors are nearly diametrically opposed in their assessment of Joyce Brown's mental condition and in their predictions as to whether she is likely to cause herself or others harm. Thus I derive little psychiatric guidance from them and therefore place great weight on the demeanor, behavior, and testimony of Joyce Brown herself.

On the stand she provided her own explanation of the street conduct upon which the hospital psychiatrists relied for the diagnosis of her . . .

She survives on the street by panhandling. She generally collects $8 to $10 a day, although she needs no more than $7 for a meal. She prefers to have no money on her person at night because it's dangerous.

With respect to her toilet habits, Ms. Brown explained, "I don't have access to toilet facilities." There being no public toilets except at Grand Central and Pennsylvania Stations, both of which are too distant from her post, she urinates and defecates on the street, though, she insists, never on herself, while covering herself with a coat. Photographs taken by a passerby offered into evidence confirm she covers herself.

Throughout her testimony, Ms. Brown was rational, logical, coherent. Her use of English, both in syntax and vocabulary, is very good and bespeaks an educated, intelligent person. She displayed a sense of humor, pride, a fierce independence of spirit, quick mental reflexes. She has, by her account, developed the needed skills for surviving on the street and it is evident she does not want her condition of homelessness to be treated or viewed as a target for insults, pity or condescension by the rest of society into whose conventional pattern of living she does not fit.

Involuntary retention of a patient for care and treatment in a hospital is warranted if the patient has a mental illness, which is likely to result in serious harm to herself or others . . .

Considering all the evidence and the contradictory expert psychiatric opinions offered, I find the proof neither clear nor convincing on the question of the petitioner's mental state. But even assuming arguendo that Joyce Brown is mentally ill, the inquiry does not stop here. The city must still prove that her mental condition is likely to result in serious harm to herself or others, as defined by statue and case law.

Is she suicidal? All seven psychiatrists agree her tests show no suicidal or homicidal ideation. The sole basis for concluding she wants to take her life is the charge she ran into moving traffic. After hearing Ms. Brown's version of the event and the NYCLU doctors, I find no reason to believe she is suicidal.

As to the likelihood she would cause herself serious bodily harm, no proof has been offered to substantiate the claim. The fear that she may provoke others to cause her harm is without substantiation in her past history.

There is no indication whatever that she ever caused risk of physical harm to others.

I now reach the question whether she has the ability to meet her essential needs of food, clothing and shelter. Can she provide herself with food? The answer is yes. She eats regularly and chooses a nutritional diet of chicken, milk, juice, and ice cream. She is not malnourished, the doctors all agree, and they all find her in good physical condition.

Can Joyce Brown provide herself with shelter? Housing in New York is an expensive commodity, so expensive that in this rich city many no longer can afford it and are driven to live on the street. Who among us is not familiar with the tattered, filthy, malodorous presence of the wretched homeless? The tired, poor, huddled masses need no longer be invited to our shores. Our society had created them at home. The blame and shame must attach to us, not to them. The predicament of Joyce Brown and the countless homeless raises questions of broad social, economic, political and moral implications not within the purview of this court.

Joyce Brown has been on the street nearly a year. She has survived, she is physically fit. She may indeed be a professional in her lifestyle. To the passerby seeing her lying on the street or defecating publicly she may seem deranged. "Bitter poverty" Juvenal wrote, "has no harder pang than that it makes men ridiculous." But how can anyone living in security and comfort even begin to imagine what is required to survive on the street? It cannot be reasoned that because Joyce Brown is homeless she is mentally ill. What must be proved is that because she is mentally ill she is incapable of providing herself with food, clothing and shelter. Yet, though homeless, she copes, she is fit, she survives.

Freedom, constitutionally guaranteed, is the right of all, no less of those who are mentally ill. Whether Joyce Brown is or is not mentally ill, it is my finding, after careful assessment of all the evidence that she is not unable to care for her essential needs. I am aware her mode of existence does not conform to conventional standards, that it is an offence to aesthetic senses. It is my hope that the plight she represents will also offend moral conscience and rouse it to action. There must be some civilized alternatives other than involuntary hospitalization or the street.

The petition is granted. An order releasing her will be signed by this court.

By the time the *Boggs* case reached New York's highest court, the case was dismissed as "moot" because the city had released Joyce Brown from custody. *In re Matter of Boggs,* 70 N.Y. 2d 972, 520 N.E. 2d 515, 525 N.Y.S. 2d 796 (1988).

The *Boggs* case illustrates that, in practice, whether a person satisfies the definitions of such legal standards as *mentally ill* and *dangerousness* is usually interpreted by mental health professionals; social workers often serve as mental health professionals that fulfill this very difficult role.

Procedural Requirements for Commitment

Whether a commitment involves institutionalization or a less restrictive alternative, a person who is committed loses liberty. This loss of liberty means that the person, often referred to as the **respondent** in court proceedings, is entitled to procedural due process protections in the commitment proceedings to ensure that the decision to commit is made fairly and accurately. Which procedural protections are afforded the respondent and the extent of the procedures, however, is generally defined by State law and varies from State to State. Several essential elements of procedural due process, which have been mandated by the courts or are set forth in statutes, are considered in this section.

Notice. Although notice is considered a fundamental element of due process, State commitment statutes may not require notice or may require only that minimal amounts of information be provided to the respondent. These statutes are based on the belief that the commitment procedure is designed to help a person with a mental illness and that the service of legal papers might only confuse and distress the person. In accordance with this belief, States may allow notice to be waived if there is a showing that it would distress the person.

Notice is usually required at several points in the commitment process, during an emergency involuntary hospitalization, and in advance of any court hearings. This notice must be given sufficiently in advance to allow the respondent time to seek assistance and prepare any response.

Although elements of notice may differ, they typically include a statement of the date, time, and place of any hearing, the alleged facts supporting commitment, the respondent's rights before and at the hearing—including any right to counsel—the names of examining physicians and all other persons who might testify in favor of commitment, and a summary of their proposed testimony. Much of this information can be provided by giving the respondent a copy of the petition and any accompanying certificates.

Any notice usually must be given personally to respondents and may additionally have to be provided to respondents' attorneys, guardians, or guardians *ad litem,* any legally responsible relatives, and, if they are currently in mental health facilities, the directors of the facilities.

Simply providing a written copy of information concerning a hearing or orally informing a person upon admission to a facility of his or her rights to a hearing is not effective notice. Notice is effective only if it is given in language understandable to the recipient and if it is given when the recipient is not overly agitated, confused, or medicated. Social workers employed by mental health facilities, because of their interaction with patients following admission, are in a position to assure that not only the respondent but also others who might assist the respondent receive effective notice.

Presence at the Hearing. States provide the respondent the right to be present at the hearing, but some States may allow the court to excuse the respondent's presence if it might be detrimental to the respondent's health. Medications may be useful to calm the respondent or stabilize the mental condition; however, they may also make the respondent appear dazed or limit the ability of the respondent to assist counsel.

Counsel. Respondents have a right to counsel in commitment proceedings under State laws. Counsel is typically provided either by the office that represents indigent criminal defendants, by an independent State agency, or by a private attorney appointed by the court. Respondents might also be provided a guardian *ad litem* to speak for the best interests of the respondent or to represent the respondent.

Trial by Jury. States may accord a jury trial to a respondent on demand. The jury may have less than twelve members and may not be required to render a unanimous verdict. In practice, requests for a jury trial are extremely rare.

Clear and Convincing Evidence. The Supreme Court in *Addington v. Texas,* 441 U.S. 418 (1979), established clear and convincing evidence as the minimum standard of proof in civil mental health commitment proceedings. The following excerpts from

Addington illustrate the Court's reasoning for establishing this standard of proof.

> In considering what standard should govern in a civil commitment proceeding, we must assess both the extent of the individual's interest in not being involuntarily confined indefinitely and the State's interest in committing the emotionally disturbed under a particular standard of proof. Moreover, we must be mindful that the function of legal process is to minimize the risk of erroneous decisions.
>
> At one time or another every person exhibits some abnormal behavior which might be perceived by some as symptomatic of a mental or emotional disorder, but which is in fact within a range of conduct that is generally acceptable. Obviously, such behavior is no basis for compelled treatment and surely none for confinement. However, there is the possible risk that a fact finder might decide to commit an individual based solely on a few isolated instances of unusual conduct. Loss of liberty calls for a showing that the individual suffers from something more serious than is demonstrated by idiosyncratic behavior. Increasing the burden of proof is one way to impress the fact finder with the importance of the decision and thereby perhaps to reduce the chances that inappropriate commitments will be ordered.
>
> The individual should not be asked to share equally with society the risk of error when the possible injury to the individual is significantly greater than any possible harm to the state. We conclude that the individual's interest in the outcome of a civil commitment proceeding is of such weight and gravity that due process requires the state to justify confinement by proof more substantial than a mere preponderance of the evidence.

However, the Court was not willing to mandate the "beyond a reasonable doubt" standard of proof used in criminal cases. It stated:

> The initial inquiry in a civil commitment proceeding is very different from the central issue in either a delinquency proceeding or a

criminal prosecution. In the latter cases the basic issue is a straightforward factual question—did the accused commit the act alleged? There may be factual issues to resolve in a commitment proceeding, but the factual aspects represent only the beginning of the inquiry. Whether the individual is mentally ill and dangerous to either himself or others and is in need of confined therapy turns on the meaning of the facts, which must be interpreted by expert psychiatrists and psychologists. Given the lack of certainty and the fallibility of psychiatric diagnosis, there is a serious question as to whether a state could ever prove beyond a reasonable doubt that an individual is both mentally ill and likely to be dangerous.

The Court, thus, turned to "a middle level of burden of proof that strikes a fair balance between the rights of the individual and the legitimate concerns of the state," noting that at the time twenty-five states used this standard of proof, defined as "clear and convincing evidence." As you can see from the opinion in *Addington,* there is nothing to prevent States from adopting a higher standard than clear and convincing evidence.

Review. As we have seen, a mentally ill person may not be involuntarily committed unless he or she presents a danger to self or others. Statutes typically provide that the need for continuing commitment be periodically reviewed by the court. The review occurs by limiting the length of time for which a person can be committed or by requiring review of commitment orders after a specified period of time. Moreover, persons who have been committed can generally request court reviews of their commitments at any point. Whether the court must consider each request for review and when a hearing must

be given on the committed persons' request depends on State law.

Commitment of Minors. As we saw in chapter 7, minors are, by definition, always under someone's care. Their parents and legally appointed guardians usually make decisions for them, including the decision to be admitted to a psychiatric facility. In *Parham v. J.R.,* 442 U.S. 584 (1979), the Supreme Court held that parents may commit their children for psychiatric care with only minimal procedural protections. The Court considered a due process challenge to the Georgia statute establishing commitment procedures for children under age eighteen. Like the statutes in most States, the Georgia statutes permitted a parent or guardian to apply for hospitalization for his or her child. The child could then be admitted by the hospital superintendent for observation. If the superintendent found evidence of mental illness and found that the child was suitable for treatment, the child could be admitted indefinitely, subject to the parent's or guardian's right to request discharge and the superintendent's duty to release a child who had recovered or no longer required hospitalization. The Court concluded the statutes were constitutional, and did not violate children's due process rights.

Our jurisprudence historically has reflected Western civilization concepts of the family as a unit with broad parental authority over minor children. Our cases have consistently followed that course; our constitutional system long ago rejected any notion that a child is "the mere creature of the State" and, on the contrary, asserted that parents generally "have the right, coupled with the high duty, to recognize and prepare [their children] for additional obligations." Surely this includes a "high duty" to recognize symptoms of illness and to seek and follow medical advice. The law's concept of the family rests on a presumption that parents possess what a child lacks in maturity, experience, and capacity for judgment required for making life's difficult decisions. More important, historically it has recognized that natural bonds of affection lead parents to act in the best interests of their children.

The Supreme Court assumed, however, that children did have a protectible liberty interest "not only in being free of unnecessary bodily restraints but also in not being labeled erroneously by some persons because of an improper decision by the state hospital superintendent." Thus, children were entitled to some due process protections before they could be committed. To determine what protections and to balance parents' rights against children's liberty interest, the Court considered and weighed the risk of error, the value of additional or different procedural safeguards, and the State's interest, including the fiscal and administrative burden that additional or different procedures would entail. The Court concluded that parents should "retain a substantial, if not the dominant, role in the decision, absent a finding of neglect or abuse, and that the traditional presumption that the parents act in the best interests of their child should apply." However, the Court also concluded that there was a substantial risk of error, and that the "child's rights and the nature of the commitment decision are such that parents cannot always have absolute and unreviewable discretion to decide whether to have a child institutionalized." Moreover, the State had certain interests, including "a significant interest in confining the use of its costly mental health facilities to cases of genuine need"; a competing but also significant interest "in not imposing unnecessary procedural obstacles that may discourage the mentally ill or their families from seeking needed psychiatric assistance"; and a "genuine interest in allocating priority to the diagnosis and treatment of patients . . . rather than to time-consuming procedur[es]." Balancing all of these considerations, the Court held that at a minimum, parents' "plenary authority" should be "subject to a physician's independent examination and medical judgment" and there should be other limited procedural protections that would "adequately" protect

the child's constitutional rights by reducing risks of error without unduly trenching on traditional parental authority and without undercutting efforts to further the legitimate interests of both the state and the patient that are served by voluntary commitments. We conclude that the risk of error inherent in the parental decision to have a child institutionalized for mental health care is sufficiently great that some kind of inquiry should be made by a "neutral factfinder" to determine whether the statutory requirements for admission are satisfied. That inquiry must carefully probe the child's background using all available sources, including, but not limited to, parents, school, and other social agencies. Of course, the review must also include an interview with the child. It is necessary that the decisionmaker have the authority to refuse to admit any child who does not satisfy the medical standards for admission. Finally, it is necessary that the child's continuing need for commitment be reviewed periodically by a similarly independent procedure. We are satisfied that such procedures will protect the child from an erroneous admission decision in a way that neither unduly burdens the state nor inhibits parental decisions to seek state help.

[It is not necessary that] the neutral and detached trier of fact be law trained or a judicial or administrative officer. [A] staff physician will suffice, so long as he or she is free to evaluate independently the child's mental and emotional condition and need for treatment. It is not necessary that the deciding physician conduct a formal or quasi-formal hearing. A state is free to require such a hearing, but due process is not violated by use of informal traditional medical investigative techniques. [W]e do not undertake to outline with specificity precisely what this investigation must involve. We do no more than emphasize that the decision should represent an independent judgment of what the child requires and that all sources of information that are traditionally relied on by physicians and behavioral specialists should be consulted.

Although we acknowledge the fallibility of medical and psychiatric diagnosis, . . . we do not accept the notion that the shortcomings of specialists can always be avoided by shifting the decision from a trained specialist using the traditional tools of medical science to an untrained judge or administrative hearing officer after a judicial-type hearing. Even after a hearing, the nonspecialist decisionmaker must make a medical-psychiatric decision. Common human experience and scholarly opinions suggest that the supposed protections of an adversary proceeding to determine the appropriateness of medical decisions for the commitment and treatment of mental and emotional illness may well be more illusory than real.

By expressing some confidence in the medical decisionmaking process, we are by no means suggesting it is error free. [But] that there may be risks of error in the process affords no rational predicate for holding unconstitutional an entire statutory and administrative scheme that is generally followed in more than 30 states. In general, we are satisfied that an independent medical decisionmaking process, which includes the thorough psychiatric investigation described earlier, followed by additional periodic review of a child's condition, will protect children who should not be admitted; we do not believe the risks of error in that process would be significantly reduced by a more formal, judicial-type hearing.

Even though the Supreme Court in *Parham* approved a statute offering few

procedural protections for minors, a State may still offer greater procedural protections. The Supreme Court in *Parham* only set forth the minimum required. In some States, minors are entitled to a full judicial hearing before they can be admitted to mental hospitals over their objections.

One should note that *Parham* applies to children whose parents or guardians seek to admit them to state hospitals, not private psychiatric facilities. While the decision might be interpreted to apply to all psychiatric admissions, the Court paid particular attention to the use of public facilities.

Consenting to Voluntary Treatment

Due process protections clearly apply to the involuntarily committed person with a mental illness. A more difficult situation may arise when a person is purportedly voluntarily admitted to a State mental health treatment facility but, in fact, lacks capacity to consent to such a voluntary admission and is subject to deprivation of liberty and subsequent treatment without consent. Such a case was confronted by the Supreme Court in *Zinermon v. Burch,* 494 U.S. 113 (1990). Excerpts of this case indicate what happened.

On December 7, 1981, Burch was found wandering along a Florida highway, appearing to be hurt and disoriented. He was taken to Apalachee Community Mental Health Services (ACMHS) in Tallahassee. ACMHS is a private mental health care facility designated by the State to receive patients suffering from mental illness. Its staff in their evaluation forms stated that, upon his arrival at ACMHS, Burch was hallucinating, confused and psychotic and believed he was "in heaven." His face and chest were bruised and bloodied, suggesting that he had fallen or had been attacked. Burch was asked to sign forms giving his consent to admission and treatment. He did so. He remained at ACMHS for three days, during which time the facility's staff diagnosed his condition as paranoid schizophrenia and gave him psychotropic medication. On December 10, the staff found that Burch was "in need of longer-term stabilization," and referred him to FSH, a public hospital owned and operated by the State as a mental health treatment facility. Later that day, Burch signed forms requesting admission and authorizing treatment at FSH. He was then taken to FSH by a county sheriff.

Upon his arrival at FSH, Burch signed other forms for voluntary admission and treatment. One form, entitled "Request for Voluntary Admission," recited that the patient requests admission for "observation, diagnosis, care and treatment of [my] mental condition," and that the patient, if admitted, agrees "to accept such treatment as may be prescribed by members of the medical and psychiatric staff in accordance with the provisions of expressed and informed consent." Two to the petitioners, Janet V. Potter and Marjorie R. Parker, sighed this form as witnesses. Potter is an accredited records technician; Parker's job title does not appear on the form.

On December 23, Burch signed a form entitled "Authorization for Treatment." This form stated that he authorized "the professional staff of [FSH] to administer treatment, except electroconvulsive treatment"; that he had been informed of "the purpose of treatment; common side effects thereof; alternative treatment modalities; approximate length of care"; and of his power to revoke consent to treatment; and that he had read and fully understood the Authorization. Petitioner Zinermon, a staff physician at FSH, sighed the form as the witness.

On December 19, Doctor Zinermon wrote a "progress note" indicating that Bruch was "refusing to cooperate," would not answer questions, "appears distressed and confused," and "related that medication has been helpful." A nursing assessment form dated December 11 stated that Burch was confused and unable to state the reason for his hospitalization and

still believed that "[t]his is heaven." Petitioner Zinermon on December 29 made a further report on Burch's condition, staring that, on admission, Burch had been "disoriented, semi-mute, confused and bizarre in appearance and thought," "not cooperative to the initial interview," and "extremely psychotic, appeared to be paranoid and hallucinating." The doctor's report also stated that Burch remained disoriented, delusional, and psychotic.

Burch remained at FSH until May 7, 1982, five moths after his initial admission to ACMHS. During that time, no hearing was held regarding his hospitalization and treatment.

After his release, Burch complained that he had been admitted inappropriately to FSH and did not remember signing a voluntary admission form. His complaint reached the Florida Human Rights Advocacy Committee of the State's Department of Health and Rehabilitation Services (Committee). The Committee investigated and replied to Burch by letter dated April 4, 1984. The letter stated that Burch in fact had signed a voluntary admission form, but that there was "documentation that you were heavily medicated and disoriented on admission and . . . you were probably not competent to be signing legal documents." The letter also stated that, at a meeting of the Committee with FSH staff on August 4, 1983, "hospital administration was made aware that they were very likely asking medicated clients to make decisions at a time when they were not mentally competent."

Burch sued the hospital and attending physicians under 42 U.S.C. §1983, which allows a plaintiff to bring suit for, among other things, deprivation of liberty without due process of law. The Court held that Burch may bring suit under this federal civil rights statute, reasoning:

Florida chose to delegate to petitioners a broad power to admit patients to FSH, i.e. to effect what, in the absence of informed consent, is a substantial deprivation of liberty.

Because petitioners had state authority to deprive persons of liberty, the Constitution imposed on them the State's concomitant duty to see that no deprivation occur without adequate procedural protections.

Burch teaches that mental health professionals have an ongoing duty in voluntary treatment settings to ensure that the mentally disabled person has the capacity to consent to treatment before being deprived of freedoms.

Managed Care

Another basic concept of the treatment of persons with mental disorders is managing the care of the mentally ill. Caring for persons with mental illnesses is expensive, especially for the chronic and persistent mentally ill population. Treatment often includes extensive hospitalizations and long-term care. These services are usually paid for by a third party, such as an insurance company or the government through Medicaid reimbursement.

Traditionally, these services were based on a fee-for-service model. In other words, the provider would bill the third party after rendering services. The fee-for-service model, however, was criticized because there was little accountability and dramatic increases in cost of care. The criticism was based on the idea that the provider was usually spending money of the third-party payer—which was seen as someone else's money—and thus had little concern about the cost or quality of services. In response to these criticisms, providers, including those for Medicaid recipients, developed managed care programs.

There are many types of managed care programs. Their common features include exclusive "provider networks," payment rates that shift the financial risk to the provider, and "utilization controls" over intensive and expensive services.[1] The managed care programs may be "capitated," meaning the provider is paid a fixed rate usually per member per month in advance of the months for care of the entire covered population. This payment system creates the incentive for the provider to treat the person with the mental illness or "consumer" in the most cost-effective, least restrictive manner. Managed care has been criticized, however, because it also creates an incentive for providers to restrict or deny services to save money.

Many States require Medicaid recipients to enroll in some type of a managed care program. These managed care programs, called Community Behavioral Healthcare Organization (CBHO), may be "carved out" of the traditional medical services providers. This means that services for the mentally ill are so specialized that they have their own exclusive networks of providers. When designed with consumer and family input, a managed care plan that serves the mentally ill population can bring about greater flexibility in the use of resources and focus on less expensive community-based services people want.[2] Savings realized from managed care plans have enabled providers to expand the range of services for the mentally ill population.

Social workers provide a valuable service to managed care programs. As case

---

1. *Managed Health Care: Effect of Employer's Costs Difficult to Measure* (General Accounting Office/HRD–94–3, Oct. 19, 1993).

2. R. Levy & L. Rubenstein, *The Rights of People with Mental Disabilities* (Southern Illinois University Press: Carbondale and Edwardsville, 1996), p. 250.

managers they can ensure that the consumer is linked to the proper system of care and services to best meet the consumer's needs. The social worker may also serve as an advocate to ensure that the consumer's needs are met.

The managed care program, however, can also create ethical dilemmas to the social worker. For example, the social worker may have to reveal confidences to the third party payer, or feel compelled to sacrifice the client's standard of care to save costs. Additionally, some managed care companies may pay a fixed case rate to the clinician who is providing the service. This method shifts financial risk to the clinician who has an incentive to provide fewer therapeutic sessions to increase the profit margin. These difficult problems will be discussed in more detail in chapter 19 in connection with professional liability.

THE COMMITMENT PROCESS FOR THE MENTALLY ILL

Emergency Commitment

States may provide for at least two types of involuntary commitment for the mentally ill: emergency commitments and commitments by court order. With an emergency commitment, an individual is involuntarily hospitalized pending a court hearing. Anyone may initiate the commitment but usually a police officer, psychiatrist, mental health professional, or physician must certify the need for such a commitment on the basis of professional judgment that hospitalization is required immediately. Especially with

managed care and advances in medication, an emergency commitment may not last very long; the committed person may be stabilized through medication and released before any formal commitment process is initiated.

Preliminary Hearings

Because an emergency commitment deprives the person of freedom merely on the basis of someone's judgment, due process would seem to mandate an immediate judicial screening of the commitment. Courts have so held, and States may require preliminary hearings with twenty-four to seventy-two hours of an emergency commitment. Other States have no such requirement, but may require a full examination by a psychiatrist within twenty-four to seventy-two hours of admission and the concurrence of this psychiatrist concerning the need for an emergency commitment to justify continued hospitalization. Typically, States so requiring also require a full hearing within a short time after the initial commitment, ranging from three to fourteen days.

While statutes may allow for commitments by court order prior to hospitalization, such commitments seldom occur. Given the requirement for commitment that there must be imminent danger or serious harm if one is not committed, almost all court ordered commitments follow emergency hospitalization.

Petitions

Court action in a mental health case is initiated by the filing of a **petition**, often naming the involuntarily committed person the respondent. The petition typically contains a statement of facts justifying the need for the respondent's commitment. The specific contents of the petition are governed by statute. Usually, the petition is a court form, which is simply filled out by hand. Often it is completed by social workers working in community mental health settings or mental hospitals. A petition may also be completed by a friend or relative of the respondent.

The petition usually must be accompanied by reports of psychiatric examinations of the respondent without reports, the judge may dismiss the case or, more commonly, may order the respondent to be examined before further court action is taken. The examination itself may require involuntary hospitalization for a certain period, generally up to one or two weeks.

The reports accompanying a petition or submitted after a petition is filed are typically called **certifications** or **affidavits**. Contents of these reports are often prescribed by statute. Generally, they must include a detailed description of the respondent's behavior that suggests that commitment is required. While a psychiatrist or a medical doctor usually must complete them, social workers are often involved either in gathering the information to be reported or in some cases making certifications themselves.

Commitment Hearings

At a hearing the party seeking to commit the respondent involuntarily is usually the hospital or a mental health professional. Counsel may represent the hospital or mental health professional

who, as we have already seen in the *Addington* case, must prove by clear and convincing evidence that commitment is necessary. Counsel may be appointed to represent the respondent, especially if he or she is indigent. States may authorize the holding of commitment hearings at the mental health facility where the respondent is residing.

Even though many respondents may object to being committed, they may not formally contest petitions. That is, respondents in commitment proceedings may waive their rights to a hearing. Whether respondents understand such waivers may be questionable if they have been medicated or if they have serious mental problems.

Testimony at a commitment hearing is usually that of mental health professionals, including social workers. There may also be testimony from the respondent's friends, relatives, co-workers, and neighbors or anyone who may have witnessed the respondent's behavior, including law enforcement officers. Those who are called to testify are subject to both direct and cross examination and must expect to justify and document any statements made in written documents they have filed with the court.

After evaluating the evidence presented at the hearing, the judge, or the jury if there is one, determines whether the respondent meets the standards for commitment. If the standards are met, the judge will determine what will be done. The judge, as has been noted, may not necessarily commit the respondent to an institution just because he or she had been found to meet the standards for commitment. The judge may commit the respondent to special agencies who will make a decision about the level of commitment or may order another disposition that requires the respondent to participate in outpatient treatment. The judge may also place the respondent in the custody of a responsible relative. When the judge makes a decision on commitment, he or she typically relies on information provided by qualified professionals, including social workers, concerning appropriate settings and treatment alternatives. Whatever order is made, there is likely to be some restrictions of freedoms. However, as we shall see, courts may be required to order the least restrictive alternative.

Social Workers' Roles

Social workers are often involved in commitment proceedings as petitioners or advocates for those who are subject to involuntary commitment. As a petitioner, the social worker is asking the court to commit a person. As an advocate, the social worker is questioning the validity of committing a person. Additionally, as we have seen, social workers often provide statutory notice or informally advise respondents of their rights.

Social workers are also involved in providing information to the court. The information might address the need for commitment or the services that should be provided if the person is committed. Social workers may make these assessments and provide reports of their evaluations to the courts. Social workers may also routinely present treatment plans to courts that are charged with ensuring that respondents are placed in the least restrictive setting. Further, social workers may prepare reports for courts that are conducting reviews of the commitments.

Social workers occasionally serve as administrative hearing officers or as qualified examiners in some jurisdictions. Administrative hearing officers review the validity of continuing commitment, and qualified examiners complete psychiatric examinations of persons alleged to be in need of commitment. The most important role played by social workers in commitment, however, may be that of interpreter. Commitment is a complicated proceeding, but all too often the professionals involved incorrectly assume that the patient and his or her family understand what is happening. Social workers can help matters by simply offering explanations, or helping the patient and the family find another way to obtain needed services. The social worker can also interpret the desires of the respondent to his or her family or friends in order to develop a mutually agreeable plan, which will make commitment proceedings unnecessary.

COMMITMENT AND TREATMENT OF THE DEVELOPMENTALLY DISABLED

Commitment statutes for mentally ill persons are generally not used for persons with developmental disabilities. Instead, such individuals may be found incompetent and have a guardian appointed for them. The guardian may, in turn, "voluntarily" admit the individuals to facilities for the developmentally disabled, with or without specific court authority. This procedure will be discussed further in chapter 15. Alternatively, developmentally disabled adults may have been placed in institutions by their parents when they were minors. They may remain in the institutions when they become adults without court review or with only minimal court review.

Even when developmentally disabled persons are subject to commitments by State statutes, such statutes may not have as many procedural protections as are required for mentally ill persons. For example, in *Heler v. Doe,* 509 U.S. 312 (1993), the Supreme Court upheld a constitutional challenge to Kentucky's commitment statutes, which required a higher standard of proof for commitment for the mentally ill than for commitment for the developmentally disabled. The Court reasoned that the risk of erroneously committing a developmentally disabled person was significantly less than of a mentally ill person because diagnosing someone with developmental disabilities can be much easier.

BASIC RIGHTS OF PERSONS WITH MENTAL DISORDERS

The Right to Treatment

Social workers need to understand the rights of persons institutionalized because of mental illnesses. Many times, the social worker's job is to inform institutionalized patients or those who face institutionalization of their rights or to interpret their rights for them. Often, only social workers are available to act as advocates for those who are institutionalized, ensuring that their rights are recognized and respected. Social workers should not recommend placement in an institution without knowing the

rights lost and retained by those in the institution.

These rights are reviewed below, but a word of caution is necessary first. You may get the impression that institutionalized mentally ill persons are well protected. In a sense they are—statutes, regulations, and court opinions have conferred many rights—but the mentally ill are vulnerable and dependent on their caregivers. In practice, they will have the rights that are granted to them by law only if these rights are respected by the institution's staff, or if they have strong and effective advocates.

Mentally Ill Persons. The Mental Health Patients' Bill of Rights expresses the "sense of Congress that each State should review and revise, if necessary, its laws to ensure that mental patients receive the protection and services they require" and that, whether they are involuntary or voluntary institutionalized, they are afforded certain rights, including "the right to appropriate treatment." 42 U.S.C. § 9501(1)(A), reaffirmed in 1984, at 42 U.S.C. § 10841. No Supreme Court case has held, however, that involuntarily committed persons with mental illnesses have a right to treatment. Some lower courts have so held. They have reassured that if a mentally ill person has been involuntarily committed under the *parens patriae* authority, treatment is an essential corollary of the commitment, while if the person has been involuntarily committed under the police power, treatment is necessary to avoid lifetime detention.

Two problems arise with the judicially recognized right to treatment: the courts' limited expertise to determine appropriate treatment and their limited ability to implement their opinions. Both of these problems are illustrated by the infamous case *Wyatt v. Stickney,* 325 F.Supp. 781 (M.D. Ala. 1971), which was one of the first cases to recognize that involuntarily institutionalized people with mental illnesses had a right to treatment. However, the court refused to determine the standards "to be used in effectuating that right." Instead, the court ordered the institutions involved in the case to develop plans themselves for providing treatment to the class when no adequate plans were developed six months after the decision, as set forth in a second decision, published at 334 F. Supp 1341 (1972), the court scheduled a hearing to allow the parties and interested experts to propose "miminum constitutional standards for adequate treatment of the mentally ill." In yet another decision, published at 344 F.Supp. 373 (1972), the court found none of the proposed standards acceptable and was forced to develop its own standards.

The court issued a detailed order mandating such matters as patients' clothing allotments and telephone privileges, hospital staff qualifications, number of staff required (e.g., ten housekeepers, fifteen food service workers, one messenger), the content of individualized treatment plans, the interval between reviews of plans, the number of tubs and showers per patient and the content of patients' records. Even this detailed order, however, and the on-going supervision of its implementation produced no magical solutions, and there were several more published and unpublished decisions in the following years.

State statutes may mandate that persons with mental disorders who are committed have a right to treatment, specifying particular aspects of that right. Where there is a statutory or judicially recognized right to treatment, there may be refinements of the right such as requirements that: 1) treatment be on the bases of individualized treatment plans with short-term, intermediate, and long-range treatment goals and projected timetables;[3] 2) there be periodic review and revision of treatment plans;[4] 3) there be patient participation in the development of these plans;[5] and, of particular interest to social workers, 4) there be provision of appropriate social services.[6]

Developmentally Disabled. Just as hospitalized mentally ill adults may have a statutory or judicially recognized right to treatment, developmentally disabled adults who are placed in residential facilities may have a right to **habilitation**, that is, training and development of needed skills appropriate to their capabilities. This right was recognized by the Supreme Court in *Youngberg v. Romeo,* 457 U.S. 307 (1982). Romeo was a profoundly retarded adult with the "mental capacity of an 18-month-old child, with an I.Q. between 8 and 10," who could not talk and lacked "the most basic self-care skills." He was committed to a State institution by his mother when he was twenty-six years old. In the institution, he "was injured on numerous occasions, both by his own violence and by the reactions of other residents to him." After his mother complained, he "was physically restrained during portions of each day." His mother sued on Romeo's behalf, seeking damages

---

3.   See *Davis v. Watkins,* 384 F. Supp 1196 (N.D. Ohio 1974).

4.   See *Wyatt v. Stickney, supra,* 344 F. Supp. 373; 42 U.S.C. § 9501(1)(B); 42 C.F.R. § 441.102(b)(2).

5.   For example, see 42 U.S.C. § 9501(1)(C).

6.   For example, see 42 C.F.R. § 441,102(b)(5).

for his injuries, for his prolonged restraint, and for the institution's "failure to provide him with appropriate treatment or programs for his mental retardation." As described by the Court:

> [Romeo's] first two claims involve liberty interests recognized by prior decisions of this Court, interests that involuntary commitment proceedings do not extinguish. The first is a claim to safe conditions. In the past, this Court has noted that the right to personal security constitutes a "historic liberty interest" protected substantively by the Due Process Clause. And that right is not extinguished by lawful confinement, even for penal purposes. If it is cruel and unusual punishment to hold convicted criminals in unsafe conditions, it must be unconstitutional to confine the involuntarily committed—who may not be punished at all—in unsafe conditions.
>
> Next, [Romeo] claims a right to freedom from bodily restraint. In other contexts, the existence of such an interest is clear in the prior decisions of this Court. Indeed, [l]iberty from bodily restraint always has been recognized as the core of the liberty protected by the Due Process Clause from arbitrary governmental action. This interest survives criminal conviction and incarceration. Similarly, it must also survive involuntary commitment.
>
> [Romeo's] remaining claim is more troubling. In his words, he asserts a constitutional right to minimally adequate habilitation. The term "habilitation," used in psychiatry, is not defined precisely or consistently . . . [but it] refers to training and development of needed skills.
>
> As a general matter, a State is under no constitutional duty to provide substantive services for those within its border. When a person is institutionalized—and wholly dependent on the State— . . . a duty to provide certain services and care does exist, although even then a State necessarily has considerable discretion in determining the nature and scope of its responsibilities. Nor must a State choose between attacking every aspect of a problem or not attacking the problem at all. [Nevertheless,] we have recognized that there

is a constitutionally protected liberty interest in safety and freedom from restraint, . . . [and that] training may be necessary to avoid unconstitutional infringement of [this interest].

The Court concluded that these liberty interests asserted by *Romeo* "require the State to provide minimally adequate or reasonable training to ensure safety and freedom from undue restraint." It then addressed the issue of the standards to employ in determining what was "undue" restraint and what training was required to prevent it. The Court stated:

> Romeo retains liberty interests in safety and freedom from bodily restraint. Yet these interests are not absolute; indeed to some extent they are in conflict. In operating an institution [for the developmentally disabled] there are occasions in which it is necessary for the State to restrain the movement of residents— for example, to protect them as well as others from violence. Similar restraints may also be appropriate in a training program. And an institution cannot protect its residents from all danger of violence if it is to permit them to have any freedom of movement. The question then is not simply whether a liberty interest has been infringed but whether the extent or nature of the restraint or lack of absolute safety is such as to violate due process.

To answer this question and to maintain the "proper balance between the legitimate interests of the State and the rights of the involuntarily committed to reasonable conditions of safety and freedom from unreasonable restraints," the Court decided that courts should not second-guess professionals or make their own decisions about treatment. The Court observed that "the Constitution only requires that the courts make certain that professional judgment in fact was exercised. It is not appropriate for the courts to specify which of several professionally acceptable choices should have been made." For a court to so specify "would place an undue burden on the administration of institutions such as [Romeo's] and also would restrict unnecessarily the exercise of professional judgment as to the needs of residents." Therefore, the Court held that, to determine what training is "reasonable,"

> courts must show deference to the judgment exercised by a qualified professional. By so limiting judicial review of challenges to conditions in state institutions, interference by the federal judiciary with the internal operations of these institutions should be minimized. Moreover, there certainly is no reason to think judges or juries are better qualified than appropriate professionals in making such decisions. For these reasons, the decision, if made by a professional, is presumptively valid; liability may be imposed only when the decision by the professional is such a substantial departure from accepted professional judgment, practice, or standards as to demonstrate that the person responsible actually did not base the decision on such a judgment. In an action for damages against a professional in his individual capacity, however, the professional will not be liable if he was unable to satisfy his normal professional standards because of budgetary constraints.
>
> In this case, therefore, the State is under a duty to provide [Romeo] with such training as an appropriate professional would consider reasonable to ensure his safety and to facilitate his ability to function free from bodily restraints. It may well be unreasonable not to provide training when training could significantly reduce the need for restraints or the likelihood of violence.

This minimal right to habilitation has been augmented by numerous statutes, regulations, and lower court cases. Of great importance, in the Developmentally Disabled Assistance and Bill of Rights Act, 42 U.S.C. § 6000, *et seq.*, Congress has provided financial assistance to State programs for the developmentally disabled, and made clear that the developmentally disabled "have a right to appropriate treatment, services, and habilitation" for their disabilities. § 6009.

In *Pennhurst State Sch. & Hospital v. Halderman*, 451 U.S. 1 (1981), however, the Supreme Court stated that this law did not create substantive rights in favor of residents of institutions. It stated:

> Congress in recent years has enacted several laws designed to improve the way in which this Nation treats the mentally retarded. The Developmentally Disabled Assistance and Bill of Rights Act is one such law. It establishes a national policy to provide better care and treatment to the retarded and creates funding incentives to induce the States to do so. But the Act does no more than that. We would be attributing far too much to Congress if we held that it required the States, at their own expense, to provide certain kinds of treatment.

Nevertheless, in order to obtain Medicaid reimbursement, a facility for the care of the developmentally disabled must provide health or rehabilitation services pursuant to an individualized treatment plan. 42 U.S.C. § 1396d (d) (1) and (2); see, generally, 42 C.F.R. Part 442, Subpart 483, which spells out specific treatment requirements.

Humane Treatment for the Mentally Ill

Treatment in the Least Restrictive Manner. State statutes and the courts have accepted the application of the least restrictive alternative doctrine to mental health commitments. This doctrine requires that courts consider less restrictive alternatives to institutionalization and order institutionalization only when no other alternatives are available or appropriate. The rationale for the application of this doctrine and the requirement that alternatives to involuntary hospitalization be considered were articulated in *Lessard v. Schmidt,* 349 F. Supp 1078 (E.D. Wisc. 1972), in which the court stated:

> Perhaps the most basic and fundamental right is the right to be free from unwanted restraint. It seems clear, then, that persons suffering from the condition of being mentally ill, but who are not alleged to have committed any crime, cannot be totally deprived of their liberty if there are less drastic means for achieving the same basic goal. We believe that the person recommending full-time hospitalization must bear the burden of proving: (1) what alternatives are available; (2) what alternatives were investigated; and (3) why the investigated alternatives were not deemed suitable. These alternatives include . . . outpatient treatment, day treatment in a hospital, night treatment in a hospital, placement in the custody of a friend or relative, placement in a nursing home, referral to a community mental health clinic, and home health aide services.

Many States statutorily require that less restrictive alternatives to institutionalization be explored and considered. Commitment to an institution is only authorized if there is no feasible alternative. For example, Michigan requires by statute that if a person is found to meet the standards for commitment, the judge must consider a report, usually prepared by a social worker at the community mental health center, on alternative treatment plans, available. Mich. Comp. Laws. § 330. 1469a.

The institutionalized developmentally disabled also have a right to humane treatment in the least restrictive setting. The Developmentally Disabled Assistance and Bill of Rights Act recognizes this right. See 42 U.S.C. § 6009(2), which requires that: "The treatment, services, and habilitation for a person with developmental disabilities should be designed to maximize the developmental potential of the person and should be provided in the setting that is least restrictive of the person's liberty."

For many disabled adults, recognition of the right to humane treatment in the least restrictive manner has meant deinstitutionalization or institutionalization in small community facilities, such as group homes. For those who remain in large institutions, recognition of the right has also meant recognition of a variety of rights, like those accorded to the mentally ill. Many of these rights are provided for in State statutes or are mandated by courts in addition to being found in the Developmentally Disabled Assistance and Bill of Rights Act.

Freedom from Restraints and Seclusion. In response to growing criticism of the use and abuse of restraints and seclusion for persons with mental disorders, a number of States and the federal government have restricted their use.[7] States may also focus on procedural safeguards before restraints or seclusion may be used. This approach is exemplified by the federal Mental Health Patients' Bill of Rights, which provides that patients should have the "right to freedom from restraint or seclusion, other than as a mode or course of treatment or restraint or seclusion during an emergency situation if such restraint or seclusion is pursuant to or documented contemporaneously by the written order of a responsible mental health professional."

---

7.   See, e.g., Ind. Code § 12-27-4-1; Cal. Welf. & Inst. Code § 5325.1; and 38 C.F.R. § 17.33(d).

42 U.S.C. § 9501(1)(F). As you saw, *Youngberg v. Romeo, supra,* considered the right of the developmentally disabled to be free of unneccessary restraint and required habilitation to minimize the use of restraint.

Institutional Employment. For many years, mental institutions routinely required patients to work: 1) for institutional rewards (e.g, "tokens" good for such things as television privileges); 2) for therapeutic reasons; 3) for minimal monetary rewards; or 4) to maintain the institution with minimal paid staff. Courts have forbidden such mandated employment for any of these reasons on several grounds.

Although courts have found that mandatory institutional employment constitutes involuntary servitude in violation of the Thirteenth Amendment to the Constitution, most challenges on this ground are unsuccessful. Work must be both involuntary and completely nontherapeutic to violate the Thirteenth Amendment. Thus, in *Estate of Buzelle v. Colorado State Hospital,* 76 Colo. 554, 491, P.2d 1369 (1971), for example, the court considered six thousand hours of work preparing food and cleaning and maintaining the hospital "related to a therapeutic program of rehabilitation and, therefore, not in violation of the Thirteenth Amendment."

Courts have found that in cases where institutionalized persons are paid less than the minimum wage for nontherapeutic work, mandatory work assignments violate minimum wage laws. Claims under the minimum wage laws are sustained where a claimant merely demonstrates that the institution derives a substantial economic benefit from the enforced employment.

Courts have held that insofar as institutionalized persons must work to secure privileges, work assignments violate the right to treatment in a humane environment. That is, the privileges should be afforded without the work. Claims using this theory are sustained if the claimant demonstrates that the mandatory work is neither voluntary nor therapeutic, is not compensated in accordance with minimum wage laws, and is of a type for which the institution would otherwise have had to pay a regular employee.

Some State statutes and regulations explicitly forbid involuntary or uncompensated work for nontherapeutic reasons (see, e.g., 405 ILCS § 5/2-106), or require "compensation in accordance with applicable state and federal labor laws." N.Y. Mental Hygiene Law, § 33.09.

Privacy. As part of a human treatment environment, persons with mental disorders generally have the right to be left alone. This right to be left alone includes times when a family member is visiting (see, e.g., Mont. Code § 53-21-142). State statutes, federal and State regulations, and court decisions have recognized this right, but the right may be qualified or strictly limited at times.

First Amendment Rights and Freedoms. Those who are committed to mental institutions should not be deprived of their essential First Amendment freedoms—freedom of speech, religion, and association, and the right to vote—merely because they are in institutions. These rights may be somewhat restricted, however, because of therapeutic concerns and institutional needs. That is, certain communications and visits may be upsetting or may threaten the security and administration of a facility.

Petitions for Redress of Grievances. Institutionalized persons with mental disorders should have the right to petition for redress of grievances. The federal Mental Health Patients' Bill of Rights recognizes:

> The right to assert grievances with respect to infringement of [any] rights . . . including the right to have such grievances considered in a fair, timely, and impartial grievance procedure provided for or by the program or facility.
>
> [T]he right of access to (including the opportunities and facilities for private communication with) any . . . rights protection service . . . [or] qualified advocate . . . for the purpose of receiving assistance to understand, exercise, and protect [his or her] rights . . . 42 U.S.C. § 9501(1)(J).

In order to facilitate rights for mentally disordered persons, the federal government provides funds to States in order to establish programs for "protection and advocacy." Many such programs employ social workers.[8]

Transfers to other Institutions. Involuntarily committed persons may be committed to particular institutions by a court or by mental health authorities, but, after a period of time, a need may arise to transfer them to different institutions. Due process protections should come into play when one is transferred to a more secure institution or to an institution far from one's friends and family. Generally, however, only minimal protections are provided to the transferred person. Nevertheless, there should be some justification for a transfer and a person being transferred should be given notice and an opportunity to be heard prior to a transfer—if not a full-blown administrative or judicial hearing. This is particularly so if an individual has been committed to a particular institution by a court.

If involuntary committed patients are released on outpatient status by an institution, they may also have a right to a hearing before they can be returned to the institution—even if they remain under a judicial commitment order.[9]

Refusing Treatment

As will be further discussed in chapter 16, medical treatment generally cannot proceed without the informed consent of the person being treated. Informed consent must be voluntary, competent, and given with knowledge of the risks of and alternatives to treatment. Giving informed consent may be problematic for persons with mental disorders and treating them may subject social workers or other professionals to liability. As we saw earlier in *Zinermon v. Burch, supra,* treatment given to a person who lacked capacity to give informed consent violated due process of law because it amounted to an involuntary commitment. Nevertheless, involuntarily committed persons may be treated. Moreover, they may not be able to withhold their consent, that is, refuse treatment. Commitment, either voluntary or involuntary, does not necessarily take away someone's right to refuse

---

8. For example, see 42 U.S.C. § 10801 *et seq.*

9. For example, see *In re Richardson,* 481 A.2d 473 (D.C. App. 1984).

treatment.[10] However, in *William v. Anderson*, 959 F.2d 1411 (8th Cir. 1992), the Court of Appeals held that a mentally ill patient could be forced to take medication as long as certain procedures were followed and, in *Kulak v. City of New York*, 88 F.3d 63 (2d Cir. 1996), a decision to involuntarily administer a drug to a patient was held to be a proper exercise of professional judgment not violating due process. In, *Washington v. Harper*, 494 U.S. 210 (1989), the Supreme Court upheld forced drug treatment of a mentally ill prisoner a long as procedural safeguards were followed.

The federal Mental Health Patients' Bill of Rights, however, recognizes a right of voluntary patients to refuse treatment except for emergencies. It provides that mental patients have the following rights:

> . . . not to receive a mode or course of treatment in the absence of informed, voluntary, written consent to such mode or course of treatment, except treatment
> (i) during an emergency situation if such treatment is pursuant to or documented contemporaneously by the written order of a responsible mental health professional; or
> (ii) as permitted under applicable law in the case of a person committed by a court to a treatment program or facility. 42 U.S.C. § 9501(1)(D).

Some courts have not recognized any right of the involuntarily committed to refuse treatment or have recognized only a limited right to refuse, asserting that if the

---

10. For example, see *Rogers v. Commissioner*, 390 Mass. 489, 458 N.E. 2d 308(1983); and *Rennie v. Klein*, 653 F.2d 836 (3d Cir. 1981). "There must be a careful balancing of the patient's interest with those to be furthered by administering the [treatment]."

purpose of an involuntary commitment is treatment, it should proceed despite a refusal to consent or an incapacity to give informed consent. For example, a Wisconsin statute provides that judicially committed mental patients do "not have the right to refuse medication and treatment" except, in limited circumstances, for religious reasons, and except for psychosurgery or electroconvulsive treatment. This statute was upheld in *Stensvad v. Reivitz*, 601 F. Supp, 128 (W.D. Wisc. 1985). The court stated; "Nonconsensual treatment is what involuntary commitment is all about."

Keeping in mind why someone may refuse treatment is important for the social worker. Obviously, some people suffer from delusions and may benefit from medications used to treat people with mental illnesses. Other people, however, may refuse treatment because they experience serious adverse side effects from medications. These effects were recognized by the Supreme Court in *Washington v. Harper, supra*, where a convicted criminal received psychiatric treatment, including the use of psychotropic drugs, instead of serving a prison sentence.

> While the therapeutic benefits of antipsychotic drugs are well documented, it is also true that the drugs can have serious, even fatal side effects. One such side effect identified by the trial court is acute dystonia, a severe involuntary spasm of the upper body, tongue, throat, or eyes. Other side effects include akathesia (motor restlessness, often characterized by an inability to sit still); neuroleptic malignant syndrome (a relatively rare condition which can lead to death from cardiac dysfunction); and tardive dyskinesia, perhaps the most discussed side effect of antipsychotic drugs. Tardive dyskinesia is a neurological disorder, irreversible in some cases, that is characterized by involuntary, uncontrollable movements of various muscles, espe-

cially around the face. The proportion of patients treated with antipsychotic drugs that exhibit the symptoms of tardive dyskinesia ranges from 10% to 25%. According to the American Psychiatric Association, studies of the condition indicate that 60% of tardive dyskinesia is mild or minimal in effect, and about 10% may be characterized as severe.

Freedom from Discrimination

The Americans with Disabilities Act (ADA) 42 U.S.C. § 12101, *et seq.*, provides people with mental and physical disabilities protection from discrimination. Congressional findings illustrate why the ADA was passed:

The Congress finds that—

1. some 43,000,000 Americans have one or more physical or mental disabilities, and this number is increasing as the population as a whole is growing older;
2. historically, society has tended to isolate and segregate individuals with disabilities, and, despite some improvements, such forms of discrimination against individuals with disabilities continue to be a serious and pervasive social problem;
3. discrimination against individuals with disabilities persists in such critical areas as employment, housing, public accommodations, education, transportation, communication, recreation, institutionalization, health services, voting, and access to public services;
4. unlike individuals who have experienced discrimination on the basis of race, color, sex, national origin, religion, or age, individuals who have experienced discrimination on the basis of disability have often had no legal recourse to redress such discrimination;
5. individuals with disabilities continually encounter various forms of discrimination, including outright intentional exclusion, the discriminatory effects of architectural, transportation, and communication barriers, overprotective rules and policies, failure to make modifications to existing facilities and practices, exclusionary qualification standards and criteria, segregation, and relegation to lesser services, programs, activities, benefits, jobs, or other opportunities;
6. census data, national polls, and other studies have documented that people with disabilities, as a group, occupy an inferior status in our society, and are severely disadvantaged socially, vocationally, economically, and educationally;
7. individuals with disabilities are a discrete and insular minority who have been faced with restrictions and limitations, subjected to a history of purposeful unequal treatment, and relegated to a position of political powerlessness in our society, based on characteristics that are beyond the control of such individuals and resulting from stereotypic assumptions not truly indicative of the individual ability of such individuals to participate in, and contribute to, society;
8. the Nation's proper goals, regarding individuals with disabilities are to assure equality of opportunity, full participation, independent living, and economic self-sufficiency for such individuals; and
9. the continuing existence of unfair and unnecessary discrimination and prejudice denies people with disabilities the opportunity to compete on an equal basis and to pursue those opportunities for which our free society is justifiably famous, and costs the Unites States billions of dollars in unnecessary expenses resulting from dependency and nonproductivity.

Disability under the ADA includes people with mental disorders and is defined as "a physical or mental impairment that limits one or more major life activities." 42 U.S.C. § 12102(2); 29 C.F.R. §1630.2. Although the ADA affects many areas, employment and public services are two of importance to social workers.

The ADA prohibits employers with fifteen or more employees from discriminating against "a qualified individual with a disability." 42 U.S.C. § 12111(5) and (8). The ADA's prohibitions apply when an otherwise "qualified" person with a disability seeks job applications, classifications, promotion, pay, or benefits and applies if the person is to be fired.

The employer may be required to make "reasonable accommodations" that do not cause "undue hardship" to enable the person with a disability to do the job. 42 U.S.C. § 12111(8); 29 C.R.F. § 1630.2. If the employee is discriminated against, a complaint must be filed with the United States Equal Employment Opportunity Commission (EEOC) within 180 days of the discriminatory act. 29 C.F.R. § 1601 *et.seq.* These provisions of the ADA will be more fully discussed in chapter 19.

Social workers involved with government agencies should be reminded that the ADA prohibits discrimination against "a person with a disability" who otherwise "meets the essential eligibility requirements" for receiving services. 42 U.S.C. § 12131(2). For example, a social services agency cannot, under the ADA, refuse to provide services to a person with a disability, yet offer similarly needed services to a nondisabled family member.

Social workers may serve as advocates for people with mental disabilities using ADA prohibitions against discrimination in public accommodations operated by private businesses. For example, the ADA prohibitions concerning public accommodations prohibit discrimination against handicapped individuals in the area of housing (as does the Fair Housing Act, 42 U.S.C. § 3601 *et seq.).*

There are other antidiscriminatory laws that apply to those with mental disorders. For example, many insurance companies placed limits on coverage for mental illnesses that did not exist for other illnesses. In response to this unequal treatment,

States enacted "parity laws" that mandate equal insurance coverage for major mental illnesses as for other serious physical illnesses. Likewise, the federal government enacted the Mental Health Parity Act, U.S.C. § 712(a)(1)(A) *et seq.,* which requires that lifetime coverage on an insurance policy and annual payment limits be the same for mental health coverage as for physical health coverage.

Services

State and federal statutes also provide benefits to ensure adequate services and treatment are provided for people with mental disabilities—including the mentally ill and developmentally disabled. For example, a federal income-support program for people unable to work because of a mental disability, called Social Security Disability Insurance (SSDI), 42 U.S.C. § 401, *et seq.,* pays social security benefits to certain people with, *inter alia,* mental disabilities who qualify based on credits earned by income or contributions. Another such program, Supplemental Security Income (SSI), 42 U.S.C. § 1381, *et seq.,* provides benefits to poor adults and children with, *inter alia,* mental disabilities that are expected to last at least one year. Medicaid, a federal program administered by States, provides among other things, mental health services for low-income people. 42 U.S.C. § 1396 *et seq.* We previously saw that many States are requiring Medicaid recipients to enroll in managed care programs. Another program, Medicare, is a federal program that provides, among other things, benefits to persons with mental disabilities who have received SSDI for at least twenty-four months. 42 U.S.C. § 401 *et seq*. Yet another program, the Individuals with Disabilities Education Act (IDEA), is a federal program administered by schools that provide services to students with mental disabilities. 20 U.S.C. § 1400. The IDEA was discussed in chapter 13.

THE INTERFACE OF CRIMINAL PROSECUTION AND COMMITMENT

A problem that has long concerned the courts is what should happen to persons who are either accused of committing a crime and determined to be incompetent to stand trial, or who are competent to stand trial but found not guilty by reason of insanity. Allowing persons presumed innocent to be held in secure institutions for an indefinite period of time seems contrary to our system of justice. Likewise, holding those who have not been found guilty by reason of insanity in secure mental institutions for a longer period of time than would have been served if convicted seems contrary to fundamental constitutional principles.

Incompetence to Stand Trial

In *Jackson v. Indiana*, 406 U.S. 715 (1972), the Supreme Court held that an in-definite commitment of a criminal defendant solely on account of his unfitness to stand trial violates due process. The Court stated that such persons cannot be detained more than a reasonable period of time necessary to determine if they will regain competence in the foreseeable future. If it is determined that they will not attain competency, the State must institute civil commitment proceedings or release them.

Not Guilty by Reason of Insanity

In *Jones v. United States*, 463 U.S. 354 (1983), the Supreme Court held that the confinement of a person found not guilty by reason of insanity for a longer period than he or she would have been incarcerated if convicted did not violate due process or equal protection guarantees. The Court also determined that the standards are procedural protections for commitment of persons found not guilty by reason of insanity could be different from and less stringent than those used for other civil commitments. In *Foucha v. Louisiana*, 504 U.S. 71 (1992), however, the Supreme Court held that the State could not commit a criminal defendant who was acquitted by reason of insanity but who has recovered from his drug-induced psychosis and had no evidence of mental disease.

15

Competency and Guardianship of Persons with Mental and Physical Disabilities

In this chapter, we will review some of the laws and processes that come into play when adults are unable to make sound decisions, care for themselves, or exercise basic rights because of severe mental or physical disabilities. When adults are incapacitated, the law may define them as **legally incompetent**. When they are so defined, a court appoints someone to make certain or all decisions for them. The name given to the person who is appointed varies, but the most common name is **guardian**. This is the term we will use in this chapter. Regardless of the terminology, the state intervenes in such instances under the *parens patriae* authority in order to protect the incapacitated person. The procedures and specific bases for intervention are governed by State statutes and vary from State to State but, in all the States, the guardianship process is undertaken to protect an incapacitated person.

We will discuss this process in general, focusing on the possible roles of social workers in the process and the rights of persons claimed to be and found to be in need of a guardian. We will also discuss alternatives to guardianship for those less severely disabled. This discussion should be important, not only to those social workers who may be directly involved with guardianship proceedings or with alternatives to guradianship, but also to the many social workers who work with the disabled or their relatives in a variety of settings and contexts.

OVERVIEW OF COMPETENCY AND GUARDIANSHIP

In order to put the discussion that follows in context, you should keep in mind the reality of guardianship. You are probably familiar with reports in the press of individuals who believe a member of their family is squandering a large estate and ask a court to find the family member incompetent. While such cases are noteworthy and perhaps illustrate the abuse of guardianship, they are not common. In the vast majority of cases, the person who is alleged to be incompetent is either developmentally disabled or seriously mentally ill, has an incapacitating condition, such as Alzheimer's disease or brain damage resulting from an accident, or is extremely elderly. The person who petitions for guardianship is typically a family member, but the family member is not trying to protect a large estate. Instead, the family member is doing what is necessary to protect and provide for the care of the disabled person.

Although guardianship proceedings, in theory, and in most cases, in fact, are initiated to protect the disabled person, it is important to recognize that a finding of incompetence and the appointment of a guardian deprive the disabled person of basic rights and freedoms. In addition, guardianship can impose a heavy responsibility on the guardian who stands in relation to the disabled person as a parent stands to his or her child. Guardianship, therefore, is not an action that should be undertaken lightly and without consideration of alternatives.

Every State has a statutory process by which a person may be declared incompetent and a guardian appointed. The terminology used in the guardianship statutes; the standards used to determine when someone is incompetent and a guardian may or must be appointed; the procedures used to determine incompetency and appoint a guardian; the procedural protections and rights afforded to the alleged incompetent; the authority, powers, and responsibilities of the guardian; and the rights lost by the incompetent differ from State to State.

The difference between jurisdictions is more marked in this area of the law than in many of the other areas of law we have considered because there are very few constitutional cases in this area and no authoritative Supreme Court decisions establishing basic substantive or procedural rights of those alleged to be or determined to be incompetent. Unlike in commitment law, where the Supreme Court has established some standards for commitment (i.e., danger to self or others) and some minimum procedural safeguards (e.g., right to proof by clear and convincing evidence), the Supreme Court has established no minimum standards or safeguards in guardianship law. Moreover, most of the scattered lower court decisions have been resolved *against* the incompetent. Despite the loss of rights an incompetent may endure, the courts have generally not seen the determination of incompetence and the imposition of a guardian as a deprivation warranting due process protection.

Legislatures have, however, begun to change guardianship laws to protect the rights of incompetents and to provide needed assistance to them without depriving them unnecessarily of the right of self-determination and of individual autonomy. Moreover, legislatures, courts, and agencies have developed several alternatives to guardianship that protect these vulnerable individuals without the loss of freedom that occurs in guardianships. We shall examine these alternatives in this chapter, but before doing so, understanding both the concept of competence and the process of guardianship is necessary.

COMPETENCY

In the United States, as we have seen, minors are presumed to be legally incompetent and are not generally entitled to make legal decisions for themselves. Instead, a minor's parent or parents will make these decisions for the minor. If a minor has no living parent or no parent capable of making legal decisions, however, a court will appoint an adult to serve as the minor's guardian.

By way of contrast, adults in the United States are presumed to be legally competent and are entitled to make all decisions for themselves. Only if they are determined to be incompetent by a court can they be deprived of the right to make their own decisions and a guardian can be appointed to make decisions for them. The determination of incompetence can only be made if the presumption of competence is overcome. In other words, an adult must be proven to be incompetent. An adult need not establish his or her own competence; it is assumed.

A definition of *incompetence*, now commonly referred to as **incapacity**, is found in statutes in all the States. The definitions vary, but generally require that a person must be incapacitated in some way, and, because of that incapacity, the person must be unable to manage property or care for himself or herself. With such a definition, evidence of impaired social skills and adaptive behavior must be presented in addition to evidence of mental or physical impairment in order to establish incompetency. Such a definition, for example, recognizes that one may be mentally ill but competent to make decisions concerning one's life, that one may be developmentally disabled but capable of caring for oneself, or that one may be extremely elderly or ill, but capable of managing one's money.

Some more modern definitions only have a functional component. For example, Florida used to define an *incompetent* as a "person who, because of minority, mental illness, mental retardation, senility, excessive use of drugs or alcohol, or other physical or mental incapacity, is incapable of either managing his property or caring for himself, or both." As of 1997, Florida had amended its statutes to use the term *incapacitated person* rather than *incompetent* and to define an incapacitated person who may be subjected to guardianship as "a person who has been judicially determined to lack the capacity to manage at least some of the property or meet at least some of the essential health and safety requirements of such person." Fla. Stat. § 744.102.

Because the right of self-determination and the right to control one's own life are considered to be basic in this country, the presumption of competency should not be lightly overcome. It should only be overcome if a person is incapable of making certain or all decisions and it is necessary to have another make the decisions to protect the incapable person. The presumption should not be overcome merely because a person might make harmful or unwise decisions. Adults have a right to be wrong. The state may intervene to protect a person incapable of making rational decisions under the doctrine of *parens patriae*, but not every personal decision that causes harm or that is unwise warrants state intervention. The state should intervene as *parens patriae* only where a person's ability to make decisions is so impaired as to substantially threaten the person's safety or welfare.

Limitations on Findings of Incompetency

Traditionally, people were assumed to be incompetent simply because they had been involuntarily committed for psychiatric care. Many States now recognize that a person may be a danger to oneself or others and thus subject to commitment, but may nonetheless be quite capable of making sound and mature decisions on a variety of matters. These States have thus clearly separated commitment and incompetence. For example, a Texas statute provides:

(a) The provision of court-ordered mental health services to a person is not a determination or adjudication of mental incompetency and does not limit the person's rights as a citizen, or the person's property rights or legal capacity.
(b) A person is presumed to be mentally competent unless a judicial finding to the contrary is made . . . Tex. Health and Safety Code § 576.002.

While historically incompetence was an all or none proposition—either a person was competent for all purposes or a person was incompetent for all purposes—many States now require that the decision on competence be related to specific circumstances. Under this approach, for example, a different standard of competency may be used to determine if an individual can decide where to live than may be used to determine if an individual can refuse life saving treatment. To give a further example, a person may be determined incompetent to manage a family business but determined to be quite competent to decide where and how to live. This approach recognizes the relativity of competence and the fact that no single test for competency for all purposes can be developed. It requires a court to consider the purposes for which competency is being tested (e.g., money management, consent to medical care, or need for assistance in daily living) and the particular facts and circumstances of each case. Using this approach, a court can, for example, find a person incompetent to manage financial affairs but competent to make decisions about medical care or daily living. It can then appoint a guardian only to manage the disabled person's estate or income. This guardian will not have the authority or responsibility to determine where the disabled person will live. It must be recognized, however, that the disabled person's decisions regarding living arrangements and life style may be dictated by the financial resources over which he or she has lost control.

Consequences of an Incompetency Determination

State laws differ on the rights retained or lost by a person found to be incompetent. Generally, after being found incompetent, the person loses the right to make significant decisions. Some rights that are lost, such as the right to decide where to live or the right to consent to medical or psychiatric treatment may be transferred to a guardian who acts as a substitute decision maker for the incompetent person. Other rights, however, are simply lost, like the right to vote.

In determining the rights that a person found to be incompetent loses, the constitutional principle of least restrictive alternative should come into play. The person should only lose those rights that he or she cannot properly exercise. But few courts have recognized the applicability of this principle in this context. Many legislatures, however, have adopted laws that recognize this principle. Instead of a court making a general determination of incompetency whenever a person is incompetent to make some decisions, the guardianship laws may provide that a court can or should determine that a person is incompetent only for limited purposes, that it can or should only deprive the person of limited rights, and that it can or should only give the guardian limited powers. In other words, a **limited guardianship** is recognized. Texas law, for example, provides for limited guardianship "as necessary to promote and protect the well-being" of the incapacitated person, and further provides the limited guardianship, shall be designed "to encourage the development or maintenance of maximum self-reliance and independence in the incapacitated person." Tex. Probate Code § 602. The statute further provides that a person for whom a limited guardian is appointed is not presumed to be incompetent, and "shall retain all legal and civil rights and powers" except those that the court designates "as legal disabilities by virtue of having been specifically granted to the limited guardian."

GUARDIANSHIP

Guardianship can best be understood as the method by which a court protects a person who has been found to be legally incompetent. After a court has found a person to be incompetent for any or all purposes, it must appoint a guardian to act in those areas where the person has been found to be incompetent. If a guardian was not appointed, there would be no one to make legally effective decisions for the incompetent person. Once appointed, the guardian acts under the authority of the court and may have to report to the court his or her actions.

Terminology

There is a distinction between a **guardian of the estate**, who is responsible for decisions relating to property, such as money, income, investments, and assets, and a **guardian of the person**, who is responsible for life decisions, such as where an incapacitated person lives, how he or she lives, or what medical treatment he or she will receive. The guardian of the estate and the guardian of the person may be different people or entities.

Some States use the term **conservator** for the guardian of the estate and others use it for the guardian of the person. Some use the term as a substitute for guardian. Some States use the terms *guardian* and *conservator* interchange-

ably, but suggest the use of the term *conservator* to avoid the stigma often associated with the term *guardian*. Other States use entirely different terms as **committee**, **curator** or **fiduciary**.

The person over whom a guardianship is imposed is usually called a **ward**. A person over whom a conservatorship is imposed is sometimes called a **conservatee**. Sometimes, the person is simply called "the incompetent" or the "incapacitated person."

The term **plenary guardian** is sometimes used to refer to a guardian who is both guardian of the estate and the person. Sometimes, it is used to describe a guardian who has full powers over a ward in contrast to a **limited guardian** who may only make certain decisions for or exercise limited authority over a ward.

Often, when a person is appointed a guardian, he or she is said to have been given **letters of guardianship** that define the authority the guardian has over the ward. If a guardianship is terminated, the letters are withdrawn.

The Guardian's Authority and Responsibility

A guardian generally has the same power to make decisions for his or her ward as a parent has to make decisions for his or her child. Like a parent with a child, the guardian must take good care of a ward and act in the ward's best interest, but unlike a parent of a minor child, a guardian of an adult has no responsibility to support a ward. Indeed, a guardian may be paid for his or her services by taking money from the ward's estate.

As we have seen, courts may specifically limit the authority of a guardian in the order appointing a guardian. States that recognize the concept of limited guardianship may provide that a guardian only has the powers specifically set forth in the order of appointment. Such States, and some States that do not recognize the concept of limited guardianship, may also have laws that limit the authority of a guardian to do certain things without a court order or express authorization, such as to commit a ward to a mental hospital or to consent to psychosurgery for a ward. These laws may be found in guardianship laws or elsewhere. For example, the Illinois guardianship law provides that no guardian "shall have the power, unless specified by court order, to place his ward in a residential facility," while the Illinois law related to mental health commitments provides that a guardian of a person who has been committed may consent to "electro-convulsive therapy, or to any unusual, hazardous or experimental services or psychosurgery" for the ward—but "only with the approval of the court." 755 ILCS § 5/11a-14.1; 405 ILCS § 5/2-110.

Some courts have held that certain rights are so important that they cannot be lost without specific authority. Thus, because of the importance of the right to procreate and raise a family, a guardian may not be able to consent to the sterilization of a ward or the relinquishment of a ward's parental rights.

Whether a guardian is a plenary or a limited guardian, a guardian of the estate or of the person, guardians may have to account to the court. That is, guardians may have to make a report, often called an **accounting**, to the court annually or at more frequent intervals setting forth what they have done for their wards. Usually, an accounting is more concerned with the ward's estate than the ward's person. Whatever reports are required by courts, however, studies have shown that guardians often fail to make reports and that courts rarely sanction guardians who neglect to make reports or pay much attention to the reports that are received—at least where only small estates are involved.

Who May Be Appointed as a Guardian?

In most States, any legally competent adult may be appointed as a guardian. Additionally, certain public agencies, private nonprofit corporations, private agencies, or even private profit-making institutions, like banks, may be appointed as a guardian under State law. A conflict of interest may arise if an agency providing residential care for a ward is appointed as a guardian. Thus, some States forbid such an appointment, but others specifically authorize it.

The wishes of the ward are typically considered in making an appointment. A relative or a friend is generally chosen as a guardian if at all possible. If no relative or friend is available, a private or public agency may be appointed. While some State statutes specify who courts may or should consider to be guardians, other statutes set forth a priority of preferred potential guardians. For example, Arizona law provides that "any qualified person" may be appointed as a guardian and that the court may consider the following persons for appointment as a guardian in the following order: 1) a person selected by the respondent if the respondent has "sufficient mental capacity to make an intelligent choice"; 2) the respondent's spouse; 3) an adult child of the respondent; 4) a parent of the respondent or a person named in a deceased parent's will; 5) any relative with whom the respondent has lived for more than six months before the petition was filed; 6) the "nominee" of a person who is caring for the respondent or paying benefits to the respondent; and 7) a person who acts as a guardian professionally. Ariz. Rev. Stat. § 14-5311. Such a priority list may serve to prevent or minimize disputes between potential guardians.

Some States have special public officials, often called **public guardians**, whose sole or chief function is to serve as guardians of an indigent or when no friend or family member is willing to serve as the guardian. Public guardians are often necessary for indigents because guardians are usually paid for their services by taking money from the ward's estate. People who are indigent by definition have no estates from which payments can be made.

As noted earlier, the guardian of the person and the guardian of the estate may be two different people or entities. It is common, for example, for a family member to be appointed as guardian of the person and a trust department of a bank or an attorney to be appointed as guardian of the estate—especially when an estate is large. Similarly, it is not unusual for a person of limited mental capacity to not require a guardian of the person but to require a guardian of the estate. In either of these cases, conflicts can arise because the guardian of the estate, who may wish to conserve the ward's assets for a variety of reasons, may refuse to pay for residential care and other services desired by the guardian of the person or by the ward. If such disputes cannot be resolved informally, the case can be brought to the court

appointing the guardian or guardians. Such action may require advocacy on the part of an interested third party, such as a social worker, because without assets, access to the courts is difficult.

PROCEDURES AND PROCEDURAL PROTECTIONS

As has been stated, guardianship actions are typically regulated by State statutes. These statutes are often found in the portion of the code that governs trusts and wills and the administration of estates after a person's death, often called the **probate** code.

A guardianship action is typically initiated by a relative of a person alleged to be incompetent. Where there is no relative, a public agency may initiate the action. In most States, the relative or other "interested person," the definition of which varies from State to State, notifies the court of the need for protection of the ward by filing a petition with the court. In some States, the petition is filed by a public attorney.

Notice

The statutes generally provide that the person alleged to be incompetent, that is, the respondent to the petition, be given full notice of the petition. The statutes also typically provide that notice be given to any person having the care and custody of the respondent and to close family members. Many States laws, however, waive the requirement of notice if the petition requests appointment of a temporary guardian who is appointed on an emergency basis. An emergency guardianship may be required when there is imminent danger that the physical or mental health or the safety of the person may be seriously impaired or that the person's property has the potential of being wasted, misappropriated, or lost.

In most States, petitions must be accompanied by certificates of qualified professionals attesting to the respondent's incapacity. A court may also order an examination of the respondent after the filing of a petition to determine if the respondent is, in fact, incapacitated. States differ on who is authorized to perform such examinations and how the examinations must be conducted. Social workers often are authorized to examine and report on mentally disabled adults, or the elderly.

Investigation

A court may appoint social workers to investigate the need for a guardianship after the petition has been filed. The investigator, who may be called a **visitor**, is charged with visiting the alleged incompetent person or may be appointed as a guardian *ad litem*. The investigator is usually required to inform the alleged incompetent person of his or her rights and ascertain his or her wishes as to the guardianship. The investigator may also be required to interview family members or professionals who have worked with the alleged incapacitated person. Upon completion of the investigation, the investigator may file a written report that recommends to the court who is in the best position to serve as the guardian and what limits, if any, should be placed on the guardian.

Washington law provides an example of how the guardianship investigation should occur. Section 11.88.090 of the Washington Code provides that a court shall appoint a guardian *ad litem* "to represent the best interests of the alleged incapacitated person." This guardian *ad litem* must be "free of influence" from anyone involved with the case and have "the requisite knowledge, training, or expertise to perform the duties required by this section." These duties include: 1) explaining "in language which [the respondent] can reasonably be expected to understand" the nature of the proceedings and the respondent's rights; 2) investigating the need for a guardian, including by talking to the respondent and to the respondent's relatives and friends, and by arranging for medical and other professional reports on the respondent's condition; 3) investigating alternative arrangements; 4) investigating the proposed guardian or, if a proposed guardian is not named in the petition, "to investigate the availability of a possible guardian"; and 5), providing the court with a written report that, among other things: a) sets forth a "description of the nature, cause, and degree of incapacity"; b) advises the court on the need for counsel for the respondent; c) evaluates "the appropriateness" of the proposed guardian; d) informs the court whether any alternatives to guardianship have been tried or may be appropriate; e) advises the court whether or not a limited guardianship is appropriate and, if so, "the limits and disabilities to be placed on the incapacitated person;" and f) tells the court of "any expression of approval or disapproval" made by the respondent on the proposed guardian or guardianship.

Hearing

If the appointment of a temporary guardian is sought on an emergency basis pending the final determination on competency, an abbreviated, probably *ex parte*, hearing may be held.

Whether or not an emergency appointment is sought, all States require some kind of formal hearing to determine competency, usually within a short time of the filing of a petition, but few specify the exact number of days. The hearings may be conducted in an informal manner and generally very few procedural safeguards are afforded to the respondent at the hearing. Although the respondent faces significant losses of basic rights, such as the right to marry, the right to vote, or the right to determine where and how he or she may live, no court opinion has declared that the respondent in a guardianship proceeding has a constitutional right to appointed counsel if he or she cannot afford one, and only a small minority of the States give the respondent a statutory right to appointed counsel. For example, see Fla. Stat. § 744.331 (2), giving the right to counsel in all cases. About half of the States do authorize the appointment of a guardian *ad litem*.

Many State statutes specifically permit the hearing to be conducted *ex parte*, that is, without notice to or the presence of the respondent, "for good cause." Washington, alternatively, allows the court "to remove itself to the place of residence" of the respondent. Wash. Rev. Code § 11.88.040(3).

About half the States permit a jury trial, but no court opinions have established a constitutional right to a jury in guardianship proceedings. A few States specifically grant the respondent a right to cross-examine witnesses. Only a few States authorize an independent examination at no cost to the respondent if the respondent cannot afford an examination. Most States permit a determination of incompetency to be made by a mere preponderance of the evidence, the lowest standard of proof. Combining this low standard of proof with the vague statutory standards readily permits a finding of incompetence.

If there is a finding of general or limited incompetence and a guardian is appointed, it would seem that the ward should be afforded periodic reviews to determine the continuing necessity of guardianship. Only a handful of States, however, provide for a full hearing to review a guardianship appointment on an annual basis. Other States provide for very limited reviews, and still other States provide for no automatic reviews. A ward may always petition for termination or modification of guardianship, but a court may be permitted to deny such petitions without a hearing; furthermore, a ward may be required to bear the burden of proving his or her competence, a difficult burden in most cases and particularly difficult where a ward, because of the guardianship, has been unable to make many important decisions on his or her own and to otherwise demonstrate competence. Once again, the advocacy of interested third parties, such as social workers, may be required in order to gain access to the courts and to assist in demonstrating competence.

GUARDIANSHIP OF VETERANS

Many States have adopted in whole or in substantial part the Uniform Veterans

Guardianship Act, which provides that the Administrator of the Veterans Administration be a party to all guardianship proceedings involving a respondent who is receiving money from the Veterans' Administration (V.A.) or who has assets purchased with V.A. funds. In addition, the Act provides that a certificate of incompetency from the V.A. is enough to establish a *prima facie* case of incompetency and puts some limits on who may be a guardian and how much the guardian may take from the ward's estate as fees. Other States have not adopted the entire Act but have incorporated some of its provisions into their laws. For example, Illinois makes a V.A. certificate of incompetency *prima facie* evidence of incompetence, 755 ILCS § 5/11a-11(g), but Illinois has not adopted the Act.

ALTERNATIVES TO GUARDIANSHIP

As we have seen, a finding of incompetence and the appointment of a guardian may result in severe restrictions on a person's rights and basic freedom of action, and most guardianship laws only offer minimal procedural protections to the person alleged to be incompetent. In addition, a person who is made a guardian assumes a significant burden, often at some personal cost. It is not surprising, therefore, that social workers and others have sought acceptable alternatives to guardianship. These alternatives, discussed in this section, would still protect those who cannot fully protect themselves, would not result in a deprivation of rights, and would avoid the costs and obligation of guardianship.

Self-Imposed Guardianship

While not truly an alternative to guardianship, in some States the person in need of guardianship may file the petition requesting guardianship. This allows the person in need of guardianship to exercise more control over the process and may avoid involuntary action later. Further, in those States that recognize the concept of limited guardianship, petitioning for a limited guardianship may preclude an action for a plenary guardian. Moreover, because of the individual planning that precedes petitioning for a guardianship for oneself, the guardian is more likely to have been identified in advance and to have agreed to serve, providing greater assurance that the guardian will, in fact, act in accord with the ward's wishes. Thus, this alternative might be appropriate in certain cases, especially those where an individual is diagnosed as having a degenerative disease or where a person is physically frail but mentally alert.

Some States provide that if a petition is filed by the person subject to guardianship, the guardian can be appointed without a finding of incompetence, thus protecting the dignity of a person who is physically frail but mentally competent. Such a procedure is illustrated in the Florida statutes, which provide: "Without adjudication of incompetency, the court shall appoint a guardian of the property of a . . . person who, though mentally competent, is incapable of the care, custody, and management of his or her estate by reason of age or physical infirmity and who has voluntarily petitioned for the appointment." Fla. Stat. § 744.341.

Less satisfactory but still helpful, one may execute a document while one is still of sound mind and while one still has full physical capacities asking that, should it ever be necessary to appoint a guardian, a designated person be selected. A court is not bound by the previous self-designation but generally will give it great weight in deciding who to appoint. This may be specified by statute. For example, see 755 ILCS § 5/11a-6, which requires a court to appoint a previously self-designated guardian if the court finds he or she "will serve the best interests and welfare of the ward."

Representatives for Receipt of Benefits

Another person may be appointed to receive the checks of someone who is receiving public benefits, like welfare or social security, and to spend the money on behalf of the actual recipient. The person who is appointed may be called a **legal representative** or a **representative payee**. The representative is not appointed by a court but by the agency that administers the benefit program; there is usually no need for a court determination of legal incompetence or even an agency determination—just a finding that such an appointment is necessary. There may be no specific procedures to follow in making the finding or the appointment.

Where an allegedly incompetent person's chief source of income is a public benefit program, the appointment of a representative payee or legal representative may sufficiently protect the person and may avoid appointment of a guardian with the resultant loss of rights. For example, a representative payee can ensure that rent is paid, that money is not wasted, and that there is enough money for food

and other necessities. No further protection may be necessary.

The appointment of a representative may not always be a good alternative to guardianship, however. Appointing a representative deprives a person of freedom of choice, yet there are few, if any, procedural safeguards in most agencies' appointment process. Moreover, agencies may not take care to select responsible representatives and may not oversee them adequately. Representatives may not act to protect beneficiaries, but rather may steal from them or otherwise take advantage of them.

Agency Agreements or Powers of Attorney

When a person is of sound mind, he or she may generally authorize another person to act for him or her in certain matters. The one who authorizes the action is called the **principal**, and the one who is authorized to act is the **agent**. Often, this authorization takes the form of a **power of attorney**, which gives the agent the authority to make certain legal decisions or even execute certain legal documents, like deeds, for the principal. An agency or a power of attorney agreement may be as broad or as narrow as the principal wishes, authorizing the agent to manage all the principal's income and property and make all important decisions or authorizing the agent to sell a specific piece of property or make a particular decision.

In order to prevent guardianship proceedings, one may execute a broad agency agreement with a person of one's choice. The agreement may specify what the agent is to do and how he or she is to do it. An agency agreement, however, including a power of attorney, must be executed while one is of sound mind, and, in most States, the agreement becomes invalid if the principal becomes incompetent, even if there is no legal determination of incompetency. To avoid this problem, most States have adopted so-called **durable power of attorney** laws. These laws still require that the principal be of sound mind when executing the power of attorney but allow the agreement to continue if the principal later becomes incapacitated. Indeed, durable power of attorney laws may specify that powers of attorney executed under the law are only effective when the principal becomes incapacitated.

Durable power of attorney laws create a workable and less restrictive alternative to guardianship, and permit one to shape the restrictions one would wish should one become incapacitated. The durable power of attorney is also relatively inexpensive to execute and avoids the formality and public disclosures of court action.

There are problems with powers of attorney, however. Some people may not recognize the power of attorney and may not permit the agent to, for example, withdraw money from a bank account or sell an investment. Because the power of attorney has historically been used to facilitate action on financial matters—not to support decisions related to personal care—medical and other service providers may be unfamiliar with powers of attorney and unsure of their effect. Further, it may not be accepted that the principal was of "sound mind," however this may be defined, when a power was executed. Finally, there are no safeguards to assure the honesty of the agent and to assure that the agent acts in the principal's best interests.

Living Wills

Often, a guardianship action is initiated after a medical crisis, and a guardian is needed to consent to or withhold consent for medical care. Such may be the case when an individual becomes comatose following an accident or in the course of an illness. Living wills provide a mechanism by which persons, while still of sound mind, can express their desires about medical treatment should they become incompetent to express them. They, thus, avoid a guardianship action and any doubts a guardian might have as to a ward's wishes. Living wills will be discussed in the next chapter.

Trusts

Trusts operate like agency agreements. They allow one person, known as the **trustee**, to control the property of another, known as the **beneficiary** or **legal owner**, which is placed in a trust or which is the subject of a trust agreement. The powers of the trustee over the trust property may be limited by the trust agreement, but generally the trustee may do anything that will further the purpose of the trust. This purpose may be stated generally as "to serve the best interest of the trust beneficiary." Usually, after property is placed in a trust, the beneficiary no longer has any power over it or only has such power as is reserved in the trust agreement.

One may put all or part of one's property in a trust at any time when one is of sound mind or one may execute a so-called living trust, which will put all or a part of one's property in a trust when a "triggering" event, such as one's incapacity, occurs. Such trusts are generally revocable at any time while a person is still competent.

The problems with trust agreements are that they only relate to property, there are often complex laws and rules that must be followed to create or administer a trust, and it is easy to make an ineffectual living trust. Still, where one has substantial property, a trust may prevent a guardianship. Moreover, one may put money or property in trust for another. Thus, a parent may specify by will that everything an incompetent child will inherit from the parent is to be put into a trust. It may then not be necessary for the child to have a guardian appointed to manage the estate and it can be managed according to the specific instructions of the parent.

Case Management and Protective Services

Many State and local mental health departments offer case management services through which a client is given assistance managing his or her daily affairs. In other States, special protective services offices have been opened to assist mental health clients or elderly clients in managing their affairs. Federal funds have been provided for such offices that may assist persons in "achieving or maintaining self-sufficiency" or in preventing "inappropriate institutional care." 42 U.S.C. § 1397(2) and (4). These funds may be used to provide "services related to the management and maintenance of the home, day care services for adults, transportation services, . . . the preparation and delivery of meals, health support services" and other services that would be provided by a guardian or that would make an appointment of a guardian unnecessary. 42 U.S.C. § 1397a(a)(2).

While case management services may be most helpful, like most other alternatives to guardianship discussed here, they are purely voluntary. If an incapacitated person is unwilling to use the services or did not chose to use one of the alternatives, coercive measures may have to be considered.

Medical Care

Earlier chapters of this text have discussed several topics related to medical care that are of relevance to social workers, including medical neglect of minors, discrimination on the basis of handicap, commitment of the mentally ill, and guardianship. This chapter discusses three additional topics: access to medical care; consent to treatment, including the right to withhold consent; and human reproduction. This chapter also discusses aspects of medical care of minors other than those discussed previously.

THE RIGHT TO RECEIVE MEDICAL CARE

The American health care system, unlike the system in many other countries, is predominantly private. America has predominantly private hospitals and doctors whose services are paid for by predominantly private insurance companies and private funds. A substantial amount of money is expended on health care by all three levels of governments; there is some direct provision of health care by governments at the federal, State, and local level; and there is government regulation of the health care system, primarily at the federal and State levels of government. But, the American health care system remains a private system.

Although there are some public hospitals and clinics in America, although some health care in America is provided to members of the public free of charge, and although the government pays for some private medical care through such programs as Medicaid and Medicare, there is no right to medical care at public expense

in America. The Supreme Court has never said there is a constitutional or fundamental right to medical care in America and no State constitution includes a right to medical care. No statutes create a system of free universal health care in America. Most Americans are not entitled by law to the services of any or a particular health care provider—at public or private expense. Indeed, in America, a private hospital or doctor, and in many instances a public hospital or a publicly employed doctor, may generally refuse to treat anyone.

There are several important exceptions to the broad statement that health care providers can refuse to treat anyone. There are, for example: federal "antidumping" requirements that a person be given emergency treatment if a failure to provide such treatment would cause serious injury or death, 42 U.S.C. § 1395dd; requirements to provide certain services imposed by funding sources; and civil rights requirements that no person be refused treatment for reasons like race, sex, or disability, such as requirements under the ADA or State civil rights laws. But, in general, even if the cost of a patient's medical care will be subsidized by the government through Medicare or Medicaid, a doctor or hospital cannot be forced to treat a patient.

Although there is no right to receive medical treatment in America, there is a common law and constitutional right to refuse treatment. Americans are considered to have a constitutional right to privacy and a common law right of bodily integrity, both of which preclude involuntary medical treatment. With a few limited qualifications and exceptions, no medical treatment can proceed in America unless the patient, or one who is authorized to act for the patient, such as a guardian or a parent, voluntarily consents to the treatment with knowledge of the risks and alternatives to treatment—that is, unless there is **informed consent** to the treatment. If a patient is treated without informed consent, depending on the jurisdiction, the health care provider may be civilly liable for assault, battery, malpractice, or negligence or may even be criminally liable.

Because the concept of informed consent and the right to refuse treatment are important to social workers, both will be discussed in some depth, first in relation to adults, and then, in the section on the medical care of children, in relation to children.

INFORMED CONSENT OF ADULTS FOR HEALTH CARE

Informed consent generally need not be in writing, but most health care providers obtain written consent as documentation. The written consent should be specific. A general consent may not be considered sufficient to establish informed consent for a specific treatment.

Informed consent has three elements: capacity, voluntariness, and knowledge.

To be competent to give informed consent to medical treatment, adults must be of sound mind. As a general matter, unless they have been declared legally incompetent, adults should be considered competent to make treatment decisions for themselves. As we saw in *Zinermon* in chapter 14, however, some adults may be temporarily incompetent to consent to necessary treatment. For example, they may be under the influence of prescribed (or nonprescribed) drugs or alcohol, in shock, unconscious, or suffering from a

mental disorder or medical condition that has affected their otherwise sound minds. In an emergency, when treatment must proceed and there is no time to get a court to appoint someone to consent to the treatment, a health care provider will usually ask the closest available relative of a temporarily incompetent patient to consent to the treatment of the patient, but, in most jurisdictions, this consent is invalid—unless the relative is a legally appointed guardian with power to consent to treatment. Only the patient or a legally appointed guardian is competent to consent to a patient's treatment. And, it should be noted, even a guardian may be legally incompetent to consent to any or to certain medical treatment for a ward as specified by law or by an order of appointment. Nevertheless, as we shall see, treating someone who is incompetent to consent in an emergency is generally considered an exception to the requirement of informed consent.

Consent to treatment must also be voluntary. That is, consent must be given freely and willingly to be valid. It also may be withdrawn at any moment. There may be questions of fraud and coercion in some cases, but generally, except for the involuntarily institutionalized, where the situation is itself coercive, there are few problems with the voluntariness of informed consent when consent is given by adults for their own treatment. There may be voluntariness problems, however, when guardians consent to treatment for their wards against the ward's wishes.

Consent cannot be informed unless one has knowledge of what one is consenting to. You would think that doctors would have to tell a patient about the nature of a proposed treatment and all the risks of, alternatives to and consequences of the treatment in order to obtain a patient's informed consent, but in many jurisdictions a doctor is only required to tell a patient what a "reasonable" or the "average" doctor would tell a patient in the circumstances. This is considered an objective test. In other jurisdictions, doctors only have to tell their patients what they need to know to make intelligent choices. In other words, the focus is on the patient, not the doctor, and the test used to determine how much a doctor must tell a patient is subjective rather than objective. But, using either test, patients need not be told everything for consent to be informed; they only must be told that which is reasonable to tell a patient in the patient's particular circumstances. Patients may even be told nothing about a proposed treatment if disclosure would be unreasonable; the informed consent requirement would not be violated if telling the patient nothing about the treatment was reasonable in the circumstances.

In certain situations, statutes, regulations, or the common law may require specific disclosures by doctors. For example, some States have statutes requiring doctors to inform women about the alternative forms of treatment for breast cancer and the risks and consequences of each form of treatment. In most of these States, women have to be provided with specific written material containing the information and must sign a form indicating they have received the material.

While social workers cannot provide medical advice any more than they can provide legal advice, social workers may help health care providers inform patients about proposed treatment, primarily by providing information about services and serving as a channel for communication. Moreover, social workers may assist health care providers determine the voluntariness and competence of a patient's consent. And when patients do not make their own decisions about their medical care, that is, when their informed consent is not required, social workers can help them understand why treatment proceeded without their informed consent. But the social workers' primary role when it comes to informed consent is assisting patients and their families decide when they should give informed consent to medical treatment. Social workers are not dispensing medical advice or interfering with a doctor's care of a patient if they help patients understand the psychological or social dimensions of their medical decisions, help them reach decisions with which they will be comfortable, and make sure that their doctors understand the decisions they have reached.

There are three main exceptions to the requirement of informed consent.

First, in an emergency, health care providers may and must dispense with informed consent. They need not wait for court orders appointing guardians to consent to treatment before providing life-saving treatment to those who cannot consent to treatment because they are, for example, unconscious after an accident.

Second, in some circumstances, treatment may be forced on people under the state's *parens patriae* authority or the State's police power. For example, as we have seen, people who are mentally ill may be required to submit to treatment for their own good or to prevent them from injuring others. Additionally, people who have been exposed to or who have a communicable disease may be treated against their will for their own good or to prevent the spread of the disease. Similarly, people may be compelled to submit to vaccinations over their objections.

Third, people may not be allowed to refuse life-saving treatment. In other words, people may sometimes be treated against their will if treatment will save or prolong their lives. That is, they may be denied what has been referred to as the **right to die**, the **right to death with dignity**, or the **right to die a natural death**.

Although social workers are usually not directly involved in the legal battles related to this last exception to the informed consent rule, they may be indirectly involved. For example, they may counsel patients who are making decisions to accept or reject treatment or they may take part in hospital committees that make decisions to provide or withhold treatment. Moreover, medical social workers' ability to find appropriate and affordable care for patients may play a significant part in the patients' decision to refuse treatment, and all social workers may be helping patients and their families and friends cope with guilt and doubt after making a decision to refuse treatment. Thus, understanding this exception is necessary for social workers.

ADULTS' RIGHT TO REFUSE LIFE-SAVING TREATMENT

The right to refuse life-saving treatment has become more and more important as technological advances permit many people who formerly would have died to live, albeit in hospitals connected to machines, and as more and more dying people go to hospitals or nursing homes instead of remaining at home. As this right has become increasingly important, the law on it has been changing and becoming more complex. This changing and complex law may be best understood if the right is examined in three contexts in which it may arise: 1) when competent adults refuse treatment; 2) when adults who are rendered incompetent by their medical condition never expressed their desires when competent; and 3) when adults who are rendered incompetent by their medical condition expressed their desires when they were competent.

Competent Adults

As a corollary to the requirement of informed consent, competent adults have a right to refuse to consent to medical treatment. But, if a refusal of treatment means death and acceptance of treatment means life, the assertion by a patient of the right to refuse may conflict with beliefs in the sanctity of life, a moral and legal abhorrence of suicide, the medical profession's obligation and desire to save life, the *parens patriae* notion that the state may protect people from themselves, and the state's desire to protect innocent third parties. Thus, competent adults' right to refuse treatment may be disputed by their relatives, friends, or doctors or by the government. Sometimes, these disputes will end up in a court. Patients may go to court to prevent or stop treatment provided against their will. Their relatives, friends, or doctors may go to court to force treatment the patients have refused or to have guardians appointed to consent to the treatment. Such disputes may also reach courts after patients have been treated against their will or have died without treatment.

When such disputes end up in court, a competent adult's right to refuse treatment is generally upheld based either on the common law right to be free of medical treatment absent informed consent to the treatment or on a constitutionally protected liberty interest in refusing unwanted medical treatment. It is, however, difficult to predict how a court will rule in a given case. As we have learned, one may be deprived of common law rights—and even constitutionally protected rights—if there is a sufficient government interest in doing so. Thus, a competent adult's right to refuse treatment may be denied:

1) if the patient has minor children or other dependents;
2) if the treatment is of minor intrusiveness or constitutes a minor invasion of bodily integrity;
3) if the proposed treatment is a generally accepted mode of treatment;
4) if the quality of life will not be adversely affected by the treatment or if the patient will not live a limited or painful life after treatment; or
5) if the treatment does not merely prolong the patient's life for a short time but actually will save the patient's life.

For example, a mother of young children who has a religious objection to a blood transfusion may be compelled to have a surgical procedure that requires a transfusion if the type of surgery is likely to save the child's life and if the surgery is both well-established and not unduly risky, such as an appendectomy. However, a competent adult's right to refuse treatment may be upheld:

1) if the patient has no dependents and his or her friends and family agree with the decision to refuse treatment;
2) if the treatment is highly intrusive, exceptionally painful, or both;
3) if the treatment is risky, experimental, has a small chance of success, or all three;
4) if the quality of the patient's life will be seriously affected by the treatment or by the medical condition even with the treatment;
5) if the treatment will only postpone imminent death; or
6) if the patient has a deeply held religious belief opposing the treatment.

For example, an elderly person with no dependents and a religious objection to blood transfusion may not be compelled to have a risky surgical procedure requiring a transfusion if the surgery is risky and has only a slim chance of arresting an advanced disease, such as a bone marrow transplant for metastasized cancer.

It may also make a difference whether there is a request to withdraw treatment (e.g., a patient asks that a respirator be disconnected) or a refusal to submit to treatment (e.g., a patient asks that she not be given a respirator). In other words, it may matter whether or not the health care provider is playing an active or passive role in causing a patient's death. Furthermore, it may matter whether the underlying medical condition or the provider's action or inaction causes a death. For example, there is a significant difference between disconnecting an intravenous feeding tube of a paralyzed patient, thereby starving the patient, and stopping a course of chemotherapy for a patient with advanced cancer.

Inaction by a health care provider that is usually acceptable is failure to resuscitate a patient who is in a permanent state of great pain or who has a terminal condition. Such a failure to resuscitate may be a spontaneous decision, but more commonly it is the result of a previous, probably written, "do not resuscitate" order, also known as a **DNR order**, or **no code**.

Actions directly causing a patient's death, for example, by giving an overdose of medication, may be called **euthanasia** or **mercy killing** if the patient was dying or in great pain, but would be considered murder under the law—generally even if a dying patient asked for the action as a means of hastening death. Assisting with a patient's suicide is generally unacceptable and prohibiting physician-assisted suicide or defining it as murder is not a violation of the Constitution. The Supreme Court so concluded in two landmark cases in 1997, *Washington v. Glucksberg*, ___ U.S. ___, 117 S.Ct. 2258, and *Vacco v. Quill*, ___ U.S. ___, 117 S.Ct. 2293, in which the Court held, respectively, that a Washington statute forbidding assisted suicide did not violate due process and that a New York statute also forbidding assisted suicide did not violate equal protection. The Court reasoned that while competent adults may have a constitutionally protected right to refuse medical treatment that could save their lives, they have no constitutional right to medical assistance in ending their lives.

In *Glucksberg*, the Court noted that there is a distinction, recognized by courts in many States for many years, "between acts that artificially sustain life and acts that artificially curtail life" (citing cases from nineteen States, including cases from Michigan involving Dr. Kevorkian) and

that while there may be a constitutionally protected right to refuse to be subjected to the former acts, there is no constitutional right to insist on a doctor performing the latter acts. The Court further noted that "the overwhelming majority of State legislatures have drawn a clear line" between these two types of acts "by prohibiting the former and permitting the latter" (citing statutes from forty-five States). The Court stated that these cases and statutes demonstrate that "even as the States move to protect and promote patient's dignity at the end of life, they remain opposed to physician-assisted suicide."

The Court noted several reasons for the opposition to assisted suicide, including a need to preserve "the trust that is essential to the doctor-patient relationship by [maintaining] the time-honored line between healing and harming," and a need to protect "vulnerable groups—including the poor, the elderly, and disabled persons—from abuse, neglect and mistakes." The Court recognized that there was a "real risk of subtle coercion and undue influence in end-of-life statutes," particularly for disadvantaged persons. Thus, even if there were a constitutional right to medical assistance with ending life, there would be reasons that would justify the States depriving individuals of that right.

You should note that the Supreme Court only held in *Glucksberg* and *Quill* that the Constitution did not prevent a State from *prohibiting* assisted suicide. The Court did not hold that the Constitution prevented a State from *allowing* assisted suicide. Indeed, the Court observed that Oregon had legalized physician-assisted suicide and implied that the Oregon law was constitutional. In other words, whether or not a

State allows physician-assisted suicide is up to the State.[1]

Incompetent Adults

Sometimes, adult patients are unable to make decisions to accept or reject medical treatment for themselves. Decisions about whether treatment should be initiated or discontinued must often be made for patients who had been competent adults but whose medical conditions have rendered them unconscious, comatose, or otherwise incompetent to make decisions for themselves. Social workers play a role in medical decision making with such patients by assisting the patients' families to make and live with decisions for the patients.

Many people believe that incompetent adults should have the same right to refuse treatment as competent adults. In other words, incompetent adults should not be prevented from exercising their right to die merely because they are incompetent. But how do incapacitated patients exercise this right and how do health care providers determine what incapacitated patients want?

As we have learned, when adults are unable to make decisions for themselves or to exercise their legal rights because they are somehow incapacitated, guardians may be appointed for them. These guardians stand in their wards' shoes, making decisions and exercising their rights for them. Thus, a guardian could make a decision to terminate a ward's medical treatment, that is, exercise the ward's right to refuse treatment. But is it consistent with the nature and purpose of guardianship for a guardian to make a decision which, not only does not protect a ward, but also may cause the ward's death? How does a guardian decide whether or not to refuse treatment for a ward? Should a guardian's exercise of a ward's right to die override the desires and ethics of the ward's health care providers? And is the informed consent of a guardian sufficient to protect a health care provider from liability if a ward dies without available treatment?

Beginning in the 1970s, courts have increasingly addressed these and other questions related to treatment of incompetent persons and the role of guardians in health care. These questions may arise in several ways. First, someone may seek to be appointed the guardian of an incompetent patient and be given authority to exercise the patient's right to refuse treatment. Second, a health care provider may seek to have a guardian appointed for an incompetent patient to authorize treatment for the patient or may otherwise seek judicial authority to provide treatment to the patient. Third, relatives or friends of an incompetent patient may sue a health care provider to stop or prevent treatment of the patient. Fourth, relatives of an incompetent patient may sue a health care provider civilly for providing treatment without the informed consent of the patient or his or her guardian or for causing injury or death to the patient by withholding treatment. Occasionally, a provider may also be criminally prosecuted for assault or battery for providing treatment without informed consent or for murder for withholding treatment from a patient who died. Finally, because of the potential for civil and criminal liabil-

---

1. Pursuant to the Federal Assisted Suicide Funding Restriction Act of 1997, 42 U.S.C. § 14401, *et. seq.*, however, federal funds cannot be used to support physcian-assisted suicide.

ity—no matter which course health care providers may wish to take—they may go to court to determine whether treatment may be provided to or withheld from an incompetent patient without incurring civil or criminal liability. That is, they may seek a declaratory judgment setting forth their rights and obligations.

When a court is asked to decide a case involving an incompetent person's right to refuse treatment, the court must first decide whether the person would have asserted the right if he or she were competent to do so. Depending on a jurisdiction's precedent, a court may use either a subjective or an objective test to decide this question. If it uses a subjective test, it will attempt to determine what the person would have wanted given the person's beliefs and attitudes when competent; if it uses an objective test, it will attempt to determine what a reasonable person in the position of the person would want. Because the court is substituting its judgment for the judgment of the incompetent person with the latter test, this test is known as a **substituted judgment** test. But the former test may also involve substituted judgment if there is no clear evidence of what the incompetent person would have wanted in his or her present situation. With either an objective or subjective test, the court is making a judgment for an incompetent person or allowing a guardian to do so.

Whichever test the court uses, if it decides the incompetent person would assert the right to refuse treatment, the court would uphold or deny the right based on the factors mentioned in the discussion of a competent patient's right to die above.

A court's reasoning process in deciding a case involving an incompetent person's

right to refuse treatment is illustrated by the landmark case, *Matter of Quinlan*, 70 N.J. 10, 355 A.2d 647 (1976). This highly publicized and very influential case involved Karen Quinlan, a young, single woman in a coma. Her father asked the court to be appointed her guardian and to be given the power to consent to the removal of her respirator. The trial court denied his request, and he appealed. In reversing the denial, the New Jersey Supreme Court noted that:

> No form of treatment which can cure or improve [Karen's] condition is known or available. As nearly as may be determined, considering the guarded area of remote uncertainties characteristic of most medical science predictions, she can never be restored to cognitive or sapient life. She is debilitated and moribund and although fairly stable . . . no physician risked the opinion that she could live more than a year and indeed she may die much earlier. Her life . . . is sustained by the respirator and tubal feeding, and removal from the respirator would cause her death soon, although the time cannot be stated with more precision.

However, Karen's doctors "asserted that no physician would have failed to provide respirator support at the outset, and none would interrupt its life-saving course thereafter. . . ." The court respected the doctors' position, but also concluded that Karen had a constitutional right of privacy that was violated by the forced treatment. It stated:

> We have no hesitancy in deciding . . . that no external compelling interest of the State could compel Karen to endure the unendurable, only to vegetate a few measurable months with no realistic possibility of returning to any semblance of cognitive or sapient life. We perceive no thread of logic distinguishing be-

tween such a choice on Karen's part and a similar choice which, under the evidence in this case, could be made by a competent patient terminally ill, riddled by cancer and suffering great pain; such a patient would not be resuscitated or put on a respirator and . . . would not be kept against his will on a respirator.

The claimed interests of the State in this case are essentially the preservation and sanctity of human life and defense of the right of the physician to administer medical treatment according to his best judgment. In this case the doctors say that removing Karen from the respirator will conflict with their professional judgment. [Karen's father] answers that Karen's present treatment serves only a maintenance function; that the respirator cannot cure or improve her condition but at best can only prolong her inevitable slow deterioration and death; and that the interests of the patient, as seen by her surrogate, the guardian, must be evaluated by the court as predominant, even in the face of an opinion contra by the present attending physicians.

[Karen's father's] distinction is significant. The nature of Karen's care and the realistic chances of her recovery are quite unlike those of the patients . . . in many of the cases where treatments were ordered. In many of those cases the medical procedure required (usually a transfusion) constituted a minimal bodily invasion and the chances of recovery and return to functioning life were very good. We think that the State's interest contra weakens and the individual's right to privacy grows as the degree of bodily invasion increases and the prognosis dims. Ultimately there comes a point at which the individual's rights overcome the State interest. It is for that reason that we believe Karen's choice, if she were competent to make it, would be vindicated by the law. Her prognosis is extremely poor—she will never resume cognitive life. And the bodily invasion is very great—she requires 24 hour intensive nursing care, antibiotics, the assistance of a respirator, a catheter and feeding tube.

Our affirmation of Karen's independent right of choice, however, would ordinarily be based upon her competency to assert it. The sad truth, however, is that she is grossly in-

competent and we cannot discern her supposed choice based on the testimony of her previous conversations with friends. . . . Nevertheless we have concluded that Karen's right of privacy may be asserted on her behalf by her guardian under the peculiar circumstances here present. . . . **[H]er right of privacy . . . should not be discarded solely on the basis that her condition prevents her conscious exercise of the choice. The only practical way to prevent destruction of the right is to permit the guardian and family of Karen to render their best judgment, subject to the qualifications hereinafter stated, as to whether she would exercise it in these circumstances.** If their conclusion is in the affirmative this decision should be accepted by a society the overwhelming majority of whose members would, we think, in similar circumstances, exercise such a choice in the same way for themselves or for those closest to them.

The court's conclusion that Karen's father could be appointed her guardian and could assert her right to refuse treatment did not resolve the case. The court noted that many questions remained, such as whether in this or like cases, the institution or withdrawal of life-sustaining procedures was the subject of medical discretion. The court stated that, in the past, courts have placed full responsibility "in the hands of the physician," but felt this placement of responsibility needed to re-examined in light of "underlying human values and rights" and that courts should "be responsive not only to the concepts of medicine but also to the common moral judgment of the community at large."

Put in another way, the law, equity and justice must not themselves quail and be helpless in the face of modern technological marvels presenting questions hitherto unthought of. Where a Karen Quinlan, or a parent, or a doctor, or a hospital, or a State seeks the process and response of a court, it must answer with its most informed conception of justice in the previously unexplored circumstances presented to it. That is its obligation and we are here fulfilling it, for the actors and those having an interest in the matter should not go without remedy.

But courts, "having no inherent medical expertise, . . . [should not necessarily] overrule a professional decision made according to prevailing medical practice and standards. Although the "modern proliferation of substantial malpractice litigation and the less frequent but even more unnerving possibility of criminal sanctions would seem, for it is beyond human nature to suppose otherwise, to have bearing on the practice and standards as they exist," courts should attempt to discern the prevailing practice and standards. In this case, the practice and standards seemed clear to the court.

We glean from the record here that physicians distinguish between curing the ill and comforting and easing the dying; that they refuse to treat the curable as if they were dying or ought to die, and that they have sometimes refused to treat the hopeless and dying as if they were curable. [M]any of them have refused to inflict an undesired prolongation of the process of dying on a patient in irreversible condition when it is clear that such "therapy" offers neither human nor humane benefit. We think these attitudes represent a balanced implementation of a profoundly realistic perspective on the meaning of life and death and that they respect the whole Judeo-Christian tradition of regard for human life. No less would they seem consistent with the moral matrix of medicine, "to heal," very much in the sense of the endless mission of the law, "to do justice."

Yet this balance, we feel, is particularly difficult to perceive and apply in the context of the development by advanced technology of sophisticated and artificial life-sustaining devices. For those possibly curable, such devices

are of great value, and, as ordinary medical procedures, are essential. Consequently, . . . they are necessary because of the ethic of medical practice. But in light of the situation in the present case (while the record here is somewhat hazy in distinguishing between "ordinary" and "extraordinary" measures), one would have to think that the use of the same respirator or like support could be considered "ordinary" in the context of the possibly curable patient but "extraordinary" in the context of the forced sustaining by cardio-respiratory processes of an irreversibly doomed patient. And this dilemma is sharpened in the face of the malpractice and criminal action threat which we have mentioned.

The court "hesitate[d], in this imperfect world," to give doctors absolute immunity from malpractice and criminal liability, but it did give Karen's and other doctors a qualified immunity that could "free physicians, in the pursuit of their healing vocation, from possible contamination by self-interest or self-protection concerns which would inhibit their independent medical judgments for the well-being of their dying patients." Moreover, the court urged the institution and use of a hospital ethics committee as a "technique aimed at the underlying difficulty." It described such a committee, quoting from a law review article, as "a regular forum" to provide "input and dialogue in individual situations and to allow the responsibility of [physicians' ethical] judgments to be shared," and further quoted from the article:

Many hospitals have established an Ethics Committee composed of physicians, social workers, attorneys, and theologians, . . . which serves to review the individual circumstances of ethical dilemma and which has provided much in the way of assistance and safeguards for patients and their medical caretakers. Generally, the authority of these committees is primarily restricted to the hospital setting and their official status is more that of an advisory body than of an enforcing body.

The court stated:

The most appealing factor in [this] technique seems to us to be the diffusion of professional responsibility for decision, comparable in a way to the value of multi-judge courts in finally resolving on appeal difficult questions of law. Moreover, such a system would be protective to the hospital as well as the doctor in screening out, so to speak, a case which might be contaminated by less than worthy motivations of family or physician. In the real world and in relationship to the momentous decision contemplated, the value of additional views and diverse knowledge is apparent.

Whether or not a hospital ethics committee is constituted, the court stated doctors should make decisions on the treatment of incompetent patients without courts.

We consider that a practice of applying to a court to confirm such decisions would generally be inappropriate, not only because that would be a gratuitous encroachment upon the medical profession's field of competence, but because it would be impossibly cumbersome. This is not to say that in the case of an otherwise justiciable controversy access to the courts would be foreclosed; we speak rather of a general practice and procedure.

And although the deliberations and decisions which we describe would be professional in nature they should obviously include at some stage the feelings of the family of an incompetent relative. Decision making within health care if it is considered as an expression of a primary obligation of the physician, . . . should be controlled primarily within the patient-doctor-family relationship. . . ."

The court concluded its opinion by ordering the following declaratory relief:

Upon the concurrence of the guardian [Karen's father] and family of Karen, should the responsible attending physicians conclude that there is no reasonable possibility of Karen's ever emerging from her present comatose condition to a cognitive, sapient state and that the life-support apparatus now being administered to Karen should be discontinued, they shall consult with the hospital "Ethics Committee" or like body of the institution in which Karen is then hospitalized. If that consultative body agrees that there is no reasonable possibility of Karen's ever emerging from her present comatose condition to a cognitive, sapient state, the present life-support system may be withdrawn and said action shall be without any civil or criminal liability therefor on the part of any participant, whether guardian, physician, hospital or others.

Quinlan has been interpreted to stand for the proposition, which has now been widely accepted, that "extraordinary measures" may be withheld from an incompetent patient if there is "no hope of recovery" or if the patient is "irrevocably doomed." This is not an easy test to apply. It raises many questions.

First, what is an "extraordinary" measure? Is a respirator, an intravenous feeding system, chemotherapy, or resuscitation an "extraordinary" measure? You probably believe that putting an artificial or a baboon heart into a human is an extraordinary measure, but would you say that a human heart transplant is extraordinary?

Second, what is "recovery?" Is life with great suffering or life in a permanent vegetative state recovery? In *Quinlan*, and in *Matter of Conroy*, 98 N.J. 321, 486 A.2d 1209 (1985), a case that involved an eighty-four-year-old woman who was "incompetent with severe and permanent mental and physical impairments and a life expectancy of approximately one year or less," the New Jersey Supreme Court stated that it did not want to consider the value of life or the quality of life or make decisions "based on assessments of the personal worth or the social utility of another's life," but it seemed to do precisely that. The Court said in *Conroy* that if the patient is suffering and the "burdens" of life outweigh the "benefits," life support measures, extraordinary or not, may be withdrawn.

Third, are doctors competent to decide if a patient is "irreversibly doomed?" In Karen Quinlan's case, the doctors were wrong when they all stated, as reported in the opinion, that she would die immediately if her respirator was removed and would die in a short time even with the respirator. In fact, her respirator was removed soon after the opinion was rendered, and she lived another nine years.

Apart from these questions, some courts have questioned the basic assumption of *Quinlan* that judges or guardians may substitute their judgments on medical treatment for those of incompetent persons. These courts have held that judges or guardians cannot assert an incompetent patient's right to refuse treatment in the absence of substantial evidence that the patient would have refused treatment. In *Cruzan v. Director, Missouri Dept. of Health*, 497 U.S. 261 (1990), a plurality opinion with two concurring opinions by two justices and two dissenting opinions joined by four justices, the Supreme Court upheld a Missouri Supreme Court decision so holding.

Nancy Cruzan, like Karen Quinlan, was a young, single woman in a "persistent vegetative state" due to an automobile accident. As described by the Court, Nancy's parents and co-guardians "sought a court order directing the withdrawal of their daughter's artificial feeding and hydration equipment after it became apparent that she had virtually no chance of recovering her cognitive faculties." Nancy's parents acted based on comments Nancy had once made that she would not want to live like a vegetable. The Missouri Supreme Court held that Nancy's comments did not constitute clear and convincing evidence that she would want to be deprived of food and water and refused to allow her parents to compel her doctors to disconnect her hydration and nutrition. The Supreme Court affirmed.

The Court reviewed *Quinlan* and many of the fifty-four cases after *Quinlan*, which had addressed the right of incompetent person's to refuse treatment. The Court observed that, in most of the cases, the courts had upheld an incompetent's right to refuse treatment, as asserted by a guardian, based "either solely on the common-law right to informed consent or on both the common-law right and a constitutional privacy right." However, in some of the cases, the courts had expressed discomfort with the idea of substituted judgment or had not allowed the termination of life-saving treatment without strong evidence of the incompetent person's desires on the subject. Thus, the Court observed that the cases on the subject "demonstrate both similarity and diversity in their approaches to decision of what all agree is a perplexing question with unusually strong moral and ethical overtones."

But, as the Supreme Court explained, the issues before the courts in *Quinlan*, the fifty-four cases after *Quinlan* or any previous Supreme Court cases were different than the issue presented by *Cruzan*.

State courts have available to them for decision a number of sources—state constitutions, statutes, and common law—which are not available to us. In this Court, the question is simply and starkly whether the United States Constitution prohibits Missouri from choosing the rule of decision which it did. This is the first case in which we have been squarely presented with the issue whether the United States Constitution grants what is in common parlance referred to as a "right to die."

The Court stated that, assuming a competent person had a constitutionally protected right to die and that the "forced administration of life-sustaining medical treatment, and even of artificially delivered food and water essential to life, would implicate a competent person's liberty interest," it did not follow that an "incompetent person should possess the same right in this respect as is possessed by a competent person." This is because an

incompetent person is not able to make an informed and voluntary choice to exercise a hypothetical right to refuse treatment or any other right. Such a "right" must be exercised for her, if at all, by some sort of surrogate. Here, Missouri has in effect recognized that under certain circumstances a surrogate may act for the patient in electing to have hydration and nutrition withdrawn in such a way as to cause death, but it has established a procedural safeguard to assure that the action of the surrogate conforms as best it may to the wishes expressed by the patient while competent. Missouri requires that evidence of the incompetent's wishes as to the withdrawal of treatment be proved by clear and convincing evidence. The question, then, is whether the United States Constitution forbids the establishment of this procedural requirement by the State. We hold that it does not.

Whether or not Missouri's clear and convincing evidence requirement comports with the United States Constitution depends in part on what interests the State may properly seek to protect in this situation. Missouri relies on its interest in the protection and preservation of human life, and there can be no gainsaying this interest. As a general matter, the States—indeed, all civilized nations—demonstrate

their commitment to life by treating homicide as a serious crime. Moreover, the majority of States in this country have laws imposing criminal penalties on one who assists another to commit suicide. We do not think a State is required to remain neutral in the face of an informed and voluntary decision by a physically able adult to starve to death.

But in the context presented here, a State has more particular interests at stake. The choice between life and death is a deeply personal decision of obvious and overwhelming finality. We believe Missouri may legitimately seek to safeguard the personal element of this choice through the imposition of heightened evidentiary requirements. It cannot be disputed that the Due Process Clause protects an interest in life as well as an interest in refusing life-sustaining medical treatment. Not all incompetent patients will have loved ones available to serve as surrogate decisionmakers.

And even where family members are present, [t]here will, of course, be some unfortunate situations in which family members will not act to protect a patient. A State is entitled to guard against potential abuses in such situations.

Similarly, a State is entitled to consider that a judicial proceeding to make a determination regarding an incompetent's wishes may very well not be an adversarial one, with the added guarantee of accurate factfinding that the adversary process brings with it. Finally, we think a State may properly decline to make judgments about the "quality" of life that a particular individual may enjoy, and simply assert an unqualified interest in the preservation of human life to be weighed against the constitutionally protected interests of the individual.

In sum, we conclude that **a State may apply a clear and convincing evidence standard in proceedings where a guardian seeks to discontinue nutrition and hydration of a person diagnosed to be in a persistent vegetative state.** We note that many courts which have adopted some sort of substituted judgment procedure in situations like this, whether they limit consideration of evidence to the prior expressed wishes of the incompetent individual, or whether they allow more general proof of what the individual's decision would have been, require a clear and convincing standard of proof for such evidence.

The Supreme Court of Missouri held that in this case the testimony adduced at trial did not amount to clear and convincing proof of the patient's desire to have hydration and nutrition withdrawn. In so doing, it reversed a decision of the Missouri trial court which had found that the evidence "suggest[ed]" Nancy Cruzan would not have desired to continue such measures . . . The testimony adduced at trial consisted primarily of Nancy Cruzan's statements made to a housemate about a year before her accident that she would not want to live should she face life as a "vegetable," and other observations to the same effect. The observations did not deal in terms with withdrawal of medical treatment or of hydration and nutrition. We cannot say that the Supreme Court of Missouri committed constitutional error in reaching the conclusion that it did.

You should note that, as in *Washington v. Glucksberg, supra*, 117 S.Ct. 2258, and *Vacco v. Quill, supra*, 117 S.Ct., in which the Supreme Court only held that the Constitution did not prevent a State from prohibiting assisted suicide, in *Cruzan*, the Court only held that the Constitution did not prevent a State from requiring clear and convincing evidence of an incompetent patient's desire to refuse treatment before allowing a guardian to refuse treatment for the patient. The Court did not hold that a State was constitutionally mandated to require such evidence. Thus, it is up to the States to decide whether someone may refuse treatment for an incompetent patient in the absence of clear and convincing evidence of the patient's wishes or, in other words, whether someone may substitute his or her judgment for an incompetent patient's, as was allowed in *Quinlan*.

However States decide this question, other questions remain. Three of the most important of these questions follow.

First, what should or can be done if a health care provider refuses to go along with a request of a legally appointed guardian for an incompetent adult to withhold or withdraw treatment? *Quinlan* said her doctors could not be forced to remove her respirator, but three New Jersey cases after *Quinlan* said doctors could be forced to withdraw treatment in similar circumstances.

Second, at what point should someone be considered legally "dead" so that treatment can be terminated without any legal questions? In the past, people were considered dead if they stopped breathing or their hearts stopped, but people can now be kept alive for years on life-support machines after they have stopped breathing on their own and people can now be resuscitated after their hearts have stopped. Should people who display no signs of brain activity but whose hearts and lungs are working with the aid of machines be considered alive? Most States have decided no. These States all recognize, in their statutes or common law, the concept of **brain death**. The precise definition of brain death is different in the different States, but basically, the definitions provide that one can be considered dead even if one is breathing and one's heart is beating with the aid of machines. Some urge a broadening of the States' definitions of brain death to include those, like Karen Quinlan, who are in a permanent vegetative state but who have some brain function, while others urge a tightening of the definitions, arguing that present definitions are contrary to religious and moral precepts and permit euthanasia.[2]

---

2. The definition of brain death is also important in relation to organ transplants. Before an organ can be removed from a person for transplant, the person must be legally dead, but often healthy organs deteriorate while a terminal patient is comatose but not brain dead. Thus, to facilitate transplants, some urge the broadening of the definition of brain dead.

Last, who may make a decision for an incompetent adult? Are courts competent to decide these matters? Are these matters best decided in adversary hearings traditionally used by courts? Should doctors be allowed to make certain decisions for incompetent adults on their own or does this give doctors too much power and ignore the right to privacy? Should guardians be allowed to make the necessary decisions or does this give guardians too much power? Should hospital ethics committees or other bodies specially constituted to make such decisions be entrusted with life and death decisions for incompetent patients as *Quinlan* urged? Should the decision ultimately be one for a patient's family? What if a patient's family disagrees among themselves?

There is one possible answer to the questions related to who should make the decision for an incompetent patient: incompetent patients may decide for themselves through a prior written expression of their desires.

Asserting the Right to Die in Advance

As indicated in *Cruzan*, courts have recognized an incompetent patient's prior expression of desires related to treatment even when such desires were not documented in writing and, in fact, were evidenced only by abstract or philosophical discussions. For example, see, *Eichner v. Dillon*, 73 A.D. 2d 431, 426 N.Y.S.2d 517 (1980). But no one can trust that his or her desires will be taken into account unless they are expressed in a written document recognized under the law—particularly if clear and convincing evidence of those desires are required.

Documents prepared by competent adults that state what life-saving or life-prolonging treatment they would like to be provided or withheld should they become ill and incompetent are sometimes referred to as **living wills**. Living wills, or so-called **natural death** acts authorize competent adults to prepare such documents. Most States have such acts. The acts may specify the contents and form of such documents, but living wills may be recognized by courts, guardians, and doctors even if they do not conform to the requirements of an applicable act and even if there is no living will act in the jurisdiction. Any sort of living will would be helpful to courts requiring clear and convincing evidence of a patient's desires or using subjective tests to determine if treatment may be withheld from incompetent adults. Of course, a living will is most likely to be effective if it is prepared in conformity with the law.

Living will acts differ. As noted, some acts require that the wills be in a particular form; they may further require witnesses or other formalities. Other acts permit any type of document and require no formalities. Some acts only authorize terminating certain types of life support measures. For example, some do not authorize the withdrawal of artificial feeding. Some acts apply only when death is imminent; other acts have a wider scope. None of the acts compel a doctor to honor a living will, but all give doctors some kind of qualified immunity, as in *Quinlan*, for honoring one.

Where a jurisdiction has no living will act or has an act that is narrow in scope and the courts are hesitant to recognize a nonstatutory living will, an alternative may be for competent adults to designate in advance guardians who are authorized to make medical decisions for them should they become incompetent and who are aware of and willing to follow their future ward's wishes. Similarly, a durable power of attorney can be given to another person for the purpose of having that person make medical decisions for oneself. Several States have passed laws to supplement their living will acts or instead of living will acts which recognize durable powers of attorney specifically for medical care.

The proliferation of living will and related acts and the increased use of living wills pose a danger that guardians, courts and health care providers may be hesitant to recognize incompetent adults' right to die if they have not executed living wills or otherwise expressed their desires in writing. In other words, they may presume that the failure to execute a living will indicates a desire to forego the right to die. Some living will acts address this problem. For example, Iowa Code 144A .11(4), provides: "This chapter creates no presumption concerning the intention of an individual who has not executed [a living will]." Eliminating the presumption as a matter of law, however, does not eliminate it as a matter of human psychology.

Even the most comprehensive living will act can only provide a partial solution to the problem of an incompetent adult's right to die. For one thing, most people will not execute living wills, and living wills do not solve the problem posed by those who are incompetent because of infancy or retardation. For another thing, even the best drafted law may still raise serious questions such as what type of treatment may be withheld or terminated and when the pro-

visions of a living will should be put into effect.

Social workers can help patients with terminal diseases who are facing incompetence, such as those with Alzheimer's or AIDS, achieve peace of mind by advising them of the availability of living wills and other means to express their desires before they become incompetent, and by referring them to lawyers who can draft effective documents for them that accurately express their desires. Social workers can also work with the families of such patients to help them understand the patients' wishes.

MEDICAL CARE OF CHILDREN

In general, minors are not considered competent to consent to their own medical treatment. The necessary informed consent for their treatment must come from a parent or a legal guardian.[3] There are, however, several exceptions to the rule that only a parent can provide informed consent for a minor child's medical care. Some of these exceptions come from the common law, some are constitutionally based and some are statutory. The four most important exceptions follow.

First, in an emergency, minors can consent to treatment for themselves or health care providers can treat minors without parental consent. Determining what is an "emergency" for the purpose of this exception may pose a problem. Some States, have statutes defining *emergency* or have

---

3. For convience, the term *parent* will be used to refer to both parents and legal guardians unless the context otherwise requires.

statutes permitting health care providers to proceed with treatment of a child without the consent of a parent whenever a failure to provide immediate treatment could have adverse effects. For example, New York law allows treatment of a minor without parental consent when "in the physician's judgment an emergency exists and the person is in immediate need of medical attention and an attempt to secure consent would result in delay of treatment which could increase the risk to the person's life or health." N.Y. Public Health Law, § 2504(4).

Second, health care providers may provide treatment of minor obtrusiveness of children without parental consent. As with deciding what is an emergency, deciding what is minor may not be simple. Treatment like the cleaning and bandaging of a child's small cut by a school nurse would unquestionably be considered minor, however.

Third, emancipated or mature minors may be permitted to consent to their own medical treatment. Emancipation is generally a statutory or common-law status with specific substantive or procedural prerequisites, but maturity is rarely legally recognized or defined. Nevertheless, courts have allowed "mature" minors to make treatment decisions under some circumstances. Of course, the older the minor, the more likely he or she is considered mature and capable of making his or her own decisions.

Fourth, older minors may be allowed to get certain specified types of treatment without parental consent, or even notification. It is thought that if they had to discuss the treatment with their parents or if they had to get their parents' consent, minors would not seek certain kinds of treatment that they should be encouraged to get, such

as treatment for substance abuse, assistance with birth control, or treatment for venereal disease. This exception may be found in statutes or regulations or may arise from constitutional interpretation.

The requirement that a parent provide the informed consent for treatment of a child poses a problem when the child opposes the treatment or when the treatment does not benefit the child. While a parent's desires will generally override those of a child, a parent may be deprived of the right to consent to treatment of a child that does not benefit the child. For example, a parent may not be permitted to consent to an organ transplant from one child to an ailing sibling. Older, mature children may be asked their wishes in such cases.

Courts may be asked to determine when a parent can withhold informed consent for treatment of a child or, in other words, when a parent has the right to refuse medical treatment for a child. As in *Quinlan*, they may be asked to give declaratory relief by parents or health care providers. For example, in *In re L.H.R.*, 253 Ga. 439, 321 S.E.2d 716 (1984), a critically ill newborn's doctor, parents, and the hospital's Infant Care Review Committee, consisting of two doctors, a nurse, a social worker, a hospital administrator, and the parent of a handicapped child, all wished to remove life support from the infant. The hospital filed a motion for declaratory relief. The case was treated as if it involved an incompetent adult, except that the parent was considered to have the right to speak for the child, and *Quinlan* was followed. The court concluded: "[T]he right to refuse treatment or indeed terminate treatment may be exercised by the parents or legal guardian of [an] infant after diagnosis that the infant is terminally ill with no hope of recovery and that the infant exists in a chronic vegetative state with no reasonable possibility of attaining cognitive function."

As we have seen, courts may also get involved in such cases through a child neglect action in a juvenile court. Most child neglect statutes include the failure to provide medical care within their definitions of neglect, but even if they do not, failing to provide such care would normally be considered a failure to provide "proper" or "appropriate" care within the purview of a neglect statute. Further, courts may get involved when criminal neglect, or even homicide, cases are brought against parents who fail to provide medical care for their children.

Some people view parental refusals to consent to treatment for severely handicapped children or critically ill newborns not as child neglect but as examples of discrimination against the disabled. They believe that rather than bringing such cases in juvenile courts under juvenile law or in criminal courts under criminal law, they should be brought as civil rights cases in the appropriate courts for such cases. Others reject the use of civil rights laws where parents refuse treatment for severely handicapped children or critically ill newborns, but would still assert that neither the juvenile court nor the criminal court is the appropriate forum for most such cases, which raise different issues than the usual juvenile or criminal court child neglect action.

Whatever the route to a court, a court that is determining when a parent has the right to refuse medical treatment for a child must weigh parental autonomy against the *parens patriae* authority of the state. Generally, a court will not allow a parental refusal to consent to stand if a child's life is at stake. However, if a proposed treatment involves considerable risk, if it may be painful, if it has little chance of success, if it is not a generally accepted mode of treatment, if the quality of life after treatment is questionable, if there is a strong religious basis for the refusal, or if an older or mature child concurs with the parental refusal, a court may tip the scale in favor of the parents' right to refuse.

As counselors to bereaved families of critically ill newborns, as counselors to families with severely disabled children, and as child welfare workers, social workers are often involved in cases involving a parent's right to refuse treatment for their children.

LEGAL ISSUES RELATED TO HUMAN REPRODUCTION

Many legal issues related to human reproduction are of concern to social workers who will work with clients, particularly teenagers, making medical decisions related to reproduction. The most significant of these issues follow.

Birth Control

In *Griswold v. Connecticut*, 381 U.S. 479 (1965), the Supreme Court held that a State violated the constitutional right to privacy when it forbade a married couple's use of birth control. In subsequent cases, the Court has struck down State laws restricting unmarried persons' and even minors' use of or access to birth control because of this right.

As with any other medical treatment, prescription birth control devices and drugs can only be provided after informed consent is given. Various State statutes, however, allow all minors or all minors of a certain age to obtain birth control without the informed consent of—and even without notification to—a parent or guardian. The Supreme Court has held that a State may not forbid "mature" minors from receiving birth control without parental consent. *Carey v. Population Services International*, 431 U.S. 678 (1977).

Sterilization

Sterilization as a method of birth control raises several legal issues. Voluntary sterilization raises issues related to access and consent. Access to voluntary sterilizations may be limited in some States by so-called **conscience laws**, allowing doctors to refuse to perform sterilization, by laws requiring long waiting periods after consent to sterilization is given, by lack of public or health insurance funding for voluntary sterilizations, and by consent requirements. A spouse's consent generally cannot be required, but parental consent may be required.

Other issues arise for involuntary sterilizations. In the past, the mentally ill and the developmentally disabled were sometimes involuntarily sterilized. Less frequently, criminals or the poor were sterilized against their will. Such sterilizations were done because of a belief in eugenics, a theory that the human "stock" would be improved if people with "bad genes" were kept from reproducing. In an early case, the Supreme Court permitted such a sterilization under the police power with the statement that "three generations of imbeciles are enough." *Buck v. Bell*, 274 U.S. 200 (1927). In a later case, *Skinner v. Oklahoma*, 317 U.S. 535 (1942), the Court struck down a statute authorizing sterilization of certain criminals, but the statute was invalidated only on the ground that it impermissibly distinguished among classes of criminals in violation of the equal protection clause. The Court recognized a right to procreate that could be violated by involuntary sterilization, but it also upheld the practice where there was a substantial state interest in the sterilization.

Only a few States currently have statutes authorizing involuntary sterilizations. These statutes have been attacked but because *Buck* and *Skinner* upheld the practice of involuntary sterilization, the legal arguments against the statutes have focused on procedural rather than substantive due process rights. That is, they have focused on the standards defining who may be involuntarily sterilized and the procedural protections for those facing sterilization.

Some recent cases have allowed lawsuits by involuntarily sterilized persons under various civil rights statutes. For example, in *Lake v. Arnold*, 112 F.3d 682 (3d Cir. 1997), the Court of Appeals held that a retarded woman who was involuntarily sterilized twenty years before (when she was sixteen) could sue her parents, the hospital, and the doctors under 42 U.S.C. § 1985, a Civil War civil rights statute aimed at those who conspire to violate civil rights. The Court reasoned that involuntary sterilization of the mentally retarded was a particularly invidious kind of discrimination against the disabled.

An important issue related to involuntary sterilizations is whether a parent or guardian can consent to the sterilization of a child or ward. Some States require a specific court order before a parent's or guardian's consent to a sterilization of a child or ward is effective or consider all such consents ineffective. A California statute that prohibited a parent or guardian from consenting to the sterilization of a child or a ward was, however, held unconstitutional in *Conservatorship of Valerie N.*, 40 Cal.3d 143, 707 P.2d 760 (1985), a case in which the parents of a sexually aggressive thirty-year old woman with Down Syndrome and an IQ estimated at 30 sought to have her sterilized, claiming that ordinary methods of birth control would not work. In response, California law now provides that a guardian can consent to sterilization of a ward, but only with court authorization after extensive procedural protections, including a full hearing. Cal. Probate Code § 1950, *et seq.*

Abortion

As you are undoubtedly aware, in *Roe v. Wade*, 410 U.S. 113 (1973), the Supreme Court upheld a woman's right to obtain an abortion, based on the right to privacy theory of *Griswold v. Connecticut*. However, *Roe* did not answer many questions related to restrictions that may be placed on abortions or that limit access to abortion. Many cases after *Roe*, in the State and federal courts, including the Supreme Court, have addressed questions related to these restrictions. For example, Supreme Court cases considered the validity of certain restrictions on late-term abortions, special requirements for informed consent to abor-

tion, and certain limitations on public funding of abortions. Whether and when a minor has a right to an abortion without parental consent or notification has also been repeatedly considered.

In 1989, in *Webster v. Reproductive Health Services*, 492 U.S. 490, in a plurality opinion with four concurring and four dissenting opinions, the Supreme Court upheld a Missouri statute severely limiting abortion and access to abortion. Three years later, in *Planned Parenthood of Southeastern Pennsylvania v. Casey*, 505 U.S. 833 (1992), in another plurality opinion with four concurring and four dissenting opinions, the Court upheld a Pennsylvania statute imposing several other restrictions on abortion. However, the Court reaffirmed the essential holding of *Roe v. Wade* and overruled a provision in the Pennsylvania statute calling for spousal notification.

The courts and legislatures are likely to continue to consider the extent of the right to abortion for many years to come.

New Reproductive Technologies

New reproductive technologies like artificial insemination, in vitro fertilization, and embryo transfer raise many legal issues.

With artificial insemination by donor, there are questions related to the child's legitimacy. Most States now provide that a child who is born during a marriage after the artificial insemination of the wife by an anonymous donor with the consent of the husband is the legitimate child of the husband, but the question of legitimacy may still arise when the donor is not anonymous. Further, there may be questions as to a known donor's responsibilities for and rights in relation to the child. With any donor, anonymous or known, there may be a question as to whether the child has a right to learn the identity of his or her natural father. Finally, questions arise as to the kind of genetic counseling that should be required before an artificial insemination may occur.

In vitro fertilization and embryo transfer may cause similar problems of parentage if an egg or sperm of a nonparent are used. Further legal problems can arise when a surrogate mother, who may or may not contribute an egg, is used in conjunction with these techniques.

Some States have enacted laws that inhibit the use of these techniques, either because of an antipathy to the techniques themselves or because of a desire to limit abortion. For example, destroying a fertilized egg may be defined as a crime in a State statute. Because many fertilized eggs must be destroyed in the process of in vitro fertilization or embryo transfer, such a law, even if it is unconstitutional may prevent use of these techniques. Their use may also be prevented by State statutes that forbid fetal research. In vitro fertilization and embryo transfer may be encompassed by such laws.

SECTION V

THE PROFESSION OF SOCIAL WORK AND THE LAW

INTRODUCTION SECTION V

As you have learned in reading this book, the law regulates the practice of social work in many ways. For example, the law determines when and how a social worker can involuntarily commit a client to a mental hospital or place a child in a foster home. In a sense, almost every law we have discussed so far indirectly affects or regulates some aspect of social work practice. Now we will to look at the laws that directly affect or regulate social work practice. We will also discuss the laws that are not directed at particular activities you may engage in as a professional social worker, but towards you as professional social worker—whether you work for a public or private agency or in the private practice.

The practice of the profession of social work is directly regulated in many States by statutes that determine who may call themselves social workers, who may practice the profession of social work, or both. We will look at these statutes in chapter 17. In this chapter, we will also consider the regulation of the profession.

In chapter 18, we will consider the laws that regulate the practice of social work by imposing legal obligations on social workers to maintain client confidences. We will also consider the professional requirements of confidentiality.

Social work practice is also regulated by laws that establish consequences when social workers, or agencies that employ social workers, do not adhere to professional norms or legal requirements. In chapter 19, we will examine these laws that define what can happen to social workers when they injure their clients through poor professional practice.

In chapter 20, we will examine the professional relationship between social workers and lawyers and how social workers may refer their clients in need of legal help to lawyers and how social workers can work effectively with lawyers to aid their clients or themselves.

This section of the text may be the most important one for the growing numbers of social workers in private practice. Indeed, many of the laws we will be discussing were developed with only these social workers in mind. For example, laws governing licensing and accountability were primarily developed out of concern that growing numbers of social workers were practicing outside of the protective confines of agencies. Issues concerning social workers in agencies, however, will also be covered.

17

Regulation of the Profession of Social Work

STATE PRACTICE ACTS

PRIVATE CREDENTIALING OF SOCIAL
  WORKERS

REGULATION OF SOCIAL WORK
  PRACTICE

REGULATON OF SOCIAL WORK AGENCIES

All States have laws regulating the profession of social work. These regulating laws define the practice of social work through a **practice act**. These practice acts generally establish the minimum requirements for practicing as a social worker and establish an oversight board that is responsible for adopting rules and regulations to implement the law. Most oversight boards will issue **licenses** or **certifications** granting authority to individuals who have satisfied the minimum requirements necessary to practice as social workers.[1] The oversight board may also limit the use of specific social work titles or the right to engage in certain social work activities to those licensed or certified.

Some States have laws establishing a list or registration of persons entitled to call themselves "therapist" or other titles. The distinction between a license, certification, or registration varies from State to State. Generally, if a State allows a social worker to practice without a license, these people may do so without having established a baseline level of competence through education, testing, and experience.

Practice acts, which are purely State law, will be reviewed in this chapter.

---

1. *Social Work Laws and Board Regulations: A Comparison Study, 1998 Edition* (American Association of Social Work Boards: Calpeper, WA), p. 5. Used with permission. The terms *license* and *certification* are the most common terms used in State practice acts to refer to the recognition to practice as a social worker. Only one State, Michigan, uses the term *registration* in this regard. This book will use *license* and *certification* synonymously from this point on.

STATE PRACTICE ACTS

As previously indicated, social work practice acts may limit the practice of the profession to those approved by the States' oversight board or may limit the use of a specific title to those certified by the State's oversight board. Licensure or certification generally mean that a person has been given authority to practice in the board's regulated area, has been granted authority to use a title authorized by the board, or both. An example of this might be a licensed clinical social worker (LCSW). Some States authorize certain persons to practice within the board's regulated area without having to be licensed. For example, a State might exempt from certification social workers employed by the department of social services. Some States also recognize different levels of social work practice. For example, Wyoming recognizes social workers with bachelors degrees as (**certified social worker** [CSW]) entitled to use *CSW* after their name, and recognizes social workers with at least master's degrees as (**Licensed Clinical Social Worker** [LCSW]) entitled to use *LCSW* after their name. Wyo. Stat. § 33-38-101, *et seq.*

States legally regulate social work practice generally based on three different competencies: education (BSW, MSW, or doctorate); experience (direct practice or supervised); and passing an examination (basic, intermediate, advanced, or clinical). Many States authorize different levels of social work practice, depending upon education, experience, and the examination passed. States may or may not recognize, through what is called **reciprocity**, a credential from another

State; recognition may also depend on the differences in requirements.

Education required is usually from a school accredited by the Council on Social Work Education (CSWE). Experience, if required, generally is postmasters or postdoctorate with face-to-face or supervised hours by a licensed professional. The required examination is usually administered by the American Association of State Social Work Boards (AASSWB).[2]

Once licensed, a person must submit to the State's oversight board. Many States require continuing education prior to the renewal of the certification. A person violating a State's licensing act or board rule or regulation is subject to grievance proceedings.

Licensing is always publicly enforced. If social workers were licensed by a State and if a woman called herself a social worker and practiced social work without a license, the State generally could bring a civil suit against her to stop her from using the title and from continuing to practice social work without a license. It could also probably bring a criminal action against her for using the title *social worker* and engaging in the unauthorized practice of social work. One of her clients, who was misled by her into believing she was licensed, could also sue her, but this private action would be additional to the possible public enforcement.

Because licensing may protect not only an occupational title, but also an occupation, a State must be able to define with a reasonable degree of specificity what licensed people in an occupation may do that no one else may do. This may be dif-

ficult for social work. No two social workers may agree on a definition of *social work* let alone a definition that does not include many counselors, psychotherapists, community organizers, or others, who legislators would not wish to prevent from engaging in social work–like activities.

The definitions of *social work practice* in State practice acts are typically broad and may encompass many people who do not really practice social work. Consider the definitions of *social work practice* in the Oklahoma and Massachusetts laws:

"Practice of social work" means the professional activity of helping individuals, groups or communities enhance or restore their capacity for physical, social and economic functioning and the professional application of social work values, principles and techniques in areas such as clinical social work, social service administration, social planning, social work consultation and social work research to one or more of the following ends: Helping people obtain tangible services; counseling with individuals, families and groups; helping communities or groups provide or improve social and health services; and participating in relevant social action. The practice of social work requires knowledge of human development and behavior; of social, economic and cultural institutions and forces; and of the interaction of all these relevant factors. Social work practice includes the teaching of relevant subject matter and of conducting research into problems of human behavior and conflict. Okla. Stat., tit. 59, § 1250.1, par. 2.

"The practice of social work," means rendering or offering to render professional service for any fee, monetary or otherwise, to individuals, families, or groups of individuals, which services involve the application of social work theory and methods in the prevention, treatment, or resolution of mental and emotional disorders or family or social dysfunctioning caused by physical illness, intrapersonal con-

---

2. *Id*. Michigan is the only State that does not require an examination.

flict, interpersonal conflict or environmental stress. Such professional services may include, but shall not be limited to, the formulation of psychosocial evaluation, counseling, psychotherapy of a nonmedical nature, referral to community resources, and the development and provisions of educational programs. Mass. Gen. Laws, ch. 112, § 130.

These definitions could encompass debt couselors or low-income tenant organizers, people who do assertiveness training workshops, run support groups for cancer patients, or operate shelters for the homeless, and numerous others not considered social workers; however, the requirement in the Massachusetts law that the services offered "involve the application of social work theory and methods" could narrow the definition to exclude such people. Do you think Massachusetts and Oklahoma would take action against such people on the basis of their laws restricting the practice of social work to licensed social workers, and that taking such action is what the legislature intended?

Social workers may qualify for other types of practice. For example, States may allow social workers to practice as marriage and family therapists if they have master's or doctoral degrees in marriage and family therapy or have completed a specific graduate-level course of study, which could be offered by schools of social work. States may also allow social workers to practice as professional counselors.

Licensing can help develop and protect the profession of social work. If charlatans and untrained and unskilled people are kept from practicing social work or using the title *social worker*, the professional reputation of social workers is enhanced and protected. Licensing can ensure that professional and ethical standards are maintained and that practitioners participate in continuing education requirements. Perhaps most important, licensing can grant official recognition that social workers have special skills and require special training and that social work is important enough to require regulation. That is, official recognition may be valued for its own sake. Moreover, official recognition may lead to other benefits. For example, for social workers in private, independent practice, certification may lead to a benefit of great importance: health insurance payment for their services.

Many States have so-called "freedom of choice" or "vendorship" laws that require insurance companies to provide coverage or reimbursement for social work services if mental health services are covered. Such vendorship laws usually apply only to certified social workers. For example, New York provides that any group insurance policy

for delivery in this state which policy provides reimbursement to insureds for psychiatric or psychological services or for the diagnosis and treatment of mental, nervous or emotional disorders and ailments, however defined in such policy, by physicians, psychiatrists or psychologists, must provide the same coverage to insureds for such services when performed by a social worker, within the lawful scope of his or her practice, who is certified . . . and in addition shall have . . . three or more years post degree experience in psychotherapy. N.Y. Ins. Law § 3221(4)(A).

The federal government also provides reimbursement to qualified clinical social workers for services provided to Medicaid and Medicare recipients. 42 U.S.C. §§ 1395l and 1395x(s)(2)(N).

Various provisions in the States' practice acts may have different impacts on the public.

Continuing education and periodic renewal requirements in many certification laws are designed to ensure competence. Confidentiality requirements, accessible mechanisms for making complaints, and provisions for thorough investigation of complaints and for suspension and revocation of licenses also protect the public. Grandfathering provisions may allow people who are practicing at the time a law goes into effect to be licensed or certified without demonstrating that they meet the law's minimum requirements. The more people grandfathered, the less protection of the public. Similarly, the more exclusions of like professionals and members of a profession from licensing requirements, the less protection to the public.

PRIVATE CREDENTIALING OF SOCIAL WORKERS

An occupation that is not licensed or certified by the State may be privately controlled and regulated. Unions, professional associations and other private organizations may grant recognition to or credential certain people who engage in an occupation. These organizations then control and regulate the occupation by granting or withholding recognition from some people.

There is extensive private regulation of the profession of social work, primarily through the Council on Social Work Education (CSWE) and the National Association of Social Workers (NASW). For example, only those who have obtained degrees from schools accredited by CSWE may get certain jobs as social workers or, in many States, get licenses to practice social work or publicly granted credentials to call themselves social workers. Only those who have master's degrees in social work from CSWE accredited schools, who have two years of postgraduate social work experience, and who pass a written examination administered by NASW may be admitted to the Academy of Certified Social Workers (ACSW) and may use the acronym *ACSW*, indicating membership in the academy, after their names.

Unlike regulation under the law, the regulation of social work through CSWE, NASW, and other private organizations is voluntary. Nevertheless, this voluntary regulation is powerful and respected in the profession. It may have great impact on those who practice or wish to practice social work. For example, membership in the ACSW may be necessary for certain public and private agency jobs, particularly at supervisory levels, to obtain consulting contracts with or referrals from public and private agencies, to receive insurance reimbursement for services rendered in private social work practice, or to attract clients.

While private credentialing may be quite important to an individual who desires to engage in a privately recognized occupation, and while NASW recognition is undoubtedly important to professional social workers, private credentialing, like the ACSW certification, is not backed by the government. There is no public enforcement of private recognition.

Private credentialing may recognize different levels of practice. For example, NASW maintains a national Register of Clinical Social Workers for master's-level social workers with specific postmaster's clinical experience. NASW has also cooperated with other private groups interested in clinical social work practice to have the American Board of Examiners grant certification as a "diplomat" in clinical social work to social workers who have an MSW and five years of acceptable postgraduate experience, have completed specific course work and passed an examination administered by the board, and have the highest-level license possible in their State of residence.

REGULATION OF SOCIAL WORK PRACTICE

Statutes or regulations, at the State, federal, or local level, may regulate aspects of the practice of social work by requiring certain training, experience, or expertise necessary to perform certain tasks. For example, a Colorado statute provides:

> A person shall not be allowed to testify regarding a [child] custody or visitation evaluation which he has performed . . . unless the court finds that he is qualified as competent, by training and experience, in the areas of:
>
> (a) the effects of divorce and remarriage on children, adults and families;
> (b) appropriate parenting techniques;
> (c) Child development, including cognitive, personality, emotional, and psychological development;
> (d) child and adult psychopathology;
> (e) applicable clinical assessment techniques; and
> (f) applicable legal and ethical requirements of child custody evaluation. Colo. Rev. Stat. § 14-10-127

Other laws may set forth standards more easily applied by a judge. For exam-

ple, the California law that sets forth standards for those who may perform divorce conciliation and mediation allows conciliation by social workers if they have a master's degree in social work and a set number of years of experience. Calif. Family Code, §§ 1745 and 1815.

Statutes or regulations often set forth requirements for employment as staff of public agencies. These requirements may be similar to licensing or private credentialing requirements or may refer to them. For example, many States set forth specific education requirements for certification as a school social worker and preclude public schools from employing school social workers who are not certified.

REGULATION OF SOCIAL WORK AGENCIES

Many of the agencies or facilities where social workers are employed, such as adoption agencies, day care centers, clinics, nursing homes, hospices, or drug rehabilitation centers, are subject to government supervision and regulation. The government may supervise and regulate even those social service agencies and facilities that are purely private or that are affiliated with religious organizations.

Other agencies or facilities where social workers are employed, for example, hospitals or mental health centers, may choose to be accredited by private agencies. The Joint Commission on Accreditation of Healthcare Organizations (JCAHO) accredits hospitals. The federal government accepts hospitals with JCAHO accreditation to serve as Medicaid providers, without additional review. 42 U.S.C. § 1395; 42

C.F.R. § 3482.1-482.66. Another private accrediting organization, The National Committee for Quality Assurance (NCQA), accredits managed care organizations.

Usually, public social service agencies need not be licensed. They are closely regulated, but any regulation may be self-regulation established by the same law that established the agency. Alternatively, a public agency established by one type or level of government, such as a town clinic, may be regulated by another type or level of government, such as a State health department.

Most private social service agencies and facilities must be licensed in order to operate. The licensing requirement is generally found in a State statute, which typically provides that a designated public agency with expertise in the services provided will license the agency or facility. For example, day care centers are typically licensed by a public child welfare agency, and a health department typically licenses nursing homes.

In order to be licensed or accredited, a private agency or facility must meet standards set forth in the licensing statute or regulations promulgated by the designated licensing agency or by the accrediting agency. The standards typically relate to a facility's physical structure or to an agency's program, the number and qualifications of its staff, or its record-keeping.

Private social work agencies are often publicly regulated, not only through licensing, but also through government purchase of service, that is, through contracts with public agencies. For example, a public child welfare agency might purchase counseling services or foster care services for its clients from a private agency. The private agency must meet certain requirements imposed by the public agency if it wishes to enter into a purchase-of-service agreement. Again, these requirements may relate to staff qualifications or record-keeping.

Public funding sources may also regulate private social work agencies insofar as specific requirements are established to receive public funds or grants. For example, there may be specific requirements to receive State funds to operate a drug abuse program or federal funds to operate a job-training program. Again these requirements may relate to staff qualifications.

Any requirements related to social work staff qualifications in licensing laws, purchase-of-service agreements, or funding programs serve to regulate the practice of social work itself. For example, if a hospice must have a staff social worker with certain training and experience in order to be licensed, that training will probably be offered in schools of social work, and social workers interested in working in hospices will have to obtain related experience to qualify for the job.

Most private social work agencies are organized as corporations, partnerships or associations. These are special kinds of entities recognized by law. An association, organization, or agency that wants to be recognized must follow the procedures and meet the requirements established by law, generally in a State statute. There may be different procedures and requirements for nonprofit versus for profit entities. This will be discussed in more detail in chapter 19.

18

Disclosure of Professional Communications and Records

Three catagories of laws prohibit disclosure of information about a social work client. The first category arises from the client's interest in avoiding disclosure of private matters. This category is referred to as **privacy** law and is based on the Constitution. The second category concerns the obligation of the social worker or other professional not to disclose records or communications about a client obtained in the course of practice. This category is referred to as **confidentiality** and is based on federal and State statutes and on the right to privacy. The third category concerns the obligation of a social worker or other professional not to disclose records or communications in a court case, particularly at a hearing or trial. This category is known as **privilege** and is based on statutes and court rules. These laws will be discussed in this chapter.

In order to understand privacy, confidentiality, and privilege laws related to professional communications and records, it is necessary to understand both the definitions of the following terms and the law related to professional relationships in general.

Records may be defined as written documentation of interactions with or related to clients maintained by a social worker or other professional; written comments; notes or observations placed in a clients' file; documents such as letters, consent forms, medical reports, or court orders included in a client's file; or the file itself.

Communications are statements made to or from a social worker or other professional in the course of practice. Communications may be from a client or other person, may be oral or written, and may be recorded in clients' records or only remembered.

PRIVACY LAW

While there is no express language so providing, the Constitution has been interpreted to recognize the general right to be left alone; this right to be left alone encompasses an interest in avoiding disclosure of private matters. *Whalen v. Roe*, 429 U.S. 589 (1977). Consequently, courts have found that government disclosure of private matters can create the basis for a lawsuit. In *Woods v. White*, 689 F. Supp. 874 (W.D. Wis. 1988), *aff'd* 899 F. 2d 7 (1990), for example, a prison inmate successfully sued prison medical personnel for discussing his positive HIV test with nonmedical staff and other inmates.

Federal and State statutes also recognize the right to privacy. The Family Educational Rights and Privacy Act of 1974 (FERPA), 20 U.S.C. § 1232g(b), for example, gives parents a right to privacy in regards to their child's educational records. Likewise, States may also give institutionalized persons, such as nursing home residents or mentally disabled persons, the right to privacy. Maryland's statute relating to hospitals, for example, specifically grants residents of an extended care facility the right to privacy. MD Health Gen. Code § 19-34(b)(2)(iii).

CONFIDENTIALITY LAWS

Confidentiality Laws Governing Social Work Practices

Confidentiality laws, which obligate the social worker not to disclose client records or communications, are generally found in federal and State statutes or regulations. The legal requirement of confidentiality in a professional practice stem from two things: the desire to preserve privacy in relationships with professionals; and the belief that if confidentiality is not assured, clients either will not seek necessary help from these professionals or will not reveal appropriate information. Thus, social workers are required to maintain confidentiality because it is considered essential to successful social work.

Social workers must be diligent in maintaining confidentiality. For example, they should not comment about clients at a restaurant, in a public hallway, in an elevator at work, or over the telephone where other people could hear. Likewise, social workers should not leave client files in a car where they could be stolen and should not communicate identifying information that is confidential by facsimile because of the risk that the information could be sent to the wrong number. It is important to realize that violating confidentiality laws may subject the social worker not only to civil and disciplinary liability but also to criminal liability. It is also important to realize that confidentiality laws apply not only to the social worker but also to persons employed by the social worker, such as support staff.

There are a number of federal and State laws that impose different legal confidentiality requirements depending on the practice setting. What follows next is a brief summary of major confidentiality laws that govern social workers in their various practice settings.

Public Social Service Agencies. Federal funding laws often contain as an eligibility requirement that a State enact confidentially laws governing the agency that is the recipient of the funding. Many public agencies that employ social workers receive federal funding and are thus governed by confidentiality laws. To receive federal funding, States have enacted confidentiality laws restricting dissemination of certain records, reports, and information concerning: 1) child abuse records and reports, 42 U.S.C. § 5106a(2)(A)(v); 2) children and families receiving foster care and adoption assistance or family preservation services, 42 U.S.C. § 671(a)(8); 3) individuals and families receiving Medicaid assistance, 42 U.S.C. § 1396a(7); 4) information concerning individuals and families receiving temporary assistance to needy families (TANF), 42 U.S.C. § 602(a)(1)(A)(iv); and 5) parties involved in paternity proceedings, or child support proceedings, or child custody determination proceedings, 42 U.S.C. § 654(26).[1]

Treatment. The identity of and diagnosis, prognosis or treatment information on persons enrolled in federally-funded alcohol and drug treatment programs is strictly confidential. 42 U.S.C. § 209dd-3; 42 C.F.R. § 2.2 *et seq.* Confidentiality is so strict that even written records must be secured. For example, the regulations governing confidentiality of records for patients enrolled in alcohol and drug treatment programs requires:

(a) Written records which are subject to these regulations must be maintained in a secure

---

1.   See *Sharing Information: A Guide to Federal Laws on Confidentiality and Disclosure of Information for Child Welfare Agencies* (American Bar Association: Washington, DC, 1997).

room, locked file cabinet, safe or other similar container when not in use; and
(b) Each program shall adopt in writing procedures which regulate and control access to and use of written records which are subject to these regulations. 42 C.F.R. § 2.16.

State practice acts or regulations adopted under the practice acts, discussed in Chapter 17, also contain strict confidentiality requirements governing treatment services. Confidentiality laws in this area may involve communications or records kept by a social worker practicing as a psychotherapist.

Federal and State laws require that information regarding treatment of the mentally disabled also be kept strictly confidential. Records must also be maintained in a confidential manner. 42 U.S.C. § 10805. As we shall see later in this chapter, State laws may provide exceptions to the confidentiality requirements, such as an authorization of disclosure to a court deciding whether to commit a mentally disabled individual.

Education. The FERPA, like other federal laws, contains eligibility requirements limiting federal funding unless schools maintain student records in a confidential manner. Thus, local schools must ensure that educational records are confidential. Such records are maintained by the educational institution and include files, documents, and other materials that contain information directly related to a student. This confidentiality requirement includes special education records. 34 C.F.R. § 303.460. The FERPA, however, grants parents access to the education records of their children.

Medical. Federal and State laws provide that most medical records and information contained in the records are confidential. For example, federal law requires that for hospitals to receive Medicare or Medicaid funds, there must be "a procedure for ensuring the confidentiality of patient records." 42 C.F.R. § 482.25. Federal and State laws also provide that information and records about persons tested for or are HIV-positive be confidential. See, e.g., 42 U.S.C. §§ 300ff-61(a); 300ff-63. Likewise, federal and State laws provide that information and records concerning sexually transmitted disease be confidential. See, e.g., 42 U.S.C. § 14011(b)(5); and Oklahoma Stat., Title 63, § 1-502.2(A).

Court Records. Federal and State statutes may provide for the confidentiality of certain court records, including court records involving juvenile delinquents, identities of victims of certain crimes— such as victims of sexual assaults or child abuse—or criminal history information. See, e.g., 42 U.S.C. § 3789g. Cases involving minors that end up on appeal may use a minor's initials instead of names of the minors to maintain confidentiality.

Exceptions to Confidentiality Laws

Even where confidentiality is legally required as a general matter for certain professions or in certain circumstances, confidentiality may be excused for certain records or communications. Indeed, a breach of confidentiality may be not only excused but also required in certain instances. Exceptions to confidentiality laws may be included as part of the confidentiality law itself or found in other laws—like child abuse and neglect reporting laws. They may also be recognized in a jurisdiction's common law on public policy grounds. The exceptions differ from jurisdiction to jurisdiction, from profession to profession, from record to record, and from communication to communication. Nevertheless, a few common exceptions should be noted.

Reporting Laws. Child abuse and neglect reporting laws are examples of exceptions requiring disclosure of an otherwise confidential communication due to society's view that protecting children from child neglect and abuse is important.

Client Waiver or Consent. It is usually permissible to disclose records and reveal communications if the client consents or waives the confidence. This consent or waiver should be in writing. The written consent must expressly authorize that a particular record or communication may be disclosed. In other words, a general consent for release of records or disclosure of information may not be valid and may not provide the social worker much of a defense if the client later disavows consenting to disclosure. The consent must always be voluntary. It may be difficult to determine the voluntariness of consent in certain situations that may be coercive by nature—such as when someone is required to execute a consent for the release of all medical records to obtain welfare benefits—or where a patient is mentally disabled. Insurance policies may provide waivers to allow the therapist to submit a claim for payment.

The federal regulations governing waiver of confidentiality for persons enrolled in federally-funded alcohol and drug abuse treatment programs are very strict and require a consent form that complies with the following example, but other elements may be added:

1. I [name of patient] Request [and] Authorize:
2. [name or general designation of program which is to make the disclosure]
3. To disclose [kind and amount of information to be disclosed]
4. To: [name or title of the person or organization to which disclosure is to be made]
5. For [purpose of the disclosure]
6. Date [on which this consent is signed]
7. Signature of patient
8. Signature of parent or guardian [where required]
9. Signature of person authorized to sign in lieu of the patient [where required]
10. This consent is subject to revocation at any time except to the extent that the program, which is to make the disclosure, has already taken action in reliance on it. If not previously revoked, this consent will terminate upon [specific date, event, or condition]. 42 C.F.R. § 2.31.

Moreover, disclosure made with the patient's written consent must be accompanied by the following written statement to the recipient pursuant to 42 C.F.R. § 2.32:

This information has been disclosed to you from records protected by Federal confidentiality rules (42 CFR Part 2). The Federal rules prohibit you from making any further disclosure of this information unless further disclosure is expressly permitted by the written consent of the person to whom it pertains or as otherwise permitted by 42 CFR Part 2. A general authorization for the release of medical or other information is NOT sufficient for this purpose. The Federal rules restrict any use of the information to criminally investigate or prosecute any alcohol or drug abuse patient.

A client generally does not need to consent to disclosure if one professional *consults* another professional in the *same* agency about a client. This occurs when the social worker or appropriate staff member reviews a file with a supervisor. A client may need to consent to disclosure to another professional, even one bound by similar or stricter confidentiality rules, such as when referring the client to another agency.

Defending a Charge of Misconduct. If a client sues a social worker for malpractice or if a grievance proceeding is initiated against a social worker, disclosure of client records may be the social worker's only defense. In such cases, courts have implied client waiver or practice acts may authorize or require disclosure.

Duty to Warn. A professional may be required to disclose confidential communications to prevent imminent harm to a third party. In the infamous case, *Tarasoff v. Board of Regents*, 17 Cal. 3d 425, 551 P.2d 334, 131 Cal. Rptr. 14 (1976), the California Supreme Court held that a psychotherapist, who was bound by statutory confidentiality laws, could be liable to the parents of a woman murdered by one of his patients because he failed to warn the woman of the patient's threat to kill her.

Court Order. Disclosure may be required by a court order. For example, a child custody evaluation may require the evaluator to submit a written report to the parties

involved in a child custody dispute. In addition, State statutes may provide an exception to confidentiality laws for prosecution of child abuse cases.

Research. Revealing records for purposes of research, program evaluation, or public statistical gathering is often permissible; however, client names and identifying information may have to be deleted.

PRIVILEGE LAW

Privileges are raised in the context of discovering and presenting evidence for hearings and trials. Hearings and trials allow a person to present evidence or facts that will allow the judge or jury to decide the truth. Attorneys have a duty to present evidence favorable to their client, including evidence from a social worker. This evidence may include client confidences. A **privilege** is an evidentiary rule based on public policy that allows a social worker or other professional on behalf of his or her client to resist legal pressure to reveal client confidences.

Confidentiality, as we have seen, concerns the ongoing obligation of the social worker or other professional to not disclose records or communications obtained in the course of practice. A privilege, on the other hand, is a legal evidentiary rule that allows the client to keep the professional from disclosing privileged communications and records. A law requiring a professional to maintain confidentiality can, but may not necessarily, accord the professional a privilege. Certain records or communications may also be privileged whether or not the professional is generally accorded a privilege. A privilege is more likely to be accorded if confidentiality has been legally recognized for the type of professional, communication, or record. It may also be more likely to be recognized if there are professional or generally recognized ethical requirements of confidentiality.

Privileges generally are considered to belong to clients, not to professionals. Professionals *must* assert privileges on their clients' behalf, but they may not assert privileges if their clients waive the privilege. In other words, a professional cannot refuse to testify if a client allows his or her testimony unless another confidentiality rule precludes the testimony.

Jurisdictions differ as to which professions are granted testimonial privileges or are bound by confidentiality laws and as to which kinds of records and communications are protected by privileges and confidentiality laws. Almost universally, lawyers are granted privileges not to testify and are bound by strict confidentiality rules, which have few and limited exceptions. Doctors generally are privileged not to testify about their patients and are bound by confidentiality rules but less universally than lawyers, and generally there are more and broader exceptions to the privileges and confidentiality rules than for lawyers. Some States grant privileges to and require confidentiality of all licensed psychotherapists whether or not they are doctors; a few States even grant privileges to and require confidentiality of psychotherapists but not doctors. The confidentiality rules and privileges may be broader for psychotherapists than for doctors. In addition, the priest-penitent privilege, which encompasses all recognized clergy, not just Catholic priests, is quite common.

A murder case, *State v. Martin*, 274 N.W.2d 893 (S.D. 1979), illustrates both how courts decide if a privilege exists and the courts' attitudes towards social workers' assertions of testimonial privileges, even in the face of a statute specifically requiring social workers to maintain confidentiality.

Lawrence Lawlor, a licensed, certified social worker, received a call at 4:45 AM from John Martin, one of his patients. Martin told Lawlor he had just killed someone. With Martin's consent, Lawlor notified the police, telling them where they could find Martin and his victim. Nevertheless, at Martin's trial for the murder, both urged that the content of the phone conversation be privileged. The trial court disagreed; Lawlor was compelled to testify, and Martin was convicted. On appeal, the South Dakota Supreme Court affirmed the conviction. The court recognized a statutory privilege for social workers as part of the practice act but that the privilege was limited to "information disclosed to the social worker in his professional capacity." The court reasoned:

> There is nothing in the record which would indicate that the conversation was made in confidence or with the expectation of confidentiality. The substance of the conversation would substantiate the lack of confidentiality, or intent thereof, since Martin advised Lawlor that he understood the need for advising the police before he furnished Lawlor his address.
>
> We can only speculate as to Martin's reasons for contacting Lawlor. Martin's family was out of state for the weekend—he had just that evening resigned from his part-time employment which had supplemented his in-

come since he was a college student—he had consulted with Lawlor as a patient for six to eight months and apparently had faith in him. Seemingly he wanted to talk with someone. In any event, the conversations offered in this case did not relate to and did not arise out of their specific relationship.

A significant Supreme Court case did extend to social workers the federal privilege rule that previously applied to psychologists and psychiatrists. Excerpts from *Jaffee v. Redmond*, 518 U.S. 1 (1996), illustrate how privileges work and the reasons for giving them.

After a traumatic incident in which she shot and killed a man, a police officer received extensive counseling from a licensed clinical social worker. The question we address is whether statements the officer made to her therapist during the counseling sessions are protected from compelled disclosure in a federal civil action brought by the family of the deceased. Stated otherwise, the question is whether it is appropriate for federal courts to recognize a "psychotherapist privilege."

Petitioner is the administrator of the estate of Ricky Allen. Respondents are Mary Lu Redmond, a former police officer, and the Village of Hoffman Estates, Illinois, her employer during the time that she served on the police force. Petitioner commenced this action against respondents after Redmond shot and killed Allen while on patrol duty.

On June 27, 1991, Redmond was the first officer to respond to a fight in progress call at an apartment complex. As she arrived at the scene, two of Allen's sisters ran toward her squad car, waving their arms and shouting that there had been a stabbing in one of the apartments. Redmond testified at trial that she relayed this information to her dispatcher and requested an ambulance. She then exited her car and walked toward the apartment building. Before Redmond reached the building, several men ran out, one waving a pipe. When the men ignored her order to get on the ground, Redmond drew her service revolver.

Two other men then burst out of the building, one, Ricky Allen, chasing the other. According to Redmond, Allen was brandishing a butcher knife and disregarded her repeated commands to drop the weapon. Redmond shot Allen when she believed he was about to stab the man he was chasing. Allen died at the scene.

Petitioner filed suit in Federal District Court alleging that Redmond had violated Allen's constitutional rights by using excessive force during the encounter at the apartment complex. . . . At trial, petitioner presented testimony from members of Allen's family that conflicted with Redmond's version of the incident in several important respects. They testified, for example, that Redmond drew her gun before exiting her squad car and that Allen was unarmed when he emerged from the apartment building.

During pretrial discovery petitioner learned that after the shooting Redmond had participated in about 50 counseling sessions with Karen Beyer, a clinical social worker licensed by the State of Illinois and employed at that time by the Village of Hoffman Estates. Petitioner sought access to Beyer's notes concerning the sessions for use in cross-examining Redmond. Respondents vigorously resisted the discovery. They asserted that the contents of the conversations between Beyer and Redmond were protected against involuntary disclosure by a psychotherapist-patient privilege. The district judge rejected this argument. Neither Beyer nor Redmond, however, complied with his order to disclose the contents of Beyer's notes. At depositions and on the witness stand both either refused to answer certain questions or professed an inability to recall details of their conversations.

In his instructions at the end of the trial, the judge advised the jury that the refusal to turn over Beyer's notes had no "legal justification" and that the jury could therefore presume that the contents of the notes would have been unfavorable to respondents. The jury awarded petitioner $45,000 on the federal claim and $500,000 on her state-law claim.

The common-law principles underlying the recognition of testimonial privileges can be stated simply. "For more than three centuries it has now been recognized as a fundamental maxim that the public . . . has a right to every man's evidence. When we come to examine the various claims of exemption, we start with the primary assumption that there is a general duty to give what testimony one is capable of giving . . . Exceptions from the general rule disfavoring testimonial privileges may be justified, however, by a "public good transcending the normally predominant principle of utilizing all rational means for ascertaining the truth."

Guided by these principles, the question we address today is whether a privilege protecting confidential communications between a psychotherapist and her patient "promotes sufficiently important interests to outweigh the need for probative evidence." Both "reason and experience" persuade us that it does.

Like the spousal and attorney-client privileges, the psychotherapist-patient privilege is "rooted in the imperative need for confidence and trust." Treatment by a physician for physical ailments can often proceed successfully on the basis of a physical examination, objective information supplied by the patient, and the results of diagnostic tests. Effective psychotherapy, by contrast, depends upon an atmosphere of confidence and trust in which the patient is willing to make a frank and complete disclosure of facts, emotions, memories, and fears. Because of the sensitive nature of the problems for which individuals consult psychotherapists, disclosure of confidential communications made during counseling sessions may cause embarrassment or disgrace. For this reason, the mere possibility of disclosure may impede development of the confidential relationship necessary for successful treatment. As the Judicial Conference Advisory Committee observed in 1972 when it recommended that Congress recognize a psychotherapist privilege as part of the proposed Federal Rules of Evidence, a psychiatrist's ability to help her patients "is completely dependent upon [the patient's] willingness and ability to talk freely. This makes it difficult if not impossible for [a psychiatrist] to function without being able to assure . . . patients of confidentiality and,

indeed, privileged communication. Where there may be exceptions to this general rule, there is wide agreement that confidentiality is a *sine qua non* for successful psychiatric treatment." By protecting confidential communications between a psychotherapist and her patient from involuntary disclosure, the proposed privilege thus serves important private interests.

In contrast to the significant public and private interests supporting recognition of the privilege, the likely evidentiary benefit that would result from the denial of the privilege is modest. If the privilege were rejected, confidential conversations between psychotherapists and their patients would surely be chilled, particularly when it is obvious that the circumstances that give rise to the need for treatment will probably result in litigation. Without a privilege, much of the desirable evidence to which litigants such as petitioner seek access—for example, admissions against interest by a party is unlikely to come into being. This unspoken "evidence" will therefore serve no greater truth-seeking function than if it had been spoken and privileged.

The Supreme Court determined that, "[d]rawing a distinction between the counseling provided by costly psychotherapists and the counseling provided by more readily accessible social workers serves no discernible public purpose." The Court then concluded the conversations between Officer Redmond and Karen Beyer and the notes taken during their counseling sessions were protected from compelled disclosure under the Federal Rules of Evidence.

In a dissent, Justice Scalia argued that there was little likelihood that a person would be deterred from seeking psychological counseling because of fear of later disclosure on litigation. Likening social worker counseling to counseling with one's family or friends, Justice Scalia also argued that the psychotherapist privilege should not apply to social workers because they do not bring a greatly heightened degree of skill that psychiatrists or psychologists possess.

Although some judges, like Justice Scalia may not be willing to recognize a privilege for social workers, and, although legislatures may not accord privileges specific to social workers, many social workers are nevertheless covered by confidentiality laws and have testimonial privileges because of statutes not addressed specifically to social workers, such as statutes that govern "therapists" or the kind of social work settings we saw in the last section.

In addition, social workers' privileges may be linked to the privileges of others. In many States, social workers that work with doctors, psychotherapists, or others who are covered by professional privileges are considered agents of the professionals they work with and are thus covered by any privileges applying to the professionals.

Whatever the source of a privilege, most statutes or common law rules creating privileges have built in or generally recognized exceptions. Some exceptions to laws creating privileges may be found in other laws. For example, almost all child abuse and neglect reporting laws specifically abrogate all or most privileges.

There are exceptions to privileges in certain types of proceedings such as civil commitments, child abuse cases, malpractice cases, or grievance proceedings against the professional who is required to maintain confidentiality. Some privileges do not apply in murder cases or in cases involving other serious crimes. Of course, because the privilege belongs to the client, the client may always waive the privilege; waivers are generally readily found by courts.

As you saw in *Jaffe*, confidentiality and privilege laws are based on the same public policy that clients should have the freedom to reveal personal information to a psychotherapist without fear of disclosure. Courts, however, are often confronted with competing public policy, such as determining guilt in a criminal case. These competing policies governing public disclosure were confronted by the California Supreme Court in the infamous Menendez brothers murder trial, *Menendez v. Superior Court*, 834 P.2d 786, 11 Cal. Rptr. 92 (1992).

Lyle and Erik Menendez, who were twenty-one and eighteen years of age, met with their therapist, Dr. Oziel, days after their parents were killed in their Beverly Hills residence. Police obtained a search warrant during an investigation of the murders to search Dr. Oziel's residence and offices. In the course of executing the warrant, police retrieved audiotape cassettes and notes of Dr. Oziel's sessions with Lyle and Erik.

Dr. Oziel filed a motion in court claiming for the Menendez brothers the psychotherapist-patient privilege regarding the items seized pursuant to the search warrant. The trial court ruled that the psychotherapist-patient privilege did not apply to the taped communications because of the *Tarasoff* duty to warn exception. The Menendez brothers had threatened Dr. Oziel, who felt he needed to warn his wife and his lover, of potential collateral harm.

The California Supreme Court generally agreed with the trial court's analysis, holding that the psychotherapist-patient privilege did not apply in a *Tarasoff* duty to warn situation: ". . . a psychotherapist's *Tarasoff* warning to the patient's intended victim is not covered by the privilege even if it relates an otherwise protected communication, provided that the conditions of the 'dangerous patient' exception are satisfied, viz., there is reasonable cause for the psychotherapist to believe that (1) the patient is dangerous and (2) disclosure of the communication is necessary to prevent any harm."

The absence of one simple overriding confidentiality or privilege law applying to social workers in many jurisdictions makes it difficult for social workers to know what must be kept confidential and when they must assert a privilege. The situation is made even more complex and difficult because, as has been stated, each confidentiality or privilege law that may apply to social workers may have conflicting exceptions based on competing policies.

For example, each State has a child abuse and neglect reporting law, which annuls all or most other confidentiality laws and testimonial privileges. All of these reporting laws apply to social workers. At the same time, the federal government imposes strict confidentiality requirements on all those who are engaged in substance abuse work if the work is connected in any way, no matter how attenuated the connection, to the federal government. Until 1986, the federal government insisted that its substance abuse confidentiality law contained no exception for child abuse and neglect reporting. Social workers who only did occasional substance abuse work with little connection to the federal government were probably unaware of the federal confidentiality requirements and of the conflict they faced; however, many social workers were aware of the conflict and were torn between their obligation to report child abuse and their simultaneous obligation to protect the confidentiality of their substance abuse clients. Fortunately, Congress resolved the conflict in 1986 by amending the substance abuse confidentiality laws to make an exception for child abuse and neglect reporting. 42 U.S.C §§ 290dd-3 and, 290ee-3; 42 C.F.R. § 2.1(c)(6).

ETHICAL AND PROFESSIONAL REQUIREMENTS

Conflicts may arise for social workers when they are asked to testify or otherwise reveal information covered by an ethical or professional obligation to maintain confidentiality, but not covered by a privilege or legal protection of confidentiality.

The NASW *Code of Ethics* contains specific provisions concerning confidentiality and privilege:[2]

> (a) Social workers should respect clients' right to privacy. Social workers should not solicit private information from clients unless it is essential to providing services or conducting social work evaluation or research. Once private information is shared, standards of confidentiality apply.
> (b) Social workers may disclose confidential information when appropriate with valid consent from a client or a person legally authorized to consent on behalf of a client.
> (c) Social workers should protect the confidentiality of all information obtained in the

---

2. *Code of Ethics* (National Association of Social Workers, 1996), Ethical Standard 1.07. Selected excerpts. Reprinted with permission.

course of professional service, except for compelling professional reasons . . .

(d) Social workers should inform clients, to the extent possible, about the disclosure of confidential information and the potential consequences, when feasible before the disclosure is made. This applies whether social workers disclose confidential information on the basis of a legal requirement or client consent.

(e) Social workers should discuss with clients and other interested parties the nature of confidentiality and limitations of clients' right to confidentiality.

*   *   *

(j) Social workers should protect the confidentiality of clients during legal proceedings to the extent permitted by law. When a court of law or other legally authorized body orders social workers to disclose confidential or privileged information without a client's consent and such disclosure could cause harm to the client, social workers should request that the court withdraw the order or limit the order as narrowly as possible or maintain the records under seal, unavailable for public inspection.

If a social worker is required to reveal client information and there is no legal protection of confidentiality or privilege that applies in the particular situation, the social worker must either violate his or her professional or personal standards or face sanctions, such as being held in contempt of court for refusing to testify or facing loss of employment. For example, in *Belmont v. California State Personnel Board*, 36 Cal. App.3d 518, 111 Cal.Rptr. 607 (1974), two psychiatric social workers, who were employed by the State welfare department to work with emotionally disturbed welfare recipients, refused to turn over information on the recipients for inclusion in the department's central data bank. Because of their refusal, they were suspended for five days without pay

for "willful disobedience." On appeal of the suspension order, they insisted that:

a special professional relationship exists between themselves and their "clients" entitling them to assume an adversary position toward their employer, the State of California, defending "the rights of their clients." They speak of a social worker's "code of ethics" designed to "protect those clients who come into professional contact with the social worker," to which they owe a higher duty of obedience than to their employer. And they argue that the Department's order [to turn over the information] tends to "seriously undercut the relationship between the patient and the psychiatric social worker," a relationship which they strongly suggest is covered by the psychotherapist-patient privilege against nondisclosure, created by [a California statute.]

Nevertheless, the court of appeals upheld the suspension, stating that the social workers were legally bound to fulfill the duties of their employment, or suffer disciplinary action.

RESPONDING TO REQUESTS TO REVEAL INFORMATION OR TO TESTIFY

As has been noted, a professional who discloses confidential or privileged information may be sued for damages. This may take the form of suits for malpractice, breach of contract, breach of confidentiality, or invasion of privacy. Furthermore, many confidentiality and privilege laws provide that their violation is a crime, a professional may be prosecuted for the crime of breach of confidentiality. Finally, a professional's license or credential may be suspended or revoked for breaching confidentiality laws. Thus, it is important that social workers do not lightly reveal information about a client or respond to requests for information without considering confidentiality, even if the request comes from a court or from a matter in court.

When someone is seeking to obtain a social worker's records for a court case, or possibly for an official investigation of some sort, the social worker may be served with a subpoena or a subpoena *duces tecum*. A **subpoena** compels the social worker to appear in court as a witness. A **subpoena** *duces tecum* (du-ches tay-kum) compels the social worker to turn over documents or records. If a social worker is served with a subpoena or a subpoena *duces tecum*, he or she should consult with a supervisor and, if possible, an agency attorney before responding. The social worker is not required to yield records just because a subpoena *duces tecum* has been issued by a court or other official body. Courts issue subpoenas without any controls; usually a clerk merely hands blank subpoenas to lawyers. Indeed, most lawyers have blank subpoena forms in their offices. One must respond to a subpoena, but one may respond by claiming confidentiality or privilege. If the claim is contested, there will be a court hearing, and a judge will decide if the claim is valid or if the records must be turned over. Indeed, failing to legally challenge a subpoena could subject the social worker to liability. This will be discussed in more detail in the next chapter.

Even if a court specifically orders a social worker to turn over his or her records, a social worker may refuse to comply with the order. He or she would then probably be held in contempt of court but

could challenge the order in a higher court or in a different court by appealing the contempt order. Courts will not hesitate to issue contempt orders against professionals who refuse to comply with a subpoena, as is illustrated in the following case, *In re Zuniga*, 714 F.2d 632 (1983), *cert. denied*, 464 U.S. 983 (1983):

Pierce is a practicing psychiatrist licensed to practice medicine in the state of Michigan. On November 24, 1982 a subpoena duces tecum was issued by the Grand Jury for the Eastern District of Michigan commanding Pierce . . . to appear and produce the following records:

"Patient files, progress notes, ledger cards, copies of insurance claim forms and any other documentation supporting dates of service rendered and identity of patient receiving said service for the years 1978 and 1979 for the following individuals and all dependents thereof covered under the individuals' Blue Cross/Blue Shield contract . . ."

The subpoena directed Pierce to appear before the grand jury on December 11, 1980. On December 3, 1980, he filed a motion to quash the subpoena in the district court. A hearing on the motion was conducted, and on February 26, 1981, [the court] issued an order denying the motion to quash. The district court, in accordance with the Government's concession, held that the records to be produced would be redacted of information other than the data showing the patient's name and the fact and time of treatment.

Pierce persisted in his refusal to produce the subpoenaed documents and the Government [sought to hold him in contempt]. Another hearing was conducted . . . [and] the court found Pierce in civil contempt and remanded him to the custody of the United States Marshall until such time as [he] purged himself of contempt by compliance.

The court of appeals affirmed the contempt, concluding that Pierce's refusal to

comply with the subpoena was unjustified. The court reasoned:

> [T]he grand jury is seeking limited informa-
> tion pertaining to individual patients. The
> identity of these patients, as indicated, is al-
> ready known to the grand jury from the insur-
> ance forms in its possession. Thus, the
> patients' interest in the privacy of the infor-
> mation is diminished.
>
> Furthermore, the information sought will
> be protected by the veil of secrecy attending
> grand jury proceedings. . . . The information
> will be disclosed only to the minimal extent
> necessary to promote a proper governmental
> interest and will not be subject to widespread
> dissemination.
>
> In sum, weighing the slight intrusion on the
> patients' privacy interest against the need for
> the grand jury to conduct an effective and com-
> prehensive investigation into alleged violation
> of the law, the Court concludes that enforce-
> ment of the subpoenas does not unconstitu-
> tionally infringe on the rights of the patients.

Unlike subpoenas, search warrants must
be complied with immediately. That is,
they cannot be contested at the time they
are served. After the execution of a warrant, a defense attorney could file a motion
to suppress any evidence seized under the
warrant, usually alleging that the warrant
was not based upon probable cause.

Frequently, social workers who work
with sexually abused children or who investigate sexual abuse allegations for a
social services department may be confronted with a subpoena or subpoena
duces tecum by a criminal defense attorney under the constitutional right to compulsory process. The Supreme Court in
Pennsylvania v. Ritchie, 480 U.S. 39
(1987), provided guidance on how such
matters should be addressed:

> As part of its efforts to combat child abuse,
> the Commonwealth of Pennsylvania has es-

tablished Children and Youth Services (CYS),
a protective service agency charged with investigating cases of suspected mistreatment
and neglect. In 1979, respondent George
Ritchie was charged with rape, involuntary
deviate sexual intercourse, and incest, and
corruption of a minor. The victim of the alleged attacks was his 13-year-old daughter,
who claimed that she had been assaulted by
Ritchie two or three times per week during
the previous four years. The girl reported the
incidents to the police, and the matter then
was referred to the CYS.

During pretrial discovery, Ritchie served
CYS with a subpoena, seeking access to the
records concerning the daughter. Ritchie requested disclosure of the file related to the
immediate charges, as well as certain records
that he claimed were compiled in 1978, when
CYS investigated a separate report by an
unidentified source that Ritchie's children were
being abused. CYS refused to comply with the
subpoena, claiming that the records were
privileged under Pennsylvania law. The relevant statute provides that all reports and other
information obtained in the course of a CYS
investigation must be kept confidential, subject to 11 specific exceptions. One of those exceptions is that the agency may disclose the
reports to a "court of competent jurisdiction
pursuant to a court order."

Ritchie moved to have CYS sanctioned for
failing to honor the subpoena, and the trial
court held a hearing on the motion in chambers. Ritchie argued that he was entitled to the
information because the file might contain the
names of favorable witnesses, as well as other,
unspecified exculpatory evidence. He also requested disclosure of a medical report that he
believed was compiled during the 1978 CYS
investigation. Although the trial judge acknowledged that he had not examined the
entire CYS file, he accepted a CYS representative's assertion that there was no medical report in the record. The judge then denied the
motion and refused to order CYS to disclose
the files.

At trial, the main witness against Ritchie
was his daughter. In an attempt to rebut her
testimony, defense counsel cross-examined
the girl at length, questioning her on all as-

pects of the alleged attacks and her reasons for not reporting the incidents sooner. Except for routine evidentiary rulings, the trial judge placed no limitation on the scope of cross-examination. At the close of trial Ritchie was convicted by a jury on all counts, and the judge sentenced him to 3 to 10 years in prison.

[It is] . . . suggested that the failure to disclose the CYS file violated the Sixth Amendment's guarantee of compulsory process. Ritchie asserts that the trial court's ruling prevented him from learning the names of the "witnesses in his favor," as well as other evidence that might be contained in the file. Although the basis for the Pennsylvania Supreme Court's ruling on this point is unclear, it apparently concluded that the right of compulsory process includes the right to have the State's assistance in uncovering arguably useful information, without regard to the existence of a state-created restriction—here, the confidentiality of the files.

This Court has never squarely held that the Compulsory Process Clause guarantees the right to discover the identity of witnesses, or to require the government to produce exculpatory evidence. Instead, the Court traditionally has evaluated claims such as those raised by Ritchie under the broader protections of the Due Process Clause of the Fourteenth Amendment. Because the applicability of the Sixth Amendment to this type of case is unsettled, and because our Fourteenth Amendment precedents addressing the fundamental fairness of trials establish a clear framework for review, we adopt a due process analysis for purposes of this case . . .

It is well settled that the government has the obligation to turn over evidence in its possession that is both favorable to the accused and material to guilt or punishment. Although courts have used different terminologies to define "materiality," a majority of this Court has agreed, "[e]vidence is material only if there is a reasonable probability that, had the evidence been disclosed to the defense, the result of the proceeding would have been different. A 'reasonable probability' is a probability sufficient to undermine confidence in the outcome."

At this stage, of course, it is impossible to say whether any information in the CYS records may be relevant to Ritchie's claim of innocence, because neither the prosecution nor defense counsel has seen the information, and the trial judge acknowledged that he had not reviewed the full file. The Commonwealth, however, argues that no materiality inquiry is required, because a statute renders the contents of the file privileged. Requiring disclosure here, it is argued, would override the Commonwealth's compelling interest in confidentiality on the mere speculation that the file "might" have been useful to the defense.

Although we recognize that the public interest in protecting this type of sensitive information is strong, we do not agree that this interest necessarily prevents disclosure in all circumstances . . . the Pennsylvania law provides that the information shall be disclosed in certain circumstances, including when CYS is directed to do so by court order. Given that the Pennsylvania Legislature contemplated some use of CYS records in judicial proceedings, we cannot conclude that the statute prevents all disclosure in criminal prosecutions. In the absence of any apparent state policy to the contrary, we therefore have no reason to believe that relevant information would not be disclosed when a court of competent jurisdiction determines that the information is "material" to the defense of the accused.

We therefore affirm the decision of the [lower] Court to the extent it orders a remand for further proceedings. Ritchie is entitled to have the CYS file reviewed by the trial court to determine whether it contains information that probably would have changed the outcome of his trial. If it does, he must be given a new trial. If the records maintained by CYS contain no such information, or if the nondisclosure was harmless beyond a reasonable doubt, the lower court will be free to reinstate the prior conviction.

This ruling does not end our analysis, because the Pennsylvania Supreme Court did more than simply remand. It also held that defense counsel must be allowed to examine all of the confidential information, both relevant and irrelevant, and present arguments in favor of disclosure. The court apparently concluded that whenever a defendant alleges that protected evidence might be material, the appropriate method of assessing this claim is to grant full access to the disputed information, regardless of the State's interest in confidentiality. We cannot agree.

A defendant's right to discover exculpatory evidence does not include the unsupervised authority to search through the Commonwealth's files . . . it is the State that decides which information must be disclosed. Unless defense counsel becomes aware that other exculpatory evidence was withheld and brings it to the court's attention, the prosecutor's decision on disclosure is final. Defense counsel has no constitutional right to conduct his own search of the State's files to argue relevance.

We find that Ritchie's interest (as well as that of the Commonwealth) in ensuring a fair trial can be protected fully by requiring that the CYS files be submitted only to the trial court for in camera review. Although this rule denies Ritchie the benefits of an "advocate's eye," we note that the trial court's discretion is not unbounded. If a defendant is aware of specific information contained in the file (e.g., the medical report), he is free to request it directly from the court, and argue in favor of its materiality.

Child abuse is one of the most difficult crimes to detect and prosecute, in large part because there often are no witnesses except the victim. A child's feelings of vulnerability and guilt and his or her unwillingness to come forward are particularly acute when the abuser is a parent. It therefore is essential that the child have a state-designated person to whom he may turn, and to do so with the assurance of confidentiality. Relatives and neighbors who suspect abuse also will be more willing to come forward if they know that their identities will be protected . . . The Commonwealth's purpose would be frustrated if this confidential material had to be disclosed upon demand to a defendant charged with criminal child abuse, simply because a trial court may not recognize exculpatory evidence. Neither precedent nor common sense requires such a result.

We agree that Ritchie is entitled to know whether the CYS file contains information that may have changed the outcome of his trial had it been disclosed. Thus we agree that a remand is necessary. We disagree with the decision of the Pennsylvania Supreme Court to the extent that it allows defense counsel access to the CYS file. An in camera review by the trial court will serve Ritchie's interest without destroying the Commonwealth's need to protect the confidentiality of those involved in child-abuse investigations.

It is far more common to seek a social worker's records informally than with a subpoena or a subpoena *duces tecum*. Someone, like a probation officer, potential employer, landlord of a client, a friend or relative of a client, or a welfare worker will telephone and ask a social worker a question about a client. Without thinking, the social worker may answer the question and thereby disclose information from the client's record. Social workers must be cautious about such casual disclosures of client records. They must respect their clients' right to privacy and be aware of any legal and ethical confidentiality requirements.

If a social worker receives a telephone call seeking information about a client or is otherwise asked to reveal information about a client, the social worker should not say anything—not even something he or she believes is favorable or of benefit to the client—without considering whether the information sought is confidential. Even revealing that the client is, in fact, a client may violate confidentiality laws. When in doubt, consult with a supervisor, or perhaps a lawyer. The social worker should also consult with the client, since the client may readily agree to the release of information, eliminating problems.

The South Dakota murder case, *State v. Martin, supra,* describes a social worker's

(Lawlor's) efforts to assert a privilege. This case provides several valuable lessons on the appropriate response to receiving a subpoena:

> At the trial, after . . . objections and records were made, Lawlor persistently, if not arrogantly, refused to testify. The trial court specifically advised and admonished the witness at an in camera proceeding. After repeated refusals the trial court quite properly found the witness in contempt. All parties were admonished not to reveal this publicly until after the trial, at which time the court would ascertain the appropriate sanctions. The trial court then indicated, over timely objections, that the witness's testimony from the preliminary hearing would be read to the jury. Upon reconvening, Martin then waived the privilege so that the witness could testify in person. He urges here that the conduct of the trial court in directing that the preliminary transcript be read in essence forced him to waive the privilege.
>
> The trial court was confronted with a witness who improperly refused to testify despite being ordered to do so. The witness had previously testified under oath at a proceeding where (Martin) had an opportunity to cross-examine him. When considering the posture of the case and the totality of circumstances before the trial court, we conclude that the court acted properly.

Based on this case, it is clear that if social workers have questions about the propriety of testifying, they should not testify at any hearing. Social workers cannot decide that their testimony at one hearing will be harmless and thus testify; such testimony may be used at other hearings and end up becoming quite harmful. Moreover, if a social worker testifies once, or even reveals information in another manner, such as in a conversation with the police, a court may rule that the social worker or the client waived any privilege

he or she may have and can force the social worker to testify at a time when he or she does not wish to do so.

Note that Lawlor had his own counsel at the preliminary hearing. While this counsel was not able to prevent Lawlor's testimony, the counsel surely helped Lawlor formulate his position. A social worker cannot rely on a client's counsel for advice. This counsel has other concerns, which may even be in conflict with the social worker's concerns. The social worker should obtain separate counsel for advice if there is a privilege and a need to assert the privilege.

Lawlor's refusal to testify at the trial was characterized as "arrogant" by the court. This perceived arrogance, whether or not it truly existed, surely hurt Lawlor. An angered judge is not likely to accord a professional privilege; any sanction for a refusal to testify is likely to be worse if a witness is perceived as arrogant.

SPECIAL PROBLEMS

Client Access to Records

One continuing problem that faces social workers is whether clients can have access to their own records. As a general matter, clients should have access to their own records, which may be considered their property. Moreover, the NASW *Code of Ethics* requires that: "Social workers should provide clients with reasonable access to records concerning the client."[3] Nevertheless, in problematic situations, a

---

3. Ethical Standard 1.08.

social worker should consider carefully and consult with supervisors before providing access. Access may be denied in certain situations—for example, if a social worker believes that a client could become emotionally disturbed if he or she saw the records. Even laws that mandate access to one's own records contain exceptions for such situations and NASW only requires "reasonable" access.

Before providing access, a social worker should carefully protect the confidences of others that may be contained in the records. For example, if a client's father said something about her, the social worker may take this out of her records before providing her access to them. The NASW *Code of Ethics* requires this.

A federal law, the Freedom of Information Act, 5 U.S.C. § 552, and similar State laws provide for access to records maintained by the government, including public social work agencies. These laws usually allow people to obtain any records maintained by a public agency, whether or not the records relate to them, unless access to one's own records would be harmful or access to records that relate to others is precluded by a confidentiality law. There may also be other exceptions to access established by freedom of information laws. Most freedom of information laws, for example, exempt from general access personnel records and records relating to litigation.

Parental Access to Children's Records

A problem that may arise for social workers is whether parents should have access to their children's records. Generally, parents are entitled to their chil-

dren's records, just as the children would be entitled to the records themselves if they were adults. Records related to birth control, treatment for substance abuse, or treatment for venereal disease are generally exceptions to this rule, however. See, e.g., 42 C.F.R. § 2.14.

A social worker who is providing psychotherapy to teenage clients may be concerned about the detrimental effect of disclosing confidential information to the parent. If a parent having legal custody requests disclosure of such information, the social worker may refuse the request, thereby requiring the parent to hire an attorney to let a court decide if the parent was entitled to this information. The social worker may also have adopted agency policy precluding such disclosure. Finally, State practice acts may not have any exception that would allow a parent to have access to this information.

As we have seen, parents are specifically granted access to their children's school records under FERPA. A social worker licensed under a State's practice act, however, that is also practicing in the school setting, should ensure that client confidentiality is protected. FERPA would allow the social worker to maintain his or her client's files apart from the official school files to maintain client confidentiality.

Media Publishing Information about Clients

Occasionally, social workers are involved in highly publicized cases, such as cases where murders occurred and surviving children are subject to child protection cases. Certain media may make repeated efforts to obtain information that is confidential. Indeed, when cases become highly publicized, child victims of abuse may suffer greatly from the public exposure. Generally, courts cannot prevent the media from publicizing information about a client legally obtained by the media, as that would be considered a "prior restraint" on the media's constitutional right to freedom of the press. See, e.g., *Oklahoma Pub. Co. v. District Court*, 430 U.S. 308 (1977). In such cases, social workers may want to request courts to close hearings from the public in order to avoid additional publicity of otherwise confidential information.

Professional Liability

As we have seen, State practice acts allow social workers to label themselves as professionals if they have demonstrated a baseline level of competence through education, experience, and testing. But whether they are licensed or unlicensed, social workers must engage in behavior that is in accordance with the profession's standard of care. If a social worker fails to do so, and if someone is injured because of this failure, the social worker may be **liable** for this injury.

"Liability . . . is a broad legal term of the most comprehensive significance."[1] It has been defined to mean, *inter alia*, "responsibility"; an "obligation one is bound in law or justice to perform"; and having "to do, pay, or make good something."[2] If one is liable for one's conduct, one is "responsible" and "accountable" for it and may be made to "make satisfaction, comprehension, or restitution."[3]

This chapter will review the kinds of activities and conduct for which social workers may be found liable and the forms that liability may take. Social workers may be liable for a broad range of professional activities. The liability may be based on an action or a failure to act, may stem from negligence or intentional conduct, and may be the result of a social worker's own conduct or the actions of others whom the social worker supervises or oversees.

The most common form and well-known of professional liability is known as **malpractice**. Malpractice means a negligent failure to perform professional obligations or in accordance with professional standards. Malpractice claims are primarily brought against social workers who are acting as therapists. As we shall see, not all States recognize malpractice claims against social workers. When someone is liable for the action of another, one is said to be vicariously liable. **Vicarious liability** for social workers generally stems from the doctrine of **respondent superior**, which in Latin means, "let the master answer," and from their position as supervisors or administrators at agencies. If there is vicarious liability, a social worker may be held responsible for the actions of another person at the agency even if the social worker had nothing to do with the conduct that caused an injury and did not fail to properly supervise. If the social worker had failed to properly supervise, he or she might be held directly liable for this failure whether or not he or she could or would be vicariously liable.

If a social worker is held liable for an injury by a court, the social worker may be required to pay for **compensatory damages**; this means monetary damages to compensate for the loss or injury suffered as a result of the social worker's conduct. The injured person may also sue for **punitive damages**; this means monetary damages to punish the social worker for egregious behavior. Punative damages are rarely rewarded.

One additional type of misconduct, **intentional misconduct**, refers to instances where the social worker engages in deliberate wrongdoing.

Professional liability insurance generally provides both legal representation and payment of damages in most civil suits based on negligence or on vicarious liability that can be brought against a so-

---

1. *Black's Law Dictionary*, 6th ed. (West: Minneapolis, MN, 1991), p. 631.
2. *Id.*
3. *Id.*

cial worker for professional activities. Liability insurance is often necessary even if malpractice claims against social workers are not recognized in certain jurisdictions or if it is difficult for the plaintiff to succeed in a malpractice suit against a social worker. This is so because payment of lawyer's fees would still be necessary to defend the lawsuit.

Individual liability insurance may be necessary for social workers in private practice but also for social workers employed at either government or private agencies. Social workers who work for government agencies, for example, may believe they are immune from lawsuits or that their agencies will represent them in any lawsuit and indemnify them if they must pay damages. State laws and policies, however, have differing provisions for representation and indemnification of government employees that may not cover individuals or certain types of cases.

Social workers who work for a private agency may believe that their agency's liability insurance policies will protect them, but many agencies have no insurance and even if they did, it may not cover employees sued as individuals.

As these examples show, a social worker's practice setting may be relevant to decisions about professional liability insurance. It also may be relevant to professional liability. Practicing alone or with others, working at a private or public agency, or working as a case worker or as an administrator may subject the social worker to professional liability in the various settings in which social workers may practice. By recognizing some of the problem areas in the various forms of practice, social workers can take steps to decrease their risk of being sued and that

suits will be successful. This is sometimes referred to as **risk management**. This chapter will also look at the liability of public agencies employing social workers, such as social services departments. Social workers employed by public agencies can assist their agencies with risk management.

PRACTITIONER LIABILITY

Civil Liability Based on Negligence

Malpractice. When someone is injured or suffers harm because of a social worker's failure to perform in a manner consistent with the standard of care of the profession, he or she may bring a malpractice action and seek monetary damages for the injury suffered.

To prevail in a malpractice action, the plaintiff must establish: 1) that a defendant owed a legal duty to the plaintiff, such as through a therapist-client relationship; 2) that the defendant's conduct fell below the acceptable standard of care; 3) that the defendant's conduct was the proximate cause of injury to the plaintiff; and 4) that an actual injury was sustained by the plaintiff.[4] **Proximate cause** refers to foreseeability and the causal relationship between an action or inaction and an injury.

Social workers are professionals who need certain skills and training. Thus, they have a duty to exercise due care in the practice of their profession may be held liable for malpractice if their conduct

---

4. Benjamin M. Schutz, *Legal Liability in Psychotherapy* (Josey-Bass Publishers: San Francisco, 1990), pp. 3, 5.

falls below the acceptable standards of care. However, the courts have not always recognized social work as a profession with professional standards of care and have been confused as to what social workers do or who should be considered a social worker. Thus, the courts have not always recognized that a social worker could be liable for malpractice. With increased recognition of social work as a profession and with increased licensing, social worker liability for malpractice may also increase.

Even if it is recognized that social workers have a duty to conform to professional standard of care, determining to whom social workers owe this duty may not be easy. For example, does a social worker doing family therapy owe a duty to each member of the family or to the family unit as a whole? What if the best plan for a family unit is to have one member of the family live apart from the family but this is not in the best interests of this particular family member? To whom does the social worker owe a duty in this situation? To give two other examples: does a child welfare worker owe a duty to a child's natural parents to reunite them with their child or to the child to keep him or her safe from all possible harm and does a hospital social worker owe a duty to an elderly, unconscious patient or to the patient's family?

Not all courts are willing to extend the professional's duty to exercise due care to those other than the client. This unwillingness may shield social workers from malpractice liability. In *Chatman v. Millis*, 257 Ark. 451, 517 S.W.2d 504 (1975), for example, a psychologist who made a recommendation in a child visitation dispute was held to have no duty to exercise due care to the parent who was not his client. The psychologist was thus relieved of malpractice liability. The facts in *Chatman* are that Mrs. Chatman was divorced from her husband, Mr. Chatman, who had visitation privileges with their two-and-a-half-year-old son, Chris. When Mrs. Chatman became concerned that her former husband had sexually molested Chris, she went to Dr. Millis, a licensed psychologist, to have him evaluate Mr. Chatman's. Dr. Millis met with Mrs. Chatman and Chris, but not with Mr. Chatman. Nonetheless, Dr. Millis wrote a letter to Mrs. Chatman's attorney in which he stated that her former husband was a homosexual and he was of the opinion "it would not be a good idea to allow Chris to continue to visit his father." On the basis of the letter, Mr. Chatman sued Dr. Millis for defamation and malpractice. The trial court dismissed the defamation claim for technical reasons and also dismissed the malpractice claim, ruling:

> that no action for malpractice exists in this state against a psychologist; that even if such an action were permitted in this jurisdiction, there would have to be a doctor-patient relationship or some similar relationship between the parties, and that . . . Chatman had never been examined by Millis, and in fact, was not even known to the doctor; accordingly, there could be no action for malpractice.

The Arkansas Supreme Court affirmed, agreeing that no action would lie in this case because Millis "owed no duty, *as a doctor*, to [Chatman], and this duty must be in existence before [Chatman] can recover because of negligence, constituting malpractice."

It is important to keep in mind that liability for malpractice does not just apply to paid professionals. For example, if a volunteer represents himself or herself as having special skills and training, he or she may be held liable for malpractice, and, if a social worker does volunteer work as a social worker, he or she would be held to the standard of care of professional social workers and found liable for malpractice. The fact that he or she was an unpaid volunteer for a client or agency would be irrelevant.

Supervisor Liability. Social workers in supervisory positions may be found directly or vicariously liable for the malpractice of supervisees and volunteers. In this regard, there are typically two types of liability claims related to supervision: clients not receiving adequate treatment and staff not receiving adequate supervision.[5]

Cohen v. State, 51 A.D. 2d 494, 382 N.Y.S. 2d 128 (1976), *order aff'd*, 41 N.Y. 2d, 1086, 364 N.E. 2d 1134, 396 N.Y.S. 2d 363 (1977), illustrates the first type of supervisor liability for a client's care. This case involves a resident of a psychiatric facility who committed suicide. The family brought a wrongful death action based on the fact that Alan Cohen, the decedent, was never seen by the attending psychiatrist, Dr. Bjork. Instead, Cohen's psychiatric care had been provided by a first year resident, Dr. Sverd. The following excerpts show how the supervising psychiatrist was found directly liable for the inadequate treatment of Alan Cohen:

Alan Cohen . . . was 23 years of age, married, and at the time of his death, April 22, 1971, he was a third year medical student at the Down-

state Medical Center University of the State of New York. Prior to admission as a medical student he had graduated from the University of Rochester, receiving a Bachelor of Arts degree, with a major in psychology.

In January, 1971, he voluntarily entered the Downstate Medical Center psychiatric department for a condition diagnosed as paranoid schizophrenia. He had prior to this admission been an outpatient at the psychiatric ward of the Kings County Hospital. Upon admission he was assigned to Ward 52, which consisted of 32 beds, with an open door, and a program organized around the concept of a therapeutic community. There were five nurses and generally five aides, together with members of the medical staff, occupational therapists, psychology staff and social workers.

As found by the court [below], the treating physician was not a qualified psychiatrist and had only just started on the many years of residency required to attain certification. In recognition of this system of having residents handle the immediate contact and treatment of patients, the defendant had an established hierarchy to provide medical care which in the decedent's case was: Dr. Bjork (attending doctor); then Dr. Rosenberg, a third year resident; and then Dr. Sverd, a first year resident and treating physician.

While this record establishes that patients were discussed at team meetings, it is not established that any evaluation of this decedent's suicide propensities was made by a qualified psychiatrist during his stay at the hospital. While there are inferences of judgment being made by Dr. Bjork, there is nothing in the hospital records to support a finding that she ever made a medical judgment fully based upon the nurses' notes and any kind of personal interview. The fact that the decedent was himself a medical student at Downstate may have influenced the staff in exercising its judgment.

While the court might have given more credence to the assertions of Dr. Bjork that she was fully informed than it did, the fact remains that the record does not contain any written evidence by her or any qualified psychiatrist as to suicidal propensities in and about the time of death. Indeed, she conceded

---

5. Frederick G. Reamer, *Social Work Malpractice and Liability* (Columbia University Press: New York 1994), p. 142.

that the decedent should not have been allowed off ward on the day of death in view of the nurses' observations.

On the whole, the record contained questions of fact as to supervision and whether or not any qualified medical judgment as to suicidal propensities and restraint was made in view of his behavior in the last part of his hospitalization. The failure to keep detailed and proper medical notes makes the present situation, under these circumstances, more than an error of medical judgment.

Simmons v. United States, 805 F.2d 1363 (1986), illustrates both direct liability for failure to supervise and vicarious liability for a supervisee's negligent care of the client.

Jerrie Simmons, a member of the Chehalis Tribe, sought mental health consultation from the Indian Health Service and was counseled by Ted Kammers, a social worker. Ms. Simmons had a history of economic deprivation and of physical, sexual and emotional abuse as a child. When she started consultation with Mr. Kammers, she was divorced and pregnant with her fourth child. Ms. Simmons saw Mr. Kammers for counseling from 1973 until August 1980 and maintained the counseling relationship through telephone contacts from then until at least July 9, 1981, the date of her last fact-to-face counseling session.

In October 1978, Mr. Kammers initiated romantic contact with Ms. Simmons during a counseling session, encouraging her to act on her professed feelings of attraction to him. In January 1979 he had sexual intercourse with her during an out-of-town trip and this romantic and sexual relationship continued during the course of Ms. Simmons' treatment.

In January 1980, the Tribal Chairwoman notified Mr. Kammers' supervisor, Victor Sansalone, of her concerns about the relationship between Ms. Simmons and Mr. Kammers. Sansalone took no action either to correct Mr. Kammers' improper counseling or to relieve him of his duties. In August 1980, Ms. Simmons moved to Seattle and began eventually to suffer a variety of emotional problems, ranging from anxiety to depression, which worsened until she was hospitalized for psychiatric treatment in May 1982. She finally attempted suicide in November 1982.

In February 1983 Ms. Simmons learned, through psychiatric consultation with Dr. Patricia Lipscomb, M.D., that her counselor's misconduct was the cause of her psychological problems and that her problems were due essentially to his inappropriate response to the normal "transference phenomenon" in therapy.

On May 23, 1983, Ms. Simmons filed [a tort claim in federal court], based on Mr. Kammers' negligence while counseling her in his capacity as a social worker employed by a United States agency.

The appellate court affirmed an award of damages in an amount of $150,000. The government argued that Mr. Kammer's improper conduct was not within the scope of his employment and thus the government could not be held vicariously liable. The court disagreed, concluding:

When the therapist mishandles transference and becomes sexually involved with a patient, medical authorities are nearly unanimous in considering such conduct to be malpractice. Dr. Brown explained at the trial that the reason sexual involvement with a patient is so harmful is due to the parent-child relationship symbolized by the transference. As she stated, were a therapist to be sexual with a client it would be replicating at a symbolic level the situation in which a parent would be sexual with a child. The kinds of harm that can flow from those sorts of violations of trust are very similar.

Courts have uniformly regarded mishandling of transference as malpractice or gross negligence . . .

For much the same reason, we believe the centrality of transference to therapy renders it impossible to separate an abuse of transference from the treatment itself. The district court correctly found that the abuse of transference occurred within the scope of Mr. Kammers' employment.

The Government also urges that the district court improperly made the employer's legal responsibility coextensive with the ethical standards of the mental health profession. However, the district court merely said that in this case a mental health counselor's conduct fell below widely accepted professional standards, and imposed derivative liability on his employer. The Government's assumption is that the court imposed liability on the employer for conduct outside the scope of employment, thus holding the employer to an ethical standard which governs off duty conduct as well as conduct within business hours. There is no indication that the district court made these distinctions. It found Kammers' conduct to be negligent in toto, and at least some of his negligent acts occurred during therapy sessions, and all arose out of the ongoing therapy relationship he had with Ms. Simmons.

The court concluded that Mr. Kammer's supervisor, Victor Sansalone, was also directly liable for Mr. Kammer's conduct. Mr. Sansalone was informed of the situation between the counselor and Ms. Simmons in January 1980. Since the counseling relationship continued until July 1981, Mr. Sansalone was negligent in failing to do anything to prevent further harm to Ms. Simmons. The court reasoned:

> Mr. Sansalone was aware of the situation. . . . [T]he district court found Ms. Simmons to have suffered psychological damage from the whole course of Mr. Kammers' conduct, at least a portion of which should have been averted by Mr. Sansalone's intervention.
> Under Washington law, liability for supervisory negligence is imposed on one who should have known of the negligent acts of a subordinate. It is arguable that Mr. Sansalone should have supervised Mr. Kammers more closely so that he would have been aware of the situation at a much earlier date.

Dangerous Clients. Based on the reasoning of the infamous *Tarasoff* case dis-

cussed in chapter 18, social workers may have a duty to warn or protect third parties of the imminent actual or implied serious threat of violence made by a client. The duty to warn or protect first requires the duty to accurately assess the danger posed by the client in areas such as:

1) the nature of the client's threat;
2) the client's potential for violence;
3) the client's current living situation;
4) the clients past history of violence;
5) the client's mental and medical status;
6) whether the client is (or should be) taking medication; and
7) whether the client is abusing drugs or alcohol.[6]

The social worker may also have a duty to protect a client from the danger of suicide. This liability generally occurs when the suicidal client was not placed in a secure setting or when the client in a secure setting was released prematurely. In *Ahille v. United States*, 482 F.Supp. 703 (N.D. Calif. 1980), for example, nurses who worked in a psychiatric ward were found liable because they authorized a patient to leave a secure ward, unescorted, even though the patient was continuing to experience significant depression and later committed suicide.

The best—and often legally required—practice to minimize the risk of liability when working with dangerous clients is to regularly consult with medical doctors and clinical psychologists.

---

6.   James Beck and Prudence Baxter, "The Violent Patient," in Lawrence Lifson and Robert Simon (eds.), *The Mental Health Practitioner and the Law: A Comprehensive Handbook* (Harvard University Press: Cambridge, MA, 1998), pp. 153–161.

Improper Assessment. Liability for improper assessment generally occurs for three reasons: 1) clinicians failed to use dianostic techniques according to the standard of care of the profession; 2) clinicians failed to make an accurate assessment based on information provided; or 3) clinicians falied to conduct further assessment that would have revealed the proper diagnosis. We have repeatedly emphasized that social workers should regularly consult with medical doctors or psychologists, especially in the more difficult cases. Many social service agencies have created multidisciplinary review teams where psychologists, physicians, educators, or other mental health professionals offer a wide range of professional expertise to evaluate a case.

Clinicians who base their diagnosis and assessment using the *Diagnostic and Statistical Manual of Mental Disorders*[7] can "demonstrate an objective basis and reasonable belief for their judgments."[8] An inaccurate assessment may result in the client not improving or additional harm to the client. Thus, if it appears that the client is not improving or not benefitting from the treatment, this could indicate the need for additional evaluations or consultations.

Consider the following example. Suppose a client during therapy reveals that a doctor engaged in nonconsenual sexual touching some fifty years earlier. Would this suggest false memory syndrome or repressed memory? What diagnostic techniques would you use according to the

standard of care of the profession? The need for consultation in difficult cases such as this example should be readily apparent.

Improper Treatment. Liability may also arise when a social worker engages in treatment either beyond his or her training or skill, or that is not according to accepted professional norms. An example of treatment that is not according to professional norms is the case *Hammer v. Rosen*, 7 N.Y. 2d 376, 165 N.E. 2d 756 (1960), where a psychiatrist treated a psychotic patient by beating her on a number of occasions. The appellate court did not hesitate in determining that the psychiatrist could be liable for such conduct, stating, "the very nature of the acts complained of bespeaks improper treatment and malpractice."

Another example of improper treatment is the case *Meier v. Ross General Hospital*, 69 Cal. 2d 420, 445 P. 2d 519, 71 Cal. Rptr. 903 (1968), a patient who attempted suicide by slashing his wrists was placed in a hospital's psychiatric wing located on the second floor. The hospitals "open door" policy was a method of treatment that provided a "homelike" atmosphere that deemphasized physical restraint. The "open door" policy allowed patients to leave the hospital, without security devices, locked doors, and barred windows. One day, the patient refused his medications and jumped out of the second floor window to his death. The appellate court held that the hospital and its staff could be liable to the patient's family in a wrongful death action.

Reporting Violations. We saw in chapter 8 that social workers have a duty to report known or suspected child abuse. As made clear in the *Landeros* case, the duty to report first requires the duty to accurately

---

7. American Psychiatric Association: Washington, DC, 1994 (4th edition).

8. R. Madden, *Legal Issues in Social Work, Counseling, and Mental Health* (Sage: Thousand Oaks, CA, 1998), p. 149.

assess child abuse. The National Association of Social Workers (NASW) states that, "All social workers need to have basic knowledge of the indicators of child abuse and neglect . . . [and] to obtain knowledge of the state's child abuse and neglect laws and procedures . . ."[9]

State reporting statutes often require the professional who reports known or suspected child abuse to file a written report. Not reporting known or suspected child abuse, especially when there is subsequent harm to the child by the perpetrator, may subject the social worker to civil and criminal liability, or to disciplinary liability by a State's grievance board.

Poor Record-Keeping. Besides being careful to practice one's profession well, the best defense in a malpractice action may be keeping good records. For example, a social worker's records can show that he or she conscientiously followed acceptable professional standards, that there was informed consent to a course of treatment, or that warnings were given, either to a patient or to a third party. Moreover, a record can show that a social worker consulted with colleagues, supervisors, or other experts. Also, adequate records can show reliance on a specific professional standard, law, or scholarly work. Additionally, adequate records show a subsequent therapist what appropriate follow-up treatment is necessary. Whenever a social worker feels that he or she is making a controversial decision, a record showing a thoughtful weighing of options and consideration of alternatives should be made.

Fear that a detailed record will later harm the client if it is subject to disclosure is not justified, especially if the record is properly subject to disclosure. The social worker does not have authority to determine what is or is not admissible in a subsequent proceeding. Instead, it is the client's attorney who has the duty to keep damaging information out.[10]

Indeed, courts have found that inadequate records themselves can form the basis for malpractice actions. If it was not written in the record, a court may very likely assume it did not happen. In the famous case, *Whitree v. State*, 290 N.Y.S. 2d 486, 56 Misc. 2d 693 (1968), for example, a negligence action was brought against the city of New York on the ground that State doctors committed malpractice against Mr. Whitree while he was confined in Matteawan State Hospital. Portions of the opinion reflect how the court recognized malpractice because of the poor record-keeping practices of the psychiatric professionals:

> Mr. Whitree was born on January 22, 1899 and was 68 years of age on the date of the trial.
>
> Whitree was transferred to Matteawan State Hospital on May 19, 1947, where he was admitted by Dr. William C. Johnston.
>
> The hospital record . . . maintained by the State for [Mr.] Whitree was about as inadequate a record as we have ever examined. We find that said record did not conform to the standards in the community; and, that the inadequacies in this record militated against proper and competent psychiatric and ordinary medical care being given this claimant during his stay at Matteawan State Hospital. We further find that the lack of psychiatric

---

9. Standards 37 and 38, *NASW Standards for Social Work Practice in Child Protection* (February 14, 1981).

10. Robert H. Woody, *Legally Safe Mental Health Practice* (Psychosocial Press: Madison, CT, 1997), p. 62. Used with permission.

care was the primary reason for the inordinate length of this incarceration, with the concomitant side effects of physical injury, moral degradation, and mental anguish. Therefore, to the extent that a hospital record develops information for subsequent treatment, it contributed to the inadequate treatment this claimant received. [Mr. Whitree's] expert doctor testified as to the inadequacies in this record. However, in our opinion it was so inadequate that even a layman could determine that fact.

The hospital record disclosed that Whitree was committed on May 19, 1947, on the strength of the court order of commitment and the Bellevue Hospital psychiatric examination which presented a diagnosis of "Paranoid Condition in a Chronic Alcoholic." It is of interest to note that none of [Mr. Whitree's] medical examinations disclosed any objective physical or physiological findings which could substantiate the diagnosis, Chronic Alcoholic. He was briefly and routinely examined by a staff physician on the admission date.

In the period May 19, 1947, through October 5, 1948, Whitree was psychiatrically examined on five occasions, of which four such examinations took place in the first four months. It is possible he was psychiatrically noted by a Dr. Willner, now deceased, during this period and into the early 1950s. However, Dr. Johnston stated on examination before trial that "Dr. Willner, he had his own way of doing things which I am sure was endorsed by the administration. Maybe a little different than mine." Apparently, Dr. Willner's method of doing things did not include making notes in the hospital record. It is this careless administrative medical procedure that, in our opinion, militates against adequate medical care. We must find that [Mr. Whitree] was not psychiatrically examined by Dr. Willner. The next psychiatric note, which was brief and unsigned, was dated January 19, 1950, almost 15 months after the October, 1948, examination. The next psychiatric note was dated April 22, 1952, almost 3 years and 3 months after the prior examination. . . . Obviously, a man who has been psychiatrically examined 7 times in 6 years, of which only 3 examina-

tions were of any depth and those in the first 4 months of this 6 year period, has not been afforded adequate psychiatric care at Matteawan State Hospital . . . On November 2, 1955, there is a note in the hospital record relating to Whitree medically. This note is so illustrative of the inadequacies of the hospital record and medical treatment that it is reproduced in full herein:

"November 2, 1955: He was sent visiting to Ward 2 at 6:30 A.M. because he was found unconscious in his bed. Physical examination showed T. 99.2, P. regular and strong B.P. 70/50, both pupils regular and contracted, left knee plantar reflexes decreased. Blood sugar 99.3%. Blood RBC 3,700,000. He: 78%. S.R. 18. Hem. 38. Patient remained unconscious until noon. His pupils then showed reaction to light and the sluggish left side reflexes disappeared. On November 3rd this patient *apparently* regained consciousness but he did not react to questioning. On November 7th, patient remained very uncooperative, used profane language to the doctors and attendants, and he claimed he was poisoned and physically abused." "November 8, 1955: This patient improved under treatment and is being returned to his own ward today."

One might fairly ask, what treatment? Were X-rays taken, were fluids induced, how often were pulse and respiration taken, were drugs given, how long was this patient unconscious, 5½ hours or 24 hours, what was done for him on the 2nd, 3rd, 4th, 5th, 6th, 7th, and 8th days of November, 1955? . . . Such a record substantiates [Mr. Whitree's] position that he was not given adequate medical care.

On September 25, 1961, after a thorough and complete psychiatric examination at Bellevue Hospital (Exhibit "14"), Whitree was diagnosed as "Schizoid Personality with Paranoid Features" and further that "He is not in such a state of idiocy, imbecility or insanity as to be incapable of understanding the charge, indictment, proceedings or of making his defense." One, of course, must realize that sanity is an area and not a point on a line. This diagnosis was one that fit within socially acceptable behavior, albeit one that most would prefer not to have. It is our opinion, and we so find, that if this man had received proper and adequate psychiatric treatment such diagnosis would have been developed much sooner; and, Whitree would have been released from Matteawan State Hospital much sooner. [Mr. Whitree's] expert gave us the opinion of three to six months after admission . . . We find that he should have been released from Matteawan State Hospital no later than May 19, 1949.

We awarded [Mr. Whitree] herein the sum of Three Hundred Thousand Dollars ($300,000.00) for all damages, as set forth above, incurred during the period May 19, 1949 through September 8, 1961.

State practice acts or State or federal statutes may define the minimum requirements for content and preservation of records. For example, social workers employed at alcohol and drug abuse treatment centers that receive federal funding (which includes most such centers) must comply with the record-keeping requirements of 42 C.F.R. § 485.60, which provides:

The facility must maintain clinical records on all patients in accordance with accepted professional standards and practice. The clinical records must be completely, promptly, and accurately documented, readily accessible, and systematically organized to facilitate retrieval and compilation of information.

Standard: Content. Each clinical record must contain sufficient information to identify the patient clearly and to justify the diagnosis and treatment. Entries in the clinical record must be made as frequently as is necessary to insure effective treatment and must be signed by personnel providing services. All entries made by assistant level personnel must be countersigned

by the corresponding professional. Documentation on each patient must be consolidated into one clinical record that must contain—

(1) The initial assessment and subsequent reassessment of the patient's needs;
(2) Current plan of treatment;
(3) Identification data and consent or authorization forms;
(4) Pertinent medical history, past and present;
(5) A report of pertinent physical examinations if any;
(6) Progress notes or other documentation that reflect patient reaction to treatment, tests, or injury, or the need to change to established plan of treatment; and
(7) Upon discharge, a discharge summary including patient status relative to goal achievement, prognosis, and future treatment considerations.

Good records should fully document the type of treatment and rationale, including: alternatives to treatment and why they have been rejected; dates and lengths of service, pertinent history, prescriptions of medication, and consultations; if client is suicidal, document all actions taken and why such actions were used, and all actions considered and why they have been rejected; written consents; lab reports; and correspondence. Remember, that there is generally no statute of limitations under the practice acts and never alter records after an adverse incident. Remember, also, to provide training to staff regarding handling of records and confidentiality.[11]

---

11.   JoAnn E. Macbeth, Anne M. Wheeler, John W. Sither, and Joseph N. Onek, *Legal and Risk Management Issues in the Practice of Psychiatry* (Psychiatrist's Purchasing Group: Washington, DC, 1994), pp. 7–6.

***Boundary Violations.* Boundary violations**, which create malpractice liability, occur when the therapist assumes more than one role with the client and, thus, oversteps the appropriate therapeutic boundary. Thus, a social worker should not treat employees, supervisors, or close friends. More significantly, a social worker should never assume an intimate relationship with a current or former client. Courts have not hesitated to impose malpractice liability against therapists in such situations—even when the intimate relationship is with a former client. For example, see *Noto v. St. Vincent's Hospital and Medical Center of New York*, 142 Misc. 2d 292, 537 N.Y.S. 2d 446 (1988). In *Horak v. Biris*, 130 Ill. App. 3d 140, 474 N.E. 2d 13 (1985), a social worker had sexual relations with the plaintiff's wife during the course of marital counseling sought by the Horaks.

> It was alleged that plaintiff went to defendant's office, at defendant's request, to receive counseling and guidance in his personal and marital relationships, ostensibly for the purpose of improving those relationships. Defendant held himself out as a social worker licensed by the State to render such assistance and insight. His license placed him in a position of trust, the violation of which would constitute a breach of the fiduciary relationship . . . Further, we think that the very nature of the therapist-patient relationship, which was alleged and admitted here, gives rise to a clear duty on the therapist's part to engage only in activity or conduct which is calculated to improve the patient's mental or emotional well-being, and to refrain from any activity or conduct which carries with it a foreseeable and unreasonable risk of mental or emotional harm to the patient . . .
>
> [The] defendant possessed or should have possessed a basic knowledge of fundamental psychological principles which routinely come into play during marriage and family

counseling. The "transference phenomenon" is apparently one such principle, and has been defined in psychiatric practice as "a phenomenon" by which the patient transfers feelings towards everyone else to the doctor, who then must react with a proper response, the counter transference, in order to avoid emotional involvement and assist the patient in overcoming problems . . . Accordingly, we believe that plaintiff's allegation of a mishandling of the transference phenomenon sufficiently alleges a breach of the defendant's duty here.

Disclosure Violations. Disclosure violations occur when a social worker discloses unauthorized confidential client communications. In the case, *MacDonald v. Clinger*, 84 A.D. 2d 482, 446 N.Y.S. 2d 801 (1982), for example, liability was based on a psychiatrist's unauthorized disclosure of personal information to the plaintiff's wife; the husband discovered the disclosure during the course of treatment. Social workers should exercise great caution concerning confidential reports that could be sent by facsimile to the wrong number. Cellular telephone calls may be inadvertently overheard by total strangers. Taking client files out of the secure office setting, then having the files lost or stolen, can both subject the social worker to civil liability or to disciplinary liability by a State's grievance board.

Managed-Care Liability. Social workers employed in a managed care setting frequently have competing interests: the financial interests of the third party payer that may limit the number of therapy sessions or level of care needed and the client's need for more therapy sessions or a more intensive level of care. Courts have begun to address these competing interests cases and found liability against the professional—either solely or jointly with the managed care entity.

In *Wilson v. Blue Cross of Southern California*, 271 Cal. Rptr. 876, 222 Cal. App. 3d 660 (1990), for example, a man being treated for major depression, drug dependency, and anorexia was admitted to a hospital on the treating physician's recommendation that he receive three to four weeks of in-patient care. The insurance company refused to pay for more than ten days of the in-patient care because the company hired to conduct utilization reviews of the "medical necessity" of the hospitalization had disagreed with the physician. Since nobody would pay for further hospitalization, the man was released. Twenty days after his release, the young man committed suicide. The trial court found that the treating physician was solely liable. The appellate court reversed, but still held that the physician could be jointly liable with the insurance company and utilization review company if there was "substantial evidence" of their negligent conduct.

As a practical matter, the physician's duty of care should have compelled him to more effectively advocate for the man's continued stay in the hospital, possibly through an internal process.

Client Transfer Liability. Social workers employed in a hospital setting must be aware of federal law that precludes hospitals from "dumping" patients who require emergency medical treatment, but cannot afford to pay for such treatment. 42 U.S.C. § 1395dd. Thus, patients admitted for an emergency mental health hold must be admitted and stabilized before being transferred to another facility, unless the patient can be transferred without further

deteriorating the patient's condition. By admitting emergency mental health patients, hospitals are obviously assuming care and control of the patient. Having assumed this care and control of the patient, the social worker employed in the hospital may be held liable under the *Tarasoff* doctrine for foreseeable harm to a third party by a client. A difficult question may arise as to how or when this *Tarasoff* liability is absolved when a client transfers to a subsequent treatment agency.

Consider the following example. Suppose Mr. Smith was admitted to a hospital on an emergency mental health hold because of schizophrenia with a delusional system involving his family. Mr. Smith was treated with antipsychotic medication, stabilized, and released. One month later, Mr. Smith was evaluated by an outpatient counseling center, who referred Mr. Smith to a consulting psychiatrist. Mr. Smith ran out of medication, but the consulting psychiatrist disagreed with the diagnosis of schizophrenia and refused to refill Mr. Smith's medication. During the following months, Mr. Smith's condition began to deteriorate; however, the counseling center refused to admit Mr. Smith on a mental health hold despite his family's request to do so. *Nine months* after he was seen by the consulting psychiatrist, Mr. Smith, while in a delusional state, kills his family. Is the consulting psychiatrist liable under the *Tarasoff* doctrine for not warning or protecting Mr. Smith's family? The Ohio Supreme Court, in the case *Morgan v. Family Counseling Center*, 77 Oh. 284, 673 N. Ed. 2d 13/1 (1997), answered this question in the affirmative. The court reasoned that a "special relationship" exists between the outpatient psychotherapist and the client:

One who takes charge of a third person whom he knows or should know to be likely to cause bodily harm to others if not controlled is under a duty to exercise reasonable care to control the third person to prevent him from doing such harm.

[The] courts acknowledge that [this] duty can be imposed not only upon psychiatrists, but also on psychologists, social workers, mental health clinic[ians] and other mental health professionals who know, or should have known, of their patient's violent propensities. The courts do not impose any single formulation as to what steps must be taken to alleviate the danger. Depending upon the facts and the allegations of the case, the particular psychotherapist-defendant may or may not be required to perform any number of acts, including prescribing medication, fashioning a program for treatment, using whatever ability he or she has to control access to weapons or to persuade the patient to voluntarily enter a hospital, issuing warning or notifying the authorities and, if appropriate, initiating involuntary commitment proceedings.

Although the outpatient setting affords the psychotherapist a lesser degree of control over the patient than does the hospital setting, it nevertheless embodies sufficient elements of control to warrant a corresponding duty to control.

Morgan teaches that significant risk for liability attaches once a therapist begins to see a client in an outpatient setting. If it is later determined that this client should be referred to another agency, there are practical ways that may help avoid risk for liability in the transfer of the client. One way is to develop contracts between agencies that define how referrals are to be made and how the subsequent agency will assume care and "control" of the client. Another way is to have clearly stated policies and procedures that define how the client is to be transferred to the other agency. These suggestions will help to ensure that potentially dangerous clients, especially

ones that may harm a third party, are always under the care and control of a qualified professional.

Civil Liability Based on Intentional Acts

As we have seen, malpractice is generally based on negligent conduct. Occasionally, however, the conduct may also be intentional. Social workers may be sued for various types of intentional conduct in combination with or instead of a malpractice action. Generally, malpractice insurance does not provide coverage for intentional wrongdoing.

Consent-to-Treat Issues. A client must have capacity and knowledge of the risks and alternatives to make an intelligent **consent to treatment**. As we saw in chapter 14 in the *Zinerman* case, liability can arise when a professional treats a person incapable of giving consent. In that case, the client should not have been treated unless procedures, such as required for involuntary hospitalizations, were followed. This first requires the professional to accurately assess the client's capacity to consent to the treatment. Likewise, liability can arise when a physician determines that a person incapable of giving consent is in need of medication. If there is no one available to consent to this treatment, having a court rule that such treatment is necessary is appropriate.[12]

The social worker practicing therapy on children may also encounter problems from parents purporting to give consent

---

12.   Donald T. Dickson, *Law in the Health and Human Services* (The Free Press: New York, 1995), p. 156.

when, in fact, the parent does not have legal authority to do so. In child custody cases, for example, the parent who was not awarded legal custody may nonetheless want a child to have therapy. A social worker who provides treatment at the direction of the noncustodial parent often faces disciplinary liability and involvement in subsequent court hearings initiated at the request of the custodial parent. The best method to avoid such problems is to request a copy of the court order granting custody, to include in the treatment records, before starting any therapy.

False Imprisonment. Liability for **false imprisonment** may occur from wrongful commitment, detention, or incarceration. A social worker could be sued for false imprisonment, for example, if she allegedly forced a client to enter a residential drug treatment program.

Invasion of Privacy or Breach of Confidentiality. Liability for **invasion of privacy** or **breach of confidentiality** cases may occur when social workers improperly release client records or reveal client communications. Social workers have also been sued for invasion of privacy, when they conduct allegedly harassing and overreaching investigations of possible child abuse. For example, see *Martin v. County of Weld*, 43 Colo. App. 49, 598 P.2d 532 (Colo. 1979).

Intentional Infliction of Mental Distress. Liability for **intentional infliction of mental distress** may occur if a client experiences trauma resulting either from a method of treatment or from certain social worker actions, such as removing children from a parent's home. A claim of

negligent infliction of mental distress may also arise. You should note that even if these claims are not recognized, a person may still recover damages for mental distress in combination with a malpractice or other claim. The court specifically noted in *Horak* that "the plaintiff would [also] be entitled to recover for emotional distress."

Assault or Battery. Liability for **assault** or **battery** occurs when one person improperly touches or threatens to touch another. Contact or threat of contact need not be considered offensive. Treating persons without their informed consent may be considered an assault or battery, as could having sexual relations with a patient or client. Even if a patient or client consents to sexual contact with a professional, the contact may be considered an assault or battery on the theory that the professional exerted undue influence over the patient or client to obtain the consent.

Breach of Contract. Liability for **breach of contract** can occur when social workers do not fulfill terms of a contract to provide therapeutic services. In *Martino v. Family Service Agency of Adams County*, 112 Ill App. 3d 593, 445 N.E.2d 6 (1982), a woman sued a marriage counselor for failing to provide competent counseling. The counselor fell in love with the plaintiff's spouse and engaged in "intimate relations" with him.

Malicious Prosecution. Liability for **malicious prosecution** can occur when social workers initiate law suits, particularly child protection actions, maliciously and wrongfully. In *Doe v. County of Suffolk*, 494 F. Supp. 179 (E.D.N.Y. 1980), a social worker allegedly filed an abuse and ne-glect action knowing full well that, ulti-mately, the child abuse case would be dismissed.

Criminal Liability

States have enacted criminal laws that target activities involving social workers. Of course, a social worker may also be subject to a grievance by the State's li-censing board if he or she is involved in criminal activity.

Sexual Assault. States statutes may pro-vide that engaging in sexual activities with a client is a criminal offense for a therapist; such statutes may provide that consent on the part of the client is not a defense. For example, see Colo. Rev. Stat. § 18-3-405.5.

Fraudulent Billing. States have enacted laws that make fraudulently billing insur-ance companies for services allegedly per-formed a criminal offense for a therapist. Social workers should keep accurate records detailing time actually spent with an individual or individuals.

Disciplinary Liability

Practice Acts and Regulations. As we saw in chapter 17, social work practice acts were enacted to allow social workers and other qualified professionals to practice under the supervision of the State's over-sight board. The practice acts and regula-tions promulgated by the State's oversight board specify minimum standards of practice that must be followed by those in

the board's regulated area. The minimum standards of practice usually include mat-ters such as the following: maintaining confidentiality, maintaining standards of care for treatment, making referrals in cer-tain cases; disclosing certain information to clients; and upholding record-keeping and supervision requirements. Addition-ally, practice acts usually include a list of prohibited activities such as the follow-ing: using of misleading advertising; committing abuse of health insurance; continuing practice if there has been a se-rious criminal conviction; habitually using alcohol or drugs; and having sexual relations with clients. For examples of such standards and prohibitions, see Ariz Rev. Stat. Ann. § 32-3251; Tenn. Code Ann. § 63-23-106; and Utah Code Ann. § 58-60-110.

If the social worker violates any provi-sion of the social work practice acts or of the regulations promulgated by the over-sight board, a grievance proceeding will likely be brought against the social worker. Moreover, misconduct is grounds for the oversight board to revoke or sus-pend the social worker's license, send a letter of admonition, or implement a pro-bationary term with certain conditions of compliance that must be met.

The standards of practice defined in the practice acts or regulations also apply to staff employed or volunteers, including students, supervised by the social worker.

The social worker should be very fa-miliar with the practice acts and regula-tions governing the standards of practice. In the area of confidentiality, for example, a State's oversight board may take formal action against a therapist who releases certain records in response to a valid sub-poena. This occurred in the following case, *Rost v. State Board of Psychology,* 659 A.2d 626 (Pa. 1995).

Polly Rost, a clinical psychologist licensed to practice in the Commonwealth of Pennsylvania, appeals from an order of the State Board of Psychology which reprimanded her for having violated Sections 8(a)(9) and (11) of the Professional Psychologists Practice Act (Act). We affirm.

This case originated in February of 1987, when an unlicensed supervisee of Rost began giving psychological treatment to S.P., a female juvenile. S.P. was treated in Rost's practice for recurring headaches that allegedly were caused when S.P. fell and struck her head at the York Jewish Community Center (YJCC). In March of 1988, S.P.'s mother filed suit against the YJCC on S.P.'s behalf, alleging that YJCC's negligence had caused her daughter physical and emotional harm.

In December of 1989, YJCC's attorney mailed Rost a subpoena requesting the treatment records for S.P. Rost subsequently provided YJCC with these treatment records. Although S.P.'s mother had previously signed a release allowing Rost to turn over the records to S.P.'s own attorney, Rost had not obtained permission to release the records to YJCC. Furthermore, Rost did not attempt to contact S.P.'s mother, or S.P.'s attorney, to obtain permission to release the records or to advise them of her intention to release the records prior to doing so. Rost did not attempt to gain permission because she believed that she was already authorized to release records to YJCC based upon the release which had previously been given to S.P.'s attorney.

On January 25, 1993, the Commonwealth of Pennsylvania, Bureau of Professional and Occupational Affairs (BPOA) issued an order to show cause in which it charged Rost with having violated three sections of the Act: (1) Section 8(a)(9) of the Act through her violation of Ethical Principle 5 of the Board Regulations governing the confidentiality of client information; (2) Section 8(a)(13) of the Act by failing to perform a statutory obligation imposed upon licensed psychologists; and (3) Section 8(a)(11) of the Act by engaging in unprofessional conduct.

On June 17, 1993, a hearing was held before Frank C. Kahoe, a hearing examiner appointed by the Board. Subsequently, on August 30, 1993, the hearing examiner issued a proposed adjudication and order in which he concluded that Rost was not subject to disciplinary action under Section 8(a) of the Act, because S.P. had waived the client-psychologist privilege by asserting a claim for emotional damages in her lawsuit against YJCC. In response, the BPOA filed a brief of exceptions. The Board disagreed with the hearing examiner's recommendation, and by an amended order dated April 18, 1994, officially reprimanded Rost for having violated Section 8(a)(9) and (11) of the Act. Rost's appeal to this Court followed.

Rost's first argument is that she did not violate Sections 8(a)(9) and (11) of the Act because she released the records pursuant to a subpoena and S.P. waived her right to confidentiality by initiating a lawsuit in which her psychological condition was at issue. In support of this position, Rost points out that the trial court in S.P.'s lawsuit against YJCC ultimately ruled that S.P. had waived her privilege of confidentiality. She further claims that S.P.'s attorney had a duty to disclose the records to YJCC during discovery. Accordingly, Rost argues that she did not violate Ethical Principle 5 of the Board Regulations, since S.P. no longer had an expectation of privacy in regard to the records.

However, we must agree with the Board that Rost's argument is misplaced. We are not faced with the question of whether YJCC should have been barred from introducing S.P.'s records at trial based on the psychologist-client privilege. That is a determination properly made by a judge and not by a psychologist lacking formal legal training. At the time Rost released S.P.'s records to YJCC, she did not seek the consent of her client, professional legal advice or the imprimatur of a judge. Rather, she unilaterally decided to release S.P.'s records.

Rost is also mistaken when she attempts to equate the psychologist-client privilege with the rule of confidentiality found in the Code of Ethics for psychologists. Although the two are similar, the privilege is limited in scope to the question of admissibility of evidence in a civil or criminal trial. In interpreting the psychologist-client privilege, we are guided by the same rules that apply to the attorney-client privilege. The privilege may be waived by the client as was ultimately found to have occurred in this case. Waiver of the privilege may occur where the client places the confidential information at issue in the case. It may also be waived where there is no longer an expectation of privacy regarding the information because the client has made it known to third persons.

Nevertheless, the Code of Ethics for psychologists imposes a duty of confidentiality which extends beyond the testimonial privilege found in Section 5944 of the Judicial Code; this duty is absolute and cannot be waived except after full disclosure and written authorization by the client. Unlike the privilege, it continues even when the information has been previously disclosed to third parties or is material to litigation initiated by the client. In the present case, Rost did not even attempt to obtain the consent of her client before releasing confidential information. Although S.P. was eventually found to have waived the psychologist-client privilege, this does not absolve Rost from her ethical duty of confidentiality. Rost had a duty to either obtain written permission to release the records from S.P. or challenge the propriety of the subpoena before a judge. Rost did neither. Instead, she unilaterally gave S.P.'s records to YJCC without consulting with S.P. or her attorney. Since the language of Ethical Principle 5 of the Board Regulations unambiguously prohibits this type of conduct, we must concur with the Board's conclusion that Rost violated Section 8(a)(9) of the Act. Additionally, we agree with the Board that Rost's breach of her duty of confidentiality constitutes unprofessional conduct in violation of Section 8(a)(11) of the Act.

Whenever a professional in possession of confidential information is served with a subpoena, a conflict naturally arises between one's duty to the courts and one's duty of confidentiality towards one's client. In this respect, Rost is no different from the numerous other psychologists, doctors, lawyers, and clergymen who receive subpoenas in this Commonwealth each year. The value of a psychologist's, or other professional's, duty of confidentiality would be illusory if it could be overridden anytime a conflicting duty arose which was thought to be more important. Although Rost may have been placed in an unfavorable position, she is not excused from following the ethical guidelines of her profession which plainly forbid her from disclosing a client's records without her consent.

Rost argues that it is unreasonable to expect a psychologist, lacking formal legal training, to know the proper procedure to follow after receiving a subpoena. Rost apparently believes that she was in an untenable position in which she would have had to either violate the rules of professional conduct or disregard a subpoena. However, this argument is flawed. Rost could have challenged the subpoena in court or obtained permission from her client before releasing the information. If Rost was uncertain about her legal rights and responsibilities, she should have at least obtained advice from an attorney instead of unilaterally releasing her client's records. As a licensed psychologist, she had an obligation to be aware of the ethical duties which govern her profession. Having received the benefits of being licensed by the state, Rost cannot now argue that she is a "layman" who lacks the knowledge and training necessary to understand and comply with the Board's regulations.

Accordingly, we affirm the order of the Board which reprimanded Rost for having violated Sections 8(a)(9) and (11) of the Act.

The *Rost* case illustrates that a State's practice act must be strictly followed. *Rost* also shows that a decision of a State's oversight board may be appealed; however, appellate courts often give much discretion to an oversight board's findings and conclusions.

Billing Issues. Disagreements with clients over billing may subject the social worker to a grievance proceeding. Obviously, unpaid bills may be written off by the social worker. If such bills are turned over to a collection agency or attorney, there may be difficulties because of the confidential nature of the relationship and the embarrassment many people feel when others learn of their emotional problems (or the mere fact that they were under treatment by a therapist.[13] These latter options are also expensive and antagonistic. Additionally, if a social worker terminates services due to nonpayment of fees, he or she risks allegations that the client was abandoned before the therapeutic services were completed.

A social worker should avoid exchanging goods or services with a client for payment of fees. This will avoid the appearance of exerting improper or undue influence. For example, see Standards 1.13 and 1.15 of the National Association of Social Workers' *Code of Ethics*.[14]

Billing problems may also arise with third party payers, such as insurance companies. A social worker should *never* file a claim for services that were never rendered. This could lead to criminal and civil liability, in addition to the likely grievance being initiated.

GOVERNMENT AGENCY LIABILITY

Social workers who work at a public agency or in a public capacity may also be

sued for violating a client's or another's civil rights under 42 U.S.C. § 1983, the federal civil rights statute discussed in chapter 5. Child protection workers and employees of public mental health or correctional facilities are particularly vulnerable to such suits, but all social workers employed in a public capacity should be aware of their potential liability for civil rights violations under the statute. **Sovereign immunity**, which is a doctrine that precludes lawsuits from being filed against the government, may serve as protection from civil rights actions filed against social workers employed at public agencies. The doctrine of **qualified immunity**, however, allows lawsuits against the government for egregious or intentional misconduct.

Chapter 8 explained the case, *De-Shaney v. Winnebago County Department of Social Services*, 489 U.S. 189, (1989), where the Supreme Court limited liability against child protection workers under 42 U.S.C. § 1983. Joshua, a four-year-old child, was severely beaten by his father and "suffered from brain damage so severe that he is expected to spend the rest of his life confined to an institution for the profoundly retarded." His noncustodial mother sued a Wisconsin child welfare agency and various agency workers for violating their due process rights under 42 U.S.C. § 1983 for both failing to remove Joshua from his father's custody and protecting him from injury despite several reports of abuse and several investigations by the agency. The Court, however, denied relief on these grounds, stating that the purpose of the due process clause, "was to protect the people from the State, not to ensure that the State pro-

---

13. Douglas J. Besharov, *The Vulnerable Social Worker: Liability for Serving Children and Families* (NASW Press: Silver Springs, MD, 1985), p. 9.

14. *Code of Ethics*, National Association of Social Workers, Ethical Standards 1.13 and 1.15 (1996).

tected [people] from each other." The *De-Shaney* Court specifically did not hold that there could be no civil liability based on negligence for the social worker having a duty but failing to protect Joshua.

Cases brought after *DeShaney* have recognized liability under 42 U.S.C. § 1983 when social workers took children into custody, for example, and placed them in an abusive foster home. Liability has also been recognized when social workers took children into custody without the mother's consent or without obtaining court approval for taking the children into custody. For example, see *Duchesne v. Sugarman*, 566 F.2d 817 (1977).

While the many forms of liability that are recognized against social workers may sound threatening, you should keep in mind that the first priority in any setting is the welfare of the client. Use of common sense, consultation with other professionals, and sound risk management techniques will enable the social worker to practice as a recognized and valuable professional.

Professional Relationships with Lawyers

Throughout this book, we have examined the many different ways that the law may impact the practice of social work and that social workers may encounter lawyers in the course of their practice. We have also seen that a social worker's clients may need the assistance of lawyers and that social workers themselves may need the assistance of a lawyer, for example, to advise them on confidentiality. It is, thus, important that social workers understand how to access and work with lawyers. This chapter will try to provide that understanding.

REFERRING CLIENTS TO LAWYERS

The Client's Right to an Attorney

As we have seen in the United States, the criminally accused generally have the right to assistance of counsel guaranteed by the Sixth Amendment to the Constitution. Although in other situations the Constitution may require or State statutes may grant the right to assistance of counsel—such as cases involving termination of parental rights, paternity actions, or civil commitments—in general, parties who cannot afford attorneys are not entitled to the appointment of an attorney at public expense.

Those who do have a right to appointed counsel, however, generally do not have a right to the appointed counsel's assistance from the outset of the legal problem. Instead, they would be entitled to the lawyer's appointment once the case is in litigation. Additionally, they will not have an attorney appointed unless the court is satisfied that they cannot afford to pay for a privately retained attorney. Thus, if the social worker has poor clients with the types of legal problems entitling them to free representation, the most the social worker may be able to do is advise them about the possibility of appointment of an attorney. The social worker should, additionally, make it clear that the client must pay attention to all court documents they receive and appear in court if they are instructed to do so in these documents. For example, the social worker can help the client understand that failing to appear could result in their arrest in a criminal case, for example.

The following example illustrates the social worker's role: suppose a client has been told he fathered a child out of wedlock and is now being asked by the welfare department to pay child support. Even if this client is entitled to appointment of an attorney, the social worker may not be able to refer him to an attorney for free advice. Instead, the social worker may only be able to advise him that, should he be sued in a paternity and child support action, he would be entitled to appointment of an attorney at no cost once the court believes he cannot afford an attorney. In such a situation, the client should be informed that he must appear in court and ask for an attorney after being served with the paternity petition. The social worker should also make him aware of the seriousness of his situation; advise him to be cautious about agreeing to or signing anything before he goes to court and consults a lawyer; and assure him that he will not suffer a penalty to exercising his right to appointment of counsel.

Publicly Funded Legal Agencies

There are various publicly funded agencies that provide free legal representation for those who cannot afford an attorney. Many jurisdictions have staffed **public defender** offices, which provide representation for indigents in criminal or juvenile delinquency cases. Public defenders usually represent defendants in such cases where incarceration is possible. Some public defender offices may also represent respondents in civil commitments, fathers in paternity actions, parents in juvenile court actions relating to abuse, neglect, termination of parental rights, or defendants, in other types of civil cases.

Public defenders may not be willing or allowed to counsel people unless and until a court appoints them, but some public defender offices will give brief advice to those who may face criminal or delinquency charges.

The federal government has provided funding for free representation of indigents in civil cases. This funding comes from the Legal Services Corporation (LSC), an independent federal agency with a board of directors appointed by the President with the approval of Congress. Both eligibility requirements for clients and restrictions on types of cases taken are established by the LSC board and promulgated as federal regulations.

Most LSC funded programs have staffed offices; some may also use a voucher system to reimburse private attorneys selected by clients. Because the voucher system may work somewhat like Medicare, it may be known as Judicare.

Most LSC funded offices programs put Legal Services, Legal Assistance, or Legal Aid in their names. Many of these programs and some of the Judicare programs have scattered local offices throughout a State. Some programs cover large portions of a State.

Because of sharply reduced funding for LSC in recent years, many LSC offices have closed or limited the types and number of cases they will handle. A few States have provided supplemental funding for LSC funded programs, but even in those States, many financially eligible clients must be turned away. Because of limited funding, LSC programs are only able to meet a fraction of the legal needs of the poor in civil matters. Nevertheless, where LSC funded offices exist, they are excellent referral sources for the social worker.

Some additional legal needs of the poor for assistance in civil matters are met by publicly funded programs providing legal assistance on special kinds of cases or for special kinds of populations. For example, federal funds for the aging may be used to fund legal assistance programs for the elderly. Some of this money is used to create special offices for the elderly in existing LSC funded programs; some is used to create independently staffed offices or offices that are part of other programs for seniors. Federal funds to assist the disabled or the mentally ill may be used to create law offices, which will provide representation in civil commitments, special education due process hearings, social security hearings, and other matters. Many of these offices are known as Protection and Advocacy offices. Other programs exist for juveniles, immigrants, or other special populations. The social worker may be able to make referrals to such programs.

Most States have programs that require attorneys to place client funds, if these funds will be held for a short time, in interest-bearing trust accounts (which are known as Interest on Lawyers Trust Accounts [IOLTAs]). The interest earned by these trust accounts are then used to pay foundations that fund legal services programs for low-income persons.

State IOLTA programs, however, were called into question by the Supreme Court in *Phillips v. Washington Legal Foundation.* ___ U.S. ___, 118 S.Ct 1925 (1998). The Court held that interest income generated by funds held in IOLTA accounts was the private property of the client; as such, it was protected by the Fifth Amendment, which provides that "private property" shall not "be taken for public use, without just compensation." This holding may result in further restrictions of funding for legal services programs for low-income persons.

Other Free Legal Services

There are also many private lawyers and organizations that provide free legal services to the poor with minimal or no public funding. Some large law firms in big cities operate special storefront offices or legal clinics for the poor. Some associations of lawyers operate programs where private lawyers volunteer to provide legal assistance for the poor. These are places to which social workers may refer clients.

A private lawyer's free service to the poor is known as **pro bono**, meaning "for the public good." Much pro bono work is sponsored by bar associations or structured law firm programs. Hopefully, the social worker may be able to locate attorneys who will do pro bono work for their clients.

In some cities, there are private legal aid societies that exist side by side with LSC funded programs. These societies receive limited or no public funds. They may just make referrals to lawyers.

Special interest organizations may also have law offices that will provide free legal representation for special cases. Usually, such offices have no financial eligibility requirements but will only take selected cases considered important to the organization or because they will set an important precedent. For example, the American Civil Liberties Union (ACLU) takes cases raising First Amendment issues, the National Organization for Women (NOW) takes cases related to women's rights, and gay and lesbian groups may take cases on gay and lesbian rights or AIDS issues.

Some special interest organizations, particularly shelters for women who are victims of domestic violence, may not have legal staff but are equipped to help people prepare and file simple legal papers, such as petitions for protective orders.

Many of the more than two hundred law schools in this country operate legal clinics where law students get academic credit and experience by handling real cases, usually for indigent people. Many of these clinics welcome walk-in clients. Experienced attorneys supervise the students. Some law students have also set up their own legal clinics where they help people with certain kinds of problems on a purely voluntary basis. Keep in mind that these clinics may be less supervised than those where students receive academic credit.

If there is no private or publicly funded program to refer a poor client, there may be lawyer referral services sponsored by a State or local bar association. These lawyer referral services usually provide an initial consultation with an attorney for a set low fee. The attorney and client then can make any financial arrangement they wish for continued representation.

Lawyer referral services usually make no representation of the quality of service provided by the participating attorneys. Because many private lawyers do not charge anything—or charge very little for an initial consultation—a client might be just as well off looking in the yellow pages of the telephone book. Calling an attorney will determine if there is a charge for an initial consultation, if the attorney will take the type of case, or if the attorney would take the cases on a contingency fee basis. Many attorneys list their specialties and rates in the yellow pages.

If a client wants to initiate certain kinds of legal actions, such as an action to obtain a domestic violence protective order, involuntarily commit or obtain a guardianship over a relative, obtain past due child support, or file a consumer complaint, the local prosecuting attorney or State attorney general's office may be willing to assist. Indeed, in some jurisdictions, prosecutors are required to initiate such actions in appropriate cases. Prosecutors may decide, however, that a particular case is not appropriate for action. If they decide to assist, their services will usually be free.

Referrals for Middle-Class Clients

Referrals are difficult for poor clients who cannot afford to pay for a lawyer, but referrals are even more difficult for middle-class clients. These clients often are unable to pay lawyer's fees that can be several hundred or even several thousand dollars for a simple case and yet they may not qualify for free legal assistance because they earn too much money.

Lawyer referral services usually have no financial eligibility requirements. This may be the best referral source for middle-class clients. Special interests organizations, like the ACLU also usually have no financial eligibility requirements, but they take only a few selected cases.

There are private for-profit law offices that provide services on simple cases for relatively low fees. Often part of nationwide or statewide chains, they may be located in shopping centers or in other community areas. On simple cases, like uncontested divorces or stepparent adoptions, these offices are more than adequate.

There are also some self-help offices that help people do their own legal work on certain kinds of cases for a small fee. In some jurisdictions, these self-help offices have been charged with practicing law without a license, but in other jurisdictions they are allowed to operate openly.

A social worker might be tempted to make referrals to friends, relatives, or acquaintances who are lawyers. Before making such referrals, however, consider the ethics of referring clients, who will pay fees to friends, relatives, and acquaintances. Social workers should also consider whether they want to be in a position of recommending a particular lawyer to a client. Moreover, if you work for a public agency, and even for some private agencies, making such referrals may be contrary to agency rules.

If a social worker works for an agency, a far better solution for making referrals may be to create an agency list of private attorneys to whom clients may be referred. The agency can inform local attorney groups that it is preparing such a list, can let any attorney who is interested join the list, and can promise to make referrals on a strict rotating basis. The agency can tell clients and attorneys that it does not certify the quality of service provided by attorneys on their list, but it does certify that these attorneys are willing to take certain kinds of cases for reasonable fees.

Because of the middle class's problem of finding and paying for legal representation, increasingly, legal insurance or prepaid plans may be in the package of benefits from work or may be purchased. For example, some auto clubs provide legal representation or assistance on auto related matters. Also, some credit card companies provide legal representation in certain situations. Plus, homeowners or automobile insurance companies may provide legal representation for injuries related to the covered home or automobile. With a legal insurance plan, one may have a choice of attorneys, but with prepaid plans one must usually go to specified attorneys. For instance, if an insurance company provides representation under a homeowners or automobile insurance policy, the company will provide the lawyer.

Whether making a referral for a poor- or middle-class client, a social worker saves the client much time and aggravation by checking first with attorney referrals to see if and when they will see the client, what they can offer the client, and what they will charge for their services.

If the social worker is making a direct referral to a lawyer, the social worker can provide the lawyer with the client's history and the history of the problem the client is bringing. This can save the lawyer time, and thus the client expense, and will allow the lawyer to prepare in advance for the first meeting with the client. Of course, the social worker may not breach confidentiality by discussing the client with the lawyer without client consent. A social worker must obtain permission from the client before any information is disclosed. Assure your client that lawyers are also bound by strict confidentiality rules.

Before making referrals to lawyers, but *without* giving clients legal advice, the social worker may need to attempt to ease the client's stress about seeing a lawyer, and help them address the emotional aspects of their legal problems. Keep in mind that lawyers might not deal with the emotional dimensions of their client's legal problems. The social worker can fill in this gap in service both before and after making the referral.

Moreover, if a direct referral is made to a lawyer, try to keep in touch with him or her to see how you may, perhaps, help the client cope with the stress of seeing a lawyer and going to court. Your assistance can make the lawyer's job much easier and the process more satisfactory for the client. Again, it is imperative that the social worker does not violate confidentiality. Disclosure should be made only with the client's consent, and although lawyers are bound by strict confidentiality requirements, they do not need to know everything about a client.

WORKING WITH LAWYERS

A social worker not only makes referrals to lawyers, but may also be getting referrals from them. Most lawyers do not have the time, the inclination, or the expertise to address client's psychosocial problems. Yet, often, resolution of these problems is crucial to the resolution of the legal problems. Thus, lawyers may need to make referrals to social workers.

The next three scenarios illustrate the need for social work referrals. First, lawyer cannot make a plan for child custody and visitation to present to a court if all the parties have unrealistic or inappropriate expectations. The lawyer might need a social worker's help to assist the client in designing a reasonable plan. Second, family's problems might not be resolved when a daughter appoints a legal guardian for her elderly mother but, helping the daughter find a place for her mother to live and get appropriate care might provide an answer. Finally, a lawyer may help a widow deal with her husband's estate after his death but may not be able to help her cope with the grief over her loss. Unless she comes to terms with her grief, she may be incapable of taking necessary legal actions. A social worker can help her get back on her feet emotionally.

Whether a social worker is in private practice or works at an agency, the social worker becomes acquainted with lawyers in the community that work with family problems. The social worker can inform these attorneys that he or she can help in numerous ways and can perform necessary services for their clients. If a social worker does get a referral from a lawyer, he or she should talk frequently with the lawyer and regularly report on the client's progress, *assuming* the client gives explicit permission to discuss his or her case with the lawyer. By keeping in touch with the lawyer, the social worker can be assured that both the legal services and social work services are coordinated, for the client's benefit. As a result, the social worker can establish a fruitful professional relationship with the lawyer.

As private practitioners, social workers may work with lawyers by participating in divorce mediation, arranging private adoptions, or finding rehabilitation services for injured clients. In addition, social workers may help lawyers interview difficult clients, investigate certain kinds of cases, and prepare witnesses—particularly witnesses that are children, rape victims, or emotionally disturbed—for the ordeal of trial. Social workers may assess cases that have psychological or social aspects or that involve other social workers, testify as an expert witness, or evaluate reports of other expert witnesses. For over sixty years, legal aid and public defender offices have employed social workers as staff members to perform such tasks. Remember that when social workers work with attorneys as colleagues, they are bound by additional confidentiality rules.

Social workers in many public agencies also work closely with lawyers as professional colleagues. For example, prosecutors bring cases to court in conjunction with and to assist child welfare workers. Social workers in community mental health programs work with public attorneys to initiate civil commitments or guardianships. In corrections, prosecuting attorneys often contract with social workers for sentencing recommendations.

Whether in private practice or employed at an agency, professionalism and an understanding of the respective roles of social workers and lawyers are the keys to successful working relationships. A lawyer will respect a social worker who asserts professionalism and independence rather than one who bends to the lawyers wishes. For example, refusing to recommend that a child be placed in the custody of a lawyer's client when such a placement would be contrary to the child's best interests may earn the social worker more respect from a lawyer than making a poor recommendation that is criticized by a judge.

Many times, a social worker's role with an attorney may be in an adversarial rather than a cooperative relationship. An adversarial relationship does not, however, need to be hostile. Indeed, animosity between the lawyer and the social worker may very well work to everyone's detriment. Again, the keys to successful performance of the social worker's job are both an understanding of the respective roles and professionalism.

OBTAINING LEGAL ADVICE

A social worker may need to obtain legal advice in the course of his or her practice. For instance, a social worker may have an ethical or legal problem and want legal consultation. Remember however, that lawyers may charge by the hour, so it is advisable to write out the issues and questions before meeting with the lawyer.

Lawyers may also provide representation in the form of litigation. If the social worker is charged with a crime, it is wise to meet with an attorney before speaking with the police or prosecutor's office to protect constitutional rights, such as the Fifth Amendment privilege against self-incrimination. And, if a social worker is being sued for malpractice, it is also wise to talk to a lawyer before any concessions are made or settlements offered.

Lawyers have different specialties or emphases; thus, depending on a social worker or the client's needs he or she may have more than one attorney working for them.

THE SOCIAL WORKER AS ADVOCATE

Although social workers want to guide their clients to independence and self-reliance, sometimes they can help clients achieve goals by advocacy that does not involve litigation—and may not even involve the legal system. For example, the social worker might talk to the management of a nursing home; help a client fill out a job application and tell the prospective employer about the client's strengths; try to convince a landlord that he should make repairs of his property on behalf of a group of tenants who are the social worker's clients; or argue for additional benefits in a managed care setting.

Sometimes, social workers' advocacy for their clients does take place in the legal system. Social workers may act as the client's legal representative with an administrative agency or in an administrative hearing. Administrative agencies often permit nonlawyers to act as legal representatives and perform an advocacy role that one would expect an attorney to perform. In some types of administrative hearings, for example, nonlawyer legal representatives may be far more common than lawyer representatives. Indeed, some nonlawyer legal representatives provide legal representation of clients as their only job.

When social workers are performing as advocates in the legal system, they must do work that they are generally not trained to do. Advocacy is very different from usual activities of social workers and advocacy skills are very different than the usual social work skills.

The social worker must also remember that typically his or her role within the legal system is *not* that of an advocate. Whether the social worker is acting as an expert witness, making a recommendation to a court, filing a petition with a court, or working with a lawyer on a case, his or her goal should be to strive for excellence and integrity in the professional role.

GLOSSARY-INDEX

This index contains references to legal and social work definitions. Some of these terms may also be found in the General Index.

TABLE OF CASES

<hr>
<hr>

All cases are alphabetized under the first proper name (or initial, where an initial is substituted for a proper name) in the case name, as follows: *Beruman, People v.; Bowers v. Hardwick; Gault, In re; Martin, State v.; Robert Paul P., Matter of Adoption of; Roe v. Wade.* Where page references are in **bold type**, the case has been excerpted, not merely referred to or briefly quoted.

INDEX

To locate definitions of legal terms or terms of art, use the Glossary Index. Court Opinions cited in the text are included in the Table of Cases. Significant statutes are listed below.